PRAISE FOR THE HARDCOVER EDITION

"Europe's Faustian bargain is the subject of Konrad Jarausch's authoritative new history of Europe. This is a history of the groundswell of material progress—from science and technology to production and consumption—and the inability to master it. The failure to meet these challenges spiraled into a devastating politics of destruction in the First and Second World Wars that was stopped only at the cost of a Cold War. Would the collapse of 1989 jump-start a new and more modest European order in a global world? *Out of Ashes* points to the lessons learned as well as to the current predicaments Europe faces."

—Michael Geyer, University of Chicago

"This is a well-written, well-organized, and detailed study of a notoriously difficult subject: Europe in the twentieth century. Jarausch deftly guides readers through the important developments that led through two wars to our unstable present."

—John Connelly, author of *From Enemy to Brother: The Revolution in Catholic Teaching on the Jews, 1933-1965*

"*Out of Ashes* is an extremely well-conceived and highly ambitious book. What Jarausch has pulled off is a fully balanced, elegantly integrated history of a long twentieth century in which the pre-1914 era and the post-1989 years are vital parts of the interpretation."

—Peter Fritzsche, author of *Life and Death in the Third Reich*

"This book is a sweeping study of twentieth-century European history, read through the lens of multiple modernities. Written by one of the leading lights of modern German and European history, *Out of Ashes* has the power to stake its place as a volume of truly lasting value."

—Belinda J. Davis, author of *Home Fires Burning: Food, Politics, and Everyday Life in World War I Berlin*

"Jarausch's book really comes into its own when dealing with the second half of the century. Here, he wonderfully pulls together various strands of the story of European integration and decolonisation, Cold War and the creation of the welfare state, deindustrialisation and globalisation."

—Srinath Raghavan, *Open Magazine*

OUT OF
ASHES

OUT OF ASHES

A NEW HISTORY OF EUROPE IN THE TWENTIETH CENTURY

KONRAD H. JARAUSCH

WITH A NEW PREFACE BY THE AUTHOR

Princeton University Press
Princeton and Oxford

press.princeton.edu

Cover photograph: Sunday volunteer workers working in the Martin Luther Platz, March
1946. Photo by William Vandivert / The LIFE Picture Collection / Getty Images.

Third printing, and first paperback printing with a new preface by the author, 2016

Paperback ISBN: 978-0-691-17307-8

The Library of Congress has cataloged the cloth edition of this book as follows:

Jarausch, Konrad Hugo.
    Out of ashes : a new history of Europe in the twentieth century / Konrad H. Jarausch.
        pages cm
        Includes bibliographical references and index.
    ISBN 978-0-691-15279-0 (hardback : acid-free paper)   1. Europe—History—20th
century.   2. Europe—Politics and government—20th century.   3. Europe—Social
conditions—20th century.   4. Social change—Europe—History—20th century.   I. Title.
    D424.J37 2015
    940.5–dc23   2014031328

British Library Cataloging-in-Publication Data is available

This book has been composed in Minion Pro

Printed on acid-free paper. ∞

Printed in the United States of America

10 9 8 7 6 5

CONTENTS

PREFACE TO THE PAPERBACK EDITION

After the completion of this manuscript, a host of problems have arisen which have cast a pall on the European future. A mountain of sovereign debt has burdened the Mediterranean countries, Russian separatists have conquered the Crimea, a strong segment of the British public wants to leave the EU, millions of refugees from Islamic countries are rushing to Europe, and transatlantic relations remain in disrepair. Due to this accumulation of troubles, media headlines have predicted that Europe is about to fall apart. While it is still unclear how certain aspects of the crisis can be mastered, the issues are being addressed and some solutions are beginning to emerge. Instead of reinforcing gloom, a historical perspective suggests that Europe has overcome similar difficulties in the past.

Contrary to predictions of disaster, the sovereign debt crisis seems at least to have been stabilized by the spring of 2016. In spite of President Alexis Tsipras's threats, Greece remains in the EU, while in Italy Prime Minister Matteo Renzo has been initiating a rigorous reform program. The German-inspired mixture of austerity and European Central Bank support, which lanced the speculative bubble, has revived modest growth in places such as Ireland and Portugal. While the human cost of restoring competitiveness through a lowering of living standards has been high, none of the countries involved have defaulted thanks to European solidarity in refinancing the repayment of faulty loans. The remaining challenge is therefore to create greater fiscal policy controls in the EU and reignite expansion so as to stop adult and especially youth unemployment.

In the embattled Eastern regions of Ukraine a cease fire also appears to be generally holding, because outright annexation might create too much negative fall-out for Russia. Vladimir Putin's brazen takeover of the Crimea with Russian special forces was a shock, since it violated international law and raised the specter of a "new Cold War." But that conquest is not likely to be reversed, since the West does not want a Third World War and the majority of the population is ethnically Russian. Hence it is more important to work on a peaceful settlement for the disputed regions in Eastern Ukraine, granting them enough autonomy to stay in the state. Moreover, Kiev has to reform itself so as to make its government truly functional. In response, NATO strategy is being revised to reassure its Eastern members and to warn Russia not to go any further.

During another crisis summit, the EU also made a special effort to avert the threatening "Brexit" by offering London sufficient concessions to maintain its special role. Egged on by the Murdoch press, British nationalists, still dreaming about the grand imperial past and claiming a special relationship to the U.S., wanted to leave. But Prime Minister David Cameron had negotiated concessions on delaying welfare payments for migrants and maintaining the pound as an independent currency in order to let the country remain in the EU. Since the UK Independence Party did succeed in persuading the British to leave the EU in the referendum on June 23, 2016, a complicated withdrawal process has to be negotiated. This disappointing demonstration of nationalist passions, which trumped rational considerations, challenges the remaining countries to explain the benefits of integration better to their citizens and to make further progress on integration unfettered by British skepticism.

An even more difficult challenge is the refugee crisis, since the tidal wave of desperate migrants from the failing states of Afghanistan, Iraq, Libya, and Syria shows little sign of abating. Touching pictures of drowning boat-people in the Mediterranean or of ragged columns marching through Balkan mountains evoke humanitarian compassion. But an increasing number of European xenophobes feel threatened and seek to keep out foreigners by burning down asylum homes. Chancellor Angela Merkel's vow "we will manage this" is beginning to fray, though thousands of volunteers are helping to take care of the newcomers. Maintaining an open door for the politically persecuted while rejecting economic migrants from "safe states" is becoming ever more difficult. The preservation of the Schengen travel freedom will require a combination of tougher border controls and integration support in dealing with the human catastrophe.

Finally, transatlantic relations seem to be stuck in misunderstanding with political elites drifting further apart on both shores of the Atlantic. At least on the Republican side of the U.S. presidential campaign, anti-European sentiment runs rampant as leading candidates portray the European welfare state as debilitating and un-American. At the same time, the European left is rejecting the Transatlantic Trade and Investment Partnership negotiations as making too many concessions to "predator capitalism." Attacking the pollution restrictions of the Obama administration as too close to the EU stance, the utilities lobby, right-wing politicians, and conservative judges continue to reject all evidence of global warming. It will take the election of a moderate U.S. president and greater agreement between EU members to renew the transatlantic dialogue and agree on a common course.

Though confronted with serious problems, the European model of chastened modernity therefore remains the right path for meeting the challenges of the future. Shocking as they are, the images of terrorist attacks in Paris have not been able to halt normal life in the French capital. Even after the Great Recession, the mixture of a market economy and a welfare state is the best recipe for prosperity as long as it keeps being competitive with global rivals. In spite of the horrendous ISIS brutality, skepticism against military adventures is wiser than seeking to solve foreign policy problems by force of arms. Though consensus building in the EU is a cumbersome process, multilateral cooperation is preferable to unilateral hegemony. Especially in the face of such new problems, the defense of human rights remains the abiding lesson of the twentieth century.

Konrad H. Jarausch
June 24, 2016

PREFACE

The ancient legend of Dr. Faustus largely anticipates the paradoxical trajectory of European history during the past century. In this tale a successful scholar makes a pact with the Devil, exchanging his soul for unlimited knowledge and worldly pleasure. After enjoying the fleeting fruits of his bargain, he is inevitably damned because his ambition violates the divine order. In Goethe's version a restless Faust seeks to understand the essence of life with the aid of Mephistopheles, destroying the innocent young woman Gretchen in the process. But in the second part of the drama Faust learns to serve others rather than just to satisfy his own desires, and finally escapes damnation owing to his ceaseless striving for human improvement. Reflecting in his 1947 novel *Dr. Faustus* on the horror of the Third Reich, Thomas Mann returned to the earlier cautionary view by presenting Adrian Leverkühn as a composer who produces beautiful music at the cost of a syphilitic madness that devours him. Hence the tale can be read as an allegory either of the quest for innovation that leads to destruction or of the search for potential redemption.

Because of its drastic reversals, the European experience of the twentieth century presents a story of unparalleled drama, ranging from suffering and self-destruction to civility and prosperity. Ushering in 1900 with high hopes for further material progress and proud of their imperial command over the globe, the European nations all too soon became embroiled in the bloodshed of the Great War that shook their confidence to the core. After a temporary respite during the 1920s, the competition between communist, fascist, and democratic ideologies led to an even more devastating Second World War and frightful Holocaust that has become synonymous with the human capacity for evil. In spite of the subsequent Cold War confrontation and the loss of the overseas empires, the devastated continent emerged out of the ashes of self-immolation to regain a surprising measure of peace and affluence. Moreover, an unforeseen peaceful revolution spread liberal capitalism to Eastern Europe as well, only to be confronted by new global problems. The interpretative challenge is to render the succession of such reversals, ruptures, and displacements intelligible.

To explain such a confusing trajectory, this book focuses on the peculiar dialectic of European dynamism that inspired both an impressive march of material progress and a frightful process of political self-destruction. Defenders of Western civilization and postcolonial critics agree that the Europeans created a protean civilization that conquered and transformed the rest of the world so as to rule and exploit it. Near the beginning of the twentieth century some social thinkers began to call the conjuncture of scientific discovery, economic development, political participation, and cultural experimentation by the term "modernity" in order to distinguish such advances from earlier traditions and to differentiate themselves from the "backward peoples" of other continents. No doubt their quest for becoming "modern" was more an aspiration than a reality, a depiction of a goal rather than a statement of actual achievement. But like the Faustian legend, this self-description stressed the incessant drive for more knowledge, material gain, and mass mobilization that would plunge the continent into catastrophe, forcing it thereafter to struggle for a return to civility.

Especially fascinating about Europe's experience of the last century are the many broken, but also touching, life stories that grew out of coping with such upheavals. For instance, about 1900 my grandparents moved from a Silesian farm to the bustling metropolis of Berlin in search of prosperity. Though my father survived military service during World War I, the family's grocery store ran into difficulties during the hyperinflation. During the depression, my parents had a hard time finding teaching positions, and my father was drafted again in the Second World War. As I described in *Reluctant Accomplice*, he died in Russia in January 1942, while his widow escaped the bombing in a Bavarian farm and resumed her teaching career in the Rhineland after the war. Since prospects in Europe looked dim, my father-in-law migrated with his family to the United States in 1948 as a captured engineer and scientist. This book charts the framework of destructive forces that killed relatives, destroyed homes, threatened livelihoods—in short turned entire worlds upside down. But it also offers an encouraging record of recovery, reconciliation, and emancipation that inspires hope for the future.

My own perspective on the European past is a transatlantic vantage point, combining both inside and outside views. I was born in Magdeburg during the Second World War and grew up in West Germany, but then moved to the United States to go to college, obtain my PhD at the University of Wisconsin, and pursue an academic career there. As part of the last generation with classical training, I learned Latin, Greek, and Hebrew in the *Gymnasium* and then added English, French, Russian, and Italian, giving me access to a range of European cultures. Beyond getting acquainted with German-speaking Europe during vacations, fellowships and family ties allowed me to live at various times also in France, the Netherlands, and Sweden. Finally, professional travel brought me from the Balkans to Britain and from Russia to Portugal. While the following pages draw on my German background and training, they are animated by a sincere desire to do justice to the different trajectories of other countries. As a Euro-American hybrid, I have for over four decades made a scholarly effort to discern "the unity within diversity" of the Old Continent's distinctive heritage.

Konrad H. Jarausch
Berlin/Washington/Chapel Hill, summer 2014

OUT OF
ASHES

Introduction

THE EUROPEAN PARADOX

Palace of Electricity, Paris World Exposition of 1900. *Source*: Brooklyn Museum.

Proud of the steady improvement in their lives, most middle-class Europeans greeted the dawn of the twentieth century with optimism. During the summer of 1900 the Exposition Universelle in Paris showcased confidence-inspiring inventions and offered futuristic designs that enthralled some fifty million spectators. Its permanent buildings and temporary pavilions at the Champs de Mars as well as the newly opened Metro underground were a strange mixture of historicism and modernity, blending an idealized past with an art nouveau present. Connected by a moving sidewalk, exhibits showed such innovations as a gigantic telescope, the diesel engine, and a fast locomotive along with photographs of big bridges and other technical accomplishments. The chief attraction was the Palace of Electricity, a shining display of artificial light that foreshadowed what one French illustrator called "the electrical life" of the future. The world fair's splendid display of "the wonders of science and technology" reinforced public "faith in uninterruptable and unstoppable progress."[1]

More critical spirits, nonetheless, warned that the "enormous mechanization of life through capitalism and the modern superstate" was creating a dangerous crisis. Scottish Labour Party leader Kier Hardie worried about the arms race on land or sea and the threat of war with new kinds of weapons, while others were more concerned about the perils of imperialism. Social commentators were divided between critics of decadence who feared "the anarchy of the masses" and writers such as Emile Zola, who loathed the pursuit of money in department stores and the heartless exploitation of laborers in the mines. The chief rabbi of Britain, Hermann Adler, feared "the recrudescence of racial antipathies and national animosities," while other moralists deplored "that infernal selfishness called by pseudo-philosophers 'individualism.'" The novelist Conan Doyle scorned "the ill-balanced, excitable and sensation-mongering press," whereas one society dame warned of the growing "laxity in the matter of marriage." Some perceptive observers sensed that beneath the thin veneer of civilization a "most terrible and malignant form of barbarism" continued to lurk.[2]

In spite of such forebodings, most commentators of the *fin de siècle* remained confident in the future, since they naturally extrapolated from their previous advances. Engineers predicted that exciting scientific discoveries and technical inventions would continue to characterize the new century. Social reformers hoped that agricultural improvements, better hygiene, and safer housing would make lives longer and more comfortable, allowing humankind finally to escape hunger and cold. Intellectuals and artists expected that increasing freedom of expression and experimentation would permit them to expand the boundaries of accepted truths and taste. Businessmen were sure that colonial conflicts would be resolved and that Europe would remain peaceful, enabling them to intensify trade and exchanges across frontiers. Even the leaders of the labor movement proclaimed: "The new century belongs to us!" Although the sociologist Werner Sombart worried about the "total transformation of all ways of life," there was much reason to believe that further progress would solve any remaining problems.[3]

THE PROMISE OF MODERNITY

The key concept that sought to capture this exciting sense of advancement was the term "modernity." Introduced by French symbolist poets during the 1870s to justify their artistic departure from the realist style, it rapidly spread as a rationale for initiating change. A decade later members of the Berlin literary scene picked up the label to legitimize naturalism as a more expressive and critical form of writing about "modern life," while some avant-garde artists in other fields embraced the notion of "modern art" in order to experiment with atonal music or abstract painting. Bourgeois intellectuals who sought to reform middle-class lifestyles similarly adopted the word, while scientists and inventors also used it to promote their discoveries. Around the turn of the twentieth century, the appellation therefore became popular in intellectual circles as a concept that suggested breaking with traditions by exploring new possibilities.[4] Initially designating innovative impulses, the clarion call of "modernity" became a code word for a liberating sense of progress.

Denoting opposition to the past, the adjective "modern" possessed a protean character, which made it difficult to pin down its precise meaning. Dictionaries suggest that the notion was originally coined in the Renaissance to designate an epoch different from the classical heritage of the ancients and also from the period of religious superstition and political confusion in between, known as the Middle Ages. The relational nature of the term that denotes difference from a preceding era provided little fixed content of its own, because the present remained a moving target, forever undergoing change. As a result of this fluidity, successive sets of cultural avant-gardes that sought to break with tradition could claim to be "modernist," no matter what their actual style. Finally, modernity might also suggest a progressive philosophical outlook, a secular stance that was dedicated to rational thought and social improvement.[5] Since these connotations tended to intermingle freely, they speeded the diffusion of the term by leaving open what was really being referred to.

In their reflections on the rapid transformation of Europe around 1900, social scientists like Emile Durkheim formulated a theory of societal evolution that stressed the process of becoming modern. The resulting notion of modernization identified essential aspects of European development such as the scientific, industrial, and democratic revolutions and universalized them into a normative construct that prescribed their outcome as desirable. Transferred to the United States by Talcott Parsons to embody the "highest aspirations of American liberalism," the concept optimistically "defined a universal, historical process through which *traditional* societies became *modern.*" During the Cold War this modernization theory became a democratic alternative to Marxist ideology by promoting economic development through unleashing the dynamic spirit of capitalism to spur a series of stages of growth. In textbooks, the concept therefore acquired a sense of sociological determinism that saw it as a universal process of change in which the Western world functioned as yardstick and developmental goal.[6]

This narrowing of modernization theory into a Cold War ideology has provoked fierce criticism from a variety of directions. Some global historians have suggested that the term should be abandoned entirely because its underlying reference to the European experience makes it too "Eurocentric." Similarly, several postcolonial anthropologists who engage in "provincializing Europe" have argued that overt racism and ruthless exploitation subverted the purportedly humane goals of the imperial modernization project. At the same time post-Holocaust thinkers such as Zygmunt Bauman have emphasized that ethnic cleansing and mass genocides contained considerable elements of modernity, revealing that what claimed to be a benign process possessed a dark underside.[7] Finally, environmental historians, sensitive to "the limits of economic growth," have stressed the inevitable ecological damage of unbridled urbanization and economic development. Taken together, these critiques have turned "modernization" from a widespread aspiration into an intellectual problem.

Instead of abandoning the notion altogether, it would be more productive to approach modernity from a critical historical perspective. Historian Jürgen Kocka correctly stresses that "there is no other concept which can encapsulate a whole epoch as suggestively, relationally and powerfully within diachronic processes of long-term change." Historicizing the term involves deconstructing its shifting meaning according to the time, place, and speaker behind it. Such a perspective uncovers a host of conflicting contemporary references to the concept as well as an amazing, but often uncritical, proliferation in the scholarly literature. More importantly, the competing liberal, communist, and fascist blueprints for economic and political development suggest a pluralization of the notion into "multiple modernities." Finally, such an approach reveals the fundamental ambivalence of the transformative changes, engendering both enormous benefits and frightful suffering.[8] Rather than positing modernity as a self-evident standard of civilization, these reflections will treat it as a complex problem to be approached historically.

In order to explore the ramifications of this concept, the following exposition will focus particularly on four central dimensions. First, it will discuss the varied meanings of the adjective "modern" as references to a historic period and an ever-changing present. Second, the text will analyze the term "modernization" as a description of the process of becoming modern, since it served as a label for political efforts to transform a "backward society," for instance in trying to turn peasants into Frenchmen.[9] Third, it will scrutinize the cultural style of "modernism" as an innovative claim of competing artistic movements that agreed only on the rejection of tradition while promoting a broad range of differing avant-garde forms. Fourth, it will explore the general notion of "modernity" as an explicit vision of the future that has served as a projection screen for a whole host of rivaling images of a better life. The multiple connotations of these closely related linguistic constructs offer important clues to the twentieth-century travails of the age-old search for progress.

Confronted with modernity's rapid innovations, Europeans experienced the dynamism of these transformations as a series of exhilarating and unsettling accelerations of changes in their daily lives. On the one hand scientific discoveries and technological breakthroughs such as the automobile and the airplane brought a proud sense of excitement, because they opened up surprising possibilities of speed and power that overcame barriers that had limited human mobility for centuries. On the other hand, such advances as the assembly line and area bombing also inspired fears because they permitted a shocking degree of economic exploitation and mass killing during warfare. Producing continual upheavals with an uncertain outcome, this unstoppable quest for progress combined intoxicating possibilities with appalling threats—creating a novel sense of turbulence that characterized twentieth-century lives.[10] Since Europeans considered themselves as the epitome of progress, the following pages will endeavor to address the multiple challenges of modernity as a frantic search for political solutions that might master its relentless drive.[11]

THE DYNAMISM OF EUROPE

By 1900, thinkers like Max Weber had already begun to wonder about the sources of Europe's exceptional dynamism, while fearing that this force might someday turn destructive. Contemporaries advanced all sorts of contradictory justifications, ranging from Christianity to racial superiority, and later scholars explained the "great divergence" in economic development with factors such as commercialization, market competition, colonial exploitation, institutional culture, and state intervention. Although other civilizations, notably in Asia, had also achieved a high level of prosperity and cultural sophistication, something happened in Europe by the end of the eighteenth century that made it possible for its nations to dominate most of the globe.[12] The African observer Cheikh Hamidou Kane marveled at the ambiguity of this "de- and constructive, violent, abhorrent and attractive power" that could kill and heal at the same time.[13] Without falling into the normative trap of Eurocentrism, the explanatory challenge remains: What made the modern Europeans so different that they were able to control the rest of the world?

One important reason was the spread of a rational outlook that produced scientific discoveries and technological innovations. No doubt, without the preservation of learning by the Church or without the transmission of knowledge from the Arab world, the "scientific revolution" would not have been possible. But the spirit of empirical inquiry emancipated itself from the authority of the classical texts and dictates of the Christian religion so as to venture beyond. While building on the reception of information from other high cultures, European thinkers developed their insights further in a series of remarkable breakthroughs that transformed their understanding of the world. The astounding burst of technical inventions from the eighteenth century onward provided a whole new range of machines, notably the steam engine, to conquer nature, improve production, and speed transport as well as communication. Ultimately this process was sustained in institutional form by the European university, which in mid-nineteenth century adopted the "research imperative" as an ethic leading to ever further discovery.[14]

Another significant cause was the emergence of capitalism and industry, which produced an unprecedented accumulation of wealth. Other civilizations like the Chinese also had extensive trading networks, but economic development in Europe eventually exceeded such models by inspiring a capitalist spirit determined to acquire ever greater profit. In a continent blessed only with modest natural resources of iron and coal, this attitude propelled entrepreneurs in search of raw materials and markets beyond their regions and around the globe, and made them create organizational forms such as the joint-stock company and the stock exchange to raise capital. Coupled with technical inventions, their quest sparked what is known as "the industrial revolution," by mechanizing textile production, digging vast underground coal mines, expanding iron foundries into steel factories, and developing steamships as well as railroads. Aided by a combination of state support and laissez-faire liberalism, the rise of capitalist industry not only facilitated the mass production of goods but also provided the material basis for European ascendancy.[15]

An important societal dimension of difference was the development of individualism and the increase in social mobility. The discovery of the "self" during the Enlightenment loosened the collective bonds of estate or corporation and endowed the individual with responsibility for the conduct of his or her own life. Unlike in African societies where tribal loyalties remained strong or in India where one's place was fixed in a caste system, traditional forms of deference weakened sufficiently in Europe to allow persons to think of making their fortune by their own exertions—thereby creating an increasing dynamic of social mobility. The hope of advancing through hard work, celebrated in Samuel Smiles' bestseller *Self-Help* of 1859, motivated countless individuals to strive to better themselves, thereby creating much energy. The search for greater opportunity also led to increasing migrations, both from the countryside to the expanding cities and across the Atlantic toward the New World. The growing restlessness of Europeans was an important psychological motivation for their dynamism.[16]

The incremental emergence of the rule of law, which eventually produced a conception of fundamental human rights, was a final, and often forgotten, factor. Even absolutist monarchs like the Prussian king Frederic the Great figured out that the advancement of commerce and maintenance of religious peace required the sanctity of contracts, the security of property, and binding legal rules of tolerance. In a series of contests between rulers and ruled, punctuated by the French and subsequent continental revolutions, subjects won a number of civic rights, protecting them from the depredations of the state. Freedom of speech led to the emergence of a public sphere, while freedom to assemble facilitated the formation of a pluralistic civil society. Enshrined in constitutions, these hard-won civil rights permitted first the middle class and eventually even the proletariat to participate in political decisions. Though the social, racial, and sexual boundaries of such citizenship remained contested, most European men no longer lived under arbitrary rule and felt secure enough by 1900 to involve themselves in public affairs.[17]

These preconditions led to the development of a novel set of political arrangements, called the nation-state, which also profoundly differed from those of the rest of the world. While Eastern Europe was still dominated by the Russian, Habsburg, and Ottoman empires, composed of different ethnicities and religions, in the wake of the French Revolution the western monarchies transformed themselves into new, more homogeneous polities, claiming to consist of a single nation. This national ideal rested on a shared language, a similar past, and a common citizenship that transcended all prior internal distinctions by creating a single body politic based on firm control of a territory, with one constitution, set of laws, coinage, and internal market, facilitating growth and trade. This imagined community proved so attractive to Italian and German intellectuals that they attempted to unify their fragmented principalities into one newly created nation-state as well.[18] By mobilizing its citizens, this new political organization grew not only more powerful than traditional empires but also proved capable of acquiring colonies overseas.

The success of the nation-state model rested in part on its unprecedented capacity for resource mobilization through an efficient bureaucracy and a universal system of taxation. In contrast to the prerevolutionary sale of offices or the Ottoman corruption by *bakshish*, the administrative corps of the nation-state was supposed to be competent and impartial, because it received a state salary and pension privileges. Offices were to be filled on the basis of certified university training in law or other disciplines instead of being awarded as a result of family connections or political patronage. Moreover, taxes would no longer be arbitrarily assessed but based on objective criteria, making the collection of revenue so reliable and transparent that governments could plan ahead. In return, citizens would be guaranteed domestic peace and equality before the law. Though not always living up to the ideal, the bureaucratization of administration proved more efficient and predictable than earlier practices, making it possible for the nation-state to expand its services into ever new domains.[19]

A second pillar of the European nation-state was a reformed military that allowed it to project an unprecedented amount of force against its enemies within or without. In contrast to the costly mercenaries of the ancien régime, the revolutionary concept of citizens in arms rested on the obligation of universal male military service. In case of attack from the outside, it allowed the creation of mass armies at a limited cost and provided the state with an opportunity to indoctrinate its recruits in their national duties. At the same time technical inventions such as the repeating rifle, machine gun, hand grenade, and heavy artillery made it possible for European soldiers to kill a much greater number of foes than with muskets and bayonets. Similarly the emergence of the gunboat, battleship, and submarine made naval warfare more lethal and permitted attacks on overseas targets, far from their home base. Finally, the meticulous logistical planning by general staffs maximized the efficiency of troop movements. Taken together, these traits were the foundation of European military superiority.[20]

The international order, dominated by these European states, consisted of an informal "nonsystem" that left nations free to compete against one another. Since previous attempts at hegemony, most recently by Napoleon, had been defeated, the continent remained fragmented into several dozen independent states. Chief among them were the five great powers who ruled their neighbors in a "pentarchy" that remained flexible enough to have dynamic newcomers like Prussia/Germany replace old declining members like Spain. The British called this system "balance of power," since they carefully watched that no continental state would become powerful enough to challenge their empire. Hence German chancellor Otto von Bismarck always wanted to be allied to two other states out of the five in order to remain secure. Conflicts among smaller countries or the big powers were resolved by international congresses or diplomatic negotiations according to the principle of compensating one state for the gains of another.[21] The system had but one fundamental flaw—its readjustment required war.

Though endowing the leading European states with unparalleled power, these dynamic developments also created enormous tensions that threatened to erupt at any moment. Perceptive critics who were troubled by a sense of impending crisis pointed to a multitude of unresolved conflicts. In the process of dividing up the globe, colonizing claims often clashed with each other as in the Sudan, while indigenous populations as in India tried to rise up against the foreigners. At home, industrialists and landowners who benefited from exploiting labor engaged in fierce class warfare with the proletariat, which was organizing into trade unions and socialist parties. In public opinion, the yellow press fostered nationalist hatred that deprecated other countries, while agitators fanned ugly racial prejudice. In the eastern empires national liberation movements tried to escape the center's domination by clamoring for self-determination.[22] At the turn of the century Europe was therefore a rapidly developing continent with enormous power, but also a society rent by deep fissures that would eventually tear its countries apart.

AMBIVALENCES OF PROGRESS

While building on previous works, this book presents a distinctive interpretation of twentieth-century European history, focused on the fundamental ambivalence of modernity. The story line of ineluctable progress, prevalent in Western Civilization textbooks, fails to do justice to the immense suffering of the world wars. Mark Mazower's inverted counterpart of the *Dark Continent*, which focuses on the enormity of the crimes of ethnic cleansing and the Holocaust, does not sufficiently explain the dynamics of postwar recovery. Neither Eric Hobsbawm's leftist lament about the defeat of the communist project nor Richard Vinen's celebration of the advances of consumer society captures the full complexity of European developments. Tony Judt's social democratic account of postwar rehabilitation comes closer to the mark, but it lacks a vital discussion of the first half of the century.[23] Stimulating in their different ways, these accounts fail to offer a comprehensive and balanced framework for discussing the disasters and the achievements of Europe during the past century.

This reflection differs from the existing literature therefore in several important ways. In contrast to other authors who start earlier or later, this book begins with the intensification of modernization that produced the apogee of European imperialist power in 1900. Instead of fading out with the youth rebellion of 1968 or the peaceful revolution in 1989, it takes the last quarter of the twentieth century seriously as an epoch with a distinctive character that needs explaining in order to provide perspective on the perplexing challenges of the present. Whereas many culturalist portrayals privilege impressions and feelings, this presentation retains a focus on politics, international affairs, and wars, while expanding the causal discussion to economic dynamics, social changes, and cultural currents. The following pages also reflect a discursive understanding of the past by framing its arguments in reference to competing views of major issues. Finally, instead of just offering a detailed narrative, this book sets out to present a consistent interpretation by exploring the struggle between competing conceptions of modernity.[24]

In order to capture the complexity of the European past, the subsequent reflection will go beyond essentialist definitions and explore constructivist and relational approaches. On the one hand it interprets the continent's dynamism as an intensive space of communication and shared experience, stemming from its ancient, Christian, Renaissance, and Enlightenment roots. On the other, it approaches Europe as a discursive construct of inside commentators and outside observers, since its center, frontiers, and values have continued to shift.[25] Attempting to avoid the usual West European bias, this synthesis gives more space to developments in Central and Eastern Europe and places the continent in a global context in order to trace its imprint upon the world as well as the world's impact upon it. In order to discern common patterns beyond the still-powerful nation-states, it also focuses on a series of major crosscutting issues such as depression or decolonization and concentrates on a handful of leading countries, while turning to smaller states at special flash points that illuminate important transnational developments. Because of the lack of a common polity before the European Union, this reflection does not pretend to present a single story of Europeanization but rather proceeds in terms of plural yet intersecting histories.[26]

Instead of looking at Europe primarily through the lens of painful memory, this account also stresses the continent's lively present. Tourists tend to be attracted by the romance of ancient cathedrals, towering castles, and splendid patrician houses of the old town centers with their cobblestoned streets. More perceptive visitors also see the many scars of war such as gaps from bombing, bullet holes in walls, military cemeteries, and memorials to the victims of bloody battles.[27] But this book argues that the continent is not just a museum, since life goes on in gleaming modern cities with elegant shopping districts, connected by high-speed rail and crisscrossed by efficient mass transit, full of well-dressed people that seem to be quite oblivious of the past. In recent years immigration has brought different colors to the faces in the crowd—head scarves and burkas mingle with miniskirts and jeans, while mosques are starting to compete with churches. This presentation therefore explores the tension between a problematic past and a promising present in order to decode the particular version of liberal modernity that is European.[28]

Such an approach raises new questions about the hopes unleashed by the drive for modernization as well as the resistance to it and the conflict between its competing ideological versions which dominated the entire twentieth century. Why did the promise of progress capture so many leaders, businessmen, professionals, and workers by suggesting a path to a better future? These advocates of change had to vanquish a whole host of defenders of tradition who rejected innovation in order to preserve their established order and lifestyle. What were the pressures that fragmented the project of advancement into liberal, communist, and fascist ideologies, each promoting a different blueprint of the future? The conflicts between these programs enhanced the malignant sides of the process, causing untold new forms of suffering in the war of annihilation and Holocaust. How did the ravaged continent reemerge out of the rubble to recover a chastened sense of modernity? By analyzing the manner in which the Europeans used the potential of progress, this book encourages a more critical understanding of the chances and dangers posed by this quest.[29]

Focusing on the ambivalences of modernity makes some well-known events appear in a new light and brings other, more neglected developments into sharper relief. It suggests that the first quarter of the twentieth century was dominated by an optimistic faith in progress due to the visible improvement of middle-class lives by science, prosperity, and peace. The deadliness of industrial warfare therefore came as an enormous shock that seemed to prove the critics of modernity right, because it inflicted immense suffering in the trenches and at the home front. Undaunted, leading politicians nonetheless proposed several competing ways out of this predicament. The liberal, communist, and fascist visions of modernization promised to resume progress, if only their prescriptions were followed. Though the transition to peace proved difficult, by the mid-1920s it seemed that conditions were improving sufficiently for hope to return. Moreover, intellectuals experimented with cultural modernism, leaving the restraints of tradition behind. Reemerging from the trauma of World War I, Europe appeared poised on the brink of additional advancement.

Such a perspective also shows the dangerous potential of modernity that brought Europe close to self-destruction during the second quarter of the twentieth century. Reversing the trajectory of development, the Great Depression sowed deep doubt about the survival of democracy. The stunning success of Stalinist modernization in the Soviet Union attracted many intellectuals from the West who praised the Soviet model of radical egalitarianism as path to the future. Other critics of democracy and communism turned to the organic modernity of the Nazis, which promised to reconcile social order with technical advancement in the people's community. The murderousness of the Second World War far surpassed the carnage of its predecessor, while the social-engineering projects of communist class warfare and Nazi ethnic cleansing as well as Hitler's Holocaust were expressions of a modernity run amuck. As a result of the intensity of the fighting, most of Europe looked like moonscape, with its dazed inhabitants struggling for mere survival. Dictatorial social engineering therefore wreaked enormous destruction.

This focus also reveals that the Old Continent did not remain prostrate but reemerged out of the ashes by embracing a conservative version of modernization in the third quarter of the century. Aided by the United States, the western part seized the chance to stabilize democracy through the welfare state, while the eastern half faced Sovietization. The resulting Cold War crises were fortunately contained by the fear of nuclear annihilation, while the loss of the colonies rid Europe of its imperial baggage. The economic integration of Western Europe showed that the lessons of nationalist hostility had been learned, while the Eastern version remained under dictatorial Russian control. In contrast to the interwar period, most Europeans accepted modernity after the Second World War, because it brought them noticeable benefits by raising living standards and improving consumption and entertainment. On both sides of the Iron Curtain politicians were convinced that they were able to realize the benign potential of progress by planning social reforms. Once again, modernization became the watchword of peaceful coexistence between competing blueprints of the East and West.

This approach finally indicates that an unforeseen cultural revolt against modernity and the transition to postindustrial society shook the recovered confidence in progress in the last quarter of the century. The youth rebellion, new social movements, and postmodern criticism rejected the rationalist synthesis of classical modernism. At the same time the economic transformation in the wake of globalization undercut the social underpinnings of social democratic planning. Facilitated by the end of the Cold War, the "peaceful revolution" of 1989 overthrew communism and thereby left only democratic modernization as model for the transformation of Eastern Europe. But new global challenges of economic competitiveness, "poverty migration," and international terrorism quickly ended the feeling of triumphalism. Around 2000 Europe faced the task of defending its own version of welfare capitalism against the hegemony of the American model and the rising Asian competitors. By highlighting the hopes and disappointments of this quest for progress, this perspective provides a fresh reading of the continental travails of the twentieth century.

Though interests are shifting toward other regions of the globe, the European case remains important because it represents a telling example of the failures and successes in confronting modernization. The rise, fall, and rebirth of the Old Continent in the twentieth century presents a highly dramatic story, driven by exceptional individuals, full of surprising twists and turns of fate. On the one hand it can be read as a cautionary tale of the terrible consequences of social engineering in Stalinist Russia and Nazi Germany, which left a trail of suffering and death on a scale that is hard to imagine. On the other hand it also offers an encouraging narrative, because it demonstrates that societies close to self-destruction can recover by learning the lessons of a murderous past and cooperating for a better future.[30] Underlining the dangers of self-destructive warfare and exploitative capitalism, the European experience finally emphasizes the importance of safeguarding the stability of democracy through peaceful cooperation and an enabling welfare state. The key lesson of a century of turmoil is therefore the need to master the dynamism of modernity in order to realize its benign potential.

Part I

PROMISE OF PROGRESS, 1900–1929

Chapter I

GLOBAL DOMINATION

South African diamond mine, 1911. *Source*: Library of Congress.

Queen Victoria's diamond jubilee, marking the sixtieth anniversary of her accession to the throne, was the symbolic climax of European imperialism. Suggested by Colonial Secretary Joseph Chamberlain, the celebration on June 22, 1897, was a splendid "Festival of the British Empire," attended by eleven prime ministers from the self-governing dominions. Barely visible in the flickering images of a film taken at the time, all of London was decked out with flags, garlands, and curious crowds, held back by soldiers in tall fur hats. Military units from all over the empire paraded on foot or on horseback through the city streets in colorful uniforms, including Canadians in red serge and Indian regiments in native garb. Led by the octogenarian queen in a horse-drawn carriage, the procession stopped in front of St. Paul's Cathedral for an open-air service. Local celebrations in Britain and the colonies marked the day with speeches and fireworks. The diamond jubilee displayed the military might of the empire and the affection of its many subjects for their aging monarch.[1]

Contemporary propagandists and later commentators never tired of touting the benefits of empire for the colonizers as well as the colonized. Writers like H. Rider Haggard penned exciting stories such as the adventures of Allan Quartermain, which were set in Africa and became the model for the Indiana Jones movies. Journalists such as a young Winston Churchill vividly described rousing colonial victories against superior numbers of dervishes without any qualms about the ethics of their slaughter. A century later the jihadist chaos has once again drawn attention to some of the advantages of imperial order when compared to the disruption caused by clashes between religions or nation-states. British historian Niall Ferguson has argued therefore that "the Empire enhanced global welfare" as an early form of "Anglobalization" by spreading liberal capitalism, the English language, parliamentary democracy, and enlightenment in schools and universities. Pointing to the benign impact of empire, he concluded that "the imperial legacy has shaped the modern world so profoundly that we almost take it for granted."[2]

Over the century mounting criticism, however, turned imperialism into one of the most hated terms in the political vocabulary.

Novelists such as Joseph Conrad portrayed European exploitation and racism in compelling stories like his novella *Heart of Darkness*. Liberals such as John A. Hobson attacked colonialism for having "its sources in the selfish interests of certain industrial, financial and professional classes, seeking private advantages out of a policy of imperial expansion." During World War I the revolutionary Vladimir I. Lenin claimed that "the economic quintessence of imperialism is monopoly capitalism" in order to argue that the chain of imperialist exploitation could be broken at its weakest link, his native Russia. Eager to have a theoretical justification for overthrowing European rule, many anticolonial intellectuals embraced this critique of exploitation in their national liberation struggles. Inspired by resentment of America's Cold War support for Third World dictatorships, much postcolonial scholarship continues to excoriate the nefarious consequences of imperialist racism and white oppression.[3]

The intensity and longevity of the normative debate about imperialism underlines the centrality of empire in modern European history. For centuries, the quest for resource-rich overseas possessions dominated the politics of western states, while the eastern monarchies similarly sought to acquire adjacent territories. Much of the raw material used by Europe's industries came from the colonies, while finished products were exported to the captive colonial markets. Many European attitudes reflected a sense of superiority over foreign "natives," while precious objects of imperial culture graced the drawing rooms of the European elite. As a result of this unequal interaction, empire was omnipresent in the metropolitan countries. At the same time, non-Europeans encountered whites first in the guise of imperial explorers, traders, missionaries, officials, or officers. Their understanding of and feelings about Europeans were therefore profoundly shaped by their experiences with imperial control and economic exploitation.[4] At the turn of the twentieth century imperialism characterized not only Europe's domination over the world but also the world's reaction to Europe.

Both as a cause and as a result, modernization was deeply involved in the imperial project, testifying to the ambivalence of its dynamism. On the one hand, European military superiority over indigenous peoples rested on the technological advances in weapons and organization that modernity offered. The restlessness that propelled exploration, the greed that motivated risk taking, the individualism that encouraged emigration, and the rule of law that made contracts enforceable were fundamentally modern. On the other hand, the imperial imprint on colonized societies was profound, spreading an exploitative form of modernization by force and persuasion around the entire globe. By creating plantations, trading houses, government offices, and military barracks as well as establishing schools, hospitals, and churches imperialists disrupted traditional patterns of life. While imperial possession reinforced the European sense of arrogance and confidence in progress, it imposed a perplexing mixture of oppression and amelioration on the colonized. It is therefore essential to recognize the deeply problematic connection between empire and modernity.[5]

CAUSES OF EXPANSION

European overseas expansion had begun in the fifteenth century with daring Portuguese and Spanish explorers like Vasco da Gama, later joined by Dutch, British, and French seafarers. This initial wave of colonialism was by and large coastal and commercial, driven by private concessions such as the Dutch East India Company. It concentrated on extracting precious metals such as silver, which were getting scarce in Europe, or on collecting spices, tea, and coffee that could not grow there. Much of the trade was also in involuntary labor, reduced to slavery, for plantation agriculture in the Caribbean or the Americas. In more hospitable regions of North America and Australia, where the climate was moderate and there were no diseases like malaria, settlement colonies also developed; these attracted religious dissidents, land-hungry peasants, and criminal outcasts.[6] This older colonialism established vast transoceanic empires, but with the rise of free trade and the abolition of the slave trade around the first third of the nineteenth century, its energy was largely spent.

From the 1870s on a new imperialism developed, based on the dynamics of European modernization, that built on earlier trends but intensified penetration and control. The term "imperialism" originally criticized Napoleon III's adventurous policy of building the Suez Canal, but once the shorter shipping route to India had turned into a "life-line of the British empire," the word assumed a more positive ring. In the ensuing "scramble for Africa" that divided the continent among European powers according to the boundaries laid out in the 1884–85 Congo Conference in Berlin, the new imperialism acquired a different character from the older pattern of colonialism. Though still propelled by scientists, missionaries, and traders, it was quickly taken over by governments and involved claiming entire territories, penetrating the back country beyond the coastlines, and establishing military security as well as bureaucratic control. This more invasive form of domination allowed plantation owners, mining companies, financial investors, and shipping lines to pursue their profits within a framework of European hegemony.[7]

In the 1920s the American political scientist Parker T. Moon tried to define the essence of this "new imperialism" by highlighting its political aspects. He considered it "an extension of political or economic control by one state over another, possessing a different culture or race, supported by a body of ideas, justifying the process." Instead of focusing on economic exploitation, this classic definition stressed a direct or indirect form of control, a difference in culture and race as well as a rhetoric promoting expansion. A more recent definition paints a more complicated picture: "Empires were characterized by huge size, ethnic diversity, a multitude of composite territories as a result of historic cession or conquest, by specific forms of supranational rule, by shifting boundaries and fluid border-lands and finally by a complex of interactive of relationships between imperial centers and peripheries." This description has the advantage of encompassing not only the maritime empires like that of Great Britain but also the contiguous land-based empires like those of Russia, Turkey, and Austria-Hungary.[8]

The renewal of European overseas expansion and territorial conquest was propelled by several complementary aspects of modernity. One often-overlooked motive was scientific curiosity in exploring the geography of unknown territories, such as David Livingstone's attempt to discover the sources of the Nile, and to map their resources so as to exploit them. Engineers were also excited about the challenges of building harbors, bridges, railroads, telegraph lines, or canals in difficult environments in order to tame an unruly nature so that Europeans could penetrate into and profit from their new possessions.[9] Moreover, a whole new scholarly discipline of ethnology developed in order to study representatives of presumably more primitive cultures, describing their strange customs and collecting their religious or secular artifacts. When these anthropologists brought some of the products and sometimes even peoples of exotic lands back home, they exhibited them in newly founded ethnology museums so that European visitors could marvel at their strange customs— and feel superior to them.[10]

Economic interests undoubtedly played a major role as well in propelling adventurers into foreign continents in the hope of making a fortune abroad. With the advent of mass production, industries such as textiles looked for new markets beyond Europe, since the meager wages paid to their own workers kept consumption low. The rise of new technologies such as electricity and automobiles also required raw materials that were not available in the Old Continent such as copper for wiring or rubber for tires. Moreover, the spread of prosperity expanded the available capital of speculators intent on making investments where the return might be double or triple that of the yield at home, even if the ventures were much riskier. These incentives motivated businessmen to establish plantations or mines supervised by whites who ruthlessly exploited native labor in order to turn a profit. To the shopper in the European metropolis, some goods like coffee, tea, bananas, oranges, and chocolate were offered in stores as "colonial wares."[11] Since creating the necessary infrastructure was expensive, most colonies operated at public cost for the sake of private gain.

Somewhat less clear are the social dynamics, connected to the rise of the masses, that lay behind the drive toward empire. One element was the fear of overpopulation that resulted from rapid increases in the last decades of the nineteenth century, dramatized by Hans Grimm's novel *People without Space* (1926). However, hopes for bettering one's life through emigration to the colonies were often disappointed owing to the hardships involved in such a move, so that the expectation of Europe's governments to clear their domestic slums through imperialism rarely panned out. Another aspect was the fierce propaganda of pressure groups such as the colonial leagues or navy leagues financed by commercial interests such as shipping lines or importers of colonial goods. With posters, pamphlets, and lectures these associations painted a glowing picture of individual opportunity in the empire, ready for the taking.[12] Finally, some European elites also sought to deflect the increasing pressures for social reform and political participation through imperial expansion, thereby making a lowly proletarian feel superior to a foreign prince.

The cultural impetus of the new imperialism was the paradoxical project of a "civilizing mission" or *mission civilisatrice*, understood as a right and duty to elevate lesser peoples to the European standard. Originally, this motive comprised the missionary aim to bring the blessings of Christianity to heathens so that they might also have a chance for salvation. In its secular guise developed during the Enlightenment, the concept also involved the propagation of a rational way of life, which Europeans regarded as the apex of human development. In his poem titled "The White Man's Burden," the British writer Rudyard Kipling provided the classic rationale for this effort by enjoining youths "to serve your captives' need." But calling the colonial peoples "half-devil and half-child" betrayed a deepseated arrogance and racism that contradicted the altruistic spirit of lifting so-called natives "out of bondage" by spreading knowledge, health, and civility. While claiming to disseminate a humanitarian vision of modernity, the civilizing ethos went only so far as to make the colonized function in the imperial system, denying them full equality.[13]

A final cluster of causes of the new imperialism involved the rivalry between the great powers, which incited countries to compete with each other in conquering and exploiting colonies lest they be left behind. A social Darwinist outlook saw international politics as a struggle for survival, forcing governments to match any presumptive gain in power or territory of a neighbor with similar increases of their own. Once an empire had been established, there was also the strategic necessity of geopolitical defense of one's possessions, demanding coaling stations for naval resupply or the annexation of further lands to improve the military position of a frontier. In 1890 the American admiral Alfred T. Mahan formulated this credo of "sea power" persuasively, arguing that empires like the British rose to dominance due to their superiority on the oceans, thereby propagating a "navalism" that dovetailed well with imperialism. Such views coalesced into a sense of national vitality, which argued in biological metaphors that the future belonged to young and growing as opposed to old and declining nations.[14]

The rise of the new imperialism in the last decades of the nineteenth century therefore resulted from the dynamism of European modernity, which propelled outward expansion. Many of the motives—such as scientific curiosity, capitalist greed, and mass politics—were driving forces of modernization. Also most of the tools of domination—such as steamers, railroads, telegraphs, and machine guns—were new technological inventions that made European countries more powerful, allowing their navies and armies to conquer new territories and bureaucracies to establish administrations to control them. Moreover, the humanitarian vision of "civilizing" the world was a modern European invention, intending to reshape the entire globe in its own "progressive" image. Taken together, these forces made the new imperialism a self-propelling process that proved so unstoppable as to overcome even the reluctance of continental traditionalists like Prince Otto von Bismarck, who had vowed "as long as I am imperial chancellor, we shall not pursue a policy of colonialism."[15] The result was the scramble that divided Africa and the rest of the not-yet-modernized globe.

PATTERNS OF DOMINATION

In hindsight it still seems baffling that a small number of Europeans managed to seize control over far more numerous peoples and vast territories by making use of the advantages of modernity. Usually the imperialists merely transformed the previous penetration of explorers, traders, or missionaries into political control by intervening in local conflicts. In India several tens of thousands of Englishmen managed to govern an entire subcontinent populated by tens of millions through a mixture of political alliances with powerful local rulers (Raj) and the occasional use of military force against their foes. In German East Africa a few thousand administrators and soldiers succeeded in subjecting a huge area, inhabited by several million tribesmen, by allying with members of previously defeated tribes. When temporary setbacks occurred, the metropole would provide additional resources or soldiers to increase the pressure. Once in power, Europeans relied on superior organization to establish peace between tribes, using economic incentives and symbolic rewards to motivate the colonized to accept their dominion.[16]

Another method was the ruthless use of military force, leading to the exceptional violence of colonial wars in which technology and organization compensated for strategic disadvantages. For instance, in the Battle of Omdurman on September 2, 1898, 8,000 British regulars, supported by 17,000 local auxiliaries, routed almost 50,000 dervishes to reestablish control over the upper reaches of the Nile. While General Sir Herbert Kitchener had powerful artillery, machine guns, and gunboats at his disposal, the caliph Abdullah's more numerous forces were equipped only with spears, sabers, and muzzle loaders. As a result about 10,000 of his men were killed, 13,000 more wounded but subsequently murdered, and another 5,000 taken prisoner. In contrast, the British suffered only 47 dead and 382 wounded in the fighting. Due to European superiority, the combat was "not a battle, but an execution." Reported by a young Winston Churchill, the smashing victory became a self-reinforcing legend of empire. Brutality against the inhabitants was therefore an essential part of establishing control with limited forces over larger numbers of natives.[17]

Another strategy was the opening of new possessions to trade beyond local exchanges by constructing an infrastructure so as to exploit colonial resources more efficiently. To allow steamships to dock, harbors such as San Juan in Puerto Rico were dredged, and quays, cranes, and customhouses were built to facilitate the transfer of bulk goods. At the same time, the interior was made accessible by converting paths into roads suitable for trucks or constructing rail-roads capable of carrying larger numbers of people and products greater distances. Trading posts would be established along such routes for supplying white settlers and selling mass-produced goods to local inhabitants. In the Congo plantations replaced subsistence agriculture in order to grow coffee or bananas in sufficient quantities to be profitably shipped. In South Africa various kinds of mines were dug in order to extract precious stones such as diamonds or metals such as copper or silver.[18] Offering a few aspects of the European lifestyle to some of the colonized, these innovations intensified the exploitation of resources and linked colonial production to world markets.

This imperial system relied on a rigid racial stratification of co-lonial society that clearly delineated the rulers and ruled. In prin-ciple, colonial society was divided into a white ruling class, an inter-mediary group of subaltern helpers, and finally a bottom rung of exploited local labor. The reality was, of course, often more complex, since a parallel local hierarchy existed that had to adapt to the new authority relationships by being fundamentally reshaped or gradu-ally dissolved. Crossovers between both realms also complicated the maintenance of distinctions, since some Europeans inevitably "went native" whereas sons of the local elite, once trained in European uni-versities, no longer wanted to play inferior roles. While some whites bonded to the landscape or established affection for local peoples, romanticized in memoirs like Karen von Blixen-Finecke's *Out of Africa*, the basic relationship between colonizers and colonized re-mained highly unequal.[19] Moreover, a complex set of customs, apart-heid laws, or the use of physical force saw to it that both worlds would generally remain separate.

Confident of bringing progress, Europeans superimposed their own institutions, manifested in colonial buildings that were a curi-ous mixture of their own and local styles. The center of an administra-tive capital such as Windhoek was usually the governor's palace, a gleaming white structure with verandas and gardens, suitable for administration as well as representation. Barracks to accommodate military or police forces sufficient to maintain order were also needed.

Since colonizers often fell ill, they had to build a hospital, staffed with white doctors and helped by black nurses. Then there were churches to minister to the colonizers and to the newly converted. European-style schools for the children of the new rulers also had to be erected, all the way from primary to secondary establishments. Finally, in especially salubrious areas. villas surrounded by greenery and staffed by numerous servants were constructed to house the whites. Bypassing the hubbub of native towns, these representative buildings of the European way of life created parallel settlements in which colonizers and colonized barely interacted.[20]

The degree of European control depended on both the pressure of imperial modernization and the level of development of the local culture. Where there was only tribal organization, the colonizers were able to take over completely, and attempts at rebellion were quickly crushed. Such a "complete dependence" characterized outright colonies like the Belgian Congo or Portuguese Angola. Where there were more developed local cultures, more complex religions, and stronger forms of political organization, European influence was more limited, allowing local structures to survive. Such "semiautonomous" regimes or protectorates existed in Egypt and Morocco, although they were formally part of the British and French empires respectively. Where the indigenous population had a long tradition of independence, considerable resources, and a high culture, these factors kept the colonizers from annexing the country, allowing imperialists only to establish coastal beachheads or exert political pressure. This loosest form of control in a "sphere of influence" was typical of China or Turkey.

European domination therefore rested on a complex mixture of imperialist power and local complicity. No doubt military force was important in the initial conquest and subsequent suppression of revolts, but it was not sufficient, because the colonies were too vast and the occupiers too few. In essence, the European generals, administrators, and planters inserted themselves into existing structures, replacing previous rulers or co-opting them into the new order, often leaving the lower levels of society largely intact. In doing so, the colonizers also used incentives such as distributing medals and titles or sharing some of the monetary gains in order to win cooperation. The establishment of military security, administrative control, and economic exploitation also required the use of local manpower in subaltern roles, which had to be trained in European procedures in order to function efficiently. The resulting colonial society was therefore a hybrid realm of exploitation and racial inequality, blending modernizing European influences with remaining indigenous traditions.

VISIONS OF EMPIRE

Beyond these structural similarities, the major European powers developed competing visions of empire, depending on their past, politics, and resources. Resting on sea power, the British Empire gathered the most extensive domains because it had begun in the seventeenth century. After salvaging control over Canada from the debacle of American independence, London managed to open up new settlement colonies in Australia and New Zealand. But the "jewel in the crown" was the Indian subcontinent owing to its vast wealth and large population, which provided the aristocracy opportunities for making fortunes. In order to safeguard imperial communication, Britain took over the Suez Canal of Egypt in the 1880s and defeated the Islamic Mahdi rebellion in the Sudan. In the scramble for Africa, London promoted a "Cape to Cairo" vision of a north-south axis of contiguous possessions, blocked only by the Portuguese, Belgians, and Germans. This paradoxical blend of economic exploitation, racial arrogance, and humanitarian rhetoric, while on the one hand abolishing the slave trade, was on the other hand quite successful at conquest and domination until running into territories already occupied by competitors.[21]

Combining personal profit with imperial ambitions, Cecil Rhodes was the quintessential British imperialist. Born in 1853 in Herefordshire into a vicar's family, he was sent to Natal in 1870 to improve his health. During later stints of study at Oxford University, he imbibed the ethos of empire. Though he succeeded as a fruit grower, his breakthrough came with the creation of the De Beers Mining Company, which managed to corner the diamond market with the help of the Rothschilds. As one of the wealthiest English businessmen in Africa, he became prime minister of the Cape Colony, where he promoted racist laws, pushing blacks off their land. Trying to expand British control over all of South Africa, he promoted the Boer Wars against the Dutch settlers in Transvaal, hastening their defeat. Blending business with politics, his British South Africa Company pushed north, opening up the Zambesi Basin and creating another colony named Rhodesia, after him. Ultimately Rhodes, wanting Britain to rule the entire world, funded scholarships to entice top American and German students to join his quest by studying at Oxford and presumably absorbing the same imperial ethos. When he died in 1902, he was both admired and reviled.[22]

The French were the chief rivals of the British, since their colonial ventures had a similarly long history and geographical scope. Although they lost their North American possessions in the Seven Years War to the British and sold Louisiana to the United States, they managed to hang on to the West Indies. But the contradiction between the Enlightenment conception of human rights and the profitable practice of slavery in the sugarcane fields came to a head under Toussaint L'Ouverture's revolt in Haiti. After this setback the French concentrated their efforts on "Mediterranean proximity," seizing Algeria in 1830. During the Third Republic, France conquered a host of other North and Central African territories and established itself in Madagascar and Indochina. In contrast to the British, who migrated in substantial numbers to several parts of their empire, large numbers of Frenchmen settled only in Algeria, leaving the other colonies and protectorates to be ruled by a thin layer of administrators and soldiers. Colonial apologists like Jules Ferry believed in the *mission civilisatrice*, spreading French language and culture regardless of skin color.[23] This promise attracted some indigenous intellectuals, even if its practice fell far short.

The lure of empire was so powerful that other newcomers also tried to accumulate their own overseas possessions. While declining countries such as Spain and Portugal sought to defend the remnants of once-extensive empires, rising nations like Imperial Germany attempted to grab whatever was left. Only unified in 1871, the Germans seized East and West Africa, Togo, Cameroon, and some smaller possessions in the Pacific. Since in Africa the Maji Maji and Herero engaged them in bloody wars, Berlin shifted its attention to the Balkans and the building of the railroad to Baghdad, seeking a sphere of influence in Turkey.[24] Though the new Italian state failed in its attempt to conquer Abyssinia, it managed to seize Libya in 1911, seeking to recapture the glory of the Roman Empire. Pushing beyond its continental conquests according to "manifest destiny," the United States also ventured into the Caribbean and the Philippines. Finally, rapidly modernizing Japan, having barely escaped outside control, now tried to establish its own Asian empire in Korea and Manchuria, defeating Russia in 1905.

The great landed empires of Eastern Europe were based on contiguous expansion but nevertheless showed many similarities to the overseas dominions. While the army played the central role and differences in religion and race between imperial and subjected peoples were often smaller, the structures of annexation, exploitation, and central control resembled the overseas pattern. The oldest and most vulnerable was the Ottoman Empire, also known as "the sick man of Europe," since it had begun to lose its possessions by 1900. In their heyday the Ottomans were an advanced military power, conquering Constantinople in 1453 and subjugating territories from the Balkans to the Maghreb across the Near East and North Africa. Though Islamic in religion, they were nevertheless tolerant to the subject peoples as long as these paid taxes and provided sons for the Sultan's elite fighting corps. By the nineteenth century, the Ottomans were increasingly threatened by Christian uprisings in the Balkans as well as by Arab insurrections. Hence in 1908 the Young Turk movement under Mustafa Kemal, called Atatürk, sought to modernize Istanbul in order to salvage the Turkish core.[25]

The even larger Russian Empire extended all the way from Warsaw in the West to Vladivostok in the East and from Finland in the North to the Caucasus Mountains in the South. The motives for expansion involved the usual mixture of economic interests in acquiring more resources, security questions of defending frontiers, and the weak organization of the neighboring territories. Since it was a land-based empire, the newly conquered regions were simply incorporated into mainland Russia, ruled autocratically by an all-powerful tsar, an imperial bureaucracy, and a huge army. The Russian ethnic core was inspired by an ideology of exceptionalism based on Greek Orthodox Christianity, claiming to represent the "Third Rome," which was Moscow. In practice, the empire was a weak giant because its population, recently liberated from serfdom, remained largely agrarian and its aristocracy was ambivalent about whether it would be better to follow European modernization or reject it for its subversive tendencies.[26] The middle class longed for greater participation in political decisions while an emerging intelligentsia attacked autocracy, orthodoxy, and hierarchy from within.

Often underestimated, the Habsburg Empire of Central Europe comprised a mixture of ethnic groups that lacked a clear majority. Its origin went back to the unification of the Austrian, Bohemian, and Hungarian crowns in 1526, which succeeded in fending off successive Ottoman onslaughts in the Balkans. During the Counter-Reformation the Catholic emperors ruthlessly suppressed Protestantism in their own lands and tried to defeat it in other German states in the Thirty Years War. Around 1900 the empire was held together by affection for its long-serving monarch, Emperor Francis Joseph, as well as by a multilingual army, a central bureaucracy, and a commercial middle class that cut across ethnic differences. Though the Austrian Habsburgs' compromise with independence-minded Hungarians in 1867 had managed to restructure the Dual Monarchy, the rise of German and Czech nationalism boded ill for its future. On the one hand Vienna became famous as the capital of *Jugendstil* and psychoanalysis, but on the other it was also a hotbed of anti-Semitism. In dealing with the Balkans, Austria-Hungary could not decide between defensive and aggressive policies.[27]

European domination was therefore not a common enterprise but rather a competitive undertaking, avoiding war only through international conferences that settled conflicting claims. In general, the western overseas empires were more modern (i.e., developed economically and liberal politically) and possessed a stronger middle class. However, as a legacy of slavery their imperial projects created a deep contradiction between their social Darwinist racism toward the colonized and the development of citizens' rights among their own populations. In contrast, the eastern landlocked empires were less industrialized and more autocratic, with most inhabitants still working on the land. Nonetheless, they, too, faced the need to modernize, which triggered a conflict between the claims of their own citizens to political participation and the demands for self-determination of the ethnic and religious groups subjected by them. While the edifice of empire still looked imposing at the turn of the century, the growth of anti-imperialist and nationalist independence movements would eventually bring it down.[28]

COLONIAL IMPACT

The impact of imperialism on the colonies was profoundly transformative, forcing a flawed form of modernization onto the reluctant subjects. Within a generation after the arrival of white colonizers the outward appearance of life changed profoundly, ranging all the way from the spread of Western clothing to the emergence of Christian symbols. The extent of the transformation varied, of course, with the level of development of the local culture and the degree of European power, triggering drastic changes in most of Africa while making a smaller impression on much of Asia, where resistance was stronger. Though some of the innovations were the result of formal compulsion by the new rulers, others developed through informal interactions between colonizers and colonized. The transformation usually began piecemeal in colonial centers but eventually spread to the entire territory, creating an unstable hybrid of old customs and new habits. Because the relationship was highly unequal, the results were also rather mixed, entailing both much brutal oppression and some humanitarian improvement.

The workplace was one problematic point of enforced modernity because it replaced traditional agriculture or crafts by toil in plantations or mines. Essential for the exploitation of these resources, male workers were usually conscripted by force, compelled to do backbreaking labor without the aid of machinery. Rather than following the rhythm of the sun or the seasons, they had to internalize Western concepts of time, with the clock or the siren determining the length of their workday. Moreover, they were forced to acquire European notions of labor discipline, working diligently until the assigned task was completed rather than taking breaks whenever they felt they needed them. For their efforts they were paid in kind or in money, barely sufficient for their survival. Whenever they slackened their labor or complained, they were brutally beaten by mostly white overseers who reinforced the racial hierarchy by doling out arbitrary punishment. In the colonies this general transition from traditional life to capitalist labor was aggravated through an even more ruthless exploitation of nature and people.[29]

The colonizer's home, where most of the women's work was done, was another place of unequal modernization. The elaborate colonial lifestyle required numerous servants to carry out the domestic tasks of cooking, cleaning, washing, gardening, and child care so as to afford the white mistresses a life of leisure. In order to function effectively, indigenous women quickly had to learn European middle-class virtues such as neatness, thrift, diligence, cleanliness, and punctuality. At the same time they needed to acquire enough knowledge of Western forms of clothing and food preparation so as to be able to fulfill their duties. While there was less physical abuse than in the fields, paternalism clearly kept servants in their place, and mistresses could be quite demanding and capricious. Moreover, sex was a continual problem since there were not enough white women to go around and domineering white males often impregnated local girls, creating a half-caste group of mulattoes caught between both races. But through social pressure white women quite effectively maintained their version of a color line in colonial society.[30]

The trading post was yet another modernizing space because it drew the local people into a monetary exchange system, albeit on rather unequal terms. Essential for supplying white settlers or engineers in the outback with their accustomed provisions, these outlets taught natives to replace traditional forms of trading goods with selling and buying for money. While in relatively developed economies local coins survived, in other places the currency of the colonizing country became the prime medium of exchange. The Western trader would offer his local customers basic implements such as metal pots and knives, seasonings such as salt, or pieces of cotton fabric as well as baubles for embellishment. In exchange he would acquire local products: cocoa beans, tea leaves, or whatever else could be sold in Europe as "colonial goods." Sometimes other intermediaries—Indians in South Africa, Chinese in much of Asia—would fulfill the Western trader's roles. But in general such trade was profoundly uneven, since indigenous people were at the mercy of the prices set by traders.[31]

The encounter with European culture in school was presumably more positive because it claimed to spread modern enlightenment among the ignorant locals. No doubt the initiation into reading, writing, and arithmetic had a liberating effect on illiterate African children, since it enabled them to access a world of learning and to meet whites on more equal terms. But much of the instruction took place in a foreign language, the tongue of the colonial teacher, especially in the higher grades. Moreover, the lessons generally celebrated the "mother country's" past and present achievements, disregarding the attainments of local culture and creating an artificial world of the *mère patrie*. At the same time, the often rigorous secularism of the teachers ridiculed traditional customs as superstition, destroying the old faith without putting anything comparable in its place. While the shift to written texts opened up realms of knowledge, it also weakened long-standing oral traditions. No wonder that colonial intellectuals often complained about being alienated from their own heritage without feeling fully at home in a Western world.[32]

The mission also purported to be a place of benign communication, since its intent was altruistic, bestowing the blessings of Christianity on heathens. At the risk of their own lives, missionaries of various denominations labored hard to break local superstitions like voodoo or animism and to replace them with the hope of salvation in the hereafter. More effective than their teaching were works of charity like Albert Schweitzer's hospital in Lambarene that combated local diseases and ministered to the poor to keep them from starvation. The baptism of converts was often a joyful act, since it initiated the new believers into a community of a more benign faith. But when

Christianity faced more highly developed religions such as Islam, Buddhism, or Confucianism, it had difficulty making inroads, since it offered little spirituality that these did not already possess.[33] Though codifying indigenous languages, missionizing was basically a condescending enterprise, presuming a superior religious insight. Moreover, the newly converted were often shocked to find out that the Europeans themselves hardly followed their Christian precepts.

The colonial office was a final instrument of bureaucratic modernization, designed to uphold European rule over a restless local population. In administrative bureaus, courts, police stations, and customhouses the colonizers had to deal with the colonized in order to assure the smooth functioning of their domain. If they wanted to survive within a white world, the colonized had to learn unfamiliar bureaucratic rules, foreign legal concepts, strange behavioral patterns, and novel economic regulations. Especially where there were only a few European administrators, the control of large territories and populations required the assistance of trained locals as lower officers who would be appointed as clerks, legal aides, policemen, and customs agents. In their work these subalterns increasingly realized that once they knew European procedures and laws, they could begin to use them for protecting their own interests.[34] But paradoxically in order to learn such ways, "Westernized oriental gentlemen" had to collaborate in upholding European domination and therefore found themselves between both cultural fronts.

The colonials' response to this exploitative modernization was therefore highly ambivalent, mirroring the contradictory nature of its mixed impact. Once the destabilizing impetus of colonization became clear, local elites rallied to defend their own traditions, sometimes in bloody uprisings, such as the Sepoy Mutiny of 1857, that were put down with great brutality. A more successful strategy was adaptation, a concerted effort to learn European ways so as to use them for the colonials' own purposes. It helped that liberal colonizers allowed sons of the local elite to attend British or French universities in order to acquire the technical skills and cultural sophistication needed for transforming their native lands upon their return.[35] In the more autocratic landed empires this process usually entailed complete assimilation to the ruling ethnicity, be it Turkish, Russian, German, or Hungarian. Both welcomed and rebuffed, the colonial intellectuals who were not content with inferior roles therefore resolved to use the very ideological appeals, organizational skills, and military techniques they learned from Europe in order to throw off colonial control.

CULTURE OF EMPIRE

Though this aspect is often overlooked, imperialism also had a considerable impact on the European countries, both speeding and hindering their own development. Some scholars argue that an "imperial culture," propagating the necessity of empire and extolling its benefits for all of society, formed in the last decades of the nineteenth century. Claiming that there was little explicit teaching of imperialism in the school curriculum, other historians have countered with the thesis of "absent-minded imperialists," which stresses that the impact of empire on the lives of average people in Europe was indeed minimal.[36] A closer look at the evidence suggests that both readings might be partially correct: A strongly committed minority of enthusiastic imperialists was directly involved in running the colonies, benefiting from them and therefore defending their importance. The passive majority with little such contact accepted the existence of empire as long as it did not become a major burden on them. Yet a small but growing band of critics also began to object to the financial costs and ethical transgressions of imperialism.

Among those susceptible to the lure of empire, European scientists who ventured abroad in search of new objects of discovery were one important group. A whole host of different disciplines was involved: Geographers mapped previously "unknown" territories, geologists explored mineral deposits, biologists catalogued new species of plants and animals, ethnologists observed customs of "primitive cultures," linguists transcribed local dialects, and medical doctors studied the causes of tropical diseases. While such research added non-European specialties to established pursuits, eventually these different subjects were combined in colonial institutes for teaching future imperialists. As Edward Said has correctly pointed out, this was a paternalistic gaze that reduced the strange "other" to an object of study. Moreover, it was the exotic difference that appealed to the general public in colonial exhibitions and newly opened ethnology museums. While many of the findings reinforced a sense of racial superiority, other research contributed to scientific discoveries that could benefit colonized peoples—making it possible, for instance, to fight tropical diseases.[37]

Businesspeople who profited from trade with the colonies were another influential set of advocates of imperialism. Some were the owners of shipping lines or railroads that carried goods and mail, thereby assuring communication between the home country and the colony. Others were the growers of spices, coffee, or fruit, as well as their retailers in Europe who depended on a steady supply of such colonial goods. Many companies sought precious minerals such as diamonds or raw materials such as copper to be refined and incorporated into countless products they sold to metropolitan shoppers. Moreover, manufacturers of mass-produced textiles and implements like pots needed the colonial markets in order to expand their production beyond what they could distribute at home.[38] Finally, even some ordinary people looked to the colonies either to make their fortune by working in imperial trade or to settle permanently abroad. Though liberal skeptics argued that these goals could be achieved more cheaply by free trade, imperialists insisted that it was necessary to have political control.

Government employees who could hope for advancement by serving abroad constituted another imperial pressure group. Navy and army officers especially looked forward to foreign adventures and counted on faster promotion than could be attained at home. In the colonies they could try out new gunboats or artillery on hapless subjects without observing the same restrictions applying to more civilized warfare in Europe. At the same time empire also offered ample opportunities for officials who might be stuck in middling ranks and could thereby leap ahead, lording it over the colonized with less-constrained authority. Sometimes these might be family misfits, sent overseas as punishment for a scandal to redeem themselves if no new shame attached itself to their name. No doubt in some postings there was the risk of disease and death, but a lavish lifestyle tended to compensate for such dangers. While scientific discovery and economic development contributed to modernizing Europe, the military and bureaucratic side of imperialism tended to reinforce conservative power structures.[39]

Those altruistic individuals who went to the colonies in order to help the indigenous people to improve their lives were a final group of pro-imperialists. Many missionaries, sent by various denominations, were motivated by a desire to bring the spiritual consolation of Christianity and to reform the morals of the local population. Similarly some doctors and nurses who staffed colonial hospitals also sought to alleviate pain and suffering among people who often lacked the scientific knowledge and the pharmaceutical means to combat disease. Some of the teachers who were willing to work in the imperial schools wanted not only to escape from the boredom of their continental lives but also to spread enlightenment among illiterate and superstitious locals. While these humanitarians also firmly believed in the superiority of European civilization, they were willing to undergo considerable privations in order to share its benefits. In contrast to the exploitative aspects of businessmen and administrators, these altruists gave imperialism a more humane face, blunting some of the criticism.[40]

Most of the Europeans who had little direct contact with empire were willing to tolerate it as long as it promised to bring more benefits than costs. In the metropoles, some inquisitive people might attend a scientific lecture, listen to an adventure story, or marvel at an exotic exhibition. Many more would buy colonial wares for daily consumption without a particular concern about their provenance. Others yet would hear political speeches celebrating new acquisitions or read imperial items in the newspaper with a sense that these colonies were interesting but far away. Or they might be asked in a church service to contribute to a missionary fund. On the whole, these slight contacts produced an awareness of a larger imperial scope beyond the nation-state but little willingness to make sacrifices for it. Europeans might be proud that their flag flew over possessions around the globe, like *la France d'outre mer*, but needed to be convinced by imperial enthusiasts that the whole enterprise was worth it. Even skeptical members of the "underclass" at home could feel themselves included as part of the "ruling class" in the colonies.[41]

Toward the turn of the century voices of criticism nonetheless grew stronger, thus calling the entire imperial project into question. These strictures were usually triggered by cases of economic speculation, instances of military brutality, or scandals due to administrative corruption. Free traders wondered whether commerce could not flourish without political possession. International commentators worried that confrontations between imperial powers, such as the encounter between Sir Herbert Kitchener and Major Jean-Baptiste Marchand in Fashoda in 1898, might lead to a European war. Spokesmen from the rising labor movement charged that the imperialist jingoism was distracting attention from the necessary reform of domestic problems. Moralists railed against debilitating vices such as opium, imported from the colonies. Sympathetic observers like Sir Roger Casement exposed the inhuman treatment of the natives in the Congo, leading to its being taken away from the Belgian king. Finally, colonial intellectuals also pointed out the glaring discrepancy between European professions of civility and practices of racist prejudice and economic exploitation. Increasingly, empire was acquiring a bad name.[42]

During its prime the "culture of empire" was nonetheless strong enough to deflect such attacks and to reinforce a popular imperialism that considered colonies the natural reward for European superiority. To counter the criticism, imperialist interests groups such as the navy leagues, army leagues, and colonial leagues as well as the missionary societies issued a stream of propaganda in posters, pamphlets, and speeches that defended the benefits of empire. It took a concerted effort to popularize the Congo and make the Belgians, except for the socialists, into proud imperialists.[43] At the same time the cultural establishment was pervaded by imperialist ideas, since children's authors spun adventure tales, playwrights used imperial settings, and journalists wrote captivating reportages. The rapid international spread of the Boy Scouts, founded in 1907 by General

Robert Baden-Powell, illustrates that the quasi-military training of boys for imperial tasks proved attractive everywhere. This diffusion of imperialist sentiment infected wide circles with a powerful blend of nationalism, militarism, and racism that would soon tear Europe itself apart.

EUROPEAN HEGEMONY

In retrospect it is difficult to recall the extent of the European domination of the world, because it has been shattered so completely that only a few traces remain. Yet any schoolchild who looked at a map in 1900 saw the globe colored in different hues, showing virtually all territories in Africa, Asia, and Australia under imperial control, with even China divided into spheres of influence. While British, French, German, Dutch, Belgian, and Italian children had to memorize the names and capitals of distant dependencies, the Portuguese and Spanish basked in memories of their earlier empires. In Istanbul, St. Petersburg, and Vienna pupils were instead required to list faraway provinces, peopled by different ethnic groups and engaging in strange religious practices.[44] The excitement of acquiring possessions was so strong that it even drew latecomers, notably the United States and Japan, into the race. The result was the establishment of a system of competing empires around the globe, centered on European states that were national and imperial at the same time.

The dynamic force that propelled this new imperialism by providing the motives, tools, and organization for expansion was European modernization. While scientific curiosity drove exploration, technological invention produced the steamships, telegraphs, and machine guns that allowed communication and control. Hope of profits motivated investment abroad, while the accumulation of capital offered the means to fund imperial ventures. Search for advancement motivated individuals to serve in the colonies or emigrate permanently, while legal codes established a framework guaranteeing white supremacy. The emergence of an efficient form of governmental organization, usually associated with the nation-state, was also crucial for the political implementation of imperial dreams. Powerful militaries

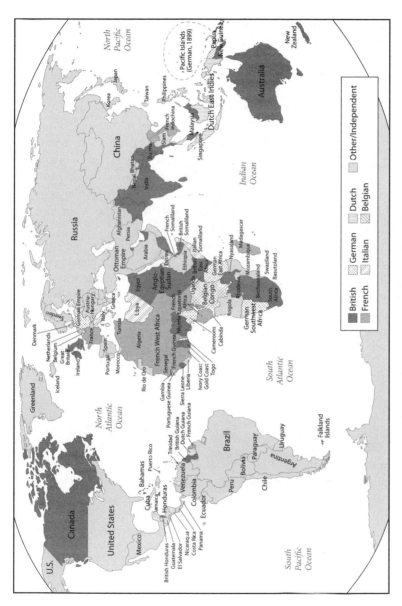

Map 1. The extent of European imperialism, 1900. Adapted from Maps.com.

using technical weapons systems were needed to conquer and hold territories, while efficient bureaucracy was necessary to administer the imperial domains. Though the symbolic trappings of empire remained neofeudal, the sources of metropolitan power were distinctly modern.[45]

The ensuing Europeanization of the world was therefore an unequal form of modernization, using a mixture of compulsion and incentive to transform the colonies. Scientific penetration, economic exploitation, colonist settlement, and political control all required the construction of an infrastructure of harbors and railroads, plantations, mines, and markets as well as administrative centers on a European model. Moreover, the exploitation of local labor also demanded a social and cultural transformation of the indigenous population, conveying the rudiments of literacy, implanting work discipline, spreading hygiene, and even preaching the blessings of Christianity. This multilevel onslaught of Western modernity destroyed traditional outlooks and behaviors, dissolved social customs and hierarchies, and profoundly unsettled the colonized peoples because it came in a violent and repressive guise that left them little choice but to comply. But some of the imported changes also offered access to European knowledge and culture, providing ideologies and techniques that frustrated colonial intellectuals would eventually use to challenge metropolitan control.[46]

Europe itself was also profoundly transformed by imperialism, which seemed a beneficial form of modernization by creating new wealth, institutions, and practices. London, Paris, and Berlin witnessed the building of new colonial offices, scientific institutions, missionary headquarters, shipping agencies, and land bureaus whose business was the connection to the empire. Zoos full of strange animals such as elephants, botanical gardens filled with exotic plants such as orchids, and ethnology museums containing strange artifacts offered Europeans glimpses of a foreign world without their actually having to go there. Exchanges traded stocks in colonial ventures, creating those great fortunes that manifested themselves in imposing Victorian mansions and town houses. Stores sold precious gems as well as colonial wares, allowing the display of imperial objects and forming new consumption habits such as the drinking of coffee, tea, and cocoa. In the busy streets, people of different skin color, practicing different religions, and speaking different languages jostled one another, and in hotels strange guests arrived wearing Indian saris or Chinese silks.[47] Faded snapshots in crumbling newspapers suggest that imperialism had penetrated European society to a considerable extent.

By its inherent brutality imperialism also fueled those destructive tensions of modernity that would eventually become its own undoing. In the international realm the race for colonies triggered a series of severe crises between the great powers, while in the colonies the resentment of subject peoples produced a chain of ugly colonial wars. Domestically, the celebration of empire fostered a climate of jingoism and racism that pitted European countries against each other and spread hatred between members of different ethnic or religious groups. In the land-based empires, efforts of the ruling nationalities to transform their multiethnic domains into more homogeneous nation-states inspired their subject groups to form national liberation movements that clamored for autonomy. In the overseas colonies the discrepancy between the professed civilizing values and repressive practices of the colonizers led intellectuals to agitate for independence from European control. Just when the edifice of imperialism looked most imposing, those cracks began to appear that would first make the land-based, and eventually also the overseas empires, collapse.[48]

Chapter 2

BREAKDOWN OF PEACE

Assassination of Francis Ferdinand, 1914. *Source*: bpk, Berlin / Art Resource, NY.

On June 28, 1914, Serbian terrorist Gavrilo Princip killed Austrian crown prince Francis Ferdinand and his wife Sophie von Hohenberg. Disregarding warnings, the royal couple was visiting the Bosnian capital of Sarajevo on the Serbian national holiday, commemorating the battle of Kosovo Polje against the Ottomans. As their open roadsters drove slowly through the crowded city streets, a bomb suddenly exploded behind them, wounding some attendants and spectators. After an angry speech at city hall, the crown prince insisted on visiting the victims at the hospital, but the driver mistook his instructions and followed the original route. When he tried to reverse course, the nineteen-year-old Serbian high school student Princip drew his pistol and shot Sophie in the abdomen and Francis Ferdinand in the throat before enraged bystanders could overpower him. Though the car sped back, medical attention came too late, since both had already lost too much blood.[1] The shock of this nationalist assassination of the Austrian crown prince triggered an international crisis that would escalate into World War I.

The terrorist attack by Serbian nationalists ruptured the ties of peace that had made modernity seem synonymous with international cooperation around the turn of the twentieth century. Believing in the dream of peaceful progress, optimists saw the world as developing steadily toward harmony and prosperity through mutual interchanges. Such a hopeful view pointed to the emergence of a network of connections between the major countries that would make war increasingly unthinkable and practically unsustainable. Many aspects of modernization such as scientific exchanges, mutual trade, individual migration, and international law were reinforcing bonds between nations. Not only pacifists like the British writer Norman Angell and the Austrian novelist Bertha von Suttner, both winners of the Nobel Peace Prize, believed that the frequent scholarly contacts, increasing volume of commerce, intensifying communication, and rising cross-border mobility were weaving a web of legal relations and reinforcing mutual understanding that would render military combat impossible.[2]

Skeptical observers, however, emphasized the negative forces of modernity that heightened conflict. Pessimists had been pointing out that some aspects of modernization such as strident nationalism, bureaucratic regimentation, rampant militarism, and great-power rivalry were increasing hostility and thereby making compromises more difficult. The yellow press was creating enemy stereotypes, political repression of independence movements was fueling resentment, and the many nations engaged in arms races on land and sea were raising international tensions by anticipating another war. As a result a darker, dystopian vision portrayed the international situation in terms of competition and struggle for survival in which only the fittest nation would prevail. Some theorists of international relations—Kurt Riezler, for instance, the adviser to the German chancellor—believed that the traditional pentarchy of nation-states was being reduced to only two or three "global powers" possessing enough resources, population, and land area to pursue world-political aims.[3] The Sarajevo assassination tipped the already precarious balance between the many rival nations toward the direction of war, precipitating Europe and the world into the bloodiest conflict of their entire history.

The "war guilt controversy" among politicians and historians who have argued about the responsibility for the outbreak of the war misunderstands this underlying reversal, which involved all the competing nations. In Article 231 of the Treaty of Versailles, the victorious Allies held Berlin responsible "for causing all the loss and damage" to which their citizens had "been subjected as a consequence of the war imposed upon them by the aggression of Germany and her allies." This legal justification for Germany's payment of reparations sparked a heated debate about culpability between revisionists and defenders of the treaty via the publication of diplomatic documents that sought either to exculpate or blame Germany. A generation later, Hitler's undeniable responsibility for unleashing World War II reinforced the impression of German guilt for the First World War, while critical postwar historians also charged Wilhelmine expansionism with being chiefly at fault.[4] Since such emotional involvement has prevented reaching a consensus about each country's precise amount of responsibility, the sterile arguments of the blame game remain trapped in a legalistic moralism.

The "raw modernity" of the July crisis rather suggests reversing the question, that is, shifting the focus from reasons for the outbreak of war to causes of the breakdown of peace. When tested by a severe confrontation in the summer of 1914, the ties of peaceful cooperation proved too weak to keep Europe out of war. The bellicose tendencies ultimately prevailed because the growing hostility between nations overwhelmed the cooperative outlook by legitimizing combat for the sake of aims that could only be reached by military force. A series of ever deeper international crises had created such a sense of antagonism between the Triple Alliance and the Entente as to make compromise seem like weakness. As a result, the leaders of the great powers made a series of disastrous decisions that escalated a local Balkan quarrel from a Serb-inspired assassination, via an Austrian punitive action, into a continental war between Germany, Russia, and France that eventually drew Britain, Turkey, and Japan into the conflict.[5] Instead of guaranteeing peaceful progress, the negative dynamics of modernity helped unleash a world war.

TIES OF PEACE

Inspired by Immanuel Kant, optimists who believed in the progress of civilization could point to an increase of internationalism that linked European countries ever more tightly around 1900. For instance, the building of railroad lines and the stringing of telegraph cables eased transnational travel and facilitated communication, binding major continental cities together to an unprecedented degree. At the same time the standardization of measurements through the adoption of the meter, kilogram, and the Celsius scale, as well as the reorganization of timekeeping through the introduction of Greenwich mean time, created a common denominator of civilization. Moreover, the creation of international organizations with local branches, such as the Red Cross, provided instruments for addressing specific problems across frontiers. Although encompassing the entire civilized world, these efforts were generally based in Europe, including the United States but excluding the colonies.[6] To hopeful observers it therefore seemed that modernization was making the continent grow together at a rapid pace.

One traditional link was the close relationship between European monarchs in the last decades of the nineteenth century. The continental aristocracy was used to serving different sovereigns, while the crowned heads tended to intermarry, thereby creating multiple cross-frontier ties. As the grandson of Queen Victoria, German emperor William II craved social recognition from his British relatives. When a new monarchy was to be established as in Greece, there was always a minor German prince ready to take up the crown. But the rise of nationalist politics articulated in a mass-circulation press increasingly forced the royal families to nationalize themselves by learning the local language and changing their original name, for example Saxe-Coburg-Gotha to Windsor. Family reunions and state visits provided ample opportunity not only for exchanging courtesies but also for discussing substantive political concerns, much to the chagrin of advisers. While the eastern courts were linked through a common interest in defending autocratic rule, clashing geopolitical interests began to strain their practical cooperation.[7]

The explosive growth of international commerce was another positive linkage between European countries. Over the whole nineteenth century the volume of world trade rose forty-three-fold, doubling in the last two prewar decades alone! This breathtaking expansion was the result of the spread of industrialization from the United Kingdom to the continent, which increased the production of goods thirty-three-fold between 1800 and 1900. In contrast to imperialist claims, well over three-quarters of this trade in mass products took place between the advanced countries rather than between the metropolitan areas and their colonies.[8] To facilitate transactions merchants created connections across frontiers, sending their sons abroad to acquire new skills and founding branches in other countries. One highly successful example of such linkages was the development of the Rothschilds from a Jewish banking family in Frankfurt to a network of leading international financiers with branches in Paris and London.[9] Such contacts created a transnational business community that thought in European or even global terms.

The advancement of trade also necessitated international cooperation in establishing a legal and organizational framework for
cross-border exchanges. For instance, Europeans were instrumental
in founding a Universal Postal Union as well as a Telegraph Union
so that letters and telegrams could move across frontiers. Through
complicated negotiations, continental governments also agreed to
respect the sanctity of commercial contracts, since these were essential for trade. Similarly, they sought to establish conventions for the
respect of intellectual property through copyright agreements so that
books could be exchanged. In order to regulate the flow of migration
by admitting people with means while screening out the undesirable
poor, governments pressed for an international system of passports
and the formulation of residence rights and duties for foreigners. Finally, they pushed for the creation of commissions regulating the
uses of seas, rivers, and canals.[10] Out of these practical concerns European states developed a body of international law that facilitated
peaceful exchange.

The emergence of a *fraternité des arts* of painters and musicians
who formed a cultural avant-garde in Europe was more spontaneous.
Since the language of art or music was universally accessible, the
freedom and stimulation of metropolitan centers attracted artists from
all over the continent, such as the Spanish painter Pablo Picasso to
Paris and the Bohemian composer Gustav Mahler to Vienna. Believing that "art knows no fatherland," creative innovators could spread
new styles like abstract painting or twelve-tone music from one
capital to another, creating a community of experimentation across
frontiers. Official exhibitions as well as independent shows, established concert halls as well as unauthorized performances, would
inform both practitioners and the public. Moreover, critical reviews
in the press also created an international debate, irrespective of the
origin of particular works. While an international art market and
concert-booking system organized such exchanges, many of the struggling artists and musicians lived a bohemian existence, irrespective
of nationality.[11]

Another area of increasing transnational cooperation among
European countries was scientific research. Though institutions like

the Deutsche Museum in Munich intended to showcase national accomplishments, the validation of scientific discoveries and technological advances required international judgment. The processes of disciplinary specialization and academic professionalization in the second half of the nineteenth century produced a community of scholars eager for international exchange of information. The formation of national scientific associations with their journals and meetings implied as a next step the creation of international bodies, organizations, and congresses in which researchers could meet and present their results to a wider public. While much of the state or philanthropic funding remained national, the most advanced facilities attracted scholars from the entire continent, moving Albert Einstein, for example, from a Swiss patent office to the University of Berlin.[12] The establishment of international prizes through Albert Nobel from Sweden in 1900 furthered such internationalization.

Holding twenty-one international congresses before World War I, the pacifists were even more explicitly dedicated to preserving peace. Toward the end of the nineteenth century the religious impulse of the Quakers gave way to a secular conviction that "war among civilized people is a crime." In France some radical republicans sought to preserve the legacy of the Revolution by advocating international arbitration while others even championed European integration. In German-speaking areas the courageous baroness Bertha von Suttner in her best-seller *Die Waffen nieder!* tried to stem the militarization of society by portraying the dreadful consequences of war from a female perspective. In England the publicist Norman Angell similarly argued in his treatise *The Great Illusion* that war was destructive even for potential winners and therefore ought to be considered irrational. Drawing much attention, such pleas attracted only the support of a dedicated minority, although they contributed to the conclusion of international conventions to regulate warfare in The Hague.[13]

The Second International of the labor movement also opposed war on the basis of Karl Marx's dictum that "working men have no country." Initially much of its energy was dedicated to overcoming the hostility between France and Germany, since union organization and party development had made the most progress there. In a series of international congresses, the theoretical minds and political leaders of the movement, including Karl Kautsky, Jean Jaurès, Rosa Luxemburg, and Vladimir I. Ulianov, called Lenin, discussed strategy, disagreeing on revolution versus evolution according to the degree of their respective repression. Through intense correspondence, articles in journals like *Die Neue Zeit*, and conversations at personal meetings they attempted to create a Marxist analysis of the development of capitalism in order to chart a united course. However, the millions of adherents in trade unions and labor parties remained more rooted in their national contexts.[14] A similar international voice for peaceful change was the international women's movement, which grew rapidly in the last decades before the Great War.

The preservation of peace in Europe was therefore not a diplomatic accident but a result of the internationalizing impetus of modernization. Through all levels of society, from the aristocracy via the middle class to the proletariat, there were influential groups that either cooperated transnationally or worked against war explicitly. Their interests were in part material, such as the advancement of trade, but in part also moral, such as the prevention of bloodshed between nations. This cooperation rested on increasing personal contacts in international meetings or at fashionable cosmopolitan spas such as Baden-Baden, Bath, Karlsbad, and Plombières. Some of the cooperation also had a competitive edge as in British-inspired sporting events like soccer or in the French-created Olympic Games, which intended to showcase individual athletes but ultimately turned into a contest between nations. By around 1900 this web of multiple ties, called by some historians the first globalization, seemed strong enough to guarantee the further peaceful progress of Europe and the civilized world.[15]

SOURCES OF HOSTILITY

In the first decade of the twentieth century critical commentators like Heinrich Mann and Romain Rolland nonetheless noted a distinctive deterioration of the international climate that raised the specter of a return of war. In part, the increase of hostility between the major

Map 2. Prewar Europe, 1913. Adapted from Institute for European History, Mainz, Germany.

powers stemmed from actual conflicts of interest be they strategic
or colonial. In part, the growing tensions also resulted from misperceptions of motives and national stereotypes that made it ever more
difficult for the customary mechanism of diplomacy to work out
acceptable compromises.[16] Some cultural critics at the same time
pointed to the deleterious effect of the hate mongering by an irre-

sponsible mass-circulation "yellow press." Such propaganda proved particularly effective when it appealed to a changed outlook that saw international politics as a struggle for survival among nations. Propelled by the negative dynamics of modernization, the creation of national enmities and a sense of existential threat were therefore an essential cultural precondition for the resumption of warfare on the European continent.

An initial source of growing hostility was the proliferation of an unbridled nationalism among the policy elites as well as the popular masses. The eighteenth-century idea of basing a state on people speaking the same language, having a shared history, and adopting a common constitution was originally a progressive notion that sought to overcome territorial fragmentation and dynastic irresponsibility. The promise of trade without tariffs and communication without barriers appealed especially to businessmen and intellectuals, while political leaders could hope for greater military strength and international influence. However, when citizens considered their own country superior to all others, this attitude became rather illiberal, "chauvinist" in the French term or "jingoist" in the British designation. The addition of a biopolitical racism turned such pride into prejudice, justifying domestic discrimination and foreign aggression.[17] Due to the spread of mass politics, a strident nationalism became an easy tool for popular mobilization against imagined enemies at home or abroad.

Another hidden assumption that increasingly influenced European elites in their prewar decision making was social Darwinism. In essence, this popular outlook transposed Charles Darwin's biological theory of evolution onto society and international affairs. Propagated by intellectuals like Herbert Spencer and Ernst Haeckel, this view emphasized that struggle between individuals would lead to a "natural selection," which would allow only the fittest to procreate and thereby help the species to survive. If applied beyond domestic eugenics to international affairs, it constructed the world as a sharply competitive place in which only the strongest nations would be able to flourish while weaker countries would inevitably decline. As a logical test of strength between countries, such a philosophy endorsed war.[18] Unfortunately the spread of this outlook coincided with the transition from a limited continental *Realpolitik* to a broader *Weltpolitik* encompassing the entire globe. This ill-fated combination gave international competition an ever more ruthless edge.

To established nations like Britain the rapidly developing Germany also appeared as a pushy competitor, threatening their comfortable economic advantage. Though the mother country of industrialization had long held a lead in production and trade, Imperial Germany was quickly catching up in volume of imports (659 vs. 525 million pounds) and exports (525 vs. 505 million pounds) by 1913. The Germans were already producing more industrial goods, and their balance of trade with the United Kingdom was turning ever more favorable. The fear of losing the economic competition because of Berlin's support of technology and protection of domestic markets created a sense of trade rivalry in London. But stratagems to conserve the lead by enforcing a stamp "made in Germany" to identify the competitor's products as inferior backfired, and British discrimination against continental exports like beet sugar raised German resentment against Britain's *Handelsneid* (trade envy).[19] While trade between both countries continued to grow, such differences, exploited by the popular press, contributed to their political alienation.

Imperial Germany's belated colonial bid was another source of friction, since it upset the established division of the world. As long as political fragmentation kept the Germans from imperial aspirations, the British, French, and Russians could concentrate on their rivalry with each other. But after its Prussian-led unification in 1871, the newly created German Reich also began to develop imperial aspirations. During the 1880s, domestic pressure for colonies grew in Berlin because, unlike the U.S. "open door" rhetoric, leading Germans thought they needed to protect their commercial interests through outright possession. Reluctantly, Otto von Bismarck did not just broker the division of Africa at the 1884–85 Berlin Congress but also acquired German colonies in East and West Africa, Togo, and the Cameroons. Not that these possessions were particularly profitable (only Togo yielded positive returns), but their very existence complicated Anglo-French designs to control the entire continent.

As latecomers, the Germans appeared in the most unlikely places, such as Samoa, and rudely insisted on a piece of the action although the others were already there. It was this combination of dynamism and pushiness that created anger abroad.[20]

As a result of growing tensions, writers and journalists busied themselves with turning former foes into friends and former friends into new enemies. For instance, British publicists suddenly painted France, which had been London's chief naval, colonial, and continental rival, in a more favorable light, transforming Paris into a center of fashion and art. Instead of reviling Napoleon's hegemonic designs, travel writers started to extol the attractions of Provence and the Riviera. In contrast, the Germans, who had been considered first cousins of the Anglo-Saxons as members of the white Protestant race, now suddenly seemed more sinister. Indeed, in his highly popular 1903 novel *The Riddle of the Sands* Erskine Childers wrote about a couple of young men who stumbled upon a German armada and foiled its plot to invade Great Britain. This riveting adventure tale magnified British fears to such a degree that the Admiralty was forced to construct several defensive naval bases in the North Sea.[21] Such spy fiction was therefore not harmless entertainment but psychological preparation for a return of war.

The concrete background to the cultural warmongering was a fierce naval race between Great Britain and Imperial Germany. Though the Royal Navy had ruled the seas for the entire nineteenth century, Emperor William II decided in 1898 that Germany also ought to have a powerful naval force to defend its colonies and bring Britain to the bargaining table. To retain their superiority, the British countered with a technological quantum leap in 1906, called the *Dreadnought*, whose stronger guns, better armor, and greater speed rendered prior battleships obsolete. Though caught somewhat by surprise, Admiral Alfred von Tirpitz clung to his goal of reaching two-thirds of British strength, thereby making it too risky for London to attack the German fleet. However, Admiral John Fisher insisted on keeping the Royal Navy stronger than the next two navies combined, redoubling British building efforts.[22] This race tested not only both countries' technical inventiveness and industrial capacity but also their ability to pay and their political resolve, requiring a huge propaganda effort to sustain its pace.

At the same time another dangerous competition for the biggest army developed between the Franco-Russian Alliance and the Austro-German Dual Alliance. Because of their declining population, the French for example insisted on universal military service, drafting 83 percent of an age cohort. In contrast, the Germans conscripted only 53 percent because the Prussian Junkers did not want to dilute the officer corps with middle-class members. With their large population, the Russians called up only 20 percent but modernized their technical capacity and enlarged the number of recruits. In 1912 General Erich Ludendorff insisted on drastically enlarging the size of the German army, but the big naval expenditures only permitted an increase to roughly three-quarters of a million soldiers. Since the expansion of the armed forces was quite expensive, the public had to be convinced by being scared with tales of imminent attack. The arms race on land followed the same pattern as on the sea—when one side raised its fighting force, the other scrambled to catch up.[23] As a result of such agitation, both parties became less and less secure.

Increasing fears and enemy stereotypes combined in literary fantasies of a coming war. General Friedrich von Bernhardi's forecast was the most notorious, since he had been a German military attaché and a general-staff historian. In 1911 he aroused a storm of controversy with the book *Germany and the Next War*, which argued in a social Darwinist fashion that "war is a biological necessity" in order to test the mettle of the nation. Not only did he proclaim a duty to wage war; he also insisted on a "right of conquest," especially by a country like Germany, which had been shortchanged in the division of the world since it had entered the arena when most areas were already claimed. Ominously anticipating later racist dreams, he saw expansion possibilities primarily in Eastern Europe. Supported by the Pan-German League, this book was quickly translated into English and French, serving as proof of German belligerence, even though it did not reflect official policy.[24] This scenario and similar tracts by authors from other nations made the outbreak of war more likely by prefiguring it.

Real and imagined dangers from rival countries were amplified by a "yellow press" of cheap dailies that relied on scandals and rumors to promote sales. The prewar years were the golden age of the newspaper, since dozens of morning and evening sheets clamored for public attention in the capitals. To be sure, each major country had a serious paper like the *London Times*, *Le Monde*, or the *Berliner Tageblatt*, which strove for accurate reporting, but even these were not above defending what they saw as the national interest. More dangerous were the mass-circulation sheets like the *Daily Mail* or the *Berliner Zeitung*, which appealed to a semiliterate public with sensationalist stories without always bothering to check their veracity.[25] In each country, the yellow press inflamed popular passions by using national stereotypes and exaggerating dangers threatening from abroad. Even children were conditioned to militarism when playing with war toys. Heightening international conflicts and creating enemy stereotypes, these negative dimensions of modernization undermined peace and helped prepare the public for war.

POLARIZING CRISES

Because there was no institutionalized form of cooperation, a series of diplomatic crises in the early twentieth century reinforced the sources of hostility. In a balance-of-power system such confrontations were considered a normal part of international affairs, since states pursued conflicting interests by negotiation or force until they met sufficient resistance. But advancing one's aims through risking conflict had serious drawbacks that became increasingly evident. Blustering during a crisis as well as disappointment in its outcome left a residue of hostility even after a solution had been found, impairing the antagonists' willingness to compromise the next time. Moreover, reaching an agreement required a mechanism such as an international conference or the mediation of some disinterested powers, which would break down if either party refused to join the talks or the potential go-betweens were themselves drawn into the conflict. The pattern of crises that developed during the last prewar years contributed materially to creating two opposing international alliances and hardening the fronts between them.[26]

By turning away from Bismarck's complicated diplomatic system, Imperial Germany itself precipitated a diplomatic revolution that would ultimately isolate it. Intent on being always *à trois* in a system of five great powers, the Iron Chancellor had complemented the Dual Alliance with Austria-Hungary by a secret Reinsurance Treaty with Russia in order to contain a revanchist France, while Britain enjoyed its "splendid isolation." The young emperor William II wanted to emancipate himself from the tutelage of this careful, if not always honest, statesman so as to pursue a navalist *Weltpolitik*, while the new chancellor Georg Leo Count von Caprivi intended to create a continental trading bloc, excluding Russia. Hoping to regain the lost provinces of Alsace-Lorraine, the French cabinet seized upon the opportunity to offer an alliance to the tsarist government stung by the nonrenewal of its pact with Germany and angry over being blocked in the Balkans by Austria. In 1892 this unlikely marriage of convenience blossomed into the Franco-Russian alliance and divided the continent into hostile camps.[27]

Resolving the dramatic Fashoda crisis, the conclusion of the entente cordiale between England and France in 1904 was another step toward polarization. In September 1898 French major Jean-Baptiste Marchand and his small detachment ran into a powerful flotilla of British gunboats, commanded by Sir Herbert Kitchener, at the town of Fashoda in the upper reaches of the Nile River in Sudan. In this encounter French designs of contiguous west-to-east expansion from Senegal to Somalia clashed with British aspirations of south-to-north control from the Cape to Cairo, propagated by Cecil Rhodes of South Africa. On learning of the confrontation, the press in both countries howled and politicians flung insults at each other, drawing London and Paris to the brink of war. But in order to gain British support against Germany, Foreign Minister Théophile Delcassé abandoned French claims and started negotiations to settle colonial disputes instead. The resulting agreement gave Britain a free hand in

Egypt and turned Morocco over to France, fundamentally changing the "frame of mind" of both countries toward each other.[28]

The first Moroccan crisis of 1905–6 cemented the two hostile camps of Entente and Dual Alliance in Europe. Irritated by France's silent annexation of this North African country, Germany protested, demanding an open door for its commercial interests. In order to test the strength of Anglo-French cooperation, Chancellor Bernhard von Bülow sent Emperor William II to Tangiers, where he gave a speech in support of Moroccan independence. This demonstrative challenge angered public opinion in Paris as well as in Berlin so much that both antagonists mobilized for war. Ultimately, the defiant Delcassé was forced out as foreign minister, and France agreed to an international conference at Algeciras. But owing to effective French diplomacy, Germany found itself isolated among the participants, supported only by Austria-Hungary. Berlin therefore had to accept a face-saving compromise that merely kept the Moroccan police independent.[29] This show of German strength ultimately backfired, since it reinforced Anglo-French cooperation and even prodded Russia to settle its colonial differences and join the Entente in 1907.

The Austrian annexation of Bosnia-Herzegovina on October 6, 1908, further strained the international situation. The Treaty of Berlin of 1878 had allowed Vienna to occupy this Ottoman province as compensation for staying neutral in the Russo-Turkish War. But a coup in 1903 brought a nationalist dynasty to power in Belgrade that agitated for a Greater Serbia with Russian support. To resolve the tensions, Russian foreign minister Alexander Izvolsky worked out a tentative deal with Austrian foreign minister Count Alois von Aerenthal allowing Vienna to annex the territory, Bulgaria to declare its independence, and Russia to receive support in its quest to open the Straits of Constantinople as exit from the Black Sea. Since the matter had not yet been settled, the Austrian annexation created massive public resentment, especially in Russia and Serbia. Seeking to end the crisis, in March 1909 Imperial Germany warned that "things would take their course" unless Russia accepted the fait accompli.[30] By forcing St. Petersburg to back down, this blunt threat permanently damaged relations with Berlin and Vienna.

Ironically even the kaiser's effort to improve Anglo-German relations through an interview with the *Daily Telegraph* in October 1908 added to their deterioration. The British journalist Stuart Wortley put several private conversations with William II together in the form of an interview, which the emperor forwarded to Chancellor Bülow for checking. It is still not clear whether the latter, who was vacationing at the North Sea, actually read the text before its release. However, the British public was outraged by the kaiser's protestation of friendship, his boast of mediation during the Boer War, and his claim that German naval armaments were not directed against the Royal Navy. All the accumulated frictions between the two countries vented themselves in a storm of English criticism. In turn, the German public was irate about the tactlessness of its monarch, and his chancellor threatened to resign from office. While a chastened kaiser thereafter meddled less in foreign affairs, the damage to the Anglo-German relationship had been done.[31]

The second Moroccan crisis of 1911 isolated Germany further, since Berlin's blustering pushed London into even closer cooperation with Paris while disappointing a belligerent public. The pretext was the French occupation of Fez and Rabat, ostensibly to help the sultan against local rebels. So as to extort compensation elsewhere, the German government sent the gunboat *Panther* to Agadir, thereby triggering British fears that it wanted to establish a naval base in the Atlantic. Though London was uneasy about the French invasion, David Lloyd George warned Berlin bluntly that peace at the price of damage to national interest and honor "would be a humiliation intolerable for a great country like ours to endure." In the ensuing negotiations between Alfred von Kiderlen Waechter and Jules Cambon, Germany conceded the establishment of a French protectorate over Morocco in exchange for a slice of Equatorial Africa to be added to its Cameroon colony.[32] While the German public construed the settlement as a diplomatic defeat, the British navy extended its protection to the French side of the Channel coast.

The Balkan Wars of 1912–13 severely tested the international fabric but remained limited to the region, because the great powers chose not to intervene directly. In the first conflict, the Balkan League of Bulgaria, Serbia, Greece, and Montenegro defeated the Ottoman Empire, and the ensuing Treaty of London ended centuries of Turkish control over the Balkan Peninsula. In the second struggle, Bulgaria attacked its former allies but was defeated with the help of the Romanians and Ottomans, losing almost all of its previous gains in the Treaty of Bucharest. The conflagration did not spread to the major European countries, since they were not ready to fight, and the Ambassadors Conferences brokered compromises.[33] The Russians found their designs to open the Straits of Constantinople frustrated and were left only with the alliance of an expansionist Serbia. The Austrians blocked Serbian access to the Adriatic coast through Albanian independence, while the Bulgarians and Ottomans now turned toward Germany. Though a major war was averted, the growing enmities structured future alignments.

While hostilities heightened, the general staffs of all major powers designed offensive war plans against their presumed enemies that dictated their actions in July 1914. Expecting a Serbian provocation, the Austrians for example prepared for war with its Russian protectors. In order to win a two-front war, Count Alfred von Schlieffen planned first to defeat France with an enveloping campaign through neutral Belgium and then to turn the German forces against the slower Russian advance. So as to recapture their lost provinces, the French designed their Plan XVII for an all-out offensive into southern Germany, hoping to win with superior élan. In order to help their allies more quickly, the Russians sped up their mobilization schedule for a campaign not just against Vienna but also against Berlin by plotting to march into East Prussia and Galicia. Finally, the British entangled themselves through staff conversations ever more deeply with defending France, though they claimed to remain neutral.[34] Though each crisis was ultimately resolved, in the summer of 1914 Europe was therefore divided into two alliances, ready to wage war against each other.

As the last in a series of increasingly hostile confrontations, the July crisis resembled previous confrontations but differed in its most important aspect—the outcome. Because of the assassination of Francis Ferdinand, it began with a local Balkan quarrel between the

Habsburg monarchy and the Serbian nationalist movement. Predictably, the alliance system quickly drew in Russia as Belgrade's patron, which in turn involved Germany as Austria's ally and France as Russia's friend. But in contrast to the previous Balkan Wars, this crisis pitted one of the major powers against a secondary client state of another great power. Overheated public opinion, fueled by an irresponsible press, made it more difficult to achieve compromises, while diplomatic decisions became constrained by the technical needs of war plans and mobilization timetables. When Britain abandoned its isolation and came to the aid of France, no major European power was left to mediate. Since Germany refused to participate in another conference so as not to be humiliated again, the modern state system had no mechanism left to stop the disaster.[35]

PROCESS OF ESCALATION

Though the previous clashes made a resort to arms more likely, it took a series of actual decisions by individual governments to start the First World War. For all the gathering storm clouds of hostility, many Europeans considered the collapse of cooperation unlikely. The progress of civilization appeared to have overcome the atavistic habit of warfare between countries, because the unprecedented level of destruction, made possible by advances in weapons technology, would discourage warfare. But the July crisis showed that the negative aspects of modernization such as nationalism, social Darwinism, and militarism had created a "shared political culture" in the European capitals that considered war a legitimate means for advancing national interest. Though pursuing conciliatory options could have stopped the outbreak, the confrontational decisions actually made left no alternative but military conflict.[36] By consistently choosing risk over compromise, the various leaders initiated a process of escalation that spread a local Balkan quarrel into a continental conflict, and led from a European conflagration to a World War.

The spark that started the conflagration was provided by Serbia, bent on creating a greater national state for the South Slavs. Surprisingly, the central role of Belgrade is often ignored, though the atrocities of the recent wars of Yugoslav succession suggest the need to reconsider this neglect. There is little doubt that the Serbian military intelligence service and Colonel "Apis" Dimitrijevic were behind the training of the youthful Bosnian terrorists, providing them with weapons and offering them logistical support. While the young men could be considered misguided idealists of South Slav nationalism, the adult backers going all the way up to Serbian prime minister Nikola Pasic knew that their order to assassinate the provincial governor Oskar Potiorek, later shifted to the Austrian heir apparent, might start a war. Though the sources are spotty, it is unlikely that Serb leaders could have done so without the assurance of Russian support. Even if some civilians developed last-minute qualms, it was ultimately their state-sponsored terrorism that made the gun, which they had helped to load, go off by itself.[37]

The tough Austrian response to the assassination created a local Balkan war, conceived as a punitive action to chasten Serbia that would also weaken Russian influence. Vienna was not merely a puppet of Berlin, since the Habsburg leadership was an independent actor who made decisions in its own interest. However, Austria's ruling councils were divided between the war party around Chief of Staff Conrad von Hötzendorff, the peace group around Hungarian premier Count Istvan Tisza, and the vacillating foreign minister Leopold Count Berchtold, who advocated a "militant diplomacy." To shore up the emerging consensus on punitive action, Austria sent cabinet chief Alexander Count Hoyos to Berlin, where he received the infamous "blank check," since Germany feared losing its last major ally. In the decisive Crown Council of July 14, Berchtold persuaded Tisza to endorse a humiliating ultimatum to Serbia, intended to provide a pretext for attack.[38] In trying to meet the South Slav irredentism by force, Vienna triggered a war to save the monarchy that instead would eventually destroy it.

The Russians' resolve to support their Serbian client in order to retain their influence in the Balkans helped escalate the conflict to the level of a continental war. Blaming the assassination on its victim, the leaders in St. Petersburg sought a counterstrategy to the Austro-German attempt to "localize" the conflict in the Balkans, because in a limited war Vienna was bound to defeat Belgrade. On the one hand Russia rallied its allies with false allegations and reassured Serbia of its assistance in case of Austrian attack. On the other, it prepared to mobilize its own forces on the Austrian frontier so as to pressure the Habsburgs to abstain from war. Although Tsar Nicholas II was willing to limit mobilization to the Austrian part of the front after an appeal from William II, Foreign Minister Sergei Sazonov and Minister of War Vladimir Sukhomlinov insisted on comprehensive premobilization, since they wanted to ready the army for a conflict with Germany.[39] It was this broader deployment of troops that meant war and prevented a limitation of the crisis, because it confronted Berlin with the need to mobilize against Russia and France as well.

German decisions remain particularly controversial since they showed a curious defensive aggressiveness that sought to secure and extend Berlin's position at the same time. Moreover, it was not clear whether the mercurial kaiser, the nervous chief of staff Helmut von Moltke, or the pessimistic chancellor Theobald von Bethmann Hollweg was really in charge. But Germany was united in supporting Austria come what may. The civilian leaders pursued a "risk policy" to test Russian intentions, which endorsed a local Balkan war and risked a wider continental war since that still seemed winnable; but they did not want a war with Britain, because that would exceed their strength. Fearing Russia's quickly growing military might and French efforts to modernize their forces, Germany saw the assassination of the archduke as a last chance to break its diplomatic "encirclement." The Schlieffen Plan's priority of an initial attack in the West forced the government to issue an ultimatum not just to Russia but also to its ally France.[40] The Germans were ready to back down only when it became clear, too late, that England would enter the fray.

Surprisingly, French actions during the July crisis tend to be overlooked although they, too, played a considerable part in the breakdown of peace. After its defeat in the Franco-Prussian War of 1870–71, one of the few constants of European diplomacy was that Paris would be revanchist, seeking to reconquer the lost provinces of Alsace and Lorraine. Because of its heritage of *grandeur* from Louis XIV to Napoleon, France also wanted to counteract the growing dominance of a more populous and industrially dynamic Germany on the continent. When labor leader Jean Jaurès was assassinated on July 31 by a French nationalist, a leading voice for peace and reconciliation was silenced. During his talks in St. Petersburg at the height of the crisis, President Raymond Poincaré did not counsel moderation but rather assured Russian leaders that France would stand by them, since he did not want to miss the opportunity to fight.[41] Disregarding the responsibility of Serbian irredentism, this desire for revenge therefore drew Paris into the conflict, completing the lineup of what thereby became a continental war.

The role of Britain has also been fiercely debated since its decision for war marked the transition to a general European conflict with worldwide implications. The majority of the Liberal cabinet under Herbert Asquith was inclined to follow the traditional detachment from continental affairs and to remain on the sidelines. But the Foreign Office under Sir Edward Grey was Francophile and therefore focused on the danger that a strengthening Germany might pose to British hegemony. Moreover, military authorities were deep into unofficial staff conversations with the French about cooperating in defense of the Channel coast. Finally, the yellow press enjoyed ridiculing William II, whose penchant for gaffes provided it with ample opportunities. Germany's violation of Belgian neutrality, required by the Schlieffen Plan, ultimately tipped the balance of opinion in the divided government and provided a convenient justification for mobilizing the public. Instead of defense of international law, it was solidarity with the Entente as well as self-interested fear of a rising naval and colonial rival that prompted London to intervene.[42]

The initial momentum of escalation brought two more countries into the war, spreading the fighting beyond the European continent. Japan had been strenuously modernizing since the Meiji Restoration following the best practices of various countries in Europe. Having already defeated Russia, Tokyo saw the European conflict in late August as chance to seize German possessions in Tsingtao as well as the Caroline, Mariana, and Marshall islands in the Pacific in order to become the strongest power in Asia.[43] Led by Enver Pascha, the Ottoman Empire had similarly been transforming itself into a modern nation according to European models of secularism, education, and economic growth. When the two German cruisers *Goeben* and *Breslau* under Admiral Wilhelm Souchon attacked the Russian Black Sea fleet as a result of a secret alliance, Istanbul joined the Central Powers in October.[44] The Turkish entry was of greater strategic significance, since blocking the Dardanelles denied Russia a warm-water shipping route to its western allies and tied down considerable Russian forces in the Caucasus Mountains.

Contrary to popular opinion, it was a collective failure of leadership rather than the actions of a single statesman like the kaiser that was responsible for the outbreak of World War I. By 1914 monarchs such as Francis-Joseph, George V, Nicholas II, and William II were too mediocre and controlled by advisers to dictate events. While military leaders such as Austrian chief of staff Conrad von Hötzendorff were more bellicose, even some generals such as his German counterpart Helmut von Moltke had second thoughts. It was rather the civilian leadership of Nikola Pasic in Serbia, Count Leopold von Berchtold in Austria, Sergei Sazonov in Russia, Theobald von Bethmann Hollweg in Germany, Raymond Poincaré in France, and Sir Edward Grey in Britain that played a crucial role. They were neither "sleepwalkers" nor "fatalists" but seasoned politicians and diplomats who pursued their own national interests to the detriment of the entire continent.[45] Not really understanding the bloody consequences of the decisions they were about to make, each lacked a sufficient sense of responsibility for the whole to be inclined to compromise.

The outbreak of the First World War was therefore not an accident but the result of a process of escalation that turned a limited regional clash into a general global conflict. At least three different levels need to be distinguished: Its origin was the Serbian-Austrian confrontation in the Balkans over the liberation of Bosnian Serbs from Habsburg rule. From this clash a continental conflict for hegemony over the European peninsula developed between the Dual Alliance of Germany and Austria on the one hand and the Franco-Russian Alliance on the other. Finally, this conflagration grew into a global naval and colonial struggle between the Central Powers plus their Ottoman ally and the British as well as Japanese. Only the Italian government broke from the Triple Alliance and waited until the spring of 1915 to enter on the side of the Entente.[46] Instead of a particular country being chiefly responsible, the conflict spread incrementally through a sequence of individual decisions, driven by specific national interests. Not stopped by common institutions or a sense of shared responsibility, this cascade of choices drove Europe into war.

Ironically, none of the belligerents ultimately achieved their aims. Realized in the creation of Yugoslavia, the Serbian dream of a greater South Slav state disintegrated with the collapse of communism. The desperate gamble to fortify the Dual Monarchy backfired with the self-determination of its constituent nationalities, which shattered the Austro-Hungarian Empire. The Russian hope for dominance over the Balkans and access to the Mediterranean crumbled in revolution, leading to the Soviet dead-end that cut the country off from liberal development. The German intention of maintaining hegemony over the center of the continent triggered another, even more deadly war and a genocidal Holocaust, dividing the country for decades thereafter. While the French succeeded in regaining Alsace and Lorraine, they paid for it by their defeat in World War II and the erosion of their great-power status. Finally even the twice-victorious British somehow lost their empire and saw the United States overtake them.[47] Could European leaders have foreseen these outcomes, they might have thought twice about their fateful decisions.

ORIGINS OF WAR

Since the impact of modernity on the transformation of international relations remains under-theorized, most explanations for the outbreak of war in 1914 fail to address its deeper causes. Oblivious to Adam Smith's aspirations to external peace, modernization theory basically focuses on domestic processes such as economic development, social mobilization, cultural experimentation, and political democratization rather than on the evolution of the international order. Two prominent schools of thought, nonetheless, confront each other: Legal scholars tend to focus on the "gentle civilizer" of international law as a method of increasing cooperation between nations by regulating their interaction with binding agreements and resolving conflicts between them through arbitration.[48] Neorealist theorists of international relations are instead skeptical of the chances of peace, because they believe that sovereign states are ready to use force in pursuing their interests in a competitive system without any central authority. Both perspectives contribute in different ways to illuminating the outbreak of World War I.[49]

Before 1914 the development of international law did make some progress, but this increase of cooperation still proved too weak to keep the great powers from resorting to war. If states shared interests, as in the delivery of the mail or the transmission of telegrams, international conventions facilitated communication between developed countries. When there were transnational problems like the care of the wounded on a battlefield, organizations such as the Red Cross provided services regardless of nationality. In spite of much skepticism, the Hague conferences also managed to codify rules of land and sea warfare because limiting the use of force might serve all parties of an armed conflict.[50] But ultimately, the maintenance of peace was consigned to the deterrence of an attack by arming oneself and seeking the help of powerful allies. While alliances stabilized the system in the short run, in the long run they drew more countries into the conflict. In the end, instruments of diplomatic negotiation, conflict resolution, and mediation by international conferences were not strong enough to preserve cooperation.

The behavior of European states in the summer of 1914 therefore more closely resembled the neorealist view, because they acted out of individual self-interest with little regard for the benefit of the whole. The ideology of nationalism put a premium on advancing one's own cause and divided the world into dangerous enemies to be combated as well as potential friends to be courted. At the same time, the mind-set of militarism considered war not just a legitimate means of politics but also a necessary instrument for pursuing one's interests. In every country the generals believed in a "cult of the offensive" and persuaded the civilian leaders that victory required adopting attacking strategies even in order to defend themselves. Finally, the widespread outlook of social Darwinism defined international relations as a struggle in which the strong nations would survive whereas the weak would be trampled underfoot.[51] Operating on the basis of such "hidden assumptions," statesmen were willing to cooperate only when it suited their interests and felt little responsibility for preserving peace for the entire continent.

In contrast to the earlier confrontations, the July crisis could no longer be resolved since all the governments involved pursued policies that risked war. After decades of peace, the danger of an outbreak of general hostilities seemed so slight that special sacrifices to maintain cooperation appeared unnecessary. Each country harbored aims of national defense, political revenge, or territorial gain that it could achieve only by facing down its enemies and threatening them with attack. All states were afraid to back down, since that would be construed as a sign of weakness by their own citizens as well as their presumed enemies.[52] Moreover, with Britain and Germany choosing opposite sides, there were no disinterested parties left that would be both willing to mediate and strong enough to impose their solution. When it came to the final decision, the European statesmen and generals considered the potential gains from war more important than the losses likely to be incurred in such a conflict. Coupled with this narrowly defined pursuit of national interest, the complacency of decades of peace made them ultimately unwilling to compromise.

Instead of leading to the further progress of civilization, the decisions of July 1914 therefore unleashed the demons of war that revealed a shockingly destructive side of modernity. The nationalist choices of the leaders turned presumably benign developments into their very opposite. Technological innovation provided deadlier weapons for the battlefield; economic development offered greater resources for fighting; social mobility subsumed individualism into mass mobilization; and increased political participation inspired more hostile propaganda. Looking inward to gain new continental possessions, the nation-states of Europe now sought to vanquish one another with the help of their imperial possessions. An efficient bureaucracy marshaled the resources necessary for combat, while a modern military worked out mobilization timetables and drew up war plans that promised easy victory.[53] Owing to the weakness of restraints and the absence of an overarching system, Europe degenerated into internecine warfare that came close to destroying the entire continent.

Chapter 3

WAGING TOTAL WAR

Trench warfare, 1916. *Source*: bpk, Berlin / Art Resource, NY.

For most soldiers, fighting in the First World War was anything but heroic. On October 29, 1914, Sergeant I. F. Bell of the Gordon Highlanders was admiring his "almost perfect trench" near the Belgian town of Ypres "when all hell seemed let loose." Suddenly the great guns roared and made the earth heave, ears ring, and eyes tear. Then "Germans sprang from everywhere and attacked us," throwing hand grenades, ducking into craters, cutting through barbed wire, tiptoeing through minefields, and ignoring dying comrades. Terrorized defenders crouched behind sandbags, countering with rifle and machine-gun fire until their barrels glowed, but were forced to fall back. In a ritual repeated a thousand times, a British officer rallied his troops, ordering them to "retake the trench" with bayonets in hand-to-hand combat. Then Bell felt a "dull thud," tumbled head over heels, and "discovered that [his] right foot was missing." The dead piled up three deep, but hardly any ground was gained. Eventually stillness returned and corpses rotted in the mud, emitting a nauseating stench. The "stark hellishness" of the scene was indescribable.[1]

Contemporaries initially referred to this conflict as the "Great War" because it ended a relatively peaceful century and involved more countries and combatants than the prior wars of national unification. Though it was essentially a struggle for European hegemony, it gradually began to be called a "world war" due to its spread to overseas powers, the involvement of the colonies, and the global ambitions of the belligerents. Since millions of fathers, brothers, and sons were lost or wounded, while many bodies were never found, almost every little village erected a monument at its center for those fallen in combat in order to have a place for patriotic remembrance. All over the continent, military cemeteries with endless rows of little white crosses recalled the enormous blood toll of a male generation, neatly separated by nationality. At famous battle sites like Verdun, memorials were constructed as focal points of annual observances by the living veterans for their dead comrades, giving meaning to their sacrifice by renewing a commitment to the national cause. Only a minority of critical intellectuals like the British feminist Vera Brittain dared question the legitimacy of warfare and argue for reconciliation instead.[2]

The concept of "total war," popularized by General Erich Ludendorff in 1935, suggested a more comprehensive mobilization and a more violent form of fighting than ever before. "The character of total war requires literally the entire power of a people." Though earlier conflicts like the Thirty Years War had already been quite bloody, the First World War shocked participants by overturning international efforts to limit combat to soldiers. Even if the effects of bombing by airplane remained slight, German retaliation against partisan attacks obliterated the distinction between soldiers and civilians, while the Allied blockade starved women, children, and the aged, making them susceptible to disease. Moreover, the manpower needs of mass armies required a more thorough mobilization of young men, the scarcity of labor led to an increasing recruitment of women, and the necessity of generating sufficient war material required the transformation of the entire economy toward military priorities. Finally, the intensification of the struggle also made generals push for the development of ever more deadly weapons, and inspired politicians to proclaim grandiose war aims that required complete victory.[3]

This first truly modern war differed fundamentally from the grand Napoleonic battles, since the industrialization of the battlefield potentiated the projection of force. The advancement of technology created more efficient killing devices such as the machine gun; factory assembly lines produced larger supplies of ammunition such as artillery shells; conscript armies fielded much greater numbers of troops; and the use of new weapons such as poison gas violated accepted international norms. Mechanized combat became so deadly as to compel the abandonment of colorful uniforms in the spring of 1915. At the same time, journalists and intellectuals mobilized the home front with propaganda; bureaucratic war-production boards tried to marshal scarce resources of steel and food; plant managers persuaded women to work in the factories, blurring gender roles; generals gradually adapted their strategy to mass combat by shifting from attack to attrition; and political leaders sought to sustain an emotionalized conflict that they could not end. Unlike the one-sided colonial wars, World War I was largely a combat between equals that claimed incredible numbers of victims, recalling the U.S. Civil War.[4]

In contrast to the simplification of computer games, modern war was not decided just on the battlefield but also in the hearts and minds of the citizens involved. Already a century earlier Prussian theoretician Carl von Clausewitz had argued that war was the continuation of politics by other means. Of course, the success or failure of military strategy continued to play a key role in the outcome of the First World War. But by becoming more total, the struggle turned into a contest for allies, with the Entente and the Central Powers trying to tip the scales by drawing other powerful countries into the conflict. The war was also a severe test of their economies, since the capacity for weapons production would be decisive in a prolonged struggle. Similarly, the First World War was a trial of political will among the belligerents to sustain the fighting in the face of horrific personal and material losses.[5] In such a multidimensional contest, only a well-organized and committed country would be able to prevail. Hence modern warfare consisted of far more than innovative weapons technology, testing the very fabric of society and politics.

SHORT-WAR ILLUSION

The public greeted the outbreak of the war in July 1914 with a mixture of enthusiasm and foreboding. In all major European cities middle-class crowds gathered spontaneously, read the latest newspaper dispatches, marched waving flags, listened to nationalist speeches, and sang patriotic songs. Inspired by professorial exhortations to national unity, university students who dominated the streets welcomed the liberation from a boring peace and the chance to prove their mettle in a historic trial of arms. Yet in working-class quarters or among national minorities, apprehension prevailed, and socialist speakers like Rosa Luxemburg called for "mass action against war." Fearing what was to come, the poor especially worried about having to bear the brunt of the fighting. Seeking to overcome their nervousness, drafted recruits scrawled "*à Berlin*" or "*nach Paris*" on their train cars, confident that they would be home by Christmas. Neither generals nor politicians imagined that the intensity of modern warfare could be sustained for more than a few months, and therefore based their decisions on ways to achieve a quick victory.[6]

Given the large superiority of the Entente over the Central Powers in population size and access to resources, the war should, indeed, have been short. The former commanded 28 percent of the world's industrial capacity compared to the latter's mere 19 percent. Moreover, the Allies had 5.8 million soldiers under arms as opposed to only 3.8 million on the other side. Owing to the Royal Navy's command of the seas, the Entente could draw on raw materials and food from all over the world, whereas the Dual Alliance lacked such essential supplies as nitrogen for explosives and fertilizer as well as iron for weapons and rubber and oil for motor vehicles. The Central Powers' only advantage was their compact land area, which offered strategists interior lines for shifting troops from one front to another. In contrast, the Entente had long communication routes between France, Britain, and Russia that complicated joint planning. Perhaps the professional training of the German military and the excellent scientific support were also somewhat helpful.[7] But because of their structural inferiority, the Central Powers were forced to take more strategic risks.

As a desperate gamble to win a two-front war, the Schlieffen Plan almost succeeded—but coming close was not enough. In principle it was deceptively simple: in a gigantic sweep the right wing of the German front would advance through Belgium into northern France in order to capture Paris. In practice it proved difficult to execute, since the Belgians tenaciously defended their fortresses (Liège, for example) and the Russians mobilized more quickly than expected, forcing Chief of Staff Helmuth von Moltke to send two army corps to defend the eastern frontier. In early September the advancing German forces, nonetheless, crossed the river Marne and threatened Paris itself. But communication confusion, troop exhaustion, overextension of supplies, and a fifty-kilometer gap in the lines made them vulnerable to Joseph Joffre's and the British Expeditionary Force's counterattack. On September 9 Generals Karl von Bülow and Alexander von Kluck therefore decided to break off the advance. Dramatized through the shifting of defenders with Parisian taxis, the "miracle of the Marne" meant that the German war plan had failed in the West.[8]

The French Plan XVII met the same negative fate, since German resistance proved much stronger than expected. Based on the "cult of the offensive" and designed to liberate the lost provinces, this strategy demanded that the main thrust take place in Alsace and Lorraine in the hope of splitting the southern German states from Prussia. Though initially the French advanced into the valley of the Rhine, capturing Mulhouse, furious German counterattacks forced them quickly to retreat. As a result of this double failure, both sides dug into trenches so as to establish impregnable defensive positions. Only in the still-open northern portion of the front could a "race to the sea" have developed, with each side trying to outflank the other so as to regain the strategic initiative. But the various German and British encircling moves in Flanders' fields canceled each other out, finally running out of space at the Channel coast. Contrary to most predictions, the war of movement ended in the West by November 1914.[9] The Germans occupied most of Belgium and northern France, but they had failed to win the war.

In the East the Russian and Austrian offensives also did not achieve their goals, bogging down along an eight-hundred-kilometer front from the Baltic to the Romanian border. Mobilizing more quickly than anticipated, tsarist armies under Paul von Rennenkampf and Alexander Samsonov invaded East Prussia, heading for Königsberg and for Danzig. Their separation gave the German defenders the chance to surround them first at Tannenberg and then at the Masurian lakes, throwing them back into Poland. In contrast to Moltke's failure in the West, this eastern victory by Paul von Hindenburg and Erich Ludendorff created a myth of their military brilliance that would have disastrous political consequences.[10] In the Serbian campaign, Austrian chief of staff Conrad von Hötzendorff underestimated his enemy; he briefly captured Belgrade but could not hold it against the fierce resistance of the defenders. In Galicia the material superiority of Russian attackers was so great that the Habsburg forces lost the fortresses of Lemberg and Przemyśl before

German reinforcements managed to recapture some of the lost ground in a winter campaign in the Carpathians.[11]

The unexpected stalemate in the West and East inspired a frantic search for allies powerful enough to tip the military balance in one side's favor. While the Turkish entry into the war weakened Russian capabilities by diverting troops to the Caucasus front, the Entente succeeded in persuading Italy to enter the fighting on its side. Nationalist agitation in Rome focused on *Italia irredenta* (Italian-speaking territories still held by Austria in Trentino, Friuli, and Istria) rather than on the French-dominated Nice or Savoy. As a result of western promises of expansion on the Dalmatian coast and of new colonies, the war party in Italy, bolstered by the socialist turncoat Benito Mussolini, decided to gamble on an Entente victory. Though the Austrians had only weak militia units, their strategic position in the first chain of the Alps appeared impregnable, forcing Field Marshal Luigi Cadorna to attack across the Isonzo River. Supported by better artillery, the Habsburg defenders just managed to redeploy enough troops from Serbia to hold off a succession of Italian offensives.[12] So the opening of a new front in southern Europe merely extended the carnage.

The initial war of movement therefore failed to bring a military decision by the end of 1914 because neither side won or lost decisively enough in order to cease fighting. On the one hand, the German advantages of tactical effectiveness and troop discipline were counteracted by the weakness of a multiethnic Austrian ally. On the other, the manpower and material superiority of the Entente was nullified by the lack of coordination in its campaigns. All the carefully developed strategic plans failed, since they privileged the offensive in order to reach extensive war aims through outright victory rather than adopting a defensive posture that was militarily more effective and politically easier to sustain. As a result, all armies incurred frightful losses, amounting to almost half their initial strength in dead, wounded, or captured. While the Central Powers had occupied most of Belgium and a good part of northern France, their advance on Warsaw was checked, and they were barely holding on in

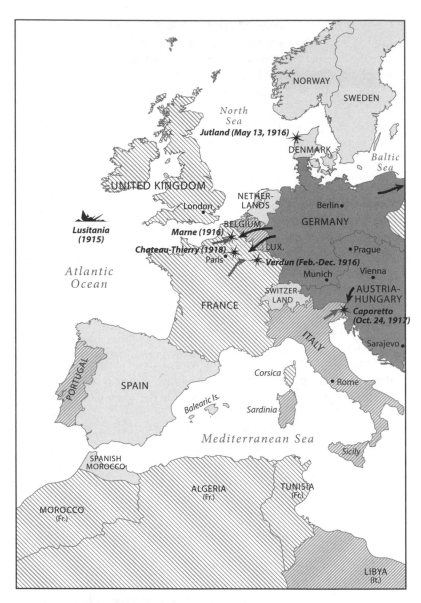

Map 3. World War I in Europe, 1914–18. Adapted from Maps.com.

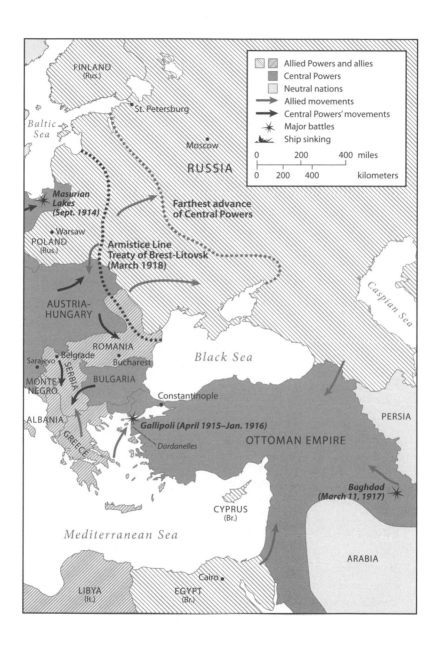

FINLAND
(Rus.)

Baltic
Sea

• St. Petersburg

• Moscow

RUSSIA

Allied Powers and allies
Central Powers
Neutral nations
Allied movements
Central Powers' movements
Major battles
Ship sinking

0   200   400 miles
0   200   400   kilometers

Masurian
Lakes
(Sept. 1914)

Farthest advance
of Central Powers

• Warsaw
POLAND
(Rus.)

Armistice Line
Treaty of Brest-Litovsk
(March 1918)

AUSTRIA-
HUNGARY

Caspian Sea

ROMANIA

Black Sea

Sarajevo • Belgrade
• Bucharest

MONTE-
NEGRO

SERBIA

BULGARIA

ALBANIA

Constantinople

PERSIA

GREECE

Gallipoli (April 1915–Jan. 1916)

Dardanelles

OTTOMAN EMPIRE

Baghdad
(March 11, 1917)

CYPRUS
(Br.)

Mediterranean Sea

ARABIA

Cairo •

LIBYA
(It.)

EGYPT
(Br.)

Galicia as well as in Italy. To everyone's surprise, modern warfare therefore turned out to become an interminable struggle.

STALEMATE IN THE TRENCHES

The rough balance of forces led to a protracted stalemate due to the construction of elaborate trenches in which defenders could weather murderous assaults. Across a no-man's-land, the contending armies faced each other in a complicated maze of observation posts, infantry trenches, communication ditches, fallback positions, artillery platforms, and staging areas. The usually three-deep lines could be dented, but rarely broken, only to be reestablished farther back. Continually tested by local forays, tactical attacks, or massive offensives, this system was itself a product of learning how to survive the deadly artillery assaults by elaborate measures to maintain fighting capacity. Only where positions were hewn into stone, as in Alsace, did they remain largely static; elsewhere they shifted with battle fortunes, creating a labyrinth of protective trenches carved out of the earth. In the East, movement reemerged intermittently when the Central Powers began to capture pieces of Poland. But in the West the experience of most soldiers, and the memory of the Great War, were characterized by this warfare in the trenches.[13]

The deadlock was not a matter of strategic choice but a result of the superior defensive power of modern weapons. Though military doctrine celebrated the spirit of offensive, in practice attacking a well-organized trench system demanded immense sacrifices of dead, wounded, and missing in action. Assault units had to cut through rolls of barbed wire and move through minefields while facing murderous machine-gun or rifle fire. After a preliminary artillery barrage tried to break resistance, attacking troops would throw hand grenades into the trenches or use flamethrowers to smoke out defenders. Often about half the attackers were already incapacitated before a unit could reach an enemy trench, where hand-to-hand combat with small arms and bayonets would ensue. Much of the killing therefore took place at a distance through artillery bombardment, machine-gun fire, or sharpshooters and therefore depended more on a sufficient supply of ammunition than on individual valor. In this impersonal, industrialized warfare the chances of survival were higher if one could hide in a well-built trench than if one had the courage to go "over the top."[14]

During 1915 the stalemate in the trenches developed into a war of attrition in which each side tried to wear down the other with massive firepower. In order to liberate northern France and Belgium, the Entente forces were compelled to attack, while the Germans could hunker down in defensive positions, holding on to their gains. The increasing numbers of British troops, led by the unimaginative Douglas Haig, tried their luck in Flanders, while the French, still clinging to Robert Nivelle's idea of *percée*, launched their assault in Champagne. These repeated offenses made only minimal gains against well-constructed German defenses, stalling with enormous losses. Similarly Austrian troops managed to hold off Italian attacks at the Isonzo front with heavy casualties on both sides. In contrast, a combined German-Austrian offensive broke through at Gorlice-Tarnów, captured Warsaw, and threw the still-sizable Russian armies back to their own frontier with Poland before it bogged down as well.[15] On the continent itself, the Central Powers therefore managed to weather all Entente assaults during the first full year of the war.

At the European periphery, the results of the fighting initially also favored the Central Powers. Since the proclamation of a "holy war" by Sultan Mohammed V had little effect, the Ottoman Empire found itself on the defensive against Arabs in the Near East, aided by the British, and against Russian forces in the Caucasus. The failure of an Allied effort to break through the Dardanelles, the straits that controlled the shipping lane to the Black Sea, was strategically more significant. In spite of fierce fighting at Gallipoli by an Australian and New Zealand expeditionary corps, the Turkish army managed to beat off the attackers and to deny the Entente this essential maritime supply line. When Bulgaria, still smarting from its losses during the Second Balkan War, entered the fray in the fall of 1915, a combined Austrian-German-Bulgarian offensive was finally able to subdue the Serbs. A Greek counterlanding of British and French forces in Saloniki came too late. Using their superiority on land, the Central Powers thereby managed to establish strategic control over the Balkans and to open a direct connection to their Turkish ally.[16]

Only in the war on the seas and in the colonies did the western Allies have the upper hand, since the Royal Navy was larger and more experienced than the German fleet. Though the kaiser's battleships sank some British cruisers, they were defeated at the Battle of the Falkland Islands, and the raiders who had destroyed some merchantmen were eventually rounded up. Commanding the Channel as well as the upper exits of the North Sea, the Royal Navy instituted a tight blockade of the Central Powers, hoping to deprive them of essential foodstuffs and raw materials. Owing to this control of the maritime supply lines, the Anglo-French colonial forces quickly captured the smaller German contingents in the colonies, with the sole exception of General Paul von Lettow-Vorbeck, who waged an elusive guerrilla war in Southeast Africa. Not willing to risk its home battle fleet, the German navy could only counter with submarine attacks on Allied battleships and merchantmen. But when over twelve hundred passengers sank along with the British liner *Lusitania*, which was probably carrying ammunition, it had to break off its indiscriminate torpedoing because of U.S. protests.[17]

During 1916, the third year of the war, both coalitions intensified the war of attrition in pursuit of outright victory. Recognizing the industrial nature of modern warfare, German chief of staff Erich von Falkenhayn sought to break the enemy's will to fight by "bleeding [him] white." Forcing the French to commit their troops, he chose to assault the fortress of Verdun, the strategic hinge of the western front, which could be attacked from three sides. German artillery pounded the forts around the city; German infantry captured the fort Douaumont and inflicted severe losses on the defenders. But declaring "they shall not pass," General Philippe Pétain organized a determined defense, hauled in supplies, and deployed colonial troops. When Falkenhayn realized that inflicting frightful losses at the cost of equal sacrifices had failed to break the French resistance, he desisted from further attack. At the same time a growing number of well-supplied British troops, aided by Canadian and Australian forces and supported by a new kind of weapon—tanks—mounted a huge offensive at the Somme. Costing nineteen thousand dead on the first day, it exerted an even higher blood toll for little territorial gain.[18] Owing to the failure of both attacks, the stalemate continued in the West.

In the East, the Russians mounted a last big offensive under Alexei Brusilov in the summer of 1916 that almost changed the outcome of the war. Drawing on their inexhaustible manpower supply and armed by a rapidly expanding industry, they attacked the German lines at Vilna, only to be eventually pushed back. But in June, when they surprised the Austrians in Galicia, the tsarist armies recaptured much of the previously lost territory. This apparent change of fortunes brought the Romanian government, hoping to extend its territory in Transylvania, into the war in August. However, the combined German, Austrian, Bulgarian, and Turkish forces subdued this new enemy and occupied virtually the entire country by the end of the year. The exploitation of Romania's rich resources of grain and oil helped the Central Powers to continue the war for two more years. Finally, the presence of Entente troops also drew Athens into the conflict, intent on recapturing some of its historic territories from Bulgaria to create a greater Greece. Ironically, the entry of further countries into the war spread the conflict without really changing its outcome.[19]

The continuation of warfare on the high seas also failed to tip the military balance. With the Royal Navy maintaining its blockade of the North Sea exits, the Kriegsmarine did not dare a challenge in unfavorable waters. The only major naval battle took place somewhat by mistake at Jutland when both forces ran into each other during fog. The German ships sank more British tonnage, but the Royal Navy maintained its command of the seas, scoring a strategic victory. Submarine warfare, however, proved more dangerous to British supply lines as long as U-boats torpedoed enemy shipping on sight, since following traditional rules by surfacing exposed the vulnerable submarines to enemy counteraction. But Americans insisted on trading and traveling in contested waters, warning Berlin against sinking liners or neutral ships like the *Arabic* or the *Sussex*. To keep the United States out of the war, the German submarine fleet therefore tried to carry on its campaign without sinking passenger ships, limiting its results.[20] Due to the lethal effectiveness of technical weapons, the stalemate unleashed horrendous violence, destroying millions of lives.

For the soldiers on both sides, the front experience was a special kind of hell that burned itself deeply into the memory of the survivors. The routine of trench warfare involved long stretches of boredom, in which the men could perfect their shelters, play cards, smoke cigarettes, and tend to their infected feet. When action started, there was frantic excitement, a heightened state of existence that proved exhilarating. The noise was overwhelming, mixing the barking of orders with the tok-tok-tok of machine guns, the whistling of mines, the dull thuds of exploding shells, and the cries of the wounded men or horses. The sight of it all was ghastly: blurry photos show bent soldiers dashing forward, bodies being torn by grenades, muddy figures crawling into craters for coverage. At night the sky was lit up with flares, illuminating an eerie scene of death and destruction. The stench of rotting corpses was overwhelming. Many soldiers could only bear the alternating emotions of fear and indifference through iron discipline, liberal doses of alcohol, or visits to brothels. The fighting in the trenches forged a close comradeship of male bonding as a survival community.[21]

WAR AIMS AND PEACE MOVES

The First World War dragged on because both sides pursued aims that could be realized only through victory, thereby condemning all secret peace feelers to failure. In order to mobilize public support, governments claimed to be defending their countries against foreign aggression and appealed to patriotism even among the working classes, previously suspect for their internationalism. At the same time military planners, economic interest groups, and chauvinist propagandists demanded tangible gains as compensation for all the material and human sacrifices incurred, drawing up vast claims that required their enemies to be completely defeated. Moreover, several secret agreements such as the Treaty of London between the Entente and Italy promised territorial annexations and other rewards for entering the war, which in some cases even contradicted each other. While the actual extent of the aims fluctuated with military fortunes, the exigencies of mass politics increasingly trapped cabinets between pursuing limited aims that might be realized and the need to whip up enthusiasm through uncompromising rhetoric.

Among the Central Powers Austria was the most vulnerable, since it faced separatist agitation from the Serbs and the Czechs. The ancient Habsburg Empire was technically a dual monarchy, ruled jointly from Vienna, supported by German speakers, and from Budapest, based on Hungarian dominance. Attacked by nationalist agitators, the multiethnic structure was held together by the aging emperor Francis Joseph, a central bureaucracy, an imperial army, and a commercial middle class in which Jews played a major role. In order to quell further agitation, the Austrian government decided to partition Serbia, although the Hungarians were hardly enthusiastic about adding more Serbs to their domain. Since the Poles in Galicia were still largely loyal to the crown because they had more freedom than their relatives under Russian or Prussian rule, Austria also wanted to expand into central Poland. Whatever the precise aims, Vienna ultimately fought for the very survival of the Habsburg state.[22] Similarly the Ottoman Empire also struggled for its continued existence against separatist movements in its domains.

German war aims were also a paradoxical blend of defense of their continental position and expansion in order to become a global player. The semiconstitutional system, headed by the volatile emperor William II, precariously balanced a strong military with a weaker civilian leadership dependent on Reichstag support. At the height of the first advance, the chancellor's secretary Kurt Riezler drew up the secret "September Program," which sought to "make the German Empire secure towards West and East." By annexing Luxembourg, Antwerp, and the iron-ore basin of Longwy-Briey, the plan tried to weaken France; by claiming a border strip in Poland and creating vassal states in the East, it intended to push Russia back; by constructing a Central European customs union, it attempted to gain economic control over the continent; and by consolidating colonies into a Central Africa, it sought to shore up the overseas possessions. Modified according to the military situation, these goals were loudly proclaimed by a war-aims movement that contradicted the claim of self-defense and rendered separate-peace attempts futile.[23]

The Entente's goals during the war were no less extensive, since they also aimed at the fundamental weakening of their opponents. Tsarist Russia was an embarrassment to its western Allies because its autocratic rule, only somewhat modified by the Duma, and its economic backwardness did not fit into the image of defending democracy. Foreign Minister Sergei Sazonov pursued "the chief aim of countering German power and its efforts at military and political dominance." Concretely, that meant annexing some Prussian territories and conquering all of Poland, assuring it some kind of undefined autonomy. The Austrian rival was to be weakened by promising "freedom and the realization of their national wishes" to the ethnic minorities, especially the Czechs. From the Ottoman Empire, the Russian leadership demanded control over the Straits of Constantinople in order to have free access to the Mediterranean, plus the cession of additional territories in the Caucasus.[24] These aims were so ambitious that Petersburg rejected all of Berlin's advances to conclude a separate peace, although it thereby risked the future of the monarchy.

In France, the war-aims debate was simplified through the national consensus of liberating the northern departments from their German invaders. Though the Third Republic was politically fragmented between a nationalist Right and an internationalist Left, all parties agreed on the restoration of the "lost provinces" of Alsace-Lorraine, responding to the wishes of the francophone bourgeoisie in spite of the reservations of much of the German-speaking populace. The return of Belgian independence and economic reparations were not controversial either. Pushed by nationalists like Georges Clemenceau, the French government secretly also aimed at annexing the left bank of the Rhine or, failing that, at least creating a separate Rhenish state and at conquering the Saar Basin, though both were indisputably German by ethnicity. Moreover, Paris also developed extensive plans for dividing the Near East into spheres of influence with the British in the secret Sykes-Picot agreement and assured Russia of support for its ambitions to seize the Straits in exchange for accepting French expansion toward the Rhine. Above all, France sought future security against Germany.[25]

The British were publicly less vindictive toward Germany but also pursued interests that would materially strengthen their position. In a constitutional monarchy, the cabinet had to pay close attention to the House of Commons, where some leftist members were less annexationist. Nonetheless, there was broad agreement on the restoration of Belgian independence, the destruction of the kaiser's fleet, and the takeover of the Reich's colonies, demanded also by the dominions. London remained noncommittal regarding boundary shifts on the continent and the Balkans, even if its rhetoric also favored national liberation movements. Instead, Britain sought to defend the Suez Canal and foster a revolt of Arab subjects against the Ottoman Empire so as to establish predominance in the Near East. In the competition for Jewish support, London also upstaged Berlin by issuing the Balfour Declaration, which supported the creation of an Israeli homeland although that clashed with promises to Arab sheiks.[26] In short, Britain wanted to eliminate German competition without too much upsetting the balance of power on the continent.

With such extensive war aims on both sides, peace moves were almost preordained to fail, since the respective conditions were too far apart for compromise. The London Agreement of August 1914 between the Entente leaders had foreclosed the possibility of separate peace—an aim consistently pursued by Berlin in order to break its diplomatic "encirclement." American mediation by President Woodrow Wilson's confidant Colonel Edward House was also doomed because its proposals, such as the restoration of Belgian independence, the cession of Alsace-Lorraine, and Russian access to the Mediterranean favored the Entente, though the military situation remained somewhat more auspicious for the Central Powers. When domestic pressure to end the war forced the German government to launch a peace offer of its own in December 1916, its conditions of returning to an improved status quo ante, circumscribed by the Supreme Command, remained unattractive to the Entente. The responses of both sides to subsequent offers by the U.S. president and the pope turned into a propaganda contest of trying to look peaceful while carrying on the war.[27]

The failure of the peace moves suggested that modern war was escaping the control of cabinet diplomacy, since appeals to mass support inflamed popular passions, rendering compromise impossible. Arguing that only tangible gains would make the blood toll worthwhile, chauvinists pressed for extensive public commitments, which effectively tied the hands of the governments among all belligerents. Annexationist war-aims demands, however, increasingly undercut the claims of national defense around which the majority of the populations had rallied in the summer of 1914. Faced with material deprivation and losses of family members, most Europeans were getting tired of the carnage, since the incompatible aims of the elites did not seem worth the additional suffering required for their accomplishment. Left-socialist and pacifist antiwar agitation therefore found more and more adherents who were willing to strike in order to end the senseless slaughter. Instead of returning to the prewar order, the frustrated governments continued to pursue outright victory.[28]

DOMESTIC MOBILIZATION

In modern warfare the home front became just as important as the actual fighting, since it offered the material and psychological support that soldiers needed to carry on. A universal male draft could function only if young men were either enthusiastic or at least willing to join a struggle in which many of them would be killed. Since the production of weapons and ammunition was essential for military success, the absence of a considerable share of the labor force had to be compensated for by employing nonconscripted men, women, POWs, or colonials. At the same time, the war required enormous amounts of money to be raised through increased taxes or public borrowing in order to finance the huge expenditures of paying for troops and their supplies. All belligerents therefore mounted propaganda campaigns to convince neutrals of the justice of their cause and to shore up the fighting spirit of their own population. Where patriotic appeals evoked little response, military censorship saw to it that no criticism would be raised or damaging information divulged.[29] Much more than earlier conflicts, World War I involved civilians at home.

After the outbreak of fighting, all belligerents tried to present a united front by suspending domestic politics so as to maximize their commitment to war. In Germany, Kaiser William II sought to overcome regional, religious, class, and ethnic divisions by proclaiming to the Reichstag "I no longer know parties, I know only Germans." Instead of locking up socialists as subversive agitators, this "truce-within-the-castle" appeal urged them to vote for war credits in exchange for having the labor movement accepted into the national community. In France, the left-center government similarly included two socialist ministers and announced a *union sacrée*, uniting all different groups in a national struggle without seeking partisan advantage. In England the competing Liberals, Unionists, Labourites, and Irish Nationalists also rallied behind the war effort, though they debated more openly about the right strategy. Even in the authoritarian Austrian, Russian, and Ottoman empires there was a similar closing of ranks, albeit with more compulsion from above.[30] This "spirit of 1914" only began to fray when the war dragged on and suffering became interminable.

The propaganda that mobilized the home front and appealed to international opinion created a veritable "culture of war," which blended patriotism with hatred. In this area, the Allies had a great advantage, since the Reuters and Havas agencies controlled the international cables that transmitted the news. The Entente succeeded in depicting the struggle as a fight between the universal values of Western civilization, based on democratic government, and Prussian militarism, exemplified by atrocities against Belgian civilians.[31] The Central Powers found themselves on the defensive in the publicity war, since they were unable to frame their cause in a general fashion by emphasizing the superiority of their own *Kultur*. Less versed in dealing with the media, the German government relied more on censorship under martial law, favoring patriotic rhetoric as "apolitical" and suppressing leftist criticism. While writers such as Maurice

Barrès or T. E. Lawrence provided support for the Entente, professors such as Werner Sombart and authors such as Thomas Mann polemicized in favor of the Central Powers.[32] In colorful posters graphic artists also reinforced patriotic appeals by painting horrifying images of the enemy.

In industrial warfare, a high-performance economy was crucial for producing the necessary weapons for fighting. The Entente powers also led in mobilizing the economy, as they had better access to resources through drawing on wealth accumulated during decades of prosperity. Owing to their control of the seas, they were able to resupply themselves from the empire and the United States, where businessmen were ready to float loans in order to make a tidy profit. In contrast to Russian ineptitude, England and France used a mixture of government control and private enterprise in order to raise their output considerably.[33] With fewer resources at their disposal, the Central Powers had to rely on technological innovation like Fritz Haber's nitrogen synthesis in order to replace raw materials with *Ersatz* products. The Berlin government used a more bureaucratic approach to coordinate production through a War Raw-Materials Department let by Walther Rathenau, and rationed food so as to hold prices down. But when the blockade tightened and the potato harvest declined by 50 percent, widespread starvation ensued in the "beet winter" of 1916–17, sapping the will to fight.[34]

Because of its larger population, the Entente also had an advantage in available manpower, which was crucial for continued fighting and arms production. The French moved almost half a million North African soldiers to the front, while Britain, helped by numerous volunteers from the dominions and the Indian army, instituted the draft in 1916. Russia had an ample supply of men but difficulty in training troops. With reserves depleted, the Germans called up the birth cohort of 1900 in 1918, since Austrian troops were ethnically unreliable and only the Turks could be counted on among the Ottoman ally. Facing enormous numbers of wounded, medical officers made heroic efforts to treat the disfigured or shell-shocked so as to save their lives and return them quickly to combat. At home, skilled industrial laborers needed to be replaced while farm workers were also in short supply. To make up these deficits, in the fall of 1916 the Berlin government proclaimed the Hindenburg Program to double arms output, which compelled all males between sixteen and sixty-five to perform some kind of national service in the factory or on the land. As a reward for cooperating in the patriotic effort, labor unions were granted new rights of representation.[35]

Though women remained excluded from combat, their contributions became increasingly important to the war effort. On the one hand they played traditional supportive roles, serving symbolically as patriotic inspiration and practically as psychological comfort by sending letters and packages. When soldiers were home on leave, wives were also encouraged to get pregnant in order to make up for the manpower losses on the battlefield. On the other hand, women gradually assumed auxiliary military functions as nurses, secretaries, or drivers in uniform, thereby freeing men for the actual fighting. More important yet was the recruitment of females for industrial production, where they replaced drafted workers in making artillery shells, machine-gun ammunition, and even actual weapons. This was tough work in noisy and ill-vented factory halls that tested physical stamina and mental commitment. While combat reinforced the distinction between male killing and female support from the sideline, the war hastened the erosion of traditional gender roles in the workplace.[36]

When the struggle entered its third year with no end in sight, public opinion became increasingly polarized between advocates of victory at any price and proponents of immediate peace. The ever larger numbers of dead, wounded, and missing as well as shortages of food and fuel raised the question of whether the sacrifices were worthwhile. Nationalists among all the belligerents stressed the need to "persevere" until a victorious end, because otherwise all the previous suffering would have been in vain. Schoolteachers tried to motivate pupils by showing the front lines with pins on maps, posters appealed for subscription to war bonds, and patriotic rallies celebrated local victories. Within the Central Powers, ineffective or unlucky commanders such as General Falkenhayn were replaced with presumed winners like Hindenburg and Ludendorff. In response to army mutinies and strikes, hard-line politicians such as *le tigre* Georges Clemenceau and the mercurial Lloyd George assumed greater responsibility in the Entente countries because they were capable of rousing the masses with patriotic appeals. Newly founded chauvinistic groups like the German Fatherland Party also tried to strengthen the will to victory.[37]

In spite of such efforts, the patriotic fervor wore off, and war weariness spread among soldiers and civilians facing death or deprivation. In all countries, the majority of the elite remained committed to annexationism while the middle class continued to respond to national appeals. But in the trenches some soldiers began to refuse orders to attack, and in the factories many laborers demanded more food, shorter hours, and better pay. The mounting criticism of the war as an imperialist struggle among independent socialists, led by Vladimir I. Lenin, Rosa Luxemburg, and Karl Liebknecht, led to the symbolic refusal of war credits by leftist parliamentarians. Promising an immediate end to the carnage, the slogan "no annexations, no indemnities" resonated ever more widely among industrial workers who broke with the suspension of politics by organizing strikes. About forty thousand French soldiers on the western front also mutinied, though their protests were put down with some concessions and force. Since the misery of the trenches and the hunger at home made patriotic rhetoric lose its appeal, the conduct of the war reached a crisis during the winter of 1916–17.[38]

ULTIMATE ESCALATION

As neither the Bulgarian nor the Romanian entry proved decisive, the totalizing logic of modern warfare finally also drew the United States, the only country left that could tip the balance, into the conflict. American opinion was, however, divided, with much of the progressive reform coalition heeding George Washington's warning against getting involved in European quarrels. In particular, many midwesterners and westerners, immigrants of Irish descent, and German-Americans were opposed to participating in a fight that looked as bloody as it seemed pointless. However, eastern elites felt a cultural affinity to Great Britain and France, while businessmen were making much money by supplying the Entente and bankers floated loans to finance such orders. British command of the sea and of the news cables meant that sentiment and material interest among an influential segment of politicians and the press swung in the direction of the Entente. Conscious of the strength of isolationist reluctance, the Democratic administration of President Woodrow Wilson sought to mediate until the submarine issue finally drew the United States into the war.[39]

Unlike the British naval blockade, the submarine was a new kind of weapon that, used without restrictions, violated the rules of sea warfare. During the naval race Admiral Tirpitz had not put much priority on its development, since the kaiser wanted to create a competitive high-seas fleet. Following the traditionally accepted pattern, submarines would have to surface, stop an enemy ship with a shot across the bow, send over a boarding party, let its sailors enter lifeboats, and only then sink it. But the cornered vessel could in turn try to outrun a slower submarine, ram it, or puncture its vulnerable hull with machine-gun or small-cannon fire. Moreover, ships of belligerent nations could change their names, add false smokestacks, or fly neutral flags to disguise their origin. Though they had some success with conventional methods, submarine commanders came to prefer a policy of sinking by torpedoing on sight, because that kept their own ship and crew safe while giving the enemy no chance to escape. The strategic aim of sinking merchant shipping was the interdiction of food and raw-material supplies, especially to Britain, which needed both.[40]

In neutral countries unrestricted submarine warfare created more resentment than a conventional blockade, since ships and crew members were lost instead of just being impounded and interned. The British stretched the rules of sea warfare by demanding that neutral vessels stop in their ports, from which they would be released only if they carried no goods for transshipment to the Central Powers. The U.S. government protested somewhat halfheartedly against such restrictions of trade. In contrast, the sinking of passenger liners like the *Lusitania* provoked a greater public outcry, because 128 American citizens went down with it, although they had been cautioned not to travel in a war zone on a British ship that might carry ammunition. In response to the further torpedoing of passenger ships, President Wilson sternly warned the kaiser that a continuation of unrestricted sinking would bring the United States into the war. Berlin therefore backed down, much to the chagrin of its own naval leadership. While the British blockade killed slowly by starvation, the loss of life by submarine warfare violated the ethics of civilization more dramatically.[41]

The German decision to resume unrestricted submarine warfare on January 9, 1917, was therefore a desperate gamble to secure outright victory. The failure of Berlin's peace offer to produce viable negotiations left the civilian leadership around Chancellor Bethmann Hollweg no alternative but to go along. While the new Supreme Command of Hindenburg and Ludendorff decided on a defensive strategy for the western front, it hoped to knock Britain out of the war by using growing numbers of submarines to interdict essential supplies of war goods, raw materials, and foodstuffs. Glad at last to be able to play a decisive role, the naval command supported the strategy, producing spurious statistics that promised that the United Kingdom would collapse within six months. The civilian experts consulted were more cautious, since they were somewhat better informed about the potential of the United States. But during the decisive meeting, the military leaders fatally underestimated American power by ignoring its war-production capacity as well as its ability to train enough soldiers to affect the outcome on the western front.[42]

The resumption of unrestricted submarine warfare triggered American entry into the First World War, which transformed the country's friendly neutrality toward the Entente into an actual cobelligerency. The yellow press had aroused public opinion with sensationalist stories about German sabotage and spies that exaggerated a few misguided incidents into a ubiquitous danger. The interception of a secret telegram by German secretary of foreign affairs Arthur Zimmermann to the Mexican government created a further outcry, because Berlin proposed an alliance and promised the restoration of territories that Mexico had previously lost to the United States.

Violating the Monroe Doctrine, this diplomatic ploy of befriending the enemy of your enemy provided President Wilson and his advisers with a public pretext to join the Allies at last in the hope of creating a new and peaceful world order. The affront of ignoring previous warnings triggered a lopsided vote in both houses of Congress in favor of entering the conflict. Claiming that "the German government has committed repeated acts of war against the government and people of the U.S.," Washington declared war on April 6, 1917.[43]

The immediate military effect of the American entry was limited, although the formal backing strengthened the Entente's resolve to continue the fight. Since it had previously engaged only in local or imperial campaigns in places such as Cuba, the Philippines, and Mexico, the U.S. Army was merely a colonial force, while the navy was rapidly growing. Though President Wilson insisted on a special role as an "associated power" so as not to be committed to the secret treaties of the Entente, his involvement put the full industrial and financial power of the United States at the disposal of the Allies. Now the navy could openly co-organize a convoy system across the Atlantic in which merchant vessels were protected by warships with sonar and depth charges, thereby blunting the effectiveness of the submarines. Finally, the army itself instituted an ambitious program of expansion that allowed it to train tens of thousands of raw recruits, which would resupply the depleted manpower reserves of the Entente with young men still willing to risk their lives in an attack.[44] Even if its initial impact remained slight, U.S. participation turned the war into a truly global conflict.

Since most fighting took place in Europe, the U.S. government mounted a propaganda campaign to unite a divided population behind the war effort. President Wilson sought to endow the conflict with a higher meaning by proclaiming that this would be "a war to end all wars," designed "to make the world safe for democracy." Moreover, his administration created a Committee on Public Information, led by George Creel, which pilloried Prussian militarism and ridiculed "Kaiser Bill" as "the Hun," referring to the emperor's ill-advised injunction to the international force to put down the anti-Christian Boxer Rebellion in China in 1900 by being as "terrible as the Huns."

Creel's effort, supported by a rabid mass-circulation press, created a veritable "war hysteria," which forbade speaking German in public, renamed streets patriotically, and changed harmless products like *Sauerkraut* into "victory cabbage." This nationalist frenzy even claimed some human lives, such as in the lynching of a hapless German-American in East St. Louis.[45] In propaganda terms, the U.S. entry transformed the war into a struggle between "Western civilization" and German barbarism.

In spite of the addition of a new belligerent, the outcome of the war remained undecided in the spring of 1917. The British continued their massive offensives in France and Belgium against the heavily fortified positions of the Hindenburg line, conquering small areas of devastated territory at enormous human cost. The Germans slowly advanced from Poland into Russia, also suffering heavy losses but capturing larger areas from the Baltic provinces to the Romanian border. Moreover, it was not yet clear whether the convoys or the submarines would win the naval struggle. In the western countries, deep political divisions over military strategy reemerged, but ultimately advocates of continued fighting prevailed. The strains were showing more clearly in tsarist Russia, where food riots tested the imperial order, and in the Habsburg monarchy, where the voices of separatist nationalism grew ever louder. The end of the war was therefore a race between the gradual collapse of Russia, leading to German victory in the East, and the arrival of American troops, helping the Entente to win the war in the West.

MECHANIZED SLAUGHTER

The "front experience" deeply scarred European intellectuals, disabusing them of their optimism about the continuation of progress. A "lost generation" of poets sought to make sense of "the pity of war." Wilfred Owen, for instance, deflated the notion of glorious death by describing the effect of a gas attack:

> If in some smothering dreams you too could pace
> Behind the wagon that we flung him in,

And watch the white eyes writhing in his face,
His hanging face, like a devil's sick of sin;
If you could hear, at every jolt, the blood
Come gargling from the froth-corrupted lungs,
Obscene as cancer, bitter as the cud
Of vile, incurable sores on innocent tongues,—
My friend, you would not tell with such high zest
To children ardent for some desperate glory,
The old Lie: *Dulce et decorum est*
Pro patria mori.

Such shocking experiences destroyed faith in a benign providence, disillusioned patriotic idealism, and undermined military discipline. Many of the greatest talents of European youths, like Rupert Brooke or Walter Flex, paid for their patriotism with their lives. Even soldiers who survived began to question not just the purpose of the war but the very values that they were presumably defending. Most writers including Erich Maria Remarque or Robert Graves left powerful indictments of warfare so as to warn against its repetition. But there were also nationalists like Ernst Jünger and Louis-Ferdinand Céline who glorified danger and the comradeship of war.[46]

In these testimonies, mechanized war appears as all-engulfing force, unleashing previously unimaginable levels of violence. To begin with, the advance of technology made weapons such as heavy artillery, machine guns, poison gas, and tanks much more destructive and deadly than ever before. The actual battlefield therefore tended to resemble a moonscape with trenches, shell craters, concrete shelters, and gun emplacements, in which houses were reduced to rubble, trees cut down to stumps, and pools filled with carcasses of horses. At about seventeen million, more people than ever before were killed outright, with equal numbers grievously wounded and others so psychologically damaged that they would wake up screaming in the middle of the night. While much of the killing was at a distance through artillery bombardment, machine-gun salvos, or rifle shots, battling in the trenches still involved hand-to-hand combat with hand grenades, sidearms, and bayonets. During this kind of fighting, most illusions of individual heroism vanished. The reality of industrial warfare turned out to be dirty, destructive, and depressing.[47]

In retrospect, it still seems amazing that soldiers continued to wage such a murderous war, facing considerable odds of getting killed in the process. Diaries and letters from the front offer some clues as to their motives. Initially there was much patriotic fervor, which made upper-class Englishmen volunteer and drove German students into death at Langemarck. But for drafted workers it was more likely compulsion that kept them in uniform, since shirking one's duty was severely punished, with deserters being shot. For a while, hatred of enemies, deprecated by names like "Jerries," "Limies," and "Frogs," spurred the fighting. Yet there were also moments of truce to gather up the wounded, and even rarer instances of fraternization such as by singing Christmas carols together, that indicated a sense of being caught in a vortex from which there was no escape. More powerful still was the solidarity with one's immediate comrades when units became survival communities where each member depended on all the others. Finally, a misplaced desire to prove one's manhood also played a role since young men did not want to be shamed in front of one another.[48]

Modern warfare also put new demands on civilians because the escalation to total war involved the home front to a much higher degree than before. According to the traditional division of labor, women were supposed to keep the home fires burning while nonconscripted laborers provided the essential supplies for fighting. But in World War I the British blockade mercilessly starved the old as well as mothers and children, while German submarine attacks sank ships with their crews and passengers. At the same time, the rise of mass politics meant that governments had to go to greater lengths to persuade the electorate of the justness of their cause by claiming that they were merely defending the *mère patrie* or *Vaterland*, though their war aims were undoubtedly expansionist. In order to break an enemy's will to fight, they therefore engaged in mutual subversion and clothed their national interest in universal language that might appeal to minorities among their foes. In this political contest the democracies held better cards than the monarchies, since the former were used to conflict while the latter counted on deference.[49]

As the initial step toward the self-destruction of Europe, World War I was "the great seminal catastrophe of the twentieth century."[50] Dragging on for four and a half years, it reduced to ashes houses in the battlefields of Belgium and northeastern France, northern Italy, the Balkans, Poland, Russia, and the Baltic. Pieces of corpses and metal scraps still surface upon plowing in battlefields like the Somme, and trees remain stunted at Verdun while the red poppies of Flanders' fields symbolize the futility of the carnage. By mobilizing troops from the colonies, the overseas empires shattered the myth of white supremacy and taught subalterns those military skills that would eventually displace them. The entry of transoceanic powers like Japan and the United States also marked the end of European hegemony in world affairs, since the conflict could not be resolved without drawing on resources and manpower from beyond the continent. Finally, the unprecedented violence of combat left a legacy of hatred that poisoned European politics for the next generation. Even if the fighting produced some technical innovations and medical advances, the negative impact of the first modern war on Europe can, therefore, hardly be exaggerated.

Chapter 4

BOLSHEVIK REVOLUTION

Lenin as revolutionary, 1920. *Source*: bpk, Berlin / Art Resource, NY.

S hortly before midnight on April 3, 1917, Vladimir I. Lenin got off the train at the Finland station in Petrograd. Just returned from Swiss exile, the little-known revolutionary issued a stirring call for a "worldwide socialist revolution." The next day Lenin elaborated his radical ideas in ten "April theses," published in the Bolshevik paper *Pravda*. Repudiating further support of the war, he called for a break with the Provisional Government so as to proceed to "the second stage of the revolution, which must put power into the hands of the proletariat and the poorest stratum of the peasantry." Since Lenin was aware that his cadre party was a small minority within the broad revolutionary movement, he urged propaganda to "enlighten the masses" that the Bolsheviks were the only group truly representing their interests.[1] With the instinct of a gifted politician, he promised abolition of the hated police, military service, and bureaucracy; nationalization of the land; and control of industrial production by the workers. To galvanize a confused Left, this improvised program justified a second, more radical revolution.

Repeated and amplified in countless articles and speeches, Lenin's vision was so appealing because it fundamentally revised Marxist theory by promising to realize the dream of a classless society immediately. Instead of waiting until bourgeois capitalism was fully developed, this situational rethinking seized upon the anarchy following the collapse of tsarism by refusing to cooperate with a liberal middle class of entrepreneurs and professionals and sought rather to put power into the hands of the long-suffering masses of soldiers, workers, and peasants, which would be represented in their grassroots councils, the soviets. Freed of the historical determinism of Marx and Engels, daring revolutionaries like Leon Trotsky and Josef Stalin could now attempt to break the weakest link in the imperialist chain by exploiting the contradictions of a still-rural but rapidly developing country like Russia. Clothed in heroic narratives from John Reed's and Leon Trotsky's memoirs to Sergei Eisenstein's films, this voluntaristic revision of structural theory acquired mythical proportions, inspiring many imitators around the globe in the decades to come.[2]

Begun with high hopes, this revolutionary form of Marxist modernization demanded an enormous effort that exacted an immense price of human suffering. Bypassing an entire stage of liberal capitalism required much compulsion and violence that contradicted its emancipatory intent. Neither the remnants of tsarist autocracy nor the bourgeois reformers would voluntarily give up their claims to power. The largely illiterate peasantry and the still semirural factory workers would have to be convinced that even when their immediate needs were satisfied, they should support a Marxist project of emancipatory egalitarianism that required a fundamental reshaping of Russian society. No doubt a growing number of Bolshevik Party members would enjoy wielding revolutionary power, while the radical intelligentsia could engage in a social experiment of unprecedented scope. But bypassing the incipient development toward a western-style capitalism and democracy meant that the minority of professional revolutionaries had to force their theoretical vision on a reluctant populace unprepared for such drastic change.[3]

During the past century, evaluations of the Russian Revolution have come full circle, largely discrediting its supporters and justifying its critics. During the heyday of the Soviet Union, celebrating the "Great October Revolution" was a patriotic ritual of praising a cast of superhuman heroes, led by Lenin. This was the founding myth upon which the communist claims of legitimacy rested, since it had made industrialization and victory in the Second World War possible. But already by then, skeptics pointed to the erasure of the Old Bolsheviks from photographs and to the promotion of Joseph Stalin in official accounts. In the West opinion was always split along ideological lines, with anticommunists, supported by émigrés and some anti-Stalinist radicals, emphasizing the repressive aspects of the regime, while many liberals were willing to concede that the Bolsheviks had, indeed, modernized the country, albeit by force.[4] More recently, the collapse of the Soviet Union has reopened the original question of whether communism was a necessary step forward or a regrettable detour, preventing a more benign development.

Shorn of their partisan posturing, the Russian revolutions were largely a struggle between competing blueprints of modernization. While Slavophiles wanted to retain the old rural order, even the tsarist autocracy realized that industrial production, social reform, and political representation had to be imported from the West to make the country competitive. However the suffering of the Great War exposed the incompleteness of this transition, creating widespread popular discontent. The February Revolution opened a path to a liberal modernity though the Provisional Government, but the ineptness of its leaders, which kept Russia in the war, discredited their effort at constitution building. Hence the paradoxical October Revolution was in part a Bolshevik military coup that inaugurated a developmental dictatorship and in part a genuine effort to empower the oppressed. Only the failure of authoritarian transformation from above and of liberal development by the middle class gave the Bolsheviks the chance to pursue their own dictatorial modernization from below.[5]

BELATED WESTERNIZATION

At the dawn of the twentieth century foreign travelers and domestic critics considered Russia the most backward of the five great powers in Europe. Even Karl Marx was skeptical of the prospect of revolution in an underdeveloped society, revising his opinion only toward the end of his life. Many indicators, indeed, supported such a bleak view. The vast country was governed by an autocratic monarch, called the tsar, supported by a cumbersome bureaucracy, huge army, and ruthless secret police. The leading stratum was the aristocracy, oriented toward the imperial court and living on the proceeds of its estates. Most of the population still resided in peasant villages, either working for the nobility or holding its property communally in the famous *mirs*. Religious life was dominated by the Orthodox Church, a staunch supporter of the traditional hierarchy. In teeming cities, the poor, illiterate masses struggled from day to day just to survive somehow in their tenements.[6] And yet such stereotypes of backwardness missed the increasing signs of a rapid development that was about to awake this slumbering giant.

Ironically the initial impetus came from the monarchy itself, which embarked on a "modernization from above" in order to make Russia competitive with the West. Defeat in the Crimean War in 1856 suggested that fundamental changes were necessary to restore its military power. In 1861 Tsar Alexander II therefore liberated twenty-three million serfs from their personal bondage, transferring their feudal obligations into monetary compensation so as to spark agricultural development. Three years later he created local bodies of self-government called zemstvos, which were composed of nobles, townsmen, and peasants, and were supposed to work on the improvement of education, medical service, transport, and agronomy. In 1874 he also introduced universal military conscription as a prerequisite for citizenship. Such promising reforms were, however, abruptly ended when terrorists of the "People's Will" assassinated him in 1881, unleashing a wave of repression that stalled further liberalization for another generation.[7] Fearing revolt, his son Alexander III and grandson Nicholas II were determined not to make additional concessions.

As a result, the push for reform shifted to economic development, in which Russia made great strides during the following decades. For instance the minister of finance, Count Sergei Witte, advocated the rapid industrialization of the country and started the building of the Trans-Siberian Railroad so as to connect European and Asian Russia. Under his auspices, numerous large factories were built, importing the newest production methods in heavy industry, machine building, and textiles from Western Europe. With an average annual growth rate of about 5 percent Russia was quickly becoming the fourth-largest industrial power in Europe.[8] Another economic reformer, Prime Minister Pyotr Stolypin, pushed for the commercialization of agriculture by dissolving the communal tenure of *obshchina* in order to make peasants individual proprietors looking out for their own gain rather than for the common good. His reforms included the establishment of large farms, the creation of agricultural cooperatives, the propagation of land improvement, and the offering of credit. These measures unleashed a surprising dynamism that put Russia on the road to catching up with the West.

This economic development created enormous social strains by forcing a rapid transition from a late feudal to an emerging capitalist system. Industrialization allowed great fortunes to be made, with which the newly rich bourgeoisie could rival the ruling aristocracy in display by constructing fashionable city palaces. The expansion of the bureaucracy and the work of the zemstvos led to the emergence of a stratum of university-trained professionals, who claimed a larger voice in addressing public concerns. Since not all graduates found appropriate jobs, the growth of education and the proliferation of print produced a critical intelligentsia that insisted on more radical changes. The commodification of agriculture created successful peasant proprietors, while pushing less-adept competitors off the land into the cities to seek their fortune. The building of large factories also necessitated the collection of a new labor force of about two million workers, which produced an incipient industrial proletariat.[9] Each of these groups had its own vision of Russia's future, which unfortunately clashed with the scenarios of the others.

Such societal tensions inspired a fierce intellectual debate about Russia's identity as an independent alternative to, or a potential member of, Europe. On the one hand, defenders of religious orthodoxy promoted the theory of a Third Rome, arguing that Moscow was the successor to Constantinople. Successive movements of Slavophiles, Pan-Slavs, and Neo-Slavs believed in a special Russian mission to unite all Slavic brethren in Eastern Europe and the Balkans. These antiwestern groups extolled the glory of the Romanov dynasty, the holiness of the Orthodox Church, and the superiority of the Russian way of life. On the other hand, numerous reformers from Peter the Great on sought to overcome local ignorance and poverty as quickly as possible by importing ideas, styles, and practices from the West. Unfortunately, these westernizers were in turn divided between evolutionary professionals who looked for liberal models of capitalist democracy and radicals who favored a more revolutionary break with the past. Since these blueprints were incompatible, it was not at all clear which of these roads Russia would follow.[10]

Marxism came late to Russia since it had to displace other rivals and the industrial proletariat still remained small. Only after the failures of the tradition of sporadic peasant revolt, the populist project of "going to the people," and the anarchist preference for terrorism could socialist alternatives gain a foothold. In 1883 the Marxist theoretician Georgy V. Plekhanov, in Swiss exile, succeed in founding a group "for the liberation of labor." When socialist ideas had spread in the intelligentsia, a Russian Social Democratic Labor Party constituted itself in 1889 and joined the Second International. After the turn of the century this radical group split into a moderate wing, led by Julius Martov, which wanted to create an open, democratic workers' party that could play a major role in advancing social reform. The more hard-line faction instead followed Lenin's idea of a cadre party of dedicated professional revolutionaries as the only means to overthrow tsarist repression. When during the 1903 Party Congress the radicals were in the majority, they called themselves Bolsheviks in contrast to the Menshevik moderates.[11]

Tensions exploded in the 1905 revolution, which provided a dress rehearsal for the overthrow of tsarist autocracy. News of defeats in the Russo-Japanese War such as the fall of Port Arthur and the loss of the naval battle of Tshushima brought public agitation to a fever pitch. When the priest Georgy Gapon led a throng of protesters to the Winter Palace in St. Petersburg, troops opened fire, killing hundreds of demonstrators. This "Bloody Sunday" sparked a wildfire of rural revolts, the burning of about three thousand noble manors, and inspired a series of strikes in urban areas. The revolt was led by the populist Socialist Revolutionaries (SRs), who invented a new institution—revolutionary councils, called soviets, in which orthodox Marxists also participated. The government responded by resorting to military force and succeeded in restoring order. But pressure from Count Witte and the public also compelled the tsar to issue an October Manifesto, creating the State Duma as the first nationwide parliament for Russia.[12] This concession did not diminish his ultimate power, but it provided an advisory body to discuss policy that could not be ignored.

During the last prewar years three modernization programs, representing the major divisions of Russian society, vied with each other for leadership of opinion. Supporters of autocracy, such as the aristocracy, the bureaucracy, the army, and the church, sought a nativist path of partial change that would enhance their country's military power without upsetting its traditional social hierarchy. With the establishment of the Duma, the rising entrepreneurs, professionals, and some reformist nobles propagated a constitutional route of enhancing economic development, strengthening the rule of law, and sharing power with the crown. In contrast to the beleaguered autocrats, most of the newly licensed parties felt optimistic about further progress toward a liberal system.[13] Finally, the exploited masses of landless laborers, industrial workers, and urban poor hoped for a revolutionary uprising that would sweep away their oppressive lords and allow them a better life. While the rural populists (SRs) called for the distribution of the land, the Mensheviks proposed social reform and the Bolsheviks propagated a real revolution.

THE IMPACT OF WAR

Contrary to patriotic expectations, the First World War had a devastating effect on Russia, ultimately toppling the tsarist system. Since Great Russian nationalists of all social classes greeted the outbreak with bursts of national fervor, the conservative government thought participation in it would strengthen the unity of the country. But despite some victories against the Austrians, the succession of defeats at the hands of the German army had precisely the opposite effect of disillusioning the people with the performance of the constitutional autocracy. Supporters of the monarchy were upset about the ineptness of the tsar and the rapidly changing cabinets; liberal members of the Duma were angry about the disorganization of the bureaucracy, which hampered the fighting; and the laboring masses in the fields and factories were appalled by the deterioration of their own living conditions. Once initial supplies were exhausted and troops decimated, the war exposed the incomplete modernity of tsarist society.[14] Instead of uniting Russians against a foreign enemy, the struggle sharpened their internal divisions.

What looked like a promising war effort at the beginning began to fall apart when the struggle continued for several years. Since the Russians had spent more on the military than the Germans, their store of weapons, including artillery, was impressive, and their mobilization plans were surprisingly effective. Almost fifteen million peasants and workers were drafted into the army, led by bourgeois officers and directed by noble generals. But when the stockpiles were used up, the troops dead or captured, and the officer corps thinned out, the tsarist state was unable to replace the losses efficiently enough. Though taxes were raised, the conversion to a war economy led to rampant inflation. Because of the drafting of farm laborers as well as the requisitioning of horses, the production of food declined drastically, eventually requiring rationing. While the large factories produced enough rifles and shells, the transportation system was unable to get them to the front in time, hampering offensives at crucial moments. Though Russia had ample manpower, it failed to organize sufficient supplies, making it incapable of sustaining a lengthy war of attrition.[15]

Successive defeats created confusion among the military leadership and undercut the morale of frontline soldiers. While the tsarist army was able to defeat the Habsburg military in the fall of 1914 and in 1916, it continued to lose against the Germans, gradually retreating from Poland and the Baltic states. The civil-society effort by a national zemstvo committee to increase weapons production and speed distribution to the front consumed vital civilian resources and exposed administrative incompetence. Rumors spread that Russian soldiers lacked rifles and were told to pick them up from their fallen comrades during attacks. Since the new recruits, rushed forward to make up the losses, were often insufficiently trained and badly equipped, they suffered frightful losses. As a result many soldiers and noncoms lost morale, sometimes disobeying orders and having to be driven forward by machine guns at their back.[16] When tales of such disasters spread to the home front, patriotism evaporated, anger at superiors grew, and a feeling took hold that only a radical change could end the ceaseless carnage.

The tsarist government proved incapable of remedying the situation, because it was itself in a state of disarray. After the fall of Warsaw, Tsar Nicholas II made the fateful decision to go to the front and assume command of the army. This choice was a mistake since he thereby became personally responsible for any defeat, while his departure left a political vacuum in the capital. Though the Duma was only intermittently in session, its spokesmen increasingly criticized the government, which was led by weak ministers like Boris Stürmer and Alexander Protopopov, whose competence was doubted even in ruling circles. In order to create a "government of public trust," the deputies organized a "Progressive Bloc"—but the tsar refused their request for parliamentarization, since it would diminish his autocratic power. The conflict deepened between the state bureaucrats, intent on maintaining control, and the representatives of civil society, who were organizing their own war-industry committees. By November 1916 frustration over the chain of such blunders had provoked the liberal deputy Pavel Miliukov to the point of shouting: "Is it stupidity or treason?"[17]

Part of the problem was the meddling of Tsarina Alexandra, who tried to run the court and government in Nicholas' absence. As granddaughter of Queen Victoria, she belonged to the highest nobility, but the Russian people intensely disliked her German birth and reticent style. Moreover, she constantly interfered in personnel decisions, appointing and dismissing favorites without sufficient concern for their abilities. The most serious problem was her association with the mystic monk Grigori Rasputin, who claimed to be able to stop the bleeding of the hemophiliac crown prince Alexei. This faith healer led a debauched life centered on alcohol and sex while bestowing favors on his relations and intervening in government affairs. But since there was no medical cure for the inability of her son's blood to clot, the desperate tsarina would not part company with him, though the capital was rife with rumors of his misdeeds. In December 1916 Prince Felix Yusupov and several other aristocrats poisoned, shot, and drowned Rasputin in order to restore some credibility to the crown.[18] But when the monk finally died, the damage had already been done.

On February 23, 1917, popular patience finally ran out. The winter had been brutally cold, and the food supply had broken down in Petrograd. With the metalworkers striking, angry housewives, joined by textile laborers, demonstrated on International Women's Day for more bread to feed their starving families, and some women plundered the bakeries for flour. On the following day the crowds grew to 150,000 people, confrontations with the police multiplied, and some demonstrators were shot. In solidarity with the protesters, the unions proclaimed a general strike, which immobilized the Russian capital, and the crowds began to shout "Down with the tsar!" "Down with the war!" Finally the absent tsar ordered the military to quell the unrest, but protesters chanted "They are shooting our mothers and sisters." Shocked by the brutality of the police and some troops who fired into the crowds, other soldiers, including the Cossack cavalry, began to change sides and shoot their officers.[19] When his army no longer obeyed, the tsar's power vanished. The bread riots and strikes had turned into a veritable February Revolution.

The fall of tsarist autocracy posed the question of how to organize the revolutionary order so as to prevent anarchy. Though loyalist chief of staff Mikhail Alekseev was ready to march on Petrograd, the spreading unrest forced him to sacrifice the tsar in order to preserve the army. Leading Duma deputies such as Miliukov and Alexander Guchkov tried to save the monarchy by transforming it into a constitutional system, but Nicholas II was so discredited that he had to resign. It was the pressure of people who had taken to the streets, organized according to the 1905 example into revolutionary councils, that dictated a more drastic change. In these soviets of deputies, elected from factories, military units, and the countryside, the agrarian populists (SRs), social democrats (Mensheviks), and radical revolutionaries (Bolsheviks) vied for power. Eventually the moderate Duma also lumbered into action and constituted a Provisional Government under the zemstvo leader Prince Georgy Lvov. In an informal division of labor, called "dual power," the Duma set out to govern and draft a constitution while the Petrograd Soviet, composed of revolutionary deputies, sought to defend the interests of the proletariat.[20]

In many respects, the February Revolution was a popular uprising like the Springtime of the Peoples in 1848.[21] The autocratic order collapsed under the strain of losing a war, since even its adherents admitted that the tsar was incompetent. The middle-class Duma, elected by restricted suffrage, simply wanted a larger voice in running national affairs but was eventually willing to gamble on a republic. It was the rebellious mass of women, workers, and soldiers demanding "Bread and Peace" that overthrew the autocracy when military discipline gave way and the rank and file, led by sergeants, took power into their hands. The bourgeois liberals merely wanted a constitution with civil rights, a market economy, and improved education, in short, a western form of modernity for Russia. Hating wartime starvation, exploitation, and death, the long-suffering masses demanded more radical changes in Russian society, but they were not so sure of how to realize their aims. Since orthodox Marxism suggested that the bourgeoisie needed to transform the country first, the soviets were initially content just to control the Provisional Government.

THE PROVISIONAL GOVERNMENT

Though the collapse of the old order provided a chance for a liberal modernization of Russia, the middle classes had to contend with the more far-reaching demands of the soviet-led masses. Possessing only a limited social base, the Provisional Government, nonetheless, had the advantage of holding the official reins of power, since the soldiers' and workers' deputies lacked practical experience, even if they had greater revolutionary legitimacy. Both agreed in early March on an informal coalition in order to realize the shared goals of introducing political freedom, guaranteeing rights of speech and assembly, amnestying political prisoners, drafting a constitution, ending discrimination, and curbing the bureaucracy and police. In his first interview as prime minister, Lvov announced optimistically: "I believe in the great heart of the Russian people ... and am convinced that it is the basis of our freedom, justice and truth."[22] Since the Provisional Government had international support, government expertise, and habits of command on its side, its eventual failure surprised observers in the Allied capitals.

The personal style and political orientation of the new cabinet represented a gradual evolution from tsarism, not a radical break with hated autocracy. Prime Minister Lvov, Foreign Minister Miliukov, and Minister of Defense Guchkov were experienced parliamentarians, used to giving speeches, drafting legislation, and negotiating compromises. Official photographs portray them as gentlemen (no women!) in dark suits, respectable representatives of property and education, with grave demeanor, conscious of their responsibility. Politically they came from the Center and moderate Right, since the limited suffrage of the Duma underrepresented the lower classes. Their prosperous lifestyle isolated them from the suffering of the Russian masses because they lived in country villas or urban apartments, supported by servants. Their political project was to westernize their country, write a republican constitution, accelerate economic development, increase literacy, and promote science—in short to transform Russians into modern Europeans.[23] Such leaders could manage a gradual transition but not a dramatic revolution.

In contrast, the revolutionary council deputies were representatives of mass sentiment who lacked the necessary experience to govern a vast country during wartime. Even the members of the Petrograd Executive Committee like Nikoloz Chkheidze and Alexander Kerensky were little known, serving as representatives of their parties such as the SRs, Mensheviks, and Bolsheviks. Snapshots show them wild-eyed with excitement, riding on trucks or haranguing crowds, wearing workingmen's blouses or military tunics and holding rifles as signs of newfound power. Though they tended to be union leaders, noncommissioned officers, or persons with some education, they were closer to the people, suffering cold, hunger, and abuse along with them. Their "order number one" therefore called for the establishment of soldiers' councils, claimed political control of the army, and abolished some excesses of military discipline. Their political ideals tended toward an egalitarian democracy with improved working conditions, enough food for everyone, and the return of peace—implying not just a political but also a social revolution.[24]

The most divisive issue between the Provisional Government and the soviets was the continuation of the war, pitting patriotic officers against defeatist recruits. Western capitals greeted the February Revolution with enthusiasm, since the collapse of autocracy in Russia facilitated their propaganda by creating a united front of democratic countries against the authoritarian Central Powers. As a bourgeois liberal, Foreign Minister Miliukov wanted to persevere until a "decisive victory," promising to abide by all international commitments in pursuit of expansionist war aims. The war-weary Petrograd

Soviet was outraged, since it saw no reason to prolong a losing conflict at the cost of further lives. To keep antiwar demonstrations from turning into a civil war, the moderate voices in the soviets proposed a compromise of "revolutionary defensism" that would continue the war to stop the German invader, while striving for a compromise peace. This crisis was finally resolved through the creation of "a coalition of reason," in which six SRs and Mensheviks like Kerensky entered the cabinet of the Provisional Government with a program of radical democratization.[25]

Just when it seemed that the government might stabilize through broadening its political base, the radical émigrés began to return and advocate a pacifist course. Exiled revolutionary leaders had watched the February Revolution with elation and frustration, eager to participate themselves. Intent on eliminating one major enemy through internal turmoil, the Imperial German government even shipped Lenin and thirty of his followers in a sealed train from Switzerland to Sweden so that they could spread his defeatist message in Russia. Others, such as the SR Viktor Chernov, the Menshevik Martov, and the Bolshevik Trotsky, came back on their own, while still others, including Lev Kamenev and Stalin, returned from banishment in Siberia. Cut off from Russian patriotism, most of the exiles had joined the left wing of the Second International in denouncing the war. Their return to Russia provided the war-weary masses with an intellectual and organizational leadership that sought to steer the soviets away from defensism.[26] While the middle class continued to support the war, the soldiers, workers, and peasants now found new arguments to oppose it.

Seeking to counter the dissolution of the army, the ambitious minister of defense Kerensky authorized another offensive in order to revive Russian confidence. As a moderate socialist and member of the Petrograd Soviet, he supported a bill of soldiers' rights but simultaneously sought to restore the authority of the officer corps. Moreover he undertook a propaganda trip to the front, in which his eloquent pleas for the continuation of fighting were received with applause. He also fired the previous chief of staff and replaced him with General Alexei Brusilov, who had been a more successful commander. On June 16, 1917, the Russian army mounted its last major attack in Galicia against Austrian troops, gained thirty kilometers—and stalled. On July 6, the combined forces of the Central Powers counterattacked and broke through, precipitating a full-fledged flight. As a result, the Russian lines disintegrated, with many soldiers, even entire units, deserting and making their way home.[27] Instead of saving the country with a revolutionary *levée en masse*, Kerensky hastened a military defeat that pulled the Provisional Government down with it.

The government similarly failed to make headway in domestic issues, since the positions of the liberal and socialist deputies were basically irreconcilable. While the middle-class ministers insisted on respect for private property, the representatives of revolutionary soviets wanted workers' protection and land for the peasants. In the factories, union spokesmen demanded an eight-hour workday, better pay, and workers' control. In the countryside, peasant councils began to grab land, animals, and tools from the nobles. At the edges of the empire, restive nationalities like the Finns, Ukrainians, and Baltic peoples declared their independence, supported by the German military. Since the bourgeois Constitutional Democratic Party (informally, Kadets) opposed the leftward drift of the government, its members resigned, precipitating a crisis that was resolved only when Kerensky became prime minister in a restructured cabinet with more ministers drawn from the Petrograd Soviet. In the Petrograd City Council election the Kadet Party shrank to 21 percent, the moderate socialists (SRs and Mensheviks) won 44 percent of the vote, but ominously the radical Bolsheviks advanced as well, to 21 percent.[28]

By midsummer signs were multiplying that the Provisional Government was failing for a number of structural as well as political reasons. Confronted by uncooperative conservatives from above and discontented radicals from below, the Russian middle class was simply not large and powerful enough to carry through a liberal modernization of such a chaotic country on its own. Even if the soviets initially refused to take power due to ideology and inexperience, they competed effectively for popular allegiance by proposing programs of more drastic changes. Added to the inherent problems of dual power were basic mistakes in policy. Most important was the decision to continue the war with another offensive, a desperate gamble that speeded the dissolution of military authority at a time when civil order was vanishing. But equally significant was the conflict between bourgeois interest in the sanctity of private property and mass desire for economic relief through social reform.[29] Failing to understand that peace and bread were more pressing needs than a new constitution, the Provisional Government threw the chance for a democratic development away.

RED OCTOBER

Since the Bolshevik seizure of power seemed to have come out of nowhere, the reasons for its surprising success are still hotly disputed. No doubt the ineffectiveness of the Provisional Government provided the opportunity for a further radicalization according to the pattern of the French Revolution a century and a quarter before. But surprisingly the popular disillusionment with Kerensky did not help the SRs or Mensheviks but rather boosted the Bolsheviks. Traditional accounts argue that the clairvoyant and ruthless leadership of Lenin, not matched by any competitor, was the key difference between them. Soviet apologists have also pointed to the growing support of the masses for the Bolshevik program of bread, land, and peace, which gave their takeover an aura of legitimacy that the others lacked.[30] In contrast, post-Soviet critics emphasize that the communist takeover was technically the result of a coup d'état. Was the "Glorious October Revolution" therefore the triumph of grassroots democracy or the putsch of a radical minority leading inevitably to dictatorship?

It is difficult to gauge the contribution of Lenin's leadership, since the cult around his personality has created a larger-than-life image of exceptional charisma. Born as Vladimir I. Ulyanov into a liberal family of teachers, he seemed predestined for a promising legal career. But when his older brother was executed for sedition, Vladimir vowed to become a revolutionary, joining the radical wing of the labor movement. To escape from tsarist persecution and imprisonment in Siberia, he went into exile in Switzerland, seeking to apply Marxist structural analysis to Russia's belated development. In the process he adopted the pen name "Lenin," developed a spartan lifestyle, and made himself into the prototype of a professional revolutionary. With various pamphlets like *What Is to Be Done?* (1902) he developed a reputation as a brilliant theorist because of his ability to relate socialist ideas to concrete political situations. By denouncing the First World War as an imperialist struggle, he impressed his comrades with his iron will and total dedication, though he continued to have difficulty in convincing them with his tactical insights.[31]

Equally important, however, was the growing appeal of the Bolshevik Party due to its uncompromising opposition to the war and its promises of food and land. In the underground, the party had attracted a bevy of talented individuals like Leon Trotsky, Joseph Stalin, Lev Kamenev, and Nikolai Bukharin. When these organizers were allowed to operate in the open, they transformed the Bolsheviks from revolutionary cadres into a mass-membership organization capable of taking power. In contrast to the SRs and Mensheviks, who were compromised by entering the Provisional Government, Lenin's party profited from its refusal to cooperate, growing from a few tens of thousands to about a quarter of a million members by midsummer. In the First All-Russian Congress of Soviets, which met in June, they still had only 105 seats compared with 285 for the SRs and 248 for the Mensheviks. But the disappointed workers, soldiers, and peasants increasingly flocked to them, giving the Bolsheviks one-third of the votes in the Petrograd City Council elections in August and half of the seats in the Moscow ballot in late September.[32]

Another crucial factor was the inability of the Provisional Government to control the soviets and maintain military discipline. When in early July a machine-gun company was ordered to the front, a throng of workers and soldiers protested, marched toward the center of Petrograd, and shouted "All power to the soviets!" Confronted with a spontaneous revolt, Lenin cautioned, "If we now seized power, it would be naive to believe that we could keep it." Since the Bolsheviks were only a small minority, he argued that they should wait until they gained more support. This refusal to lead the crowds saved the Provisional Government for another day. But Kerensky also faced a threat from the right. In August, frightened middle-class parliamentarians and tsarist officers persuaded General Lavr Georgiyevich Kornilov to save the country from impending catastrophe by restoring law and order. When he heard rumors that the military was prepared to take power, Kerensky had to call on the workers and soldiers to stop the troops from reaching Petrograd. Such crises demonstrated that the government was being ground down between the political extremes.[33]

By mid-September Lenin judged the time ripe for a Bolshevik-led uprising. From the security of Finland, he exhorted his followers: "The Bolsheviks, having maintained a majority in the Soviets of Workers' and Soldiers Deputies of both capitals, can and *must* take power into their own hands." Afraid that Kerensky might create a legitimate government if the Constituent Assembly met to approve a democratic constitution, Lenin claimed a popular mandate: "The majority of the people are *on our side.*" Unwilling to observe democratic formalities, he proposed an "armed uprising in Petrograd and Moscow" to overthrow the parliamentary regime: "History will never forgive us if we do not assume power now." Fearing that a premature putsch would defeat the revolution, Kamenev warned: "*No, a thousand times no.*" But after a fierce debate Lenin convinced him as well as other reluctant party leaders, and preparations for the seizure of power began.[34] This gamble rested on the calculation that the Bolsheviks could dominate the new military revolutionary committees that had assumed control of all troop movements around the capital.

Ironically, the Provisional Government itself provided the pretext for the uprising in late October. Having heard that something was afoot, Kerensky ordered two Bolshevik newspapers shut down, intending to arrest the leaders of the Petrograd Military Revolutionary Committee. Claiming "Petrograd is in danger! The revolution is in danger! The people are in danger!" the Bolsheviks appealed to the soviets to fight the threatening counterrevolution. On the evening of October 24, 1917, Lenin urged his party dramatically: "The government is tottering. One must give it the *coup de grace*, cost what it may. Delaying action means death." Directed by Trotsky, the Petrograd Military Revolutionary Committee therefore ordered the Red Guards, a paramilitary organization of Bolshevik volunteers, to seize the train stations, power company, postal and telegraph office, state bank, and strategic streets and bridges. When Kerensky fled in a U.S. embassy car, the uprising had succeeded without bloodshed, since the Provisional Government could not marshal any military force to defeat it. Contrary to later legend, the other ministers also surrendered in the Winter Palace without a fight.[35]

The Bolshevik leaders wasted no time in exploiting their victory by dominating the Second All-Russian Congress of Soviets. On the morning of October 25, a flyer signed by the Petrograd Military Revolutionary Committee announced that the Provisional Government had been overthrown: "State power has passed into the hands of the organs of the Petrograd Soviet of workers' and soldiers' deputies." As justification the revolutionaries claimed: "The aims for which the people have fought, immediate conclusion of a democratic peace, abolition of landed property rights of estate owners, workers' control of the production, creation of a soviet government—all that has been secured." Received by stormy applause in the headquarters of the Petrograd Soviet, Lenin explained that this was "the third Russian Revolution," which would ultimately lead "to the victory of socialism." Though the Bolsheviks held only 338 of 739 seats in the All-Russian Congress, a clear majority of deputies supported the creation of a soviet government. Elated, Trotsky taunted the losing Mensheviks: "Go where you belong, onto the rubbish heap of history!"[36]

The Red October was therefore a minority coup d'état that claimed to be a popular revolution from below. In contrast to 1905 and February 1917, the Bolshevik seizure of power was not a spontaneous grassroots revolt but a carefully planned and well-executed putsch by a radical party. Lenin could point to indications of growing public support for demands of peace, bread, and land, which had increased the Bolshevik voice within the revolutionary councils all over Russia and gained them majorities in the military revolutionary committees that controlled the troops around Petrograd and Moscow. But in terms of democratic theory, the Bolshevik takeover was not a revolution *by* but *for* the people. Lenin and his party would not be bothered by the formal mechanisms of democracy, since in a Rousseauian sense they believed they knew what was good for the Russian people and were therefore willing to force them to follow their lead.[37] While the Bolshevik coup threw their own country into turmoil, and its violence frightened the European middle classes, among war-weary soldiers and workers the October Revolution served as a beacon of hope for peace and equality.

SOVIET POWER

Their seizure of power confronted the Bolshevik leaders with the challenge of actually governing a chaotic country and implementing socialist modernization. Even experienced Marxists like Plekhanov were skeptical that they could hold on to political power, since "in the population of our state, the proletariat forms *not the majority, but the minority.*" To overcome such hesitation, Trotsky argued "what has happened was an uprising and no conspiracy," since the Bolsheviks acted on behalf of the "masses of the people." Trying to consolidate power, Lenin quickly constituted a new government, a council of people's deputies (*soviet narodnykh kommissarov*), called Sovnarkom, which claimed to represent the soviets.[38] In the deepening anarchy of tsarists and parliamentarians preparing for a comeback and moderate revolutionaries smarting over being outmaneuvered, this self-proclaimed socialist regime sought to establish its authority by popular laws and use of force. Since it was barely able to control the streets of the capitals, the new Sovnarkom, or Soviet, government faced a tough task in maintaining power and putting its program into practice.

The first effort to gain the support of war-weary soldiers was the decree on peace of October 26. This proclamation called on "all the belligerent peoples and their governments to start immediate negotiations for a just, democratic peace." The Bolsheviks adopted the Menshevik slogan of "no annexations, no indemnities," adding to it the self-determination of various nationalities, and the repudiation of "secret diplomacy," which voided tsarist treaty commitments.

Delighted to get rid of one important enemy, the German government accepted an armistice and entered into negotiations on November 19. When it became clear that the Soviet side was playing for time, hoping for revolution among other belligerents, Berlin concluded a separate peace with Ukraine on February 9, 1918. A furious Trotsky walked out, declaring "no war, no peace," but the Germans called his bluff and resumed their offensive, forcing the Soviets to sign the peace treaty of Brest-Litovsk on March 3, 1918. Getting "breathing space" in order to consolidate the revolution by leaving the war cost Russia the independence of Finland, the Baltic States, Poland, and Ukraine.[39]

Other moves to reward Bolshevik followers were the decrees on land and on workers' control. Proclaimed immediately, the former abolished all private property in the countryside, turning the noble, church, and crown domains over to peasant councils, called *volost'*. In effect, this measure legalized an ongoing process of expropriation, allowing peasants to govern themselves. Politically, it was a brilliant move because it stole the chief plank from the populist SRs, but economically it was of dubious value, since the distribution of land fragmented holdings and privileged self-sufficiency rather than creating a secure food supply for the cities. The latter order established "workers' control over industry" through "elected committees supervising production and management," which gradually transferred ownership of large enterprises to municipalities or the state.[40] The fulfillment of other trade-union demands like the eight-hour workday and the introduction of mandatory health insurance helped the workers, like the farmers, to accept direction from the Bolshevik-controlled government, though the Soviet regime soon curtailed such newly won gains.

The Bolsheviks also resorted to dictatorial means in the name of "revolutionary class struggle." Within the soviets, they outflanked and divided their competitors by stealing their programmatic thunder. To control public opinion they also prohibited the publication of all press organs critical of their policies, abolishing the very rights that they had demanded from tsarist autocracy. In early December they started to round up leaders of the Kadet Party and uncooperative SRs or Mensheviks as "counterrevolutionaries." By founding their own secret police, called the Cheka, they established a police state. Its head, the fanatical Felix Dzerzhinsky, repudiated "revolutionary justice," since he believed "now there is war—face to face, a struggle to the end. Life or Death." Since Lenin did not want to go back to parliamentarianism, he suppressed the Constituent Assembly, the hope of all moderate reformers. Aware that they had won only 175 out of 707 assembly seats while the SRs had received 370, the Bolsheviks simply locked out the delegates after the first day, aborting the experiment in Russian parliamentary government.[41]

The ensuing Civil War, immortalized by Boris Pasternak, speeded the establishment of a Bolshevik dictatorship by unleashing untold terror on the people caught between the fronts. The dissolution of the Constituent Assembly indicated that the Soviet regime could be overthrown only by the use of force. Although the western Allies landed some troops in northern and southern Russia to safeguard their military supplies, they could not really decide whom to support. During 1918 a series of confusing engagements developed in which German occupiers, the Ukrainian Rada, the Czech legion, and SRs in Samara played a role. During the following year White Russian generals Aleksandr Kolchak, Anton Denikin, and Pyotr Wrangel mounted concentric offensives toward Moscow, but lack of coordination led to their successive defeats. Energized by the tireless Trotsky, the Red Army, newly constituted out of former tsarist officers and revolutionary soldiers, triumphed over all enemies, reconquering Ukraine in 1920.[42] This force even grew strong enough to fight the reconstituted Polish national state to a draw in a full-scale conventional war.

War communism radicalized the Soviet regime further by emphasizing that "order and discipline" were needed to assure its survival. Since industrial and agricultural production plummeted while inflation soared, a barter economy developed in which grain had to be requisitioned by force and goods traded in a black market. Concurrently the Cheka grew by leaps and bounds, accusing and imprisoning thousands of victims without any recourse to law. Opportunists now also thronged to the Bolshevik Party, since it had acquired a monopoly of political power. When the soldiers of the Kronstadt naval base protested for a return to the original revolutionary aims of freedom and equality, the Soviet government ruthlessly suppressed the revolt, discrediting itself in the process.[43] Even Lenin realized that these draconian measures threatened to alienate the very workers and peasants that the regime claimed to represent. As a result, he reluctantly allowed the reintroduction of some market incentives in his New Economic Policy, while at the same time strengthening internal controls over the members of his party.

Though the Soviet government barely hung on at home, its message of peace and equality resonated in Europe, inspiring workers and soldiers among all belligerents to demand an end to the slaughter. Afraid of pacifist and socialist contagion, the continental governments redoubled their propaganda efforts to counter the strikes and demonstrations. But Bolshevik hopes for help from a "world revolution" were disappointed. While antiwar slogans hastened the collapse of the Central Powers, Soviet-style republics arose only briefly in Munich and Budapest. To isolate the rest of the world from the revolutionary virus, the Paris Peace Conference created a cordon sanitaire of independent states between Russia and Central Europe that built on the Brest-Litovsk Treaty. Promoting revolution through the foundation of the Comintern in 1919, the Soviet government remained an international outcast without recognition or treaty relations. Only when it proved impossible to settle debts between the former Allies in 1922 did the pariahs Berlin and Moscow sign a neutrality treaty at Rapallo, canceling each other's financial demands and starting covert military cooperation.[44]

Ultimately, the reasons for the survival of the Bolshevik minority dictatorship were more complex than either popular legitimacy or ruthless compulsion. Contrary to allegations of a capitalist conspiracy, it was the ineptness and lack of coordination of their enemies that gave the embattled Soviet leaders a lease on life. No doubt the early decrees on peace, land, and workers' control also fulfilled the wishes of a war-weary, land-hungry, and exploited populace in the metropolitan centers and sprawling countryside of Russia. The systematic suppression of real or imagined counterrevolutionaries by the Cheka and the defeat of various White or Green (local peasant) forces by the Red Army also played an important part. Moreover, Lenin's tenacious will and pragmatism in adjusting policy and the iron discipline of a growing Bolshevik Party in meeting the postrevolutionary challenges contributed as well.[45] In spite of many actual disappointments, the vision of a socialist modernity—living in peace, providing enough food, and offering easier work—retained some appeal, because it promised to propel the former tsarist empire into a better future.

REVOLUTIONARY UTOPIANISM

In the early twentieth century, Russia had to choose between several paths toward modernity, each offering a particular combination of advantages and costs. After losing the Crimean and Japanese wars, supporters of tsarist autocracy like Count Witte understood that the country needed to develop economically in order to strengthen its military and remain competitive with other powers. While freeing the serfs dissolved the traditional rural order of noble estates and peasant communes, the rapid industrialization from the 1890s onward created a new urban proletariat. The challenge of a defensive, partial modernization was the need to enable economic development without upsetting social hierarchies or weakening tsarist administrative control. The paradoxical project of trying to catch up with western progress while maintaining a different Slavic identity foundered during the First World War, since this contradictory system proved unable to sustain a war of attrition. Autocratic "modernization from above" therefore created increasing contradictions that brought the tsarist system down with it.[46]

The creation of a parliamentary government after the February Revolution of 1917 opened up a different possibility for gradual, democratic development led by the middle class. The Provisional Government consisted of experienced Duma deputies who intended to draft a western-style constitution in order to safeguard the rule of law and self-government. Supported by leading businessmen and professionals, they could draw on the organizational expertise of civil society working in the zemstvos. Their economic program sought to free individual initiative though a competitive market, sparking further dynamic growth. Abhorring anarchy, this scenario was, unfortunately, fixated on creating a constitution and protecting private property rather than responding to popular demands for increasing the food supply and distributing land to the peasants. But the fundamental error of the Provisional Government was its decision to continue the war, which cost it the support of the weary masses. By pursuing a nationalist course, the fledgling bourgeoisie gambled away the chance for a liberal development toward modernity.[47]

The failure of these alternatives opened the door for the radical attempt at modernization by revolution from below. The Bolsheviks won the competition among the socialist parties since they presented a program that promised to fulfill the immediate wishes of the masses. The populist SRs mainly agitated for the distribution of land, while the Mensheviks only wanted to moderate the necessary capitalist development by social reform. It was Lenin's revision of Marxism in *The State and Revolution*, calling for a socialist revolution to establish a dictatorship of the proletariat, that provided the theoretical justification for the Bolshevik seizure of power in Russia. Moreover, his pragmatic decision not to force the issue in early July but to wait until the situation had deteriorated further in late October proved ultimately correct.[48] Though the Bolsheviks started the year as a minority even within the soviets, their slogan of "Bread, Land, and Peace" appealed to the workers, peasants, and soldiers, steadily increasing their following. The success of their coup gave them an opportunity, inconceivable by orthodox Marxist theory, to realize their socialist dreams.

The Bolsheviks understood that they could retain power in the long run only if they succeeded in modernizing the economy in order to make their social program palatable for the masses. Lenin himself believed that "Communism is the Soviet power plus electrification of the whole country." In February 1920 a Soviet commission, supported by scientists and engineers, therefore started to implement the "GOELRO plan" for Russia's electrification by building a network of thirty regional power plants, harnessing hydropower as well as using coal. This gigantic effort would raise the power output more than fourfold from the last prewar year to 8.8 billion kilowatt-hours within a decade. With such rapid electrification Lenin wanted to promote "the organization of industry on the basis of modern advanced technology," linking town and country in order "to overcome, even in the most remote corners of the land, backwardness, ignorance, poverty, disease, and barbarism."[49] This was a classic statement of the communist path to modernity, which promised to improve the lives of the masses by introducing industrial technology.

Revolutionary modernization offered Russia the chance of rapid development—albeit at tremendous human cost. Leaping over the entire stage of historical development described by Marx as bourgeois capitalism and democracy required much compulsion, since processes like the spread of literacy that elsewhere had taken several generations had to be compressed into a few years. For the Bolsheviks, aided by the intelligentsia, the design and construction of a new Soviet society was a heady project, justifying their dictatorship in moral terms. But the majority of the people did not necessarily buy into this utopian transformation, wanting just to carry on their normal lives in predictable circumstances. All too soon it became apparent that the compulsory effort to reach modernity had a negative side: forced labor in industry, widespread hunger in the countryside, and a network of prison camps all over the country. Since it is difficult to tote up the balance between this appalling suffering and the actual improvement of lives, judgments about the October Revolution will remain controversial for a long time to come.[50]

Chapter 5

DEMOCRATIC HOPES

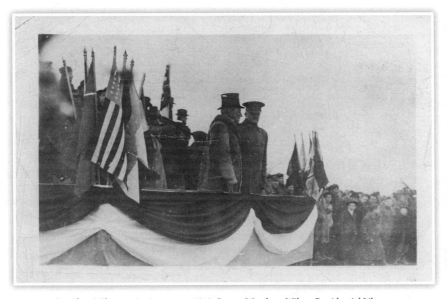

President Wilson reviewing troops, 1918. *Source*: Woodrow Wilson Presidential Library.

On January 8, 1918, Woodrow Wilson addressed a joint session of Congress with a democratic program that sought to counter Lenin's revolutionary message. With great eloquence, the president proposed "fourteen points," prepared in secrecy, that outlined a path toward making the world "fit and safe to live in" by ending the Great War. Not being a party to secret interallied agreements, the former law professor appealed to the war-weary peoples on both sides of the front with proposals that encapsulated progressive thinking about the preconditions for a more peaceful world. His first demands centered on open diplomacy, freedom of the seas, free trade, and disarmament—noble sentiments that would also benefit American interests. The next points outlined territorial conditions that favored the Entente without humiliating Germany needlessly—the evacuation of Russian territory, the restoration of Belgium, and the return of Alsace-Lorraine to France—while promising "autonomous development" to Austrian and Ottoman subjects. The capstone of such "a just and stable peace" was to be "a general association of nations"[1]

As a representative of democracy, the American president cut an imposing figure, looking both stern and inspiring. Hailing from a Scotch-Irish family, he was a sober Presbyterian but also an inspiring public speaker. After obtaining a doctorate in law from Johns Hopkins University, he had joined the Princeton University faculty and written about congressional government. Becoming its president in 1902, he had expanded the faculty and modernized the curriculum, calling on students to dedicate themselves to the service of the nation. Entering politics as a member of the progressive wing of the Democratic Party, he had been elected governor of New Jersey in 1910. Only two years later he had succeeded in winning the presidency as a result of his reputation for personal honesty and willingness to engage in reforms, formulated in his program of "New Freedoms." In 1916 he had been reelected to a second term, largely because he had kept the country out of the war. As a democratic theorist and an experienced politician, Wilson brought the idealism of the progressive movement to the task of pacifying war-torn Europe.[2]

To supersede traditional power politics, the president's "war aims message" addressed three problem areas that he considered essential for creating a stable postwar order. First, since the returning soldiers claimed participation rights as citizens, internal peace demanded the expansion of parliamentary self-government. Responding to the rise of mass politics required domestic reforms in Western Europe and revolutionary changes in Central and Eastern Europe. Second, inspired by the spread of national aspirations, the emerging nationalities clamored for a chance to create-nation states of their own. This goal ultimately implied the dissolution of the multiethnic tsarist, Austrian, and Ottoman empires. Finally, the advance of transnational trade and communication called for an institutionalization of international cooperation in order to make the new countries work together. Ironically this imperative required limiting the nation-states' recently gained sovereignty. These principles envisaged a fundamental revision of the domestic and international order—but they were more moderate than the Soviet program because they did not necessitate a social revolution.[3]

Though some skeptics were horrified, President Wilson's program inspired widespread hope among the exhausted populations of the belligerents by offering a compromise to end the war. Defenders of the traditional order like the British diplomat Harold Nicolson condemned Wilson's new diplomacy of "open covenants of peace" as naive, incapable of producing lasting solutions. Bolshevik radicals like Leon Trotsky considered this bourgeois program too halfhearted to get at the social roots of the imperialist problem.[4] But the democratic Left on both sides of the front thought the territorial provisions constructive, since they suggested a moderate way to break the deadlock of excessive war aims. Offended by the chauvinist rhetoric of war propaganda, critical intellectuals were also intrigued by the innovative principles, which presented a blueprint for constructing a lasting postwar European order. Finally, once they realized that they could no longer win the war, German leaders grasped at Wilson's outstretched hand to avoid the harsher terms that they feared from their continental antagonists.[5]

The Wilsonian vision formulated a liberal path toward modernity that sought to restore hope in progress through democratizing Europe. Responding to the popular claims for democracy, his advocacy of self-government intended to reenergize the drive for parliamentary systems that would allow the masses to participate in politics. At the same time the American president's support of self-determination tried to liberate subject populations from autocratic control, encouraging the creation of ethnically based national states. Embodying aspirations of bourgeois internationalism, the plan of a League of Nations attempted to prevent another world war and reinforce the ties of peace by creating an institution to adjudicate disputes. On the one hand, this inspiring vision was directed against autocracy, championing the replacement of the land-based empires by democratic nation-states. On the other hand, Wilson's approach offered an alternative to Bolshevik social revolution by insisting on free trade and private property.[6] This liberal program therefore proposed a moderate blueprint for peace and prosperity.

GERMAN COLLAPSE

For democracy to spread, the authoritarian alternative of modernization, represented by the Central Powers, first had to be defeated on the battlefield. The Allies ostensibly fought for universal values of Western civilization, interpreted as individual liberty, parliamentary government, and market competition, even if imperialism, racism, and exploitation marred their practice. In contrast the German-led coalition claimed to embody a deeper version of *Kultur*, characterized by bureaucratic authority, military efficiency, and social welfare. Already in 1915 the Norwegian-born sociologist Thorstein Veblen pointed out the discrepancy between the scientific and technological modernity of Imperial Germany and the lagging development of self-government, which retained ultimate power for the kaiser and gave the military a larger voice than in the democracies. Instead of treating the West as standard and arguing that this difference represented a "partial modernization," it is more illuminating to view the German model as an alternate path within the broader western tradition.[7] Responding more flexibly to the strategic challenges, social leveling, and erosion of authority, the liberal variant ultimately proved superior to the authoritarian version of modernity.

While the Allied leaders could confidently wait until their material advantage prevailed, the German Supreme Command risked a desperate gamble to snatch victory from the jaws of defeat. Having been intent on strengthening the antidemocratic forces at home by conquest in the East, strongman Erich Ludendorff saw the Russian collapse as a chance to move fifty divisions to the West before American reinforcements arrived and the morale of his troops crumbled. He believed that "the situation among our allies as well as the condition of the army demanded an offensive which would bring a quick decision." On March 21, 1918, the German army launched a series of four attacks on the western front, hoping to divide the British and French and capture Paris. With new tactics such as shock troops and rolling artillery bombardments, the attackers crossed the Allied trenches and made impressive gains, creating the illusion of repeating the initial advance of 1914. But the final offensive on July 15 failed to achieve its aim, since the Allied lines were dented but never completely broken. By gambling on victory the Germans lost, since they spent their last reserves.[8]

The failure of the Ludendorff offensive hastened the end of the war in the West and South, because it returned the strategic initiative to the Allies. While both sides incurred roughly equal losses, the Central Powers had greater difficulty in replacing men and weapons than the Entente. At long last the Allied resources in war matériel and manpower proved stronger than the military training of Berlin and its allies. With the German submarine threat blunted by the convoy system, increasing amounts of shells, guns, trucks, and other weapons reached the western front. Moreover, converted passenger liners shipped growing numbers of newly trained troops, eager to fight, from the United States to European battlefields. In contrast to the dispirited French and British veterans who merely sought to survive, farm boys fresh from Iowa still obeyed orders when told to "go over the top" and attack the German lines, no matter what the cost. Finally, advances in military technology such as the introduction of about eight hundred new tanks as an infantry-support platform also turned the tide.[9]

The Allied Hundred Days Offensive of the summer and fall of 1918 proved decisive in bringing the war to a surprisingly swift conclusion. Already in mid-July, French general Ferdinand Foch had mounted an attack close to Reims that recaptured some lost ground. But when five hundred British tanks struck at Amiens, they overran weakened German divisions and forced a hasty retreat, making August 8 a "black day for the German army." This unexpected defeat convinced Ludendorff that the war could no longer be won, since not only were his divisions depleted but also his soldiers were listening to the peace propaganda of the radical Left and were increasingly unwilling to fight. With renewed vigor the attacking Allies reconquered the German salients of the spring, forcing the deteriorating enemy forces to retreat to the fortified Hindenburg Line. Though suffering heavy casualties, the combined Allied assaults eventually breached that desperately defended trench system as well. By the end of September the Entente's unstoppable advance and the crumbling of Berlin's allies made clear to the Supreme Command that the war was lost.[10]

The realization of impending defeat, long hidden by positive military bulletins, finally forced the leadership of the German Empire to sue for peace. In July 1917 a critical Reichstag majority had already voted for a resolution that called for a peace "without annexations and indemnities." Because of their military failure, the quasi-dictators Hindenburg and Ludendorff could no longer prevent calls "for a complete change of the system" toward parliamentary government led by a reformist chancellor, Prince Max of Baden. Admitting that "the continuation of the war should be abandoned as hopeless," they had to accept a civilian proposal "to approach President Wilson with the request for an armistice." Feeling betrayed by their officers, German sailors and soldiers began to abandon their discipline and also demand an immediate cessation of hostilities.[11] As a result the German army, though still occupying parts of northern France and Belgium, had to capitulate because it was unable to continue the fighting. A combination of Wilsonian hopes from above and Leninist propaganda from below ultimately made Berlin call for a cease-fire.

Signed in a railroad carriage near Compiègne, the armistice agreement of November 11, 1918, only terminated the official hostilities; it did not end international and domestic violence. The stringent military terms of withdrawing the German forces to their home bases, interning the navy, and surrendering all heavy war matériel were designed to prevent a renewal of armed resistance.[12] But the uncertainty of boundaries in Central Europe and the Balkans spurred continued fighting by Free Corps (local militia units) seeking to secure territory in mixed ethnic areas. Moreover, the Russian Civil War, Allied intervention in Russia, and the Soviet-Polish War extended major combat in Eastern Europe for several years. Some regions that wanted to secure their independence, such as the Ukraine, changed hands several times. At the same time communist uprisings in Budapest and Munich as well as right-wing military coups such as the Kapp Putsch in Berlin projected violent conflicts into the domestic arena. Contrary to the mythology of Armistice Day celebrations, it still took almost half a decade for the last fighting to subside in Europe.[13]

After the nightmare of war had finally ended, winners and losers alike faced an enormous challenge in converting the machinery of war back to peacetime uses. Estimates suggest that some 10 million soldiers had died in combat and another 23 million had been wounded while roughly 7.5 million civilians had perished, creating an irreparable demographic loss.[14] On the one hand, demobilization involved the complicated logistics of bringing troops home and getting them out of uniform. The task of turning trained killers into nonviolent civilians also turned out to be quite difficult. In order to provide jobs for veterans, regulated economies had to shift from war production back to the making of consumer goods, reconverting steel helmets into cooking pots. On the other hand, expectations for a peace dividend were enormous in the victorious countries, while the defeated had to accept the losses incurred. Citing their physical and mental sacrifices, returning soldiers as well as women of the home front demanded and won greater recognition by gaining more political rights and social services. The transition to peace proved difficult, since the elites wanted to restore prewar hierarchies, while the suffering masses called for democratic reform or socialist revolution.[15]

DEMOCRATIC PEACEMAKING

The conditions of the armistice, negotiated between the United States and the Entente, already foreshadowed the contradictory character of democratic peacemaking. Prompted by a desperate Supreme Command, the German government had appealed to Wilson in early October for an armistice on the basis of his fourteen points. But the president made it clear in several notes that German troops would have to withdraw completely from Allied territory and that the kaiser would have to abdicate. Negotiations between Wilson's emissary Colonel House, Clemenceau, and Lloyd George were even more complicated, since the French and British leaders initially refused to be bound by the American peace conditions. However, when they learned of a softening interpretation worked out by "The Inquiry," a group of U.S. academics and diplomats preparing the peace conference, the European Allies accepted the fourteen points, believing that they could modify them to suit their own interests. The tough military provisions were drafted by General Foch, including the occupation of the left bank of the Rhine and the continuation of the blockade.[16]

This pattern of blending Wilsonian principles with nationalist aims continued during the actual Paris Peace Conference. Begun in earnest on January 18, 1919, the negotiations were dominated by the leaders of the three major "Allied and Associated Powers," Clemenceau, Lloyd George, and Wilson, although representatives of Italy, Japan, and a host of smaller nations also sought to influence the decisions. Most specific terms were hashed out in committees, besieged by petitioners like Ignace Paderewski, pleading for the restoration of Poland, or Tomáš Masaryk, calling for the creation of Czechoslovakia. The French public wanted to obtain security against renewed German aggression through territorial gains, diplomatic assurances, and economic concessions. British opinion was more interested in

Map 4. Postwar Europe, 1921. Adapted from Institute for European History,
Mainz, Germany.

retaining naval supremacy and gaining additional colonies, while the
U.S. delegation focused on the creation of a Covenant of the League
of Nations. Not consulted about any of the provisions, the representatives of the new democratic Germany were confronted with a final
draft and forced to sign by an ultimatum on June 28.[17]

The Versailles Treaty imposed considerable losses on Germany
of one-seventh of its prewar territory and one-tenth of its popula-

tion. France regained the provinces of Alsace-Lorraine, assumed control over the coal-rich Saar Basin, and insisted on a fifteen-year occupation of the left bank of the Rhine. Similarly ignoring ethnic composition, Belgium obtained new territory in Eupen-Malmedy. In Schleswig there was a plebiscite in which the northern third voted for a return to Denmark. In the East, the conflict between national origin and free access to the sea was resolved by turning over the ethnically mixed province of West Prussia to an independent Polish state, making the German port of Danzig an international city, thus cutting off East Prussia from the Reich, and by dividing the coal mines of Upper Silesia mostly according to the results of a plebiscite. Moreover, the port city of Memel and its hinterland were given to Lithuania. As neither the German-speaking Sudetenland nor Austria was allowed to join the Reich, nationalists could argue that self-determination was only applied to Germany's detriment.[18]

The other members of the Central Powers were compelled to accept even more draconian terms, since new national states were primarily created at their expense. In response to nationalist agitation, the treaties of St. Germain and Trianon broke up the Austro-Hungarian Empire, claiming to divide the ethnically mixed areas of East-Central Europe according to national lines. This principle left a small ethnically German state of Austria and an equally reduced Hungary, with three million Hungarian speakers under the control of its neighbors. The Treaty of Neuilly forced Bulgaria to cede some border provinces to the newly constituted Yugoslavia. The Treaty of Sèvres dissolved the Ottoman Empire, severing its Arabic provinces as League of Nations mandates and retaining only an ethnically Turkish rump. This decision created a bloody conflict with Greece ended only by the 1923 Treaty of Lausanne, which stipulated an exchange of population, expelling hundreds of thousands of Greeks from Asia Minor and Turks from Greece. Geographic ignorance and special pleading created new borders that remained a source of hostility.[19]

The East European settlement was also hampered by the absence of Russia from the conference table due to the fear of revolutionary contagion by communism. In principle, the Allies repudiated the punitive Treaty of Brest-Litovsk, but in practice they were compelled to withdraw their interventionist forces and accept some of its provisions by recognizing the independence of Finland and the Baltic states. The peace conference instead supported the creation of three new barrier states of Poland, Czechoslovakia, and Yugoslavia as well as the expansion of Romania in order to prevent the restoration of Austria-Hungary and to counteract German influence in the region. At the same time, these new states were to serve as a cordon sanitaire, keeping Central and Western Europe from being infected by the virus of communism. But these newly drawn borders put about thirty million people into nation-states whose language they did not speak and to which they did not wish to belong. For instance, Italy reclaimed some ethnic compatriots in Istria but also gained a strategic frontier in South Tyrol that was indubitably German-speaking.[20]

In order to prevent a resumption of the fighting, the losing countries were also thoroughly disarmed, although the victors failed to reduce their own forces in a similar manner. French insistence left the Weimar Republic with an army of only one hundred thousand men without an air force, tanks, heavy artillery, poison gas, or a general staff. While the left bank of the Rhine was occupied, the right bank was also demilitarized. After the crews scuttled sixty-six German warships at Scapa Flow, British pressure permitted only a small coastal-defense navy with fifteen thousand officers and sailors and required all submarines to be handed over. Austria and Hungary were allowed dwarf armies of thirty thousand men respectively. These drastic reductions left the losing countries virtually defenseless and fueled resentment in former military circles, which found themselves suddenly unemployed. Because the new states of Poland and Czechoslovakia were rearming with about half a million soldiers each, this one-sided disarmament created a huge imbalance of forces in the center of Europe. Moreover it sparked constant conflicts over securing its enforcement.[21]

Perhaps the most contentious issue of the entire treaty system was the question of reparations, since chauvinistic opinion in Britain as well as the rebuilding of France demanded "Germany must pay." In order to have a legal basis for this claim, John Foster Dulles suggested a statement of German responsibility for the outbreak of the war that became Article 231, the infamous war guilt clause. Complicated by the issue of inter-Allied debts, the Paris debates concentrated on three issues: how to assess the civilian damage caused, how much Germany might be expected to pay, and how the spoils ought to be divided. Adopting a fixed-sum approach, the peacemakers could not agree on an amount and on the number of years, postponing the final decision until 1921. The initially suggested sum of 269 billion gold marks seemed disappointingly low to the vindictive winners and astronomically high to the losers, who would be saddled with payments until 1999. Triggered by John Maynard Keynes' resignation from the British delegation, the debate about the justice of reparation payments poisoned postwar politics for years.[22]

The final problem of the Paris Peace Conference was the disposition of Germany's colonies and Turkey's provinces, demanded by imperialist interests and British dominions. Justifying the transfer of control by a trumped-up charge of German malfeasance, negotiators made the former colonies "mandates" of the League of Nations, establishing three levels of tutelage, deeply disappointing the anticolonial intellectuals who had hoped for immediate self-determination. While France and Britain split Togo, the Cameroons, and East Africa, Japan received the Chinese port of Tsingtao. South Africa gained Southwest Africa while Australia got New Guinea and New Zealand obtained Samoa. In the Near East the Ottoman provinces were generally turned into new states that were theoretically on their way to independence but practically divided between French dominance in Syria and Lebanon and British preponderance in the rest of the Arabian Peninsula.[23] Clashing with Arab aspirations, the 1917 Balfour Declaration that promised "a national home for the Jewish people" in Palestine proved particularly troublesome.[24]

Judging by their effect on subsequent developments, the Paris treaties remain a flawed system, since they combined innovative Wilsonian impulses with retrograde nationalist clauses. Propelled by a vengeful public and spurred on by militant advisers, Clemenceau and Lloyd George ignored calls for moderation and subverted universal aspirations for the sake of their own national interests. Though he understood that "if we humiliate the German people and drive them too far, we shall destroy all form of government and Bolshevism will take its place," the U.S. president also wanted to punish Prussian deceit after hearing of the harsh Treaty of Brest-Litovsk.[25] The Wilsonian program of domestic democracy, national self-determination, and international cooperation might have provided a constructive order for a postwar Europe, but its modification and one-sided application undercut its credibility. Many concrete difficulties in applying the ideas of the new diplomacy could not have been foreseen. But their halfhearted implementation, at once too harsh to be accepted and too conciliatory to be enforced, ultimately proved to be their undoing.

ADVANCE OF DEMOCRACY

Allied victory provided Europe, nonetheless, with a golden opportunity to choose the liberal vision of modernity by advancing self-government and self-determination within a cooperative international order. While the western Allies felt vindicated, eastern democrats could use the collapse of the multiethnic empires to promote self-rule through drafting republican constitutions. At the same time local nationalists were able to go beyond autonomy and create a series of new nation-states, legitimized by their own rather mythical view of history. Such steps turned ancient social hierarchies upside down, putting the former subjects such as Poles or Czechs on top, since their previous German or Hungarian masters now found themselves as minorities without state support. Yet in order to realize such ambitious aims, the new democracies had to overcome the legacy of underdevelopment, the devastation of war, and the disruptions of the postwar transition.[26] Their state-building had to create new governmental structures, ranging from police to military, from postal clerks to tax collectors, and from parliament to diplomacy.

Since Allied propaganda had claimed the Allies were fighting for democracy, the collapse of the autocracies strengthened the appeal of parliamentary government as a superior political system in the West. But the untold sacrifices of the war also induced veterans and suffragettes to claim new political rights as a just reward for proving their citizenship during the conflict. The smaller, neutral democracies such as Switzerland and the Scandinavian countries simply reaffirmed their forms of self-government, somewhat extending participation. In Britain, the Representation of the People Act of 1918 abolished property restrictions, giving all men over twenty-one years the right to vote and enfranchising women over the age of thirty. The French Third Republic already had a broad male franchise, though it took until 1944(!) for women to be granted the vote. At the same time various provisions to help veterans, the wounded, and war widows also started the move toward the modern welfare state. But more far-reaching demands of workers for social reforms or control of factories were generally turned down, preserving the capitalist class system relatively unchanged.[27]

The dozen new democracies from the Baltic to the Balkans entered the postwar period with high hopes that independence would give their people a better life. No longer would they be lorded over by bureaucrats who spoke a different language; now they could finally govern their own affairs. All of them drafted ambitious constitutions that sought to create nationally minded citizens, ready to participate in the new order. However, reality turned out to be rather sobering. Except for Hungary, all the new states were saddled with minorities that clamored for autonomy, that wanted to belong to a neighboring country or create their own state. The new tariffs that were supposed to shield domestic industry interrupted old trade routes, stifling commerce and economic development. Moreover, the building of national schools, hospitals, and police stations required enormous sums of money that had to be borrowed abroad. As their populations were unused to self-rule, within two decades all the new democracies save Czechoslovakia turned into nationalist authoritarian regimes like Poland under General Józef Piłsudski.[28]

In defeated Germany, democracy also triumphed as the November Revolution of 1918 overthrew the monarchy. When sailors in the ports of Wilhelmshaven and Kiel heard that they were to embark on a final battle against the British Royal Navy, they mutinied, seeing no point in a heroic gesture at the end of a lost war. Since workers in the factories went out on strike as well, the discredited kaiser was forced to abdicate, fleeing ignominiously by train to Holland. In Berlin, the Spartacists and shop stewards hoped to create a revolutionary regime of workers' and soldiers' councils modeled after the Bolshevik example. To forestall such radicalization, the moderate Social Democrat Philipp Scheidemann exclaimed dramatically from the balcony of the royal palace on November 9, 1918: "The old and rotten, the monarchy has collapsed. The new may live. Long live the German Republic!" Outflanking the Council of People's Deputies, his colleague Friedrich Ebert, the chancellor of the new republican government, eventually restored order in the capital with the help of the army and the support of the business community.[29]

Stabilizing the embattled Weimar Republic was a difficult but not impossible task. Away from popular passions in the birthplace of German classicism, liberal parliamentarians like Hugo Preuss created an advanced constitution that included proportional representation and gave women the vote. But the cabinet was shocked by the harsh Versailles peace terms, since it had hoped for more generosity from the victors in support of German democracy. On the right, the fledgling republic was besieged by revanchist nationalists who forged a "stab-in-the-back legend," claiming that the army had been defeated by subversion at home, and rejected democracy as an accomplice of the Allies. On the left, communists and anarchists fomented rebellion in industrial areas, hoping to seize power and install a Soviet-style regime. Moreover, the paramilitary Free Corps roamed the streets, killing Karl Liebknecht and Rosa Luxemburg while claiming to uphold order and defend the frontiers in the East. Nonetheless, the republic survived its turbulent beginnings, supported by the working class, and eventually gained a measure of grudging respect.[30]

Democracy faced an equally uncertain future in the new states of Austria and Hungary, which had never before existed in this form. German-speaking Austria found itself with an outsized capital of Vienna, polarized between Christian Social middle-class and Social Democratic working-class parties. The majority of the Austrian parties wanted to join the Weimar Republic, but the Treaty of St. Germain prohibited this obvious solution, as it would have strengthened

Germany. Cut off from its prior trading partners through nationalist tariffs, Vienna remained dependent on western loans. Happy to be at last independent, Hungary, however, mourned the loss of about one-third of its ethnic population due to the unfavorable borders drawn by the Treaty of Trianon. A communist rebellion under Béla Kun took over Budapest in 1919, but eventually the Romanian army restored counterrevolutionary order. In January 1920 right-wing forces seized control and allowed Admiral Miklós Horthy to rule as regent for the next two decades. The one-sided application of self-determination thus created two revisionist states, unhappy with the peace.[31]

The major exception to the sweep of democracy after World War I was the Soviet Union, which promoted itself as an egalitarian alternative to the Wilsonian vision. Lenin never tired of denouncing parliamentary government as a bourgeois sham, while claiming to be protecting civil rights against tsarist persecution. Instead of striving to enlarge political participation in a capitalist system, the Bolsheviks emphasized the need to end economic exploitation in order to obtain social justice as prerequisite for democracy. While this objection to western class hierarchies carried some weight, the Soviets practiced a "dictatorship of the proletariat" after the revolution, claiming that they needed to use force to achieve social change since they were besieged by class enemies. Promoted zealously by the Comintern, the Communist International organization founded in 1919, this rationalization appealed to disenchanted intellectuals and suffering workers in the West who welcomed a critique of capitalist exploitation.[32] While it inspired some local uprisings, the communist radicalization of socialism never quite attracted enough support to displace more moderate conceptions of democracy.

The postwar wave of democratization yielded disappointing results, since most new regimes foundered on insufficient preparation and adverse circumstances. In Central and Eastern Europe, an educated minority that had felt shut out in the previous empires seized control of the bureaucracy in the name of self-government, while the agrarian majority merely longed for a better life. The combination of democracy with nationalism incited an endless set of conflicts as the minorities within nations created by the peace fought the efforts of the new governments to enforce linguistic and cultural uniformity.[33] The customs borders of a dozen new national states also disrupted trading patterns, and the costs of state-building bankrupted the new regimes. Finally, the weakness of civil society, prevailing intolerance, and lack of democratic habits created a hankering for strong leadership. Born in revolution or defeat, democracy faced enormous hurdles in postwar Europe. At best, the new nation-states responded to desires for self-determination while offering a glimpse of what democracy might become under more favorable auspices in the future.[34]

TRAVAILS OF THE VICTORS

Even the victorious powers were soon disappointed in democracy, since they found the rewards for their sacrifices inadequate and the postwar transition difficult. The better life that propaganda had promised failed to come, and many of the spoils that secret treaties had envisaged proved unattainable. Moreover, the conversion from a wartime to a peacetime economy turned out to be more time-consuming, costly, and disruptive than imagined. The demand for consumer goods, which had been pent up during the fighting, initially resulted in a buying spree that produced a short-lived postwar boom. But public borrowing to pay for the wartime expenses contributed to a substantial inflation, and once savings were used up the lack of buying power led to a recession when returning veterans struggled to find civilian jobs. Shifting the cost onto the defeated enemies also proved illusory, since reparations payments were smaller than expected and a self-righteous U.S. Congress insisted on the repayment of inter-Allied debts. Within a few months the elation of victory turned into frustration, unleashing domestic strife and blocking international compromise.

Because of its domestic divisions, the constitutional monarchy of Britain experienced an especially trying transition. The Welsh prime minister Lloyd George promised soldiers a land "fit for heroes to live in" during the 1918 khaki election. His coalition of Liberals and Conservatives scored an impressive victory, allowing him to sponsor social reforms such as extending education, providing public housing, increasing the coverage of unemployment insurance, and raising pensions. But in October 1922 the Conservatives, disliking such measures, deserted him, while Labourites agitated for further reforms, replacing the Liberals as the main opposition party during the next election. Their talented but somewhat muddled leader Ramsay Mc-Donald formed the first Labour government in 1924, only to be replaced by his predecessor, the hard-liner Stanley Baldwin, who in turn lost the 1929 election so that McDonald returned with a national-union government in 1931.[35] During the interwar years the United Kingdom remained split between a defensive Conservative Party and a reformist Labour Party, with neither strong enough to govern effectively.

Political and social tensions came to a head in the general strike of May 1926. Though British mines had become less productive and the return to the gold standard made coal harder to sell, miners demanded better pay and more services. Appointed by Baldwin to address the problem, the Samuel Commission recommended ending government subsidies and cutting wages for miners by 13.5 percent. Horrified, the unions protested, and, after last-minute compromise attempts failed, the Trades Union Congress (TUC) called a general strike that turned out three million workers, bringing transportation to a standstill. Fearing anarchy, the Conservative cabinet quickly organized emergency services, strikebreakers, and a militia to maintain law and order. When the courts issued injunctions against sympathy strikes of other unions, the TUC called off the general strike after nine days, grudgingly accepting the reduction of wages.[36] The confrontation showed that British society was polarized between a laissez-faire-oriented middle class and a growing labor movement, whose radical members were dreaming of a social revolution.

The future of Ireland was a similarly intractable issue, since it provided an inflammatory mix of nationalism, religion, and social resentment. Inspired by sectarian hostility between Protestants and Catholics and aggravated by tensions between absentee landlords and local laborers, the Irish independence movement contested British control over the green isle. In 1914 Charles Stewart Parnell's agitation succeeded in winning home rule, allowing the formation of Irish volunteers to fight in World War I. But when the radical nationalists rose on Easter of 1916, the British put them down with brutal force, making the Sinn Fein Party's campaign for independence more popular. A key problem was the future of the six Ulster counties that were dominated by Protestants. In 1921 Lloyd George brokered an Anglo-Irish Treaty that allowed the twenty-six Catholic counties under Eamon de Valera to become independent, retaining Northern Ireland and making the Irish Free State a dominion. While this proved to be a workable compromise, it failed to eliminate the mutual hatred between Ulster Protestants and Catholics that would keep bloodshed continuing for decades.[37]

Though its reputation was enhanced by victory, France also confronted external dilemmas and internal confusion. The price of glory, with about 1.5 million dead and 3.5 million wounded, had sapped a population of about 40 million, which was only two-thirds the size of Germany's 62 million. To combat this relative demographic weakness, nationalist hard-liners sought to provide security by enforcing the clauses of the Versailles Treaty to the last letter so as to provide security against a resurgent Germany. In contrast, more flexible leaders of the Left searched for a rapprochement with the Weimar Republic in order to reduce the strain of defense expenditures. Rebuilding the devastated infrastructure, economy, and housing of northern France produced enormous costs that could not all be shifted to the defeated enemies, but tax incentives for reconstruction also created a spurt of industrial modernization. Ironically, even the celebrated reintegration of Alsace-Lorraine proved troublesome, since this partly German-speaking region wanted to maintain some autonomy vis-à-vis the central government, especially in religious affairs.[38] The basic challenge confronting Paris was therefore finding a way to preserve the fruits of victory without overextending itself in the process.

The Third Republic failed to come up with a clear solution, since the balance of forces between the nationalist Right and the internationalist Left was roughly equal. Wags claimed that Frenchmen had their revolutionary heart on the left but carried their wallets on the right. Combining various splinter parties, the nationalist hard-liners formed a loose *bloc national* while the reformists created a *cartel des gauches*. In the parliamentary musical chairs, the tough prime minister Clemenceau, who had pushed for punitive terms at Versailles, was replaced in 1921 by the conciliatory Aristide Briand. But he was ousted a year later by the bellicose Raymond Poincaré since he seemed to have been too soft on Germany. When the latter's reparations policy proved to be a fiasco, the moderate leftist Eduard Herriot assumed power in 1924, only to be replaced once again by Poincaré in 1926. Since the latter succeeded in resolving a fiscal crisis by devaluing the franc, he governed until 1929.[39] This succession of leaders created a zigzag course domestically and internationally that prevented finding a cure for the internal division and structural weakness of the country.

Faced by a dynamic German neighbor, France, weakened by war, struggled hard to preserve its hegemony over the continent. The October Revolution had eliminated Russia as a reliable ally, since bourgeois Paris feared that the Bolshevik virus might spread to its own workers. Moreover, restraint in enforcing the peace was predicated on continuing U.S. involvement and British support, both of which looked increasingly questionable as time went on. To replace these partners, France created a web of alliances with Poland, as well as with the so-called little Entente of Czechoslovakia, Yugoslavia, and Romania. This ingenious policy proved, however, rather expensive, since these clients required massive subsidies to pay for their domestic development and military strength. Even when France tried to enforce the timely payment of reparations as in the January 1923 occupation of the Ruhr Basin, the intervention backfired. Owing to Berlin's "passive resistance," Paris found it impossible to dig coal with bayonets and eventually had to break off the venture. Hence maintaining dominance stretched French resources to the breaking point.[40]

Instead of offering multiple benefits, victory in the First World War created unexpected new problems for the winning countries. Being victorious reinforced a western sense that liberal modernization was the right path, since democracy had beaten autocracy in the end. Tangible spoils like territorial gains, new colonies, greater military security, and less economic competition were also gratifying.

But domestically, victory reaffirmed not only parliamentary government but also capitalist exploitation and class hierarchy, contrary to the claims of veterans for extending the suffrage, providing social reforms, and creating greater equality. While the peace treaties offered a blueprint for a new international order composed of democratic nation-states, they also perpetuated wartime enmities by triggering a protracted conflict over enforcing their provisions.[41] The settlement sparked enormous resentment among those who felt disadvantaged by it, precluding its acceptance as a constructive plan for the future of Europe. High hopes therefore soon turned into keen disappointment—even among the victorious states such as Italy.

INTERNATIONAL COOPERATION

Creating a lasting peace entailed not only ending the fighting but also retying the ruptured bonds by creating a modern international order to prevent a recurrence of the carnage. The multiple steps toward reconciliation had to overcome many obstacles. While the American and British occupation troops were quickly withdrawn, the French and Belgians stayed in the Rhineland until 1930. The propaganda apparatus that had vilified the enemy during wartime also had to be dismantled. Though the kaiser was not tried, the "war guilt controversy" continued with mutual accusations for years. Cooperation in international associations had to be restored by readmitting, for instance, delegates of losing countries to scientific organizations dominated by the victors. Finally, the blockade had to be ended and free trade across the frontiers resumed. But economic revival was hampered by conflicts over the suspension of enemy patents and the sequestration of companies, let alone the entire reparations muddle. Undoing the aftereffects of war and resuming friendly exchanges was therefore a lengthy process, hampered as well by the influenza epidemic of 1919.[42]

The organization that was supposed to solve the problems caused by the peace settlement and enhance international cooperation was the League of Nations. It was founded in 1919 as an intergovernmental structure, headquartered in the neutral Swiss but French-speaking city of Geneva. As an association of sovereign states, it was led by a secretary-general, dominated by an Executive Council of permanent countries and rotating seats, and supported by a General Assembly in which all members had a voice. The work of the Permanent Secretariat was aided by subsidiary institutions that organized cooperation in particular areas such as the Permanent Court of International Justice, the International Labor Organization, the Health Organization, and the Refugees Commission. Aimed at preventing another world war, the Covenant of the League sought "to achieve international peace and security" through open diplomacy, disarmament, and negotiation as well as arbitration. This new institution, the particular brainchild of President Wilson, was a bold attempt to transcend balance-of-power politics through formalizing international cooperation.[43]

In promoting peace the League had only a limited success, since crucial states did not belong and its decisions were dominated by the victorious powers. The U.S. refusal to join was a serious blow, while the initial exclusion of Germany and Russia failed to represent two of the most problematic powers in its deliberations. Tied to the Versailles Treaty, the League guaranteed the independence of Danzig, supervised the French occupation of the Saar Basin, and provided cover for the reassignment of the colonies through the mandate system. In some conflicts like the disposition of Upper Silesia, it managed to organize plebiscites and determine the ultimate division of the province between Germany and Poland. In minor questions like the border dispute between Greece and Bulgaria in 1925, the League succeeded in mediating between the conflicting parties. But when national interests of big countries were at stake or in minority conflicts within states, the League proved generally helpless, since recalcitrant members could ignore its decisions, confident that these could not be enforced militarily.[44]

To counteract their exclusion, the outcasts Germany and Russia concluded a friendship treaty in the Italian spa of Rapallo in April 1922. The agreement, negotiated by Foreign Ministers Walther Rathenau and Georgi Chicherin, upset the victors of the war because it showed that the Weimar Republic and Soviet Russia were not entirely dependent on their goodwill. The text of the treaty was innocuous enough, since it merely waived "their claims for compensation for expenditure incurred on account of the war," in effect mutually canceling German demands for losses due to the October Revolution and Soviet requests for reparations for Berlin's military occupation. The agreement further promised to restore normal diplomatic relations and to resume economic cooperation, which both countries sorely needed in order to repair the damage from war and revolution. More ominous, however, was the concurrent promise of secret military cooperation, which allowed the Reichswehr to circumvent the disarmament clauses of Versailles and gave the Soviets access to German airplane, tank, and submarine technology.[45]

The most controversial issue that hindered international cooperation was the question of reparations. When the Reparations Commission set the amount at 269 billion gold marks, the German public was shocked, and even some foreign economists considered the sum excessive. Although Berlin might have been able to pay by raising taxes and lowering the living standards of the German people, the demand put the democratic government on the defensive, so that it dragged its feet regarding in-kind deliveries. The subsequent Ruhr occupation inflamed nationalist passions by increasing the pace of the runaway inflation that undermined the mark while also straining French resources. This deadlock could only be broken by American mediation. Under the leadership of the Republican banker and later U.S. vice president Charles G. Dawes, a compromise was worked out that cut the total amount in half and reduced annual payments to 1 billion marks, rising to 2.5 billion within five years. This sum would be raised by new taxes and U.S. loans. Chaired by Ramsay McDonald, the 1924 London Conference ratified this agreement, thereby ending the stalemate of the Ruhr occupation.[46]

This solution improved the international climate sufficiently to allow further steps toward cooperation with the Locarno Treaties of 1925. Concluded between German foreign minister Gustav Stresemann, British foreign secretary Austen Chamberlain, and French prime minister Aristide Briand, these nonaggression treaties ratified the western frontiers established at Versailles. At the same time the arbitration agreements with Poland and Czechoslovakia opened the door to peaceful treaty revision in the East. This compromise reassured the western powers of their possessions but also rewarded German "fulfillment policy" with the hope that the eastern losses would not have to be permanent, thereby frightening Poland. The conciliatory "spirit of Locarno" ushered in a period of cooperation between Germany and France that allowed Berlin to enter the League of Nations in 1926. Moreover, it made possible the withdrawal of French and Belgian troops from the Rhineland in 1930 ahead of schedule.[47] Though its goodwill proved fleeting, Locarno showed what interwar reconciliation might have achieved, had it been tried more earnestly.

The lessening of tensions in Europe also made it possible to resolve the thorny reparations issue by further scaling down the winners' demands. Most impartial observers had come to agree that the burden was too onerous for the German government, allowing the Weimar Republic to be attacked by the Right for selling out. In 1929 an international commission headed by the U.S. industrialist Owen Young therefore proposed a plan that reduced the total amount to 115 billion marks, payable in fifty-nine years, with only one-third of the two-billion-marks payments due each year while the rest might be postponed.[48] The Wall Street stock-market crash proved even this sum to be unrealistic, leading President Herbert Hoover to proclaim a one-year moratorium in 1930 in the hope that regular payments could later be resumed. But the Great Depression was so destructive that a 1932 conference in Lausanne lowered the amount by another 90 percent, and when raising even this sum seemed impossible, Germany was allowed to default. Only one-eighth of the total was ever paid, with the Federal Republic completing the last installment in 2010!

Though popular passions made reconciliation difficult, the gradual rapprochement in the second half of the 1920s showed that cooperation was possible if it was earnestly attempted. Commemorating the millions of dead and maimed soldiers by constructing war memorials and holding veterans' parades kept the hatred of former enemies alive. Many problems, like the new borders and ethnic minorities, were intractable under the best of circumstances. None-theless, the League of Nations provided a promising forum for inter-national debate and conflict resolution as long as the contending parties were willing to submit to its decisions. The victors gradually realized that making concessions would increase the losers' desire to abide by the remaining terms of the settlement, while it slowly dawned on the defeated that they might be able to modify some clauses by accepting the rest of the peace treaties. Narrowing this gap of distrust required a drawn-out diplomatic process, supported by positive media coverage. After Locarno such progress seemed within reach, yet it remained fragile when tested by new upheavals.[49]

LIBERAL RECONSTRUCTION

The Wilsonian program was an innovative effort to create a liberal order for postwar politics that was undermined by incomplete im-plementation and inherent contradictions. The principle of self-government responded to popular aspirations for greater partici-pation by introducing democratic constitutions. The promise of self-determination reacted to nationalist agitation by suggesting the establishment of nation-states for aspiring ethnic groups. The pro-posal to organize international cooperation sought to overcome the bellicosity of balance-of-power politics by creating an institution that would render war superfluous. Though appealing, these progressive initiatives would create many new problems. The cultural legacies of authoritarianism could subvert democratic self-government. Mixed ethnic settlements would trigger minority conflicts and border quar-rels. Intent on preserving their new sovereignty, independent states might cooperate only when it suited their interests. Though his vi-sion addressed key problems of modernity, Wilson failed to realize its potential destructiveness.[50]

The spread of democracy to Central and Eastern Europe offered the former subjects of the landed empires an unprecedented chance to determine their own affairs. The overthrow of the tsarist, Habsburg, and Hohenzollern monarchies finally realized the aspirations of the national movements inspired by the ideals of the French Revolution but stymied by the failure of the 1848 revolutions. The tenacity with which the old order defended its control so as to maintain its privileges had allowed only partial progress toward self-government.[51] It took the defeat of the authoritarian regimes to create an opportunity for expanding political participation into full representation. In the fierce ideological conflicts after the war, the democratic alternative initially prevailed everywhere except in the authoritarian Hungary and the radical Soviet Union. But many enfranchised citizens were not ready to exercise their newly won rights, since they lacked experience with self-government. The pressures of civil war, economic disruption, and populist nationalism all too quickly turned the new democracies into little dictatorships.[52]

The creation of a dozen new national states as a result of the Paris peace treaties was also a great advance for self-determination by allowing different ethnicities to govern themselves. From the Baltic to the Black Sea, former subjects of Russian, German, and Hungarian rulers were now free to form their own national states in which they could realize their dreams of independence. This liberation from previous masters meant being able to use their own language in public affairs, teaching their children their cultural heritage in schools, and receiving international respect like older established nations. But the minority safeguards of the League of Nations were inadequate to cope with the ethnic mixture in East-Central Europe, in which Germans, Jews, and Slavs lived together in cities like Prague. Nationality censuses became ethnic battlegrounds, since claims to power or borders depended on the identification of citizens with a specific language. The one-sided implementation of self-determination to weaken the Central Powers and the exclusion of Soviet Russia also created fierce disputes that would later lead to ethnic cleansing.[53]

The establishment of an international organization in order to mediate conflicts and avoid another world war also seemed to be an excellent idea. In effect, the foundation of the League of Nations took up the legacy of the Congress System in a more formal and liberal fashion a century later. Creating a forum for international public opinion to discuss the world's problems, reinforcing legal guidelines for the intercourse between nations, and addressing specific issues such as the protection of labor were honorable goals that would lessen tensions between countries. But defenders of national sovereignty managed to subvert the initiative by insisting on the veto right of the great powers, excluding the defeated enemies and the Soviet Union, keeping the United States from joining, and tying the League to enforcement of the controversial peace treaties. While the League did manage to settle a series of border conflicts through plebiscites and succeeded in civilizing international debates, it failed disastrously in dealing with those disputes between the major powers that would unleash another world war.[54]

The effort at democratic modernization at the end of the First World War proved therefore at once attractive and disappointing. The defeat of the Central Powers created a historic chance for building a peace on the principles of democracy, self-determination, and international organization. Because of these attractive ideas most citizens in Central and Eastern Europe chose Wilson's liberal program of reform over Lenin's communist promise of revolution. But nationalist fervor and conservative opposition among the victorious Allies made the implementation of these ideals in the Paris peace treaties rather one-sided, favoring the victors in virtually every disputed case and thereby fanning lasting resentment among the losers. Moreover, the inherent difficulties of creating self-government in countries not quite ready for it, establishing national states in mixed ethnic areas, and founding an international organization without ceding sovereignty limited liberal modernity to the West. The Wilsonian vision continued to inspire democrats thereafter, but it would require further improvements in order to prevail in the end.[55]

Chapter 6

FASCIST ALTERNATIVE

Fascist march on Rome, 1922. Left to right, Italo Balbo, Benito Mussolini, Cesare Maria de Vecchi, and Emilio De Bono. *Source*: bpk, Berlin / Art Resource, NY.

On March 23, 1919, several hundred ex-socialists, syndicalists, futurists, and veterans gathered in Milan to found a new movement, the Fasci di Combattimento. Ambitiously its leader, the journalist Benito Mussolini, who had supported Italy's entry into the war, proposed "to lay the foundation of a new civilization." To overcome "the limited horizons of various spent and exhausted democracies" and counter "the violently utopian spirit of Bolshevism," he called for an "Italian revolution." His ragtag program proposed a national assembly to reform the state, an eight-hour workday, labor participation in management, the formation of technical councils, and anticlerical policies. Later additions included old-age and health insurance, confiscation of uncultivated land, a steep tax on war profits, seizure of church property, and the militarization of the nation. The "antiparty" movement's name hailed from the Roman *fascio*, a bundle of rods and an ax carried by magistrates as sign of office.[1] This inauspicious beginning marked the birth of a new ideology that evolved into a third version of modernity competing for the future of Europe.

The fascist vision was an unlikely combination of nationalism and socialism that sought to harness the two great ideological forces of the twentieth century. One cornerstone was an exalted "integral nationalism," championed by Charles Maurras, who placed his own country France above everything else. The publicist Enrico Corradini picked up this nationalist message, arguing "Italy is, materially and morally, a proletarian nation" that must catch up with more fortunate countries in terms of prosperity and empire. The poet Filippo Tommaso Marinetti championed similar ideas in his manifestos for "futurist" art, announcing: "We will glorify war—the world's only hygiene—militarism, patriotism, the destructive gesture of freedom-bringers, beautiful ideas worth dying for, and scorn for woman."[2] Such rhetoric appealed to Italians who were frustrated by the gap between their country's illustrious past and its disappointing present. Inspired also by social Darwinism, these ultranationalists dreamt of a national rebirth that would provide a sense of community at home and restore imperial domains abroad.

The other foundation was a warped form of socialism that deviated from classical Marxism by embracing syndicalism. The inspiration was Georges Sorel, a French theorist, who advocated direct action, the energizing myth of a general strike, and workers' control of the factories, celebrating violence both as a means and as an end. Such ideas appealed to Arturo Labriola and those Italian socialists who were impatient with Marx's insistence on developing bourgeois capitalism before a revolution could come about. The syndicalists agreed with socialism in hating exploitation and inequality as well as in hoping for a revolutionary transformation that would give the proletariat power. But they disagreed with the Socialist Party of Italy (PSI) by propounding a productivist creed of industrialization and putting the nation above social class in order to create a national community. As a result, these nationalist syndicalists also supported Italian imperialism and the country's participation in the First World War.[3] Rejecting socialist internationalism, they were therefore ready to make common cause with radical nationalists.

Equally opposed to democracy and communism, fascism attempted to project an alternate modernity, stressing the rebirth of the Italian nation. It originated in a modernization crisis of the Italian state, aggravated by the strains of the First World War and the difficulties of the transition to peace. Though its rhetoric and symbolism invoked the grand legacy of the Roman Empire, many characteristics of the movement such as mass mobilization, the leadership cult, male bonding, exaltation of youth, and aestheticization of politics were quite modern. Moreover, fascist beliefs such as hypernationalism, militarism, natalism, and expansionism attempted to fashion a positive synthesis out of problematic elements of modernity. These confusing traits added up to "a form of revolutionary ultra-nationalism for national rebirth that [was] based on a primarily vitalist philosophy, [was] structured on extreme elitism, mass mobilization and the *Führerprinzip*, positively value[d] violence as end as well as means and tend[ed] to normalize war and/or military virtues."[4] Above all, fascism was a style and feeling rather than a systematic ideology.

To understand the perplexing appeal of fascism as an alternative to liberalism and socialism, it is imperative to distinguish between the polemical and analytical usages of the concept. Part of the problem is the tendency of the antifascist Left to call everything that it opposes on the right "fascist." This indiscriminate polemic blurs the considerable difference between fascist systems, based on mass mobilization, and traditional authoritarian regimes, relying primarily on the monarchy, church, army, and bureaucracy. Bad as they were, Franco and Salazar were neither Mussolini nor Hitler. Another part of the confusion results from the lack of distinction between the specific Italian version of fascism and a wider, generic meaning of the term fascist, which designates the spread to other countries of new right-wing movements that shared many beliefs. Although the National Socialists were inspired by Mussolini's example, they soon went beyond it, propounding a more racist and deadly version of a similar ideology.[5] Such distinctions aside, the sudden emergence of a modern version of right-wing politics threw Europe into renewed turmoil.

ITALIAN BACKWARDNESS

Until the middle of the nineteenth century, Italy was, in Prince Metternich's sarcastic phrase, not a state but a geographic expression. Cut off from Europe by the Alps and surrounded by the Mediterranean, it enjoyed a mild climate, but its fertile land had been overused and contained few natural resources like coal or iron. The grand Roman past was but a distant memory, kept alive by physical ruins, though the common language had dissolved into rival dialects. The city of Rome remained the seat of the papacy, but the Catholic Church was not content to be a spiritual force and also meddled in secular politics. After the barbarian invasions during the migration of the peoples, the country had fragmented into principalities, alternately dominated by the Spanish, French, and Habsburgs. While city-states like Venice, Florence, and Milan were renowned for their wealth and culture, the Italian Peninsula remained politically disunited. Moreover, the social differences between the industrious North and the agricultural South were enormous, while overpopulation forced countless generations to emigrate all over the globe.[6]

Italy only became a nation state in 1861 owing to a fortuitous combination of ideology, insurrection, and diplomacy. Napoleonic occupation sparked some liberalizing reforms and inspired an intellectual Risorgimento that renewed Italian pride and made unification a political dream of intellectuals. The republican writer Giuseppe Mazzini issued poetic calls for action followed by students, but the various local insurrections, including the revolutions of 1848, ultimately failed, forcing him to live in British exile. More successful was the romantic revolutionary Giuseppe Garibaldi, who overthrew the Bourbon dynasty in Naples with a ragtag army of peasants, malcontents, and adventurers, thereby becoming a national legend. But it was the reformer and diplomat Count Camillo Cavour, prime minister of Piedmont-Sardinia, who managed to unite Italy. With the help of French armies and Bismarck's acquiescence this liberal constitutionalist toppled the Austrian princes in 1861, conquered Venice in 1866, and occupied Rome in 1870, incorporating all liberated provinces save Trentino and Trieste into an expanded Piedmont.[7]

The new Italian state was a constitutional monarchy that gradually evolved into a parliamentary government. Based on the *statuto* of 1848 the king had ultimate authority, but Vittorio Emmanuele II was an insignificant man, so that power gradually devolved onto the ministers and deputies. Since suffrage was initially limited to only 2 percent of the males, its extension became a constant bone of contention. With over two-thirds of the population still in agriculture and illiterate, politics was a game for the men of property and education, as the declining nobility were mostly content to enjoy the rents from their estates. Parliament was divided between a Conservative-Liberal faction that wanted to preserve its privileges, while making only a few concessions, and a Democratic-Radical wing that agitated for more popular rights but often lacked electoral support. By following the practice of *transformismo*, the governing elite sought to co-opt its critics by giving them a share of power in order to silence them.[8] As a result, politics remained remote from the daily lives of most Italians who struggled to survive, often in abject poverty.

The Catholic Church rejected the emerging nation-state because it was inspired by liberalism. Resenting the loss of his temporal possessions, Pope Pius IX declared himself "a prisoner in the Vatican" and refused to come to terms with the new national government that installed itself in Rome. It did not help that Cavour and the liberal founders confiscated church property and insisted on establishing the state's authority over teaching in primary schools and over marriage by requiring a civil ceremony. As a result the pope and the curia hardened their "antimodernist" stance, reaffirming doctrines such as papal infallibility and the immaculate conception of Mary as well as issuing a Syllabus of Errors that attacked secular progressivism. Though religious ritual still governed the rhythm of daily life of parishioners, the Vatican forbade its flock to participate in national elections! While the clergy retained much local power, the refusal of the curia to recognize the national state prevented the formation of a conservative party until after the First World War, when the Partito Popolare Italiano was founded in order to make the Catholic voice heard in politics.[9]

The new state was also hampered by the slowness of its economic development. Though most Italians still tilled the land, the yields of growing cereal, wine, or olives were low except in some favored areas like Tuscany, sufficing at best for subsistence or supplying local markets. In the middle and South, the dominant latifundia produced commercial crops with sharecroppers but often cultivated depleted soils with age-old methods that were not particularly productive. While Italy had many accomplished artisans, industrialization came late because there were few natural resources aside from hydropower and sulfur, and too much of the available capital was invested in land. In Lombardy and other northern provinces machine-driven factories gradually emerged to produce textiles made of wool, cotton, or silk. To tie the country together the government supported the building of railroads, which required impressive engineering feats so as to overcome numerous geographic obstacles.[10] Hampered by ingrained conservatism, Italy began industrializing rapidly only after 1896, developing its own steel, shipbuilding, and automobile industries.

Social protests against such conditions were endemic both in the countryside and in the cities. The South witnessed a mixture of rebellious brigandage, Mafia crime, and rural theft. In the 1870s the exiled Russian revolutionary Mikhail Bakunin inspired an anarchist movement that attempted local insurrections and turned to political assassination. With the growth of an industrial working class in the North, Marxist socialism also began to develop in the 1880s, split between a "legalist" branch (POI) and a revolutionary wing (PSRI). Guided by the Milanese sociologist Fillippo Turati, various groups combined in 1892 in order to found the Socialist Party of Italy (PSI) following the successful example of the German Social Democratic Party. Backed by chambers of labor (syndicalist workers' councils) and a rapidly expanding set of trade unions, this new party managed to survive several waves of government repression. By 1900 the PSI had grown so successful at the polls that the cabinet, prodded by Giovanni Giolitti, reached out to Socialist deputies in order to reconcile them to the state. Nonetheless, the conflict between reform and revolution continued unresolved.[11]

Hoping to become one of the great powers, Italy succumbed to the lure of imperialism, though its objects were poorly chosen and expensive. In 1890 the Roman government proclaimed its authority over Eritrea on the Horn of Africa where traders had established a foothold. Inspired by dreams of recapturing the glory of ancient Rome, it also annexed Somalia in 1905. But these two new possessions embroiled it in a conflict with the king of Ethiopia, who defeated an Italian detachment in 1887. In order to avenge this loss, Prime Minister Francesco Crispi pushed for control over the entire Ethiopian Empire, but in 1896 the Abyssinians killed about five thousand Italian soldiers and took two thousand prisoners at Adowa. Undeterred by this signal defeat, his successor Giolitti attacked the Ottoman Empire in 1911 and succeeded in subduing Libya after a bloody campaign. This policy of prestige created a huge budget deficit and failed to relieve Italy's population surplus, since emigrants preferred other destinations such as America.[12] Imperialism was, therefore, a disastrous course that devoured resources and fed chauvinist arrogance.

Supported by a wave of nationalist euphoria, Italian participation in the First World War exposed the structural weaknesses of a country that was still catching up to modernity. The initial decision for neutrality was a compromise between adherents of the Triple Alliance and advocates of liberating *Italia irredenta*, that is, unredeemed Italian territories, from the Habsburg yoke. Since the Entente promised

Istria, Trentino, and Dalmatia as well as colonies, Prime Minister Sidney Sonnino, following the maxim of *sacro egoism*, signed the Treaty of London and entered the Great War in May 1915. But hopes for quick victory over the multiethnic Austrian forces were dashed in the trenches of Friuli, and the army was routed at Caporetto in 1917. Though industrial companies like FIAT expanded rapidly during the war, troop morale was low because soldiers were poorly trained and failed to understand the cause they should die for. Only able to beat the Austrians in October 1918, the ineptly led army had six hundred thousand killed and more wounded. The unnecessary suffering deepened the divisions between a skeptical majority and an interventionist minority.[13]

POSTWAR CRISIS

Facilitated by such modernization problems, fascism was a product of the postwar crisis of parliamentary government. Although Italy received most of the territories promised in the Treaty of London such as Trentino, veterans were disappointed that they did not include the Dalmatian coast and new colonies. Angry that their hopes were not fulfilled, nationalists complained of a *vittoria mutilata*, a mutilated victory. The delineation of the new frontier toward Yugoslavia was most controversial, since many cities were inhabited by Italians while the surrounding countryside in Istria and Dalmatia tended to have Slovenian or Croatian majorities. In order to put pressure on Rome, the diminutive poet Gabriele d'Annunzio gathered a legion of about two thousand ex-soldiers, deserters, and desperadoes, and occupied the port of Fiume, today known as Rijeka. There he established a theatrical regime, full of proclamations and parades, inventing fascist traits like the raised fist and the "corporate order." Eventually the navy evicted him, but Fiume remained an Italian city, showing what a determined right-wing militia could accomplish.[14]

The Nitti and Giolitti cabinets proved unable to manage the economic transition to peacetime, allowing a sense of panic to spread through the middle class. With guns, ammunition, and ships no longer in demand, some firms that had produced war matériel collapsed. The demobilization of veterans created about two million unemployed, while inflation rose to about 600 percent of 1914 prices. Inspired by the revolutionary example of the Bolsheviks, workers responded to the deepening recession with increased militancy. A rash of strikes immobilized production, food riots broke out, and factories were occupied for weeks. In the countryside peasants seized the land, breaking up the large holdings of the latifundia. When the government tried to appease popular demands by conceding the eight-hour workday and increasing social insurance, the propertied feared that their possessions would be taken or taxed away. The introduction of universal suffrage had transformed the cozy game of elites into mass electoral contests with uncertain outcome.[15] Instead of restoring stability, the politicians failed to find a way out of the postwar chaos.

This turmoil provided a chance for populist newcomers like the journalist Benito Mussolini. He was born in 1883 in a modest house in Predappio, a small town in the Romagna. His father, a blacksmith, was an anticlerical republican and socialist who named his son after the Mexican revolutionary Juárez. An unruly boy, Benito showed enough intellectual promise to be sent to a Catholic school where, after several scrapes, he received a teaching certificate. Too restless to fit into the routine of an elementary schoolteacher, he went to Switzerland where he came into contact with radical ideas. After completing his military service, he became a journalist and joined the Socialist Party, rising rapidly to become the editor of the main paper, called *Avanti*, owing to his fiery rhetoric. After the outbreak of World War I, he broke with the PSI because he passionately argued for intervention, founding a new paper, this time titled *Popolo d'Italia*. A postwar police report described him as "an emotional and impulsive person" and "a good speaker" who was "very intelligent, shrewd, cautious, thoughtful, with a good understanding of men."[16]

Mussolini was not a systematic thinker but rather an impressionable, largely self-taught intellectual who dramatized popular slogans with an emotional rhetoric. In his autobiography he claimed not to believe in book learning and to have had only one teacher: "The book of life—lived." Many of his impulses derived from the poverty of his origins, the anticlericalism of his youth, the conflicts with authorities as a young man, and the exciting adventure of war as a man. Nonetheless, his political speeches were laced with references to exploitation from Karl Marx, direct action from Georges Sorel, the need for an elite from Vilfredo Pareto, the power of will from Friedrich Nietzsche, and the malleability of the crowd from Gustave Le Bon. These half-digested notions instilled in him a deep hatred of the Italian political class, be it liberal, Catholic, or socialist. Considering himself "a fighter in my newspaper office," he celebrated the "spirit of national solidarity," exalting in "the victory for the whole Italian race." By 1919 Mussolini was therefore an ex-socialist and integral nationalist who considered himself "desperately Italian."[17]

The fascist movement, founded that spring, combined the competing groups among the interventionists on the Italian left. The name "fascist" denoted a number of nationalist factions such as followers of d'Annunzio, syndicalists inspired by Sergio Panunzio, futurists led by Marinetti, as well as decommissioned shock troopers. Mussolini's idiosyncratic combination of egalitarianism and nationalism resonated especially with these students and officers who were disappointed in the peace and often without work. Financed by industrial interests who feared to lose business by the conversion to peace, the *Popolo d'Italia* stridently criticized the socialists and promoted a productivist and hierarchical agenda in order to achieve a national rebirth. To intimidate their many enemies the fascists formed paramilitary squads that could beat up their opponents or raid rival newspaper offices of the PSI. By dint of his revolutionary rhetoric, personal magnetism, and organizational skill Mussolini gradually succeeded in integrating various leftist and nationalist groups and created a mass movement of malcontents intent on overthrowing the parliamentary regime.[18]

The allure of fascism derived from a pervasive sense of male bonding that made the renewal of Italy seem like a manly adventure. Wearing black uniforms and armed with clubs and revolvers, the *squadristi* emulated the military in structure, appearance, and bearing. Since many were returning veterans or youths who had missed the excitement of the war, they craved the comradeship of the trenches and the closeness of the fighting community. Their imagination was full of liberal and socialist threats, demanding heroic action in order to rescue Italy from disintegration. This task demanded not persuasion but physical violence as "righteous force," legitimizing the street battles with communist workers for control of public space. Fascists saw themselves as a political elite, which, free from the outworn dogmas of its opponents, held the key to the future, inventing its actual course from day to day by "will and power." In this Manichaean universe, there was no place for women or tender feelings. Following the call of their *duce* (leader), many fascists therefore elevated male toughness to the level of an ideology.[19]

Much of the popularity of fascism in the postwar chaos stemmed from its struggle against socialism, which won it the sympathy of an anxious middle class. The PSI victory in the 1919 election and the creation of a Communist Party inspired a host of local insurrections that conjured up the specter of a general revolution. When peasant leagues sequestered property, fascist squads endeared themselves to landowners by descending in force, beating up socialist leaders, and returning the land to their prior proprietors. Similarly, when communist workers went out on strike, fascist militia would swoop into a town, round up the ringleaders, and restore production under somewhat syndicalist auspices. Even if they then expected protection money, a grateful bourgeoisie would comply, considering the blackshirted street fighters, or Blackshirts, the smaller evil. Local police and the military tended to look the other way when fascist retribution got out of hand, since it claimed to be serving the restoration of law and order.[20] As a result of protecting property, fascism began to turn more to the right, compromising with the powers that be.

Mussolini correctly sensed that the weakness of liberal parliamentarianism provided an opportunity that fascism could exploit in more conventional terms. After having been utterly defeated in the first postwar election, he redoubled his efforts by writing inflammatory editorials in the *Popolo d'Italia*, later claiming "our democracy of yesterdays had died; its testament had been read; it had bequeathed us naught but chaos." The Duce also reveled in raucous mass meetings, shouting down his opponents, and haranguing his followers with slogans, dramatized by exaggerated gestures. His steady litany of antiliberal and antisocialist articles as well as revisionist orations deploring the injustice of the peace treaty slowly began to attract youthful but more sophisticated followers like Italo Balbo and Dino Grandi, who would play important roles. Feeding on chaos, the fascist movement gained thousands of members each month, making it increasingly confident. The dual strategy of fostering street violence and pursuing political organization was bearing fruit, because the defenders of democracy proved singularly inept.[21]

SEIZURE OF POWER

Since Italian politicians misunderstood the depth of the modernization crisis and the difficulties of postwar adjustment, they were unwilling to take the drastic measures needed to meet them. In the early 1920s, parliamentary politics was dominated by three parties: the newly founded Popolari, representing political Catholicism with about 100 seats; the bourgeoning Socialists, torn between revolutionary rhetoric and reformist practice with about 150 seats; and the slowly eroding liberal centrists, supported by the secular middle classes with about 90 seats. The fascists formally entered this arena in 1921 as the Partito Nazionale Fascista (PNF). But preoccupied by parliamentary maneuvering, the leaders of the three major parties—Don Sturzo, Turati, and Giolitti—ignored Mussolini as a populist upstart, confident that they could contain him by co-opting his movement. Like the rest of the Italian establishment the crafty Giolitti consistently underestimated their threat and put the Fascists onto his list for the 1921 election, earning them 178,000 votes and 35 seats.[22] Confronted with mounting labor unrest and increasing street violence, the parliamentarians continued to play musical chairs, oblivious of the gathering storm.

The fascists' growing success confronted Mussolini with the challenge of turning popularity into power within a parliamentary system that he claimed to detest. Attracting followers from rural laborers, urban workers, and the lower middle class, the fascist movement swelled to about two hundred thousand members by the fall of 1922, making it increasingly difficult to control.[23] For a while Mussolini sought to play the parliamentary game by cooperating with his sworn enemies, the Socialists, against the weakened liberal-centrist government, but his militias refused to follow him. In late 1921, when he formalized the movement into the PNF, he turned the unruly *squadristi* into its militia arm. Gradually, by a combination of agitation and violence, the Fascists began to gain control of important cities such as Ferrara, Cremona, Parma, Ravenna, and Livorno. At last waking up to the danger, the Socialists called for a general strike—but it was an abysmal failure. Though the Duce now openly demanded a dictatorship, the bourgeois parliamentarians were still seeking to pull him over to their side. By the fall of 1922 his ascent to power seemed inevitable—the only question was whether through invitation or force.

The famous "March on Rome" that overthrew liberal parliamentarianism was mostly a well-calculated bluff. While Mussolini was still secretly negotiating about participating in a solution to one of the periodic ministerial crises, he grandiloquently threatened civil war in the PNF Congress in Naples: "Either they will give us the government or we shall seize it by descending upon Rome!" To underline his determination, he roused his faithful followers to a fever pitch with editorials, but he himself stayed in the background in Milan. Instead, he ordered his lieutenants to organize columns of about thirty thousand armed *squadristi* and converge by truck or train on the Italian capital. At last the government of Liberal Party prime minister Luigi Facta realized it was facing "a revolutionary attempt" and tried to "maintain public order by any means and at any price." Though King Vittorio Emmanuele III did not like the Fascists, he refused to proclaim martial law so as to avoid bloodshed, offering a nervous Mussolini "the responsibility of forming a Ministry." Relieved that his gamble had succeeded, the Duce greeted the parading columns: "I was then triumphant and in Rome!"[24]

Technically, the new cabinet with Mussolini as prime minister, formed on October 20, 1922, was a coalition in which the Fascists were a minority, reflecting their lack of parliamentary strength. Glossing over the limits of his power, Mussolini called for the creation of a unified national government in order to end the fighting between factions and to reconcile all Italians. Aside from him the cabinet contained only three Fascists, two Popolari, four Liberals, one Nationalist, and three nonpartisan personalities such as the philosopher Giovanni Gentile. After a rousing speech by the prime minister, Parliament confirmed the new government with the lopsided vote of 306 to 116 and 7 abstentions. With all the bourgeois parties supporting Mussolini, only the Socialists and Communists (PCI) dared to oppose his new regime. As a reward for the support of the Blackshirts, who expected a social revolution, he created a national militia, paid by public funds that provided jobs in exchange for respecting law and order. Moreover, Mussolini also absorbed the Nationalist Association Party en bloc as well as numerous careerists into the Fascist Party, thereby broadening his popular base.[25]

Dispensing with parliamentary concerns, the Duce set out to manufacture a popular mandate that would cement his power against any challenge. To overcome the political fragmentation of proportional representation, he hit upon the ingenious expedient, codified in a voting law proposed by Fascist Giacomo Acerbo, that would give any party that received at least one-quarter of the popular vote two-thirds of the seats in the Chamber of Deputies, creating a stable majority. When the Holy See ordered the Popolari to abstain, the Fascists, supported by Liberals and Nationalists, won the decisive vote on the Acerbo Law that emasculated Italian democracy. After some minor foreign-policy successes Mussolini called for his first election in April 1924, carefully constructing a cabinet list that blended Fascist activists with traditional politicians. This combined ticket was overwhelmingly approved with 66.3 percent of the popular vote, electing 374 deputies of whom 275 were Fascists and decimating the various opposition groups. Distancing himself from the intransigent radicals in the PNF, Mussolini now called for "order, hierarchy, discipline" so as to repudiate "the putrid body of the Goddess Liberty."[26]

The final blows were the decapitation of the labor movement, the destruction of parliamentary opposition, and the muzzling of the press. When the Socialist Giacomo Matteotti attacked Fascist violence and corruption in the Chamber of Deputies, he was murdered by the Fascist secret police on June 10, 1924. Though Mussolini shifted the blame to his underlings, the opposition deputies seceded from Parliament according to an old Roman custom and retired to the Aventine Hill, hoping to block further legislation. But the boycott failed to rouse the populace or force the elite to abandon the adventurer, since even the philosopher Benedetto Croce praised fascism for its "love of Italy." As a result, the Fascists abolished freedom of the press partly by government decree and partly by pressuring the owners of newspapers to dismiss liberal editors like Luigi Albertini. When evidence implicated him in the Matteotti murder, Mussolini dramatically assumed "full responsibility for all that has happened," claiming that he alone could give Italy "peace and tranquility." Instead of toppling him, the Matteotti crisis marked the transition to open dictatorship.

The establishment of dictatorial rule was a gradual process, propelled by a mixture of Fascist coercion and public compliance. The seizure of power was a blend of constitutional legality, in the appointment of Mussolini as prime minister, and concession to the extraparliamentary pressure of a violent mass movement. The collaboration of the establishment was essential, since the liberal and national elite cooperated under the illusion that Mussolini could be contained according to the recipe of *transformismo*. Engineered by incessant propaganda in the press and mass meetings, popular acclamation for the nationalist coup forced the hand of skeptical politicians who did not want to stand in the way of a national renewal. With a mixture of incentives and repression, the Fascists divided and immobilized opponents in the labor movement and among democratic intellectuals who found themselves deserted by the public. Mussolini's government rested on an uneasy compromise between established institutions like the monarchy, church, and army as well as newly invented Fascist bodies like the PFN, the Blackshirt militia, and the secret police.[27]

Mussolini's successful seizure of power galvanized youthful members of the European Right by presenting a model that combined tradition with modernity in a novel blend. Born in the male comradeship of the trenches, his action-oriented movement sought on the one hand to restore conservative values such as order and hierarchy, social community, and national power. On the other, fascism was profoundly modern in its admiration of technology, use of electronic media, and youth orientation, thereby conveying an image of dynamism that defenders of the old order lacked. All over Europe from Norway to France, from Portugal to Romania, the fascist rejection of the discredited traditional authorities appealed to young neoconservatives casting about for an alternative to Marxism and liberalism that might offer a better way into the future.[28] Though the movement owed much of its character to the specific postwar confusion of Italy, its foreign admirers included the racist rabble-rouser Adolf Hitler, who understood the exciting novelty of fascism sufficiently to attempt to repeat Mussolini's coup a year later in the Munich Beer Hall Putsch.

THE FASCIST STATE

While it incorporated many traditional elements, the fascist dictatorship differed from conventional authoritarian regimes by being more modern and intrusive. With typical exaggeration Mussolini himself claimed: "The Fascist conception of the state is all-embracing; outside of it no human or spiritual values can exist much less have value. Thus understood, Fascism is totalitarian, and the fascist state—a synthesis and a unit inclusive of all values—interprets, develops and potentiates the whole life of the people." Marking the contrast to the limited obedience demanded by kings, priests, or generals, Mussolini used the neologism "totalitarian" to describe his more far-reaching attempt not just to rule politically but also to restructure society all the way down to the private sphere.[29] Fascism therefore set out to mobilize the masses in order to transform the country fundamentally, creating a proud and powerful national community that would be capable of gaining Italy its rightful place of honor among European nations. To achieve this ambitious aim, Mussolini used a whole repertoire of innovative measures for making Italy fascist.

Since its doctrine remained fuzzy and its policies malleable, fascism might best be understood as political theater, an ever-changing self-dramatization arranged by Mussolini. At its core was the cult of *il duce del fascismo*, the fascist leader whose carefully staged charisma inspired a whole nation to follow. Since Mussolini was a small man, he stuck out his chin, puffed up his chest, planted his arms on his hips, strode with large steps, and assumed dramatic poses, such as sitting on a horse or flying an airplane, to indicate extraordinary vision and strength. Reviewing columns of Blackshirts, he would raise his fist in a Roman salute to show his authority over his followers. Sometimes he mimicked the great statesman, dressed in an elegant tuxedo, surrounded by admiring women, to underline his machismo. On special occasions he would appear on a balcony of the Palazzo Venezia and address the crowd with inspiring phrases, supported by exaggerated gestures. Propagandists never missed an opportunity to disseminate his portrait into schools or to capture his exploits in newsreels designed to teach the populace that "Mussolini is always right."[30]

Fascism also introduced new syndicalist and corporatist institutions to discipline labor and circumvent Parliament. The syndicates were a kind of trade union that replaced the Marxist organizations, negotiated contracts with employers, and represented labor interests while domesticating them at the same time. With the improving economy they even managed to push through modest improvements in pay, leisure hours, and family allowances. Inspired by hierarchical elements of Catholic social theory, the better-known corporations were a reprise of medieval organizations that brought employers and employees together at the negotiating table so as to overcome class conflicts. Founded in 1926, the corporate structure was expanded into a National Council of Corporations four years later and eventually subdivided into twenty-two different occupational groups. In 1939 a Grand Council of Fasces and Corporations was set up that transformed the legislature into an entirely fascist deliberative body.[31] Claiming to present an alternative to capitalism or communism, this corporatist structure served as a fascist tool to control the country and rubber-stamp Mussolini's policies.

Fascist efforts to transform Italy culminated in repeated campaigns to modernize the economy and revitalize society. While free trade had created an initial boom, the collapse of the lira forced

Mussolini into a drastic upward revaluation aided by steep tariffs in 1925. To counter the high price of imported cereals, he launched a "battle of grain," pushing for higher domestic yields in order to achieve autarchy. He also initiated a public-relations effort to stem the flight into the cities by glorifying the benefits of rural life. Moreover, the dictator sought to combat the decline of the birthrate by giving prizes to women who bore many children and raising taxes on bachelors! A grand program of public works sought to drain the Pontine Marshes, build roads, and provide rural electrification. Finally, Mussolini encouraged the creation of semipublic companies such as for oil refining (AGIP) and created an Institute for Industrial Reconstruction (IRI) as a government-controlled investment bank. Promoted with great fanfare, such propaganda-drenched campaigns scored some visible gains but failed to correct the underlying weakness of the economy.[32]

Mussolini's greatest success was the solution of the "Roman question" through reconciliation with the Catholic Church in 1929. The emasculation of the Liberals paved the way for a compromise between the state and the papacy, ending a struggle that had poisoned relations since 1871. Though Mussolini was an atheist, he understood the necessity of bringing Catholics into the fascist camp; while Pius XI was not enthusiastic about fascism either, he feared the socialists and communists even more. Spurred by conciliatory gestures like the rescue of the papal bank, the conclusion of the two Lateran treaties took three years of negotiations. The first recognized the Vatican as an independent state and paid 1.75 billion lira as compensation for the loss of its temporal possessions. The second defined the role of Catholicism as "the sole religion of the state," resolving the conflict between church and civil marriage, making religious instruction mandatory in schools, and allowing organizations such as the Azione Cattolica (Catholic Action) to survive.[33] This concordat was crucial in cementing Mussolini's rule through the blessing of the church.

Ideological indoctrination focused primarily on the young, since Mussolini believed that youth held the key to the future as celebrated in the party song "Giovinezza." In 1926 the Fascists founded the official youth organization Opera Nazionale Balilla, modeled after the Boy Scouts, which combined attractive leisure activities with militarization and propaganda. Starting at age six, there was a level for each age up to the *avanguardisti* at age twenty-one, while parallel groups were set up for girls. Once at the university, young fascists continued in the Gioventu Universitaria Fascista (GUF), which similarly blended ideological indoctrination with social activities. The public schools also stressed political education so that every pupil would become a proud, fascist-minded Italian upon graduation. When university professors were compelled to sign an oath of allegiance "to the country and to the Fascist regime," only twelve of about twelve hundred refused, and these were subsequently dismissed.[34] This strenuous effort succeeded in creating a veneer of fascist orientation among the young, but the vagueness of the ideology itself prevented a deeper conditioning.

For adults the Fascists created new forms of popular culture and mass leisure, offering cheap recreation to tired workers so as to gain their loyalty. Mussolini was quick to recognize the propaganda potential of radio, which grew from modest beginnings in 1924 to one million sets in 1938, eagerly listened to in trattorias and homes. Similarly, Fascists encouraged sports, such as the car race Mille Miglia, the bicycle competition Giro d'Italia, and the soccer World Cup, which Italy won in 1934 and 1938. The key institution was the Opera Nazionale Dopolavoro, a network of "after work" clubs that attracted four million members by 1939. By offering facilities such as bars, libraries, and sports fields as well as cheap vacations, dancing, and even welfare handouts, this state- and business-supported leisure organization was quite popular, since it provided inexpensive recreation otherwise beyond the reach of many ordinary Italians. It was always accompanied by a political message, but that could be endured if one wanted to take advantage of a particular activity.[35] Fascism owed much of its popularity to such "soft stabilizers" of the regime.

As a dictator Mussolini wanted not only to be loved but also feared, since he believed that the affection of a crowd, like that of a woman, was basically fickle. While his popularity increased until 1936, Fascist power also rested on repression, a dark underside that often escaped foreign observers. The path to power was already paved with the victims of *squadristi* violence and the torture or murder of numerous enemies. In 1926 the secret police Organization for Vigilance and Repression of Anti-Fascism (OVRA) was reorganized and politicized in order to hunt down opponents more effectively. Many leaders of competing parties such as the Catholic Don Sturzo, the Liberal Gaetano Salvemini, and the Socialist Pietro Nenni were forced into exile. But even there they were not safe, since Carlo Roselli, a particularly determined dissident, was assassinated in Paris. Others, like the historian Luigi Albertini, languished for years in fascist prisons, which is where the communist intellectual Antonio Gramsci compiled his pathbreaking notebooks before he died in 1937.[36] Though the Italian fascists killed fewer victims than the Nazis or the Soviet communists, their dictatorship also rested on ruthless oppression.

PRESTIGE AND EMPIRE

The strengthening of the nation served one overriding goal—Italian expansion abroad, reviving the glories of the Roman Empire. The country's central position in the Mediterranean offered multiple targets on its immediate frontiers, the Balkan region, and the African continent. But its limited resources required a cautious search for allies, while Mussolini's lack of international experience and impulsive temper complicated this quest for increasing Italian prestige. In his foreign policy, the Duce therefore vacillated between playing the statesman charming foreign visitors and the dictator blustering toward presumed inferiors. True to its origin as a protest movement against the peace terms, the Fascist regime openly worked toward the revision of the Versailles Treaty system, irritating the French. At the same time Mussolini tried to make Italy into a leading regional power by bombing Corfu in 1923, annoying the British. Moreover, he also succumbed to the lure of empire, though the "pacification" of Libya proved costly and dragged on until 1932.[37]

As long as he could play a central role, Mussolini was, however, willing to stabilize Europe by suggesting a four-power directory in 1933 in order to contain the Nazi threat. Pleased that Hitler's seizure of power had followed his own example, the Duce sought to defuse the international situation by going outside the League of Nations and suggesting direct negotiations between the leading continental countries to settle various disputes. Though the embassies in Berlin sent alarmist reports about Nazi revisionism, the leaders in Paris and London were unwilling to confront Germany by force. As a result, Mussolini could act as mediator between the wartime victors and the defeated, since the Fascists were also unhappy about the peace treaties and sought diplomatic methods to revise the Versailles settlement. Though irritated by the Italian strongman, the western leaders were willing to make some concession to his vanity in order to keep Hitler in check.[38] Even if his initiative quickly failed, the Duce continued to pose as a statesman who was increasing Italian prestige.

By 1935 Mussolini felt confident that rearmament had proceeded far enough for Italy to avenge the defeat of Adowa by invading Ethiopia, the last piece of unclaimed Africa. Marshal Badoglio's attack on Abyssinia involved over half a million soldiers, required a sustained naval effort to supply the troops through the port of Massawa, and provided a training ground for five hundred military aircraft. After almost a year of bloody fighting, the combination of bombing and mustard gas finally broke the Ethiopians' resistance. As a result of the victory, Mussolini proudly proclaimed the founding of a "new Italian Empire" from the balcony of the Palazzo Venezia to cheering crowds. This imperialist adventure was a public-relations success at home, increasing the Duce's popularity. But the brutality of the warfare against the overmatched Ethiopians produced a wave of international revulsion and isolated Italy diplomatically when the League of Nations proclaimed economic sanctions against it.[39] Moreover, the break with the West openly aligned the Fascists with the National Socialists in threatening the peace of Europe.

The resulting delusion of grandeur drew Mussolini into the Spanish Civil War, where he supported Francisco Franco's uprising against the legitimate authorities of the Spanish Republic. In spite of the western nations' official nonintervention policy, Italy and Germany aided the reactionary coup, while the Soviet Union and the French Popular Front helped the Republican forces. The Duce's reasons for intervening remain somewhat murky, stemming from ideological affinity and from his interest in dominating the Mediterranean. But in contrast to Hitler's limited engagement with the Condor Legion, Mussolini sent seventy thousand regular soldiers, dressed as volunteers. Moreover, Italy provided four hundred planes, two hundred bombers, and fourteen hundred pilots who played an important role in the struggle against the International Brigades, which were eventually controlled by Moscow's communist regime. Though taking credit for the advance of Franco's forces, Mussolini underestimated the length and cost of the struggle, which severely strained his resources, already overstretched by the conquest of Ethiopia.[40] Italy gained nothing from the intervention but rather was driven into Hitler's arms by it.

Mussolini's hankering after prestige hastened the diplomatic realignment of the 1930s that precipitated the Second World War. Though the Duce considered himself to be the leader of the international fascist movement, the mounting cost of his wars as well as the ostracism of the West compelled him to sign a friendship treaty with Nazi Germany in October 1936. Grandiloquently he dubbed it the Berlin-Rome "Axis," because Europe was supposed to revolve around it. A year later Mussolini signed the Anti-Comintern Pact with Germany and Japan, creating a front of aggressively revisionist powers, ostensibly to combat Bolshevism. In 1938 the Italian dictator could no longer prevent the German annexation of Austria, since now he depended on Hitler's good will. The climax of his international role was the Munich Conference, where he pulled a proposal, drafted by the German Foreign Office, out of his pocket that avoided war by turning the Sudetenland over to Germany. With the bridges to its former allies burned, Italy endorsed the tripartite Pact of Steel in 1939, establishing a military alliance of dictators.[41]

Mussolini's growing stature encouraged a veritable fascism tourism, attracting a motley group of admirers, commentators, and academics eager to discover the secret of Italy's revival. Foreign high-society ladies flocked to Rome to marvel at his machismo magnetism. Nosy journalists like Emil Ludwig sought out the Duce to record his views, publishing long transcripts of their conversations. Misguided writers like George Bernard Shaw defended fascism by claiming that "Mussolini, without any of Napoleon's prestige, has done for Italy what Napoleon did for France." Somewhat naively, U.S. ambassador Richard Washburn Child introduced his autobiography by asserting that "the Duce is now the greatest figure of his sphere and time." Finally, conservative politicians like Winston Churchill praised the dictator: "The Roman genius impersonated in Mussolini, the greatest law-giver among living men, has shown to many nations how they can resist the pressures of Socialism and has indicated the path that a nation can follow when courageously led."[42] Often repeated, such acclaim was bound to go to the Duce's head.

Fascism's presumed triumphs also contributed to spreading its message abroad, since this movement seemed to offer a dynamic alternative to moribund democracy and egalitarian communism. Initially Mussolini had been skeptical about exporting his ideas, but flush with success he predicted during the 1930s that all of Europe would be fascist within a decade. Creating a Fascist International similar to the Communist International would have been a contradiction in terms, since its hypernationalism resisted transnational organization. But even in Western Europe some intellectuals in the Action Française, the British Union of Fascists, and the Spanish Falange shared many of its right-wing tenets. In Eastern Europe, radical movements such as the Arrow Cross or the Iron Guard found adherents, especially in the authoritarian states of Hungary and Romania, because of their revisionist aspirations as well as ethnic tensions. Fascism had its greatest impact on the confused German right: the National Socialists imitated many of its traits such as the leadership cult and militia violence.[43] But only in the Weimar Republic did fascists manage to seize power on their own.

In contrast to the *resistenza* myth of widespread opposition, antifascism remained relatively weak until 1938 owing to the regime's apparent popularity. The bourgeois parties were discredited, while remnants of Marxist groups fought each other. Only the communists retained an underground network of several thousand members. The political émigrés in Paris like Count Carlo Sforza or Gaetano Salvemini debated endlessly but received little support, and found hardly any audience within Italy. Some older scholars like Benedetto Croce and Luigi Einaudi also kept a certain distance from the regime, while younger intellectuals formed the group Giustizia e Liberta, which openly criticized the dictatorship. People who were especially close to the Catholic Church remained impervious to fascism's ideological appeals, and there was much popular grumbling. But active opposition remained small, since the secret police ruthlessly suppressed dissent. Though Mussolini survived a handful of assassination attempts, a broad-based antifascist resistance coalesced only during the unpopular Second World War, when partisans engaged in military attacks.[44]

FASCIST REGENERATION

Not merely a reactionary movement, fascism was rather a populist effort to respond to the modernization crisis of Italian society. In structural terms, fascism arose from Italy's belated transformation from an agrarian to an industrial order, which created deep class divisions and regional disparities between the industrializing North and the agricultural South. In actual politics, it stemmed from the difficulties of transition from war to peace, since Parliament failed to provide an adequate livelihood for the newly enfranchised masses, and to counteract the disappointment created by exaggerated expectations of a favorable peace. The timid Liberal and Catholic politicians were incapable of upholding public order against the violence unleashed by communist attempts to seize factories and right-wing efforts at retaliation. To revitalize a floundering Italy, the fascist movement promised social justice at home and imperial power abroad through a confused blend of futurism, nationalism, and syndicalism.[45] It was the failure of parliamentary government to resolve Italy's long- and short-range problems that gave this populist newcomer a chance.

Mussolini's key contribution was the invention of a modern form of right-wing politics that did not just proclaim a national renewal but actually seized power and governed for several decades. The fascists responded to the erosion of deference to traditional authorities by creating a new kind of mass movement that claimed to represent the entire national community. To inspire his following, Mussolini systematically constructed a cult of leadership, which endowed the Duce with superhuman qualities that would enable him to divine the collective will and put it into practice. Fascism also made imaginative use of media such as the press, the radio, and newsreels in order to broadcast its message to a much larger number of people than ever before. At the same time it set out to control and indoctrinate the entire country through its fashioning of mass-membership organizations. Finally, Mussolini had no qualms about using violence to suppress internal enemies.[46] These innovative features went considerably beyond the traditional methods of authoritarian regimes by aiming at a more total control of society.

Many of the actual policies pursued by the fascists were also modernizing—even if their purpose was to increase national strength rather than to provide greater welfare or enlightenment. Though invoking the glories of the past, Mussolini and other fascist leaders were fascinated by the speed and movement of modern technology— they could be seen flying in airplanes and driving fast cars, sometimes risking their lives. Even the campaign for ruralism was not motivated just by nostalgia but also by the desire to raise agricultural yields so as to achieve self-sufficiency in food. The nationalist attempt to improve infrastructure through constructing new roads, railroads, dams, and power lines not only tied the country together but also brought material progress into remote areas. The militarist project of creating an independent defense sector, capable of producing battleships and fighter planes, also required an expansion of heavy industry as well as an advancement of engineering capacity that benefited civilian users. Though its ends were often irrational and its measures inefficient, fascist practice worked somewhat like a developmental dictatorship.[47]

In the realm of culture, fascism promoted its own version of modernism as a style that blended references to the glorious past with technological visions of the future. While fascists rejected liberal decadence and communist materialism, they sought to offer an alternative form of spiritual regeneration through a broad range of competing efforts. In architecture the fascist style was a curious amalgamation of historical citations and experimental building techniques, tending toward the monumental, suggesting national unity and power. In the fascist mass spectacles, invocations of Roman greatness mingled with contemporary devices such as amplified sound, projected light, and choreographed motion, creating a sense of drama that appealed to the emotions. Even in daily consumption fascists did not sponsor a return to handicrafts but rather the design of new industrial products to fulfill mass wishes for a better life. Though the proper balance between historicizing (*Strapaese*) and futurist (*Novecento*) priorities remained contested, all fascists agreed on the basic project of fashioning a new man through "aestheticizing politics."[48]

Fascism was therefore not just a regressive throwback, as claimed by the Left, but an alternate variety of vitalist modernity that promised to control rapid and disorienting change. Though popular in the West, the equation of modernization with capitalist democracy is misleading, as it fails to acknowledge that communism and fascism attempted to develop competing models that avoided the liberal defects of exploitation and degeneration. Part of the confusion arises from Mussolini's constant invocation of *Romanita* in his speeches, the use of ancient symbols and the references to former glory. But in spite of this mythicizing, the aims of strengthening the national community biologically and militarily as well as the means of mass mobilization and propaganda were quite modern. The fascist vision appealed to international intellectuals like Ezra Pound and Louis-Ferdinand Céline because it promised to heal the crisis of modernity through fashioning a dynamic national community.[49] Tragically, the realization of these confused ideas would create even more suffering, as they would lead to repression at home and aggression abroad.

Chapter 7

MODERNIST PROVOCATIONS

Bauhaus modernism, 1929. *Source*: bpk, Berlin / Art Resource, NY.

An unprepossessing handbill invited visitors to the "first international DADA-fair" in Berlin in July 1920. Founded in revulsion against the First World War in Zurich's Café-Voltaire, this experimental art movement shocked viewers by creating a "new reality" that represented the chaos of modern life. Reacting as well to the advent of photography, artists like Georg Grosz and John Heartfield radically rejected the tradition of creating beauty, preferring instead to picture the victims of war with brutal honesty and to assemble everyday objects in startling patterns. Slogans like "art is dead" and provocative collages composed of scraps lined the exhibition's walls, culminating in an effigy of a Prussian officer with a pig's head dangling from the ceiling. Offended by the nihilist, communist, anticlerical, and antibourgeois thrust of this parody, the Reichswehr tried to have the show shut down, but the artists were acquitted. In many ways Dadaism was the most radical expression of twentieth-century revolt against convention that according to Raul Housman created "the beginning of modern art [on an] international scale."[1]

In contrast, scientists and engineers clung to their belief in progress, manifest in the construction of the German Museum of Science and Technology. Conceived by Oskar von Miller before the war, its neomedieval halls showing "masterpieces of science and technology" opened in May 1925 with a festive parade of engineers and artisans throughout the streets of Munich. The exhibits began with early discoveries but focused on the astounding inventions of the last decades of the nineteenth century, ranging from electrical motors and chemical dyestuffs to automobiles and airplanes. The museum's design promoted a heroic conception of technology by focusing on inventors, portrayed as daring explorers of new knowledge and creators of improvements that would benefit mankind. While they celebrated the achievements of the German genius, the displays also acknowledged the international character of scientific advancement.[2] Appealing especially to the curiosity of the young, this largest museum of science and technology in the world represented some of the machines that spearheaded technological innovation.

At the same time Central European intellectuals sought to come to terms with modernization in order to find "more natural and humane forms of existence under modern conditions." Fascinated by the ambivalent effects of metropolitan existence on the human spirit, sociologist Georg Simmel pondered the centrality of money. Distinguishing between organic community (*Gemeinschaft*) and faceless society (*Gesellschaft*), Ferdinand Tönnies feared that "the entire civilization has been turned upside down by a modern way of life, dominated by civil and market society, and in this transformation civilization itself is coming to an end." Economist Werner Sombart instead celebrated the dynamism of capitalism, contrasting creative entrepreneurs with avaricious traders whom he associated with the Germans and British respectively during the First World War. The most original thinker was Max Weber, who interpreted the confusing changes unleashed by industrialization as processes of rationalization and bureaucratization. But like his Wilhelmine peers, he viewed the impact of modernity with profound ambivalence, unsure whether it would be beneficial or problematic.[3]

These contradictions inherent in the encounter with modernity culminated in "Weimar culture," which has become a cautionary symbol for the dangers of artistic extremism.[4] The epithet is not entirely unjustified, since the collapse of the empires prompted intellectuals and artists from Central and Eastern Europe to flock to Berlin, making it a hothouse of experimentation and controversy. Moreover, the fragility of the first German democracy politicized cultural manifestations to a greater degree than concurrent movements in Paris or London, since Weimar culture appeared to involve the whole future of the defeated country, turning conflicts of style into clashes over ideology. The eventual collapse of the republic added an air of tragedy to its intellectual endeavors, while the "flight of the muses" to escape Nazi persecution dispersed creative refugees all over the world, where they spread some of Weimar's innovations. Though the German context therefore looms large in the subsequent discussion, the cultural confrontation with modernity was a Europe-wide phenomenon with similar battles taking place everywhere.

The explosion of modernist culture in an exciting variety of movements and styles produced a severe ideological backlash. Already in the last decade before 1914 an avant-garde revolt sought to escape the stifling confines of the traditional canon. The suffering of the First World War deepened the sense of dissonance, hastened the rejection of received rules, and radicalized the attack on bourgeois (im-)morality. With the return of peace and prosperity, a popular-culture industry also emerged to entertain the masses, giving modernization an upbeat face. Capturing control of some institutions, leftist innovators succeeded in creating lasting achievements in the style of classical modernity. But traditionalist commentators complained about urban alienation, religious leaders denounced decadence, and elitists deplored the decline of standards. Moreover, neoconservative ideologues searched for an antimodern form of modernity.[5] The artistic experiments therefore provoked fierce conflicts, in which the ideological extremes crushed the democratic vision between them.

MODERNIST REVOLT

At the dawn of the twentieth century many intellectuals grew frustrated with the hierarchical structure and conventional style prevalent in European capitals. While the landed and industrial elites were still firmly in control, the masses of ordinary people, organized in the labor movement, clamored for more political rights. Though bourgeois virtues of cleanliness, self-discipline, and hard work remained dominant, women activists began to rebel against Victorian patriarchy and the double standard in sexual affairs. Even if the churches were still highly esteemed, scientific discoveries such as the theory of evolution were undercutting biblical authority, and technical inventions such as electrical light were changing daily lives, raising hopes for further improvements. Whereas most architects continued to rely on historical precedents such as the neogothic, more daring designers and painters too started to search for novel forms of expression such as the decorative art nouveau style.[6] It was this contradiction between an apparently immutable order and a growing sense of movement that inspired the modernist revolt.

Much of the confidence in the beneficent character of modernity stemmed from the spectacular advances of science during the last decades of the nineteenth century. The biological discoveries of British explorer Charles Darwin presented a rational explanation of the origin of species that conflicted with the religious account of creation. The advances in physics by Franco-Polish researchers Pierre and Marie Curie opened a door to the phenomenon of radiation while the studies of German inventor Werner von Siemens made it possible to transmit and harness the power of electricity. At the same time the investigations by French doctor Louis Pasteur and the German physician Robert Koch confirmed the existence of bacteria and inaugurated the treatment of infectious diseases previously thought incurable. Finally, the observations of Austrian psychiatrist Sigmund Freud on the neurotic behaviors of his patients uncovered a realm of the subconscious, helping to deal with psychic disorders. This list of breakthroughs could be extended in many other directions, including the chemical experiments that produced aspirin.[7]

Technological inventions also contributed to the sense of progress, since they profoundly changed the quality of daily lives. The building of municipal sewage systems removed effluent from the streets, and the supply of clean water improved public health. The construction of power lines made it possible to light homes and shops, ending the tyranny of the night and changing circadian rhythms in the metropolis. The establishment of telephone connections initiated communication over long distances, facilitating business deals and personal contacts. The laying of rails for streetcars and the digging of tunnels for subway systems made it possible to move around in the burgeoning cities, while the linking of towns by railways reduced travel time between more distant places. The invention of bicycles and cars provided individual mobility and generated a new sensation of speed.[8] By overcoming age-old constraints, such technological developments speeded up time and shrank distance, conflating modernity with rapidity and motion that called for new forms of cultural expression beyond the canon of tradition.

One sign of revolt was the secession of painters from the official academic salons in order to break with the convention of representation and free the play of color and line. When the Parisian art academy's jury rejected impressionist paintings, Edouard Manet founded an independent Salon des Refusés in 1863 to show canvases dappled with light to the public. In subsequent decades the sculptor Auguste Rodin and the painter Pierre-Auguste Renoir also organized independent exhibitions for innovative works to circumvent the control of the art market by conservative academicians. Supporting the Fauves' experimentation with bold colors and the Cubists' venture into abstraction of lines, this independent exposition showcased painters such as Henri Matisse, Paul Cézanne, and Paul Gaugin, who transcended traditional assumptions of what constituted beauty. In 1897 the Viennese artists Gustav Klimt and Otto Wagner similarly seceded from the Austrian art academy, proclaiming "to every age its art and to art its freedom." Championed by Max Lieberman, the rebellion of the painters spread to Berlin, opening the door to an explosion of expressionism that became known as "modern art."[9]

The composers' abandonment of harmony, which introduced the shrill dissonances and hectic rhythms of metropolitan life, was another indicator of modernism. In an overripe late Romantic fashion, Richard Strauss' expansion of the tonal vocabulary still contained flashes of humor and stunning harmonic resolutions that charmed the public. Similarly Gustav Mahler's interminable symphonies, with their threatening dissonant crescendos, were balanced by pleasing strains of folklike melody. But Claude Debussy's subtle experiments with shading moods and fluctuating impressions often abandoned the canon of classical forms. Finally, Arnold Schoenberg completely rejected the restraints of tonality and ventured into "a vivid, uninterrupted succession of colors, rhythms and moods" that shocked audiences accustomed to more pleasing symphonic styles. While his daring experimentation with atonality attracted devoted followers like Anton Webern and Alban Berg, the cerebral character of such "modern music" left many concertgoers bewildered, appealing only to a small coterie of the initiated.[10]

Yet another form of rebellion against the bourgeois order and respectability was the staging of social and psychological dramas. In realistic plays such as *A Doll's House* and *Hedda Gabler* the Norwegian author Henrik Ibsen criticized the middle-class family by revealing the disastrous consequences of a patriarchal domination that confined women to domesticity while allowing men sexual license.

In a more lighthearted vein, the Irish playwright and cofounder of the Fabian Society George Bernard Shaw also ridiculed the deleterious effects of the British class system by exposing its hypocrisy in a string of well-received comedies such as *Arms and the Man* and *Pygmalion*. With stark naturalist language the German writer Gerhard Hauptmann similarly exposed the heartlessness of the capitalist system in his accusatory play *The Weavers*, which dramatized the hopeless resistance of Silesian artisans against the industrial competition.[11] While Shaw's productions used irony to ridicule prejudices, Ibsen's and Hauptmann's frontal assault on bourgeois sensibilities associated naturalist drama with scandalous provocations.

In a more muted fashion novelists also sought to escape narrative conventions by writing about taboo subjects and exploring subjective consciousness. In Germany the critic Heinrich Mann incurred the wrath of the censor by his satire of Wilhelmine arrogance in *Professor Unrat*, later made into a famous movie, *The Blue Angel*, with Marlene Dietrich. In France, the prolific André Gide sought to free himself from moralistic constraints in novels such as *L'immoraliste*, an audacious confession exploring his own homosexuality, the same "gross indecency" for which the British playwright Oscar Wilde was imprisoned. In Austria Arthur Schnitzler experimented with stream-of-consciousness narration in his short story "Leutnant Gustl," probing the psychic disorders that led Viennese to suicide. In Britain the self-taught D. H. Lawrence also began to explore the passions aroused by human sexuality so frankly in books like *Sons and Lovers* that many critics denounced them as pornography. By abandoning realist restraint, such "modern literature" went beyond moral edification, openly confronting social problems and plumbing the depth of the psyche.[12]

The prolific artist Pablo Picasso exemplified many innovations and some problems of the artistic revolt. Born in 1881 in Malaga, the child prodigy grew up in Barcelona, where he became an accomplished draftsman. His early paintings of the blue and rose periods still used representational techniques, only exaggerating color and line so as to create a haunting beauty. But upon moving to Paris, Picasso became involved in the experiments of the avant-garde, gradually abandoning recognizable subjects for a freer play of shapes and shades. Transiting into abstraction, he became one of the pioneers of cubism in the last years before the Great War, playing with subdued colors and complex forms that transcended the iconic tradition. Celebrated as pioneering innovation, his daring paintings sold well, making him rather rich. Nonetheless, he became a communist and painted a big canvas that denounced the Nazi bombing of Guernica in the Spanish Civil War. Living a bohemian life with successive wives and mistresses, Picasso was admired and reviled as a master of modernism who revolutionized artistic expression.[13]

SHOCK OF WAR

World War I intensified the assault on tradition, because the experience proved so utterly wrenching that it could not be expressed in any acceptable form. Huddled in muddy trenches, soldiers felt reduced to automatons, forced to follow incomprehensible orders, so that their horizon shrank to a constant struggle for survival, relieved only by a cigarette or a drink. Participating in mass murder and witnessing the indignity of mass death produced a loss of youthful innocence—life could never again be just beautiful and benign. The impersonal nature of killing and dying in mechanized combat gradually destroyed illusions of heroism that might have elevated the suffering as sacrifice for one's country. Finally, the pitiful gains of many attacks and the unending prospect of further fighting raised troubling questions about the entire meaning of the conflict. Artists like Otto Dix struggled to find images for conveying the horrors of the "front experience," which exposed the destructive side of modernity as a force beyond individual control.[14] Even among intellectuals at the home front, the war left deep scars that took decades to heal.

The Great War contributed to discrediting science and technology, since their effects turned out to be deadly rather than benevolent. In the industrial form of assembly-line killing during the war of attrition, it was not individual valor but collective action and the amount of available matériel that decided the outcome. Introduced in 1915, the use of poison gas produced a slow death by a burning of the lungs that permanently scarred its few survivors. At the same time the laying of explosive mines in oceans and unrestricted use of the submarine sank ships without warning, leaving sailors helpless against such danger from the deep. While the novel threat of bombing from airplanes left soldiers defenseless on the ground, the new weapon of the armored and self-propelled tank terrified infantrymen in their trenches. Even the improved medical treatment available in field hospitals only patched up wounded bodies for renewed military duty, while psychological therapy for the "shell-shocked" served to send the mentally ill back to the inferno of the front. No wonder that after 1918 cultural imagination began to portray machines as a mechanized menace.[15]

World War I therefore transformed the language and style of battle descriptions from tales of heroic adventure to accounts of senseless suffering. The celebratory tone of official war reporting proved incapable of conveying the agonizing experience of trench warfare. Many of the letters from soldiers on the front lines studiously avoided any detail of the horrifying circumstances of the fighting, creating a profound chasm between the actual battlefield and the home front, which was deluged instead with hollow phrases of war propaganda. While patriotic writers like Walter Flex or Rupert Brooke initially tried to romanticize the struggle, the grossness of the actual trench experience forced British "war poets" such as Robert Graves and Wilfred Owen to strive more honestly to find words and images adequate for what was essentially indescribable. Verse written under the impact of combat therefore slowly transformed from celebration of patriotic valor to shocking portrayal of the meaninglessness of the suffering.[16] These literary efforts to express such sensations enhanced modernist trends by dissolving form and meaning.

Since photography proved superior in portraying the horrors of the front, the war also enhanced the artistic turn away from classical styles of representation. In contrast to traditionally composed canvases of grand battle scenes, attempts to visualize trench warfare showed devastated landscapes with bodies strewn aimlessly about. More haunting yet were the portraits of George Grosz, who dramatized the disfiguring impact of war on the human form. The war experience reinforced the repudiation of realism, begun by Henri

Matisse and the Fauves in compositions of intense hues that were no longer designed to produce photographic likeness. The fighting also accelerated the trend toward abstraction pioneered by French painter Georges Braque and Russian exile Wassily Kandinsky, who stressed the importance of bordering color with geometric lines, rejecting classical perspective. Finally, the trench experience also validated the expressionist impulse of German artists like Emil Nolde to give free play to emotions in vigorous colors and strong strokes.[17] Hence World War I validated modernist experimentation in nonrepresentational styles.

The terrifying roar of the front and the din of the mechanized cities also inspired a progression from dissonance to cacophony in music and dance, tempered only by the incomprehension of the concertgoing public. As early as 1913 Russian composer Igor Stravinsky and ballet master Sergey Diaghilev had shocked Paris with a frenzied production of *Le sacre du printemps*, whose cascading rhythms and shrill chords suggested an orgiastic primitivism. The war itself inspired composers like Leoš Janáček, Béla Bartók, and Maurice Ravel to transform their own folk tunes into less-structured and more abstract forms. Stravinsky's injunction "il faut absolument être moderne" dominated the postwar scene, inspiring all sorts of experimentation from Eric Satie's subtle collages to Jean Cocteau's posturing in favor of "MUSIC FOR EVERY DAY." The encounter with jazz further expanded the melodic and rhythmic vocabulary, inspiring such different composers like Darius Milhaud and Kurt Weill. While Paul Hindemith was arguing "beauty of sound is beyond the point," Schoenberg and his disciples pushed fearlessly into a new universe of the twelve-tone system.[18]

In literature, the war experience accelerated the dissolution of the linear forward-through-time narrative focused on character development, by suggesting associative patterns that explored the nonlinear shifts and leaps of consciousness. The hypersensitive French novelist Marcel Proust constructed his grand fifteen-volume masterpiece *In Search of Things Past* as an introspective quest to discover his protagonist's experiences in Paris society through an examination of memory. The imaginative Bohemian Jewish-German writer

Franz Kafka also described the absurdity of life through brilliant metaphorical texts like *The Metamorphosis*, which both baffled and intrigued his readers through his refusal to offer a clear-cut message. At roughly the same time the Irish Catholic avant-garde writer James Joyce, during self-imposed exile in wartime Zurich and postwar Paris, evoked his native Dublin with a stream-of-consciousness technique of great complexity in his towering work *Ulysses*, full of classical allusions and wry humor that initially got it banned for indecency in the United States and United Kingdom.[19] These modernist texts not only shocked the authorities with their frankness in sexual matters but also opened up new realms of the previously unthinkable and unspeakable.

The aftermath of the war also turned the utopia of a liberating urban life into a dystopia of the threatening, exploitative megalopolis. The 1927 movie *Metropolis*, directed by Fritz Lang, revolved around the conflict between capitalists and proletarians in a futuristic city dominated by the big "M-machine." Focused on the love between the son of the chief exploiter and a young working-class woman, the convoluted plot conveyed the message that "the mediator between the head and hands must be the heart!" While the film had a happy ending, its pioneering special effects, including a "machine man," a Tower of Babel–like skyscraper, and the use of mirrors, suggested that the metropolis, dominated by machines, was a pitiless place. Similarly in his 1929 sprawling novelistic collage *Berlin Alexanderplatz*, Alfred Döblin recounted the futile struggles of the worker Frank Biberkopf, who ultimately falls victim to the indifference of the merciless class system.[20] In such films and novels the metropolis alienated and devoured its inhabitants, since its impersonality, social tension, and mechanization were ultimately dehumanizing.

Throughout the 1920s intellectuals also debated the meaning of the First World War, because they derived contradictory lessons from its carnage. In his autobiographical novel *Storms of Steel*, decorated German officer Ernst Jünger portrayed the brutality of the fighting as an exhilarating adventure that inspired heroism and comradeship, toughening men in the face of danger. In contrast, Czech writer Jiři Hašek created a timeless simpleton character with his ironic depiction of the misadventures of the *Good Soldier Svejk* who somehow survives his troubles, thereby satirizing the incompetence of the Austro-Hungarian army. Although he had served only briefly before being wounded in 1917, German journalist Erich Maria Remarque presented a devastating portrayal of the war's inhumanity in *All Quiet on the Western Front* by recounting the experiences of a young recruit whose entire cohort got wiped out. While British writers like Siegfried Sassoon and Vera Brittain clashed over whether to celebrate bravery or decry the slaughter, their conflicting accounts agreed on the increased murderousness of modernity.[21]

APPEALS OF POPULAR CULTURE

The spread of mass culture seemed to present a more optimistic aspect of modern life, since it offered the toiling masses affordable diversion and leisure. As a consequence of rapid urbanization, a secular popular culture centered on pubs, voluntary associations, spectacles, and parades gradually supplanted traditional rural, agricultural, and religious folk customs. During the late nineteenth century the perfection of inventions such as the linotype press, record player, film projector, and radio receiver provided new sensory experiences to inform and entertain the elites. When mass production made these machines cheap enough to reach the general public, a growing culture industry emerged that began to democratize their content and style.[22] Gradual gains in free time and improvement in living standards among the lower classes inspired the development of leisure pursuits like professional sports and mass tourism that expanded recreational possibilities. The high costs and potential profits associated with these changes, however, raised questions of political control and intellectual quality that proved difficult to resolve.

One important innovation was the development of a mass press that could enlighten as well as agitate the public. As the spread of literacy increased the number of readers, the development of the linotype press facilitated production, the practice of advertising lowered costs, and the establishment of news services like AP, Reuters, Havas, and WTB provided content. In the big cities dozens of morning and evening newspapers competed with one another, offering different levels of information, amusement, and commentary. The addition of graphics, caricatures, and photographs enhanced the visual appeal of illustrated magazines. While tabloids like the *Daily Mail* and the *Berliner Zeitung* titillated mass audiences with screaming headlines, primitive content, and blatant prejudice, more serious papers like the *London Times, Le Monde,* and the *Berliner Tageblatt* offered a restrained appearance, reliable information, and sophisticated reflection.[23] For their daily subscribers these newspapers created a new intellectual space, broadening their horizons from neighborhood to city and from region to country.

The first machine that brought music or speech into people's homes without requiring a live performance was the record player. As a replacement for player pianos or music boxes, Thomas Alva Edison invented the phonograph in 1878, which worked by converting grooves etched on a wax cylinder into sound waves. A decade later Emil Berliner shifted the recording medium to a flat rotating disk, made from shellac and standardized at 78 revolutions per minute so as to produce superior sound. During the 1920s the use of electrical devices such as microphones and electric motors as turntable drivers further improved the quality of sound reproduction. The big record companies such as Columbia, Victrola, Pathé, and Deutsche Grammophon offered a broad spectrum of styles from classical music and opera for the connoisseur down to vaudeville tunes for the shopgirl. The mechanical capacity to make music circumvented the need for laborious study of an instrument, offering unrivaled artistic performances. But once the recording industry discovered that it could sell more popular songs than highbrow compositions, it shifted to producing banal hits to entertain the masses.[24]

Motion pictures were another technology that opened new worlds of fantasy by transcending the still pictures of the *laterna magica*. In Lyon the brothers Lumière added the capacity of projecting motion on a screen to Edison's invention of recording images on film. In Berlin the first short movie was shown in 1895 in a vaudeville theater, and soon directors such as Edwin S. Porter began to experiment with showing sketches from daily life or even telling stories as in *The*

Great Train Robbery of 1903. The key to success was the establishment of filmmaking studios, the printing of numerous copies of new releases, and their distribution to special movie theaters, which could charge less than traditional theaters offering live staged productions, thereby acquiring a mass audience. While Hollywood produced exciting Westerns, glamorous variety shows, and Charlie Chaplin comedies for a broad public, continental studios such as UFA in Babelsberg strove for artistic quality in expressionist films like *The Cabinet of Dr. Caligari*.[25] Especially after the arrival movies with sound, called "talkies," in the late 1920s, the audience loved the new medium, since it combined verisimilitude of appearance with imaginary content.

By broadcasting programs directly into people's homes, radio was yet another technology that transformed cultural habits. Building on wireless telegraphy, Guglielmo Marconi and others developed the technology, which was first tried in England around 1900. Because of the cost of establishing transmitters, the limited signal range, and the need for listeners to purchase sets, radio broadcasting only took off in the 1920s, but then developed quite rapidly. In Europe the problem of financing the service was solved by levying user fees. Keenly aware of the medium's potential to shade news and commentary in their favor, governments maintained legal control, setting up public bodies like the British Broadcasting Corporation (BBC). In the beginning the programming, limited to major cities, aimed at an elite audience with sophisticated content, but the production of more affordable receivers forced stations to adjust their offerings to the simpler tastes of the masses. Dictators like Stalin and Mussolini were especially keen on supporting wireless transmission because radio promised to distribute their propaganda to a much wider audience than print.[26]

Increases in disposable time and income also triggered the development of mass leisure, especially the expansion of sports. Originating in the British public schools, athletic competition was supposed to build character, but it could also entertain spectators. While the elites preferred expensive games like tennis, sailing, and horseback riding, the less well-off adopted cheaper pursuits like hiking, swimming, bicycling, and kayaking. Centered on the disinterested "amateur," the Olympic movement appealed to the upper classes, whereas spectacles such as boxing, bicycle racing, and soccer attracted popular crowds. The large gate receipts at such events made it possible for participants to professionalize by training exclusively for competition. Successful athletes like German boxer Max Schmeling and Italian bicycle racer Fausto Coppi became stars, admired by thousands of fans. Understanding the propaganda value of sports, the dictatorships fanned nationalist passions in international competitions like the Olympic Games and the soccer World Cup, interpreting the medals won by their countries' athletes as proof of the strength of their regimes.[27]

Easy transportation and paid vacations also contributed to the emergence of mass tourism to famous cities or to natural sites so as to broaden the mind or restore the body. In Britain entrepreneurs like Thomas Cook went beyond the traditional religious pilgrimages or the grand tour of nobles, enticing the middle classes to travel abroad as a form of diversion. Increasing free time and a bit of loose change gradually allowed even the lower classes to venture beyond their homes to nearby lakes and forests to refresh themselves on weekends. Cheaper railroad and steamship fares made it possible for people of modest means to travel longer distances to spectacular mountain ranges like the Alps or to newly built seaside resorts. While nature lovers often put up with spartan accommodations, the majority of tourists insisted on luxury, inspiring the development of an entire new industry of hotels, museums, and other attractions.[28] Once again, the communists and fascists quickly realized that offering cheap vacations through youth organizations such as the Komsomol and clubs for adults such as the Dopolavoro would make their ideologies more popular.

A final aspect of popular culture was the transformation of gender roles due to the cultural construction of the "new woman," propagated by feminists and the media. While upper-class suffragettes demanded educational equality and political rights, lower-class women increasingly ventured out of the home to work as salesgirls or secretaries before marriage. All classes of women wanted to free themselves from Victorian corsets and bustles, while replacing elaborate coiffures with simpler bobbed, androgynous haircuts. By gaining the right to vote in Britain and Germany in 1919, women organized politically and influenced social policy, though hopes for liberalizing divorce laws and legalizing abortion were mostly disappointed. But in the illustrated press and film, the image of the self-confident, slim, smoking "flapper" became a fashionable icon that urban girls strove to emulate. This female liberation from some prior constraints also required a redefinition of the male role away from patriarchy and toward partnership in marriage.[29] Reinforcing each other, the new century's myriad technological advances and stylistic developments created a novel popular culture that endowed being modern with a positive appeal.

CLASSICAL MODERNITY

During the relative stability of the mid-1920s artists experimented less frenetically than in the immediate postwar period, searching instead for stable forms to express the modern condition. In Central Europe the result was a turn to a new sobriety, a *neue Sachlichkeit*, which no longer tried to shock but rather to express the essence of modernity. Because technical inventions, industrial production, and metropolitan life seemed here to stay, people had to get used to living with their noise, speed, and excitement. In contrast to the rural rhythm of the seasons, the seeming disorder of urban life required a different kind of aesthetic to express its own feelings and experiences. Since escaping into decorative beauty seemed unsuitable for an age of speed and power, a new matter-of-factness would more adequately capture the rational spirit of technology. This changed mood favored reportage as accurate description and photography as reliable reproduction of reality. While not ending experimentation, the spirit of objectivity dampened the profusion of styles, producing some remarkable works of lasting artistic merit that found a classical form for modernity.[30]

The surprising discoveries of nuclear physics exposed the contradiction between uncertainty and rationality in scientific research.

Already around 1900 in Berlin Max Planck had explored the basic constitution of matter by discovering the discontinuity of radiation, which he formulated in mathematical terms as a "quantum." Half a decade later Albert Einstein, working in a Swiss patent office, claimed that light was both a wave and a particle, leading him to propose the special theory of relativity, expressed in the famous formula $E = mc^2$. After the war, Niels Bohr in Copenhagen expanded on these insights, further probing the composition of the atom. At the same time Werner Heisenberg in Göttingen found a statistical way to explain the discrepancy between atomic measurements, concluding in his "uncertainty principle" that "to measure is to disturb."[31] While the exploration of the structure of the atom appeared to destroy the mechanical order of the Newtonian universe, the mathematical tools used to describe subatomic particles reinforced faith in the power of human reason.

The same spirit of rational inquiry also transformed industrial production according to the principles of "Fordism," a neologism coined by Antonio Gramsci. Prosperity advanced not only by technical inventions but also by greater efficiency in manufacturing, which lowered prices and made products accessible to a wider public. In order to increase productivity by eliminating waste, Frederick Winslow Taylor promoted "scientific management," conducting time-and-motion studies of industrial workers. In Detroit Henry Ford applied this approach to the production of automobiles, breaking down each step into standardized routines and facilitating the assembly of parts by a moving line. As a result, he was able to produce cars, notably the famous Model T, more cheaply than his competitors so that millions of people could buy them. Such rationalization treated humans as machines and threw redundant workers and engineers out of work, as ridiculed in the Chaplin movie *Modern Times*. But the introduction of these American methods in Europe also advanced mass consumption and spurred the motorization of broader segments of the middle classes.[32]

Inspired by such ideas, the new objectivity found its classical expression in the International Style of the Bauhaus. In 1907 the architect Hermann Muthesius had founded the German Werkbund in

Munich to promote the marriage of craftsmanship with industrial design. After the war Walter Gropius created a school for architecture and other arts first in Weimar, then in Dessau, and finally in Berlin in order to construct cheap, mass-produced, and yet attractive buildings and consumer products: "We want an architecture adapted to our world of machines, radios and fast cars." This new aesthetic, formulated by an extraordinary group of architects, furniture designers, interior decorators, and painters claimed that form should follow function, making use of new materials such as concrete, steel, and glass. Without recourse to historic models, the resulting buildings had clean lines, open spaces, and large windows, looking rational and practical. Though the Bauhaus members built only a few edifices, architects like Mies van der Rohe would spread its International Style abroad as refugees from the Nazi regime, making the Bauhaus style synonymous with modern architecture.[33]

The turn to objectivity had a less distinctive impact on painting, since different stylistic impulses continued to compete with one another. Of course, the return to matter-of-factness encouraged the realism of Otto Dix, Käthe Kollwitz, and Max Beckmann, who criticized social injustice. Other artists such as Fernand Léger and Lyonel Feininger also maintained stylized versions of the human form or presented crystallized views of seascapes, aiming at an expanded version of representation. Symbolists such as Giorgio de Chirico used realistic surfaces in order to transcend reality, a trend pushed further by surrealists like Max Ernst and Salvador Dalí. But the dominant impulse of modernism was the reduction of recognizable forms to mere allusions that stood as magical shorthand for reality, as in the works of Joan Miró and Paul Klee. Painters such as Piet Mondrian went even further in distilling their pictorial language to pure line and color, abandoning any reference to something recognizable. Similarly, the sculptors Constantin Brancusi and Jean Arp worked with gleaming steel or polished stone, creating abstract forms that signaled modernity.[34]

On the stage the new matter-of-factness left a stronger imprint by inspiring the "epic theater," promoted by the director Erwin Piscator and the playwright Bertolt Brecht. Rejecting the emotionalized melodrama of expressionism, their approach strove for simplicity, clarity, and critical distance in order to leave spectators no doubt about their social message. While Piscator used the Berlin Volksbühne (People's Theater) to spread Soviet ideas to a broader audience, Brecht tried to write plays that would entertain and provoke at the same time. Somewhat of a rascal and a womanizer, Brecht tried to reconcile his Marxist social conscience with his fascination for American capitalism. Many of his plays and poems were cowritten by his devoted secretary Elisabeth Hauptmann or his wife, the actress Helene Weigel. Nonetheless, his musical collaboration with the composer Kurt Weil in the *Rise and Fall of the City of Mahagonny* and in the *Three Penny Opera* produced works that were fresh, diverting, and critical of modern society at the same time. At their best, Brecht's plays like *Mother Courage* transcended their ideology by capturing timeless human suffering.[35]

The *neue Sachlichkeit* affected literature by rehabilitating more narrative writing styles that nonetheless explored social and psychological questions. In France the public read the psychological novels of the Catholic François Mauriac, while in Britain readers found comfort in the intricate family sagas of John Galsworthy. In Austria Robert Musil and Joseph Roth eloquently described the cultural reasons for the collapse of the Habsburg Empire, while in Switzerland Hermann Hesse plumbed the adolescent psyche. The most ambitious of these writers was the German Thomas Mann, who in 1901 broke onto the literary scene with his first work *The Buddenbrooks*, a sensitive portrayal of the decline of a patrician family in his home city of Lübeck. In his monumental work *Magic Mountain* of 1924, he created the figure of Hans Castorp, who debates the future of European civilization with representatives of Western rationalism and Eastern mysticism in a Swiss sanatorium. Although Mann had touted the superiority of German *Kultur* during the First World War, he reluctantly embraced the Weimar Republic, defending it against the onslaught of the Right.[36]

A final achievement of the mid-1920s was the critical theory of the Frankfurt School, which provided a compelling reflection on the modern condition. The sociologist Max Horkheimer directed the Institute for Social Research, founded in Frankfurt in 1923, which attracted a group of stellar intellectuals such as Theodor Adorno, Erich Fromm, Herbert Marcuse, and Walter Benjamin for a time. Disappointed by the rigidity of communism and the timidity of social democracy, institute members sought to free the Marxist impulse from dogmatism by engaging social thinkers like Sigmund Freud and Max Weber. To create a convincing blueprint for emancipation and enlightenment, they developed a "critical theory" of thinking dialectically about such topics as economic exploitation and cultural stultification. Confronting the aesthetic pretensions of modernism, the Frankfurt School criticized the culture industry as a new form of subjugation of the masses through shallow entertainment.[37] This quest developed fascinating insights into the ambivalence of modernity, seeking to reinforce its positive potential through critical reason.

ANTIMODERNIST BACKLASH

Frightened by the speed of change, many Europeans rejected modernity and resented modernism as its cultural expression. Conservative religious groups abhorred science, preferring to place their faith in scripture instead. Artisans disliked machine technology, priding themselves in their skilled craftsmanship. Critics of capitalism denounced industrialization, looking back to a more stable corporate order. Psychologists worried about the neurasthenia of urbanization and longed for a healthier rural life. Members of the embattled elites feared the rise of the masses and denounced the loss of deference and hierarchy. Idealists attacked the rise of materialism, altruists complained about the spread of hedonism, moralists condemned the prevalence of licentiousness, and sexists deplored the advance of feminism. Finally, defenders of taste decried both the experiments of the avant-garde and the crudeness of popular culture. Feeling provoked, a host of traditionalists attributed the collapse of conventions, values, and order to modernism, symbolized by the Jews, and loathed its effect as chaos to be halted at any price.[38]

Among the leaders of antimodernism were members of the clergy, on the defensive against the claims of science that undercut biblical authority by providing an alternate explanation of creation.

The Catholic Church, especially, warned against the heresy of modernism in doctrinal statements, because it was afraid that the unrestrained application of human reason would destroy the basis of faith. In 1910 Pope Pius X required all clergy and religious teachers to swear an oath rejecting the modern idea "that dogma may be tailored according to what seems better and more suited to the culture of each age," reaffirming instead "the absolute and immutable truth preached by the apostles." Mainstream Protestantism was somewhat more open to scientific inquiry, but even there many neoorthodox theologians called for a literal reading of scripture and a return to Martin Luther and other reformers. Various sects were even more hostile to rational thought, completely withdrawing from the contemporary world or awaiting the Second Coming, which they believed to be imminent.[39] For believers more open to modern thinking this ongoing conflict created a permanent dilemma of how to reconcile science with religion.

In contrast, racists claimed to draw on scientific inquiry when trying to justify the hoary prejudice of anti-Semitism with new biological arguments. One of its pioneers was the French nobleman Arthur de Gobineau, who celebrated the superiority of the Aryan race over its black and yellow competitors. When combined with social Darwinist notions of the "struggle for survival," such racial thinking legitimized the imperialist rule of the white race over the rest of the globe. In contrast to the religious form of Judeophobia, science-based anti-Semitism no longer allowed conversion to Christianity as an escape but instead considered Jewishness to be ineradicable. By proclaiming "the Jews are our misfortune," the National Liberal German historian Heinrich von Treitschke had popularized such biological resentment in academic circles.[40] The British Wagner devotee Houston Stewart Chamberlain further justified the primacy of the Aryan race in his anti-Semitic *Foundations of the Nineteenth Century*. After the First World War, such confused notions encouraged a transnational eugenics movement that sought to improve racial stock through sterilization.

Proponents of cultural pessimism criticized modernist experiments as a decline of standards and coherence, calling for a reinvigoration of tradition. Already during the last decades of the nineteenth century critics like Matthew Arnold in Britain had rejected Victorian optimism. In Germany the philosopher Friedrich Nietzsche deprecated contemporary education as superficial and weakening, calling instead for a new race of supermen in order to master the challenges of the future. Other popular intellectuals like Paul de Lagarde and Julius Langbehn attributed the malaise of modernity to Jewish emancipation, holding it responsible for cultural decadence.[41] After the war the historian Oswald Spengler popularized such ideas by depicting in his *The Decline of the West* the cyclical rise and fall of civilizations and arguing for a fusion of Prussianism and socialism as cure for the modernist ills. In Britain the poet T. S. Eliot, in his famous canto *The Wasteland*, echoed a more sophisticated skepticism about the decline of European culture, while the philosopher Arnold Toynbee presented a history of world civilization in the same pessimistic vein.

Many cultural elitists deplored the vulgarity of popular culture's catering to the masses, which would allow the public to be manipulated for sinister ends. In his 1896 bestseller *The Crowd: A Study of the Popular Mind*, the French physician Gustave Le Bon warned against the loss of rational control within a crowd, since "the collective mind" would inevitably lead to primitivism. A generation later the Spanish philosopher Ortega y Gasset expressed such phobias even more persuasively in his treatise *The Revolt of the Masses*. As a Castilian educated in Germany, he deplored the rise of "mass man," extending this figure from the proletarian rabble to the middle-class functionary, a theme already intoned by the French philosopher Julien Benda in his essay on the treason of intellectuals. In his denunciation of "homogenized mass society" Ortega summed up a series of cultural fears about the loss of standards in "mass culture," tending toward the sentimental and primitive.[42] Ironically, these neoconservative critics of *Vermassung* through Americanization provided intellectual justification for just those trends of totalitarian manipulation that they claimed to oppose.

Other thinkers tried to restore order in the chaos of modernity by supporting irrational or authoritarian solutions. The deliberately obscure German philosopher Martin Heidegger rejected the entire

Western philosophical tradition, arguing instead for a more existential reflection in *Being and Time*, his chief work of 1927. While some of his formulations (man's responsibility for his own existence, for example) were open-ended, other statements on technology and the superiority of imagination to reason showed an antimodernist penchant that contributed to undercutting progressive thought. Similarly, in his commentaries on liberal democracy the brilliant legal theorist Carl Schmitt stressed the power of the state, its freedom to declare an emergency, and the division into friend and foe as the essence of politics. In the crisis of the Weimar Republic this kind of legal decisionism favored the authority of the executive vested in the president over the deliberation of Parliament, legitimizing the suspension of constitutional rights.[43] No wonder both thinkers became favorites of intellectuals troubled by modernity.

During the 1920s neoconservative critics rejected both liberalism and communism, searching for a third way that might reconcile nationalism and socialism. The French writer Maurice Barrès was one influential forerunner, because he propagated an integral nationalism, spurned the Third Republic, and embraced a biological anti-Semitism. His associate Charles Maurras went even further, founding an antirepublican movement in the Action Française, which instilled generations of intellectuals with right-wing ideology. In Germany the historian Moeller van den Bruck propagated the idea of a national revolution through the founding a Third Reich behind an inspiring leader—a prophecy that the Nazis were only too happy to endorse. An even more radical Fighting League for German Culture polemicized against racial degeneration through the rise of "subhumans," calling for a cultural rebirth from ethnic roots. Similarly, the Austrian Catholic philosopher Othmar Spann called for a corporate state as an alternative to failed democracy and bloody Bolshevism.[44]

Ironically most of these antimodernists were themselves a product of the tendencies they detested, since they used modern arguments and methods to combat modernity. While thinkers like the French writer Drieu de la Rochelle hated scientism, industrialism, materialism, feminism, liberalism, and socialism, they also knew that they could not just go back to a mythic rural past but had to find solutions within their own time. In order to reach this goal, the neo-conservatives selectively appropriated modern elements such as the quasi-scientific justification for racial anti-Semitism, hoping to create a right-wing mass movement strong enough to erase degeneration and revitalize their nations. In deploring excesses of experimentation their writings also often employed avant-garde styles, and they were not shy about using contemporary media to propagate their ideas. Instead of returning to an earlier romanticized order, they strove to create an alternative future—dynamic, virile, and inspiring. By stressing youth, action, and danger, the revolt against modernity was therefore shot through with the very elements that it sought to repudiate.

CULTURE WARS

Inspiring an explosion of creativity, the encounter with modernity between 1900 and 1930 left behind some remarkable cultural achievements that have enriched human understanding. The scientific breakthroughs in nuclear physics altered our sense of the universe, the medical discoveries of bacteria made it possible to cure many diseases, and the technological advances such as the automobile and the telephone improved transportation and communication. In music, Stravinsky's rhythmic explorations, in painting Picasso's cubistic canvases, in sculpture Brancusi's shining steel, in theater Brecht's epic plays, in literature Mann's magisterial novels, in architecture the Bauhaus style, just to mention a few works, were successful efforts to use the stylistic freedom of modernism coupled with a measure of self-restraint to explore new dimensions of the human condition. In such innovative works artists radically questioned man's destiny and yet found forms of a simplicity that could only be called classical. Impressive as it was, this explosion of creativity proved, nonetheless, unable to stop the descent into another catastrophe.[45]

The provocation of modernist style and content triggered an intense ideological struggle in which the future of human civilization seemed to be at stake. The revolt against tradition saw itself as a progressive attempt to break with convention and overthrow censorship in order to establish new forms of artistic expression and address previously taboo subjects. The shock of the Great War forced intellectuals to choose between hypernationalism and internationalism by asking them to decide whether to uphold or dismantle the myth of heroic combat. With the return of peace, the advent of a technologically inspired popular culture posed novel questions about the commercialization of its contents and the vulgarity of its styles. At the same time, the conflict shifted the control of cultural institutions such as museums and concert halls, with the innovators gaining a partial foothold but defenders of tradition vigorously fighting back against the new barbarians.[46] As a result, promoters of innovation generally allied themselves with the parties of the Left while defenders of tradition flocked to the movements of the Right.

Though the avant-garde modernists struck a revolutionary pose in fighting against the constraints of bourgeois culture, they fundamentally disagreed on how to supplant it. For bohemian intellectuals it was easy enough to applaud Kurt Tucholsky's satires of the German ruling classes because they were witty and imaginative. Due to the widespread suffering of the war, the pacifist message of the French author Romain Rolland also fell on willing ears after 1918. Moreover, the triumph of the Soviet Revolution inspired hopes for ending exploitation, even if it could land imitators like the radical poet Ernst Toller in jail. But leftist critics bitterly disputed whether they should speak for the oppressed or let workers themselves produce art as in the *proletkult* movement of the Soviet Union. Supporting communism also raised the question of artistic independence, since the party preferred to dictate the production of agitprop posters or shows simple enough to mobilize the proletariat. While the trenchant critique of the Left resonated among intellectuals, its innovative artists failed to find a form and message that would reconcile freedom with equality.[47]

The antimodernists similarly agreed on the need to combat "cultural Bolshevism" but were divided about how to accomplish that aim. Since they still controlled many cultural institutions, defenders of tradition like the Austrian writer Hugo von Hofmannsthal could try to hold the line, hoping that the avant-garde onslaught would pass. In this defensive stance, they appealed to the religious and conservative parties to safeguard the influence of the churches and defend the curricular canon. But a younger generation realized that the war had so discredited the monarchs, generals, and bishops that it was foolish to expect their return. Instead these neoconservatives embraced the message of the youth movement that rejected the decadent habits of urban life such as alcohol, smoking, and sex, longing for a romantic return to a healthier existence through hiking in the countryside.[48] Like the German Free- Corps fighter Ernst von Salomon, this new Right called for a "conservative revolution" so as to found an alternate vision of community. But their fantasy would turn out to be even more destructive in fascism.

In these culture wars, democrats were assaulted from both sides and eventually crushed between them. When French intellectuals founded a Human Rights League during the Dreyfus Affair, many artists rallied to defend the rights of citizens wrongly accused. Led by republican politicians such as Ferdinand Buisson, this group went international in 1922, seeking to foster cooperation in the spirit of the League of Nations.[49] The German branch was supported by the publicist Carl von Ossietzky, editor of the *Weltbühne*, as well as by the pacifist Ludwig Quidde. But since the Bolshevik Revolution in Russia for a time fascinated even the likes of British philosopher Bertrand Russell, and the rise of fascism in Italy captivated such an eminent literary figure as the American poet Ezra Pound, democrats found themselves between both political extremes. In Weimar a moderate group of "republicans by reason" such as the German historian Friedrich Meinecke sought to defend the constitution. But because modernist artists wanted to be more radical, while neoconservative intellectuals looked for a national rebirth, most of the creative spirits failed to come to the defense of democracy.[50]

Part II

TURN TO SELF-DESTRUCTION, 1929–45

Chapter 8

DEVASTATING DEPRESSION

Depression soup kitchen, 1930. *Source*: bpk, Berlin / Bayerische Staatsbibliothek, Munich / Art Resource, NY.

On May 11, 1931, the Creditanstalt informed the Austrian government that it was bankrupt, setting off a run on its deposits. The biggest Viennese bank could no longer meet its obligations, because it had taken on too much debt by swallowing a competitor two years earlier and French depositors were withdrawing their assets in order to keep Austria from joining a customs union with Germany. Though the City of London offered a fresh loan, the Viennese government collapsed, and the panic spread to smaller institutions, making one banker shoot himself and another try to jump into the Danube. A month later when rumors claimed that one of its key debtors, the textile company Nordwolle, had become insolvent, the Darmstädter Nationalbank also came under pressure, triggering another run in Germany, the biggest continental economy. On July 13 the Berlin government saw itself forced to declare a bank holiday, stopping all financial transactions for two days.[1] Almost two years after Black Thursday, the stock-market crash in New York, these bank failures brought the financial crisis to Europe with a vengeance.

The banking collapse turned a cyclical economic contraction into a larger and longer downturn that worried observers like President Herbert Hoover called "the Great Depression." As a result of wartime overproduction, agricultural and raw-material prices had already fallen by roughly one-third during the previous decade. But after Black Thursday, the major lenders in New York and London stopped issuing credit and started to recall their short-term loans from Europe, forcing $2 billion to flow out of Germany during six weeks in the summer of 1931 alone! In the worsening business climate, coal and steel production dropped by 40–60 percent, and world industrial output shrank by 30 percent. European trade fell from $58 billion to $21 billion between 1929 and 1935. As a result, more than twenty million Europeans became unemployed.[2] The linkage among financial, agricultural, industrial, and trade losses amplified a normal recession into a depression of a length and magnitude that had previously seemed unimaginable. Caught unprepared, governments were at a loss as to how to break its devastating grip.

The question of how to respond to the Great Depression sparked a fierce ideological debate between monetarists and Keynesians that still dominates economic explanations. On the one hand, the central bankers, led by Sir Montagu Norman of the United Kingdom, insisted on defending the gold standard as a guarantee of fixed exchange rates in order to facilitate international trade. The American financier Andrew Mellon considered the depression to be an economic punishment for the excessive speculation of the 1920s, advising Wall Street to "purge the rottenness out of the system," that is, let the overextended speculators fail rather than try to rescue them through government intervention. On the other hand, British economist John Maynard Keynes, supported by the trade unions, argued for countercyclical government spending in order to restart the economy. During recessions, he argued, it was necessary for governments to borrow money and undertake public projects to put people back to work, providing buying power that would revive business by increasing demand. Convinced that "this time is different," neoliberal economists continue to blame the Federal Reserve for failing to limit the money supply, while left-wing commentators criticize the "gold standard mentality" as cause of the deflationary policies of the national governments.[3]

More than any other interwar event, the Great Depression turned European development from peaceful optimism into bellicose pessimism by halting the material progress of modernity. The practical impact on the millions of unemployed was severe, because they had to struggle for their very survival at a time when public assistance was cut back. The psychological effect on their more fortunate neighbors was equally unsettling, since these had their salaries cut and feared losing their jobs, living standards, and security. A whole generation of high school and university graduates, who seemed to have no future due to the loss of jobs and lack of hiring, blamed "the system" for a plight for which they did not feel responsible. With no end of the downturn in sight and international cooperation collapsing, many commentators began to ask, with Austrian economist Joseph Schumpeter: "Can capitalism survive?"[4] Because the Soviet Union made great strides in industrialization during the Great Depression and even Fascist Italy seemed to escape its worst effects, the slump triggered a crisis for the democratic path of modernization.

By reversing the trajectory of material progress, the Great Depression reinforced those negative aspects of modernity that brought Europe to the brink of self-destruction in the subsequent decades. The difficulties of economic adjustment after the First World War and the effects of hyperinflation delayed the postwar recovery and limited the return of prosperity to merely half a decade. The depth of the subsequent disruption caused by the bank failures disappointed hopes in the resumption of progress, creating a climate of fear in which individuals, companies, and countries scrambled to survive by following their immediate self-interest: reducing consumption, production, and international commerce in a self-reinforcing downward spiral. Massive unemployment increased tensions between the social classes, since the unions clamored for public assistance while the struggling business community refused to help. The disruption of international trade and credit strengthened an economic nationalism that prevented cooperation and encouraged autarchy. Making the leftist and rightist dictatorships appear more dynamic and effective, the liberals' refusal to engage in public works discredited democracy, setting Europe on a disastrous course.[5]

POSTWAR DISRUPTION

Already during the Versailles negotiations in 1918 John Maynard Keynes, as adviser to the British delegation, warned that the consequences of a harsh peace would be disastrous. While he criticized the terms as generally unfair and in violation of the prearmistice agreement, the brilliant Cambridge economist was especially concerned about the demand for large reparations, cautioning against their inflationary effect. Moreover, he also called for a cancellation of inter-Allied debts as an American contribution to a war that Washington had joined only in April 1917. While Keynes, as a disappointed Wilsonian, may have been unrealistic about what was possible in the heated postwar atmosphere, he was on the mark with his criticism of the economic results of Versailles. "But who can say how much is endurable, or in what direction men will seek at last to escape from their misfortunes?"[6] With about one-quarter of its gross domestic product destroyed, continental Europe needed a plan for economic recovery and international cooperation rather than the creation of divisive borders and high expenditures for military security.

Repairing the appalling physical destruction was a daunting task in itself. The battlefields ranged from northern France, Belgium, and northern Italy to Poland, Russia, and the Balkans, not to mention the Near East and the colonies. The trench systems, artillery barrages, and air bombardment of modern warfare had created a moonscape full of shell craters, waterlogged ditches, felled trees, destroyed buildings, and human as well as animal cadavers. Reclaiming the land for planting and rebuilding the houses for living was a major challenge. In France alone 23,000 factories, 5,000 kilometers of railroads, 200 mine shafts, 742,000 houses, and 3.3 million hectares of farmland had to be reconstructed at a cost of 80 billion francs.[7] While the richer countries of the West could finance such a public effort, in the East and the Southeast newly created states like Poland and Yugoslavia had few resources and capabilities for meeting this difficult challenge. Even if the reconstruction created temporary jobs, the expenditure required to return standards of living to prewar levels was enormous.

Including both military casualties and deaths from indirect warfare against civilians, the demographic losses were also severe—and largely irreparable, since the dead could no longer sire children. Most estimates suggest that between 9.4 and 11 million soldiers and 7 million civilians perished during the First World War, while almost twice that number were mutilated by wounds. Germany alone lost 2,037,000 men, Russia another 1,811,000, France 1,398,000, Austria-Hungary 1,100,000, Britain 733,000, and Italy 651,000. This carnage cost France and Germany about 10 percent of their workforce, Italy and Austria-Hungary 6 percent, and the United Kingdom 5 percent. Moreover, the neglect and destruction of crops and the naval blockades caused widespread starvation, which the Quaker Herbert Hoover and the American Relief Administration sought to alleviate by shipping millions of tons of grain to war-torn Europe. Finally, the influenza pandemic of 1918 claimed millions of additional lives in a population weakened by fighting and famine.[8] In demographic terms, the First World War caused a deep, permanent gash on the male side of the European population tree that hindered the recovery.

The economic warfare and the creation of new states also redirected and disrupted international trade. The war itself reshaped exchange patterns, interrupting continental business while enriching the neutrals and overseas countries. The peace treaties made things worse by carving up the German, Austro-Hungarian, Russian, and Ottoman empires and increasing the number of European countries from twenty-four to thirty-eight, which used twenty-seven different currencies. Intent on asserting their sovereignty and on incorporating their newly won territories, these East-Central European and Balkan states hardened their borders by levying tariffs in order to raise revenue. Such custom barriers interrupted ancient trade routes, while much of the lending sought to shore up diplomatic alliances rather than following standards of profitability. President Wilson's hope for free trade was therefore quickly dashed by the increasing barriers of economic nationalism. As a result world trade had sunk to 53 percent of the prewar level in 1921 and did not recover to the pre-1914 amount until the end of the decade.[9]

These structural problems were aggravated by interminable political wrangling over reparations and inter-Allied war debts, which complicated loans for recovery. In the heated postwar atmosphere, the Reparations Commission found it impossible to determine scientifically how large the actual damages were and what Germany could realistically be expected to pay. The sum of 132 billion gold marks determined at Spa in 1920 seemed too large to Berlin, while the actual annual payments of about one billion pounds appeared too small to Paris. At the same time the U.S. government was unwilling to forgive its loans to the Entente countries for the purchase of war matériel that had fueled a boom in the United States, though these could have been considered a financial contribution to the struggle. The refusal to recognize a linkage between reparations and war debts created a circular bind: though their economy was recovering, the defeated Germans did not want to pay reparations, which the victorious European Allies needed for repaying their U.S. debts.[10]

Because of this deadlock, the reparations quarrel blighted prospects for full recovery.

The wartime damage was so severe and long lasting that it ended the European dominance of the world economy. Already during the First World War military conscription, the requisitioning of horses, the use of fertilizer as gunpowder, and the destruction of land shifted agricultural production to the wheat fields of Canada and the cattle ranches of the American West. At the same time the Entente's need to procure war matériel transferred financial leadership from London to New York, making the unprepared United States "the world's banker" and requiring it to play a crucial role in European recovery. Although the continent reclaimed its productive capacity after the end of the carnage, the European share of world trade fell from 36 percent in 1914 to 24.4 percent in 1936. The nationalist preoccupations of the peacemakers largely ignored the economic dimension in drawing up boundaries and insisting on reparations and inter-Allied debt payments that poisoned the international climate. Europe lost almost a decade in growth, hastening its decline when compared to the booming United States and the rising Soviet Union.[11]

The war and its aftermath also interrupted the spread of globalization, which had linked European countries and the rest of the world more closely at the turn of the century. In almost all indexes of production or trade, the First World War created a jagged drop, breaking the line of long-range progress. After the war the curves once again moved in an upward direction, but they started from a lower beginning point and only reached prewar levels during the late 1920s, lagging behind where they would have been if peace had continued. The gradual pacification of the continent and the return of the gold standard did help reenergize international exchanges. But the wartime distortion and the postwar rebuilding changed the perspective from free trade to protectionism, since each country was preoccupied with rebuilding its economic base and getting ahead as quickly as possible. By weakening the links of finance and commerce between the advanced countries, the wartime exertions and difficult transition to peace interrupted the momentum of economic progress, which had hitherto made modernization appear in a positive light.[12]

RUNAWAY INFLATION

The postwar disruption of European economies was compounded by inflationary pressures that eroded the buying power of the major currencies. Having lost only half the value of the pound by the end of the war, Great Britain was better off than its neighbors, whose purchasing power declined three- or fourfold. Since much financing of the war had come through public borrowing in the hope of shifting the cost to the losers, governments were tempted to run their currency-printing presses so as to retire the bonds at lower cost. The returning veterans also demanded social services for their wounded comrades, and for war widows and orphans, as well as unemployment assistance as long as they were searching for work. With conversion from war production to peacetime consumption taking some time, the pent-up demand, delayed building, and reconstruction fueled a short-lived boom, which chased a limited amount of goods, allowing producers and shopkeepers to raise their prices.[13] Since wage adjustments rarely kept up, inflation seemed a relatively painless way to lower living standards—as long as it could somehow be kept under control.

But in Germany, Austria, Hungary, Poland, and Italy, the bankers failed to curb the rise in prices, allowing a hyperinflation to develop, which not just depreciated but actually destroyed the currency. The most dramatic example was the reichsmark's loss of purchasing power, which accelerated geometrically from 1913:

1918	245%
1920	1,400%
1921	3,500%
1922	147,000%
1923	126,000,000,000%

The printing presses could hardly keep up with the production of new bills containing ever more zeroes when prices first rose monthly, then daily, and in the end even hourly. People had to go shopping immediately after getting paid, since their wages would have lost too much of their buying power by the end of the day. Handling the money got so unwieldy that distraught Germans used backpacks and even wheelbarrows to take the inflated paper to the stores. This runaway inflation also destroyed the convertibility of the currency, since by the fall of 1923 it took four billion reichsmark to purchase merely one dollar![14]

The hyperinflation had a drastic, albeit contradictory, effect on society. On the one hand, debtors profited, because it practically wiped the slate clean when they could repay their loans with depreciated currency. Moreover, for people with tangible assets such as factories, stores, houses, or land it was a boon, since their values were not affected by price rises. But on the other hand, citizens who had lent money or invested in the stock market took a loss, because their paper holdings increasingly became worthless. Moreover, everyone on fixed income like rentiers, pensioners, or public officials suffered grievously, since the buying power of their remittances rapidly evaporated and salaries were only slowly adjusted, falling ever more behind the steep rise in prices. Even if some individuals who managed to turn their assets into dollars grew richer, wide circles of the middle class lost confidence in an economic system that cheated them out of their life savings and eroded their current earnings.[15] No wonder voters flocked to extremist parties that promised to restore economic security.

This German inflation spiraled completely out of control through the struggle over reparations, which led to the French occupation of the Ruhr Basin. When Berlin fell behind with the delivery of 135,000 telephone poles and 2.1 million tons of coal, the hard-line Parisian premier Raymond Poincaré decided on January 11, 1923, to send troops into this industrial region, seizing "productive pledges" to assure future compliance with reparations. Fearing French separatist designs on the Rhineland, the Berlin cabinet proclaimed a policy of "passive resistance," consisting of labor strikes, bureaucratic noncooperation, and occasional acts of sabotage. The occupiers created a mine administration company (MICUM) that extracted coal from belowground by forced labor, killing over 130 people in retaliation. In order to keep up the resistance, the German government paid the lost wages to the strikers, further running the printing presses and accelerating the devaluation of the reichsmark.[16] Neither side wanted to back down, because the Ruhr struggle was a symbolic contest about observance of the peace treaty.

It took U.S. mediation with the Dawes Plan to break the deadlock and return Europe to the road toward stability. Only gradually did Washington realize that its financial stakes on the continent required an active policy of mediation in order to revive its largest market. Moreover, the French leaders slowly understood that a punitive policy toward their neighbor overstrained their resources, imperiling their own currency. Finally, the Berlin cabinet under Gustav Stresemann also recognized that nationalist posturing was futile, called off the passive resistance, and issued a new currency, the rentenmark, which would be backed by the productive assets of the country. Owing to Anglo-American pressure to treat Germany more fairly, the London Conference worked out a compromise in April 1924, named after the U.S. banker Charles G. Dawes: in exchange for a gradual withdrawal of French troops, Germany promised to pay 1 billion marks during the first year, rising to 2.5 billion annually thereafter.[17] Only the experience of hyperinflation convinced Paris and Berlin that treaty fulfillment would have to be tied to a partial revision of the terms.

Five years after the end of the war the reparations settlement finally stabilized the European financial system, albeit at considerable cost. With the Gold Standard Act of May 1925 Great Britain returned to prewar parity, as Chancellor of the Exchequer Winston Churchill claimed, in order to "facilitate the revival of international trade" and restore its "central position in the financial systems of the world." France and several dozen other countries followed suit, reviving economic confidence and facilitating American loans. Yet the price of stabilization was high, since the return to the gold standard overvalued the British, French, and other currencies by 10–20 percent, making their goods less competitive.[18] Moreover, the cost of the war, the ensuing disruption, and the hyperinflation had impoverished wide circles of Europeans previously living on capital, receiving fixed pensions, or dependent on public salaries. The psychological legacy of the postwar difficulties was a deep-seated fear of inflation and a hardening of laissez-faire orthodoxy that would make future crises more difficult to resolve.

FLEETING PROSPERITY

In Europe the "golden twenties" were limited to the half decade between 1924 and 1929, when a brighter future seemed to be dawning at last. Driven by new industries such as chemicals, electronics, cars, and airplanes, production indexes rose by about one-quarter, while international trade actually returned close to prewar levels. Though still higher than before, unemployment generally declined, allowing more workers to share the fruits of the recovery. With increasing tax receipts, national governments could undertake welfare measures such as extending unemployment insurance, while municipal administrations embarked on public housing and transportation projects. Intent on making housekeeping easier, women could buy new products such as electrical stoves, vacuum cleaners, and refrigerators. In the fast-paced metropolitan centers, a quest for romance drove flappers into dance halls to meet young men in search of diversion. The pleasure seeking memorialized in the musical *Cabaret* suggests that the second half of the 1920s was an exciting time, when people assumed that progress had resumed.[19]

Much of the expansion was based on American loans, which provided credit for rebuilding European industries. From 1899 on the United States had experienced a spectacular period of growth due to its mastery of mass production and only peripheral involvement in the First World War. A good part of the available capital was looking for investment opportunities abroad, where yields would be higher than at home. With the return to the gold standard, Europe appeared to be a safe enough bet, especially since its bankers shared the same laissez-faire philosophy. From 1925 to 1929 about 5.1 billion dollars were invested in the Old Continent, over half of it in Germany. Most of the money went into modernizing industries under pressure to generate enough tax revenue for financing reparations payments to the victors, but some of it disappeared in municipal improvements. Moreover, many loans were short term and used to refinance older debts that had come due—thereby creating a revolving door of credit that kept spinning only as long as new funds flowed in.[20]

Another problem was the fall in raw-material and agricultural prices that cut their average values in half by 1930. By expanding exploration and mining, the enormous demand for war matériel during the Great War had increased the output of raw materials, driving down their prices once the military demand vanished. At the same time the need for food encouraged an increase in the output of wheat and beef in the United States, Canada, Argentina, and Australia. which flooded the postwar market, while European farmers struggled to resume their own production. The result was a glut that depressed prices, helping urban consumers by lowering their food costs. But in rural areas like Schleswig-Holstein the surplus also created a severe agricultural crisis, spawning radical populist movements that demanded protection from cheaper foreign competition. Governments responded with drastic increases in tariff levels for foodstuffs so as to shield their domestic producers.[21] While the fall of raw-material and food prices favored industrialists and consumers, it also reduced the ability of a significant part of the population to buy manufactured goods.

Industrial output did grow substantially in the second half of the 1920s, but European expansion remained sluggish and uneven when compared to the concurrent upsurge in the United States. Many older factories were hampered by their obsolete equipment, with little incentive to invest as long as the overseas colonies or the creation of cartels provided a secure market. Of course, there were also dynamic new industries like automobile manufacturing, in which some giants like Renault, Austin, and Opel catered to the middle class while luxury car makers such as Jaguar, Ferrari, and Mercedes appealed to the elite. But motorization during the 1920s remained limited to less than one-fifth of the population because of its high cost. Moreover, industrialists also had to contend with a stronger labor movement that used strikes to force such concessions as the forty-eight-hour week and increases in wages. For European industry the twenties offered opportunities for conversion back to peacetime production and expansion into new product lines, while at same time accelerating the loss of its world-leading role to the United States.[22]

Competing with the more dynamic American economy required the introduction of the gospel of "industrial efficiency" into European business. Only by copying Henry Ford's innovation of the assembly line could continental manufacturers hope to produce their cars as cheaply as the subsidiaries of the Ford Motor company in Europe. Searching for profit, many industrialists also embraced the time-and-motion studies of Taylorism, which promised a "scientific management" of large companies by cutting out redundancies and waste. Interested businessmen and engineers like Ferdinand Porsche therefore visited the United States in order to see with their own eyes what they could do in order to advance the "rationalization" of their companies. For the blue- and white-collar workers involved, such "Americanization" usually meant being dismissed from their job and becoming unemployed even during the best period of recovery.[23] While rationalizing efforts made production more efficient, such measures also created a widespread sense of insecurity, since it was not clear who might be the next to lose his job.

Many of the loans also went into reforming municipal infrastructure, resuming prewar aspirations to make urban centers more livable. Such efforts involved extending the public-transportation network by adding more subways, rapid-transit trains, tramways, and bus routes in order to satisfy the rising demand for mobility. The British "garden-city" movement of Ebenezer Howard inspired continental attempts to provide cheap housing in a parklike setting, allowing tired workers to escape their noxious slums. A curious combination of life reformers, artists, and trade-union members promoted such "greenbelt" projects in the hope that planned cooperatives could strengthen the sense of community and provide a healthier lifestyle than overcrowded tenements.[24] Local governments therefore created parks, built swimming pools, and constructed schools in order to counteract the negative effects of urbanization. While these laudable attempts generated jobs and improved the quality of life for people with modest means, they also required considerable public borrowing that would one day have to be repaid.

During the second half of the 1920s many Europeans grew hopeful that they might have overcome their war-related troubles and resumed the prior progress toward a beneficent modernity. In contrast to the previous disruptions, the visible signs of recovery gave ordinary citizens a sense that "normalcy" was returning, which would allow them to get on with their private lives. As a result of the rise in wages, consumers became more confident and willing to buy from grand department stores like Harrods in London, Galleries Lafayette in Paris, and the Kaufhaus des Westens in Berlin. With more money in their pocket, Europeans could eat better, purchase new consumer goods like cameras, and afford entertainment such as movies. And because of their reduced working hours, they could also go on vacations farther away from home. Advertisements in glossy magazines catered to these emerging tastes, while movie stars and sports heroes presented role models for a better life. It is this glittering surface of urban leisure that has become enshrined in the popular memory as the "golden twenties."[25]

The fleeting return of prosperity, however, failed to address the underlying structural problems that weakened the European economies in international and social terms. On the one hand, the expansion was largely built on American lending, which began to dry up in the second half of 1928, already bringing the German economy to the brink of a recession. On the other hand, by the 1920s industrialists had figured out how to organize mass production efficiently, churning out an ever greater number of consumer goods. But the continuing inequality in the distribution of income made it impossible for the laboring masses to buy enough of these products, creating a severe problem of underconsumption. While the rise in wages and the gradual extension of unemployment insurance increased demand somewhat, such measures were insufficient to absorb all the new consumer goods.[26] In spite of such unresolved problems, optimism was widespread that the "politics of prosperity" would continue, resuming at last the prewar advance of progress, which would realize the promise of modernity.

THE GREAT SLUMP

Such optimism notwithstanding, the U.S. stock-market crash on October 29, 1929, initiated a severe downturn in Europe, which surpassed the normal recessions of the business cycle in depth and duration. Already declining because of the Federal Reserve's tightening of credit, on the "most devastating day in the history of the New York stock market" shares plunged downward by 11 percent, altogether losing 40 percent of their nominal value by mid-November. Once the drastic drop began, panicked investors started selling their stocks, since they had speculated on margin that the upward direction would continue. Now frantically trying to avoid losing not just their recent gains but their original capital, they hurried to divest themselves of their holdings, thereby accelerating the market collapse. From a high of 381.17 points on September 3, 1929, the Dow Jones average fell to a low of 41.22 by July 1932—an unprecedented decline of almost 90 percent! While French bankers smirked that this was an overdue lancing of an abscess, the stock-market crash destroyed continental business confidence, since New York had become the financial capital of the world.[27]

The bursting of the speculative bubble created an international financial crisis by inducing U.S. investors to recall their short-term loans to European governments and businesses. Having overextended credit to stock-market speculators, American banks themselves began to fail, with 1,300 going under in 1930 and another 2,300 closing their doors in 1931. In order to shore up their own balances, U.S. financiers recalled $4 billion from Germany and another $1.3 billion from Austria in the months after the stock-market crash. These precipitous capital outflows transmitted the banking crisis to Europe, contributing to the failure of the Creditanstalt and the Danatbank in the summer of 1931. It did not help that the German government tried to use the financial troubles to end reparations, while France insisted on observing the letter of the Dawes Plan and the British sought to defend the gold standard of the pound. The disagreement among continental leaders led to a standstill agreement regarding

German loans, halting debt service.[28] Since international lending dried up, the transatlantic circulation of capital stopped.

The deflationary effect of misguided monetarist policies turned a cyclical recession into an unprecedented depression. According to the liberal orthodoxy of laissez-faire, dominant in the City of London, governments were supposed to stay out of the economy while the maintenance of the gold standard required balanced budgets. Since the contraction of business lowered tax receipts, most politicians thought they had no choice but to lower expenditures, canceling projects and reducing social services, just when they were most needed. In Germany the Brüning government therefore embarked on a drastic "austerity policy" that cut the salaries of public employees by as much as 30 percent, dismissed officials, and froze hiring of replacements in order to reduce the payroll. Looking to defend their own farms and factories, many states raised tariffs, instituted import quotas, and resorted to currency controls, thereby hampering international trade. The German cuts in expenditure, the British defense of the gold standard, and the French insistence on balanced budgets deepened the downturn, creating a vicious cycle, spinning downward at an ever greater pace.[29]

In the deteriorating economic climate businessmen lost confidence and started to retrench, thereby further aggravating the crisis. When loans dried up, new investment came to a complete halt. Declining sales forced companies to reduce their own costs, forcing them to take additional rationalization measures and lay off nonessential workers. While the one-fifth drop in wholesale prices also lowered the cost of foodstuffs and raw materials, the evaporation of business profits demanded shutting down all peripheral activities that did not pay for themselves. Owing to the pressure on their own balance sheets, companies started to recall outstanding debts, jeopardizing the survival of firms that were unable to meet their obligations. No doubt some branches that produced consumables were less affected, since customers had to continue eating and wearing clothes, but whole industries like car making, steel production, and shipbuilding were in dire straits. In the windows of marginal shops, "going out of business" signs multiplied, while mismanaged larger enterprises went bankrupt at an alarming rate.[30]

The ensuing collapse of industrial production reached astounding proportions, especially in those countries that were most heavily industrialized and involved in international trade. Compared with the 1929 figures, by 1932 industry output was virtually cut in half in the United States (53 percent), Germany (53 percent), and the smaller states of Central Europe like the Netherlands (47 percent), Austria, and Czechoslovakia, whose economies were closely intertwined. Less affected were France (72 percent) and Belgium, which formed a "gold bloc," as well as Britain (84 percent) due to its preferential commonwealth trade and devaluation of the pound. Other countries that managed to isolate themselves, such as the Swedish welfare state and the militarized Japanese economy (98 percent), were hardly affected at all. Finally, Soviet Russia, in the midst of its first Five Year Plan, actually experienced an impressive growth spurt (183 percent) while capitalist states suffered.[31] Where the depression hit hardest, economic activity almost ground to a halt.

Government cutbacks and business layoffs produced an unprecedented amount of unemployment that overstrained the still-limited welfare systems. While figures understate the true extent, since they measure only the registered jobless, they indicate a drastic situation: In Germany, the hardest hit, the number of unemployed rose from about 1 million in 1927 to 6.12 million in 1932, in contrast to only 12 million people who were still employed. Among the neighboring countries the situation was hardly better, and even in Great Britain 3.75 million workers were out of a job in 1933. These numbers do not even include the underemployed, on short hours, who were just barely hanging on. About half of the labor force was therefore in dire straits. Unemployment hit especially the industrial areas; the young, who found no jobs; women, who lost their service positions; and the old, who were forced to retire before their time. In the Weimar Republic as many as 2.03 million workers were dependent on welfare support, while religious relief efforts and private charities were unable to care effectively for the rest.[32]

According to contemporary studies like Paul Lazarsfeld's investigation of Marienthal, the effect of unemployment was the progressive destitution of the bottom third of the population. Indebted farmers who could no longer make a living because of falling agricultural prices were forced to sell their meager holdings and become landless laborers. Jobless industrial workers quickly spent their savings and desperately tried to grow some food or tobacco in urban garden plots (*Schrebergärten*) where available. While the more fortunate would be fed in soup kitchens, others were even reduced to begging when municipal relief efforts failed. With all resources devoted to procuring nourishment for bare survival, clothing deteriorated visibly, and health care had to be neglected. Even if outright starvation was relatively rare, public-health doctors found that especially children were seriously undernourished. No wonder vagrancy and suicides increased everywhere.[33] Such early sociological investigations sought to galvanize the public to offer more effective help.

By dramatizing the demoralizing effects induced by the Great Depression, writers also sought to arouse sympathy. In Germany the journalist Hans Fallada wrote a bestseller in 1932 with the apt title *Little Man, What Now?* In simple everyday language he described the social descent of a lower-middle-class salesclerk who was fired from his job in a clothing store and could no longer support his wife and small child. Since many readers could imagine the experience of a loving couple struggling against hopelessness, the book became popular although it failed to offer a way out of the predicament. In contrast, the British writer George Orwell five years later offered both a documentation of the suffering of Lancaster miners and a spirited appeal for socialism in *The Road to Wigan Pier*. The first part of the volume was a graphic description of the terrible effects of unemployment on the families of coal miners, living in abject poverty, while the second section attacked middle-class complacency. Distributed by the New Left Book Club, Orwell's message argued that only socialism could end the widespread destitution.[34]

These reports described the psychological impact on the unemployed workers as devastating. By being thrown out of their job, they lost not only lost their income, status, and security but also their self-respect and manhood when they could no longer provide for their families. Since personal identity was defined by a person's work, being deprived of this essential marker had a demoralizing effect. Most unemployed went through a sequence of stages, starting with initial unconcern about finding another job, progressing to impotent anger against the injustice of being fired, leading to frantic activity to find another position, but ending after repeated failures in fatalistic apathy. While they were even more at risk, women became more powerful in the family, as it was their ingenuity and parsimony that kept everyone alive. Most jobless workers blamed employers for sacking them and criticized the government for not helping effectively. Not finding another job and living on the dole created passivity. As one jobless man put it, "These last few years, since I've been out of the mills, I don't seem able to take trouble somehow. I've got no spirit for anything."[35]

Since appeals to charity as well as trade-union initiatives failed to alleviate the suffering, the unemployed could only protest, demanding direct material aid and insisting on a reversal of deflationary policies. With millions of the jobless available as scabs, labor unions hardly dared to strike. Distressed workers therefore appealed to the public authorities of Manchester in May 1932: "We tell you that hundreds of thousands of the people whose interest you were elected to care for are in desperate straits. We tell you that men, women and children are going hungry. We tell you that great numbers of your fellow citizens, as good as you, as worthy as the best of us, and as industrious as any of us, have been and are being reduced to utter destitution." The petition went on to warn of the dire consequences and demand a change of policy: "We tell you that unemployment is setting up a dreadful rot amongst the most industrious people in the body politic. We tell you that great measures of relief are needed and that it is absolutely essential … to provide a vast amount of public work."[36] The labor movement called for public expenditures to alleviate the symptoms of the depression and social reforms to eliminate its causes.

One consequence of the insecurity and suffering was a decided radicalization of European politics. To begin with, many afflicted citizens considered capitalism itself to be the culprit, because they believed that greedy speculation and heartless profit seeking had triggered the Great Depression. If an unemployed worker realized after months of seeking another job that "there was nothing to be had" in spite of his best efforts, it was logical for him to conclude that something more fundamental must be wrong with the system. Moreover, the deflationary policies and inadequate relief measures discredited democratic governments, which proved incapable of stopping the downturn and were incompetent in alleviating its pain. Older men therefore began to doubt their longtime political affiliations, dropping their memberships in parties and trade unions. Feeling shut out from the workforce, the young increasingly listened to the radical slogans of the communists or the fascists, who strove to abolish both capitalism and democracy.[37] Even in established parliamentary states, the Great Depression raised doubt about the survival of democracy.

The inability of parliamentary governments to end the depression provided critics from the Left and the Right with ample opportunity to denounce democracy as incompetent. Leftist intellectuals like the writer Kurt Tucholsky satirized the insensitivity of military and moneyed elites to proletarian suffering and looked for revolutionary solutions to economic problems. Waged in the name of humanitarian values, this attack on popular self-government proved difficult to refute. Rightist thinkers like jurist Carl Schmitt, who considered politics a form of muted civil war, ridiculed the ineffectiveness of parliamentary debate and pronounced "mass democracy" unfeasible. Such neoconservative theorizing also claimed to act for the people in striving for a more forceful and authoritarian form of government. Against such widespread denunciations, defenders of democracy like the legal theorist Hans Kelsen had a difficult time justifying the slowness of public deliberation and the difficulty of finding compromises.[38] By discrediting liberalism, the depression reinforced the drift toward dictatorial versions of modernity.

UNEVEN RECOVERY

Recovery from the depression remained painfully slow, since it required rethinking its causes and finding practical remedies. Denouncing the neoclassical assumption that the market would right itself through austerity, the Cambridge don John Maynard Keynes argued vigorously in his 1933 treatise *The Means to Prosperity* that government needed to take a more active role. Unemployment could be ended only by public pump priming in order to restimulate demand, and the borrowed funds that might be needed for such stimulation could be repaid when the economy was once again flourishing. Socialist theoreticians like former German finance minister Rudolf Hilferding and the Swedish sociologist Gunnar Myrdal also argued that a government stimulus was necessary to break the downward cycle. Only when politicians who were unwilling to change course like the "hunger chancellor" Heinrich Brüning in Germany and the ineffective president Hoover in the United States were removed from office could prosperity return.[39] Overcoming the depression therefore required a change of public mind and new leadership.

An initial step toward improvement was cutting away the tangle of reparations and war debts that inhibited the restoration of international finances. Just before the Wall Street crash, a committee headed by the American banker Owen D. Young had proposed to scale back German obligations to 112 billion gold marks to be paid off during a period of fifty-nine years, with half the annual amount of 2 billion fixed and the other depending on capacity. When U.S. loans dried up, President Hoover was forced to broker a one-year moratorium on German reparations in the summer of 1931, since Berlin's bank failures made it impossible to continue regular installments. Finally, the Lausanne Conference of 1932 reduced German obligations by a further 90 percent in order to assure at least some payment. But at the same time Hoover, the Congress, and the U.S. public refused to cancel the inter-Allied war debts, which would have cut the Gordian knot. As a result, the multilateral effort of the World Economic Conference in the summer of 1933 to reduce tariffs and encourage international trade failed, and countries thereafter pursued nationalist policies.[40]

Another move toward recovery involved abandoning the gold standard, which had kept currency values artificially high and made European goods less competitive. In the summer of 1931 a run on the pound triggered a sterling crisis, since London's loans to Germany were frozen and the British economy had lost its invisible earnings abroad. Ramsay MacDonald's Labour cabinet fell over the reduction of unemployment benefits, and the succeeding national government was dominated by conservatives like Philip Snowden as chancellor of the exchequer. Nonetheless, the speculative pressure forced Britain to abandon the gold standard on September 20, 1931, shocking the world of international finance. During the next six months the pound, originally valued at $4.86, lost about 30 percent of its value, making English products more competitive in foreign markets and thereby dampening the effect of the depression among the countries of the sterling bloc. While Japan followed suit, other states like the United States and Germany feared inflation and resisted devaluation, thereby deepening the depression.[41] Because of this chain reaction, the British abandonment of gold ended an era.

Countries like France, which clung stubbornly to bullion, experienced even greater difficulty in coping with the depression as a result of their procrastination. Initially Paris was hardly worried, since France was less industrialized than Britain or Germany and had more small farms as well as greater financial savings, making the downturn less marked. In order to reassure the class of rentiers, French cabinets constructed a "gold bloc" to defend the currency and instituted deflationary measures. Their inability to end the depression eroded parliamentary stability and encouraged rightist protests in the wake of the Stavisky scandal. By 1936 the social suffering grew so severe as to sweep Léon Blum into office with a *front populaire*, supported by all leftist parties from the Radicals and Socialists to the Communists. Trying to "restore consumer purchasing power," Blum finally devalued the franc, instituted a forty-hour work week, and modestly raised wages with the Matignon Agreement. Though the Popular Front managed to regain full employment, productivity lagged, and production grew only slowly. Therefore the Daladier cabinet returned to more orthodox policies without improving the result. By increasing the ferocity of social conflicts, the depression fatally weakened French democracy.[42]

The only democracies that actually prospered during the depression were Sweden and to a lesser degree its Scandinavian neighbors.

This positive record was the result of Rudolf Kjellen's conservative corporatism, stressing national cooperation, and of the Social Democrats' abandonment of the class struggle. Instead, in 1928 Per Albin Hansson suggested the concept of a *folkhemmet*, arguing that the country ought to be run like a good "people's home" with everyone having a decent chance in life, regardless of social origin. Concretely this program envisaged a planned economy, which would be controlled by government regulation, and the extension of welfare benefits such as unemployment insurance and the construction of subsidized housing. By ending industrial strife, this approach built on a secularized search for social consensus, which characterized Swedish Lutheranism.[43] Expanded by successive Social Democratic prime ministers, the Swedish welfare-state model offered a third way between capitalism and communism.

The most radical response was the nationalist program pursued by the Nazi government that took power in Germany on January 30, 1933. One of its first measures was the institution of a Reich Labor Service (RAD) that compelled young men and women to spend one year in physical labor.[44] A second step was the initiation of vast public works, such as the building of superhighways (the famous *Autobahnen*) and also military defenses such as the *Westwall*. Another policy was the initially clandestine but eventually open rearmament project, a massive effort to produce weapons systems such as tanks, airplanes, and battleships forbidden by the Versailles Treaty. A fourth approach was the striving for autarchy, which entailed subsidizing domestic production and raising tariff walls in order to become self-sufficient in food and raw materials. A final move was the signing of bilateral trade agreements to create a German sphere of influence in East-Central Europe. Though financed by borrowing and by freezing wages, these measures returned full employment and restored production, making Germany look more dynamic than its democratic competitors.[45]

Owing to the depth of the depression, the recovery took years to accomplish, since it was not clear which measures would be most effective. In response to the breakdown of international finance and trade, most countries first sought to save themselves, devaluing their currency, controlling exchange rates, raising protective tariff walls, or resorting to barter. This nationalistic response actually prolonged the agony. When laissez-faire belt-tightening failed to produce a rebound, most European states reluctantly switched to deficit financing in hopes of reversing the deflationary spiral. Social democratic governments in France and Sweden engaged in social reforms so as to stimulate demand by strengthening buying power. The fascist dictatorships instead opted for public-works programs and extensive rearmament, while the Soviet Union sought to industrialize. Ultimately it was the rise of military expenditures that speeded the recovery. Only the outbreak of the Second World War ended the depression—but at what a terrible price![46]

DOUBTING DEMOCRACY

It is hard to exaggerate the disastrous effect of the Great Depression, because it turned European development from a positive course to a negative direction. The great slump shattered the growing optimism that the Old Continent was healing the wounds of the First World War and resuming the progress of modernity. At the same time the breakdown of international cooperation strengthened the forces of nationalism, which pursued selfish economic policies at the cost of hurting their neighbors. In Berlin and Vienna, the depression toppled democratic governments, initiating authoritarian regimes that would eventually turn into a brutal National Socialist dictatorship. Since the industrializing Soviet Union escaped the effects of the downturn completely, communism attracted western intellectuals who doubted whether their divided democracies could survive. As "the seminal macroeconomic event of the twentieth century," the Great Depression triggered the reversal from a promising postwar trajectory to another gloomy prewar period, in effect marking the decisive turning point of the interwar era.[47]

Oral testimonies of the 1930s indicate that contemporaries experienced the depression as "hard times" of intense suffering and disorientation. Although living costs dropped by about one-fifth, salaries and wages of those who could hold on to jobs declined even further, forcing them to get by on less and making them worry about the future. Even harder hit were the unemployed, since public assistance barely sufficed to keep body and soul together. After their meager savings were used up, there remained nothing but "the lowest depth of misery and degradation." Picking up cigarette butts to roll their unburned tobacco into smokes, standing in soup-kitchen lines, and begging in the streets somehow passed the time. For men, used to being able to provide for their families, joblessness meant shame, shifting power to harried women in their search for scraps of food. The proud solidarity of union membership evaporated, because the abundance of desperate laborers made strike threats ring hollow. Moving testimonies show that the depression had a severe impact on personal lives, upsetting plans and forcing a struggle for sheer survival.[48]

When neither economic initiatives nor political measures seemed to work, rampant despair cast doubt on capitalism and democracy. Because the self-healing forces of the market failed to reverse the downturn, many victims gave up hope in recovery and turned against the entire capitalist system, decrying it as heartless. Due to the ineffectiveness of political remedies, long-suffering citizens also lost faith in the ability of democracy to solve their economic problems. Liberal middle-class appeals for further belt-tightening fell on deaf ears when there was nothing left to economize. The pleas of Catholic and Protestant leaders to help the unfortunate by benevolent gifts seemed inadequate, since the scale of the need vastly exceeded the capacity of religious charity. Similarly social democratic proposals of job sharing or of increasing public assistance were hardly more convincing, as they appeared only to spread the misery without curing its cause.[49] Because of the close connection between the market economy and parliamentary government, the deep crisis of capitalism helped discredit the democratic version of modernity.

The apparent inability of democratic leaders to find solutions to the predicament drove millions of disappointed Europeans into the arms of the totalitarian ideologies that proposed alternative visions of progress. One beneficiary was communism, since the planned economy of the Soviet Union seemed impervious to business cycles.

Stalin's collectivization and Five Year Plans produced spectacular growth rates just when capitalist economies were in the greatest difficulty. Scores of leftist intellectuals like Sidney and Beatrice Webb therefore admired Russia and enthusiastically endorsed the Soviet experiment, ignoring the immense human cost of the purges and the gulag. To sympathetic heirs of the Enlightenment, the communist utopia offered a better road to modernity, since it promoted rational planning, social equality, and economic security at a time when the West was struggling. The French pacifist Romain Rolland expressed the sentiment of many European writers, artists, and commentators when he described the Soviet Union as "the hope, the last hope for the future of mankind."[50]

Another profiteer was fascism, since its rejection of both democracy and communism promised to restore a mythical sense of community. In Italy Mussolini, for all his own difficulties, put on an impressive show of national strength that impressed even Winston Churchill. In Nazi Germany, the recovery appeared to proceed faster and more successfully than in hesitant Britain or troubled France, creating an image of dynamism that attracted impatient bourgeois youths from all over the continent. Cultural pessimists like Oswald Spengler, anti-Semitic writers like Louis-Fernand Céline, and misguided poets like Ezra Pound looked to Hitler to stem disorder, defend elite standards, and restore national community. Disturbed by the dissolution of order and hierarchy, neoconservative thinkers like the philosopher Martin Heidegger imagined the fascist movement as a cure to the decadence of liberal civilization.[51] These sympathizers tended to overlook the fact that the Nazis were themselves conflicted over whether to revive older traditions or to promote another organic, even more deadly, version of modernity.

Chapter 9

STALINIST MODERNIZATION

Steel mill at Magnitogorsk, 1929. *Source*: Bundesarchiv Bildarchiv.

In late April 1929 the All-Russian Communist Conference approved "a vast project entailing a huge five-year industrialization program," known as the Five Year Plan. This ambitious measure sought to realize Lenin's dream "to remake primitively agrarian Russia into an industrial super-state." Breaking the logjam of the New Economic Policy, Soviet leader Josef Stalin tried to resume the push for modernization by collectivizing agriculture and increasing industrial production with new vigor. After outmaneuvering Leon Trotsky's leftist "deviation," his initiative would also cement his power as general secretary of the Bolshevik Party by distancing him from rightist critics like Nikolai Bukharin who were too timid to increase the tempo of industrialization. "Without foreign capital," Stalin boasted, "we are accomplishing the unprecedented feat of building up heavy industry in a backward country." During the revolution's anniversary he claimed that Russia would soon win the competition with capitalism. "Then we can see which country can be called backward and which the vanguard of human progress."[1]

Foreign visitors were impressed by the "attempt overnight to industrialize the most backward land in Europe." U.S. journalist Hubert R. Knickerbocker marveled at the ambitious goal of doubling "power, oil, coal and steel production" within five years. He was amazed by the effort to build "in Magnitogorsk a steel plant that will produce within two and one half years a yearly output of 2.5 million tons of steel and iron," one-third of the entire production of Great Britain! He also inspected "the Soviet's largest tractor factory, now in the process of construction" at Chelyabinsk, scheduled to turn out fifty thousand tractors a year to mechanize the collective farms. Moreover, he stopped at the gigantic hydroelectric dam of Dnieprostroi, being built with the help of an American engineer, which would multiply electricity production. Pushed forward with "zeal and terror" by the party and the Komsomol, this exciting effort demanded "very severe sacrifices" from the population already afflicted by "poor nourishment, wretched clothing and overcrowded living quarters." The Five Year Plan was, in effect, "a method for Russia to 'starve itself great.'"[2]

Since the bold plan did succeed in transforming the Soviet Union, grateful supporters praised its author, the Georgian-born dictator

Josef Stalin, as one of the great statesmen of the twentieth century. Even during his lifetime, his accomplishments—the survival of an independent communist state, the modernization of a backward country, the victory in the Great Patriotic War against Nazi aggression, and the conquest of a Soviet Empire—inspired a cult that praised him as *vozhd*, an incomparable leader endowed with superhuman wisdom and foresight. Schools, party organizations, and an entire city, Stalingrad, received his name, while all over Eastern Europe huge statues celebrated his presence. Poets like A. O. Avidenko composed rapturous hymns to "Stalin, our inspired leader," and painters portrayed him in white uniform receiving flowers from awed schoolgirls. When he died, millions of people wept. The Stalin cult has left deep traces in Russian memory. About half of the youths in recent surveys still considered him a great man, and about one-third of the population said that they would vote for him, were he still alive.[3]

The enormous bloodshed connected with Stalin's name has, nonetheless, also inspired a chorus of criticism, which has accused him of mass murder. Ukrainians charge that the millions of kulaks who perished during the collectivization famine were killed on purpose in a systematic genocide by starvation (*Holodomor*). Followers of Trotsky accuse Stalin's henchmen of forcing Old Bolsheviks to confess that they were capitalist spies in the show trials. The families of millions of professionals who disappeared in the dungeons of the NKVD (People's Commissariat for Internal Affairs) or died from slave labor in the gulag archipelago still wonder about what became of their members during the Great Purges. Finally, the victims of Soviet repression in the satellite countries emphasize the brutality and arbitrariness of Stalinist control over Eastern Europe. As a result, intrepid dissidents like Andrei Sakharov, historians like Roy Medvedev, and writers like Alexander Solzhenitsyn have stressed the incredible human suffering connected with Stalin's name. In the West anticommunist intellectuals have summarized Stalinist crimes in a shocking *Black Book of Communism* as well.[4]

Over two decades after the dissolution of the Soviet Union, the connection between communist modernization and mass suffering remains in dispute. In spite of the end of Cold War animosities and access to previously secret documents, defenders of Russian pride like President Vladimir Putin and critics of Soviet crimes such as the human rights group Memorial continue to disagree about the nature of Stalin's legacy. At its core, the debate revolves around the necessity of violence during Soviet modernization. Even if official statistics were often unreliable, the Five Year Plans undoubtedly industrialized Russia in a hurry by providing investment goods for industry, transport, and armament. Yet at the same time, it is equally indisputable that many Soviet citizens suffered through self-exploitation and that the paranoia that accompanied the great transformation cost millions of innocent lives. At the heart of this paradox lies the question of the relationship between the two sides of Stalin's Russia—industrialization and repression. This mixture of enthusiasm and fear came to be typical of the entire Soviet communist experiment.

LENIN'S LEGACY

Bolshevik ascendancy in Russia was the achievement of Vladimir Ilyich Lenin, who masterminded the October Revolution and presided over the subsequent consolidation of power. Both friends and foes recognized him as an outstanding personality, attributing to him charismatic qualities that set him apart from other socialists. As an eloquent speaker he not only convinced a reluctant Central Committee of his own party but also swayed large crowds to follow his views. Modest in his personal lifestyle, he exemplified the discipline of a dedicated professional revolutionary that he demanded of his followers, living entirely for the cause. Well read in western languages, he possessed a commanding intellect that allowed him to revise the Marxist classics according to the situation in Russia, cloaking his policy choices in the mantle of socialist theory. But he was also a pragmatic leader, making concessions to adverse circumstances while persisting doggedly in the pursuit of his utopian goals.[5] This unique blend of theory and pragmatism inspired a loyal following in his party and undying hatred from his enemies.

In a series of pamphlets Lenin developed an interpretation of Marxism that applied its ideological insights to the rapidly industrializing but still-rural Russia. In 1902 he argued in *What Is to Be Done?* for the need to establish a vanguard party of professional revolutionaries in order to establish state capitalism, skipping the bourgeois stage of development. More importantly, in 1916 in *Imperialism: The Highest Stage of Capitalism*, Lenin interpreted the First World War as a capitalist struggle for world domination, triggered by the conflict over colonial exploitation. Since the proletariat in the advanced countries was corrupted by the spoils of imperialism, the revolution would have to develop in the weakest link of the global capitalist system—namely, in Russia. This theoretical innovation justified the Bolshevik seizure of power in 1917, as further explained in *State and Revolution* of the same year, in the hope of sparking a world revolution of the oppressed. These additions to Marxism, driven by the need to justify action against both tsarism and the Provisional Government, expanded the original socialist theory into Marxism-Leninism.[6]

According to Lenin the Bolshevik Party had to lead the dictatorship of the proletariat, since it alone had a correct understanding of the imperatives of history. With the bourgeois stage of capitalist development not yet completed in Russia, only a Marxist vanguard could be trusted to act on behalf of the workers, peasants, and soldiers in accomplishing the overdue modernization of the country. By fulfilling the most pressing desires of a war-weary populace, the promise of "peace, bread, and land" resonated especially in the bigger cities and industrial centers, as increasing election returns and rising membership figures of the Bolshevik Party indicated. But Lenin had no compunction in ousting the hated Menshevik rivals and in dividing the agrarian Socialist Revolutionaries in order to put his own followers in control of the soviets. The new dictator ruthlessly employed the revamped secret police, called Cheka, to persecute, imprison, and murder regime opponents, meeting White violence with Red Terror.[7] From the beginning, Bolshevik rule was Janus-faced, claiming to act for the proletariat and repressing all dissent.

In crucial areas, Lenin, nonetheless, was pragmatic enough to make concessions in order to preserve Soviet rule. One contested issue was the nationalities question, driven by the desire of ethnic groups in the Russian borderlands to throw off the yoke of tsarist domination. Aware that they needed to respond somehow, the Bolsheviks reluctantly included the right to secession in their program, allowing the Finns, Poles, and Balts to form their own states. For other nationalities like the Ukrainians, the party proposed cultural autonomy rather than actual independence, permitting them to practice their languages and religions as long as they were located on a definable territory. By repudiating Russian chauvinism, this compromise intended to keep them within a new Soviet state, administered from Moscow. But this left the problem of the Jews unresolved, since despite the vociferous demands of the Bund, they did not have a specific settlement area on which to base their autonomy. In the constitution of 1924 these autonomous local republics were to be combined in a somewhat federal but still-centralized Union of Soviet Socialist Republics (USSR).[8]

A similar partial retreat from the initial radicalism was the New Economic Policy (NEP), begun in 1921. Emergency measures of the Civil War such as food requisitioning and rationing could not be maintained against popular resentment in the long run. Disregarding the anger of socialist zealots, Lenin therefore pleaded for the reintroduction of "local exchanges," permitted the private sale of food, allowed the revival of limited commerce, and authorized the resumption of small-scale manufacturing. These concessions neither dismantled the nationalization of industry nor did the profiteering "NEP men" signal a return to capitalism, but they did help revive economic activity, which had almost ground to a halt due to the fighting and the radical restructuring. On the one hand the breathing space of the NEP allowed some intellectual experimentation and expansion of education, but on the other the party continued to persecute the church and censor cultural life. Saving the Soviet regime, the concessions of the early twenties were therefore a perplexing mixture of returning to private initiative and maintaining rigid Bolshevik control.[9]

Overworked by having to make all major decisions, Lenin suffered a stroke in May 1922 that left him partially paralyzed. Under the solicitous care of his wife, Nadya Krupskaya, he stabilized somewhat but remained an invalid who vacillated between full capacity and mental confusion. As the prospect of recovery receded, the day-to-day business of government had to be carried out by the Bolshevik leadership such as the newly named general secretary Josef Stalin. Resting in a dacha outside Moscow, Lenin tried to remain in touch through visits of his comrades but grew increasingly irritated over losing control of public affairs. As a result of clashing cultural styles and differences on the nationality issue, he began to resent Stalin's actions as high-handed and to worry about his rivalry with the "excessively confident" Trotsky. He therefore dictated a note, known as his testament, warning that Stalin had "concentrated boundless power in his hands" and was "too crude" to continue in his office. But since the secretaries informed him of it, Stalin limited the transmission of this last message to the party leadership.[10]

When Lenin finally died of a heart attack in January 1924, Stalin was quick to claim the mantle of close associate and true successor. In a quasi-religious move, the Politburo decided to embalm the corpse and put it on display in a mausoleum on the Red Square in Moscow. Since Trotsky was vacationing in the South to recover from influenza, Stalin played the central role in the funeral of the Soviet state's founder, celebrating the very man who had tried to remove him from office. He praised Lenin's "legacy of fidelity to the principles of the Communist International," pledging "we swear to you, comrade Lenin, that we will not spare our own lives in strengthening and broadening the union of laboring people of the whole world." With this state funeral Stalin inaugurated the cult of Leninism, casting himself as its high priest. Stalin had Petrograd, the former tsarist capital, renamed Leningrad and sought to systematize the doctrines of the founder in a series of lectures by claiming: "Leninism is the theory and tactics of proletarian revolution in general and the theory and tactics of the dictatorship of the proletariat in particular."[11]

Lenin left a highly problematic legacy for Soviet Russia in which constructive and destructive elements were closely intertwined. His insistence on a cadre party of professional revolutionaries had created a powerful instrument, and his theoretical analysis of a socialist revolution in a backward country had provided the justification for the Bolshevik seizure of power in 1917. But the lack of economic development, the weakness of civil society, and the rejection of democracy had turned Soviet rule into a minority dictatorship, resting on propaganda and violence against class enemies and socialist competitors. During the Civil War and foreign intervention, Lenin's pragmatic decisions and the support of some workers and peasants managed to retain Bolshevik power, but the dream of a communist world revolution faded as attempts in Bavaria and Hungary to emulate the Soviet example collapsed. Moreover, by the early 1920s the Bolsheviks realized that they had to retract some of the radical measures of war communism and to make compromises like the NEP, which allowed the grand project of communist modernization to stall.[12]

STALIN'S RISE

Lenin's unlikely successor turned out to be Josef Dzhugashvili, known by his revolutionary pseudonym as Stalin, the man of steel. Several reasons militated against his success: He was not even a Russian, since he was born in Georgia and spoke with a heavy accent throughout his life. Moreover, Stalin was a dry and uninspiring public speaker, unlike the flamboyant Trotsky, who could galvanize entire crowds. In contrast to the polished internationalist Grigori Zinoviev, he was a provincial figure, having gained his merits in the struggle against tsarist repression within the country. Though he also absorbed the dictates of the Marxist classics, he was not really a theoretician but rather a revolutionary fighter and organizer who only rarely tried his hand at theory. While he belonged to the inner circle of Bolsheviks, the comrades resented his domineering personality; he had never completely outgrown the cunning, vindictiveness, and violence of his Caucasus background. As a result, he was much less known to the Russian public than his leading competitors.[13] But being continually underestimated was one of the secrets of his success.

Stalin was born on December 6, 1878, in the small town of Gori in Georgia. His alcoholic father Besarion was a cobbler, while his affectionate mother worked as a seamstress and spoiled her son. To give him a better chance in life, she sent him to an ecclesiastical school where he was a promising pupil, although in his free time he also tried to become a street tough, wanting to dominate his friends. Having survived smallpox and a carriage accident, he then studied at the Orthodox theological seminary in the capital of Tiflis in order to become a priest. There he received a classical education, learned to speak Russian, explored Georgian literature, and wrote poetry, calling himself "Koba" after a romantic mountain rebel. Since he chafed at the harsh discipline of the priests, he left the seminary just before his final examinations in order to become a political activist, initially fighting against tsarist repression as a Georgian nationalist. While writing incendiary articles and organizing popular resistance, he also started to study the Marxist classics, since they appeared to offer a radical and yet scientific blueprint for rebellion.[14]

Gradually the impetuous Dzhugashvili turned into a Russian socialist leader, noted for his daring exploits and revolutionary commitment. Though the moderate Mensheviks were popular in the Caucasus, he joined the radical Bolshevik faction, led by Lenin. "Koba" spent his days as an agitator in the oil port of Baku, haranguing the workers and writing articles for the underground press. In the 1905 revolution he achieved some regional notoriety for his support of armed insurrection and revolutionary dictatorship, was elected to the Stockholm Party Congress, and came to the attention of Lenin. During the following repression he went underground, funding his agitation through bank robberies. Whenever the tsarist policemen of the Okhrana caught up with him, they sent him to Siberia, but he escaped each time. Coming from the fringes of the empire, he proposed regional self-rule as a solution to the nationalities problem in *The National Question and Social Democracy*. Though he adopted the pseudonym "Stalin" as proof of revolutionary toughness, in 1913 the Okhrana once again exiled him to Siberia, where he languished until 1917.[15]

The February Revolution finally gave him a chance to resume radical politics, which he seized with alacrity. Back in Petrograd, he attacked the Provisional Government in *Pravda* editorials, siding with the Soviet of Workers' and Soldiers' Deputies and opposing the "revolutionary defencism" of the Mensheviks. Impressed by Lenin's explosive "April theses," Stalin embraced the strategy of realizing socialism without waiting for the bourgeois stage of capitalist development: "We must reject the outmoded idea that only Europe can show us the way. There is dogmatic Marxism and there is creative Marxism. I stand on the ground of the latter." Even if he disagreed with Lenin on subsidiary points like the nationality question, Stalin resolutely advocated armed insurrection, helping to convince the doubters in the Politburo: "The existing government of landlords and capitalists must be replaced by a new government, a government of workers and peasants."[16] When the Bolshevik coup succeeded in October 1917, he was rewarded for his support by being named commissar of nationalities in the new Soviet government.

Overshadowed by Leon Trotsky in the Civil War, the Georgian outsider arrived in the inner Bolshevik circles because of his dedication and pragmatism, often serving as Lenin's lieutenant. In the hot dispute about whether to accept the harsh peace terms of the German Supreme Command, Stalin grudgingly supported signing the Treaty of Brest-Litovsk in the hope that it would allow the consolidation of Bolshevik power in the Russian core lands. When White armies under General Anton Denikin threatened from the south, he was sent to the strategic city of Tsaritsyn on the Volga River in order to stabilize the front, clashing with Trotsky over the disposition of troops. In requisitioning grain, he moved with ruthless violence, intimidating the farmers and distributors so as to secure supplies for the starving northern workers. Originally opposed, he supported Lenin's attack on Poland in the hope of sparking sympathetic revolutions in Central Europe, which contributed to the subsequent military disaster. While pursuing his policy of regional autonomy, he advocated brutal force to reconquer Soviet border regions such as the Ukraine.[17]

Though rivals like Trotsky, Kamenev, and Zinoviev held the better cards, Stalin ultimately prevailed in the succession struggle. Since they were more inspiring speakers and more accomplished theoreticians, the other Bolshevik leaders were better known to the public. But they failed to seize various opportunities offered by Stalin's mistakes to discredit him. In contrast, Stalin was cunning, plotting his ascendancy with care, wrapping himself in the mantle of Lenin and understanding politics not as an ideological game but as a personal contest for power. Using his office as general secretary, he built up a cadre of loyal followers upon whom he could rely in an emergency. Control of the Workers' and Peasants' Inspectorate allowed him to oust the supporters of his rivals by charging them with malfeasance. Even more decisive was the ebbing of the revolutionary tide outside Russia, which rendered Trotsky's faith in "permanent revolution" irrelevant. Instead, Stalin's advocacy of "socialism in one country" promised the consolidation of Bolshevik power—a course party members considered more realistic.[18]

With his promise of building socialism in Russia, the centrist Stalin succeeded in isolating and expelling his chief rivals from the party. As long as the Soviet Union was the only communist state threatened by international opposition, the Bolsheviks closed ranks behind their general secretary. During the winter of 1923–24 Stalin succeeded in disciplining the "left opposition," accusing it of "factionalism" and removing many followers of Trotsky from their offices, charging them with "petit bourgeois deviation." When Kamenev and Zinoviev accused him of putting himself above them by "creating a theory of 'the leader,'" Stalin began to criticize his remaining rivals in public. Matters came to a head in the spring of 1927 when the "united opposition" demanded a more revolutionary foreign policy, rapid industrialization, and democracy within the party. This open challenge to his power prodded the general secretary to have Trotsky and Zinoviev expelled in October and Kamenev in December.[19] By eliminating his chief competitors, Stalin became the sole dictator of Soviet Russia for the next generation.

THE GREAT CHANGE

Once he had secured power, Stalin embarked on a giant modernization project to propel the Soviet Union into the front ranks of developed countries. By abandoning the tenuous compromise of the NEP, the general secretary resumed the radical project of creating the necessary underpinnings for a socialist utopia by revolutionizing agricultural and industrial production. The materialist determinism of Marxism suggested that Russia first had to pass through the bourgeois stage of high industrialization before it could construct a truly egalitarian society without exploitation and suffering. Impatient with the slow advance during the NEP, in which free markets coexisted with government control, many Bolsheviks wanted to force the pace of economic development by expanding the scope of state planning and party initiative in order to begin to realize the promise of communism in a hostile world. In the process of outmaneuvering his party rivals, Stalin hit upon a high-speed alternative to capitalist development that provided the Soviet Union with an industrial base for its own defense and appealed to other developing countries as a way to catch up to and surpass the faltering West.[20]

The circumstance that triggered the transformation was a shortage of grain deliveries, produced by the party's interference with consumer-goods production. Since there were few attractive products to buy, many peasants hoarded their grain in the winter of 1927, resulting in a 30 percent decline of provisions although the preceding harvest had been bountiful. Outraged by such noncompliance, Stalin and his associates embarked on a train trip to Siberia in January 1928 to extract the missing grain supplies by force—reenacting the model of the Civil War. When he encountered local resistance, Stalin summarily ordered the wealthy peasants, called kulaks, to be shot in order to teach the rest to obey Soviet orders. Returning with a trainload of requisitioned supplies to Moscow, the general secretary then persuaded the Politburo, over Bukharin's protests, to start a collectivization campaign in the countryside and authorize Gosplan (the State Planning Committee) to draw up plans for a rapid industrialization.[21] This change of course set in motion a huge effort to lay the economic groundwork for the construction of socialism.

The collectivization of agriculture was an attempt to modernize the largest sector of the economy through increasing the scale of operations and mechanizing production. The revolutionary distribution of land to the peasants had created many smallholders who were content to be self-sufficient rather than producing for the market. Hence the creation of collective farms was an attempt to pool land and livestock holdings so as to increase efficiency and raise production. Echoing the traditional peasant commune, two types emerged: The sovkhoz was a state farm in which the peasants were reduced to the status of laborers in the countryside. The kolkhoz rented the land from the state and agreed to deliver a fixed quota at harvest time, allowing a bit more initiative to its members in their garden plots. These new collective farms were supported by Machine Tractor Stations that sought to raise productivity by introducing machinery into farming. Occurring in capitalist countries via individual bankruptcies, in Russia the consolidation and mechanization of agriculture was mandated from above by the Bolshevik Party.[22]

To overcome the reluctance of the wealthy peasants, Stalin authorized class warfare in the countryside through systematic dekulakization. When farmers refused to join the collectives, he vowed to "break their resistance, eliminate them as a class." As a result hundreds of thousands of peasants were arrested or murdered in cold blood, whether they were willing to comply or not. Following Lenin's dictates, Stalin wanted to transform the social hierarchies in the countryside by getting rid of the successful farmers, intimidating the middling peasants, and persuading the landless laborers that their future lay with farming collectively. In the middle of the night, urban shock brigades would assemble villagers, pull out the kulaks and their families, throw them out of their homes, and resettle them in Siberia or make them disappear, never to be seen again. In the Ukraine, this dekulakization was particularly brutal, since it took place during the famine of 1932–33 and was aggravated by bureaucratic indifference and ethnic hostility. Recent research by Ukrainian historians claims that the systematic killing, called Holodomor, cost between 2.4 and 7.5 million people their lives.[23]

The use of such force soon produced results, fundamentally changing the face of Russian agriculture. In 1928 only about 1 percent of peasants worked in collective farms. Targeting the grain-producing areas, the Bolsheviks compelled about one-quarter of the farmers within the next year to sign up. In spite of widespread resistance, the process continued inexorably, since Stalin wanted to supply the industrializing cities and sell surpluses abroad. By 1932 three-fifths of the peasants found themselves in collective farms, and by 1936 over

90 percent had joined. While the chaos in the countryside reduced agricultural output by one-fifth, collectivization did allow the party to control deliveries to the cities. Eventually the increase in the size of fields and the numbers of livestock as well as the use of machinery and chemical fertilizers did raise production and freed up much labor. But the loss of individual ownership cut emotional ties to the land, and the sense of a "second serfdom" made agriculture a perpetual problem for the Soviet state. The ruthless force employed during collectivization left a deep trail of sorrow among its millions of victims.[24]

Simultaneously Stalin unleashed an even more ambitious effort in the first Five Year Plan to transform the Soviet Union into a fully industrialized economy within half a decade. In 1928 the Shakhty trial of engineers at a Caucasus coal mine on sabotage charges revealed the Bolsheviks' growing impatience with the slow pace of Russian industrialization. As a result the economists of the Gosplan began to project more ambitious targets of growth, which were ratified in the Party Congress of May 1929. Their plan aimed at the "very rapid expansion in the economy's stocks of fixed capital, along with an increase in the size of the labor force." In other words, Stalin proposed the speedy creation of capital goods as a basis for further industrialization rather than the fulfillment of consumer desires. The entire economy was supposed to double its output within five years at a time when the most advanced western countries were losing half their industrial production! The Five Year Plan's drive for speedy industrialization provided the Bolshevik Party with a positive vision of actually creating a better future.[25]

In practice, the Five Year Plan rather resembled a series of improvised local initiatives, focused on prestigious objects such as dams and factories to propel industrialization. By setting ambitious goals, the planners hoped to motivate managers and workers to undertake a gigantic effort to move the country forward. In the "optimal variant," industry would expand 285 percent, transport 197 percent, construction 353 percent, and even housing by 151 percent between 1928 and 1933. With the help of American and German engineers huge projects were undertaken, such as the building of a new center in Nijni-Novgorod to produce cars according to Ford blueprints. In Azbest, outside Sverdlovsk, the production of asbestos in the largest open-pit mine in the world would be multiplied fivefold. To provide the necessary energy, coal mining in the Donbas region and oil production in Baku had to be increased as well. Linking these centers, miles of new railroad had to be built, canals constructed, power lines laid. The entire Soviet Union began to resemble a gigantic construction site. One U.S. visitor noted: "The goal is constantly being pushed forwards, always a little beyond human capacity."[26]

The method used to achieve such bold aims was the partly voluntary, partly compulsory exploitation of labor rather than the use of machinery. To inspire workers, the Bolsheviks celebrated Alexey Stakhanov, a jackhammer operator who was supposed to have mined 102 tons of coal in less than six hours—without explaining the special preparations for his feat. Compelled by iron discipline, Russian workers put in twelve-hour days, six days a week, laboring under incredibly harsh conditions beyond their physical capacity. The party mobilized hundreds of thousands of volunteers, especially from the youth organization Komsomol, to continue working after hours and on weekends, shovel in hand. When self-exploitation did not suffice, the state turned to prison and forced-labor-camp convicts, using them especially for the construction of railroads and canals. The contribution of tens of thousands of hapless gulag inmates to the success of the Five Year Plan is often forgotten in Soviet lore. "Socialist industrialization" was a bargain of enduring present suffering so as to reap future benefits. And yet the people labored on.[27]

Because of its improvisational nature, the first Five Year Plan yielded rather mixed results. While Soviet media were full of statistics showing astounding growth rates, their reliability is doubtful since they were meant to signal success rather than reflect reality. Even if the official claim of 213 percent growth is discounted, western economists admit that Russian industry grew by at least 150 percent within the first five years of the plan. Transport exceeded its target, and construction rose rapidly initially, then stalled for several years, only to resume growth by the mid-1930s. In contrast agriculture contracted by one-fifth, and housing increased only 12 percent, much less than the rise in the urban population, thereby aggravating the shortage. Instead of gradually expanding all sectors, the Five Year Plan shifted resources to capital goods, creating the basis for further industrialization. As a result, the economy continued to grow throughout the 1930s at an annual rate of about 10 percent, though actual living circumstances improved more slowly. Anticipating success, Stalin proudly proclaimed in June 1930: "We are on the brink of our transformation from an agrarian to an industrial country."[28]

Feeding on the excitement of visible progress, the dual policy of collectivization and industrialization transformed the entire face of Russia. Tactically, Stalin intended the renewed initiative to reshape the Soviet economy as an effort to consolidate his power by showing that he was a true Leninist who had not given up on "industrialization, electrification, mechanization." Strategically, he saw the double push as an effort to overcome Russian backwardness, which had been the downfall of the tsarist empire, and to create an impregnable fortress of Soviet communism that could withstand any capitalist onslaught. Operationally, both projects were closely intertwined, since collectivization needed industrial products like tractors, while industry had to absorb the agricultural labor that had become redundant. Psychologically, after half a decade of stagnation, the great change promised that the party would recapture its original utopian enthusiasm by returning to the inspiring task of shaping the country's future.[29] In building dozens of places like the new steel city of Magnitogorsk, communists could finally realize their dream of constructing an entirely modern society.[30]

REIGN OF TERROR

Though the transformation of Russian society seemed to be succeeding, Stalin was not content with proclaiming victory. Instead he unleashed the Great Purge. No doubt compulsory collectivization and speeded-up industrialization had created numerous enemies who resented the disruption of their lives. There were also remnants of the tsarist regime who had not fled into western exile and still hoped for an overthrow of Soviet rule. Moreover, there were countless disappointed radicals who resented the dictatorial turn of the revolution—even some of the Old Bolsheviks criticized individual policies as excessive. But Stalin's personal paranoia exaggerated the dangers of such "anti-Soviet elements," seeing everywhere capitalist saboteurs and fascist spies who plotted to overthrow the system or to defeat it in a future war. Fearing his revolutionary comrades as rivals to his own power, the dictator began to suspect them of his own brand of treachery.[31] Instead of opting for a political process of convincing the multitude of critics by successful policies, Stalin chose repression, authorizing a witch hunt unparalleled in history.

The purges began with the December 1, 1934, assassination of Sergei Kirov, whose popularity had become annoying to Stalin. At the previous Party Congress the Leningrad party chief had been re-elected with many more positive votes than General Secretary Stalin. Since various accomplices of the murderer Leonid Nikolaev were immediately killed, it is not clear whether the Soviet dictator personally authorized the elimination of his rival. But Stalin and his associates immediately used the incident to unleash the NKVD against presumed moderates in the party and suspected opponents in the populace. Without any respect for "socialist legality," the secret service arrested suspects, interrogated them, and extorted confessions; it put the victims on show trials and swiftly carried out their sentences, which ranged from forced labor to summary execution. According to NKVD figures a staggering 1,575,000 people were detained, of whom 681,692 were shot, during 1937 and 1938 alone! Stalin's nasty comments and signatures on lists of condemned enemies prove that the dictator was personally in charge.

The most shocking aspect of the terror was the conduct of show trials in which Old Bolsheviks absurdly accused themselves of betraying the revolution. Between 1936 and 1938 secret police chief Genrikh Yagoda and state prosecutor Andrey Vyshinsky staged three major trials in Moscow. The first was directed against the "Leftist-counter-revolutionary bloc" headed by Lev Kamenev and Grigori Zinoviev; the second against the "anti-Soviet Trotskyite-centre" represented by Karl Radek; and the last against the "bloc of Rightists and Trotskyites" led by Nikolai Bukharin. Concurrently another secret trial of Red Army commanders, including Mikhail Tukhachevsky, decimated the military leadership. An amazed public witnessed the contrition with which Lenin's old associates confessed to imaginary crimes against the revolution, deviation from the Bolshevik Party, and treason to the Soviet state. These well-rehearsed self-incriminations were coerced by physical torture, intimidation of family members, and the fear of being expelled from the party.[32] In spite of Stalin's promises of leniency, all the 139 accused revolutionary leaders were ultimately shot.

The Great Purge soon engulfed the entire Russian society in a frantic effort to eradicate all "anti-Soviet elements." A prime target was the intelligentsia, with about two thousands artists imprisoned and the poet Osip Mandelstam and the writer Isaac Babel perishing. Subsequent decrees on "mass operations" also targeted the "ex-kulaks and criminal elements," with several hundred thousand killed. So-called "former people" such as members of the tsarist bureaucracy, White army officers, and Orthodox clergy were equally at risk, since their Soviet loyalty was suspect. But nonpartisan engineers and bourgeois specialists, essential for industrialization, were also accused of being insufficiently enthusiastic. Accused of being foreign-security threats, representatives of other nationalities like Poles or Germans were decimated as a group as well. Most absurd was the persecution of communist exiles from the West, crowded into Hotel Lux, who were often denounced as fascist spies.[33] No accusation appeared too far-fetched to be believed. Once someone had gotten in the hands of the NKVD, there was little hope for escape.

Propelled by a limited number of fanatics, this widespread reign of terror also relied on the voluntary cooperation of large segments of Soviet society. Led by the zealot Nikolai Yezhov, the secret police masterminded the repression in order to increase their power. But local party officials also raised its target figures, seeking to deflect suspicion from themselves by overfulfilling quotas of suspects. Eager propagandists supported their efforts by playing on popular fears of counterrevolution and inciting suspicion of foreign subversion. As a result many ordinary Russians denounced their neighbors out of personal envy or turned in fellow workers for anti-Soviet jokes. While people lived in permanent fear of being hauled away by NKVD men, they also contributed to the magnitude of the victimization by betraying their own friends in a desperate effort to save their own skin. Once suspects were in custody, a troika of secret police, prosecutors, and party members saw to it that they were speedily condemned.[34] The Great Purge was an orgy of self-immolation that belied communist claims of humanitarianism.

Those not killed outright were sent to concentration camps, immortalized by Aleksandr Solzhenitsyn as the gulag archipelago, a vast penal system covering the entire Soviet Union. Having been imprisoned themselves under tsarism, the Bolsheviks likewise jailed numerous enemies, expanding the camps in 1929 to mobilize forced labor for industrialization projects like the White Sea canal. During the Great Purge, the number of inmates swelled from one million to over eight million, not counting the administrative exiles. The moving descriptions of survivors paint a picture of a hellish life in barbed-wire enclosures and overcrowded barracks, with endless physical work at the mercy of brutal guards. While recalling the Nazi concentration camps, the gulag differed by the arbitrariness of its definition of "enemies" and by its primarily economic function. Death through contagious disease, labor in lethal mines like Kolyma, and widespread starvation were incidental rather than systematic, though victims numbered in the millions. Such dehumanization was even more intolerable for being perpetrated by what claimed to be a humane ideology.[35]

The purges were not just a regrettable aberration of an emancipatory project but an essential concomitant of Stalinist modernization. Though the rapid transformation of Russia probably required some compulsion, Stalin's arbitrary violence went far beyond anything needed for overcoming inertia. Defending socialism, left-wing intellectuals like Sidney and Beatrice Webb in Britain, Jean-Paul Sartre in France, and Bertolt Brecht in Germany refused to acknowledge the terror that accompanied the "great change." Only when former communist Arthur Koestler revealed such duplicity in *Darkness at Noon* did the public realize that the Old Bolsheviks were compelled to confess to undermining the Soviet Union so as to render the revolution a last service—though the charges against them were patently false. Even after the publication of Solzhenitsyn's powerful indictments, it took years of debate for impartial observers to acknowledge the extent and systematic nature of communist killing.[36] Eventually the evidence became incontrovertible that under Stalin modernization and murderousness went hand in hand.

STALINISM

Stalin's personality and policies put their stamp on the development of Russian communism so strongly that his name came to characterize the entire system during his lifetime. Both acolytes like Lazar Kaganovich and critics like Leon Trotsky began to speak of Stalinism in the early 1930s in order to praise or condemn his policies. Ironically, the epithet hardly indicated a theoretical contribution, because Stalin's writings such as the *Short Course* of party history remained meager, mostly just summarizing Lenin's doctrine and justifying his own decisions. Instead Stalinism usually refers to the perplexing blend of policies such as forced development and the accompanying terror. To supporters, the notion implies an elaborate "cult of personality," praising the Soviet leader and his accomplishments to the skies. To the critics, the concept instead suggests a form of communist dictatorship that is particularly brutal and paranoid, a style of intolerant rule beyond any legal restraint. Used both in political propaganda and in historical analysis, Stalinism is a slippery term with contradictory meanings—just as the subject itself.[37]

Somewhat surprisingly for a communist movement, a veritable cult developed that praised Stalin's wise leadership as a symbol of Soviet progress. The celebrations began with his fiftieth birthday in 1929, which the party paper *Pravda* marked with eulogies. Though Stalin stayed out of the limelight during the most difficult years of the great change, by the mid-1930s his portrait, whether a copy of a painting or of a photograph, started hanging not just in party offices but in government bureaus, joining and eventually replacing pictures of Lenin. Frequent newspaper snapshots in different official and private poses got the public used to having Stalin in the center of the action, gradually elevating him above other party leaders. Dressed in a revolutionary tunic, he was often shown with a pipe, making him look both folksy and benign. From 1937 on, the figure of Stalin also began to appear in Soviet films on the revolutionary struggle, extolling his contributions in contrast to the misdeeds of former rivals. By his sixtieth birthday, portrayals became even more imposing looking, cloaking him in an aura of sacrality that marked his unquestioned ascendancy.[38]

Everyday life under Stalin was nonetheless a rather prosaic struggle to survive in which the regime's promises of socialist abundance rang increasingly hollow. No doubt many Russians appreciated the visible progress represented by new factories, apartments, and subway systems. Moreover, they were proud of scientific advances, military parades, and athletic victories. But the abolition of the market created endless shortages, forcing shoppers to stand in line for food, clothing, and consumer goods. The collectivization of agriculture propelled surplus farm laborers into the cities and aggravated housing shortages by crowding families into small flats. The massive industrialization created smokestack factories that demanded repetitive physical labor and polluted the environment around them. The expanded bureaucracy produced a stream of regulations that could only be circumvented by personal connections, called *blat*. The close surveillance of the secret police also stifled personal initiative and independent thought.[39] While opening new opportunities, Stalinism, nevertheless, fell far short of its ambitious rhetoric.

But winning the "Great Patriotic War" enhanced the cult of Stalin, making him into a superhuman leader, the perspicacious *vozhd* who saved the Soviet Union from Hitler's hordes. With "immodest modesty" Stalin posed in military uniform with Red Army cap, suggesting his genius as military commander even though his credulity had brought him close to losing the entire war. More frequently, portraits also showed him as a renowned international statesman in the company of the great world leaders, deliberating about the future of defeated Germany. To mark his achievement the city on the southern front that had stopped the Nazi advance renamed itself Stalingrad. Both within the Soviet Union and in the East European capitals, sculptors erected larger than life statues of Stalin to mark their gratitude for the liberation and their subservience to his dictates. Everywhere in the Soviet Empire schools and factories vied to bear his name. Poets like the East German Johannes R. Becher wrote "high hymns on Stalin's heroism."[40] Hence communism turned into Stalinism, making the two indistinguishable in their followers' minds.

During the postwar decade the negative features of Stalinism deepened, because now Stalin's despotism could reign unchecked. As supreme leader he balanced the party against the state, and with all rivals eliminated only lieutenants like Vyacheslav Molotov and Andrei Zhdanov remained to do his bidding. Like an emperor he controlled an enlarged Soviet Union and lorded it over the East European states, reduced to hapless satellites. The international communist movement looked to his guidance, and western journalists treated "Uncle Joe" with respect, whatever their private opinion. As unquestioned dictator, Stalin ruled arbitrarily, following his own whims, drinking with and degrading his associates at his own pleasure. This omnipotence brought out a cruelty and brutality that destroyed his immediate family and those of others around him. Opposing any relaxation of control in the Soviet Union, the aging dictator suspected conspiracies around him, revealing anti-Semitic prejudices and fearing western influences in a so-called "doctors' plot."[41] The starving populace had to rebuild war-torn Russia in an atmosphere of darkening gloom.

Stalin's death on March 5, 1953, remains somewhat shrouded in mystery. After one of his all-night dinners in his dacha outside Moscow he apparently suffered a stroke, falling to the ground, drenched in his own urine. But his entourage was so afraid of the wrath of the ailing dictator that it took them until the next evening to call in medical help. When alerted, associates like the chief of the secret police Lavrenti Beria only had him cleaned up and put to bed, thinking that he was drunk. When physicians arrived the next morning, Stalin, who had sunk into a coma, was apparently already too far gone to be saved. The official postmortem contradicts the rumor that the despot was poisoned, concluding that he died of natural causes, because he was already seventy-four years old and in poor health. As a consequence of his habits of excessive eating, drinking, and smoking, he had a massive hemorrhage, though he might have ingested some toxic substance as well. The Soviet state radio interrupted its programming and announced melodramatically: "The heart of the collaborator and follower of the genius of Lenin's work, the wise leader and teacher of the Communist party and of the Soviet people, [has] stopped beating."[42]

The demise of the Soviet dictator was greeted with a mixture of sorrow and relief, which reflected the conflicting emotions evoked by his rule. Taken by surprise, shocked subordinates prepared a state funeral befitting a hero of the Soviet Union. Communist leaders like Zhou Enlai, Palmiro Togliatti, and Maurice Thorez attended the elaborate ceremony, and even western leaders such as President Harry Truman and former prime minister Winston Churchill telegraphed their condolences. Hundreds of thousands of Muscovites watched the military cortege take the coffin to Lenin's Mausoleum at the Red Square, where the embalmed body lay in state, wearing a military tunic in a bed of flowers. The party manager Georgi Malenkov, Foreign Minister Molotov, and secret police chief Beria delivered the eulogies, testifying to their importance as Stalin's close collaborators.[43] While millions of Russians genuinely wept over the loss of their leader, equal numbers of his victims rejoiced that their brutal despot was finally gone.

After Stalin's death Soviet politics largely revolved around the memory of the deceased dictator. His successor Nikita Khrushchev based his claim to power on a limited de-Stalinization by distancing Soviet communism from its most egregious crimes. In a secret speech during the Twentieth Party Congress he accused Stalin of murdering his associates, of military errors, and of postwar despotism.[44] But his effort to detach Soviet modernization from Stalinist excesses was doomed to failure, because both were too deeply intertwined. The dictatorship of the proletariat was a central tenet of the Marxism-Leninism that was only exaggerated by the Great Purge. The breakneck speed of industrialization, the Russian victory over Nazi aggression, and the establishment of the Soviet Empire were such popular achievements that later leaders were loath to criticize them. After the interlude of de-Stalinization, Leonid Brezhnev therefore returned to an orthodox line that seemed neo-Stalinist in style and intent. Mikhail Gorbachev's effort to shed this oppressive legacy logically had to lead to the dissolution of the Soviet Union itself.[45]

STALINIST DEVELOPMENT

In many ways Stalinism was a gigantic social experiment of forced modernization that propelled a developing but still-backward Russia into the twentieth century. In trying to create the "new Soviet man," the Bolsheviks embarked on a systematic campaign to spread literacy and numeracy by mass education, to eradicate disease by public hygiene, and to replace religion by advancing science and technology. While justified as catching up to the West in order to become militarily secure, the Soviet effort went far beyond that goal: it aimed at a utopian transformation of humankind. In the minds of propagandists communist modernity promised to cure capitalist evils like exploitation and unemployment by ending class warfare through social equality. This was the historic task of the party, which would not just allow socialism to survive in Russia but also make a leap into the future that would benefit all of suffering humanity. Such noble aims, enshrined in the 1936 constitution, inspired some artists like the writer Maxim Gorki and the filmmaker Sergei Eisenstein and attracted support from many fellow travelers abroad.[46]

Unfortunately this modernization project was carried out in a Stalinist manner with a mixture of revolutionary enthusiasm and dictatorial repression. The setting of optimistic targets in the Five Year Plans was supposed to spur extraordinary efforts to achieve them. The one-sided focus on heavy industry was intended to provide the means for building the infrastructure that would allow further industrialization. The collectivization of agriculture was designed to assure a secure food supply and to liberate farm labor for work in factories. The gigantism of many construction sites, claiming to be the world leader in size, was aimed at leapfrogging intervening stages of development. The endless reporting of success statistics of overfulfilling the plan was an attempt to convince a skeptical public that the march of progress would soon yield improved living conditions. While many party members, engineers, and intellectuals were enthralled by the challenge of remaking an entire society, ordinary workers had to be compelled to exploit themselves for the future, and millions of forced-labor camp inmates had no choice but to toil in order merely to survive.[47]

As "the most important socioeconomic experiment of this century," the Soviet administrative-command economy succeeded to a surprising degree in transforming the face of Russia. While the Politburo set the general targets, the Gosplan broke them down into practical increments, the ministerial officials directed their implementation, and the local party leaders made sure to realize them. In dealing with stubborn reality, there was some possibility of adjustment and bargaining—but no concessions were possible regarding the fundamental goal of modernizing the Soviet Union. The result of this planning process was an allocation of scarce resources toward heavy industry, defense, and further growth at the cost of housing or consumption, privileging the goals of the Russian state over the needs of its citizens. Such forced development produced a great leap forward, industrializing the Soviet Union within a decade, but it also created accompanying distortions in an inefficient agriculture and a wasteful gulag.[48] Producing dramatic progress, the Stalinist model impressed many contemporaries with its unexpected success.

The enormous human cost, however, undercut the moral legitimacy of this compulsory economic development. Forcing the speed of industrialization was possible only through denying consumption and exploiting labor, a strategy justified by the claim of bringing about a better future. But the rampant bloodshed of dekulakization during collectivization, the mass killing of party faithful and specialists in the Great Purge, the annihilation of the millions of prisoners by overwork in the gulag, the indiscriminate killing during ethnic cleansing and nationalities relocation were unnecessary excesses of Stalinist murderousness. Proud of the great transformation, many Russian nationalists under Putin are still in deep denial, refusing to confront Stalin's unsavory past. Many leftist intellectuals remain more reluctant to acknowledge the victims of their ideology's social engineering than to decry the numbers of dead attributed to their fascist enemies. While exact figures are difficult to substantiate, the international scholarly consensus now estimates twenty million victims of Stalin during peacetime alone.[49] Has the time not come to acknowledge their untold suffering?

Ultimately Stalinist excesses discredited the communist version of modernization, compromising an emancipatory project through inhumane policies that contradicted its noble aims. While the attempt to shake tsarist Russia out of its backwardness was legitimate, the effort to launch a utopian leap into a more just and egalitarian society failed even by Marxist standards because of Russia's underdevelopment. Lenin's erection of a "dictatorship of the proletariat" logically led to compulsion and killing, since it represented the rule of a committed minority over a skeptical majority. Stalin's subsequent great change required even more force to compel collectivization and industrialization, mingling enthusiasm and repression. Even if his paranoid personality exaggerated the problem, the murderousness of Stalinism was a structural result of imposing a communist project on an unready population. Ultimately, forced modernization blocked the possibility of a more gradual development, vitiating its humanitarian goals through inhumane methods. Instead of inaugurating a better future, Stalinist development produced a novel kind of hell.

Chapter 10

HITLER'S *VOLKSGEMEINSCHAFT*

Nazi Party Congress, 1934. *Source*: Library of Congress.

On January 30, 1933, German radio broadcast the momentous news that Adolf Hitler had just been appointed chancellor. Due to the failure of the preceding minority cabinets, which he had supported by his emergency decrees, President Paul von Hindenburg had entrusted the government to the leader of the largest Reichstag party. In Berlin, nationalists and Nazis were overjoyed by their joint seizure of power, gathering before the presidential palace and staging a gigantic demonstration. "Throngs of singing and chanting civilians jubilantly hailed the storm troops who had gathered in the Siegesallee for a torchlight parade." Onlookers were impressed when "column after column, with waving swastika banners, swung through the Brandenburg Gate down Unter den Linden, which was jammed by jubilant crowds of Nazi sympathizers." The Republican aesthete Count Harry Kessler marveled at "the pure carnival atmosphere." But many workers tried to resist, sometimes even by force, while intellectuals like the literature professor Victor Klemperer had dark forebodings: "It is a disgrace which grows worse every day."[1]

The National Socialists (NSDAP; informally, Nazis) were anything but a normal party, since they considered themselves a radical movement, pursuing a "program of cultural and social regeneration." Founded in Munich in the wake of Germany's defeat in the First World War, the NSDAP embodied the multiple resentments of the Right against the humiliating Treaty of Versailles and the politicians of the Weimar Republic that sought to fulfill its terms. But the Nazis differed from conventional conservatives by not wanting to go back to the empire; instead they sought to recapture that feeling of national unity which had inspired the war effort and to create a true people's community, erasing class distinctions, religious differences, and regional divergences. As a reborn nation, Germany would then be strong enough to risk another trial of arms that would bring ultimate victory. Ironically, it was an Austrian-born failed artist by the name of Adolf Hitler who led the movement by styling himself as its charismatic *Führer*, a leader with superhuman insight.[2] This was therefore a dynamic right-wing movement that set out to remake Germany fundamentally.

Because of National Socialism's irrational nature, opinion has been deeply divided about its actual character and its relationship to modernity. Especially in Germany many leftist intellectuals consider the Nazis a quintessentially reactionary movement according to the standards of western democracy or Marxist theory. They like to cite Hitler's personal distaste for the degeneracy of "modern art" as well as much propaganda rhetoric by Alfred Rosenberg with an anticapitalist, anti-Semitic, anticommunist, and antiurban bent. Moreover, the positive appeals to order, stability, and community suggest a world of small towns and the countryside, ideologically glorified by Walter Darre's "blood and soil" fantasies. From a western vantage point that equates modernization with the advancement of individual freedom and equality, the racial hatred and genocidal practice of the Nazis seem deeply antimodern, like a flight into an imaginary past. The antifascist perspective therefore asserts that "National Socialism has not accelerated the modernization of Germany, but rather has hindered it."[3]

Yet less-ideological commentators insist that the Nazi rejection of modernism was itself a product of modernity since they also embraced it selectively. Already at the time Thomas Mann pondered the "mixture of robust modernity ... combined with dreams of the past," deriding Nazi views as "a highly technological romanticism." Since leaders like Hitler, Speer, and Goebbels were fascinated by the likes of Mercedes cars, Junkers airplanes, and UFA films, one attempt to resolve the paradox of murderous irrationalism and fascination with technology is the concept of "reactionary modernism." Another approach asserts that the biopolitical engineering with which the SS tried to reshape the physical body and the racial composition of the nation was based on faith in science, exaggerating tendencies such as eugenics present in other countries as well. For all their rhetorical denunciation of decadence, the Nazis also vastly expanded the reach of the media by creating a popular entertainment and consumer culture.[4] While National Socialism rejected urban decadence, such features suggest that it was ultimately searching for its own alternative vision of an "organic modernity."

The Nazis' simultaneous rejection and embrace of modernity holds the key to their puzzling seizure of power in a country that prided itself on its contributions to European culture. In parts of the Islamic world and among skinheads the Nazi swastika still exerts a prurient fascination, while no theory, such as that of Hitler's missing testicle, seems to be too far-fetched to be believed. On the one hand it is important to remember that Hitler profited from the failure of liberal democracy in the Weimar Republic, which allowed him to exploit the Great Depression demagogically. Moreover, fear of a Bolshevik-style revolution drove many voters into the Nazi camp because they promised to offer protection against communist leveling. On the other hand, the Nazis themselves used up-to-date techniques to broadcast nationalist appeals to their male and lower-middle-class supporters, promising them a strong and harmonious national community. Once in power, the NS dictatorship also employed a modern mixture of incentives and repression to cement its popularity. And yet, even after such rational considerations, an element of inexplicable mystery tends to remain.[5]

AGONY OF THE REPUBLIC

Dramatized in Christopher Isherwood's *Berlin Stories*, the fate of the Weimar Republic reads like an ancient tragedy, beginning with hope and ending in disaster. In retrospect, the failure of the first German democracy looks almost overdetermined, since its endless problems appeared to doom it from the start. Many factors seem to explain the collapse such as the lack of a social revolution, the resentment of a punitive peace, the ambivalence of the Reichswehr, and the flaws in the constitution. Intellectuals therefore like to invoke the "Weimar analogy" to warn against the danger that democracy will erode if authoritarian tendencies are not stopped from the start. Nonetheless, Weimar culture continues to exert a strange fascination as an extraordinary moment of modernist experimentation that inspired innovative styles all over the world due to its forced dispersal. In order to do justice to the modernizing potential of the Weimar Republic, it is necessary to put aside the teleological fixation on its ending and also to examine its chances for success as well as appreciate some of its lasting contributions.[6]

Ending four and one-half years of war, the November Revolution of 1918 inspired hopes for peace, political participation, and social equality. Virtually overnight, the revolt of war-weary sailors, soldiers, and workers overthrew the imperial structure, discredited by defeat: "The Kaiser has abdicated. The revolution has been victorious in Berlin." Led by the radical Spartacists and shop stewards, the hungry masses wanted to create a Soviet-style council system in order to expand participation and social equality. But ultimately the moderate majority of the Social Democrats (SPD) won out, insisting on the creation of a democratic republic, headed by a parliamentary government. Newly elected president Friedrich Ebert of the SPD negotiated a compromise with the army leadership, which promised to tolerate the republic, while unions and employers agreed to treat each other as legitimate social partners. The January 1919 election therefore returned a left-center majority for the Constituent Assembly in Weimar, which drafted a progressive constitution that guaranteed extensive civil rights.[7]

Yet social cleavages and political divisions deepened, bringing the country to the brink of civil war. Following the Soviet model, the Spartacists staged an ill-advised uprising in Berlin that the government put down with military help, culminating in the murder of their leaders Karl Liebknecht and Rosa Luxemburg. The announcement of the Versailles Treaty's harsh terms and the accusation of war guilt created "incredible dejection" across all party lines, leading to the fall of the cabinet and strengthening the hand of obdurate nationalists. Emboldened by the paramilitary units of the Free Corps, East Prussian bureaucrat Friedrich Kapp launched a right-wing putsch ostensibly to restore order, which failed due to the resolute resistance of the trade unions. Hence the major political parties created uniformed auxiliaries like the veterans' Stahlhelm, the Socialists' Reichsbanner, the Communists' Rotfront, and the Nazis' Sturmabteilung (SA) to battle for control of the streets. Although the government survived these challenges, the proliferation of extremist violence weakened the republic, since it was never able to assure security.[8]

After weathering such unrest, the first German democracy consolidated during the mid-1920s under the capable leadership of Gustav Stresemann. While unpopular policies cost the Weimar coalition of working-class Social Democrats, bourgeois Democrats (DDP), and the Catholic Center Party its parliamentary majority, the national-liberal middle-class German People's Party (DVP) took up some of the slack, shifting the cabinets to the center-right of the spectrum. Though Stresemann had been a rabid nationalist and supporter of the kaiser, political realism made him moderate his views sufficiently to accept the republic and help negotiate the Dawes Plan, which ended the hyperinflation and produced a more tolerable reparations schedule. In contrast to much of the elite, he saw international reconciliation as the best way to revise the onerous clauses of Versailles, cooperating in the spirit of Locarno with French statesman Aristide Briand.[9] While the leftist Communists and the right-wing German National People's Party continued to reject democracy, the economic recovery helped stabilize the republic politically.

Weimar's halcyon years made possible exciting experiments in democratic modernity that sought to better the lives of the toiling masses with all sorts of innovations. Leftist politicians sponsored social reforms such as reducing the length of the workday and extending unemployment benefits. Progressive architects like Bruno Taut built improved workers' apartments, using green spaces for more "light and air" than in the usual dingy rental flats. Socially concerned doctors campaigned for improved hygiene, seeking to decrease mortality by public support for preventive medicine. While advertisers promoted an androgynous "new woman," sexual reformers like Magnus Hirschfeld campaigned for access to contraception and decriminalization of abortion as well as homosexuality. At the same time philosophers like Martin Heidegger, artists like Georg Grosz, and intellectuals like Carl Schmitt explored the contradictions of life in the metropolis.[10] With their boldness, these emancipatory initiatives, daring experiments, and ideological discussions created a sense of unprecedented social and cultural modernity.

The Great Depression not only ended the hopeful mood; it also dealt German democracy a blow from which it did not recover. In some rural areas like Schleswig-Holstein the fall of agrarian prices sparked a protest movement against the Weimar system that used terror to destabilize the countryside. In the cities, unemployed workers flocked to the radical Communists while the Social Democrats had difficulty in maintaining their support by promising additional welfare measures. Faced with the threat of destitution, much of the middle class abandoned its allegiance to democracy, while many members of the economic, military, and administrative elite campaigned for an authoritarian dictatorship. When the unemployment insurance fund went bankrupt owing to the huge number of jobless, the grand coalition under SPD chancellor Hermann Müller fell apart, since it could not agree on how to meet the emergency: The Left wanted to raise business taxes; the bourgeois right insisted on cutting benefits. Hence President Paul von Hindenburg appointed the conservative Center Party politician Heinrich Brüning chancellor.[11]

Since austerity measures and revisionist confrontation remained unpopular, the republic gradually turned into an "authoritarian democracy." When the electorate rejected Brüning's policies in July 1930 by dramatically increasing the number of NSDAP and Communist (KPD) seats, he resorted to paragraph 48 of the constitution, which envisaged rule by presidential decree in case of a national emergency. Since deflationary measures failed to end the depression, Hindenburg lost patience, because the Junkers around him opposed Brüning's plan to distribute land to the unemployed in the East. In May of 1932, the president appointed Catholic nobleman Franz von Papen, whose dashing bearing was matched by his political incompetence, as chancellor. But when he lost the July election and failed to get parliamentary backing, the president was at his wit's end. Egged on by his conservative camarilla, the octogenarian Hindenburg named the head of the Reichswehr, General Kurt von Schleicher, as chancellor in December.[12] Within two years a struggling parliamentary democracy had turned into an autocratic presidential regime.

The Weimar Republic failed because of a combination of underlying structural problems and short-term contextual causes. As the cliché of the "Republic without republicans" indicates, only the working class and the liberal *Bürgertum* were ready for self-government, since many members of the elite remained hostile to mass participation. Negative circumstances such as military defeat, an onerous peace treaty, hyperinflation, civil strife, and the Great Depression did not help endear democracy to the population either. Moreover, mistaken policies, ranging from the confrontation over reparations and foreign-policy revisionism to the failure to dismiss the old elites, the toleration of private armies, and the austerity response to the depression, contributed to the collapse. As a result, citizens who had reserved judgment about parliamentary government distanced themselves from it when they felt disappointed that it could not deliver on its promise.[13] In the end, Weimar's fall was merely the German variant of a more general rejection of democratic modernity in the interwar period, though it had more disastrous consequences by far.

FÜHRER FROM THE FLOPHOUSE

The ascent of a "bizarre misfit" like Adolf Hitler to power in a cultured country like Germany continues to strain credulity. His central role in the rise of the Nazi movement can be attributed to his exceptional abilities, the cult of the Führer, and the polycratic competition between collaborators that reserved all decisions ultimately for him. Though he was often underestimated by his competitors, part of his success was also due to his extraordinary personality, a strange mixture of talents and liabilities. Highly effective as propaganda, the Charlie Chaplin parody in *The Great Dictator* has actually made understanding Hitler's ascendancy more difficult by ridiculing his odd mannerisms. But poking fun at his outlandish personality traits fails to clarify the reasons why so many people would go along with such an exalted individual. To explain this surprising bonding, Max Weber's notion of "charismatic authority" offers an important clue, because it links an aura of leadership with a mass following.[14] The secret of Hitler's success lay in the peculiar relation between his personality and the public.

Since Hitler mythologized his background, it is necessary to recall a few simple facts. He was born in 1889 as the son of an Austrian customs official in Braunau on the Inn River. Unlike his authoritarian father, his mother was a simple, doting woman who failed to discipline the young Adolf. In the provincial town of Linz, he attended the *Realschule* with a modern curriculum, though he dropped out after his father's death in 1905. After two years of idleness, punctuated by a passion for Wagner operas, the eighteen-year-old moved to the capital of Vienna, where he twice failed the entrance examination to the Austrian Academy of Fine Arts. Stymied in his grandiose plan to become an artist, he used up his inheritance after his mother's death by refusing to take on regular work. When his money ran out, he was reduced to poverty, an unkempt young man with lice-infested clothes, sleeping in hostels and selling postcards and paintings. Though a bequest from an aunt improved his situation, he remained a déclassé bohemian who listened to the anti-Semitic rants of Georg von Schönerer and read rightist pamphlets full of hatred for the Reds and Slavs.[15]

The outbreak of World War I suddenly gave his life new purpose and direction, since Hitler was swept up by the national enthusiasm. In order to evade military service in Austria, which he considered moribund, he had previously moved to Munich, where he eked out a modest existence as a painter. In early August 1914, he volunteered for the Bavarian army and was inducted into the List regiment, which became his physical and psychological home for the next several years. At the western front, he served as a dispatch runner, carrying messages from regimental headquarters to the trenches and back, a dangerous undertaking in which he was wounded. Though brooding and moody, he felt secure in the comradeship of his fellows, serving with enough courage to be promoted to corporal and earn the Iron Cross first and second class. In October 1918 he was gassed, experiencing the end of the war in a military hospital in Pasewalk. The unexpected defeat shattered his nationalist universe, robbing his life of structure and meaning.[16] Distraught, he sought explanations for the disaster, blaming the Left and the Jews.

Back in Munich, the thirty-year-old Hitler became a beer-hall orator who galvanized a crowd with his simple, emotional harangues. The Bavarian capital was torn between the council republic of left-socialist revolutionaries and counterrevolutionary forces of local and national reactionaries. In this chaos, Hitler became an informant of the nascent Reichswehr, discovering a talent for speaking in propaganda courses designed to keep the troops loyal. In September 1919, he attended a meeting of the radical German Workers' Party, which he joined as number 555, sensing that he might play a leading role in this small organization. In the fragmented scene of competing right-wing movements, Hitler quickly made a name for himself with his impassioned rhetoric that attacked communists and Jews, calling for a national rebirth. The twenty-five-point party program was a mélange of various resentments, blending nationalist with anti-Semitic and anticapitalist themes. As a result of his rhetorical ability as "a drummer" Hitler quickly took over the control of the renamed National Socialist German Workers Party (NSDAP).[17]

Emboldened by growing success, Hitler in November 1923 decided to launch a putsch in order to topple the government in Berlin. His fiery speeches had attracted followers such as the lawyer Hans Frank, flying ace Hermann Göring, and Captain Ernst Röhm, who created the paramilitary SA, swelling the party's ranks to about fifty thousand members. After Mussolini seized power in Rome, Hitler began to style himself as Führer and decided to follow his example, since the Ruhr struggle against French occupation and the hyperinflation had made the national government look ineffectual. On November 8, 1923, Hitler stormed into a mass meeting in the Bürgerbräukeller and tried to compel leaders of the conservative Bavarian government who were there to join him in proclaiming a national revolution. But when the Reichswehr balked at his coup and the regional reactionaries rejected his demands, a debacle ensued. On the following morning the police fired on the Nazi demonstration on the way to the Feldherrnhalle, killing fourteen insurgents. Marching in front with Ludendorff, Hitler barely escaped alive, only to be imprisoned in the Landsberg fortress.[18]

The failure of the Beer Hall Putsch forced Hitler to switch to a legal strategy after his release in December 1924. He used his time in prison to formulate his worldview in *Mein Kampf*, a turgid collection of anti-Semitic and anti-Bolshevik ravings as well as nationalist attacks on the peace treaty and calls for "living space." During the consolidation of the republic, he refounded the NSDAP under his own leadership and made it preeminent among the competing right-wing groups. With the help of Gregor Strasser's organization and Joseph Goebbels' propaganda, he also expanded the reach of the party into northern Germany. Initially the strategy of a legal quest for power yielded only local gains such as twelve Reichstag seats in the 1928 election. But soon the Great Depression sparked so much rural radicalism and urban despair that membership numbers swelled and donations multiplied. The breakthrough came in September 1930, "a black day for Germany," when the NSDAP jumped to 107 seats. Two years later street violence and incessant agitation against the "Weimar system" helped the party to obtain 37.1 percent of the vote, winning 230 deputies' seats.[19]

Once the Nazis were the largest party, any solution to the government crisis had to include them in some fashion. But President Hindenburg was suspicious of the Austrian upstart while Hitler wanted nothing less than the chancellorship and control of the government. This stalemate was broken only when the number of Nazi seats decreased to 196 in the November election, suggesting that the peak of their popularity might have passed. Outmaneuvered by Schleicher, his predecessor Papen finally realized that he could return to power only if he accepted Hitler's leadership. In complicated negotiations between the NSDAP leaders, Hindenburg's circle, and the conservatives, a compromise was eventually reached: Hitler would become chancellor, but only the jurist Wilhelm Frick and Göring would join him as Reich and Prussian ministers of the interior. Papen would be vice-chancellor, supported by the reactionary press tycoon Alfred Hugenberg and a bevy of conservative noblemen. Ironically, this NSDAP and DNVP coalition seemed almost to be a return to democracy, since it represented just over two-fifths of the popular vote.[20]

Part of Hitler's success was therefore due to his extraordinary personality, which set him apart from other politicians. Caricatures of the man with the mustache, burning eyes, and fixed expression overlook that his speaking ability enthralled crowds, his emotional intensity inspired a movement, and his personal magnetism attracted followers. After lengthy hesitation, he often guessed right in his political gambles. Critics correctly pointed out that he was an odd person: moody, lazy, brooding, and given to fits of temper. With his vegetarianism, refusal to smoke and consume alcohol, and disinterest in womanizing, he deviated considerably from the machismo image expected of politicians. But somehow he managed to turn his liabilities into assets, transforming difference into evidence of superiority so as to justify his ascendancy and expect devotion. Facilitating his rise, bourgeois patrons like the Bechsteins helped refashion his appearance, behavior, and speech patterns so as to make him look more impressive. Finally, the photographer Heinrich Hoffmann contributed to the Führer myth by picturing him in various studied poses, suggesting a modern style of leadership.[21]

APPEALS AND FOLLOWERS

Another secret of Hitler's success was the pervasive sense of crisis, which made his extremist ideology appear as the only way out of a threatening catastrophe. Under normal circumstances, the strident simplifications of his rhetoric would have repelled sensible voters, but during the depression and the disintegration of the republic, his message found increasing resonance. Nazi appeals were a collection of resentments against what seemed to be going wrong in Germany, augmented by a pseudophilosophical rejection of negative aspects of modernity. But Hitler also offered a positive, if rather hazy, vision of national rebirth and people's community that promised to lead the country into a better future. Much of the propaganda was contradictory, appealing to different groups, and difficult to pin down because of its irrationality, but the very actionism radiated a sense of resolve, finally, to do something that would improve the situation.[22] Rejecting the squabbling of democracy and the violence of Bolshevism, the Nazis proposed a different, more organic modernity for the national community.

Much of Hitler's invective was directed toward mistakes of the recent past and the predicaments of the present. He derided the November Revolution as "the greatest villainy of the century" and explained the defeat of the army, "victorious in a thousand battles," as a result of "internal decay." In social Darwinist terms he argued: "The deepest and ultimate reason for the decline of the old Reich lay in its failure to recognize the racial problem and its importance for the historical development of the peoples." He railed against the "shameful peace" of Versailles, signed by the "November criminals" who created the weak Weimar Republic, leading to "a rampant degradation, which gradually consumes our entire public life." As an ardent nationalist Hitler deplored how the German people had been "mugged by a pack of rapacious enemies from inside and outside," and tried to rouse them to militant resistance. The misery of the Great Depression, which caused "fighting for the daily bread of this people," could only be cured by conquering "necessary space" to live in.[23] Such resentments were shared by an increasing number of confused patriots.

Hitler's ambition, nonetheless, aimed at providing a deeper understanding of Germany's malaise in order to offer a more lasting cure. Departing from the premise that "it is the highest task of politics to preserve and continue the life of a people," he claimed that maintaining biological health required safeguarding the "racial purity" of the nation. In a terrible misreading of history, he argued that all high cultures had collapsed because "the originally creative race died out from blood poisoning." In Germany, he saw the superior Aryan race beset by two mortal enemies—the Jews and the Bolsheviks. Lacking a territory of their own, the former were by definition a "parasite in the body of other nations" and thereby ultimately destructive. Inspired by Jews, the Marxists were also violently corrosive of civilization, since they focused on social leveling. His other objections to capitalism and feminism were derived from these presuppositions, even if such deductions were hardly logical.[24] With his racist nationalism Hitler rejected the entire thrust of emancipatory progress, derived from the Enlightenment.

In much vaguer terms than his phobias, Hitler also tried to sketch a positive image of national rebirth, centered on the notion of a "people's community." Germany could only be revitalized by obeying the dictates of "racial hygiene," creating a body politic cleansed of biological and racial inferiors. In order to regain the health of its blood, the nation had to live on the soil, tilling the land and drawing strength from it. In contrast to bourgeois hierarchy and Marxist class struggle, the *Volksgemeinschaft* would treat all members equally, while respecting a hierarchy of achievement. By repairing the effects of urban decadence, the national community would also recover its fighting prowess, making it capable of enduring the necessary battles. In this partly military, partly biological enterprise, gender roles were clearly defined, with men as warriors and women as reproducers of the race. Seeking to recapture the emotional unity of the Great War, such a nation transformed would leave behind the partisan squabbles of democracy and dedicate itself to achieving greatness by working together with enthusiasm.[25]

A "truly German democracy" was supposed to combine atavistic myths with modern innovations in a novel blend that would make the nation more powerful. At its head would be the freely elected leader, obligated "fully to assume all responsibility for his actions and omissions." The Führer's vision would be propagated by a political movement of dedicated followers, creating a dynamic bond of national resolve. The masses had to be won over by propaganda, since they were like women, easily swayed and dominated by an iron will. Of course, all enemies such as Jews and Bolsheviks would be ruthlessly excluded. A new elite would arise to implement this combination of visionary leadership and popular acclamation, capable of highest achievement and ready for heroic action. In such a conception, science and technology played an important role by providing tools for propaganda, rearmament, and biopolitics. This entire concept of the *Führerstaat* was an effort at social engineering that was distinctly modern, even if it proposed an illiberal racial alternative to the democratic and Marxist ideologies.[26]

The followers who joined the NSDAP began as a small band of extremists but eventually grew to a virtual cross section of German society. During the initial struggle only convinced reactionaries dared to commit to a party that was considered part of the radical fringe. The Nazis attracted some workers, but more came from the lower middle class and marginal members of the elite. From the late 1920s on, the Great Depression drove new converts to National Socialism, mostly recruited from the middle class, which feared social descent, and from among the young, blocked in their careers. After the 1932 electoral triumph many opportunists, hailing from the administrative ranks, professions, and technical pursuits, flocked to the swastika banner, wanting to join a movement that looked like the wave of the future. Finally, once in the saddle the Nazis could use the lure of privilege to attract members from the previously skeptical elites and could rely on their own youth organization as a recruiting ground. Containing over eight million members by 1945, the Nazi Party systematically moved from the fringes into the center of German society.[27]

Nazi electoral support similarly expanded from a limited core to a mass following approaching a people's party through appeals to the losers of modernization and to protest voters. The NSDAP made some inroads among blue-collar workers but could never win over the majority of the proletariat. Its nucleus was instead composed of struggling small farmers, shopkeepers, and independent artisans, complemented by white-collar employees who were especially battered by the economic crisis. Moreover, the party also found a surprising amount of support among university students, civil servants, and in affluent districts where the nationalist message resonated. While the young were especially susceptible, a considerable number of retirees also voted for the party, and women, who were underrepresented among the members, cast their ballots for Hitler as well. The typical Nazi follower was therefore a young Protestant World War I veteran with limited education. The NSDAP especially managed to mobilize many formerly apolitical voters who were strongly dissatisfied with the Weimar Republic.[28]

In essence, National Socialism offered a more dynamic and modern version of the radical Right by using the economic and political crisis of the republic to broaden its appeal. In spite of all propaganda efforts, most of the working class remained committed to the Social Democrats, while the unemployed tended to vote Communist. Similarly, religious authority immunized the Catholic milieu somewhat against nationalist appeals, so that many of its faithful remained skeptical. In contrast, the democratic and liberal middle-class parties crumbled, first transforming themselves into special-interest groups and then fading entirely from the scene, as they lacked an encompassing vision. The German National People's Party failed to profit from the chaos, because it was too backward looking, hoping to bring the kaiser back and revive the discredited empire. The Nazis instead projected an image of dynamism, ready to shape the future by promising a national renewal that would restore external power and heal internal rifts.[29] This combined message of past resentment and future hope captured an increasing number of Germans.

NATIONAL REVOLUTION

While the "national renewal" was mostly a propaganda show, Hitler managed to establish a dictatorship with surprising speed and thoroughness, outwitting his opponents and partners. Since he was only the chancellor of a coalition government in which the DNVP held a strong majority, the traditional elites were confident they could control the agitator. Skeptics predicted that "the apparition will not last long, since the Nazis and Papen-Hugenberg are bound to clash." But the SA terror against communists and Jews in the streets, abetted by Göring's Prussian police, proved that this was an illusion, because the Nazis refused to respect any legal limits. Intimidated by the outpouring of nationalist propaganda, cowed opponents just disappeared, making a few critical speeches without daring to organize mass resistance or a general strike. During the first weeks Hitler quickly gained the backing of the business community and the army leadership, persuading Hugenberg to agree to the dissolution of the Reichstag. Under the cover of a "national revolution," the Nazis set out to establish a racial dictatorship.[30]

The Reichstag fire presented Hitler with an unplanned chance to expand his power by suspending civil rights and arresting the Marxist opposition. On the evening of February 27, 1933, the young Dutchman Martinus van der Lubbe set fire to the parliament building in protest against the lawless violence of the Nazis. Although nobody believed the charge of "Communist arson," the quickly assembled Nazi leaders recognized the act as "a heaven sent, uniquely favorable opportunity" that allowed them to issue an emergency decree "For the Protection of People and the State," which simply abolished all civil rights enshrined in the Weimar Constitution. Göring not only "had the entire Communist Reichstag caucus, but hundreds, even thousands of Communists arrested all over Germany" as well as many Social Democrats and trade-union leaders locked up and the leftist press forbidden. As a result of such repression, the election campaign turned into a highly uneven contest. When the votes were counted on March 5, the Nazis had won 43.9 percent and the DNVP 8 percent, barely constituting an absolute majority.[31]

The Enabling Act of March 23 formalized the National Socialist dictatorship, since with it the Reichstag practically abolished itself. Encouraged by the "inordinate electoral victory," the Nazi terror in the streets continued: "Nobody breathes freely any more, no free word is spoken or printed." Yet Hitler also strove for a veneer of legality, meeting with the aged president Hindenburg in the garrison church in Potsdam in order to symbolize the reconciliation between Prussian traditions and the radical volkish movement. Moreover, he harangued the Reichstag in a bid to change the constitution fundamentally by adding the seemingly innocuous clause that "laws of the Reich may also be enacted by the government of the Reich." Though the Nazis promised to leave the Reichstag and the president untouched, this stipulation transferred legislative power to the cabinet, thereby legalizing dictatorial rule. In order to preserve the Catholic Church, the Center Party joined the Nazis and the Conservatives in the decisive vote of 441 to 94. Only the Social Democrat Otto Wels had the courage to warn against the disastrous abolition of humanity, freedom, and justice.[32]

A mixture of violent intimidation and voluntary cooperation Nazified German society during the spring and summer of 1933 in a process called *Gleichschaltung*, or coordination. First, the national government seized control of the various states by appointing Reich governors. Then all opposition parties reluctantly dissolved themselves, since they had become superfluous. Moreover, the once-mighty trade unions fell into line by joining the celebration of May 1 as "day of national labor." At the same time, the universities purged themselves of democrats, Marxists, and Jewish professors, while professional associations expelled Jews, forced liberals to resign, and elected nationalist officers who transformed their organizations into Nazi auxiliaries. Even the Catholic Church signed a treaty with the Third Reich in which the Vatican permitted the dissolution of its civic associations so as to preserve its religious core. Typical of rising nationalist intolerance was the "action against the un-German spirit," organized by the Nazi Student League, which burned thousands of books by leftist authors like Karl Marx, Heinrich Heine, Sigmund Freud, Bertolt Brecht, and Kurt Tucholsky.[33]

The bloodbath of June 30, 1934, resolved growing tensions between the continuation of the revolution and the pursuit of respectability. Though Hitler sympathized with the radicalism of many followers who beat up Marxists and harassed Jews, killing about five hundred to six hundred people, expediency also dictated that he maintain the goodwill of the established elites and of foreign observers who abhorred violence. One problem was the head of the SA, Captain Ernst Röhm, who flirted with a "second revolution," hoping to initiate an egalitarian nationalism. A second challenge was the increasing skepticism of the conservatives, voiced by Vice-Chancellor Papen's warning against trying to live in "a continuous revolution." When the army chiefs protested against turning the SA into a national militia, Hitler was forced to act. In a "night and fog" action he had the SA leadership executed, while the Gestapo killed conservatives like Schleicher and old rivals like Strasser. Claiming to have stamped out a treasonous conspiracy, Hitler combined his office with the presidency upon Hindenburg's death in August.[34] Now he finally reigned supreme.

The so-called Röhm putsch sent a chilling message to the populace that nobody would be safe in the Third Reich. Among the party faithful the wanton butchery enhanced the Führer myth, because he had elevated himself above all competitors. But the murders struck terror into the hearts of NSDAP opponents such as Heinrich Brüning, Willy Brandt, and Walter Ulbricht, who sought refuge in exile. From abroad they tried to set up resistance organizations, waiting in vain for the Third Reich's collapse. The book burning forced writers like

Bertolt Brecht and Thomas Mann to leave the country, while the university purge expelled eminent scientists such as Albert Einstein and historians like Hajo Holborn, costing Germany some of the best and brightest minds. In the Reich citizens had to learn how to mouth Nazi slogans so that they would not be reported by the countless zealots enforcing nationalist conformity. While the administrative, business, and military elites still enjoyed some latitude, and writers might choose "inner exile," ordinary democrats, socialists and communists were constantly afraid that denunciation would land them in a concentration camp.[35]

Hitler's dictatorship rested not only on repression but also on popular gratitude for the economic recovery, for which he claimed credit. Economists still dispute which of the policies actually worked, but it is undeniable that full employment returned fairly rapidly. In grapeshot fashion, the Nazis launched numerous measures, ranging from public works such as building the high-speed *Autobahnen* to subsidies for regular construction and reviving industrial investment. Wages initially remained frozen, but the return to work raised the living standards of households that had barely survived the depression and made the Führer popular. Propaganda coups like the production of an affordable radio set, called *Volksempfänger*, and the design of a people's car, named *Volkswagen*, also improved the mood. Most importantly, the massive, initially clandestine, and then open rearmament program, financed by public borrowing with the infamous "Mefo bills of exchange," contributed to the recovery.[36] Though not accepting all facets of National Socialist ideology, many Germans nonetheless appreciated the improvement in their material circumstances.

The final consolidation of Nazi power therefore turned out to be surprisingly easy. With the opposition exiled, fragmented, or driven underground, Hitler replaced the last members of the conservative elites during 1937 and 1938 with hardly a ripple. In short order he fired the financial wizard Hjalmar Schacht, pushed out the army leaders Werner von Blomberg and Werner von Fritsch on trumped-up sexual charges, and dismissed the experienced diplomat Konstantin von Neurath. Their replacements—Walter Funk, Wilhelm Keitel, Walther von Brauchitsch, and Joachim von Ribbentrop—were second-rate NSDAP cronies. Skeptics of National Socialist policy like General Ludwig Beck and Leipzig Mayor Carl Goerdeler remained isolated, since the domestic recovery and foreign-policy successes supported Hitler's leadership claims. Only emigrants like Sebastian Haffner could warn the world of the Nazis' murderous character, hoping to undermine their power from without. Inside the Third Reich, intrepid communists and socialists tried to organize an underground resistance, but their efforts yielded few tangible results.[37] Within half a decade, Hitler had established a single-party dictatorship.

THE PEOPLE'S COMMUNITY

Chief among the soft stabilizers of National Socialist rule was the rhetoric of the "people's community," implemented by an array of subsidiary organizations. Even Germans otherwise opposed to National Socialism shared the aspiration of national harmony superseding class, religious, and regional differences. Goebbels' propaganda ministry ceaselessly put out slogans like "community comes before the individual" and "one people, one Reich, one Führer" to emphasize national unity, expressed symbolically by eating a simple dish of stew one day a week. No doubt reality never quite lived up to this image of classless solidarity, but the constant repetition of the ideological mantra had some effect, even on the industrial working class. The young were especially susceptible to appeals to idealism, since the need to belong to the *Volksgemeinschaft* was drummed into their heads in school and the Hitler Youth. Of course, such an inclusive vision presupposed the exclusion of Marxists, Jews, and other enemies. Reports from the security service and Socialist exiles agree that the national community was both a propaganda claim and a partial reality.[38]

One integrative force was the Nazi Party, which celebrated its unity in the annual rallies held in the medieval city of Nuremberg. Memorialized by Leni Riefenstahl's seductive reportage in *Triumph of the Will*, these congresses were carefully orchestrated, quasi-religious ceremonies in which the Führer and his followers of all ranks, from gauleiter to *Blockwart*, reaffirmed their emotional bond. Arriving by airplane, Hitler would drive in an open Mercedes through the jubilant throng to the parade ground. There tens of thousands of eager members of the party, Hitler Youth, and other National Socialist organizations would welcome him with roaring applause, while the paramilitary units of the SA, SS, and the Reich Labor Service paraded before his reviewing stand. Excitement would reach a fever pitch when the leader himself finally addressed the eager crowd with his strange intonation, exaggerated gestures, and magnetic intensity. The gigantic spectacle was designed to renew the members' dedication to the Nazi cause, strike terror into the hearts of their enemies, and impress the outside world with the resurgence of German power.[39]

The German Labor Front (DAF), which absorbed the socialist, Catholic and liberal trade unions, was another important organization supporting the people's community. The DAF was the creation of Robert Ley, a corrupt alcoholic and philanderer, who strove to fashion an empire of control and service for labor. The revised charter of 1934 envisaged a "factory community," headed by employers as plant leaders with whom workers as followers were to work harmoniously. Instead of being divided along the collar line, manual laborers and office employees were now to cooperate for the common good. To create a hardworking and docile labor force, the German Labor Front not only suppressed any lingering remnants of Marxist agitation but also offered a series of positive incentives. One policy was the campaign for Beauty of Work, which tried to render the workplace more attractive. Another effort was the Strength through Joy program that offered affordable leisure activities and subsidized vacations so as to restore energy.[40] Though some workers resented being muzzled, many also took advantage of such National Socialist initiatives.

The Hitler Youth sought to carry the nationalist and racist message to the younger generation through exciting programs and ceaseless propaganda. Begun as the youth group of the party, it gradually expanded into a compulsory association for children aged ten to fourteen (Jungvolk) as well as boys (HJ) and girls (BdM) aged fourteen to eighteen. In part, its campfire romanticism was a remnant of the volkish Youth Movement, which had made hiking and camping popular around the turn of the century. In part, its paramilitary preparation was a copy of the forbidden Boy Scouts that drilled the young in discipline and prepared them to fight through adventurous war games. Starting with only a few hundred in the early 1920s, the HJ mushroomed under Baldur von Schirach to eight million members by 1940. The heavy demands on time created continual conflicts between the HJ and the schools whenever teachers insisted on their academic subjects rather than glorifying physical athleticism and mental toughness. While a few rebels like the "swing youths" resisted, the Hitler Youth succeeded in indoctrinating many young Germans.[41]

In spite of Nazi misogyny, women were also an important part of the "people's community," since their biological and social contributions assured the continuation of the master race. On the one hand, the uniformed columns of the National Socialist movement rested on male bonding, with a sexist sense of superiority. To ease unemployment, women were forbidden to be "double earners" with state-employed husbands and were limited to 10 percent of the enrollment in the universities, relegating them to the sphere of "children, kitchen, and church." On the other hand, Hitler's eugenic obsession with declining birthrates made their reproductive role more significant, creating a female realm that extended the family into society. Under Gertrud Scholz-Klink the National Socialist Frauenschaft built up a Nazi women's league that engaged in "administering welfare services, educational programs, leisure activities, ideological indoctrination and consumer organization." Contrary to movie clichés, the Nazis were not prudish about sex, as long as it did not involve miscegenation.[42] Hence women were not just victims but also important accomplices of the regime.

The most popular National Socialist organization was the Nazi People's Welfare (NSV), which strove "to augment and further the vital healthy forces of the German people." The NSV started as an effort to help indigent party members but gradually developed into the central welfare association of the Third Reich, growing to seventeen million members by 1943. Led by Erich Hilgenfeldt, it replaced the socialist *Arbeiterwohlfahrt*, directed state welfare efforts, and coordinated the religious charities and the Red Cross. Concretely, the NSV campaigned to improve the situation of "mother and child" by providing counseling and trying to assure sufficient nutrition and health through better hygiene and subsidized vacations. Organizationally separate but propagandistically related were the huge annual collections for the Winter Aid program that appealed to the public for donations so as to assure heat and food during the coldest months of the year. At the same time the NSV also policed the exclusion of racial inferiors and "asocial" persons from reproduction. The goal was less to help needy individuals than to create a healthy body politic.[43]

Excluded from the imagined "national community" were the political and racial enemies who bore the full brunt of Nazi terror. Hitler's unbounded hatred for the Left made the "elimination of the Marxist poison from our national body" a top priority, leading to the arrest, imprisonment, and death of known communists. Based on Nazi anti-Semitic racism, the persecution of the Jews was another important goal, leading to a legal purge of public service, the universities, and the professions as well as a grassroots boycott of Jewish business. Victor Klemperer felt as if he were back in medieval Romania: "An animal is not more outlawed and hunted." Since the Gestapo had fewer than twenty thousand agents, it relied on ordinary Germans to denounce their communist or Jewish neighbors as "enemies of the people." Improving on initial SA efforts, the SS constructed three chief concentration camps (*Konzentrationslager*, or KZ) in Dachau, Buchenwald, and Sachsenhausen to contain the increasing number of those who might "endanger state security."[44] By discrimination, repression, and violence the Nazis created a countercommunity of political and racial victims in the KZ.

Those Germans who were not ostracized generally developed positive feelings about the Nazi project of a *Volksgemeinschaft*, since it contrasted with the divisiveness of the Weimar Republic. One important reason was the notable improvement of living conditions that made even workers consider the prewar years of the Third Reich as "a good time." Another cause was the tangible benefit derived from some programs, which made the compulsion and indoctrination of the National Socialist organizations bearable. The 1936 Olympics in Berlin, which showcased Nazi accomplishments through new facilities like the one-hundred-thousand-spectator *Olympiastadion* and impressed even foreign visitors, were a case in point. In spite of the controversy over the barring of Jewish athletes and Jesse Owens' spectacular victories, the Germans could point proudly to their winning a total of eighty-nine medals, which was considerably more than the fifty-six of their closest competitor, the United States.[45] With such a mixture of control, incentive, and propaganda, Hitler succeeded in constructing a dictatorship of the right, resting largely on popular acclaim.

ANTIMODERN MODERNITY

The debate about the relationship between National Socialism and modernity remains sterile as long as it continues to be moralizing rather than analytical. By conflating progress with the advancement of democracy, western intellectuals have tended to denounce fascism as a reactionary "utopian antimodernism." No doubt many pronouncements by Hitler, Rosenberg, and other National Socialist ideologues demonstrate that the Nazis rejected the Enlightenment heritage in its capitalist, democratic, and Soviet communist guise while railing against "modernist" culture. Yet when the adjective "modern" designates a historical period, then National Socialism clearly does belong to the recent era. And if one concedes with sociological theory that development involves "multiple modernities," which include not only remnants of tradition but also rejections of some of its features, then the Nazi project can be understood as "proposing a radical alternative to liberal and socialist visions of what form modernity ideally should take."[46] Even if it may seem paradoxical, the National Socialists did develop their own version of modernity.

Hitler and his henchmen denounced the destructive consequences of democratic and Marxist modernization in the strongest terms. They hated democracy because it "produced an abortion of filth and fire," had stabbed the German army in the back, accepted the humiliating Versailles Treaty, and sapped the nation's strength by pacifism. Similarly they loathed the "Marxist world pest" as "spiritual degeneration" because Soviet Russia was ruled by "blood-stained criminals" who were "the dregs of humanity" and had "extirpated millions of educated people out of sheer blood lust." The Nazis reserved their harshest invective for the common source of both rival ideologies: "the Jewish drive for world conquest" and "racial bastardization" that threatened the country by denationalizing it and polluting its blood.[47] Such emphatic rejection of the western and Soviet rivals, however, called for the elaboration of a superior alternative that would not just escape into a mythical volkish past but revitalize the nation in the future. Designed to heal the wounds made by its competitors, this warped National Socialist vision might be called "organic modernity."

Above all, the Nazi project of an alternative future sought to reconcile man with the machine in a creative union, redounding to national glory. For all his disparagement of experimental art, Hitler also used the adjective "modern" when talking positively about science and technology in the service of a revitalized nation.[48] Making only halfhearted efforts to return the country to a rural past, the Nazi leadership was fascinated by novel machines such as radio transmitters, jet airplanes, and ballistic rockets and sponsored the first experiments with television. In spite of their anti-intellectualism, National Socialist leaders also supported research in weapons development for the sake of rearmament, racial science as basis for cleansing the national body, and volkish history in order to construct claims for expansionist foreign policy. In gigantic building projects like the canopy of the Tempelhof airport, Third Reich planners used "modern" techniques of steel and concrete construction while covering the facade with limestone. In designing the network of *Autobahnen*, they similarly tried to fit highways harmoniously into the landscape.[49]

A central aspect of organic modernity was the biopolitical effort to purify and strengthen the *Volkskörper* in a gigantic social-engineering project. This "biologization of the social" stemmed from the writings of physicians and culture critics who decried the nervousness, disease, degeneration, and declining birthrates attributed to the unhealthy lifestyle of the city. The Nazis embraced this international eugenic critique and pushed it in a racist direction by trying to combat negative tendencies such as inherited diseases through sterilization and prohibiting "inferior stock" such as asocial individuals and Jews from reproducing with Aryans. At the same time, they also sought to foster positive reproduction through programs like the SS *Lebensborn*, increasing marital and extramarital birthrates through incentives, reducing infant mortality, and curing venereal disease through improved preventive healthcare.[50] Unconstrained by civil rights, such state intervention into individual sexuality, gender roles, and public health was a modern project of social medicalization, supported by academic research that acted in the name of racial purity and national strength.

Finally, the charismatic reshaping of German politics also aimed at providing a new and harmonious form of right-wing politics appropriate to the mass age. The Führer's power rested not only on the propagation of the Hitler cult but also on a mystical willingness of a large part of the population to suspend criticism and accept his leadership. By "working toward the Führer," the party acted as a crucial intermediary, since it interpreted his will and implemented his dictates, often even before they were announced. The state and its bureaucratic organs had no choice but to accept the direction of the Nazi Party and to play a subservient role. The individual citizen was compelled to trust the leader and, whenever called upon, applaud his decisions while trying to achieve the goals suggested by his superior wisdom. Prohibition of dissent and persecution of opposition were justified by eliminating the factionalism and squabbling of parliamentary debate. From Goebbels' propaganda to Himmler's SS henchmen, the structure and instruments of governance constituted a thoroughly modern consensus machine.[51]

Chapter 11

UNLEASHING WORLD WAR II

Munich Conference, 1938. At the Munich train station: *Left to right, front,* Joachim von Ribbentrop; *behind and right,* Heinrich Himmler; *front,* Edouard Daladier; *behind and right,* Hermann Göring; *front,* Neville Chamberlain; *behind and right,* Galeazzo Ciano; *front,* Hitler talking to Mussolini. *Source*: bpk, Berlin / Bayerische Staatsbibliothek, Munich / Heinrich Hoffman / Art Resource, NY.

On November 5, 1937, Hitler secretly harangued the military leadership in the Chancellery about the need for "the acquisition of greater living space." Calling this rant "his last will and testament," the Nazi dictator argued that neither autarchy nor increased participation in the world economy would be able to "secure and … preserve the racial community." Since the country would not provide enough food for a growing population, "Germany's problem could be solved only by the use of force, and this was never without attendant risk." This bald statement signaled his decision in favor of another war. The question was no longer if, but rather when and how. "It was his unalterable determination to solve Germany's problem of space at the latest by 1943–45," since rearmament would reach a peak and he might not live much longer. Overriding the objections of his military advisers, the Führer proposed defeating Czechoslovakia and Austria with "lightning speed" so as to keep other countries on the sidelines.[1] These notes, taken by his adjutant Friedrich Hoßbach, would serve as proof of Hitler's will to war at the Nuremberg Tribunal.

In contrast to the acrimonious debate about the responsibility for World War I, there is therefore no such discussion concerning the origins of the Second World War. The evidence is overwhelming that Nazi Germany was the driving force that precipitated Europe into another bloodbath far more horrible than the first, if that were possible. The few revisionist attempts to absolve the Third Reich or shift the blame to mistakes in western diplomacy have been dismissed as irrelevant or worse.[2] While the ideological expansionism of Soviet dictator Stalin and the inflexibility of Polish foreign minister Józef Beck contributed to the breakdown of peace, they played a minor role compared to Hitler's initiative. In part, the Nazi dictator followed a series of intentional steps, seeking to overthrow the restrictions of Versailles, restore Germany's continental position, and conquer living space in the East. In part, this aggressiveness was also a function of the polycratic dynamism of the Nazi system, in which various groups egged one another on and ambitious rearmament needed a victorious war to finance its cost.[3]

Since the French were preoccupied with the Popular Front, the responsibility of dealing with Hitler fell upon the shoulders of British prime minister Neville Chamberlain. Born in 1869 into a leading political family, he received a public-school education and later went into business. Entering politics for the Conservative Party at the age of forty-nine, he quickly became minister of health and then chancellor of the exchequer, pushing for imperial tariff preferences and fiscal austerity in response to the Great Depression. When Stanley Baldwin resigned in 1937, the industrious and decent Chamberlain became prime minister, hoping to concentrate on further domestic reforms. But a resurgent Nazi Germany forced him to turn to foreign affairs, where he searched for a way to avoid war by accommodating Berlin's justified complaints.[4] His hands were largely tied because opinion was deeply split between authoritarian conservatives and leftist pacifists who wanted to preserve peace on one side, and nationalists like Winston Churchill along with antifascist Labour intellectuals on the other who warned that only firmness could prevent the coming storm.

Chamberlain's lack of success with a conciliatory policy raises the controversial issue of appeasement in dealing with the expansionism of a rogue regime. Since concessions did not stop Hitler's drive, resisting aggression became the key lesson of the Munich Conference during the Cold War and beyond, invoked by statesmen from Harry S. Truman to George W. Bush. However, a simplistic application of this analogy has sometimes also precipitated war when further negotiations might have preserved peace and succeeded in bringing about change without human cost. The British Left has been correct in discrediting appeasement by pointing to the fascist sympathies of some its leading advocates, but the conservative counterargument that compromises with Hitler rectified shortcomings of the Versailles Treaty or bought time for rearmament of the Royal Air Force cannot be so easily dismissed.[5] While appeasement toward the more limited ambitions of Imperial Germany might have prevented World War I, toward the Third Reich's racist expansionism it indubitably hastened the Second World War.

Liberal internationalism failed to maintain interwar peace because of the inherent contradictions of the "Paris system" and the ruthlessness of its Nazi and Soviet antagonists. The imposing edifice of the League of Nations reflected the increase in international cooperation due to the advance of communication, trade, and investment. But the consecration of "population politics" at the peace conference also made nation-states more powerful in pursuing their self-interest and in seeking to homogenize their populations, creating endless minority conflicts. Rejecting the western vision of peaceful interaction, both communism and fascism pursued their own antiliberal versions of an international order, since they saw the world in terms of class or race struggle.[6] In seeking to advance their competing ideological projects, they eagerly exploited the internal divisions of the democracies on the issue of war as well as the flaws of the peace settlement that created widespread ethnic resentment. When the West proved too weak to stop aggression, Hitler and Stalin colluded in unleashing another world war.

RETREAT FROM INTERNATIONALISM

Starting with high hopes of fostering Christian brotherhood and international law, the League of Nations was an admirable effort to create a modern international system. In effect, the Geneva institution was an Anglo-French attempt to formalize cooperation so as to avoid the recurrence of war by amicable resolution of conflicts. While the United States refusal to participate and the exclusion of Germany and Russia limited the League's purpose to enforcing the peace treaties, its Assembly did provide a new forum for debating contested issues that gave international public opinion a chance to be heard. Moreover, the growth of an institutional infrastructure from its secretary-general to the Council, Permanent Secretariat, and various commissions introduced a new player capable of articulating the general interest as opposed to national agendas. Finally, with the eventual accession of Weimar Germany and even of the Soviet Union, this international organization included all major European countries. Though consisting of sovereign nation-states, the League had a chance to strengthen cooperation and prove its worth by its actual performance.[7]

The League's primary aim was the provision of "collective security" through the resolution of international conflicts short of war. Its mediating commissions scored some successes in disputes over boundaries after World War I, for example, leaving the Aaland Islands with Finland, partitioning Upper Silesia according to a referendum between Germany and Poland, and ceding the port of Memel to Lithuania. Similarly, in conflicts between smaller countries such as Greece and Bulgaria, a stern warning from Geneva was sufficient to end the hostilities in 1925. The high-water mark of its pacifist internationalism was the Briand-Kellogg Pact in 1928, which insisted that countries "condemn recourse to war for the solution of international controversies" and "renounce it as an instrument of national policy." The only exceptions were acts of self-defense or the use of military force in support of League of Nations decisions. Intended as an effort to prevent war by international law, the treaty was signed by some forty states, but as the declaration of intent lacked an enforcement mechanism, it largely remained "a pious aspiration."[8]

At the same time, the League also provided an array of useful services to the international community by addressing problems that cut across national lines. One important associated institution was the International Labor Organization, headed by the socialist Albert Thomas, which campaigned for the improvement of working conditions through the introduction of the eight-hour workday and the abolition of child labor. The League's Health Organization fought epidemic diseases such as typhus, leprosy, malaria, and yellow fever. In response to several million displaced persons, the League also created a Commission for Refugees, headed by the explorer Fridtjof Nansen, which repatriated thousands and issued passports to stateless persons. Similarly, the League established a Committee on Intellectual Cooperation under the author Henri Bergson so as to improve the situation of intellectuals, facilitate international exchanges, and protect the rights of authors. Efforts such as the campaigns against opium and slavery made the League appear helpful for addressing problems that transcended national frontiers.[9]

In spite of promising beginnings, a series of policy failures, such as the lack of protection for minorities and the authorization of population transfers, undercut liberal internationalism and eroded the League's authority. The Paris treaties' creation of eight new East-Central European states produced twenty-five million citizens of ethnicities or religions different from the majority in those countries, all clamoring for their own rights. The new national states set out to "nationalize" their minorities by enforcing their own language and expelling unwanted ethnicities. Focusing on individuals, the peace discussions failed to agree on a general safeguard for different groups owing to the objections of British imperialists. A series of minority treaties with individual countries like Poland called for full protection of all inhabitants "without distinction of birth, nationality, language, race or religion." But the lack of any concrete enforcement mechanism and the acquiescence in the forced removal of unwanted populations like the Greeks from Turkey vitiated the force of these treaties.[10] Fierce disputes over the treatment of ethnic minorities therefore poisoned international relations thereafter.

Another disastrous setback was the lack of agreement on disarmament, which triggered a new arms race culminating in World War II. Not just war-weary pacifists but also hardheaded bankers wanted to reduce the numbers of costly arms, seeking to outlaw weapons of attack. The losers of the First World War also called for military equality through a reduction of armaments among the victors, since the German Reichswehr was limited to one hundred thousand men, while Czechoslovakia alone had an army five times that size! In 1932 a World Disarmament Conference convened in Geneva to debate how to reduce the stockpiles of arms and balance forces on the continent. Afraid of a revival of German power, the French adamantly refused to give up any of their advantage in military strength, while the British and the Americans also balked at reducing their superiority in sea and air power. The deliberations produced many pious speeches such as the McDonald Plan but no agreement on specific action. Frustrated by such equivocations, the Japanese and the Germans withdrew their delegates, turning to rearmament instead.[11]

The international effort to reverse the disruption of trade during the Great Depression also failed disastrously at the World Economic Conference in London during the summer of 1933. As a result of domestic pressures and divergent analyses, the advice of the preparatory committee of experts against tariffs, quotas, unbalanced budgets, and inflation was simply ignored. While the French insisted on maintaining the gold standard, the British hoped to reflate their economy through devaluation. The incoming Roosevelt administration in the United States sent mixed signals, in favor of going off the gold standard and proposing tariff reduction but refusing to compromise on inter-Allied debts. In spite of the common interest in reviving international exchanges, FDR ultimately refused currency stabilization, preferring to stimulate American business through an easy-money policy. Sir Herbert Samuel, leader of the British liberals, concluded pessimistically: "The crux of the whole problem was that no proposal could be made in the interests of the whole of Europe which was not against the individual interests of almost every country in Europe."[12]

The first violation of its Covenant by a major power showed that the League could muster only moral condemnation and remained essentially powerless in the face of aggression. On September 18, 1931, hotheaded Japanese officers bombed a railroad track near Mukden, using the incident as a pretext to occupy Manchuria, an important resource-rich province in northeastern China. With its forces in retreat, the Kuomintang government of China protested the invasion to the League of Nations, which condemned the Japanese action by a vote of forty-two to one. In order to get to the bottom of the conflicting claims regarding the incident, the League sent a commission, headed by Victor Bulwer-Lytton, which reported that the Japanese were, indeed, responsible for the affair so as to erect their own puppet state, named Manchukuo. Though the United States refused to recognize the new regime, Britain and France, preoccupied with their domestic troubles, were loath to send an expeditionary force to the Far East on behalf of the League. Critics therefore concluded caustically that "in the face of the first serious challenge" the League of Nations had capitulated ignominiously.[13]

Underway before the Nazi seizure of power, the retreat from liberal internationalism had psychological, structural, and practical causes. The high hopes for an era of peace that animated the first postwar years recorded some initial successes but gave way to disappointment when the League proved incapable of dealing with a series of intractable problems. It did not help that the Covenant required unanimity in the Council in order to take action; also lack of taxation and of military force limited the League to being an intergovernmental body without the essential attributes of state power. Initially the new institution was too much tied to the enforcement of a contested peace to endear it to the losers, since it seemed to follow a double standard in applying the principle of self-determination. Ultimately, however, it was the preservation of national sovereignty that allowed the major powers to reject League of Nations interference in their own affairs. The accumulation of such unresolved issues undermined the effort to create a peaceful international order by discrediting the effectiveness of the League.[14]

REVISIONISM AND REARMAMENT

Undoubtedly, it was Adolf Hitler who pushed a reluctant Europe toward a new war in order to reverse the German defeat. Only four days after seizing power, he informed the army and navy chiefs of his aims during a dinner: First, he would attempt to undo the political division of the country by eliminating Marxism and get the nation ready for "the idea that only a struggle can save us." Second, he wanted to "battle against Versailles," throwing off the restrictions of this onerous peace. Third, he proposed to reinvigorate the economy by rural settlement rather than by increasing trade. Fourth, he promised to build up the armed forces in order to be able to fight for his ultimate goal—"the conquest of living space in the East and its ruthless Germanization." From the beginning of his chancellorship, Hitler therefore pursued a long-range design aimed at successively repudiating Versailles, gaining hegemony over Europe, and conquering racial living space in the East.[15] Even if this chilling vision need not be interpreted as a fixed plan, it suggested an ambition that went far beyond merely revising the terms of a punitive peace.

Unaware of the radicalism of Nazi aspirations, Germany's European neighbors failed to react decisively to the establishment of Hitler's dictatorship. Though a stream of negative news about the persecution of communists and Jews issued from Berlin, many observers assumed that things would calm down again and the conservative majority of the cabinet would rein in the SA. Forced to read the rambling *Mein Kampf*, the ambassadors sent alarmist reports back to their capitals, but most political leaders in Paris and London were unwilling to take such warnings seriously. At home, they were faced with large leftist peace movements that wanted to avoid another war at all costs, while some conservatives admired the vigor with which Mussolini and Hitler claimed to have restored domestic order. The French clung to a defense of Versailles, the British were willing to allow some treaty revision in order to rectify its mistakes, and the Soviets intended to continue their cooperation with Berlin. Since their separate concerns prevented joint action, the moment passed when an incipient catastrophe might easily have been averted.[16]

To shield his secret rearmament, the Führer pursued a duplicitous policy that heightened the confusion among his international antagonists. While he piously announced that "the new Germany desires bread and peace," he continued to spring diplomatic surprises on Europe that tested the limits of what his neighbors would tolerate. During the summer of 1933, Hitler went along with Mussolini's plan of a four-power directory of Britain, France, Germany, and Italy to negotiate a peaceful treaty revision. But after the failure of disarmament talks he left the League of Nations in October and had the repudiation of collective security overwhelmingly ratified by a plebiscite. To calm international suspicion of his territorial aims, he then surprisingly signed a Non-Aggression Pact with Poland in January 1934. But during the following summer he shocked the world by supporting a Nazi putsch in Vienna, which failed because Mussolini upheld Austrian independence by sending a couple of divisions to the Brenner Pass.[17] Still charmed by Hitler's personal magnetism, foreign visitors like the historian Arnold Toynbee tended to ignore his growing bellicosity.

During these diplomatic maneuvers, Hitler forced the pace of rearmament in order to gain parity with the victors and to acquire the military means for future expansion. Going beyond the defensive weapons allowed by Versailles, the Wehrmacht secretly developed a broad array of offensive capabilities by designing, testing, and producing new tanks, mobile artillery, dive bombers, and quiet submarines. At the same time, Nazi Germany circumvented the personnel restrictions by paramilitary training in the Reich Labor Service and Hitler Youth, although Hitler refused to merge the SA with the regular army. The surprisingly positive outcome of the Saar plebiscite in January 1935 further emboldened the dictator, since 91 percent voted for a return to Germany in spite of all the leftist warnings against National Socialist repression. Tired of having to conceal what most journalists already knew, Hitler announced the reintroduction of the draft in order to increase the Wehrmacht to thirty-six divisions with 550,000 men and to construct a modern air force.[18] This repudiation of the military clauses of Versailles in March 1935 was an open challenge to the international community.

Shocked by this flouting of restrictions, the western powers finally made some effort to contain the Nazi threat. French prime minister Pierre Laval persuaded the British and Italians to meet at Stresa and to condemn "the unilateral violation" of international treaties. At the same time Russia, worried about Berlin's anticommunist rhetoric, joined the League of Nations, signing a treaty with France. But this emerging front crumbled when Great Britain chose to conclude a separate agreement with Germany, limiting the latter's naval buildup to 35 percent of the size of the Royal Navy. Searching for imperial glory, Mussolini moreover invaded Ethiopia, unleashing air bombardments and artillery barrages upon the hapless Abyssinians. International opinion was horrified by the cruelty of modern warfare and demanded sanctions against Italy. When it leaked out that Foreign Secretary Samuel Hoare and Laval had offered Mussolini Ethiopian territory in order to keep him on their side against

Map 5. German expansion: territorial changes, 1935–39. Adapted from Militärgeschichtliches Forschungsamt, Potsdam, Germany.

Germany, collective security was further discredited. Hence the chance for anti-Nazi cooperation evaporated.[19]

Sure of the disunity of his foes and conscious of growing military might, Hitler then undertook another gamble, essential to his preparation for war. Still bogged down in Abyssinia, Italy had inched closer to Germany, while Britain seemed unwilling to defend the peace settlement. On March 7, 1936, Hitler therefore sent twenty-two thousand Wehrmacht troops into the demilitarized zone along the Rhine and Ruhr with orders to retreat should they encounter resistance.

The Rhineland Germans were jubilant, but the French were appalled, frantically trying to decide whether to use force to defend the glacis in front of their eastern frontier. In the end Hitler's pacifist smoke screen, promising future cooperation and even mentioning the possibility of a return to the League, managed to draw both Paris and London into negotiations. Due to the timidity of the western powers, who looked impotent, the German gamble of reoccupying the Ruhr Basin, the forge of war, succeeded. Now a gloating Führer, convinced of his own infallibility, once again turned peaceful and welcomed the world to the Berlin Olympics.[20] Another opportunity to stop aggression was lost.

Learning that western protests could be ignored, Nazi Germany began to prepare openly for another bid for European hegemony. By proclaiming a Four Year Plan under Göring in September 1936, Hitler tried to lay the foundation of a largely autarchic war economy, rapidly increasing the production of essential strategic goods: synthetic oil, aluminum, nitrogen, and the like. At the same time he forced the pace of rearmament, initiating a vast expansion of all branches of the Wehrmacht that increased military expenditures from 746 to 17.247 million reichsmark between 1933 and 1938. Defaulting on foreign debt, the financial wizard Hjalmar Schacht devised an ingenious method of borrowing vast sums with industrial exchange bills that would need to be repaid—by the defeated enemies after a victorious war. The resurgence of Germany produced a diplomatic realignment by the proclamation of the Berlin-Rome Axis, with Italy as junior partner, and the signing of the Anti-Comintern Pact, including Tokyo, in late 1936.[21] With their elaborate security system lying in shambles, the western powers had no choice but to rearm frantically as well.

The Spanish Civil War further clouded the international situation, since it exposed the weakness of the western democracies. On July 17, 1936, a collection of Spanish monarchists, Catholics, and Falangists initiated a military coup against the socialist government of the Second Republic. For prestige reasons Mussolini came to the aid of the nationalist leader General Franco, while Hitler also sent his Condor Legion and some Luftwaffe dive-bombers in order to test the new weapons systems in combat conditions. Helped by leftist volunteers of the International Brigades, the Republicans fought back, creating a protracted and bloody struggle in which white terror against workers was matched by red atrocities against priests and landowners. Horrified, the western powers pushed the League of Nations to proclaim a nonintervention policy, which prohibited weapons deliveries to the republic and forced it to rely on aid from the Soviets, who ignored the ban. After three interminable years, Franco was finally victorious.[22] Both fascists and communists gained prestige in this ideological struggle that inspired many writers and intellectuals.

Thus, within a relatively short time, Hitler succeeded in realizing his initial goal of escaping the restrictions imposed by the Versailles Treaty. Combining protestations of peace with surprise coups, the Nazi dictator in effect reaped what Weimar democrats had sown, namely, an adjustment of peace conditions in Germany's favor. The West loudly protested his repeated violations of international treaties—but remained unwilling to enforce their observance by a creditable threat to go to war, since most of their citizens wanted to preserve peace. Most Nazi opponents also underestimated the radicalism of the Nazi danger and failed to understand that its racist expansionism would attempt to shatter the European balance-of-power system altogether. The French hunkered down in a defensive Maginot Line mentality, while the British were ready to make concessions to assuage their feelings of guilt over the harshness of the peace treaty. Meanwhile the Americans were hiding in isolationism. Appealing to western guilt about the severity of Versailles, the Führer as modern dictator could exploit with impunity the western reluctance to go to war.[23]

THE *ANSCHLUSS* OF AUSTRIA

The first application of Germany's resurgent power was the annexation of Austria, its southeastern neighbor. For centuries Vienna had been the center of the Holy Roman Empire of the German Nation, only to be excluded from the creation of a German national state by military defeat at the hands of Prussia in 1866. Moreover, the country was Hitler's birthplace, cultural home, and political environment during his formative youth. The German-speaking Habsburg core lands only became an independent state through the St. Germain peace treaty in 1919 in order to deny the provinces to a defeated Germany. In Vienna a strong pan-German movement clamored for union with Berlin, and most of the political parties in Austria did not really want to be in a country of their own with an outsized capital, supported only by western loans. But the victorious Allies disregarded a parliamentary vote for union with Germany in 1919 and once again during the last years of the Weimar Republic.[24] The argument for joining Austria to Germany therefore seemed like a liberal claim of national self-determination that was hard to refute.

The collapse of Austrian democracy weakened the case for continued independence by disappointing the country's western sponsors. Even beyond the vocal pan-German minority, Austrian politics were deeply polarized by ideology. On the extreme right were the *Heimwehren* under Prince von Starhemberg, local militias who resented the loss of Südtirol (Alto Adige) to Italy. In the center-right stood the Christian Social Party, led by Ignaz Seipel, which propagated a Catholic conservatism and drew its support from the smaller towns and the countryside. The left-center was occupied by a vigorous Socialist movement, directed by Otto Bauer, which represented the urban working class and transformed Vienna into a model of public housing and other social services. Further left was a small group of Communists. After becoming chancellor in 1932, the Christian Social Engelbert Dollfuss unleashed the military and police, defeating the Socialists and their Republikanische Schutzbund militia in bloody street battles. Then he set up an Austro-fascist state, a clerical-authoritarian-corporate regime following the Italian example.[25]

Because of the crudeness of its methods, the initial Nazi attempt to incorporate Austria into the Third Reich nonetheless failed disastrously. The growth of Hitler's NSDAP and its auxiliaries also attracted sympathizers in Austria, mostly from the ranks of the disgruntled middle class and from among the German nationalists. On July 25, 1934, 154 Austrian SS men stormed the chancellery and shot the diminutive dictator Dollfuss (a.k.a. "Millimetternich"), letting him bleed to death. Though the Nazis managed to seize the national radio transmitter and the railroad station, the Austrian army and police suppressed the uprising in the provinces. Angered that his Viennese protégé had been assassinated, Mussolini sent several divisions to the Austrian frontier to warn Hitler against a takeover. As a result the defenders of independence rallied around Kurt Schuschnigg, the new chancellor, and Nazi Germany was forced to back down. Though the Führer lost face by having to deny any involvement, it was only the Duce's threat that preserved Austria, since the western powers failed to react.[26]

Undeterred by this setback, Hitler continued to pursue the goal of uniting all ethnic Germans through a mixture of subversive action and diplomatic pressure. In order to hurt Austria's economy, Berlin imposed a minimum fee of one thousand marks to deter potential tourists from vacationing there. Though forbidden, the Austrian branch of the Nazi Party continued to grow, supplementing its propaganda with terrorist attacks. The Socialists also agitated in the underground against the government, because they were still smarting from their military suppression. Finally, as a result of his Ethiopian and Spanish adventures, Mussolini became so dependent on German support that he could no longer guarantee Vienna's independence. Acting on this increasing pressure, in July 1936 Hitler managed to compel Schuschnigg to sign a friendship treaty, which proclaimed that Austria was part of the German nation, amnestied seventeen thousand Nazis, relegalized the party, and accepted National Socialist representatives into the government. Although Schuschnigg sought to defend a "free and German Austria," his domestic and international support crumbled.[27]

By early 1938 Hitler felt diplomatically and militarily strong enough to dare forcing the actual annexation of Austria. Ambassador Papen persuaded Schuschnigg to visit Hitler at his spectacular mountain retreat outside Berchtesgaden in mid-February. Though initially polite, the Führer accused Austria of having betrayed its century-old German roots and blustered that his patience had run out. When the Austrian chancellor refused to buckle, Hitler threatened to send the Wehrmacht across the frontier unless the local Nazi leader Arthur Seyß-Inquart was made minister of the interior and put in charge of the police. Bereft of diplomatic support and harassed by Nazi fanatics from below, Schuschnigg finally capitulated and signed the Berchtesgaden agreement. But when he returned to Vienna and received some domestic reassurances, he hit upon the desperate stratagem of calling a plebiscite for "a free and German, independent and social, Christian and united Austria." Appealing to all political groups, this was a formula to which virtually all patriotic citizens were bound to agree.[28]

Livid over this unexpected resistance, Hitler abandoned all caution and resorted to outright threats. While he demanded the cancellation of the plebiscite, to which a cowed Schuschnigg finally agreed, Göring called for the Austrian chancellor to resign in order to have Seyß-Inquart take control of the government. Concurrently the local Nazis staged an uprising, overthrew the legitimate authorities, and raised swastika flags on official buildings. Hitler then had the Austrian party leaders issue a call for assistance from the Reich to which he eagerly responded, since British ambassador Neville Henderson had signaled that London would not interfere. On March 12, 1938, sixty-five thousand Wehrmacht troops and police officers with heavy weapons invaded Austria. Though some of the tanks broke down, the Germans encountered no resistance but rather were welcomed by cheering crowds. A few days later in Vienna an overjoyed Hitler proclaimed "the entry of my home into the German Reich." After a barrage of nationalist propaganda, over 99 percent of Austrian voters ratified the incorporation into Germany with a plebiscite.[29]

The pan-German enthusiasm began to cool, however, when the Austrians realized what it was like to live under a Nazi dictatorship. The Law on the Reunification of Austria with the German Reich formalized the incorporation that made Austrians full citizens, with all rights and obligations. Almost immediately, the Nazi police arrested 72,000 patriots, leftists, and Jews as enemies so as to gain control. Around 700,000 Austrians, that is, 8 percent of the population, nonetheless joined the NSDAP out of conviction or opportunism. But about 250,000 Jews, deprived of their civil rights overnight, bore the full brunt of the discriminatory Nuremberg laws. Eventually the new *Ostmark* (Eastern March) was subdivided into seven administrative districts, called *Gaue*, and Vienna lost its privileged position as the capital. For the strained German economy, Austria was a valuable prize, increasing output by 8 percent and adding crucial iron ore deposits. The *Anschluss* was therefore a curious mixture of voluntary accession and compulsory occupation.[30] This success reinforced Hitler's conviction that the West would protest but ultimately refuse to fight.

THE MUNICH CONFERENCE

The next Nazi target was Czechoslovakia, but it was a much harder nut to crack. The former Habsburg lands of Bohemia, Moravia, and Slovakia were strategically important, since their geographic position pointed them like a dagger at the heart of the Third Reich. During the First World War Tomáš Masaryk and Edvard Beneš so ably represented the burgeoning Czech national movement in the West that their extensive claims for the creation of an independent western Slavic state were accepted at the Paris Peace Conference. The new country of Czechoslovakia, which combined the Czech and Slovak populations, was the only functioning democracy that had survived in East-Central Europe into the 1930s. Moreover, it was linked to France by the treaty system known as the "Little Entente." Finally, Czechoslovakia had an industrial economy and a sizable army, supported by well-designed border fortifications.[31] The new state had only one weakness, which proved fatal—after the *Anschluss* it was surrounded on three sides by territories of the Third Reich, ranging from Silesia, via Saxony and Bavaria, all the way to Austria.

The lever Hitler used to unhinge Prague was a 2.5-million-strong minority called Sudeten Germans, after a local mountain range. After 1918, German speakers, who had been the ruling class of the Habsburg realm, suddenly found themselves at the mercy of a much larger Slavic population that held political power. Many Sudeten Germans, some of whom also lived dispersed in cities of the interior, resented now having to learn the Czech language, while witnessing the diminution of the medieval German university of Prague by the expansion of a rival Czech institution. As a result, many ethnic Germans rallied in self-defense around the Sudeten German Party, which captured forty-four of the sixty-six German seats in the Czech parliament, with the rest going to Social Democrats and Communists. When their leader Konrad Henlein came to Berlin for support, Hitler realized that he could destabilize Czechoslovakia by always asking for more ethnic autonomy than Prague could concede. In response to rumors of an imminent invasion, the Czech government mobilized its troops in May 1938, forcing a furious Führer to deny such plans.[32]

During mid-September Hitler increased diplomatic pressure, precipitating a severe international crisis by preparing for war. In a bellicose speech at the Nuremberg party rally, he proclaimed the goal of bringing the Sudeten Germans "home into the Reich," asking openly for the cession of their territories. While the French were willing to fight and the Russians mobilized some of their forces, British prime minister Neville Chamberlain sought to placate the Nazi leader by addressing his justified grievances. First he met Hitler in Obersalzberg, where both agreed on the need for self-determination of the Sudeten Germans to take place through a plebiscite, much to the horror of the Prague government. Cleverly the Führer also got the Hungarians and Poles to raise territorial claims against the Czechs. Instead of being grateful, Hitler then increased his demands during a second meeting in Bad Godesberg and issued an ultimatum, calling for immediate transfer of the disputed territories. In spite of this affront, Chamberlain remained willing to go the extra mile in order to preserve peace, calling on Mussolini to mediate.[33]

Improvised on September 29, the infamous Munich Conference was a last-ditch effort by the British government to avoid the impending war. It was a classic meeting of European great powers—on one side France and the United Kingdom as victors of World War I, and on the other Italy and Germany as the chief revisionists. The United States had excluded itself because of its isolationism, while Russia was not invited, still being considered too subversive. Moreover, the representatives of the Czechoslovak government were left to worry in the lobby without being consulted about which parts of their country were being bartered away. At the decisive moment, Mussolini pulled a proposal out of his pocket that had been prepared by Ernst von Weizsäcker of the German Foreign Ministry: The German army would immediately occupy the Sudeten areas, the signatories would guarantee the rest of the Czechoslovak state, and Germany would be prepared to sign a friendship treaty with Great Britain. When he learned of the terms, Czech president Beneš was devastated, but he accepted the agreement as the lesser of two evils.[34]

The Munich Conference was the high-water mark of appeasement since it represented a sincere effort to avoid another world war by meeting legitimate German grievances. Seeing it as a courageous attempt to banish the shadow of Versailles from international affairs, the British public was immensely relieved when Chamberlain announced back in London that he had won "peace for our time." Even Daladier was welcomed enthusiastically at Orly airport on returning to Paris. But the steep price for the temporary respite was the partial dismemberment of one crucial client state of the peace treaty. The attempt at conciliation did buy the western powers another year to complete their rearmament, and when war proved inevitable it banished all public doubts about its necessity. But the surrender cost them the support of the Czechs and the Soviet Union, which appeared to be willing to fight. Though he got all he claimed, Hitler was nonetheless furious that the war he wanted had been snatched from him at the last minute. The next time around, he would not be induced to compromise.[35]

Germany's March 1939 annexation of the rest of the Czech lands destroyed the illusion that the Nazi beast might be tamed. After the occupation of the Sudeten regions, Hitler ordered preparations for a police action to take over the Czech state's Slavic core, rendered defenseless by the loss of its frontier fortifications. Meanwhile the Poles and Hungarians also rose to the bait, taking Teschen and Slovak border areas in the First Vienna Award, a sequel to the Munich Agreement that further partitioned Czechoslovakia. Capitalizing on internal tensions between Czechs and Slovaks, on March 14, 1939, Hitler pressured Prime Minister Josef Tiso to declare the independence of a Slovak rump state—under German military control. A day later he bludgeoned aging Czech president Emil Hacha, with the threat of bombarding Prague, into "laying the fate of the people and the country into the trustworthy hands of the Führer of the German Reich." The creation of the Czech protectorate was an important strategic gain, since it shortened German frontiers and provided new fuel to an overheated Nazi economy. On March 23 Hitler added insult to injury by ordering German troops from East Prussia to occupy Memel, a port city contested between Germany and Lithuania.[36]

Marking the transition from self-determination to outright expansion, the Prague coup triggered shock and outrage in the western capitals. Even Italian foreign minister Ciano called Hitler "unreliable and false," while British ambassador Henderson concluded that "with the occupation of the rest of Czechoslovakia Hitler has crossed the Rubicon." Prime Minister Chamberlain felt personally offended and warned Hitler against renewed aggression, a more truculent stance long advocated by his conservative rival Winston Churchill. Moreover, the British government increased the pace of rearmament, ordering thousands of additional Spitfire airplanes and, in close consultation with the French, drafted a diplomatic response. When Mussolini was foolish enough to invade Albania over Easter, Britain and France in a diplomatic revolution unilaterally guaranteed Poland, Romania, Greece, and Turkey against fascist aggression.[37] Due to an excess of cynicism Hitler never quite understood that by abandoning any pretext of ethnic self-determination, he undercut the continuation of appeasement and forced the western countries to fight.

Tangled up in ideological disputes, the "Munich analogy" has often been misused from the Cold War to Iraq because it rests on a simplistic understanding of appeasement. The rapid failure of the promised peace has made the Munich Agreement seem like a craven surrender to dictatorial bullying. Though honorable in intent, British policy was based on a fundamental misreading of Hitler's racist imperialism that ignored his anti-Semitic and anticommunist persecution and treated him as if he were a democratic statesman, that is, a reasonable leader interested in a limited correction of the peace treaty.[38] The lesson of Munich is, therefore, not the neoconservative call to reject negotiation and compromise outright, but rather the need to make sure of the other party's character: If one is dealing with a decent opponent who is willing to obey international law and respect treaty obligations, then concessions may well avoid unnecessary armed conflict. But if one confronts a murderous dictator, intent on self-aggrandizement, then it would be wiser to stand firm. Neither toughness nor conciliation is correct in itself—the choice always depends on the context.

THE DANZIG DISPUTE

Ironically, Nazi Germany had a better case in the Danzig quarrel, which triggered World War II, than with the annexation of Czechoslovakia. In order to give the new Polish state access to the sea, the Versailles Treaty had stripped the mixed-ethnic provinces of Poznań and West Prussia from Germany and added them to Poland (a.k.a. the "Polish Corridor"), thus separating East Prussia from the rest of Germany as an enclave surrounded by Polish and Lithuanian territory. Though over 90 percent German-speaking, the port of Danzig at the mouth of the Vistula River was turned into a "free city" administered by the League of Nations. Nonetheless, Poland built a more up-to-date deepwater harbor of its own, away from the river delta, in Gdynia. But in a 1922 plebiscite the Slavic population of Masuria voted to stay with East Prussia. This complicated arrangement might have worked under feudalism, but during modern nationalism it proved a source of continual conflict. Seizing on local discontent, Hitler called for a return of Danzig to Germany and the construction of an extraterritorial rail and road link through the Polish Corridor to East Prussia.[39] Both of these demands appeared reasonable enough in themselves.

Seeing these claims as an attack on its regained sovereignty, the Polish government refused any concessions so as not to become Nazi Germany's junior partner. Led by the fiercely nationalist General Piłsudski, Poland had barely survived a war with the Soviets in the East and become rather authoritarian in structure. Unsure of their loyalty, the Poles sought to nationalize the diverse German, Jewish, and Ukrainian minorities, expelling those Germans from Poznań and West Prussia who were not willing to accept Polish rule and citizenship. The proud foreign minister Józef Beck overestimated his country's military strength and put too much faith in Anglo-French assurances that these allies would help defend Poland against a German attack. Though frantically preparing for the coming conflict, western generals were instead pursuing a defensive strategy in which Poland would bear the brunt of the attack without receiving much active help. After Hitler abrogated the Non-Aggression Pact, negotiations between Berlin and Warsaw stalled, since both sides suspected each other of acting in bad faith.[40]

While countries armed at a furious pace, in the spring of 1939 European diplomats still sought to stave off the inevitable or at least improve their chances during the fight. Considering his rearmament sufficient and fearing that the other powers would eventually catch up, Hitler in early April authorized his general staff to plan for an attack on Poland, called Operation White, on September 1, 1939. Though doubtful of Rome's military value, Berlin also signed an alliance with Fascist Italy, called the "Pact of Steel," with much ballyhoo on May 22. Concurrently the western powers were negotiating with the Soviet Union for an antifascist defensive alliance on the basis of Soviet foreign affairs commissar Maxim Litvinov's appeals to collective security. But the Polish government feared that Red Army troops, once in their country, might not leave again and so refused the necessary permission for their transit to the German frontier. Hastened by Soviet suspicion of western capitalism, the breakdown of the Anglo-French talks with Russia removed the threat of reviving the World War I constellation, which Hitler had vowed to avoid.[41]

On August 24 a stunned world learned instead that Nazi Germany and the Soviet Union had signed a Treaty of Non-Aggression. After years of anticommunist propaganda in Germany and of antifascist agitation by the Comintern, the agreement between the ideological enemies shocked not only their followers but also neutral commentators who had considered such a move unlikely. Yet there were a number of reasons for its conclusion: In the Rapallo Treaty of 1922 the Weimar Republic was the first state to recognize the Soviet

Union and to establish economic relations as well as clandestine military cooperation. Moreover, on-again, off-again trade talks between Berlin and Moscow during the spring had presented Stalin with an alternative, should the Anglo-French negotiations for an alliance with the Soviet Union break down. An agreement with the Germans would reduce Russia's diplomatic isolation and give the Red Army time to recover from Stalin's purge of its officer corps. For the Nazis such a deal would avoid the danger of a two-front war. Finally, the grudging respect between the dictators also made the Hitler-Stalin pact seem more reliable.[42]

Unknown at the time was the treaty's secret annex, which divided Eastern Europe from the Baltic to the Black Sea into spheres of influence between Nazi Germany and the Soviet Union. Until the 1980s the Soviets denied its existence, since it showed that Stalin was as ruthless as Hitler in despoiling his neighbors. This proposed territorial division was highly favorable to Moscow, showing that German foreign minister Joachim Ribbentrop had to offer considerable incentives to Vyacheslav Molotov, his Soviet counterpart, in order to conclude the bargain: Finland, Estonia, Latvia, and Bessarabia were assigned to the Soviets, restoring much of the tsarist domain lost in the Treaty of Brest-Litovsk. In its fourth division, Poland was to be split between both countries along the rivers Narev, Vistula, and San. West-central Poland and Lithuania, plus Vilna, were to be controlled by Nazi Germany, recovering the territory of the Second Reich and advancing somewhat in the direction of the border strip claimed by annexationists during World War I.[43] This cynical bargain not only obliterated *Zwischeneuropa* as a buffer zone between the German and Russian empires; it also removed the last obstacle to the outbreak of the war.

In the final countdown various mediators desperately tried to prevent another war—but their efforts foundered on Hitler's determination for aggression. Within Germany officers around former chief of staff Ludwig Beck and diplomats around State Secretary Weizsäcker did not want to fight, and even some Nazi leaders like Hermann Göring were unenthusiastic. Unlike its equivocation in 1914, the British government sternly warned Berlin to be under no illusions, while French diplomats hoped to deter the Germans by signaling that they would stand firm. Intent on keeping England out of the war, Hitler clumsily made a sweeping offer to respect the integrity of the British Empire, guarantee the western frontiers, and limit German armaments if London would give him a free hand in the East. But Britain signed a formal alliance with Poland on August 25, while Mussolini evaded his treaty commitment by asking for excessive military help from Berlin. Since the Warsaw government continued to refuse tangible concessions, all-last minute mediation efforts by the Italians, the Swedes, and the pope eventually failed.[44]

In the early morning hours of September 1, 1939, German radio tersely announced the start of hostilities with Poland: "Since 4:45, we are returning fire." The aging cruiser *Schleswig-Holstein* had shelled Polish ammunition dumps at the mouth of Danzig's harbor, while SS men in Polish uniforms had faked a raid on the German radio transmitter in Upper Silesia, leaving one prisoner dead, to convince a reluctant nation that it had to respond to a foreign attack. But few were fooled by such a transparent propaganda ploy, since it was all too clear that Hitler had been pushing for war. In contrast to 1914, hardly anyone in Europe was elated; instead the mood was somber and apprehensive, since the memory of the First World War and the development of new weapons suggested that the second conflict would be more deadly yet. Even when fighting had started, there were some last-ditch efforts to contain it, but the diplomats had no chance. After two days of agonizing debates, Britain and France issued ultimatums to Germany and declared war on September 3.[45] There was no doubt that Hitler's expansionism had plunged Europe once again into war.

The second bloodbath within one generation was not completely inevitable. French field marshal Foch called the interwar period a "twenty-year armistice," suggesting that both world wars might just have been one long Thirty Years' War. But that evaluation is too cynical, since two decades of peace did present real chances to avoid a recurrence of fighting through the League of Nations. First, it took the collapse of German democracy to give a fanatic like Hitler the opportunity to seize power and push for a renewed struggle to reverse the verdict of Versailles. Second, Allied statesmen reacted with an unfortunate sequence of toughness against Weimar, appeasement to ethnic revisionism, and finally steadfast resistance against Nazi expansionism, which actually encouraged the aggression that it was designed to prevent. At the same time American isolationism, Soviet opportunism, and Polish self-importance played into the Nazis' hands. While the blame for the catastrophe must clearly lie on Hitler's shoulders, the misguided efforts of his opponents contributed to the failure of stopping his murderous designs.[46]

RIVAL INTERNATIONALISMS

Unfortunately the transformation of foreign relations during the interwar era failed to create a modern international order strong enough to maintain peace against fascist revisionism. In contrast to the nineteenth century, the development of mass politics, be they democratic or dictatorial, greatly expanded the concerned public and gave more weight to popular feelings. At the same time inflation and depression added economic interests advocated by powerful pressure groups to the mix, complicating agreement on contentious issues. Through mass-circulation newspapers, radio broadcasts by statesmen, and newsreels shown before movies, the media began to intrude to an unprecedented degree, emphasizing outward appearances and symbolic gestures over rational assessments. Finally, wartime propaganda and the ensuing competition of Wilson, Lenin, and Mussolini made international relations highly ideological, dedicated to advancing their competing worldviews. Each of these competing modernities had its own method of diplomacy and vision of international order that rendered peaceful cooperation difficult.[47]

The democratic conception of the West envisaged peace through compromise, institutionalized in international law and the League of Nations. Following the imperative of economic liberalism, it advocated free trade rather than tariff barriers in order to benefit participants by reducing the cost of exchanges. Domestically, this view supported various forms of self-government, ranging from constitutional monarchy to participatory democracy. Internationally, it championed self-determination through the dissolution of the Central and

East European empires into independent nation-states. In order to resolve potential conflicts, this system would be stabilized by an institutional form of collective security through the League of Nations, designed to resolve conflicts through arbitration and prevent the outbreak of another large-scale war in Europe. No doubt this Wilsonian dream was an appealing vision that inspired hopes in a war-torn continent.[48] Unfortunately, it was also somewhat compromised by being tied to American economic interests and the maintenance of what the losers considered to be an inequitable peace treaty.

The chief competitor of the western democratic system among intellectuals and the working class was socialist internationalism, enshrined in the Second International and the Moscow-dominated Comintern. This vision grew out of Marxist critiques of nationalism and appeals to solidarity among the dispossessed of the world. Its focus on the class struggle as vehicle for human progress made it more conflictual, since it suggested the necessity of fighting against the oppressors with organization and strikes before reaching the utopia of a classless society, where all contradictions would be non-antagonistic. The domestic method for getting to this blissful state was highly contested between champions of revolution to overthrow the capitalist bourgeoisie or evolution through trade unions and parliamentary representation. Internationally, socialism proclaimed its adherence to peace, even if that meant being ready to use force to defend the dictatorship of the proletariat. Attractive as it was for many thinkers and labor organizers, this conception was, however, tainted by Stalin's ruthlessness and paranoia, undercutting the Soviet promise of a federation of nationalities.[49]

Surprisingly enough, the radical nationalists also had their own conception of international relations, even if they were unable to work together effectively. The authoritarian regimes and fascist movements were intensely nationalist, believing in the primacy of their own ethnicity and doing everything to advance the power and glory of their nation. Domestically, they rejected both moribund parliamentarianism as decrepit and revolutionary socialism as divisive. Consequently, such hypernationalists saw the world in terms of social Darwinism as a struggle for supremacy in which only their own superior race could win against various "degenerates" such as Jews and Slavs. Concretely that meant contempt for international cooperation and an instrumental view of treaties, which were to be observed only as long as they served the nationalists' own interests. Exploiting the ethnic contradictions of the Paris treaty system, the Nazis envisaged the targets of their racist expansionism primarily in the weak, newly created states in the East.[50] For the fascists war was not an evil to be avoided but a necessity to be glorified.

The clash of such fundamentally incompatible visions of international order rendered well-intentioned efforts to preserve peace through accommodation futile. By promoting self-government at home and free trade abroad, liberal internationalism primarily served the national interests of the British and Americans. But in order to realize the peaceful potential of cooperation, the League of Nations had to develop beyond defense of the Versailles settlement, thereby alienating France. The socialist vision of revolutionary internationalism also inspired postwar hopes for peace, but its revolutionary militancy and dictatorial practice in the Soviet Union rendered it internationally more unreliable than the pacific version of moderate social democracy in Scandinavia. Ultimately it was, however, the hypernationalism of the Nazis that plunged the world into another war by cleverly employing the language of self-determination to justify the *Anschluss* of Austria and the Sudetenland before showing its true colors as racist imperialism. The horrible specter of Nazi enslavement left other Europeans no choice but to fight.

Chapter 12

AXIS CONQUEST

Blitzkrieg in France, 1940. *Source*: Bundesarchiv Militärarchiv.

During a brief ceremony on June 21, 1940, elated Wehrmacht leaders handed the defeated French generals the terms of the armistice on the western front. To "right an old wrong" Hitler chose the same railroad car in the forest near Compiègne in which the Germans had surrendered to General Foch on November 11, 1918. In the presence of the Führer, General Wilhelm Keitel explained to General Charles Huntziger the severe conditions designed to "prevent a resumption of the fighting," to facilitate "the continuation of the war against Britain," and to lay the basis for a hegemonic peace. Three-fifths of France would be occupied, all refugees had to be turned over to the Germans, the war costs were to be borne by the losers, captured soldiers would remain POWs until the end of the fighting, and the rest of the country was to become a *zone libre*, governed from Vichy. Having at last reversed the defeat of World War I, Hitler seemed "afire with scorn, anger, hate, revenge, triumph." After a futile attempt to soften these terms, the humiliated French envoys had no choice but to accept the "very hard conditions" the next day.[1]

Surprised by the speed and thoroughness of the victories, neutral observers attributed the German success to a novel conception of mobile warfare, called *Blitzkrieg*. Witnessing "Hitler's amazing, awe-inspiring armed forces in action," U.S. journalist Louis P. Lochner explained this innovative method as a revolutionary combination of "terrorizing Stukas" in the air and "speedy mechanized units" on the ground, striking "quick as lightning." Frustrated by the immobility of the trenches, military theorists from Captain Basil H. Liddell Hart to Colonel Charles de Gaulle had tried to develop a new way of breaking through enemy lines that proved particularly attractive to the German command, since it restored the initiative to the attacker. In practice, this kind of warfare consisted of air reconnaissance and dive-bombing, followed by massed tank assaults and supported by mobile infantry to cut into an enemy's rear with pincer movements, encircle defenders, and force their surrender.[2] Because the Wehrmacht had only a limited number of tanks and mechanized infantry divisions, it was their concentration that made the sudden attacks successful.

Astonished by its effect, later analysts have emphasized the military and political advantages that the blitzkrieg synthesis offered to the expansionist Nazi dictatorship. Short attacks allowed the only partly rearmed Wehrmacht to concentrate its mechanized forces on a few sectors of the front at a time. The speed of the strikes tended to isolate a particular victim, preventing what Hitler wanted to avoid—a two-front war. At the same time, slashing supply lines, sowing confusion, and discouraging defenders in order to hasten their surrender led to the capture of large numbers of troops and matériel. Winning such limited wars against one opponent after another made it possible to husband scarce resources of oil and steel, exploiting the defeated enemies in order to carry the war to the next victim. Finally, the relentlessness of the advance, magnified by weekly newsreels, also generated a sense of Nazi momentum that enticed hesitant allies like Italy to join the fray.[3] Though critics have started to question the novelty and singularity of the lightning-war strategy, they have hardly been able to deny its surprising success.[4]

The general who contributed most to this innovative form of warfare was the tank commander Heinz Guderian. Born into a West Prussian officer's family in 1888, he was educated in military academies and served as an intelligence specialist in World War I. Put in charge of a transportation unit, he closely studied the potential of armor from the writings of British theorists like J.F.C. Fuller. Convinced that the use of tanks as spearheads made it possible to exploit the storm-trooper breakthroughs, he argued for building an independent *Panzer* force. Hitler endorsed the idea of creating armored divisions so as to overcome the static nature of trench warfare. In actual combat Guderian proved to be a daring commander, leading the Wehrmacht's breaking of the French lines at Sedan and the subsequent push to the Channel coast. His insistence on electronic communication between tanks, their massed and mobile use, and close dive-bomber support proved to be a magic formula. While Guderian was a model professional officer, he was also a moral failure by not questioning the criminal use to which his talents were put.[5]

The key to the Wehrmacht's initial success was therefore the creativity and ruthlessness with which it exploited the offensive possibilities offered by "modernest warfare" [sic]. As all belligerents had similar weapons at their disposal, their tactical use by the Germans made the difference by creating an image of invincible force bearing down on its hapless opponents. Since every major combatant possessed an advanced industrial economy, Germany's only advantage was its head start in war production, which devoured more than 20 percent of its GNP in 1939. Because all countries involved in the war also controlled extensive media such as radio stations, newsreels, and newspapers, the Nazis led merely in the shamelessness of their propaganda toward their own and other audiences, which seemed credible at least for a while. Another important difference lay in the inhumanity of the National Socialist dictatorship, which had no compunction about killing for political ends whether it involved enemy soldiers or civilians. But overall, it was the marshaling of the most modern weaponry and tactics for attacking purposes that contributed to the Nazis' early victories.[6]

INITIAL INVASIONS

Nazi Germany's "flagrant, inexcusable, unprovoked act of aggression" against Poland was immediately recognized as the start of another world war. In contrast to the widespread enthusiasm of 1914, American journalist William S. Shirer found "no excitement, no hurrahs, no cheering, no throwing of flowers, no war fever, no war hysteria" in Berlin.[7] Remembering the terrible suffering of the Great War, most adults were reluctant to obey the call to arms and willing to do their duty only when they had no other choice. Pointing to the Third Reich's inferiority in population size, economic production, number of troops, amount of weapons, and reliability of allies, commentators expected the combined Polish, French, and British armies, supported by their colonies and dominions, to win the renewed contest, if only they were really willing to fight. In contrast, Nazi Germany could merely count on novel weapons technology, militarized attitudes, well-trained soldiers, daring leadership, and ruthless policies. The speed and extent of the Wehrmacht victories during the first half of the war therefore caught everyone by surprise.

Though the number of soldiers on either side looked about even, the Polish campaign turned out to be amazingly brief and successful

■ Germany and annexations	▢ Operational areas	
■ German occupied areas	▢ Neutrals/states not officially parties to the war	
▨ Italy and Italian occupied	▨ Grand Alliance	
▨ Axis Allies and their occupations	▨ Territories occupied by the Western Allies	

Map 6. Nazi domination: Europe at the beginning of December 1941. Adapted from
Militärgeschichtliches Forschungsamt, Potsdam, Germany.

for the German army. Part of the reason was the technical superiority of its newer airplanes, tanks, and artillery; another part was its favorable strategic position, which had the defenders surrounded on three sides. Wehrmacht corps under Generals Fedor von Bock, Walther von Reichenau, and Gerd von Runstedt attacked from East Prussia, Silesia, and Slovakia, while the Polish generals sought to stop them at the frontier and withdrew to a better defensive position behind the Vistula and the Bug only when it was too late. Though Poland's western Allies declared war, they failed to mount a relief offensive, while the Soviet Union attacked from the rear on September 17 as well. Polish soldiers fought gallantly, but they were clearly outgunned, with one army after another surrounded and compelled to surrender. When Lublin fell on September 23 and Warsaw capitulated five days later, effective resistance ceased. While the German invaders also incurred substantial losses, within four weeks they had conquered their eastern neighbor.[8]

The invasion of Poland also marked the beginning of the ideological war of annihilation, still somewhat uncoordinated but nonetheless deadly. Owing to the swiftness of the German advance, overrun Polish defenders continued to fight behind the lines, precipitating brutal antipartisan reprisals. When "liberated" by the Wehrmacht, ethnic Germans also retaliated by killing more than fifteen thousand Poles in revenge for Polish atrocities against about one-third that number of *Volksdeutsche*. The mass murders committed by seven SS *Einsatzgruppen*, mobile killing units charged by Heinrich Himmler with subduing hostile elements in the rear of the advancing troops as well as with the eradication of the intelligentsia in order to break the back of Polish nationalism, were even more systematic. The twenty-seven hundred men of these roving death brigades rounded up and shot more than fifty thousand professors, doctors, lawyers, teachers, priests, and political leaders—an unprecedented bloodbath designed to reduce the Poles to the role of passive serfs. At the same time the ethnic Germans, military, and SS also killed about seven thousand Jews, hastening the flight of survivors to Soviet-occupied territory.[9]

In contrast, the western front remained strangely quiet for the first seven months, leading pundits to wonder about "the phony war." While the Allies vastly outnumbered German forces by about a hundred divisions to twenty-three, they failed to assault the *Westwall* except for one diversionary attack at the Saar. Instead, the French huddled behind their own fortified border, called the Maginot Line, which stretched all the way from the Swiss to the Belgian border. Building on the experience of trench warfare, it was a marvel of concrete bunkers, artillery turrets, machine-gun nests, and anti-tank obstacles, supported by underground troop quarters, ammunition dumps, and communication lines. Waiting for the buildup of the British army and trusting in the power of the Royal Navy, General Maurice Gamelin decided to keep three-quarters of a million soldiers in a defensive posture, hoping to defeat the Germans by letting them attack. But not even the impatient Hitler was foolhardy enough to comply, since he first needed to resupply his troops. Since there was little action in the West, the Poles received no aid, and the opportunity for defeating the Nazis passed.[10]

On November 30, 1939, the Soviet Union surprisingly attacked Finland, starting what is commonly called the Winter War. Behind the cover of the German invasion of Poland, Moscow had been collecting its spoils as stipulated in the Nazi-Soviet Pact by occupying eastern Poland, trying to regain its tsarist possessions. Though formerly a Russian province, independent Finland resisted Stalin's attack by fighting valiantly and ingeniously in the snow. Western public opinion was outraged by this communist aggression, struggling for some way to help the Finns, while Berlin stood passively by in order not to offend its eastern partner. Vastly underestimating the resolve of Finnish resistance, the Soviets bungled the initial offensives against the Mannerheim Line and lost about two hundred thousand men. But eventually their numerical superiority and heavier weapons began to tell, allowing the reinforced Red Army to breach the defensive positions. Compelled to surrender over 10 percent of their Karelian territory and 30 percent of their economic resources in the peace treaty of March 15, 1940, the courageous Finns nonetheless managed to preserve their independence.[11]

Before risking a western offensive, Hitler decided to strike in Scandinavia, invading Denmark and Norway on April 9, 1940. The German navy had long coveted North Atlantic bases like Trondheim that would allow it to break out of the confines of the North Sea. At the same time the iron ore from the Swedish mountain at Luela, crucial for the war effort, had to be shipped through Narvik when the Baltic Sea was frozen during the winter. British destroyers were intent on interdicting this supply line, forcing German freighters to maneuver within the three-mile line of the coast—the farthest extent of Norway's jurisdiction. Controlling the exit from the Baltic, Denmark merely had the misfortune of being on the way to its northern neighbor. Admiral Erich Raeder was concerned that the Royal Navy would mine the Norwegian coastal waters regardless of neutrality conventions and might even prepare a landing in order to assure itself of that country's "favorable neutrality." Though the operation was a logistical nightmare because of the small size of the German navy, Hitler authorized the gamble, hoping that surprise and the support of Norwegian Nazi leader Vidkun Quisling would carry the day.

The occupation of Norway turned out to be a race between the Royal Navy's laying of mines and the German landing of troops. Encountering little active resistance, the Wehrmacht overran Denmark within six hours on April 9, 1940. With the help of the remaining ships of the Kriegsflotte and heavy air support, between fifteen and twenty thousand German troops—infantry hidden in merchantmen as well as hundreds of paratroopers—landed in Norway as well. Bypassing the superior Royal Navy, the invasion achieved virtually complete surprise and managed to overcome locally fierce resistance, capturing not only the capital Oslo but also the ports of Bergen, Trondheim, and Narvik along the coast. Five days later British forces succeeded in a counterlanding, seeking to rout the entrenched occupiers with larger numbers, since a good part of the German naval forces such as the new cruiser *Blücher* and ten destroyers had been sunk during the invasion. But in the fierce fighting the Wehrmacht troops, supported by some local collaborators, held on, and in early May the British withdrew, abandoning Norway to Nazi rule.[12]

At the end of the first winter of World War II, Hitler could congratulate himself on "a brilliant military performance," even if the main challenge still lay ahead. Assaulting one weaker victim after another with more advanced weapons and greater ruthlessness in fighting, the Nazis had overrun Poland and conquered Denmark and Norway. These initial victories improved the strategic position of the Wehrmacht and the Kriegsflotte in the coming struggle for continental hegemony with bigger foes. But the attack of Poland had also embroiled Germany in a European war with France and Britain, supported by their colonies and dominions. At the same time, Neville Chamberlain resigned as prime minister after the bungling of the Royal Navy in the Norway campaign. This put the more resolute Winston Churchill into 10 Downing Street—who galvanized the nation's fighting spirit with his promise of "blood, toil, tears, and sweat" until Britain achieved "victory at all costs." Finally, with German resources stretched to the breaking point due to losses and economic bottlenecks, France still held out behind the formidable Maginot Line. While the opening victories had created the myth of an irresistible blitzkrieg, the outcome of the war was far from decided.[13]

VICTORY IN THE WEST

The German attack on France on May 10, 1940 was an even bigger gamble than the invasion of Norway, since the western Allies were better prepared and had larger resources. On both sides, recollections of the Great War's stalemate in the trenches led the generals to expect a protracted struggle. Moreover, the strategic situation favored the defense, because the Maginot Line looked impregnable, while the Belgian and Dutch neutrals north of the line were protected by major rivers such as the Rhine, Meuse, and Schelde, which were difficult to cross. Also, in contrast to the prior blitzkrieg victims, the western Allies had a considerably larger number of tanks (4,200 to 3,254), airplanes (4,469 to 3,578), and divisions (151 to 135) at their disposal, not to mention the Royal Navy ships that commanded the sea. Finally, their general staffs had had sufficient time to study the new tactics of the Wehrmacht and to devise countermeasures. Even the Nazi propaganda machine predicted, in typical hyperbole, that the battle would "decide the future of the German nation for the next thousand years."[14] Nonetheless, the Germans were again quickly victorious.

One key reason was the abandonment of the original plan of attack through the Low Countries, which the Allies expected, as it would repeat the thrust of the previous war's Schlieffen Plan. It appeared only logical that the Germans would bypass the Maginot Line and concentrate on sweeping through the less-fortified neutral countries of Holland and Belgium in order to conquer the Channel coast and carry the fight to England. The need to resupply and disagreements among the German planners forced the operation to be postponed successively from fall to spring, while intelligence leaks and the Allies' capture of part of the plans from a staff officer in a downed airplane in Belgium made a fundamental revision necessary. The new strategy, advocated by Erich von Manstein, proposed to launch the assault through the mountainous territory of the Ardennes so as to skirt the French defenses and make "a sickle cut" toward the Channel coast, separating the Low Countries from the Anglo-French forces. This risky alternative restored the element of surprise, since the deceived Allies rushed their main troops to Holland and Belgium to save their client states.[15]

Another cause of the Wehrmacht's success was the speed, size, and firepower of the assault on the Low Countries, which terrorized the defenders and caught them off guard. Paratroopers and glider landings spearheaded the initial attack, seizing many bridges and airfields in spite of some severe losses. The regular ground forces quickly followed, cutting off Holland two days later. When the city of Rotterdam refused to surrender, the Luftwaffe mounted a devastating attack that annihilated the old town and cost many civilian lives. In panic, the Dutch surrendered on May 15, but Queen Wilhelmina went into exile to continue the fight. Belgian resistance lasted just a few days longer. On May 16 General Erich Hoepner's tanks broke through the defenses of the Dyle-Breda position, which had been reinforced by Allied troops. Brussels fell a day later, and on May 28 the surrounded Belgian army surrendered, with King Leopold III going into captivity with his troops. Though the Allies had expected the direction of the assault, they were unable to stop the German steamroller.[16]

Finally, the concentration of superior German force on the main point of attack, compounded by Allied errors, sealed their fate.

Considering the Ardennes "impassable for tanks," the French defended the area at the northern end of the Maginot Line only with inferior strength. Though the narrow roads, deeply cut valleys, and extensive forests created logjams, panzer units succeeded in crossing the Meuse as early as May 14. Sending reinforcements north had left too few armored and infantry divisions to stop the advance, and Gamelin had to admit to an exasperated Winston Churchill that he had no reserves left at all. Though Hitler got increasingly nervous that the overstretched pincers might be cut off, excited tank commanders including Guderian and Erwin Rommel pushed ahead with "reconnaissance in force," wreaking havoc in the Allied rear. In spite of counterattacks by General de Gaulle and the British, the Wehrmacht reached the Channel on May 20, encircling most of the French in Flanders and pinning the British to the coast. Due to the massing of tanks and close air support, Hitler had won another gamble.[17]

Sure of victory, the German leadership then made a major blunder that resulted in the "miracle of Dunkirk," and which still remains somewhat of a puzzle. On May 24 General von Runstedt ordered the German units to stop their pursuit of fleeing British and French, allowing them to construct a defensive perimeter around the one remaining Channel port under their control. No doubt the tank divisions had incurred significant losses, needing to resupply and repair so as to recover from the rapidity of their advance. Moreover, Hermann Göring promised Hitler that the Luftwaffe would deliver the "coup de grace" by bombarding the penned-in enemy—but bad weather kept his bombers on the ground for several decisive days. During this respite the Royal Navy launched a daring rescue operation, requisitioning all manner of craft from battleships to civilian sailboats in order to evacuate 338,226 Allied soldiers to Britain. This resolute action saved the core of the British army and some French units, turning military defeat into a propaganda victory through Churchill's impassioned promise that Britain would never surrender.[18]

The subsequent battle for France rapidly turned into a rout, since the "complete breakdown of French society" prevented the organization of an effective defense. Though the new commander Maxime Weygand decided to hold the line along the World War I trenches of the Somme and Aisne, he lacked sufficient manpower and armor, because he did not dare denude the Maginot Line. On June 5, the Wehrmacht attacked from the northeast with Army Group B striking to the west around Paris and Army Croup A rolling up the eastern defenders in the fortified positions from the rear. After intense fighting, both pincer movements broke through the defensive lines. On June 10 Mussolini, who had been nervously waiting to see which side would win, also invaded France in order to get his share of the spoils. Declared an open city, Paris fell on June 14, and three days later Guderian reached the Swiss frontier, trapping three-quarters of a million French soldiers in the Maginot Line—since their heavy guns could only fire eastward! Having fled to Bordeaux, the dejected French government had no choice but to sue for peace.[19]

Put in force on June 25, the armistice contained severe conditions that divided France and reduced the "free zone" to subservient status in spite of its titular neutrality. As long as the war against Britain lasted, three-fifths of the country would be occupied, while Alsace-Lorraine reverted back to the Reich. The occupation costs were to be borne by the French, and one million POWs would remain imprisoned until the end of the war. The French navy was to be disarmed, but since it had escaped to North Africa, the British sank most of its ships lest they fall into Nazi hands. The new government, established in the spa town of Vichy, would retain a force of one hundred thousand men, exactly what the Weimar Republic had been allowed. In these humiliating circumstances, the rump parliament created a more conservative, Catholic, and authoritarian constitution under the World War I hero Marshal Philippe Pétain. This so-called Vichy government sought to "alleviate the misfortune" of the French nation by collaborating with the victors as much as it had to. This rationale was denounced from London by the Free French leader Charles de Gaulle.[20]

The stunning victory over France cemented Hitler's self-confidence, increased his popularity at home, and fueled hatred abroad. Silencing domestic critics, Nazi propaganda touted the modernity of the military and the Führer's genius as "the greatest commander of all times." Foreign admiration of "the magnificent machine" of the Wehrmacht neglected to point out the considerable losses of 714 tanks and 1,236 airplanes in France, not to mention some forty thousand dead. Though there was less random violence than in the East, during the heat of the fighting German soldiers also committed war crimes, and resistance members as well as Jews soon felt the brunt of Nazi persecution. The success also put much of the raw material and production resources of France at the Reich's disposal, easing some economic strains through exploitation and the requisitioning of slave labor. Strategically, the possession of the Atlantic coast and of the airfields close to the Channel improved the German position in the coming battle with Britain. Drawing Italy into the contest, the fall of France marked Germany's ascendancy over continental Europe.[21]

EXTENDING THE WAR

By rallying Britain to resist, Winston Churchill denied Hitler victory and thereby prolonged the war. Born in 1874 into an aristocratic family of politicians, the unruly young Winston was trained in military school. Multitalented, he tried his hand at journalism but became a controversial Conservative politician, rising to various government offices such as first lord of the Admiralty and chancellor of the exchequer. His rampant imperialism and reactionary views on domestic issues put him into the wilderness in the 1930s, blunting his insistent warnings of the Nazi menace. Only on May 10, 1940, was he chosen as prime minister of the National Union government in order to mobilize the British populace with his unbending will and strengthen the French resolve to fight. Endowed with great oratorical power, he vowed "we shall fight on the beaches, we shall fight on the landing grounds, we shall fight in the fields and in the streets, we shall fight in the hills; we shall never surrender."[22] His close relationship with U.S. president Roosevelt was another asset, as it guaranteed the Lend-Lease help, essential for the island democracy to hold out alone.

In the struggle against Britain, the German navy proved an utter disappointment. The prohibitions of the Versailles Treaty had effectively retarded the development of new battleships, leaving the Kriegsmarine much smaller than the Royal Navy. Though inflicting some damage, its battleships, notably the *Graf Spee* and the *Bismarck*, were quickly scuttled or sunk. Realizing that he could not compete with England in this way, Hitler switched priorities to building submarines in order to mount a counterblockade against merchant shipping. While the infamous U-boats had some success, such as sinking the battleship *Royal Oak* in home waters, they were clearly incapable of controlling the surface of the sea. Outnumbered by the British and heavily damaged in the Norwegian campaign, the German navy simply did not have enough ships left to carry the forty divisions across the Channel that the planners of Operation Sea Lion required for an invasion of Great Britain.[23] In spite of all the investment of money and resources in preparing an amphibious assault, the mere twenty-some miles of water between Calais and Dover ultimately proved an insuperable obstacle.

Between July and October 1940 the Battle of Britain turned into a contest for air superiority, since the German navy would require control of the skies to implement its invasion plans. Technically, the opposing aircraft such as Messerschmitts and Spitfires were roughly equivalent, with the former being faster but the latter more maneuverable. Bombers like the Heinkel 111 and the Junkers 88 needed fighter cover, because their slower speeds made them easy targets. Once again the strategic situation favored defense, since German planes had enough fuel for only about an hour over Britain, whereas shot-down defenders could parachute to safety over their own territory. Moreover, the attackers' range was limited to the southern and central part of the United Kingdom, leaving the airfields and factories in the North out of reach. While German pilots were better trained and used more effective formations, British radar tracking proved superior, allowing a more flexible and instantaneous response due to an early warning of attacks. The ensuing dogfights over Britain therefore became the first battle entirely waged in the air.[24]

Numerically the combat with the Royal Air Force (RAF) was a virtual draw, but this result represented a strategic defeat for the Luftwaffe, since it failed to gain air superiority. After initial success over the Channel, the Germans launched their "eagle attack" in mid-August, trying to destroy radar installations and enemy fighters, but switched thereafter to airfields and airplane factories and finally to civilian targets such as Coventry. Between July 10 and October 31 the RAF lost 544 pilots and 1,547 planes, while the Luftwaffe had about 2,000 crew killed and 1,733 aircraft shot down. The German air force consistently underestimated its opponents and found some of its planes, including the Stukas and twin-engine Messerschmitt 110 fighters, unsuitable. Moreover, neophyte British pilots fought rather bravely, their replacements were trained more rapidly, and factories produced 50 percent more planes than in Germany. By mid-October, it was clear that Göring was unable to fulfill his promises, forcing Hitler to break off the attacks.[25] Mislabeled as "the blitz," the Battle of Britain, against an adversary of equal modernity, was the Nazis' first real defeat.

The Italian entry into the war extended the conflict into North Africa when Mussolini invaded Egypt in mid-September 1940. Hoping to reach the Suez Canal, the fascist forces made some gains against the British, then dug in at Sidi-el-Barrani. But General Archibald Wavell counterattacked so successfully as to dislodge and defeat the invaders, taking 130,000 prisoners. To avoid the loss of the Libyan colony, Hitler came to Mussolini's aid by dispatching the Afrika Korps under the command of Erwin Rommel in January 1941. The German troops succeeded in restabilizing the front, initiating a hit-and-run contest with General Bernard Montgomery called the "desert war." Its daring exploits have become romanticized in fiction, since the protagonists treated each other with a dash of chivalry missing from other battlefields. Rommel eventually captured the port El Tobruk, but the goal of cutting "the life-line of the British Empire," the Suez Canal, continued to elude him. Since Hitler did not believe in African colonies, he put insufficient resources into this campaign, and Islamic uprisings in Syria and Iraq failed to threaten Allied control.[26]

Another Italian blunder pulled the Wehrmacht into the Balkans, although Hitler had not intended to commit troops there, preferring diplomacy instead. On the one hand, Russia occupied the Baltic states, Bessarabia, and northern Bukovina during the French campaign, seeking to convert its sphere of influence into direct control. On the other, Berlin tried to secure its fuel supply by a "weapons for oil treaty" with Romania and by sending troops; Hitler also signed an alliance with Bulgaria and stationed forces there as well. Intent on recapturing the eastern part of the Roman Empire, Mussolini attacked Greece with massive force on October 28, 1940. But spirited defense and British help pushed the Italian invaders back into Albania. In early April 1941 a putsch overthrew the Belgrade government since it seemed to be too pro-German, abrogated its treaty commitments, and sought help from the Soviet Union. Though Berlin had so far tried to mediate territorial disputes on the Balkans, local conflicts and growing tensions between the big powers precipitated Hitler's impromptu decision to secure his southern flank by military force.[27]

On April 6, 1941, the Wehrmacht attacked Yugoslavia and Greece from bases in Austria, Hungary, Bulgaria, and Romania. Although both countries fought valiantly to preserve their independence, German superiority in armor and airplanes made the Balkan campaign another classic blitzkrieg operation. After Belgrade had fallen to a concentric assault on April 17, Yugoslavia capitulated, only to be divided into an independent Croatia, ruled by the pro-Nazi Ustasha, and a remnant of Serbia, which lost its border regions to the other German allies. Since Greece was supported by several British divisions, the fighting there took another ten days until Athens was occupied on April 27 and the British withdrew their forces. Finally, a daring parachute attack secured German control of the strategic island of Crete, which dominated Mediterranean shipping lanes. While the victories had been as swift as usual, the Balkans tied down a large German occupation force, since the underground resistance waged a fierce partisan warfare, leading to ugly reprisals.[28] Moreover, this diversion delayed the German campaign against Russia by six crucial weeks.

The aftermath of the victory in the West proved disappointing to Hitler since the conclusion of hostilities continued to elude him. Thanks to Churchill and the British refusal to panic, London remained unwilling to settle, while the tenacious defense of the RAF gave the overconfident Luftwaffe a bloody nose. Instead, the grandiloquent incompetence of its Italian ally drew the Third Reich into peripheral theaters from North Africa to the Balkans, devouring resources and manpower without bringing much strategic gain. In the spring of 1941 the Wehrmacht was still capable of beating less-modern continental enemies in blitzkrieg fashion, but the German population grew restive, since all the victory fanfares had not ended the war. While offering the economy additional resources, the territorial gains nonetheless diluted German military strength by demanding the stationing of occupation forces for control. After having conquered the southeastern part of the continent, the Führer once again faced the Napoleonic dilemma of whether to seek an arrangement with the British or march on into the East.[29]

LIVING SPACE

Though it ultimately turned out to be a disaster, Hitler's decision to invade Russia had both ideological and economic motives. Since the Nazis believed that Germany was overcrowded, their remedy was not the acquisition of colonies in Africa, deemed unsuited for white settlement, but conquest of agrarian living space in Eastern Europe, from the Baltic to the Ukraine, whose inhabitants would need to be displaced. While Berlin's continental bloc with about three hundred million people looked impressive on paper, it lacked essential raw materials and foodstuffs such as grain, iron ore, and oil, all of which had to be imported. The Soviet Union had been a reliable partner in delivering the missing resources but was asking for arms and finished goods that might one day be turned against Germany. Since so many Red Army generals had been killed in the Great Purge, the German command underestimated its fighting power based on its mediocre performance in the Winter War. Lacking the patience and factories to outproduce the British and their American helpers in airplanes and ships, Hitler turned his Wehrmacht to the one remaining target—Soviet Russia.[30]

Begun in the early morning of June 22, 1941, Operation Barbarossa largely achieved tactical surprise because it proceeded in classic blitzkrieg fashion as a series of deep thrusts by three army groups surrounding the defenders and forcing them to surrender. The Soviets' building of the Molotov Line in its new western territories following their decision on a strategy of forward defense also played into German hands. Stalin ignored reliable intelligence reports of the attack, considering them disinformation, including even a pointed warning by the spy Richard Sorge. The confident and battle-tested Wehrmacht invaded with about three million German and six hundred thousand allied soldiers, but from the beginning it possessed fewer tanks, airplanes, and cannon than the Red Army. In March 1940, Hitler had characterized the coming struggle to his generals as an ideological "war of annihilation," calling for the extermination of communists and Jews. Though the defenders fought courageously, the Germans succeeded in overrunning western Russia from Riga to Odessa, capturing millions of soldiers in the pockets of Bialystok, Minsk, and Smolensk.[31]

Euphoric over such huge victories, the Nazi attackers were confident that they could end the campaign before the onset of winter. But the Soviets created a State Defense Committee to coordinate their efforts, and Stalin called for a "Great Patriotic War" in order to rouse patriots and the Orthodox Church to fight for Mother Russia rather than for communism. On July 12, Britain and the Soviet Union also signed the alliance treaty that had previously eluded them, and the United States gradually extended its Lend-Lease program to include Russia, sending crucial matériel at the moment of highest need. Meanwhile, to secure the coal and oil supplies of the Donbas and link up to his Finnish allies, Hitler diverted part of the Wehrmacht from the attack on Moscow to thrust south into the Ukraine and also north to encircle Leningrad. This strategic shift yielded 660,000 POWs in the pocket of Kiev and another 600,000 in the area of Vyazma and Bryansk. Confident that with such incredible losses there would no longer be enough Red Army troops left to resist, the German command announced at a press conference on October 10, 1941, that the war had been won.[32]

When the attack on Moscow finally began ten days later, the Germans came tantalizingly close but failed to capture the capital.

The sight of Guderian's and Hoepner's tanks about twenty miles north and south of the Kremlin created a mass panic, arrested only by force of the NKVD. But fall rains stopped the supplies of the Wehrmacht by turning the interminable dirt roads into mud, making them impassable. In mid-November a desperate Stalin ordered the Red Army to burn all villages, fields, and factories close to the front lines in order to deny the invader the possibility of resupplying from the land. Moreover, winter arrived about a month early, with temperatures dropping as low as –35 degrees Celsius, immobilizing the tanks in their tracks due to congealing oil, jamming the artillery cannons, and freezing the limbs of soldiers without proper winter clothes. Finally Soviet general Georgy Zhukov also drew reserves away from Asia and threw every last man into battle, willing to take heavy casualties for the sake of the fatherland.[33] By December the awful weather and fresh defenders had stopped the seemingly inexorable German advance.

The following Russian counteroffensive almost unhinged the entire eastern front, since it sent the outworn German attackers into full-fledged flight. Stalin had ruthlessly moved most war production behind the Ural Mountains, out of reach of the Luftwaffe. Some Russian weapons like the Katyusha rocket thrower and the T-34 tank were superior to anything the Wehrmacht could muster. Though often insufficiently trained, Soviet troops, fearing to be shot when retreating, fought with grim determination for "Holy Russia." In contrast the depleted invaders suffered from the cold, broken-down equipment, and overstretched supply lines. Suddenly thousands of German soldiers found themselves surrounded and desperately tried to break out. In mid-December Hitler took personal command of the eastern front and issued a "stand or die" order, calling for fanatical resistance. Though the Russians had lost about six million in dead, wounded, or POWs, the roughly one million German casualties seemed to make more of a difference. Only with its last reserves did the Wehrmacht restabilize the front—albeit one hundred miles to the west.[34]

Part of the Nazi failure was also political, because the brutal treatment of Russian POWs and civilians alienated the local population.

At least in the Baltic states and the Ukraine, the Germans had initially been welcomed as liberators from Stalin's yoke. But indiscriminate repression, economic exploitation, and mass murders by the SS *Einsatzgruppen* made it abundantly clear that they had not come as friends. Both by circumstance and design, the starvation of Russian POWs in the winter of 1941–42, which killed over two million soldiers as well as many civilians in Belarus, sent a chilling message that the Brown conquerors were even more ruthless than the Red commissars. Though many prisoners were willing to join the anticommunist Russian Liberation Army of General Andrey Vlasov, Hitler was never ready to offer them an attractive goal of a post-Communist state. Instead, the ruthless murder of Communist Party members and Jews inspired a partisan movement that hid in the forests and disrupted German supply lines. Hence the Nazis failed to take advantage of the widespread anticommunism, ethnic hatred, and religious resentment that might have helped their cause.[35]

Since Hitler still sought to win the war in the East, he mounted a final offensive in Russia during the summer of 1942. After beating back a Soviet attack at Kharkov, the Wehrmacht strove to secure Ukrainian grain and Caucasus oil as prerequisite for the continuation of the war. Waging fierce battles, the Germans took the Crimea in early July. A first thrust moved southward toward the Caspian Sea, reaching Mount Elbrus, the highest peak in the Caucasus, on August 21, 1942. A second, more eastward offensive approached the industrial city of Stalingrad, which controlled the Volga crossing, at the end of the same month. In tough house-to-house battles, the Wehrmacht managed to capture most of the city but could never quite gain complete control, suffering heavy losses in the process. While this dual advance gained a lot of territory, it stretched supply lines even further and necessitated a defensive posture in the central and northern part of the interminable Russian front. The German military machine could still win battles, but it was no longer able knock a major opponent like the Soviet Union out of the war.[36]

The Russian campaign stopped the German advance across Europe and transformed the character of the warfare, ultimately leading to Hitler's fall. Begun as yet another blitzkrieg, the struggle turned precisely into the kind of war of attrition between major industrial powers that a midsize, even if militarized continental country such as Germany could not win. Hitler's boundless expansionism had created a two-font war by forcing the British Empire and the Soviet Union into a reluctant alliance strong enough to withstand the Nazi attack. First the Luftwaffe failed to gain air superiority over England, and then the Wehrmacht met its match in the cold of the Russian winter. The German leadership continually underestimated the size of the country, the number of Red Army soldiers, the quality of Soviet arms, and the Russians' capacity for suffering. Any other country would have succumbed to such an assault.[37] While German soldiers posing in the Caucasus Mountains or the desert at El Alamein made catchy propaganda photos, this was as far as they would get. The tide of war was about to turn.

GLOBAL STRUGGLE

Propelled not just by Nazi Germany but also by Fascist Italy and militarist Japan, the war gradually developed into a truly global struggle, drawing in virtually all major countries. Lacking a master plan, the nationalist expansionism of the Axis powers had connected separate theaters of war into one worldwide conflict. In ideological terms, the National Socialist, communist, and liberal democratic visions of modernity were vying for primacy. In economic terms, industrialized warfare demanded resources from around the globe that were easier to obtain for the western sea powers than for the land-based fascists. In diplomatic terms, two large multistate alliances were fighting each other, since not just the British Empire and the Soviet Union but also the Nazis could draw on the help of allies and client states in Europe and Asia. Finally, in military terms, troops from the Canadian and Australian dominions as well as soldiers from colonies in India and Africa lined up against regular forces and volunteer SS units from all over Europe. More encompassing than the first time, the second clash became truly a world war.[38]

Once the League of Nations was emasculated, it became ever more difficult to remain neutral during the worldwide conflict. Surrounded by Nazi-held territory, democratic Switzerland mobilized its militia-style army but did much financial business with its German neighbor and became a haven for spies. Social Democratic Sweden, cut off from the world by the Wehrmacht, was compelled to sell its iron ore, timber, and other industrial products to Berlin, while serving as a refuge for escaping Jews. Though Italian Fascist and Nazi troops had helped him win his military coup, General Franco kept Spain out of the war as a result of American diplomatic pressure, only allowing volunteer units like the Blue Division to fight in Russia. Hitler was similarly disappointed that the right-wing dictator Antonio Salazar did not permit Portugal to join the Axis, even if it supplied valuable tungsten. The Irish Free State refused to side with England, while Turkey also stayed out of the war. As long as the Nazis were winning, the continental neutrals cooperated with them, but once the fortune of battle turned, they started to help the Allies as well.[39]

Japanese aggression against China created another regional war in Asia that was initially only loosely linked to the European conflict. Already in July 1937 an incident in Peking had triggered a full-scale invasion by the Japanese army against the Nationalist Chinese regime of Chiang Kai-shek, leading to the occupation of a huge swath of territory around Shanghai and Nanking. After the attack on China, Japanese troops in Manchuria got embroiled in protracted border clashes with the Red Army in Outer Mongolia in which they suffered a surprising defeat. In line with the Ribbentrop-Molotov Pact, Tokyo therefore signed its own nonaggression treaty with the Soviet Union in April 1941. Pushed by its ambitious navy, the Japanese government instead began to turn southwestward in order to take advantage of the defeat of the colonial powers by securing oil-rich Indonesia from the Dutch, taking over French possessions in Indochina, and threatening British control of India. After Japan signed the Tripartite Pact with Germany and Italy in September 1940, each power continued to pursue its own national priorities.[40]

President Franklin Delano Roosevelt watched the European and Asian dictators with growing apprehension, since his hands were tied by the prevailing isolationist sentiment in the United States. The

Republican Party's repudiation of the League, the revisionists' criticism of the Versailles Treaty, and the suffering of the Great Depression had turned the American public inward. Disliking Germans ever since his childhood vacations, and having served as assistant secretary of the navy in World War I, Roosevelt began to warn in October 1937 that aggressors would have to be "quarantined." In order to circumvent the Neutrality Acts designed to keep the country out of war, he authorized an ingenious "cash and carry" policy in November of 1939 that would allow the Allies to buy weapons and thereby improve U.S. business. Declaring America an "arsenal for democracy," FDR then swapped fifty old destroyers for British naval bases and started systematic rearmament. In March 1941 he maneuvered a the Lend-Lease Act through Congress to support Britain and safeguarded transatlantic shipping lanes with naval escorts just short of war.[41]

Hitler deeply resented the increasing flow of aid in raw materials and weapons from the United States to his opponents. In part, he was fascinated by America's size, speed, inventiveness, and economic power, attributing such dynamism to the Aryan roots of the white population. He found much to admire, such as the efficiency of Fordist mass production, the glamour of Hollywood movies, and the high living standard of regular citizens. At the same time, he was repelled by the diversity of immigration and the mixture of blacks, Hispanics, and Asians, considering the country a racial hodgepodge that could only breed decadence. When transatlantic hostility grew, the Führer began to denounce New York more openly as the center of the "world Jewish conspiracy" that was opposing his plans at every turn. Since the Nazi leader expected a future intercontinental showdown with the United States, he tried to expand the German power base—its territory, industry, and resources—so as to get ready for such a conflict. While some Luftwaffe and Kriegsmarine officers dreamt of a direct attack on the United States, such a transatlantic invasion remained utterly beyond German military capacity.[42]

The Japanese attack on the U.S. naval base at Pearl Harbor on December 7, 1941, finally drew the Unites States into World War II as a full-fledged belligerent. Since the British and French armies were engaged in Europe, the American Pacific Fleet was the only sizable force standing between Japan and its goal of establishing a Southeastern Resources Area in Asia. The numerical equality of Japanese and American forces in aircraft carriers, battleships, and destroyers suggested to Admiral Yamamoto that a stealth attack would be the best way to eliminate the opposing fleet once and for all. Since U.S. commanders could not imagine such a strike, their defenses were lax. Hence successive waves of Japanese airplanes, dropping specially designed torpedoes and armor-piercing bombs, wreaked terrible havoc, sinking or damaging all eight American battleships along with several cruisers and destroyers, not to mention numerous naval aircraft. The shock of such an unexpected assault inspired an angry resolve to fight. Congress declared war on Japan by a vote of 470 to 1 the very next day. While FDR railed against "a day that will live in infamy," Berlin, too, was completely surprised.[43]

Three days later Hitler inexplicably declared war on the United States, turning an undecided contest into certain defeat for Germany. Since he had not informed Tokyo about his attack on Russia, the Japanese did not alert him to their strike against the U.S. Navy, absolving him of any obligation. In fact, the consultation within the Axis was so poor that there was no overall strategy, though a joint attack on Russia might have yielded Siberian resources for Tokyo and toppled Stalin in the bargain. Although he had some sense of the productive capacity of the United States, the Führer ignored the warnings of his economic advisers and, judging by current troop strength alone, disastrously underestimated its military potential and political resolve. Perhaps he persuaded himself with the thought that the declaration of war only formalized an informal war already taking place on the sea, allowing German U-boats to sink American vessels on sight. Ignoring the huge disparity between the resources and industry of the two countries, he gambled on winning while he was still ahead.[44] With one stroke, this erroneous decision hastened his own doom, while it solved FDR's long-standing problem of wanting to fight in Europe but not having enough popular support to do so.

The Japanese attack and the German declaration of war on the United States closed the circle of combatants, creating a truly worldwide contest. The separate expansionist designs of the fascist regimes had cemented an unlikely Grand Alliance between liberal democracy and communism that was ideologically disparate but nonetheless worked well enough against a common threat. No doubt the attacking dictatorships had a well-oiled war machine, fierce fighting spirit, and valuable combat experience that gave them advantages in the short run. But the various defenders possessed a larger population, bigger economy, and more resources that, once fully mobilized, would allow them to prevail in a drawn-out conflict.[45] Initially, the Japanese repeated the pattern of blitzkrieg successes by conquering a good part of Southeast Asia, helped by anticolonial resentment. But when it became clear that the new conquerors were even more exacting than the old imperialists, local populations turned against them. In this global struggle of competing modernities, the fates of Europe and of Asia were now closely joined.

LIGHTNING WARFARE

Already during the struggle, military writers had begun to debate the characteristics of modern warfare, which had increased its intensity and violence even in comparison with the horrors of the First World War. One new element was the greater killing power caused by advances in weapons technology such as bombers, tanks, and mobile artillery, though the relative advantages of one side over another tended to remain fleeting. A second dimension was a more massive propaganda that turned the contest into a struggle of ideologies, depersonalizing enemies and motivating mass armies to sacrifice for their cause. A third novelty was the systematic use of terror against civilian populations through bombardment from the air or indiscriminate reprisals, which created panic and induced surrender. A fourth dimension was the more thorough mobilization of the economic basis for mass-producing weapons, feeding the population, and maintaining morale. A final factor appeared to be the respective nature of the political systems, which gave the dictatorships an important edge in unleashing attacks but also rendered them vulnerable in defeat.[46]

During the first half of the war Nazi success rested on a new synthesis of combat elements, called blitzkrieg, which was especially suited to Germany's rapid rearmament but limited resources. According to American eyewitnesses, the concerted use of technically advanced weapons like armored tanks, dive-bombers, and mobile artillery proved so intimidating as to be well-nigh irresistible. The novel tactic of breaking through defenses with a superior concentration of force, then cutting communication and supply lines as well as surrounding defenders in pockets, resulted in the capture of huge numbers of POWs. Moreover, the strategy of picking off one presumably weaker opponent after another permitted a series of brief campaigns, which prevented effective aid by potential allies and left the victim little choice but to surrender. Finally, the consistent use of terror against civilians and the propagandistic exploitation of victories created a climate of fear and a sense of invincibility that made resistance seem pointless. During the initial phase of the war, this improvised attacking formula worked so well as to surprise even its inventors.[47]

The western democracies developed a different style of warfare that favored defense, since it was constrained by parliamentary oversight. During the respite offered by the Munich Agreement, Britain and France rearmed to such a degree that they had a clear superiority in available weapons and troops, usually a sufficient deterrent against attack. But their passivity left the overmatched Poles in the lurch, and the concentration of the RAF on defending Britain also did little to stem the panic of the Low Countries. Immobilized by internal division and self-doubt, the French, though an even match on paper, mistook the main thrust of the German assault, remained behind the Maginot Line, used their weapons badly, and lacked the fighting spirit to stand up to the confident invaders. That left Great Britain behind the Channel to carry on the fight, ably defended by its navy and air force. Increasing material help from the United States as well as assistance from the empire made up for the defeat on the continent. The greater appeal of freedom and the superiority of resources also boded well in an extended struggle.[48]

The Soviet Union produced yet another way of fighting modern war that was initially disastrous but gradually became unstoppable as the conflict wore on. At the beginning Stalin's dictatorial control almost lost the struggle because of his incredulity about a German attack and his decimation of the officer corps in the purges. But eventually his orders to relocate industry and exploit the gulag made it possible for Russia to survive. The Communists relied on seemingly inexhaustible mass armies that continued to amaze the invading generals: "Whenever one dozen [divisions] is destroyed, the Russians put another dozen in its place." The Soviets' simpler but more durable technology was well suited to the Russian climate and easy to produce in great numbers. As relic of the Civil War, the Soviets also used political commissars for ideological mobilization and reactivated dormant feelings of nationalism. Finally, the Soviet military operated with an utter disregard for individual lives, accepting untold casualties. While Red Army attacks were rather methodical, their unrelenting pounding eventually wore down the Wehrmacht.[49]

Though the Nazi synthesis was initially effective, the transformation of the conflict from short bursts to a prolonged war of annihilation blunted the blitzkrieg approach. Putting a premium on control of resources and industrial production, the prolongation of the struggle shifted the balance of power to the Grand Alliance, which had a larger population and bigger economic base. Lacking oil and other raw materials, the Nazis tried to develop substitutes such as hydrogenation from coal, but such replacements were costly. While the exploitation of the continent through slave labor and extraction of resources did enable Germany to continue to fight, the ruthlessness of repression made the Nazis "bitterly hated" and inspired an ever-growing resistance movement. Even though some German weapons were technically superior at the outset, the Allies began to surpass them in both quantity and quality by the middle of the war.[50] Ironically, Hitler ultimately became a victim of his own success formula: By its risky strategy of attack to compensate for material inferiority, the Third Reich created a superior Grand Alliance that would defeat it in the end.

Chapter 13

NAZI HOLOCAUST

Selection at Auschwitz, 1944. *Source.* bpk, Berlin / Auschwitz, Poland / Art Resource, NY.

On September 28, 1941, posters ordered "all Jews living in the city of Kiev" to gather the next day, ostensibly for resettlement. In retribution for the sabotage killing of German officers, the SS forced the remaining Jews in the Ukrainian capital to march to the edge of the city, verify their identity, give up their valuables, and take off their clothes. Members of *Einsatzgruppe* C, made up of German security police, SS troops, and Ukrainian auxiliaries, led them in groups of ten to the edge of a ravine and shot them, dumping their bodies below. Surprised by the large number of victims (33,761), the executioners continued to kill for thirty-six hours, murdering "all of them, without exception—old people, women and children." Only twenty-nine individuals, including Dina Pronicheva, managed to escape and tell about the slaughter, though photos taken by guards also attest to its gruesome reality. In a moving poem and a somber symphony, Yevgeny Yevtushenko and Dimitri Shostakovich sought to preserve the memory of this massacre. As one of the largest killings, Babi Yar has become emblematic of the initial "holocaust by bullets."[1]

Inspired by increasing ethical concerns, the concept of the Holocaust has come to represent the Nazis' Judeocide during the past several decades. Especially in the United States this approach has filled the need to honor the memory of survivors, support the state of Israel, and sidestep the guilt of not having accepted enough refugees. Precisely because the mass murder did not take place in North America, intellectuals could elevate it into a generalized secular standard of inhumanity by linking it to Raphael Lemkin's neologism of genocide. Though it took an entire generation to end the postwar silence, the Holocaust perspective thereafter quickly institutionalized itself through the founding of the U.S. Holocaust Memorial Museum and the establishment of numerous chairs in Holocaust studies at universities. This proliferation has also swept away the stubborn remnants of right-wing Holocaust denial. While the Holocaust sensibility has provided an effective bar against forgetting, its penchant for metahistorical moralizing has also tended to place its stylized narrative of good and evil beyond human understanding.[2]

A more historical approach instead recontextualizes the genocide in Eastern Europe by emphasizing the antimodern modernity of the ethnic cleansing, anti-Semitism, and war of annihilation. The orgy of mass killing was part of a broader project of racial imperialism that intended to conquer space for agrarian settlement. In practice, that social Darwinist aim meant that the local Poles, Ukrainians, and Belarusians needed to be forcibly evicted or reduced to slavery to make place for Aryan farmers. Widespread anti-Slavic prejudice among Germans made this policy popular, since it appealed to a sense of superiority and satisfied an expectation that the spread of their *Kultur* would colonize the inferior East. Moreover, it promised that new resources such as Ukrainian grain and Caucasus oil would enable the Third Reich to compete in future struggles on a global scale. Millions of Jews were, however, in the way, since their pale of settlement was precisely that area in eastern Poland and western Russia that the Nazis hoped to conquer.[3] The systematic mass murder was therefore part of a project of creating an Aryan racial empire.

This spatial imperialism was compounded by a peculiarly modern form of anti-Semitism. Such prejudices had deep roots in a Christianity that charged the Jews with the killing of Christ, with ritual murder, and with usurious greed. But emancipation had removed the legal constraints of the ghetto, allowing the Jewish minority to enter professions beyond money lending. Their relative success in medicine, law, or journalism and their ostentatious accumulation of wealth spurred widespread envy among a radical fringe of Christian competitors. The crucial shift in rhetoric was the pseudoscientific basis of a new racism that claimed a fundamental biological difference that could not be erased by conversion or secularization, trapping Jews forever in otherness. Holding them responsible for the ills of modern civilization, the new Judeophobia clamored for their expulsion. Not a generalized "eliminationist anti-Semitism" but rather Hitler's obsession and the Nazi seizure of power propelled the escalation from social discrimination to physical genocide.[4]

The ideological war of annihilation between National Socialism and communism rendered ethnic cleansing and racist murder possible in practice. By removing diplomatic and moral constraints and abolishing the distinction between combatants and civilians, the murderous modernity of warfare on the eastern front facilitated the implementation of racial genocide. For each side, Nazis or Bolsheviks, those on the other side were the key enemy to whom no quarter was to be given. Moreover, the policies of "scorched earth" to deny the conqueror any resources and of "living off the land" so as not to overburden supply lines unleashed waves of destruction that eliminated the very resources from which the survivors would have to live, precipitating hunger and disease. The Jews and Slavs of the "bloodlands" had the misfortune to be caught in this ideological clash, changing their rulers from Soviets to Nazis and back, depending on military fortunes.[5] The unprecedented brutality of this struggle inevitably led to an abandonment of moral limits and civilized restraints—showing modernity's cruelest face.

NAZI WAR AIMS

By the summer of 1941 Hitler had reached the zenith of his power, allowing him to announce ever more openly the aims for which he had launched the Second World War. In the pace of eight short years he had thrown off the onerous restrictions of Versailles, managed to reunite most German speakers such as Austrians, Sudeten Germans, and West Prussians in the Greater Reich, and established hegemony over the European continent by conquering Poland, Scandinavia, France, and the Balkans while seeming to be on the verge of defeating Soviet Russia as well. Adherents of traditional *Realpolitik* among the elites were astounded by this strengthening of Germany's international position. Even radical nationalists like the Pan-Germans had to acknowledge that virtually all their aims had been achieved. And yet the Führer was not content with consolidating such signal successes; he interpreted them only as the springboard for ever greater efforts. Transcending conventional hegemony, these ideological aims continued to drive the Nazis onward and made the war even more murderous.[6]

For Hitler the central purpose of the conflict was "expansion of living space in the East" in order to stabilize control over the continent and enable the Reich to compete on equal terms in world politics. Considering Germany a continental power, he was skeptical of overseas possessions and preferred instead to colonize the Slavic East, since he considered the Western European countries too firmly established. In a way, this project sought to resume a mythical *Drang nach Osten*, celebrated in Prussian fiction and history, which glorified the Teutonic Knights as carriers of Christianity and law. The lure of living space also built on the visions of the Baltic Germans, who sought the Reich's support against the more numerous Russians and Lithuanians, Latvians, and Estonians. During the First World War the German army under Ludendorff had already controlled vast stretches of Poland, Belarus, and the Ukraine, only to withdraw as a consequence of its defeat in the West.[7] Conquering and colonizing the agrarian East would broaden the resource base Germany would need for the global competition against world powers like the United States and Russia.

Sharpened by decades of fierce struggles between nationalities, Nazi colonization took a more radical form than conventional conquest and occupation, aiming at nothing less than a reversal of ethnic balances. Skeptical of the value of industrial production, Hitler, Heinrich Himmler, and Walter Darré considered agrarian settlement the source of national power, envisaging a belt of German farm villages running all the way to the Crimea. This gigantic *Umvolkung* project sought to collect all dispersed ethnic Germans from the East so as to resettle them in West Prussia and the Warthegau, thereby re-Germanizing these ethnically disputed territories. However, shifting the demographic composition required the removal of the current inhabitants, such as Poles and Jews, by means of ruthless ethnic cleansing to create room for German colonists. Safeguarding Aryan racial domination moreover necessitated the systematic killing of Slavic elites so as to reduce the rest to passive slave laborers, incapable of resisting their conquerors. Using force rather than assimilation, this social-engineering project proceeded with frightening brutality.[8]

A related biopolitical aim was the "solution of the Jewish question" in order to remove an influence that Nazi leaders held responsible for the cultural and social degeneration of modernity. Though building on a tradition of religious anti-Semitism, the secular version of Judeophobia was a product of the emancipation that had brought civil equality to Jews in Central Europe.[9] During the financial crisis of the early 1870s, critics like Heinrich von Treitschke had attributed the crash to unscrupulous Jewish speculators, while cultural pessimists like Julius Langbehn accused the Jews of undermining German *Kultur*. In the universities nationalist students in the Vereine Deutscher Studenten raised the anti-Semitic banner, spreading prejudice among future professionals.[10] Nevertheless, the efforts of agitators like Otto Böckel to found an anti-Jewish party failed owing to the resistance of assimilated Jews in the Centralverein (a civil-rights group) and of liberal Germans in parties of the Left. But once concocted, the anti-Semitic poison spread to ever wider circles, making Judeophobia socially acceptable.

Anti-Semitism did not put the Nazis in power, but their control of the government removed all restraints to pursuing Judeophobic policies in Germany. No doubt radical hatred of Jews was one of the attractions for many Old Fighters who joined the fledgling Nazi movement in the early 1920s. One of the worst, the Franconian Julius Streicher, edited an anti-Semitic sheet full of pornographic cartoons of lurid Jewish men defiling innocent Aryan girls. Another rabid racist was the agronomist Heinrich Himmler, who organized the Schutzstaffel (SS) as an ideological elite within the paramilitary thugs of the SA.[11] Though many Germans disliked the crudeness of anti-Semitism, the seizure of power allowed the Nazis to spew hate phrases, boycott Jewish stores, and assault their hapless Jewish neighbors. In the spring of 1933 the Hitler government issued a series of anti-Semitic decrees in order to purge the bureaucracy and the free professions of Jews while denying Jewish students access to higher education. Accompanied by spontaneous pogroms, these official measures sought to reverse the liberal gains of civic emancipation.[12]

The Second World War made it possible for Hitler and Himmler to escalate their anti-Semitic discrimination, designed to trigger emigration, into ghettoization as a prelude to mass murder. The Nazis systematically increased their pressure from the initial denial of livelihood, via the deprivation of citizenship in the 1935 Nuremberg Laws, to the physical threats in the November 9, 1938, pogrom known as the *Kristallnacht* (Night of Glass) because of all the broken shop windows. Forcing them to leave their possessions behind, this increasing persecution drove a quarter million German Jews, about half of the total, to emigrate, if they were lucky enough to overcome the reluctance of other countries to accept them as refugees. The *Anschluss* of Austria and the takeover of Czechoslovakia added several hundred thousand Jews, but the unleashing of the war soon afterward shut most doors to escape. The conquest of Poland brought several million additional eastern Jews under Nazi control, terrorized by SS violence that pushed some into Soviet territory. Their temporary confinement in urban ghettos left open the question of their ultimate fate.[13]

Temporarily suspended by the Nazi-Soviet Pact, Hitler's final ideological aim was the elimination of communism at home and in Russia. Like other German nationalists, the Nazis hated the Bolsheviks as defeatists who had contributed to losing the First World War and as revolutionaries who threatened national unity through class warfare. After the Reichstag fire the Gestapo focused most of its energy on suppressing communist resistance among the workers as the only serious domestic threat. Internationally, Hitler saw Stalin as a rival dictator and Bolshevism as a mass movement of comparable attraction that needed to be defeated in order to stop its subversive influence. Though the two totalitarian movements shared some characteristics, their enmity was logical because both coveted the same East European territories of the Baltic states, Poland, Belarus, and the Ukraine for their imperial designs. Predicting a "clash of ideologies" in his briefing of military leaders, Hitler called for utmost brutality in the struggle against the Soviet Union, ordering the elimination of the intelligentsia and the political commissars.[14]

The anti-Slavic, anti-Semitic, and anticommunist phobias converged and mutually reinforced one another, leading to an unprecedented bloodbath in Eastern Europe. In the warped Nazi perception an ideological crusade was needed against the Bolsheviks, who ruled the Russian Slavs, since they were dominated by Jews. While known communists and Slavic intellectuals were to be killed, the remaining population had some chance of survival if it proved compliant and worked hard in the fields and factories. The fate of the Jews was even more horrible, since they faced complete extermination once the various plans for resettlement in Madagascar or behind the Urals had failed. Stretched for manpower, the Nazis sought to exploit local ethnic conflicts in order to mobilize auxiliaries like the Arajs commandos in Latvia and the Trawniki guards in Poland. But ultimately Hitler's chilling vision of establishing Aryan hegemony through mass murder proved self-defeating since it did not leave any space for potential collaborators.[15] While other pressure groups in Germany pushed for further war aims such as African colonies, the deadly core of the Nazi ambition lay in reshaping the East.

NEW ORDER

Military victories allowed Hitler to transform the face of Europe, imposing a mixture of German domination and Nazi ideology on the continent. In theory, everything was organized according to the *Führerprinzip*, the leadership principle by which authority flowed down from the top. In practice, Hitler created a series of competing domains in which Alfred Rosenberg and Himmler vied for ideological control, Hermann Göring and Fritz Todt competed for economic ascendancy, and so on. Though usually compliant, the military retained some degree of organizational and operational independence, but it had to compete with the growing Waffen-SS. Entrusted with providing security and seeing itself as the new ideological elite, Himmler's SS created a parallel universe of concentration camps. By anticipating Hitler's wishes, the bureaucracy as well tried to retain some degree of competence and order in a dynamic situation, while business leaders were only too happy to exploit the resources of conquered territories. As European hegemon, the Third Reich was a contradictory blend of dictatorial control and polycratic chaos.[16]

Like other conquerors before him, Hitler fundamentally redrew the map of Europe, surrounding Greater Germany with circles of occupied territories, allied countries, and neutrals. To begin with, the Nazis reannexed the disputed provinces of Alsace and Lorraine from France, and extended Germany's eastern borders beyond prior possessions such as Danzig, Upper Silesia, West Prussia, and Poznań to include about half of ethnic Poland, planning additional annexations after the war. While leaving South Tyrol to Mussolini, these territorial gains broadened the economic base but introduced a considerable number of non–German speakers into the Reich. Respecting the national states of Western Europe, the Nazis controlled occupied France, Belgium, Holland, Denmark, and Norway through a mixture of military governors and civilian administrators. But in Bohemia, the government-general of Poland, the Baltics, the Ukraine, and the Balkans, Hitler instituted imperial commissars in order to rule directly from Berlin. Hence the Nazis governed occupied Europe through a confusing tangle of military and political authorities.[17]

Often forgotten is the significant role of allies in extending the reach of the Third Reich into areas beyond direct German control. While the touted Axis with Italy and Japan turned out to be more formidable on paper than in practice, it nonetheless spread the war into the Mediterranean and into Asia, tying down huge Allied forces to combat it. More often than not Mussolini made his own decisions and had to be bailed out by German troops. Though the Japanese military decided to settle its border disputes with Soviet Russia rather than to support the German attack, it posed a formidable threat to the colonies of Western European nations and to the United States that took years to overcome.[18] On the continent Finland and the Balkan countries of Hungary, Bulgaria, and Romania chose to ally themselves with Nazi Germany, partly for reasons of ideological affinity and partly for the sake of gaining territorial spoils. Finally, authoritarian puppet regimes like those of Slovakia and Croatia owed their entire existence to the destruction of the Versailles-mandated barrier states. Even the various neutral countries collaborated to a considerable extent with Berlin, facilitating German ascendancy.[19]

The most complicated mixture between outside control and continued independence developed in France. The northern three-fifths of the country along the Atlantic coast was occupied by the Wehrmacht as a staging area for the naval war while the rest of the free zone was governed from the spa city of Vichy, which also retained civil authority over the occupied zone. Technically, Vichy France continued to be an independent country, recognized even by the United States. After the armistice in June 1940 conservative opponents of democratic modernity in France proclaimed an authoritarian constitution, ending the Third Republic, and made the World War I hero Marshal Philippe Pétain head of state. Seeking to establish an order based on "god, family and fatherland," his reactionary regime cooperated officially with the Third Reich so as to preserve the substance of the nation until a time when the country could become truly independent again. The British sinking of a French fleet at Mersel-Kébir facilitated Vichy's cooperation with Berlin. In retaliation for the Allied landing in North Africa, however, the Germans occupied the free zone in November 1942, preparing to repulse an invasion by fortifying the coast and controlling the hinterland.[20]

Like the citizens of all other occupied nations, the French faced the difficult choice of whether to "collaborate" or resist. Unable to openly refuse orders, most apolitical Frenchmen coped with the curfews, shortages, labor conscriptions, and political restrictions as best as they could. Opportunistic businessmen could make great profits from supplying the German war machinery. But providing raw materials and finished goods for Berlin also involved Prime Minister Pierre Laval's government in repressive, exploitative, and anti-Semitic measures. Some rightist youths were so caught up in the ideological appeals of the Nazis and attracted by the deadly romanticism of the SS that they volunteered to fight for the Third Reich. In Paris, the Francophile ambassador Otto Abetz sought to draw intellectuals like Louis-Ferdinand Céline into cultural collaboration with Germany, though the military administration instituted a draconian regime. Capitalizing on his compatriots' disenchantment, General Charles de Gaulle's proclamation of the Free French movement in

London exile inspired a resistance movement, headed by Jean Moulin, that deeply split the country's loyalties.[21]

This organizational patchwork allowed the Nazis a ruthless exploitation of resources in a *Grossraumwirtschaft*, an economy of large enough scale to sustain what had turned into a war of attrition from the fall of 1941 on. In defeated countries Agriculture Minister Herbert Backe's emissaries fanned out to seize foodstuffs for supplying the German military and civilians at the expense of starvation among the defeated. Industrial giants such as the Krupp steelworks and the chemicals conglomerate IG Farben requisitioned companies and raw materials with scant regard to property rights or fair contracts in order to meet the rising production targets for weapons and ammunition. With military losses averaging fifty thousand dead per month, the dwindling supply of industrial and agricultural labor became a key bottleneck. At first workers were recruited voluntarily. But when the terrible conditions of long hours, insufficient food, and housing in camps became known, labor boss Fritz Sauckel had to use force to round up prospects, mistreating them brutally. By the end of the war the mixture of POWs and slave laborers reached a staggering 7.9 million—a crucial workforce that kept the Nazi war machinery rolling regardless of human cost.[22]

The domination of continental Europe was essential for continuation of the war and realization of the Nazi aims of settlement, Judeocide, and the defeat of communism. Since not even an expanded Germany was strong enough to fight against Britain, Russia, and the United States at the same time, Hitler sought to mobilize the entire continent. To make up for limitations in resources and manpower, the Wehrmacht had to exploit the raw materials, industrial production, and agricultural produce of new provinces, occupied territories, allies, and neutrals. In order to foster voluntary collaboration, the Nazis increasingly claimed to be defending "fortress Europe" against the communist menace of Bolshevik hordes, but endemic shortages of food and war matériel forced them to resort to ever more violent compulsion, which could only inspire hatred and resistance. German control of the continent modernized Europe in an exploitative form, centralizing its economic resources under the command of Berlin.[23] Moreover, it emboldened Hitler to undertake the even more gigantic project of cementing German hegemony by colonizing the East.

ETHNIC CLEANSING OF SLAVS

Though the term ethnic cleansing only originated in the Yugoslav Wars of the 1990s, the concept accurately describes Nazi policies in Eastern Europe. Hitler aimed at nothing less than "the planned deliberate removal from a specific territory [of] persons of a particular ethnic group, by force or intimidation, in order to render that area ethnically homogeneous." The German description of anti-Semitic policies as designed to make the country *judenrein* employs precisely this image of cleansing an area of Jews. Moreover, "means of murder, torture, arbitrary arrest and detention, extra-judicial executions, rape and sexual assaults, confinement of civilian population in ghetto areas, forcible removal, displacement and deportation of civilian population, deliberate military attacks or threats of attacks on civilians and civilian areas, and wanton destruction of property" were employed by the SS, Wehrmacht, and local auxiliaries in Eastern Europe from 1939 on.[24] Ethnic cleansing was both the aim and the method by which the Nazis wanted to eliminate the Jewish and much of the Slavic population to make room for German settlement.

The Master Plan East, a secret blueprint for Germanization sketched out in 1940, outlined the dual goal of eliminating the local inhabitants and implanting German-speaking settlers in Eastern Europe. SS bureaucrats like Hans Ehlich in the Reich Main Security Office (RSHA) and academics like the Berlin agronomist Konrad Meyer collaborated in the *Generalplan Ost*, drawing up grandiose visions of enhancing Germandom without regard for existing populations. With chilling radicalism, such concepts envisaged the removal of about forty-five million inhabitants, four-fifths of the Poles and half of the Russians, leaving the remainder as an enslaved workforce. At the same time, the plan called for the settlement of eight to ten million Germans as *Wehrbauern*, armed farmers, who would defend the colonial territories and absorb the Slavic natives. The conquerors would not be squeamish in the methods of removal, ranging from expulsion to the Far East to extermination for those who had nowhere to go. While some of the plan's racist rhetoric seems fanciful, many of its policies were implemented, turning it into gruesome reality.[25]

The key instrument of Germanization was ethnic selection, designed to recover German blood while weeding out opponents and racial inferiors. Made official for annexed territories in 1941, this classification was called the Ethnic German List (*Deutsche Volksliste*), constructed by SS officials of the Reich Commissariat for the Strengthening of Germandom. On the basis of documents and interviews, ethnic Germans without citizenship were divided into four categories: (1) *Volksdeutsche*, who had supported the Reich; (2) *Deutschstämmige*, who were of ethnic descent; (3) *Eingedeutschte*, who needed to recover their roots; and (4) *Rückgedeutschte*, who were willing to become Germans. While German communists and other opponents of Nazis were mercilessly sent to concentration camps, certified ethnic brethren could count on numerous benefits such as acquiring citizenship—though the men had to serve in the military. SS officials found out that making these selections was quite difficult, as there was no firm ideological or biological basis beyond behavior and appearance. Not surprisingly most of the 2.7 million members of the list in 1944 were in the vague third category.[26]

The systematic decimation of the Polish elite and the persecution of Jews began not after but during the German victory over Poland. SS *Einsatzgruppen* moved behind the advancing Wehrmacht columns, ostensibly to secure the rear against sabotage but in fact to begin mass killing. Rhetorically, such murder was motivated by revenge for some anti-German atrocities committed by Poles, which were inflated by Nazi propaganda. In practice, the killing targeted the Polish political elite and intelligentsia, tens of thousands of whom were murdered in order to prevent any resistance. Moreover, the murders also involved Jews as racial inferiors or potential opponents. Incarceration in work camps and in ghettos prompted hundreds of thousands to flee eastward—only to be killed or imprisoned by Stalin's henchmen. The attack on the Soviet Union extended Nazi repression to the Baltic states, Belarus, and the Ukraine, focusing especially on Communist commissars and cutting off any escape routes for Jews. Organized reprisals against partisan attacks proved a license for soldiers to retaliate against civilians without any scruples.[27]

More deadly yet was the starvation by neglect and design that threatened Slavic and Jewish civilians and Russian prisoners during the winter of 1941–42. To stretch the insufficient food supply, the Nazi leadership put priority on maintaining the fighting power of the Wehrmacht as well as the morale of the home front—a ruthless choice that amounted to a "hunger plan" toward the occupied population and POWs in the East. The decision to supply the troops from local resources rather than via the long transportation routes from home required extracting food by force, leaving civilian rations disastrously short of survival needs. Due to a lack of preparation and empathy, the surprisingly large number of Red Army prisoners overwhelmed the German capacity to receive, feed, and process them so that untold individuals succumbed to starvation. Moreover, during the siege of Leningrad, which lasted more than two years, the German-Finnish command used hunger as a deliberate weapon. Those weakened by insufficient nutrition were especially vulnerable to the development of epidemics like typhoid fever. Over five million civilians and POWs therefore died "a silent death" from hunger.[28]

Another, similarly inhumane method to further ethnic cleansing was "death through labor" under intolerable conditions. To compensate for German workers fighting and dying at the front, millions of young Poles, Jews, Russians, Belarusans, and Ukrainians were requisitioned to work in armament factories or on farms. In Himmler's vast SS concentration-camp universe, many prisoners were forced to do heavy physical labor for scraps of food that did not suffice to keep them alive. In factories in the Reich, slave laborers sometimes encountered slightly better conditions if industrialists appreciated their skills. But weakened from malnutrition, they also perished in large numbers since they were incarcerated, compelled to labor long hours, and exposed to bombing attacks. Only if they worked on a friendly farm did they have a chance to survive. In defiance of economic logic, the slave laborers were insufficiently fed and yet expected to produce as much as comparable German workers.[29] Although two-thirds of the German workforce eventually consisted of slave labor, hundreds of thousands were literally worked to death.

For all their murderous effort, the Nazis had relatively little to show in terms of successful Germanization. The SS office for the Strengthening of Germandom tried to collect ethnic Germans from language islands all over occupied Eastern Europe, for example, bringing farmers who had lived for centuries in Transnistria at the Romanian border back into the Reich. Displaced from their rural roots to an urban culture, these resettlers faced a difficult adjustment. Altogether about 867,000 ethnic Germans were thus returned to Germany proper. It was even more difficult to motivate potential settlers to take up abandoned Polish farms in West Prussia or the Warthegau, since these often did not measure up to German standards. While the Volksdeutsche Mittelstelle put out colorful brochures with smiling farmers in their new homes, the reality was disappointing since the newcomers had to cope with different crops, unfamiliar livestock, and a hostile climate. Altogether about 723,000 settlers moved to the new provinces—a far cry from expectations that had been ten times as high.[30] Moreover, they were all uprooted by the Red Army in 1944–45.

It is largely forgotten that about half the victims of Nazi ethnic cleansing were Slavs killed to make room for erecting a German Empire in the East. According to one rough count, about one hundred thousand members of the Polish elite were murdered from 1939 on in order to break the back of any potential resistance. Another 4.2 million Soviet POWs as well as Russian, Belarusan, and Ukrainian civilians perished as a result of starvation during the German occupation. And finally about seven hundred thousand partisans and noncombatants were shot as reprisals for resistance against German forces in Warsaw and Belarus.[31] These staggering numbers, amounting to about five million dead, do not include other civilian deaths from fighting, which ran several million more. Since the carnage occurred away from western media and most of the populations did survive, the silent deaths from hunger are less well remembered. Yet these casualties were not just collateral damage of savage fighting but rather the logical result of seeking to create a modern racist utopia by changing the nationality balance of Eastern Europe.

GENOCIDE OF JEWS

The most radical form of ethnic cleansing was the genocide of the Jews, since it aimed not just at displacing but at exterminating an entire population. Conceptualizing the memory of Judeocide, the neologism *genocide*, enshrined in a United Nations convention in 1948, refers to all "acts committed with intent to destroy, in whole or in part, a national, ethnical, racial or religious group, as such." The difference between the decimation of the Slavs and the genocide of the Jews lay precisely in the radicalism of the Nazi project to annihilate all Jews under their control, once there were no more avenues left for emigration or expulsion. Though discrimination and persecution had already forced half of the German, Austrian, and Czech Jews to flee, the victories over Poland, France, the Balkans, and the initial success of the attack on the Soviet Union brought approximately five million more Jews under Nazi control. While the food shortages and settlement plans encouraged harsh measures such as compulsory labor, in the end it was the biopolitical crusade to eliminate "the Jewish virus" that motivated this mass murder. The genocide therefore grew out of the ethnic cleansing but went far beyond it.[32]

The euthanasia program by which Nazi doctors murdered incurably ill and disabled Germans was the precedent that pioneered the genocidal killing method. Hitler authorized the "mercy death" of "life not worth living" in order to improve the composition of the Aryan race and to save labor and food during the war. In accordance with the international eugenic movement in the United States and in Sweden, the racial hygienists initially just sterilized the hereditarily ill, depriving about 330,000 Germans of the ability to reproduce. But the victory over Poland offered Nazi doctors a chance to murder the institutionalized in a program that they then extended to the Reich. Initially children and adults were killed with injections, but eventually they were gassed in vans by carbon monoxide. Medical records indicate that the T-4 program killed 70,273 individuals. Though the

Nazi physicians used deception, church leaders and family members protested so loudly that Hitler stopped the killing in August 1941. But the example had been set, and some two hundred thousand more concentration-camp inmates were murdered by war's end.[33]

The policy of ghettoization facilitated the subsequent murderous campaign by removing Jews from their surroundings and concentrating them within designated enclaves in Polish or Russian cities. In September 1939, Gestapo chief Reinhard Heydrich ordered Jews to be collected in urban centers and then shipped from Germany and Western Europe to the East, reviving a medieval practice in a more horrible way. These designated Jewish quarters were administered by local *Judenräte* (Jewish Councils) that played an ambiguous role both as self-defense organizations and as transmitters of Nazi orders. Living conditions in the ghettos of Warsaw, Lodz, or Minsk, to name just a few, were simply atrocious, since hundreds of thousands of people were crammed into too little space, food rations were insufficient, and contact with the outside was barred by walls or barbed wire. In the midst of such hunger and disease, a rich personal and cultural life nonetheless flourished during this strange time, suspended between a normal past and a deadly future. For the SS, the ghettos were a convenient source of labor and a stopgap device, which indicated that the Nazis had not yet made up their mind.[34]

Harsher yet was the confinement in concentration camps (KZ), because it stripped the inmates of every shred of human dignity. Pioneered by the British in the Boer War, imprisonment in improvised enclosures made it possible to control large numbers of enemies. Begun with the establishment of Dachau in 1933, the system spread to Buchenwald, Sachsenhausen, Bergen-Belsen, Ravensbrück, and beyond, imprisoning German communists and other regime opponents, gays, gypsies, and foreigners as well as ordinary criminals. Before 1939 Jews were incarcerated to prompt emigration, whereas during the war they were imprisoned to provide slave labor in quarries or underground mines to build V-2 rockets and so on. While all inmates were overworked, starved, and beaten, the Jews, identified by their yellow star, were at the bottom of the hierarchy, subject to harassment even by fellow prisoners. Eventually thousands of camps

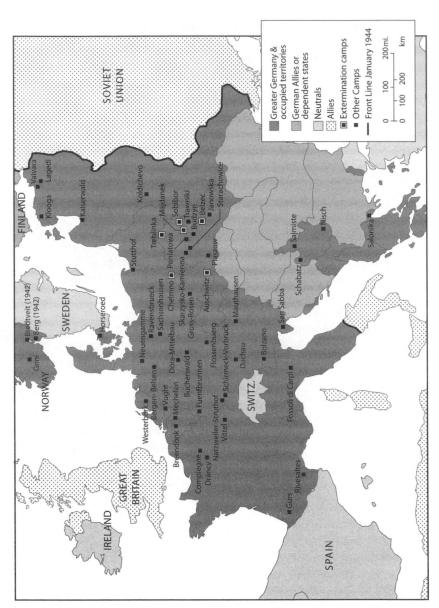

Map 7. Concentration camps, 1943–44. Solid squares represent camps. Because of map scale, not all camps can be shown or labeled. Camps operated by German-allied or dependent states are not shown. Adapted from National Holocaust Memorial Museum, Washington, DC.

sprang up in the Reich and the occupied territories, in which human skeletons in striped garb ceaselessly toiled for their Nazi masters. No wonder that the suffering was immense and death rates were high.[35]

The actual genocide began with the "Holocaust by bullets" in the fall of 1941, when the Nazis murdered masses of eastern Jews by conventional methods. Although the timing and content of Hitler's order of the "final solution of the Jewish question" remain disputed, it is undeniable that the attack on the Soviet Union provided the SS with a cover to implement its anti-Semitic fantasies, initially in an improvised fashion but eventually in a quite systematic manner. In a procedure repeated hundreds of times, one of the infamous *Einsatzgruppen*, composed of SS, security police, and local auxiliaries, would sweep into a town, round up all the Jews it could discover, march them to a forest, force them to dig their own graves, and then execute them with individual shots or machine-gun fire. Often rear Wehrmacht units would also lend logistical help.[36] A mixture of ideological conviction, group pressure, and liberal doses of alcohol seems to have motivated ordinary policemen to follow their deadly orders, though many did not like murdering helpless women and children. During this incredible killing spree in the winter of 1941–42, about 1.8 million Jews perished.[37]

With Operation Reinhard mass killing shifted to extermination camps, establishing a new form of assembly-line murder. In January 1942 the Wannsee Conference of SS and government leaders discussed plans for a comprehensive solution to the "Jewish question in Europe." On Himmler's personal orders new killing camps were established in Chelmno, Belzec, Sobibor, and Treblinka, all located in eastern Poland in wooded areas at the end of railroad spurs. Regularly trains with cattle cars would bring new victims; the able-bodied might be selected to work, but the rest would be forced to undress, stripped of valuables, and marched into "delousing showers," where they were killed by inhaling Zyklon B gas. After twenty-five to thirty minutes their desperate cries and struggles would cease and the bodies be cleared out and thrown into mass graves or burned in special crematoriums. Over time, this terrible "special treatment" was perfected so that it took only several dozen SS personnel, local guards, and Jewish work details to accomplish the killing. In this merciless manner the East European ghettos were emptied and an additional two million Jews murdered.[38]

In a letter to his family of August 1945 the Belgian survivor Charles Katzengold has left a graphic account of such an ordeal. Caught as a resistance operative in October 1941, he was deported to "the famous concentration camp Auschwitz." Stripped of his belongings and hair, he was tattooed on his left arm and brutally beaten on his arrival, thereby "beginning to learn the other side of existence." The camp leader left no doubt about their fate: "Jews you have not come here to live but to die." In Birkenau, a subcamp within Auschwitz, he was forced to build barracks and dig ditches under "absolutely inhumane conditions." Harassed by vermin, lacking water, and continually beaten, his fellow prisoners perished like "snow in the sun." Since he knew various languages, he was fortunate enough to be selected as a secretary for the camp administration, but typhus reduced him to "a living skeleton" weighing less than fifty kilos. His situation improved somewhat when he became a camp guard (kapo), receiving better food and clothing. But with the approach of the Red Army he was sent on a death march for seven hundred kilometers on foot in the middle of the winter, which only 122 of the six thousand prisoners survived. In Auschwitz "men, women, children, all went to the gas chamber, and rare, very rare were those who came back."[39] Such individual testimonies, written immediately after liberation, are irrefutable evidence of the mass murder of the Jews.

Though most notorious, Auschwitz was rather an exception, since it had already opened in the spring of 1940 and combined several purposes. Located in territory annexed to the Reich, the *Stammlager*, based on military barracks, was initially a prison for Polish opponents and Russian POWs. The huge addition of Birkenau was the actual extermination site, where Jews were brought in from all over Europe to be killed by poison gas. The third complex, Buna-Monowitz, was a large work camp with forty-eight outposts in which inmates labored for German firms like the synthetic gas producer IG Farben. About 90 percent of the roughly 1.1 million people who were murdered in Auschwitz were Jews. With impending defeat, the

SS tried to cover the traces of its crime, sending the inmates on death marches before the Red Army liberated the camp on January 27, 1945.[40] Unlike the victims of the pure killing camps, some writers like Elie Wiesel, Primo Levi, and Tadeuz Borowski managed to survive this hell and leave shocking portrayals of the brutality of the SS guards, the corruption of the kapos, and the suffering of the inmates. "Humanity? Humanity is not concerned with us. Today anything is allowed. Anything is possible, even these crematoria."[41]

The medical experimentation performed in concentration camps on helpless inmates without their consent was especially revolting. Physicians proved quite susceptible to Nazi ideology, because their eugenic notions overlapped with racial biopolitics. Moreover, the armed forces were interested in testing exposure to cold, immersion in seawater, high-altitude responses, the impact of injuries, and amputation or transplantation methods on actual subjects in order to develop measures to protect their own troops. Some Nazified doctors were only too glad to undertake such "research," since the KZ inmates were human material that could not protest the pain, disfigurement, and death visited upon them. Most notorious was Dr. Mengele of Auschwitz, who conducted almost fifteen hundred twin experiments on Romani (Gypsy) children, injecting them with dyes to change their eye color, sewing them together, and so on. Since the results of such horrific studies were reported in journals, the professional leadership was complicit in such science run amok. This reversal of the Hippocratic Oath transformed humane healing into medical torture.[42]

In spite of instances of heroic resistance, it was the compliance of most victims that made the final solution possible. The majority of Jews failed to fight against their impending destruction because they hoped to survive by following orders, while they were certain to die if they did not. Of course, widespread intimidation by the SS, its auxiliaries, and the Wehrmacht made opposition seem pointless. Moreover, to facilitate deportation to the camps, the Nazis used deception in promising resettlement, work opportunities, and medical treatment. The hostility of the local populations and the indifference of German soldiers also rendered trying to find and join the resistance difficult. And there was always the hope that by cooperating as a member of a *Judenrat*, kapo, or part of a special assignment within the camp like Irmgard Mueller one might see another day. But in truth all too few fortunate individuals who succeeded in joining the partisans or were hidden by Christian families were ultimately able to survive.[43] Given this horrible situation, the courage of the participants in the Warsaw ghetto uprising in 1943, some concentration-camp revolts, and the partisan struggle was therefore truly admirable.[44]

The genocide of Jews, this Holocaust, or Shoah, was therefore the result of a fanatical anti-Semitic crusade, escalating from discrimination via ghettoization to extermination. According to the count of the Nuremberg Tribunal, substantiated by more recent research, the Nazis and their local auxiliaries killed just under six million Jews, approximately two-thirds of the roughly nine million in occupied Europe who did not manage to escape.[45] This Holocaust went beyond ethnic cleansing for *Lebensraum*, since it included the Jews from western countries like France and Holland. The Shoah was also singular because the SS tried not just to reduce but to eradicate an entire racially defined group. Hitler's fanatical Judeophobia exceeded all rational calculations, because devoting considerable resources to the elimination of racial enemies that might have been employed as slave labor even appeared counterproductive to the war effort.[46] While being part of the general drive to create a Greater German Empire through eastern settlement, "the final solution of the Jewish question" ultimately became an ideological end in itself, rupturing all civilized bonds.

PERPETRATORS, COLLABORATORS, AND RESISTERS

The implementation of ethnic cleansing and genocide required hundreds of thousands, if not millions, of willing helpers from Germany and all over Europe. In order to minimize their own participation, many collaborators afterward put the blame on Hitler and his henchmen, the SS or the NSDAP, a strategy that facilitated the reintegration of most collaborators into postwar society. While some claimed to have followed "superior orders," others asserted merely to have "done their duty," while yet others argued that they had only "tried to survive" themselves. Yet the exonerative strategy of stating "we did not really know" about the Nazi crimes remains unconvincing, because the disappearance of Jewish neighbors, the existence of concentration camps, the eastern settlement schemes, and the perpetration of war crimes were common knowledge, even if the full extent of the Holocaust remained shrouded in secrecy. The popular preference for not really wanting to know and the willingness to continue to function within the Nazi universe remains hard to explain in retrospect.[47]

On one end of the spectrum were the fanatical National Socialist activists who admired the Führer and believed in the murky ideology of the movement. Many of these, like the lawyer Roland Freisler, were Old Fighters who had joined the party out of conviction before 1933, when it was still problematic to be considered a Nazi. Though some even rose to the rank of gauleiter, these ideologues and thugs were increasingly replaced by the new SS elite of technocrats with academic training such as Werner Best, who were competent professionals and ruthless anti-Semites at the same time. Members of this "uncompromising generation" had embraced the National Socialist movement during the crisis years of the Weimar Republic and thought of themselves as the masters of a New Europe, dominated by the Greater German Reich.[48] In other countries, many rightist youths also flocked to the fascist banners, seeing Hitler and Mussolini as dynamic leaders of the future. Even if their intense nationalism made the creation of a "Fascist International" difficult, they were willing to aid the racial cleansing of their countries, hoping to carve out a leading role in Nazi Europe.

Less rabid, but still crucial, was the complicity of nationalists or opportunists, since their expertise kept the war effort going. Even if they were disdainful of Nazi excesses, many lawyers, professors, and engineers continued to put their knowledge at the service of the Third Reich because they believed in a Greater Germany. Diplomats like Ernst von Weizsäcker, generals like Erwin Rommel, and conductors like Wilhelm Furtwängler were willing to collaborate and provide a respectable front for a disreputable regime. Once the likes of philosopher Martin Heidegger or the writer Ernst Jünger had endorsed Hitler's dictatorship, their subsequent second thoughts could no longer undo the damage. Similarly, scores of opportunists also jumped onto the Nazi bandwagon as long as it rolled victoriously along. The hope of acquiring Jewish businesses, gaining occupation loot, or exploiting conquered resources drew many industrialists such as Alfried Krupp and Friedrich Flick into working for the Third Reich. But when battlefield defeats and Allied bombing suggested that the war was lost, it was too late to repent; they were trapped.[49]

The apolitical majority of the population in the Third Reich and occupied Europe simply tried to lead a normal life under abnormal circumstances, remaining preoccupied with their private affairs. Concretely that meant doing one's job within the Nazi system as well as one could without running afoul of the little dictators, such as the *Blockwart* of one's street or the party representative in one's firm. Assuring survival also required nominal concessions like paying dues to National Socialist professional associations, donating during collections for the Winter Aid, sending children to the Hitler Youth, or displaying enthusiasm at a political rally. One might even try to take advantage of some Nazi entertainment or Labor Front vacation offers. At the same time, such conformists could tell Hitler jokes or ridicule the SA thugs in private so as to keep their emotional distance from the boorish Brownshirts. Though the "reluctant loyalty" of the majority never ran very deep, its surface compliance sufficed to keep the war effort going and allowed the Nazis to pursue their murderous dreams.[50]

Some groups within Germany and citizens in occupied countries proved more impervious to Nazi ideology and practice, as suggested by the concept of *Resistenz*. Catholics traditionally lived in a church-dominated subculture, which was authoritarian and patriotic but, like Bishop Clemens von Galen, rejected the secularism of the National Socialists. While many Protestants sympathized with the Nazi-inspired German Christians, a substantial minority followed Dietrich Bonhoeffer and the teachings of the "Confessing Church," which rejected the Germanic neopaganism of the regime. Similarly, the dissolution of the trade unions could compel workers to join the German Labor Front, but it was unable to eradicate Marxist solidarity toward the multiple victims of the system. Though some young women fraternized with Wehrmacht soldiers, most of the people in occupied countries hated not just the Nazis but resented all Germans as overlords. Even when skeptics did not dare engage in open acts of defiance, an attitude of noncompliance, such as listening to the BBC, kept alternate views alive in spite of Gestapo control.[51]

Active resistance was a courageous choice that involved risking one's life, since it required a strong commitment to humanistic values that rejected Nazi repression and genocide. In the occupied countries increasing numbers of nationalists and communists engaged in sabotage and partisan warfare. Encouraged by the Free French, an underground maquis, for instance, attacked German outposts and helped the D-Day invasion with intelligence. While Russian and Yugoslav partisans troubled German supply lines, the most spectacular effort was the uprising of the Polish Home Army, which tried to liberate Warsaw in August 1944 but was betrayed by the Red Army.[52] Within Germany, it was difficult to stand up to the regime as long as Hitler kept winning. But impending defeat and knowledge of atrocities eventually inspired some conservative officers and politicians to attempt to overthrow the National Socialist dictatorship. Unfortunately the bombing attack, carried out by Klaus Schenk von Stauffenberg on July 20, 1944, failed to kill the Führer, leading to the death of thousands of conspirators in retribution.[53] Such resistance was a heroic demonstration of morality, but it alone could not bring the Nazis down.

MURDEROUS MODERNITY

The brutality of the Holocaust, broadly defined, poses a fundamental challenge to the Western master narrative that views modernization as a civilizing process. If since the Middle Ages Europeans had been progressing toward a reduction of violence, as Norbert Elias has argued, the sudden relapse into utter barbarity during the Nazi dictatorship is hard to explain. In order to maintain the optimistic Whig interpretation of ineluctable progress, democratic intellectuals have tended to claim that the Germans deviated from this liberal development, following a special path in an antimodern direction. But the Polish Jewish sociologist Zygmunt Bauman has challenged this self-exculpatory view, which understates Western imperialist crimes; instead, he claims that "the historical study of the Holocaust has proved beyond reasonable doubt that the Nazi-perpetrated genocide was a legitimate outcome of rational bureaucratic culture." By producing a sense of "moral indifference" among the perpetrators and conferring "moral invisibility" on the victims, modernity itself was to blame: "Both creation and destruction are inseparable aspects of what we call civilization."[54]

In order to resolve this paradox, it is necessary to stop treating the Holocaust as metahistorical morality tale and to reinsert it into its actual historical setting. Hitler unleashed his wars of aggression primarily as an effort to gain hegemony over the European continent in order to strengthen Germany's base for global competition. The ensuing mass murder of civilians was the result of Nazi dreams of eastern settlement, which required the ethnic cleansing of the existing residents so as to create space for German colonists. The persecution of millions of Jews caught in ghettos and concentration camps stemmed moreover from a post-Jewish-emancipation form of racial anti-Semitism which, by arguing biologically, cut off any escape by religious conversion or sociocultural assimilation. Finally, the ideological war of annihilation against communism and the Soviet Union facilitated mass killing because the savagery of the fighting ruptured all moral restrains. By involving local auxiliaries and extending into the Balkans, the Nazi campaign of mass murder interwove these three separate strands in a more complex fashion than is commonly remembered.[55]

Many aspects of the Nazis' orgy of destruction had, indeed, antimodern overtones in intention as well as in practice, supporting the interpretation that the Holocaust was a terrible reversion to ancient barbarism. Much of the cultural energy of National Socialism stemmed from a rejection of decadence that was symbolized by Weimar's experimental, urban modernity. At the same time the cult of violence and male bonding, derived from the Great War, invoked images of Germanic tribalism and medieval knighthood so as to constitute a new racial elite. Moreover, the entire project of agrarian settlement in the East was based on a romantic and anti-industrial understanding of national power as directly issuing from "blood and soil." The racist prejudice against Slavs and the hatred of Jews had ancient roots that appealed to irrational feelings of German superiority and revived anti-Semitic fears of ritual murder. Finally, the initial method of killing by bullets was a rather primitive form of butchery. All such aspects suggest that the National Socialist repudiation of the standards of civilization must have been a murderous relapse into barbarism.[56]

Yet other, even more important indicators demonstrate that the mass killing of Poles, Jews, and communists was part and parcel of the Nazis' effort to construct an alternate, organic form of modernity. The persecution of ideological and racial enemies within and without was the result of a massive propaganda effort that desensitized perpetrators and dehumanized potential victims. At the same time, the form of assembly-line killing in the extermination camps with the sequence of cattle cars, selection, undressing, and poison gas had an almost Fordist quality, possible only in an industrialized century. Moreover, the systematic organization of discrimination, persecution, and extermination, supervised by such deskbound killers as Adolf Eichmann, required an elaborate bureaucracy to plan each step. The academic support by scholars involved in Jewish research or doctors conducting experiments on human subjects was another aspect of quasi rationality. Finally, the genocidal effort of ethnic cleansing and racial purification was one of those great social engineering projects conceivable only with the hubris of an age infatuated by ideology.[57]

This frightening modernity of the Holocaust reveals a fundamental rupture of civilization that contradicts optimistic expectations of continued progress. The ideologies of nationalism, racism, and fascism so callously dehumanized Poles, Jews, and communists that they became mere numbers that could simply be erased.[58] Even such an advocate of the civilizing process as Norbert Elias was forced to admit that "the highly organized and scientifically planned extermination of whole population groups ... does not appear to be entirely out of place in highly technicized mass societies." While wholesale murder has a long history beginning with the ancient Assyrians, the Nazi ethnic cleansing, racist genocide, and political violence added another, even more lethal chapter due to its technical tools, bureaucratic methods, and ideological goals. Instead of bringing continued progress, the modern condition now threatened the very survival of humanity with its unprecedented capacity for murder.[59] Though the courageous resister Sophie Scholl of the White Rose represents the humane values of progress, the ruthless Auschwitz killer Rudolf Höß typifies more clearly the murderous potential of modernity.

Chapter 14

BITTER VICTORY

Dresden bombing inferno, 1945. *Source*: bpk, Berlin / Carl Weinrother / Art Resource, NY.

On April 25, 1945, an American reconnaissance patrol met advancing Soviet troops in the vicinity of the medieval city of Torgau at the Elbe River. Though Wehrmacht remnants fought desperately against the Red Army so they could surrender to U.S. forces, the Sixty-ninth Infantry Division of the First Army succeeded in linking up with the Fifth Guard Army of the First Ukrainian Front, thereby effectively cutting Nazi Germany in two. On the next day, Second Lieutenant William Robertson ceremoniously shook hands with Lieutenant Alexander Silvashko on the destroyed bridge. The official photo of their smiling encounter, taken indoors a day later, was flashed around the world. U.S. correspondent Andy Rooney witnessed the fraternization of the elated troops at an impromptu concert by a female singer just freed from a POW camp by Russian soldiers, who accompanied her with harmonicas pillaged from the Hohner factory nearby.[1] Though little known, this meeting at the Elbe signaled the joint Soviet-American triumph over the once-vaunted German army, and thereby the end of the Second World War in Europe.

Taking two and one-half years from Stalingrad to surrender, the ultimate victory of the Allies was perhaps less daring than Hitler's exploits but nonetheless all the more definitive. In retrospect it may seem inevitable that the change of the war's character from blitzkrieg to attrition should have favored the Grand Alliance, but for the participants the outcome remained long in doubt. Only through strenuous efforts at innovation did the Allies succeed in overtaking the German lead in technology, since the latter's "miracle weapons" were finished too late to affect the outcome. No doubt the combined manpower, production capacity, and resources of the British, Soviets, and Americans were considerably larger than the matériel that Hitler's generals could extract from occupied Europe, but these advantages needed to be deployed effectively in battle. While the British and the Russians were already fully engaged in the field when Germany declared war on the United States, the Americans, shielded by the Atlantic, had yet to mobilize their industries and train their troops effectively.[2] Allied victory was therefore no foregone conclusion but the result of an enormous concerted effort.

In the wake of this success, fierce arguments have developed about who deserves the actual of credit for the victory. Having absorbed countless self-congratulatory movie portrayals and specials on the History Channel, western audiences firmly believe that the D-Day landing in Normandy was crucial, largely ignoring the Soviet contribution. Based on their much larger losses, Russians and East Europeans in contrast point to the relentless assault of the Red Army as the decisive factor in winning the "Great Patriotic War." Within the western countries, the British are convinced that they deserve praise for holding out alone, the French think that only the *résistance* and General de Gaulle liberated Paris, and the Americans, of course, believe that they played the most important part of all. Finally, interservice rivalries also muddy the waters, since the air force stresses the effect of strategic bombing, the army emphasizes land battles, the navy points to the sinking of submarines, and the intelligence services tout their code breaking. What gets lost in these arguments is the way in which these aspects had to fit together to succeed.[3]

Although the "Grand Alliance" between Britain, Soviet Russia, and the United States fought for humanitarian aims, the desperate nature of the struggle brutalized Allied warfare to such an extent that they also engaged in some morally questionable acts. Winston Churchill's and FDR's Atlantic Charter of August 1941 propounded high-flung principles by rejecting territorial gains and calling for self-determination, free trade, cooperation for social welfare, and liberation from want and fear as well as freedom of the seas and disarmament. But the Red Army had no compunction about murdering up to twenty thousand Polish officers, while the British and U.S. air forces invented a new kind of firestorm bombing against cities like Hamburg and Dresden, dramatized by Kurt Vonnegut and W. G. Sebald,[4] which killed tens of thousands of civilians from the air. Moreover, the Americans dropped two atomic bombs to compel Japan to surrender. The high price of achieving victory through Red Army atrocities and systematic bombing of noncombatants threatened to erode the very values for which the Allies claimed to be fighting.[5]

Ultimately the success of the Grand Alliance derived from the superiority of communist and democratic forms of modernity over their dictatorial Nazi rival. While the organic modernity of the Nazi dictatorship possessed initial advantages in attacking its neighbors, in the long run it lacked the resources and political appeal to compete on the battlefield with the unlikely combination of forces of liberal capitalism and dictatorial communism. In spite of Stalin's paranoia and mistakes, the Soviet Union ultimately produced more effective weapons and inspired more sacrifices for "Mother Russia" than the Third Reich could muster for the "fatherland." Though democratic decision making was more cumbersome, Britain held out against Nazi air and submarine attacks. Requiring time to mobilize and placing a high value on human lives, the United States eventually brought its greater air and sea power to bear on the continent, while its armed forces were also engaged in the Pacific against Japan. The reasons for the victory of the antifascist alliance therefore lay in the greater efficacy of the communist and democratic visions of modernity.

TURNING THE TIDE

After the Allies stopped the Nazi advance, war nonetheless continued until the Axis powers were completely defeated, since both sides rejected a compromise settlement. Similar to Napoleon, Hitler needed to keep fighting in order to legitimize his rule, while the horrendous crimes of ethnic cleansing and racial genocide closed the door to any negotiated conclusion. To avoid another "stab-in-the-back" myth, the western Allies also proclaimed an "unconditional surrender" policy at the Casablanca Conference in January 1943 in order to make sure that Germany would never rise again. This formula was supposed to reassure the Soviets, who were bearing the brunt of the fighting on land, that the Anglo-American Allies would not conclude a separate peace in spite of their frustrating delay in invading France. Discouraging the anti-Nazi resistance movement within Germany, the refusal of an armistice forced the war to go on until Nazi Germany and its allies were finally conquered by force of arms.[6] Since most casualties occurred in the last six months of the fighting, it also meant that millions more people would have to be killed.

The battle that turned the tide in the East took place at Stalingrad, which became legendary because of the fierceness of the fighting and the number of casualties, approaching two million. Once known as Tsaritsyn, this city was an important industrial center that controlled the Volga crossing and shielded the routes to the oil fields in the Caucasus. After relentless Luftwaffe attacks, the German Sixth Army under General Friedrich Paulus reached its outskirts on August 23, 1942. Owing to the desperate resistance of the Soviet soldiers, militia members, and civilians, including women, the Wehrmacht tactics of mobile tank and *Stuka* (dive-bomber) warfare soon proved useless. The savage house-to-house fighting that developed in the burned-out hulks of buildings and factories, conducted by small arms, sniper fire, and mortar grenades, neutralized the tanks and artillery. In spite of incurring big losses, German forces gradually gained control of 90 percent of the city on the west bank. Realizing its symbolic significance, Stalin committed all available reinforcements, making this the decisive battle for superiority on the southern front.[7]

On November 19 the Red Army launched a well-planned counterattack that cut through both German flanks, therefore bottling up the invaders in Stalingrad. After resupplying and deploying his defenders on the eastern bank of the Volga, Marshal Georgy Zhukov shattered the overstretched Romanian, Hungarian, and Italian forces north and south of the city. With a gigantic pincer movement, emulating blitzkrieg tactics, he cut the Sixth Army off from the rest of the German lines. Though some of his officers wanted to break out of the pocket, Hitler refused, since Göring assured him that the Luftwaffe could keep supplying the encircled army, while General Erich von Manstein also argued that he would be able to relieve them by a ground attack. Obsessed with not withdrawing, Hitler announced in a rabid speech at the Berlin Sportpalast that the Germans would never leave, thereby publicly committing himself. As a result about twenty-one divisions with some 250,000 German soldiers and auxiliary forces found themselves trapped, not only without a way out but also with slim prospects of relief. What started out as a great Wehrmacht victory was turning into a crushing defeat.[8]

The Red Army prevailed at Stalingrad by employing more equipment, fighting harder for its imperiled homeland, and making superior tactical decisions. The German air force proved incapable of supplying the encircled army with sufficient ammunition, fuel, and food in order to keep it in fighting shape, losing about one-third of its eastern-front planes. Moreover, the Soviet commanders anticipated Manstein's relief offensive in December and stopped it well short of linking up with the Sixth Army. When the Red Army tightened its ring, the former attackers now became defenders in a destroyed city, bereft of any resources to sustain the fighting. With the arrival of winter, they not only starved but also froze. Nonetheless, the ferocious house-to-house combat continued with both sides giving no quarter and suffering intensely. Russian diary entries and last letters flown out to Germany show the increasing confidence of Red Army soldiers and the growing desperation of the Wehrmacht.[9] On February 2, 1943, Paulus finally disregarded Hitler's order and surrendered with less than half of his original troops still alive. In Stalingrad the Nazi war machine met its match, never to recover.

As a substitute for opening a second front in Europe, as Stalin kept demanding, the western Allies tried to relieve the pressure on the Soviets by landing in North Africa on November 8, 1942. An unregenerate imperialist, Churchill had long been pushing for Operation Torch in order to secure British supply lines in the Mediterranean and to make sure that the French colonial forces, including sizable naval units, would not support the fascists. The Allies landed tens of thousands of troops in the Moroccan and Algerian ports of Casablanca, Oran, and Algiers, intending to push on to Tunisia. Still trying to remain loyal to the Vichy government, French troops initially resisted, but they were rapidly overwhelmed by the superior naval, air, and ground forces of the combined British and American assault. Though Admiral Darlan and General Giraud wavered, eventually most of the French troops joined the Allies when Hitler ordered the occupation of the rest of mainland France.[10] Even if only a sideshow to the continental battles, the North African landing, which secured control of the Mediterranean shipping lanes, was the first success on land for the western Allies.

The North African campaign was significant because it drove the Axis forces out of Africa and opened the door for a subsequent attack on the European mainland. By October 1942 British general Bernard Montgomery had succeeded in defeating the legendary Afrika Korps under Erwin Rommel, the "Desert Fox," in the Second Battle of El Alamein, stopping once and for all the German threat to Egypt and the Suez Canal. A month later the successful landing opened a second North African front, pressuring German and Italian forces from two sides. After building up their strength, the British and Americans broke the stalemate with their April offensive, sending the fascists into full flight. Though the Axis lacked the airpower and shipping to defend the Italian colonies in North Africa, Hitler repeated the Stalingrad mistake and refused to pull out as many men and as much matériel as possible. On May 13, 1943, the remaining Germans and Italians surrendered in Tunis, giving up 275,000 POWs at one stroke. Many of them were fortunate enough to be shipped to the United States, where they waited out the rest of the war in relative comfort. The African fiasco was another drastic Axis defeat that opened the door for the Allies to invade Italy.[11]

Though thousands of miles apart, the Stalingrad and North African successes decisively changed the trajectory of the war from Axis aggression to Allied victory. In the desperate battle at the Volga River, the Wehrmacht and its allies were beaten at their own game, outgunned, outfought, and outmaneuvered, losing both the strategic initiative and their faith in ultimate victory. For all the exploits of the Desert Fox, the German-Italian forces were also defeated in the North African campaign, due to inferior weapons, lower numbers. and embattled supply lines. Furiously seeking to stave off complete disaster, the Nazi master propagandist Joseph Goebbels spoke on February 18, 1943, to a selected audience in a Berlin arena. He acknowledged a broad "crisis" on the entire eastern front, praised the trapped "heroes of Stalingrad" as defenders of European culture against the Jewish-Bolshevik threat, and appealed to everyone not to lose faith in the Führer and to redouble their efforts. Raising passions to a fever pitch, he queried rhetorically: "I ask you: Do you want total war? If necessary, do you want a war more total and radical than anything that we can even imagine today?" The electrified crowd shouted back "Yes! Yes!" and broke into "unending stormy applause." But feverish fanaticism would prove unable to stop superior force.[12]

WEARING DOWN THE REICH

The Allied victories during 1942–43 revealed the superiority of communist and democratic modernity in a drawn-out struggle of attrition. While lightning strikes favored the well-oiled Nazi war machine, the prolongation of the conflict brought the Allied advantage in resources, manpower, and weapons into play. For the Axis powers, Albert Speer tried to organize production more efficiently and to increase the exploitation of conquered Europe, but crucial raw materials under his control, such as oil, were limited, and hydrogenation of synthetic fuels from coal remained costly and time-consuming. In contrast, the Allies were able to rely on a surprising increase in output of war matériel by Russian factories hastily relocated east of the Ural Mountains, continued British manufacturing supported by the British Empire, and the enormous capacities of the United States, once fully converted to Fordist mass production of military goods.[13] It took time to coordinate these efforts, to train the troops in the available arms, and to employ new weapons successfully on the battlefield. But ultimately this discrepancy proved decisive.

Production figures show the drastic extent of Allied superiority, which continued to increase during the second part of the war while Axis production could not keep up. The basic size of the competing economies was disparate enough: In 1942 the Allied GNP per person was 2.4 times larger than that of the Axis, and this advantage grew to 3.1 times during 1944. Similarly Allied countries made 2.9 times more steel than the Axis powers, increasing to 3.4 times three years later. As a result the Allies outproduced their fascist enemies in all significant weapons categories: From 1942 to 1944 the Allies manufactured 184,200 tanks compared to only 39,600 of the Axis, giving them a 4.7-fold edge. In fighter airplanes the difference was somewhat smaller, 299,500 versus 114,600, yet still amounting to 2.6 times greater. But in artillery the gap was once again larger, 1,209,000 versus 395,000, that is, 3.1 times larger. In other weapons such as rifles, machine guns, and so on the Allied advantage was generally around threefold.[14] Moreover, the quality of Allied arms gradually caught up and in some cases, such as the Russian T-34 tank, even proved superior.

The German command sought to compensate by using submarine warfare so as to keep the Allies' superior amounts of supplies from reaching the battlefield. Britain proved particularly vulnerable to a naval counterblockade, since it received 75 percent of its food, 95 percent of its petroleum products, and 30 percent of its iron ore by sea. Moreover, all American war matériel had to be ferried across the Atlantic. While the Royal Navy quickly managed to sink German battleships like the *Bismarck*, Churchill worried about the U-boats, whose stealthy attacks came close to interdicting British shipping. Since Hitler had not realized the significance of this weapon despite the pleas of Admiral Karl Dönitz, the Germans initially had merely fifty or so submarines at their disposal, only one-third of which could be on station at any time. Preying on convoys with "wolf-pack" tactics, the U-boats nonetheless managed to sink about seven million tons of commercial shipping in the crucial year of 1942 alone. As the official history of the Royal Navy commented afterward, the Battle of the Atlantic turned into "a close struggle for bare survival."[15]

Though Dönitz built up his fleet, during 1943 the Allies quelled the submarine threat by shattering German confidence through the sinking of 242 U-boats. This success was largely due to the strategic help of the United States, which provided longer-distance cover, and the occupation of Iceland, which allowed airplanes to patrol the North Atlantic routes. Changed tactics, such as more warship escorts for convoys, the use of planes to drop depth charges, and the development of sonar and radar to spot submarines, shifted the odds against the attackers, who thereafter failed to return from every third mission, on average. The mass-production techniques of U.S. shipyards also allowed more standardized "liberty ships" to be built each month than could be sunk by enemy raiders. German countermeasures, such as speeded-up building programs, an improved design for the snorkel, allowing boats to remain submerged longer, and the construction of supersubs, came too late. Though the submarines sank altogether almost 15 million tons of shipping, the Allies built 46.5 million tons at the same time. Allied antisubmarine measures were so effective that the U-boats became "iron coffins," suffering overall losses at an incredible rate of 75 percent.[16]

The Allied leadership in turn resorted to strategic bombing in order to hamper German war production and undercut morale. Initially the British flew raids in retaliation for attacks on England and as a psychological boost, showing that they were serious about fighting the Nazis. When daytime attacks incurred too many losses because of fighter harassment and antiaircraft guns, the RAF switched to dispersed nighttime raids on military and civilian targets that were less precise but safer. The U.S. Air Force preferred attacking strategic targets during daytime instead, hoping to knock the Germans out of the war by destroying ball-bearing and synthetic-fuel plants and puncturing reservoir dams. Although carpet bombing by thousands of planes created enormous damage on the ground, it also proved quite dangerous for the air crews, leading many planes to crash. To reduce such losses the British and Americans developed a new strategy of starting "firestorms" by dropping incendiary bombs on the crowded medieval parts of cities that would burn thousands of houses and civilians.[17] Doing much damage, these devastating attacks nonetheless failed to break German morale.

Though at first disappointing, saturation bombing eventually helped win the war by limiting Germany's war production and bringing its transportation to a standstill. German defenses such as the interceptor aircraft and the fifty thousand flak guns all over the Reich were initially fairly effective in punishing attackers, causing the loss of about eighty-one thousand pilots and aircrew. Meanwhile civilians huddled in air-raid shelters, praying not to be hit, and then workers quickly rebuilt destroyed factories or relocated them in the safer countryside. But these countermeasures could not keep pace with the relentless Allied attacks. Even if they were unable to interdict war production completely, the massive raids on Hamburg and the Ruhr Basin that cost tens of thousands of German civilian lives did slow increases of war production after May 1943, thereby depriving the Axis of potential arms. Ultimately, however, it was the destruction of the railroads, bridges, and canals that brought down the Third Reich. Altogether the bombing razed scores of ancient cities like Cologne and killed about six hundred thousand civilians, going vastly beyond what could be called "collateral damage," since the one thousand bomber raids also involved an element of revenge.[18]

The intelligence war also strongly favored the Allied side owing to the breaking of the German code, called Enigma. In the beginning the Nazis could rely on human information from fascist sympathizers and had some success in deciphering British codes, but it took too much time for the information to be useful in the field. In contrast, the Polish secret service had procured a copy of the German encrypting machine, an electromechanical typewriter that could produce 1,253 trillion permutations. The subsequent capture of a trawler and submarine gave the Allies access to the key tables, enormously facilitating their task. At Bletchley Park in the United Kingdom an entire unit worked on decoding Enigma intercepts (classified as *Ultra* Secret), helped by the brilliant mathematician Alan Turing and other Cambridge dons. Since most military orders were telegraphed through the airwaves, German messages could be intercepted, sent to "Ultra," and decoded within a few hours.[19] This deciphering in real time was an enormous operational advantage, since the Allies were apprised of German plans and devised countermeasures without the enemy being aware of it.

Finally, the Allies also proved more adept at psychological warfare than the Nazis because they employed modern advertising methods and appealed to more humane values. The Third Reich controlled its media through the Ministry of Public Enlightenment and Propaganda, headed by Joseph Goebbels. He excelled at mass rallies and press direction, but when he found it hard to keep emotions at a fever pitch by these methods, he turned to entertainment as a morale booster during the war. In contrast, the decentralized effort of the Allies relied more on a "strategy of truth" and the self-mobilization of the media. Helped by Weimar émigrés, Hollywood movie directors produced a stream of propaganda films on government orders and also as commercial ventures. Both sides sent entertainers to the front, whose songs sometimes even cut across the front lines, like Lale Anderson's "Lili Marleen." In the contest between pro-Axis radio propagandist Lord Haw-Haw and pro-Allied commentator Sefton Delmer, the BBC ultimately had the upper hand because its news reports proved more reliable.[20]

LIBERATING THE WEST

The military leader who brought the superiority of Allied modernity to bear on the battlefield was General Dwight D. Eisenhower. He was born into a poor but devout German-American family and grew up in rural Kansas. As a West Point graduate, he became an engineer and tank commander during World War I without seeing frontline duty. As his leadership potential was gradually realized during the interwar years, he was put in charge of general-staff planning for a victorious strategy against Japan and Germany during World War II. In 1942 he was appointed commander of U.S. troops in the European theater and after the successful operations in North Africa elevated to supreme commander of Allied forces in Europe a year later. Eisenhower was a careful planner, a capable organizer, and a persuasive mediator in disputes about strategic questions such as whether to establish a second front in France, the Balkans, or Italy. Less flamboyant than Douglas MacArthur or George S. Patton, the affable "Ike" nonetheless became the mastermind of Anglo-American victory.[21]

On July 10, 1943, a combined British-American force invaded Sicily with 160,000 troops, ferried on three thousand vessels. Having gained control of the air and seas, the Allies quickly increased this army to 450,000 men, who routed Italian and German defenders within thirty-eight days, though the personal rivalry of vainglorious generals such as Montgomery and Patton complicated the operation. The Italians lost 132,000 men and the Germans 32,000 men killed, wounded, or captured, but the Wehrmacht managed to withdraw 53,000 other soldiers to the mainland. The political repercussions were even more important than control of the island. In a surprise move, the Fascist Grand Council voted seventeen to nine to oust the dictator Mussolini and install Marshal Pietro Badoglio as prime minister. Even the Duce's son-in-law, Foreign Minister Ciano, agreed to depose him. While publicly proclaiming his Axis loyalty, Badoglio secretly negotiated an armistice with General Eisenhower, signed on September 3. The Allied strategy seemed to be paying off when Italy officially switched sides and declared war on Nazi Germany on October 13.[22]

Yet the Italian campaign turned out to be disappointing because it resulted in endless fighting, which proved a diversion from rather than a decisive contribution to ending the war. Landing at the tip of the Italian boot at Salerno, Taranto, and Bari, the Allies liberated the South without encountering much resistance and pushed on to Naples. But an irate Hitler refused to give up and quickly ordered the confused Italian forces to be disarmed and interned. Under the command of Field Marshal Albert Kesselring, the Germans, now freed from negotiating with their Italian partners, quickly scratched together another army that fought with skill and determination. Moreover, in a daring mission on September 12, 1943, SS *Obersturmbannführer* Otto Skorzeny freed Mussolini from captivity on Gran Sasso Mountain and brought him back behind German lines. Though broken, the Duce reestablished an Italian puppet government, the so-called Republic of Salo, which continued to fight on the German side and pursued even more radical Fascist policies. The Allied advance thereafter bogged down, taking almost two more years to reach Lombardy.[23]

The ground war in Italy saw some ferocious fighting because the difficult terrain negated most Allied advantages. The Apennine Mountains and the narrowness of the long peninsula made it possible for the defenders to construct formidable positions like the Gustav Line, which had to be taken by infantry assault. American forces trying to bypass such defenses by landing farther up the peninsula, behind German lines, got bottled up in the Anzio beachhead, near Rome, while the monastery on top of Monte Cassino changed hands several times in fierce combat. Declared an open city to save its treasures, Rome was finally liberated in June of 1944 and Florence captured in the fall. But the Wehrmacht always succeeded in reestablishing another defensive position such as the Gothic Line, supported by artillery. Because the D-Day landing in France diverted experienced troops, it took until April of 1945 for the Allies to finally break through into the plains of Lombardy and for the Germans in Italy to surrender. On either side the struggle cost over 50,000 lives and over 330,000 casualties.[24] The Italian campaign contributed to the attrition of Nazi Germany by tying down troops but failed to be decisive in the end.

Only the invasion of France delivered the crushing blow that opened up the road to Nazi Germany and established a second front in Europe equal to the front in the East. So much has been written and so many movies made about Operation Overlord that it is hard to distinguish fact from fiction. The attack was delayed because the German defenses of the *Westwall* looked so formidable that the Allies decided not to land at the Pas de Calais right across the Channel but rather chose the more lightly defended Normandy coast instead. Marshaling an armada big enough to be confident of victory took, nonetheless, many months to complete. On June 6, 1944, the biggest invasion force ever, consisting of twelve thousand airplanes, seven thousand ships, 17,000 paratroopers, and 160,000 soldiers transported by boats finally hit the beaches from Utah to Sword. Though the American, British, Dominion, and French armies of 2.8 million in thirty-five divisions were vastly superior in number, the landing was nonetheless a military challenge because they needed to ferried across the treacherous channel. Wading to shore, the first waves of attackers had to scale steep cliffs in order to silence the big guns in pillboxes, firing from above. While Wehrmacht defenders fought tenaciously, Hitler held his armored reinforcements back because he believed that the main cross-Channel invasion would come elsewhere. This crucial delay allowed the landing forces to establish and secure their initial beachheads.[25]

After two months of struggling through hedgerows, the Allied breakout into Brittany opened northern France to the invading forces. In a logistical masterpiece, the Anglo-American troops built two provisional harbors through which they landed a million soldiers within ten days, thereby achieving numerical superiority on the battlefield. While Montgomery was pushing east along the coast, U.S.

general Omar Bradley broke through the German lines to the south-west in early August, trapping German garrisons in the important ports of Cherbourg, Brest, and St. Nazaire. Instead of organizing a retreat, Hitler ordered German divisions to counterattack south of Caen, where Patton's forces encircled them in the pocket of Falaise, pulverizing helpless tanks with airpower. Though many Germans escaped, forty divisions were destroyed and fifty thousand men captured, freeing the way to the French capital. On August 15, the Allies landed a second invasion force on the Mediterranean coast in Provence, which began racing up the Rhone Valley to threaten the Wehrmacht from the rear. Disobeying explicit orders, General Dietrich von Choltitz surrendered Paris on August 25, sparing the French capital destruction by declaring it an open city.[26]

The rest of France was liberated in short order, but then a pause slowed the Allied advance for several months. The surviving German units hastily withdrew toward their own border, while the Allies mopped up the Wehrmacht pockets holding on to the French ports. Crossing river estuaries, the British and Canadians conquered most of Belgium in September. But Holland remained in Nazi hands, slowly starving, because its source of food was cut off. Although some generals were pressing to continue a rapid advance, Eisenhower, who was responsible for overall strategy, realized that the Allies had outrun their supplies and needed to rest and repair before the final push into the Reich. Even though German resistance stiffened once again in places like the Hürtgen Forest, the Allies gradually managed to reach the Siegfried Line, the fortified border of the Reich. In October they captured Aachen, the first German city to fall into Allied hands, and installed an occupation regime. While Montgomery's attempt to secure the Rhine crossings in Operation Market-Garden fell short, the Allies had liberated all of France in half a year, a truly impressive feat.[27]

The Allies won the French campaign because they succeeded in translating their material superiority into battlefield performance. Though they also suffered heavy casualties, the Allied armies routed the Wehrmacht by destroying eighteen hundred tanks, killing 240,000 Germans, and taking 350,000 prisoners. Several reasons explain their triumph: They held a clear command of the air as well as the seas; they possessed more tanks, cannon, and even jeeps; and they had larger numbers of troops at their disposal. In the savage fighting, their soldiers also acquired that battle hardness necessary for defeating an experienced enemy, who was gradually losing faith in his own superiority. The Ultra intercepts let the Allied commanders know in advance what their enemies were planning, making a crucial difference in preparations for D-Day. They could draw on a multinational force with units from Poland, Canada, and Australia fighting side by side. Finally, local resistance movements like the French maquis supported their advance with intelligence and partisan attacks.[28] No wonder democratic modernity ultimately prevailed.

WINNING THE EAST

In spite of the important contribution of the western Allies, the Second World War was ultimately decided on the eastern front, where the scale of the battles was larger, the losses on both sides were greater, and the psychological effects more discouraging for the Wehrmacht.[29] It is understandable for Anglo-American veterans to insist on their own bravery and for novels, films, and television specials to celebrate the liberation of France. In contrast, the East European sites were remote, few western journalists were attached to the Red Army, and no battlefield tourism has developed that might be comparable to that of Normandy. Only in the former Soviet Union are the exploits of the Russian commanders regularly commemorated on May 9 of each year, bemedaled Red Army veterans praised, and huge monuments erected to recall the millions of dead. While German officers and soldiers attributed their defeat to the superior matériel of the West, they continued to wonder about their inability to stop the Russian advance in the East. The Red Army ultimately triumphed because the communists had also developed an invincible version of military modernity.

The Battle of Kursk, the largest tank engagement ever, provides some clues. In the aftermath of Stalingrad the Red Army had captured this important railroad hub, thrusting far into the German lines.

But holding on to Orel in the North and retaking Kharkov in the South, the Wehrmacht intended to straighten out its front by pinching off the Russian salient. On July 5, 1943, 2,900 German tanks, 10,000 artillery pieces, and 900,000 troops attacked 5,100 Russian tanks, 25,000 cannons, and 1.9 million soldiers. While making some initial gains, Operation Citadel soon bogged down because the Red Army defenses were too formidable. Though the Germans used some of their newest weapons and best units, the Russian lines proved impenetrable, since the defenders were willing to die in larger numbers than the attackers. Unable to achieve a decisive breakthrough, Hitler abandoned the attack, having lost 3,000 tanks, 1,400, planes and half a million men dead, wounded, or captured. While it suffered even greater losses, the Red Army gained the strategic initiative, pushing the Germans back to the Dnieper River by early fall.[30]

The victory at Kursk showed that the Soviets had succeeded in blunting German blitzkrieg tactics with deep defense, relying on superiority in numbers and matériel. From 1942 on, the Russians outproduced the Reich in crucial armaments such as numbers of tanks, artillery, and airplanes. Moreover, they were helped by American Lend-Lease supplies, ranging from jeeps to infantry boots. While some of the new German weapons like the Tiger tank were superior, they often broke down in the field, whereas the Soviet T-34s proved more suited to the Russian climate, and the Wehrmacht had no defense against the Katyusha rocket launchers. With sufficient preparatory time, the Red Army also developed a method for stopping the German tank spearheads with minefields, coordinated artillery, and deep deployment, supported by airpower. In infantry combat, Russians, fighting for their homes, were more ready to sacrifice their lives, wearing down resistance by attacking in endless waves.[31] Though sustaining heavier losses, the Red Army had grown capable of defeating the Wehrmacht in open field battle by the summer of 1943.

On the twenty-seventh anniversary of the October Revolution, Stalin described the offensives that liberated Russia and drove the Nazis from Eastern Europe during 1944 as the "ten great blows." In its inexorable advance the Red Army used its superiority in manpower (6.5 million to 4.3 million), tanks (5,600 to 2,300), guns (90,000 to 54,000), and airplanes (8,800 to 3,000) to good advantage. The Soviets mounted the first offensive along the Dnieper River to liberate the Ukraine from occupation and exploitation. Next they attacked in the North, freeing Leningrad from its encirclement, which had cost 1.1 million lives largely due to starvation. Then they switched to the South, moving toward Odessa and the Crimea, forcing those Axis forces to surrender. Thereafter they again moved north against Finland, compelling Germany's ally to sue for peace. But they struck the most important blow on the central front in the Bagration offensive, when the Red Army encircled thirty German divisions at Minsk, recaptured Belarus, and thrust deep into Poland. Though stubbornly fighting, the Wehrmacht proved incapable of stopping this methodical advance.[32]

The basic pattern of combat was repeated time and again in a lethal dance that followed a fixed choreography. Helped by partisan harassment, the Red Army would build up its forces, attack on a front of a hundred miles or so, break through the lines in several places, stream forward, and rout the defenders. Ignoring the advice of his generals, Hitler would refuse to retreat, issuing "scorched earth" and "stand or die" orders in a frantic effort to stabilize the front. The Soviet troops would bypass German "hedgehog" positions to be eliminated later and continue to surge ahead until encountering a new defensive line constructed by Axis reserves far in the rear. This systematic approach was never daring enough to unhinge the entire eastern front in one bold stroke, but it ultimately shattered the morale of the Wehrmacht, which, try as it might, proved unable to stop the continual Russian advance. Sarcastically the demoralized soldiers encouraged each other with slogans like "Forward comrades, we have to retreat!" While withdrawing, the Germans exacted fearsome losses from the Russians, but these were never big enough to halt the advance.[33] Hitler's stubborn refusal to adopt a flexible defense hastened his defeat.

On August 1, 1944, the Polish Home Army, an underground resistance movement led by General Tadeusz Bor-Komorowski, rose up in Warsaw in order to chase the Nazis out and liberate the capital before the Russians arrived. Without any heavy arms, tens of thousands Polish patriots battled against the occupiers in city houses and sewers, fighting spiritedly to regain their freedom. Though the Red Army had reached the eastern bank of the Vistula, the Russian generals failed to cross over to relieve the embattled Poles. Stalin did not want an independent, nationalist Polish government, preferring instead the communist puppets of the Polish Committee for National Liberation, whom he had just installed in Lublin. For sixty-three days the Poles battled mechanized forces and ruthless SS troops in fierce house-to-house fighting, but they were eventually forced to surrender, since the Red Army provided neither air cover nor ground support. About sixteen thousand Polish resistance fighters were killed and another six thousand wounded, though the Germans also suffered heavy casualties. During the uprising 85 percent of the city was destroyed, and two hundred thousand civilians died.[34]

The concurrent Soviet offensives during 1944 targeted the Balkans and the Baltic countries instead so as to drive the Germans out of their eastern conquests and split off their allies. The summer attack in southwestern Ukraine encircled about twenty German and Romanian divisions trying to defend the vital oil fields and thereby forced Romania to switch to the Allied side. Crossing the Danube, the Red Army then compelled Bulgaria to capitulate and linked up with Tito's partisans to liberate Belgrade in October. As a result, Nazi occupiers in Greece were cut off, while Soviet armies began to lay siege to Budapest in December. During the fall the Red Army also recaptured the Baltic states such as Estonia, Latvia, and most of Lithuania, trapping the German Army Group North under Guderian in Courland because Hitler refused his pleas to withdraw. Finally the Soviets also chased the remaining German troops out of Finland, forcing them to flee into Norway.[35] These Soviet victories dissolved the Nazi alliance system by overthrowing pro-fascist governments and forcing countries to change sides.

The collapse of Hitler's empire plunged Eastern Europe into a chaotic transition, marked by conflicting emotions of joy and fear. The liberated Slavic populations celebrated the arrival of the Red Army, and the freed concentration-camp survivors were relieved that their ordeal was finally over. But those countries like Hungary and persons like the Russian soldiers of the Vlasov army, who had collaborated with the Germans, experienced the arrival of Soviet troops as new repression, characterized by violent retribution. Facing defeat, the civilian German occupiers started to flee in droves, trying to relocate their war industries and salvage some of their spoils by returning to the Reich. At the same time non-German collaborators also sought to escape, since they feared the vengeance of the partisans or the resistance who now gained control. Order dissolved in the dangerous interregnum between the departure of the Wehrmacht and the arrival of the Red Army, a time when authority vanished and private scores could be settled. In this confusing transition, nationalist leaders and socialist functionaries began to quarrel over the future orientation of their liberated countries.[36]

FORCING SURRENDER

Allied advances from the West and East to the borders of the Reich initiated the final round of the war for control of Germany itself. Russian atrocities in East Prussian districts, which were reconquered by the Wehrmacht, allowed Goebbels to proclaim an *Endkampf* in order to mobilize all possible resources for staving off the impending defeat. Nazi leaders still hoped for miracles either from the arrival of new, more powerful weapons or from a breakup of the enemy coalition after FDR's death, as in the Seven Years' War. National Socialist Party fanatics were ready to perish in a Wagnerian Götterdämmerung, taking the entire country down with them, while ordinary Germans were beginning to make plans for life after the Third Reich and imprisoned members of the resistance were praying for liberation before it was too late.[37] In contrast, Allied commanders were confident of ultimate victory, wondering only whether the Russians or the Americans would be the first to arrive in Berlin. Meeting at Yalta in February 1945, Roosevelt, Churchill, and Stalin already started to stake their claims for a coming postwar order in Europe.

Nazi hopes for so-called miracle weapons were not entirely misplaced, but these potentially deadly arms arrived too late and in too small numbers to affect the outcome. Surprised by the quality of Allied arms, German engineers improved existing designs, constructing prototypes of a superheavy tank, the Maus. At the same time, they also ventured into entirely new areas. Messerschmitt started to develop turbojet fighters like the Me 262, which were much faster than piston-engine aircraft. But a combination of lack of jet fuel, pilot losses, and transportation bottlenecks kept most of these planes from flying and deciding the outcome of combat in the air. Another such project was rocket development, headed by Werner von Braun, who designed ballistic missiles capable of crossing the Channel and delivering payloads of up to one thousand kilos of explosives. Used against London, the V-2 terrorized the British capital but was not precise and numerous enough to make a strategic difference. Fortunately, the Nazis did not assign the development of atomic bombs sufficient priority to produce an operable weapon for mounting on missiles by the end of the war.[38]

Running out of manpower, a frantic Hitler tried to raise a national militia in October 1944, called the *Volkssturm* according to the Prussian precedent of 1813. Since the regular replacement process of the *Ersatzheer* (army reserves) no longer produced sufficient soldiers to make up for the millions of dead, wounded, and captured, he ordered the Nazi Party to organize a paramilitary defense force by mobilizing all males from sixteen-year-old boys to sixty-year-old grandfathers in a last-ditch attempt to boost morale. Lacking sufficient uniforms, the militia was identified by black armbands and supplied with rifles, submachine guns, and antitank grenades. Harangued by party functionaries but badly trained, these civilians were ordered to create antitank barriers and destroy bridges so as to defend their towns. Some of the thrown-together units were even sent to the front in order to stop the Russian advance. Looking bedraggled, this *Volkssturm* was a far cry from the confident Wehrmacht troops of five years earlier. Instead, it was a pathetic effort to stop the invaders that had little military value and only increased the number of pointless casualties.[39]

The Allies were surprised that many Germans continued to fight in the face of certain defeat. Not all of them did, since in the West some courageous commanders surrendered their cities rather than have them destroyed, while entire units deserted. But especially in the East, the Wehrmacht battled desperately because its soldiers instinctively feared that they would suffer retribution for their wartime atrocities. Many were also scared of the roving police squads of the army and SS, called *Kettenhunde*, who combed the front and the rear, summarily shooting anyone accused of defeatism. Invoking the threatening vengeance by the Soviet Army's "Asiatic hordes" with examples of real Red Army atrocities, Goebbels appealed not only to fanatical Nazis but also to ordinary Germans to defend their homes. Finally, soldiers above all battled from a "feeling of loyalty, a sense of responsibility and comradeship" in an unspoken survival pact that made them dependent on each other.[40] As a result, a strange disconnect developed between the growing realization of impending doom and the continued commitment to fight. Cynical veterans quipped: "Enjoy the war, the peace will be terrible."

In the West, the Battle of the Bulge, the final German counteroffensive, temporarily halted the invasion of the Reich. Hoping to repeat his initial success, Hitler gambled his last reserves on a daring plan to split the British and American forces by again attacking in the Ardennes and recapturing the port of Antwerp. Starting on December 15, thirteen Wehrmacht divisions with about 340 tanks and 1,600 cannon assaulted a weakly defended section of the American lines, achieving complete tactical surprise because of the bad weather that inhibited air reconnaissance. Though unanticipated resistance by American GIs slowed the Germans down, they advanced about fifty to seventy miles, surrounded a U.S. airborne division in Bastogne, and got about halfway to the Channel coast. But eventually the offensive stalled, and American counterattacks, led by General Patton, managed to push the Wehrmacht back, with each side losing about one hundred thousand men.[41] By the end of January 1945, the Allies were once again advancing and threatening the Siegfried Line. By using up his last available armored forces and Luftwaffe planes, Hitler left the door to Germany proper wide open.

The ensuing conquest of western Germany turned out to be surprisingly easy, since the depleted and demoralized Wehrmacht offered only sporadic resistance. The Allies breached the fabled *West-*

wall of bunkers, pillboxes, and tank traps in February 1945. Advance units of the Ninth Armored Division captured the bridge at Remagen and established a beachhead on the east side of the Rhine, while General Montgomery managed to cross at Wesel and Rees. As a result, the British enveloped the Ruhr Basin, the industrial forge of Germany, from the north, while American armor surrounded it from the south, closing the trap at Lippstadt on April 1. Though clearing the pocket took another three weeks, the Allies captured over 325,000 prisoners and drove Field Marshal Walther Model to commit suicide. Since the Germans were no longer capable of a coherent defense, Eisenhower readjusted his plans, pushing forward toward Leipzig in order to link up with the Red Army at the Elbe River. While the British fanned out to conquer the northern plain, American units turned southward to prevent the establishment of a Nazi mountain redoubt.[42]

In contrast, the final offensive of the Red Army in the East involved much heavier fighting with huge losses on both sides. Soviet forces had about a six-to-one advantage in manpower, tanks, airplanes, and guns, but the Wehrmacht defenders bitterly battled for every kilometer of German soil. On January 12, Marshal Zhukov started the Vistula-Oder offensive, finally taking Warsaw, then overrunning Pomerania and rapidly advancing to the Oder River, cutting off East Prussia, which held out until early April. In the South the Red Army captured Budapest in February and moved on to Vienna, which surrendered in mid-April. In the ensuing Battle of Berlin a confident Red Army of about 2.5 million soldiers as well as twenty thousand tanks and self-propelled artillery faced a ragtag force of regular army, SS, *Volkssturm*, and Hitler Youth units of about one-fifth its size. When Soviet troops started their final offensive on April 16, they crossed the Oder River to the north, the middle, and the south and encircled the Reich's capital, trapping the rest of the Wehrmacht at the Seelow Heights, their last defensive position.[43]

Holed up in the *Führerbunker* in central Berlin, a desperate Hitler could no longer stave off his downfall. Declaring cities like Breslau as fortresses did prolong local resistance but also assured their destruction through bombing and artillery fire. Having lost seven hundred thousand soldiers in January and February on the eastern front alone, the Führer could only move paper armies about that lacked equipment and fighting strength. Beating back General Walther Wenck's relief attempt, the Red Army began to shell the city of Berlin, advancing inexorably in bloody hand-to-hand combat toward the center. After marrying Eva Braun, a despondent Hitler committed suicide on April 30, blaming the "world Jewish conspiracy" for the defeat in his testament. While Nazi leaders like Goebbels followed his example or sought to hide like Himmler, remnants of German forces tried to break through to the West. Ending the pointless bloodshed, General Helmut Weidling finally surrendered Berlin on May 2. Glad that the fighting was over, survivors in the city now experienced some of the rape, pillage, and murder that the Nazis had themselves committed all over the continent.[44]

The capitulation of the remaining German forces ended World War II in Europe after almost six years of incredible suffering and bloodshed. Though the Wehrmacht still controlled Norway, Denmark, pieces of northern and southern Germany, Courland, Bohemia, as well as parts of Austria and northern Italy, the meeting of U.S. and Russian forces at the Elbe and the fall of Berlin signaled that further resistance was pointless. Various regional commanders therefore surrendered to the advancing Allies from May 1 on. Bypassing Göring and Himmler as traitors, Hitler had appointed Admiral Dönitz his successor as president, who vowed "to save Germany from destruction by the advancing Bolshevik enemy." But when Eisenhower insisted on "unconditional surrender," General Alfred Jodl agreed at Reims that "all forces under German control [were] to cease active operations at 23:01 hours Central European Time on May 8, 1945."[45] Not to be outdone, Marshal Zhukov repeated the ceremony with Field Marshal Wilhelm Keitel in Berlin-Karlshorst a day later. The second time around, there was no doubt that conquered Germany had definitely lost the war.

CAUSES OF VICTORY

Pitting the three great ideologies of the twentieth century against each other, the Second World War was in many ways a conflict for control of Europe between opposing visions of modernity. Instead of just competing for electoral success, the fascists, communists, and democrats engaged in mortal combat, trying to prevail by force rather than by propaganda. Conventional explanations of Allied victory stress the heroism of the troops, the brilliance of strategic decisions, the superiority of weapons, and the wealth of economic resources. Other interpretations instead focus on Axis blunders in arms development, choice of strategy, or political coordination.[46] But on a deeper causal level, the outcome was also determined by the differing potential of the conflicting modernities, because their implications determined the military capabilities and policy decisions of the combatants. It was the particularly aggressive expansionism of fascism that forced its communist and democratic competitors into collaborating in spite of their fundamental ideological differences. But in the end this unlikely Grand Alliance did prevail.

Though seemingly dynamic, the organic modernity of the Nazis ultimately proved self-defeating because it fundamentally disregarded human life. In the chaos after World War I and onward through the Great Depression, fascism appeared as the wave of the future by promising to create a national community with forceful action. Indeed, this vision appeared to have many advantages: the leadership principle allowed for quick decisions, the public acclamation suggested unity, the militarization of the economy prepared for war, the cult of manliness extolled sacrifice for the fatherland, and the racist rhetoric identified scapegoats on whom failures could be blamed. But the Nazi system also had large flaws that proved deleterious: Hitler's charisma permitted no correction of his political and strategic errors, the suppression of dissent eliminated alternatives, the racist persecution wasted manpower, and the ruthless exploitation of the conquered countries inspired resistance. Mistaken strategies and lack of resources as well as disregard of allies and obsequious subservience were no accident but rather the logical result of the basic character of Nazi ideology.[47]

In spite of social upheaval and intense suffering, the resiliency of communist modernity surprised not only the Russians themselves but also astounded foreign observers. Initially, Stalin's dictatorial paranoia and the bloodletting of the Great Purges, especially among the Red Army generals, brought the Soviet Union to the brink of collapse in 1941. But the preceding collectivization and industrialization had created an economic base, educational reforms had trained capable weapons designers, and the decision to shift production behind the Urals had allowed Russia to outproduce Germany. Moreover, Nazi aggression forged political unity by inspiring Soviet citizens to fight for the motherland, the *rodina*, no matter what they thought of communism or the Bolshevik Party. The existential threat of ethnic cleansing also roused members of other nationalities and even some women to take up arms, with about twenty-seven million sacrificing their lives. While western Lend-Lease helped, the emancipatory core and rational bent of Marxist ideology, which harked back to the Enlightenment, made it easier to believe in the justness of its cause.[48]

The democratic version of modernity, which in the depression seemed to be on its way out, also proved more capable of sustaining the conflict than its critics had predicted. No doubt France collapsed from internal weakness and British appeasement hardly prepared the United Kingdom for the assault of the Luftwaffe and the raids of the U-boats. But the appointment of the brilliant orator Winston Churchill helped stiffen the Royal Air Force and Navy's resistance enough to hold out. While isolationism made it difficult for President Roosevelt to help Britain, the Japanese attack on Pearl Harbor as well as Hitler's declaration of war spurred the United States to mobilize on an unprecedented scale. Though it took considerable time to make a difference, the addition of huge American manpower, massive Fordist war production, and Hollywood's propaganda effort eventually helped reverse the tide of war. But in the end, it was the defense of the ideal of freedom, the public debate to correct mistakes, and the ability to coordinate strategic decisions between the United

States and the United Kingdom that inspired domestic determination and gained international support.[49]

For the relieved survivors of May 1945, liberation from Nazi tyranny nevertheless left a bitter taste, since the paroxysm of violence among the contending ideologies came close to destroying Europe during the war. Within the continent alone the fighting had killed about forty million soldiers as well as civilians, with many more wounded and traumatized. Moreover about another thirty million uprooted people were on the move, with survivors leaving the concentration camps, DPs trying to get back home, POWs released from prison camps, and ethnic Germans fleeing from the East. Prefigured by the brutality of the First World War, ideological propaganda, bureaucratic planning, and technological innovation had produced a peculiarly modern murderousness. To defeat the vicious fascist aggressors, even the Allies had felt compelled to resort to methods that might be considered a violation of human rights such as the firestorm bombing of German cities and the use of nuclear bombs against Japan. Scorched-earth tactics, saturation bombing, and racial genocide had unleashed so savage a violence that it left much of the European continent in ashes.[50]

Part III

SURPRISING RECOVERY, 1945–73

Chapter 15

DEMOCRATIC RENEWAL

Aneurin Bevan visits a patient of the British National Health Service, 1948. *Source*: Central Manchester University Hospitals NHS Foundation Trust.

In February 1945 the leaders of the victorious powers met at Yalta, in the balmy climate and scenic surroundings of the Crimea, in order to consult on the transition to peace. "Waging a fierce struggle for the shape of the post-war world," they were an impressive group, consisting of Winston Churchill, the indomitable conservative from London; Franklin Delano Roosevelt, the ailing president from Washington; and Joseph Stalin, the revolutionary dictator from Moscow. In the hope that Allied cooperation would carry over from the conduct of the war, the trio of statesmen discussed the establishment of the United Nations, Russian participation in the defeat of Japan, and Polish frontiers. The conference signaled their "inflexible purpose to destroy German militarism and Nazism in order to ensure that Germany will never again be able to disturb the peace of the world." In "liberated Europe" the victors hoped "to solve by democratic means their pressing political and economic problems." Euphorically, all agreed that the postwar order of European peoples should be based on "democratic institutions of their own choice."[1]

The task of restoring self-government was daunting because much of Europe lay in utter ruin. News photographs show that except for some fortunate stretches of untouched countryside, the combination of saturation bombing and savage ground fighting had reduced most larger cities to moonscapes of gutted buildings in which a few forlorn souls made their way through piles of rubble.[2] With water mains ruptured, power lines cut, railroad tracks destroyed, bridges broken, and roads clogged, the most important task was to restore basic services and to provide enough food and fuel to assure the survival of the remaining inhabitants. Disposing of the physical remains of the dead so as to prevent epidemics and coping with the psychological traumas of mass murder and mass death by finding a way to mourn the losses posed other existential challenges. In order to pacify wartorn society and help restore civility, the rampant violence needed to be reigned in and bonds of sociability retied. But above all, new forms of domestic and international politics had to be developed so as to prevent another relapse into barbarity.

Renewing democracy was also complicated by the erosion of cooperation in the Grand Alliance, since the victory over Hitler revived prior differences. After all, it was the fascist menace that had forced the competing ideologies of liberal democracy and Stalinist communism into an unlikely wartime alliance that they had been unable to negotiate on their own. In spite of goodwill between soldiers and ideological affinity among intellectuals, the defeat of the Nazis removed the shared objective, allowing the divergence of political cultures and national interests to resurface. Intensive consultations notwithstanding, the western powers and the Soviet Union failed to conclude World War II with a peace treaty, since they were unwilling to compromise on their different interpretations of a postfascist order. Instead, Poland was moved west and Germany became divided along the lines of military occupation after U.S. troops withdrew from Leipzig in exchange for a share of control over Berlin.[3] For the western countries this separation into contrasting spheres had the advantage of giving democracy a second chance.

Ironically, the greater physical destruction and loss of life during the Second World War inspired a more intensive soul-searching than after the First about how "to create conditions for a genuinely democratic government." Among the victors, the U.S. leaders decided to remain involved in international affairs in order to help advance capitalism and democracy; the British public resolved to soften the class antagonisms of its parliamentary monarchy by extending the welfare state; and the French tried to stabilize their republican government. Shocked by the totality of the defeat and the depth of their own suffering, the losers in Germany and Italy also sought to forswear force and to democratize their societies on the western pattern that had proven superior.[4] Though hardly visible to contemporaries, such collective learning processes reversed the direction of European development away from catastrophe toward civility, making 1945 the hinge around which its trajectory turned. While the Cold War initially obscured this qualitative change, the second half of the twentieth century turned out much more prosperous and peaceful for Europeans then the first.

The method that resurrected Western Europe after 1945 was a paradoxical form of conservative modernization that attempted to revive traditions while moving forward at the same time. Much of the physical rebuilding tried to resurrect as many houses and factories as possible in order to reconstruct the previous environment. Conservative parties also sought to restore prewar patterns of family life, religious values, and social deference so as to re-create order and stability according to accustomed norms. But at the same time, postwar Europeans continued to be enamored of technological progress, admiring the automobiles, refrigerators, and television sets that improved their mobility, consumption, and entertainment. Moreover, leftist parties pushed for social reforms and the artistic avant-garde resumed its experimentation in music and architecture, making modernism the dominant artistic style of western democracy.[5] In many ways this attempt to recover the benign potential of modernity helped Europe to rise like a phoenix from the ashes, but its inherent contradictions also created those tensions which would inspire the revolt of 1968.

UBIQUITOUS DEVASTATION

The joyful victory celebrations in the Allied capitals were an emotional release that helped revive spirits for the grim task of reconstruction ahead. When an AP broadcast reported that the war in Europe had ended, over a million New Yorkers gathered in Times Square to dance, shout, and cavort in the streets. After the announcement of the unconditional surrender, enthusiastic crowds also assembled in Moscow's Red Square, forming an impromptu parade to fete the victorious Red Army soldiers. A couple of weeks later fifty thousand troops paraded through Paris, cheered by over two million spectators seeking to reaffirm the recovery of French independence. During an official celebration in London in August, the king urged the British to work for peace, declaring: "Our sense of deliverance is overpowering."[6] In defeated Germany the Nazis feared retribution, but the liberated camp inmates were overjoyed, while most citizens were just relieved to still be alive. Victors and losers alike, however, faced the enormous challenge of repairing an unprecedented amount of physical and psychological devastation.

The destruction of Europe in 1945 was much greater than in 1918, since more areas had been involved in the fighting and new weapons proved much more lethal. Where there had been little Allied bombing or German ground fighting, stretches of the countryside and towns such as picturesque Rothenburg, in Bavaria, escaped largely unscathed. But the relentless bombing attacks had reduced the city centers of Rotterdam and Coventry, for instance, as well as the downtown areas of Cologne, Hamburg, and Dresden to heaps of rubble, in which streets lined by shattered buildings disappeared under mountains of debris. The artillery barrages and scorched-earth tactics of the Red Army and the Wehrmacht had destroyed not just military targets but also civilian neighborhoods, and house-to house-combat in Stalingrad and Warsaw had left hardly a building standing. As a result, in a wide swath from France to Norway, from Italy to the Balkans, from Germany to the Soviet Union, housing stock, factories, railroad tracks, highways, and bridges lay in ruins. In the areas most affected, it appeared to American observers that the entire infrastructure of modern civilization had been destroyed.[7]

The horrendous death toll during World War II was also more than twice as high as during the First World War. Approximately 40 million Europeans perished as a direct result of the fighting, with the Allies suffering about twice as many military and almost fifteen times as many civilian casualties. With about 26.6 million dead, Russia lost the most people, followed by Germany with between 6.7 and 8.8 million killed and Poland with between 5.6 and 5.8 million murdered. In relative terms, more than 16 percent of the Polish population died, almost 14 percent of the Russians perished, and 10.5 percent of the Germans lost their lives. While about 30 percent of Wehrmacht soldiers fell in battle, the much larger Red Army had a casualty rate of about 25 percent. Due to the war of annihilation, about half the dead were civilians, with recent estimates of the Holocaust ranging between 4.87 and 5.85 million.[8] Falling especially on men between ages eighteen and forty-five, this carnage left 1.6 women of marriageable age for each surviving male. The mass deaths thus propagated as children that were never born, so that the war left a deep and continuing gash in the population structure of the main combatants.

At the same time European streets and trains were clogged with an unending stream of prisoners of war, liberated slave laborers, and ethnic Germans expelled from the East. The several hundred thousand Allied POWs were only too glad to be free, but millions of Wehrmacht soldiers soon took their place in the camps, some of whom remained in Russian and French captivity for years. Moreover, the about seven million slave laborers and concentration-camp survivors were classified as "displaced persons," or DPs, waiting to be returned to their countries of origin. While western politicians wanted to send them back, many DPs no longer had a home to go to, and others who did nevertheless refused to be sent back to cities now in a different state under communist rule, hoping for emigration papers instead. Finally, the fear of Red Army atrocities and the subsequent expulsion from their former residences in Eastern Europe and the territories conquered by Russia and Poland sent twelve million ethnic Germans on desperate treks toward the West.[9] Only the organization and food provided by the United Nations Relief and Rehabilitation Administration helped stave off a greater humanitarian catastrophe.

The disruption of the European economy and Allied punitive policy toward Germany also slowed down the recovery. Since essential goods were in short supply, rationing continued as well into the postwar years, thereby inspiring a black market in which heirlooms were bartered for food, with U.S. cigarettes such as Lucky Strikes serving as currency in the West. The lack of livestock, fertilizer, and manpower limited food production to only two-thirds of prewar levels, drastically dropping calorie intake and leading to widespread starvation. The destruction of the transportation network kept coal from being delivered to factories, reducing industrial output to about half the peacetime amount. Scouring parks and woods for anything to burn, many Europeans froze during the bitterly cold winter of 1946–47. Moreover, the demilitarization of the German economy through widespread dismantling of factories also incapacitated the industrial heartland of Europe, inhibiting the restoration of international trade. Finally, labor calls for socialization and bureaucratic planning further slowed the revival of the postwar economy.[10]

Another poisonous legacy complicating reconstruction was the widespread hatred that stoked demands of revenge for past injuries. Not just the actual Nazi and fascist perpetrators but Germans and their auxiliaries in general became international outcasts, with little sympathy for their postwar plight. Allied newspapers seriously discussed radical proposals such as shooting the entire officer corps of the Wehrmacht for its alleged crimes. While some punitive politicians suggested partitioning the defeated country, others like the U.S. secretary of the Treasury Henry Morgenthau proposed stripping it of industry in order to reduce its entire population to mere agricultural subsistence.[11] Within the liberated states, the resistance movements similarly called for a strict reckoning with collaborators who had profited from doing business with the despised enemy. Popular passion fed spontaneous acts of violence against Germans and those who had done their bidding, often ignoring the rule of law. This understandable insistence on retribution not only vented pent-up anger but also created a climate of fear that hindered recovery.

A final difficulty was the widespread corruption of values that left a trail of debilitating cynicism, especially among the disenchanted young. The barbarity of the warfare shocked European thinkers because the veneer of humanist civilization had proven too thin to prevent horrible atrocities. Many conservative defenders of cultural tradition were tarnished by their cooperation with fascism, undercutting their appeals for a restoration of order and authority. But leftist admirers of revolution also lost credibility owing to their association with Stalinist repression, weakening their calls for socialist reform. Many intellectuals therefore flirted with nihilism or sought to find a reaffirmation of life in the existentialism promoted by Jean-Paul Sartre and Albert Camus. Less blemished than most other institutions, religion made a popular comeback since for many the present misery could be endured only with a transcendent faith.[12] Stripping off their uniforms or reemerging from bomb shelters, many among the younger generation did not know where to turn and withdrew from public affairs in an effort simply to rebuild livable cities and resume private careers.

Magazine reports, nonetheless, demonstrate that life continued among the ruins, revealing the tenacity of the human spirit amidst shocking devastation. Snapshots picture half-destroyed houses, where interior rooms turned into balconies allowed washing to be hung out to dry or tobacco to be grown in planters. They show women in drab smocks and head scarves clearing the rubble from streets and chipping mortar from bricks so that they could be used for rebuilding. Photos portray hollow-cheeked men in torn uniform coats picking through the ruins of factories, seeking to salvage pieces of equipment in order to resume production. They depict crowds gathering in black markets, intent on converting family china into scraps of edible food. But they also show laughing girls swimming in lakes, ignoring the fresh birch-wood crosses with steel helmets on top that marked the graves of victims of the final battles. And they capture cheerful U.S. soldiers distributing chocolate candy from their jeeps to curious children playing in the rubble.[13] It was this elemental drive to go on living that inspired the effort to reconstruct a more benign modernity.

PEACE WITHOUT TREATY

The main political difference between the end of the First and the Second World War was the lack of a formal peace treaty with the chief enemy, the German Reich. Since the war against Japan had yet to be won, the victorious Allies postponed final decisions at the July 1945 Potsdam Conference until the end of the fighting in Asia. Instead, provisional border changes were agreed upon and an occupation regime instituted in which each of the "Big Three" powers—the United States, Britain, and the Soviet Union—possessed ultimate authority over its occupation zone. The Paris Peace Treaty of February 1947 formally ended the war with the former Nazi allies Italy, Romania, Hungary, Bulgaria, and Finland, imposing territorial losses and reparations to help rebuild their ravaged neighbors. When negotiations for a peace treaty with Germany began thereafter, the ideological differences and diverging interests between the victorious powers had grown to such an extent that the Soviet Union and the United States could no longer agree on terms. Instead, the makeshift arrangements governing the border shifts and occupation zones gradually became permanent, initiating a profound division of Europe that would last for almost five decades.[14]

American Zone
French Zone
British Zone
Soviet Zone
Saarland

★ Seat of the Allied Control Council for Germany
• Headquarters in the Zones of Occupation
▨ Territorial losses sanctioned by Potsdam Agreement
── Border of the German Reich 1937

Map 8. Occupied Germany, 1945. Adapted from German Historical Institute, Washington, DC.

The provisional postwar order was the result of intensive wartime consultations within the Grand Alliance, formalized in summit meetings. At Tehran in November 1943 Churchill, Roosevelt, and Stalin discussed war strategy and the invasion of France in order to create a second front. The Bretton Woods meeting of 1944 set up an International Monetary Fund and a Bank for Reconstruction and Development so as to restore international trade, and the subsequent conference at Dumbarton Oaks established the United Nations to replace the defunct League of Nations. Many of the crucial decisions, such as the initial partition of Germany into three occupation zones, the division of Berlin into sectors, and the creation of an Allied

Control Council, were prepared by staff talks in the European Advisory Commission in London. In February 1945 the Big Three met again at Yalta and accepted Poland's westward displacement, German dismemberment, and Russian control over the liberated states in East-Central Europe. These interim arrangements reflected the Red Army's territorial occupation, which left the West little choice but to accept.[15]

Before a settlement could be reached, the last German ally, Japan, had to be defeated in the Far East. Assembled at Potsdam, the leaders of the Grand Alliance also insisted on the unconditional surrender of the Japanese imperial army. In order to increase the pressure on Japan, the United States began to draw down its European forces, shifting them to the Pacific. Moreover, Washington asked Stalin for help, inviting the Red Army into Manchuria, where it not only attacked the Japanese enemy but also began supplying the Chinese Communist uprising led by Mao Zedong and Zhou Enlai. In order to avoid a costly invasion of the main islands of Japan, the U.S. Air Force dropped atomic bombs on Hiroshima and Nagasaki on August 6 and 9 respectively, which completely devastated these two cities, killing several hundred thousand inhabitants. This unprecedented attack on their homeland convinced the militarist leaders of Japan to sue for an armistice on August 14, finalized in a ceremonial surrender on board the battleship *Missouri* on September 2. After costing fifty-five million lives, the Second World War had finally come to an end.[16]

Still inspired by an antifascist consensus, the Potsdam Conference during the second half of July 1945 made the territorial decisions that shaped the postwar order of Europe. As host of the meeting in a Russian-held city, Stalin was in the driver's seat, the more so since Churchill had lost his election to Clement Attlee and Harry Truman, FDR's successor, had little diplomatic experience. It was only logical that Germany would be stripped of its Nazi conquests, returning the country to its 1937 borders. Concretely that meant reestablishing Austrian independence and returning the Sudetenland to Czechoslovakia, Alsace-Lorraine to France, and West Prussia to Poland. More momentous was the Soviet annexation of eastern Poland and of half of East Prussia (*oblast* Kaliningrad), which pushed the reconstituted Polish state westward to the Oder and Neisse rivers, giving it the other half of East Prussia around Gdańsk. This border shift triggered the expulsion of 12.5 million Germans, to be conducted in an "orderly and humane manner," but which killed about half a million on the way. Reflecting the Red Army's advances, these territorial revisions left the Soviet Union in control of Eastern Europe.[17]

The chief aim of Allied policy toward Germany was the prevention of another world war by stripping the defeated country of its military capacity. In an unprecedented step, the Allies deposed the post-Hitler government of Karl Dönitz and dissolved German statehood on June 5, taking the administration of Germany into their own hands by creating an Allied Control Council (ACC). What was left of German territory would be split into four occupation zones, with Russia in control of the East, Britain of the industrial Rhine-Ruhr area, and the United States of Hesse and Bavaria, while a French zone was carved out of the border area in the Saar, Palatinate, and Württemberg. Berlin, the capital, was to be administered jointly by all victorious powers, which in fact created a West Berlin island in the middle of a Soviet-occupied sea. All war-making potential was to be eliminated through the dismantling of industries and through the payment of $23 billion of reparations in money and in kind, with about half the amount going to Russia. Based on the assumption of continued Allied cooperation, these severe provisions barely left the Germans enough resources to survive.[18]

The subsequent punishment of German allies restored much of the interwar map but preserved the Soviet conquests achieved during the Molotov-Ribbentrop Pact. In spite of changing sides, Italy was stripped of its gains and colonies, while Austria got off lightly as "the first Nazi victim" so as to shore up its independence. Slovakia was reincorporated in Czechoslovakia; similarly Croatia was reassigned to Yugoslavia. Hungary lost its territories gained from the Vienna awards, while the Romanian province of Moldova was annexed by Russia. Finland was also forced to cede some border areas. At the same time, the former Nazi allies had to pay considerable reparations to the neighbors whom they had previously despoiled. In undoing the Nazi order, these territorial decisions restored the interwar state system on the Balkans, favoring the pro-Allied resistance movements and reviving the barrier states of the Versailles Treaty.[19] Although the pro-western exile governments of all these areas insisted on holding free elections to determine their postwar course, the liberation of their states by the Red Army meant that East-Central Europe would fall under Soviet domination.

Ever so gradually these provisional arrangements became permanent, shaping Europe for most of the second half of the twentieth century. Elated over their joint victory, the Allies agreed on a negative program of destroying the Nazi system and preventing the revival of Germany, but the postponement of final decisions revealed disagreements on positive plans for the future. The unequal contributions of the Soviet Union and the western powers to the defeat of the fascist enemy left the Red Army in Eastern Europe and the Balkans, while the Anglo-American forces dominated Western Europe, the Mediterranean, and Scandinavia, with Germany split in half. The longer the military occupation lasted, the more the interpretations of the antifascist consensus diverged, since "democracy" meant control by the Communist Party in Russia while it signified free elections in the West. Once both sides had started to transform the areas under their control in their own image, there was no turning back. The result of the temporary solutions of 1945 was therefore the long-term division of Europe into eastern and western spheres of influence.[20]

During the Cold War the Potsdam decisions sparked much controversy over their substance and interpretation. Pro-democratic groups in Eastern Europe felt abandoned, since the feeble protests of the western governments proved unable to deter Soviet repression. Refugee groups in Germany clamored for the borders of 1937, yet ethnic cleansing was turning Germany's lost territories into western parts of Poland and Russia. Moreover, Soviet propaganda kept accusing the West of violating the Potsdam agreement by ceasing to provide reparations and rebuilding only its own occupation zones. Agreed upon before the liberation of France, the apportionment decisions of the European Advisory Commission had undoubtedly favored the Soviet Union. Moreover, General Eisenhower's insistence on establishing logistics and fear of friendly fire had slowed the western Allies' advance; he had failed to appreciate that military possession would guarantee postwar control.[21] Since the Russians conquered Eastern Europe, while the Anglo-Americans liberated the West, their forces met in Central Europe, dividing the continent and creating a competition that prevented the establishment of a truly peaceful postwar order.

REBUILDING DEMOCRACY

In Western Europe the Allied victory gave proponents of democratic modernity a second chance to fashion a more representative and stable political system than had existed in the interwar period. During the struggle, the tenacity of Britain's parliamentary government and the support of New Deal America's resources had ultimately proven superior to fascist dictatorship. The British and American publics therefore considered the parliamentary system vindicated, while liberation allowed continental Europeans like the French, Belgians, Dutch, Danes, and Norwegians to rebuild their prewar institutions so their citizens could once again govern themselves. Nonetheless, political commentators heatedly debated the lessons of the prior disenchantment with democracy so as to make it more resilient in the face of political extremism. Moreover, the bourgeois nationalists and working-class communists, the dominant forces within the resistance movements, battled over implementing their competing visions of the postwar world.[22] The challenge of modernizing democracy was to make it more socially inclusive and politically responsive to its citizens.

A prerequisite for rebuilding democracy was the purge of native fascists and Nazi collaborators from politics and society. The pent-up resentment against Nazi repression exploded in a populist *épuration* in France, killing about ten thousand collaborators. The minority who had actively resisted seized the chance to settle accounts and to take over power as the sole political force endowed with antifascist legitimacy. Vindictive crowds gathered in French streets to shave the heads of women who had slept with the enemy, making them wear placards that proclaimed "I am a Nazi whore." In Norway occupation children were taken away from their biological mothers and reassigned to foster parents so as to eradicate the shame of cohabitation. While some prominent collaborators were summarily lynched, others were tried for treason and either executed or given lengthy prison sentences. Such cases of retaliation against collaborators were justified by the concept of a "militant democracy" defending itself against extremist enemies. Only gradually did it dawn on the righteous avengers that restoring the rule of law also required their own observing of legal rules.[23]

American elites lent a helping hand in restoring democracy, since they had learned from the interwar debacle that they needed to stay engaged in Europe in the spirit of "democratic internationalism." With about 50 percent of the world's industrial production, the United States had become the dominant western power because it had remained relatively unscathed from the fighting with losses of 418,500 men, which amounted to only 0.32 percent of the population. Repudiating the legacy of isolationism, both political parties understood their responsibility for rebuilding the Old Continent so as to prevent another calamity. This new commitment also made economic sense, because ravaged Europe would be a profitable market for U.S. business if only it possessed sufficient credit to purchase such goods. In spite of the necessary drawdown of a draft army, the United States left a sizable occupation force in Germany, which provided its neighbors with security and assured Washington a voice in decisions regarding Germany's future. Finally, the exhausted continent was eager for Hollywood-style entertainment and receptive to the prosperity of the "American way of life."[24]

In victorious Britain, the electorate chose to reaffirm democracy by a massive expansion of the welfare state. In a stunning upset, they dumped the fiery wartime leader Winston Churchill in July 1945 and brought the Labour Party into power in order to end wartime austerity as quickly as possible, organize an equitable recovery, and soften the sharp edges of class hierarchy. Exhausted from fighting, the majority chose the vision of a "cradle to grave" system of social security sketched by the Beveridge Report of 1942. While rather uncharismatic, the new prime minister Clement Attlee embarked on a program of nationalization, converting wartime coordination into public ownership by taking over such industries as mining, power, and the railroads. At the same time the Labour government expanded access to education and built more public housing. The creation of "a comprehensive scheme of insurance" culminated in the establishment of the National Health Service in 1948, which provided medical care free of charge.[25] Though Great Britain was virtually bankrupt and rationing continued for years, the expansion of the welfare state rewarded the ex-soldiers for years of sacrifice and advanced social peace through greater equality.

In liberated France the military hero Charles de Gaulle pushed for the establishment of a more stable parliamentary system than had prevailed in the highly polarized Third Republic. Born in the industrial North in 1890 to a devout Catholic professor's family, he was trained at the military school of St. Cyr, served with distinction in World War I, but was captured by the Germans. During the interwar period, he advocated the buildup of armored forces, which he successfully commanded in World War II. After the defeat and surrender of France, he fled to Britain and rallied the Free French troops against the Nazi invaders. Angered that he was not treated as an important cobelligerent by the Anglo-Saxons, he made a triumphal entry into liberated Paris in 1944, claiming the mantle of national leadership. His authority was, however, contested by the resistance fighters of the French Communist Party (PCF), who had borne the brunt of the struggle within occupied France. The new constitution of the Fourth Republic, ratified in October 1946, strengthened the executive and finally gave women the right to vote. But when de Gaulle resigned in a huff, the previous parliamentary instability returned. Nonetheless, the rebuilding succeeded in achieving the overdue modernization of the economy.[26]

The smaller West European countries similarly reemerged as nation-states with democratic governments after the Second World War. In the Netherlands Queen Wilhelmina returned from exile, and a constitutional monarchy was restored on the previous pattern. In Belgium King Leopold III had to abdicate because he had collaborated too much with the Nazi occupiers. Both countries together with Luxembourg formed the Benelux customs union in 1948 in order to speed economic recovery through the construction of a broader market. In Scandinavia the Danes and Norwegians also revived their national states as functioning democracies. With Finland forced to sign a neutrality treaty, efforts at cooperation resulted only in the creation of a Nordic Council as an interparliamentary consultative body, which created a joint labor market and free passage across borders but fell short of a real customs union. Though understanding that small states such as theirs had been unable to resist Nazi aggression, their citizens preferred to return to their prior institutions and were willing to engage only in limited cooperation.[27]

Distancing themselves from various levels of collaboration with the Third Reich, the neutrals retained their independence and reinvigorated their democracies. Switzerland had to pay compensation for profiting from the Nazis' looting of banks and withdrew into political isolation while participating in the economic revival. Similarly Sweden reemphasized its neutrality during the Cold War, preferring instead to perfect its domestic welfare state, which set a global standard for social support. The Irish Free State was initially shunned for having maintained its distance to Britain, since it was preoccupied with liberating Northern Ireland. Having refused to join Hitler's war, the Spanish dictator Franco survived in isolation as punishment for his pro-fascist leanings. But during the Cold War the United States renewed contacts with his anticommunist regime and invited autocratic Portugal into NATO, the U.S.–Western Europe military alliance, since the Iberian Peninsula was important as a naval staging area. In general, the neutrals abandoned their earlier ties with Germany and reoriented themselves culturally toward the victorious Anglo-American model.

In Western Europe the liberation restored democracy through a novel mixture of tradition and modernity. The prewar institutions of representative government and nation-states reemerged with only minor modifications, since their citizens viewed them as having been vindicated. But after the flirtation with fascism had turned out to be disastrous, the bourgeois center-right repudiated authoritarianism and embraced the new movement of Christian Democracy, which sought to reconcile religious and humanistic values with parliamentary institutions. Yielding to labor pressure, governments also extended the welfare state, providing a stronger social safety net so as to cope with the demographic consequences of the war and provide buying power for the masses during the process of economic recovery. Though there was much sentiment for socialization, the influence of the United States and fears of communist expropriation allowed capitalism to return in a regulated fashion that limited the vagaries of the market. Abandoning prior skepticism, western intellectuals resumed with intense interest their discussions about renewing democracy.[28]

REHABILITATING ENEMIES

Allied policy toward the defeated enemies envisaged a deeper intervention than in 1918 in order to eliminate any possibility of another world war. Initially, graphic reports about the brutality of the war of annihilation and the atrocities of the Holocaust inspired a punitive approach that would inflict retribution on the losers and reduce their population to a survival level. Moreover, there was a clear consensus that perpetrators had to be prosecuted, the entire fascist apparatus dissolved, and the military establishment disbanded. But occupation practice soon made it clear that in taking over a country, the Allies had also assumed the responsibility for feeding and policing the vanquished population—which could turn out to be costly unless it was permitted to rebuild. As a result, public sentiment in the western capitals gradually swung toward a more therapeutic approach, seeking to rehabilitate the erstwhile antagonists.[29] Viewed with suspicion by the Soviet leadership, this shift from punishment to reconstruction offered the defeated a chance for recovery that many of them embraced with enthusiasm.

The treatment of the chief enemy, Germany, was initially quite harsh in order to emphasize the totality of its defeat and prevent any possibility of revanchism. Inspired by a punitive spirit, the Joint Chief of Staff directive 1067 emphasized that "Germany will not be occupied for the purpose of liberation but as a defeated enemy nation."[30] The Potsdam Agreement insisted on "demilitarization" in order to dismantle the Wehrmacht and erase the militarist spirit by civilizing the country. It also called for "denazification" so as to dissolve the Nazi Party and discredit its ideology by vetting all members and functionaries in civil tribunals. The International Criminal Tribunal and other war-crime trials sentenced 668 political, military, and economic leaders to death and about four thousand to incarceration. Finally, the Potsdam decisions proposed a "decartelization," breaking up the monopolistic structure of the heavy steel, machinery, and chemical industries and the banks so as to prevent the production of arms. Only after these preconditions were fulfilled did they mention the possibility of democratization, hinting at eventual rehabilitation.[31]

With his "speech of hope" Secretary of State James F. Byrnes signaled a switch of U.S. policy toward reconstruction in September 1946. The head of the American Military Government in Germany, General Lucius D. Clay, was convinced that U.S. taxpayers would have to pay for meeting the survival needs of the defeated country unless the Germans were allowed to raise their level of industrial production. When Washington pushed for cooperation between the occupation zones, the Soviets refused, since they were intent on introducing socialism into their area. In March 1948 Ludwig Erhard, a liberal economist who headed the Economic Council, gambled on a currency reform, devaluing the old reichsmark by ten to one, which reignited economic growth. Together with the lifting of economic controls the western powers allowed the resumption of political life, first on the local and then on the state level, by reconstituting political parties and holding elections.[32] They also promoted cultural reorientation by licensing media, instituting exchange programs, and sponsoring America Houses as positive examples of democracy. Hence the western zones began to recover with surprising speed.

In the spring of 1949 this dynamic of western reconstruction and Soviet refusal to cooperate led to the founding of a separate West German state, called the Federal Republic of Germany (FRG). Combining the three western occupation zones, this new creation was the culmination of a political revival that had started with local efforts at self-government in which proven antifascists took over the administration of cities so as to organize relief and rebuilding. Eventually local elections led to the establishment of federal states, loosely modeled on the tradition of regional representation. These postwar leaders met in a constitutional convention at Herrenchiemsee in 1948 in order to work out a democratic political order under the supervision of the western Allies. Their product, the so-called Basic Law, was a provisional constitution that sought to correct the mistakes that had overthrown the Weimar Republic. This second, more successful attempt at democracy instituted a federal system of about a dozen states, a 5 percent hurdle for a political party to win parliamentary representation, a constructive vote of no confidence, and a ceremonial presidency.[33]

In a tight election, Konrad Adenauer, the leader of the Christian Democratic Union, won the chancellorship with the help of minor conservative parties. He was born in 1876 into a devout Catholic family and trained as a lawyer, already gaining political notice in Imperial Germany. Intensely disliking Prussian authoritarianism, he was a successful mayor of Cologne who was twice briefly incarcerated during the Third Reich. As a committed anticommunist, he was instrumental in broadening the appeal of the prewar Catholic Center Party by merging it into a general Christian Democratic Union that also appealed to Protestants as a moderate middle-class party. Unlike his Social Democratic rival Kurt Schumacher, who put a premium on preserving national unity with the Soviet zone, the septuagenarian Adenauer favored western integration as a way of regaining political sovereignty. Carefully, he balanced the reintegration of former Nazis with restitution payments to Israel. Under the patriarchal leadership of "Der Alte" (the Old One) and buoyed by the Economic Miracle, the Federal Republic gradually became the first successful democracy in German history.[34]

Thanks to its change of sides, Italy got off more easily and was left rather to its own devices in reviving its parliamentary tradition. Its territorial losses in Gulia and Trieste were limited, and Allied occupation remained transitory. Already in 1946 a referendum abolished the monarchy, and by 1948 a new republican constitution was adopted. Since the papacy had rescinded its ban on politics, the Catholic and conservative party Democrazia Cristiana overwhelmingly won the first postwar election under its leader Alcide de Gasperi. Nonetheless, it was continually challenged by a large Communist Party, which attacked the corruption and clientelism typical of Italian elites, calling for more radical social reforms. This endemic cultural conflict was immortalized in the movie comedy *Don Camillo and Peppone*. During the 1950s the country also experienced its own economic miracle in the North and center, which left behind the agricultural regions of the Mezzogiorno. But in contrast to Germany, the Italian public was reluctant to confront its collaboration with fascism, hiding instead behind the myth of a general *resistenza*.[35]

The Austrian case was similarly paradoxical, since the country was treated both as a perpetrator and a prey of National Socialism. Already in 1943 the Allies proclaimed Austria to be the first Nazi victim, promising to restore its independence, but nonetheless returned South Tyrol to Italy. Though the Red Army conquered Vienna, the country was divided into four occupation zones, with the capital coadministered like Berlin. The Russians ruthlessly exploited the eastern regions, which hampered their efforts to gain political control. As a result the local Communists lost the November 1945 election to the conservative Austrian People's Party (ÖVP) and the Social Democratic Party (SPÖ), which together dominated Austrian politics in the following decades. In order to prevent the Federal Republic of Germany's entry into NATO in 1955, Soviet diplomats surprisingly offered to withdraw their troops if Austria were to embrace neutrality. The state treaty, also signed by the western Allies, finally ended the occupation and reestablished the independence of the country on the Swiss model.[36] As a result, the Austrian public was not really compelled to reckon with its own Nazi complicity.

With some justification, the rehabilitation of these former enemies of western democracy features prominently among the successful cases in the nation-building literature. In contrast to 1918, the defeat of 1945 had been so total as to exclude thoughts among the vanquished of reversing the outcome. The policy of the western Allies was just the right mixture of toughness to purge fascists and their collaborators as well as assistance to put the affected countries back on their feet. Unlike in later failures, there were also strong pro-democratic minorities in these Central European states who were eager to resume the tradition of prior self-government. Helped by the expansion of the welfare state, the speed of economic recovery associated capitalism with prosperity instead of with depression, thereby making democracy seem more attractive. Finally, the Cold War confrontation facilitated the acceptance of the penitent sinners into the western camp. The restoration of democracy among the defeated countries was therefore due to a rather exceptional set of circumstances that could not easily be replicated elsewhere around the globe.[37]

INTERNATIONAL COOPERATION

A final lesson of the Second World War was the need to modernize international organization by strengthening cooperation so as to prevent another such catastrophe. The collapse of world trade during the Great Depression suggested the importance of reviving transnational exchanges as a basis for economic recovery. The horrendous suffering of the war also encouraged efforts at solving political disputes so that a similar resort to force could be avoided in the future. Concretely, initiatives to weave a tighter organizational web developed on three competing levels: The optimism of the Grand Alliance encouraged global solutions such as the founding of the United Nations, the creation of the International Monetary Fund, and the establishment of regulated exchange rates in Bretton Woods. When East-West tensions prevented universal approaches, the focus shifted to transatlantic initiatives such as the Marshall Plan or the North Atlantic Treaty Organization, which provoked mirror-reverse counterparts in the Council for Mutual Economic Assistance and the Warsaw Pact. Finally, the pan European vision of the anti-Nazi resistance movements inspired the initial postwar initiatives at European integration.[38]

Surprisingly enough the nation-state reemerged unscathed from World War II although its sovereignty had proven unable to stave off economic depression and military aggression. While critical intellectuals continued to predict its imminent demise, neither transnational capitalist trade nor communist internationalism convinced citizens to give up on the nation as key political unit. The failure of the Nazis' bid for imperial domination had restored the attractiveness of Wilsonian self-determination along the lines of the state system established after the First World War. In victory or defeat the nation remained the legitimate frame of reference, since it provided the collective identity to be celebrated in shared triumph or the solidarity to be embraced in common suffering. When they lost their overseas possessions, the colonial powers also simply chose to fall back on the existing nation-state. Even the American "empire by invitation" and the Soviet satellite system nominally respected the separate statehood of its clients.[39] Regional, continental, or global cooperation was therefore possible only between sovereign countries, which remained an obstacle limiting its effectiveness.

The chief innovation that was supposed to guarantee "peace and security" was the creation of the United Nations (UN) as an improved successor to the League of Nations. President Roosevelt promoted the establishment of such an organization so as to perpetuate the cooperation of the twenty-six nations that were fighting the Axis. In the Dumbarton Oaks Conference between August and October 1944 China, Britain, the United States, and the USSR hammered out the basic structure of the UN General Assembly, Security Council, International Court of Justice, and Secretariat. A subsequent meeting of fifty nations in San Francisco drafted the United Nations Charter, signed on June 26, 1945, which sought "to save succeeding generations from the scourge of war," reaffirmed "faith in fundamental human rights," tried to strengthen "international law," and promised "to promote social progress." Going far beyond Europe, this global initiative intended to provide "collective security" by discussing problems and mediating disputes. President Truman therefore welcomed the United Nations as a "solid structure upon which we can build a better world."[40]

Though limited by the veto power of the five permanent members of the UN Security Council and often deadlocked by Cold War rivalry, the United Nations nonetheless proved useful for addressing a number of international problems. In the immediate postwar period the UN Relief and Rehabilitation Administration (UNRRA) assured the survival of starving Europeans by providing food, fuel, clothing, and shelter. Drawing on the horrible prewar and wartime experience of dictatorial repression and mass murder, the United Nations also adopted the Universal Declaration of Human Rights in 1948. Two years later it took advantage of the Soviet Union's temporary boycott of the Security Council to organize the defense of South Korea against aggression from the Communist North. Though it proved incapable of preventing the Suez crisis of 1956, the United Nations did stabilize the Near East by providing a peacekeeping force. Finally, in reinterpreting the trusteeship mandate as a call for independence, it facilitated decolonization by accepting newly independent states as members.[41] While the New York location of the UN headquarters showed that Europe was no longer the center of world affairs, many UN initiatives benefited the Old Continent.

The Marshall Plan, which provided American aid for the recovery of the war-torn European economies, was even more successful. On June 5, 1947, Secretary of State George Marshall promised in a speech at Harvard University that the United States would "assist in the return of normal economic health" to Europe in order to alleviate the suffering, which increased the appeal of communism. Initiated in 1948 and formally named the European Recovery Program, the Marshall Plan was a product of enlightened self-interest, since it committed American financial resources but called on the European nations themselves to cooperate in creating an organization (OEEC) to administer the program. Ignoring lingering hatreds, Washington included Germany as the industrial heart of the continent, but the Soviets forced their satellites to rebuff the offer as capitalist enslavement. The $13 billion in credits offered to the western countries bought American food and industrial products, thereby benefiting U.S. producers, while at the same time making essential materials available for repairing infrastructure and modernizing factories. Though economists are still disputing its precise effect, the Marshall Plan's message of hope accelerated recovery, triggering the postwar boom.[42]

Another transatlantic link was the North Atlantic Treaty Organization (NATO), which responded to European security fears in the Cold War. When Soviet occupation forces temporarily blocked the western Allies' access to Berlin in 1948, Britain, France, and the Benelux countries concluded a West European Union to defend themselves against possible Russian attack. In April 1949 the addition of the United States, Canada, Italy, Portugal, Norway, Denmark, and Iceland enlarged this cooperation, signaling an American commitment to the defense of Europe. The first NATO secretary, Lord Ismay, succinctly quipped that the alliance pursued the triple purpose "to keep the Russians out, the Americans in, and the Germans down." The Chinese military support of Communist North Korea during the Korean War inspired closer military cooperation in NATO's command and field operations, creating a ground force large enough to stop potential Soviet aggression into Europe, supplemented by extensive airpower and naval support. After the French rejected the European Defense Community, West Germany was included in the alliance in 1955 in order to make use of its manpower potential. Though dominated by the United States, NATO provided a stable form for West European defense.[43]

Seeking to overcome historic enmities, the West Europeans also took initial steps toward political integration so as to revive their prostrate continent. In 1946 Winston Churchill dramatically suggested in Zurich to build a United States of Europe in order to assure a more peaceful future—though he also ruled Britain out. Adherents of national sovereignty founded the Council of Europe in 1949, which tried to improve cooperation between nation-states in the area of human rights by establishing an international court in Strasbourg. Advocates of supranational integration like Altiero Spinelli instead founded a Union of European Federalists (UEF) in December 1946 in Paris. Believing that only the creation of a European federation would be able to guarantee peace and progress in the future, they campaigned for transforming the Council of Europe into a constituent assembly for a European state. Though thousands of intellectuals and citizens supported the UEF's petition for a federal pact, this project was too visionary to succeed. While these initiatives suggested the goal of integration, the path to realizing it remained unclear.[44]

Propelled by the shock of the war, the impulse for international cooperation grew stronger after 1945, but it failed to produce a modern order that would guarantee peace in Europe and the world. The retention of the nation-state as the basic unit of politics meant that insistence on national sovereignty would hamper all efforts to collaborate. The concurrent establishment of global (UN), transatlantic (Marshall Plan), and European (Council of Europe) initiatives created a series of overlapping institutions with competing jurisdictions that often failed to work together. Moreover, the deepening ideological conflict between communism and capitalism divided Europe into Soviet and western spheres, limiting organizational innovations like NATO and the Warsaw Pact to separate blocs and inspiring hostility between them. Within this confusion, some visionary Europeans like Jean Monnet searched for more far-reaching solutions that would eventually develop a momentum toward unifying the European continent.[45] While the necessity of greater cooperation was evident, it was not at all obvious which of these forms would win out.

REVITALIZING DEMOCRACY

During the postwar years most Europeans simply longed for a return to normalcy, so that their personal lives could resume without being disrupted by forces beyond their control. In many ways people wanted to get back to the "good times" of the prewar, interwar, or even imperial years when they had earned enough in order to enjoy life without having to fear for the next day. The prevailing wish for peace and prosperity required the restoration of order and stability, based on accepted authority rather than experimentation with new forms of government. In the western democracies this meant a strengthening of parliamentary institutions, while among the defeated countries it required the reintroduction of self-government, derided by fascists and communists alike. Older leaders such as Charles de Gaulle, Konrad Adenauer, and Alcide de Gasperi were therefore quite popular, since they epitomized a continuity reaching all the way back to the halcyon years before the First World War. No wonder that in the reconstruction of democracy much effort was devoted to restoring what had been lost in the interval.[46]

At the same time, however, the push for modernization continued, since mass death and mass murder had made it patently impossible to recapture an earlier way of life. Even if science had been associated with destruction, technological advances such as the introduction of television and the development of jet airplanes continued unabated. In spite of preservation efforts, it was simply too expensive to rebuild city centers according to medieval patterns with narrow cobblestone streets when the use of automobiles demanded broad thoroughfares. In spite of the reassertion of patriarchy, many women who had worked in war production or cleared the rubble were unwilling to return to the hearth and subordinate themselves to their husbands coming home from the front. Overcoming the resistance of cultural traditionalists, modernist styles like abstract paintings, absurdist plays, and twelve-tone music captured the galleries, theaters, and concert halls. To remain viable, democracy therefore could not just be restored in its somewhat elitist prewar guise, but had to update its form in order to come to terms with demands for broader participation.[47]

One way of revitalizing parliamentary government was to reform those structural weaknesses that had led to its demise in many countries during the interwar period. Participation could be enlarged by abolishing the remaining property-ownership restrictions on voting and giving women greater rights like the vote, as it happened in France. Constitutions might be altered to make governing more predictable by introducing hurdles against the representation of splinter parties or by allowing the prohibition of antidemocratic extremists, as was done in Germany. Political leaders could also pay more attention to shifts in public sentiment outside parliaments through the novel method of opinion polling, as they began doing in the United Kingdom. Election campaigns might use new methods of appealing to the public, such as through American-style advertising rather than by drafting elaborate party programs. Interest groups like farmers could learn that influencing the legislative process would be more profitable than trying to destabilize elected governments by populist opposition. Finally, strengthening the executive as in the Federal Republic's "chancellor democracy" and the presidential system of the French Fifth Republic would create more political stability.[48]

Another method of making democracy more modern was the broadening of its social base through the expansion of the welfare state. Recalling government coordination of the wartime economies, the unions, intellectuals, and leftist media clamored for the nationalization of key industries after 1945. But American counterpressure, exerted through the Marshall Plan, kept key countries like the Federal Republic of Germany from socializing production, promoting instead the dynamism of free-market competition. Nonetheless, Britain and France embarked on major extensions of the welfare state after the war in order to reward both soldiers and civilians for the sacrifices they had made for the national cause. Even the center-right Christian Democratic parties in Germany and Italy were willing to extend benefits beyond pensions, unemployment insurance, and health coverage to help the many war victims such as widows, orphans, veterans, and expellees. By lessening inequality, such social measures reduced class warfare, saved capitalism, and thereby strengthened public commitment to democracy.[49]

The successful renewal of democracy after the Second World War therefore rested on a mixed welfare-state and free-market model that became distinctly European. The revival of parliamentary institutions was easiest in those western countries which had gradually developed traditions of self-government, whether they formally remained constitutional monarchies like Great Britain or republics like France. But the reintroduction of democracy into the defeated nations also made gradual progress through the conversion of middle-class and conservative voters who had formerly supported fascism to Christian democracy. The postwar recovery of democracy was moreover facilitated by the lobbying of the labor unions and the social democratic parties for the extension of the welfare state, since it created a social basis for citizenship. The abhorrent example of Stalinist communism as well as American pressure and aid kept the dynamic competition of the market sufficiently alive to spark the postwar boom.[50] Though varying considerably in detail, the second time around European postwar democracy would prove more resilient and stable than ever before.

Chapter 16

DICTATING COMMUNISM

Hungarian Uprising, 1956. *Source*: Magnum Photos.

On the morning of March 10, 1948, Czech foreign minister Jan Masaryk was found dead in the courtyard of Czernin Palace in Prague. His corpse lay fourteen meters below the bathroom window of his official residence, in which a Bible was opened to a passage in Galatians referring to the comfort of the Holy Spirit. According to acquaintances, he had been quite depressed after the Communist takeover two weeks before, which had marginalized him and the aging president Edvard Beneš. The police declared the death a suicide, but the public suspected that he had been murdered by Soviet agents—a theory later supported by forensic evidence. The exact circumstances of this new defenestration, which recalled the outbreak of the Thirty Years' War, remained one of the mysteries of the Cold War. But whether suicide or murder, Masaryk's death clearly signaled the end of the Communist Party's cooperation with bourgeois partners and the transition to open dictatorship under Klement Gottwald. The death "came as a great shock to the whole Western World," as it indicated "a policy which was to destroy the last vestiges of freedom" in Eastern Europe.[1]

Military victory provided the Soviet Union with the opportunity of dictating communism to its conquered territories and satellites. The success in defeating German aggression reaffirmed the correctness of communist ideology, proving its superiority to National Socialism and cementing Bolshevik dictatorship for another half century. The advance of the Red Army into the heart of Central Europe not only demonstrated the rise in Soviet power but also created an armed occupation that could be turned into political domination. Watching impotently from the outside, western governments were reduced to issuing paper protests, since they lacked the means to influence developments on the ground. In the East, however, many people from the Baltic to the Black Sea were grateful to be liberated at last from Nazi servitude and annihilation, while intellectuals admired the speed and extent of Soviet modernization. In short, at the end of the war Stalin could finally begin to implement what his rival Trotsky had earlier demanded—he could export revolution beyond the borders of the Soviet Union.[2]

Central European émigrés and western critics attacked the establishment of Soviet hegemony over Eastern Europe by coining the concept of "totalitarianism." Philosopher Hannah Arendt was struck by the antidemocratic similarities of the dictatorial methods employed by both the Nazis and the Soviets. Political scientist Carl Friedrich listed a series of characteristic traits shared by both systems such as a dominant ideology, a mass party led by a dictator, the use of terror, a monopoly of force and propaganda, as well as the control of a planned economy. Disappointed by the suppression of freedom in communist countries, British writer George Orwell dramatized mechanisms of repression in his dystopian novel *Nineteen Eighty-Four*. In practical politics, President Eisenhower in 1959 created the National Captive Nations Committee, an advocacy group that agitated for the eventual liberation of East European countries from Soviet domination.[3] Since the charge of totalitarianism justified switching enemies from National Socialism to communism, the word itself became a powerful weapon in the ideological battles of the Cold War.

Liberal intellectuals and communist sympathizers countered that the concept of totalitarianism obliterated the differences between types of authoritarian regimes and simplified the complexity of their dynamics. Stressing the Enlightenment roots of the socialist utopia, leftist commentators pointed to the consistent antifascism of the communists in order to highlight their ideological hostility to National Socialism. Scholars sympathetic to the Soviet project stressed instead the weakness of the tsarist state, the popular participation in the revolution, and the relative normalcy of most lives among ordinary people in the USSR. Intent on maintaining a critical stance toward the West, social reformers cited the improvements in living conditions, welfare provisions, health care, and educational opportunities under communism that created greater social equality than under capitalism. Comparing the actual functioning of the Soviet and fascist dictatorships, they emphasized the differences in their ideology, longevity, and murderousness. Against the repressive picture, they suggested a more nuanced image of the Soviet Union that also acknowledged some of the progressive features of its "welfare dictatorship."[4]

The notion of "Sovietization" offers a way out of the interpretative dilemma because it shifts the focus of debate to the transformation of Eastern Europe according to the model of Soviet modernity. While the concept originated as a Cold War accusation, its analytical use provides an eastern counterpart to the way in which "Americanization" has been employed for describing changes in the West. Sovietization draws attention to the hegemonic influence that the Soviet Union exerted on its satellite states, extending from the political rhetoric and form of leadership to the structure of the economy, the pattern of social interactions, and the cultural style. Moreover, it emphasizes the mixture of *compulsion* (such as the dictates of the Cominform, the orders of the military, or the demands of Russian and local joint economic companies) and of *voluntary imitation* of customs (such as wearing Russian fur hats, drinking vodka, or eating dishes like *solyanka* soup). Sovietization therefore addresses the various ways in which the communist project of modernization sought to transform Eastern and Central Europe in the postwar period.[5]

COMMUNISM REAFFIRMED

The Soviets' hard-won victory in the "Great Patriotic War" over the German invaders seemed to prove the ideological superiority of communism over Nazism and capitalism. Stalin's wartime appeals to socialist internationalism and Russian nationalism merged both sentiments indissolubly into a new Soviet identity. The expansion of the Soviet Union into the Baltic states, a slice of Finland, eastern Poland, half of East Prussia, and Bessarabia offered tangible proof, since it restored the geographic reach of the tsarist empire and extended Russian influence into the center of Europe. In massive monuments, ranging from the Mamayev Kurgan memorial in Stalingrad to Berlin-Treptow, the Soviet Union celebrated the courage of its soldiers and its military victory. On May 9 of each year, ritualized parades recalled the triumph with bemedaled war heroes reviewing goose-stepping troops and endless rows of tanks and missiles.[6] With these commemorations the Communist leadership crafted a self-approving narrative of victory over fascism that, in the sad words of the dissident Efim Etkind, cemented its dictatorship for another half century.

The challenge of the postwar rebuilding in the East was, nonetheless, even more difficult than in the West, because the war of annihilation had left greater destruction behind. Much of the land between the Volga and the Elbe rivers had been twice fought over, and the successive scorched-earth policies of the Russian defenders and the retreating Wehrmacht had devastated fields as well as factories. Moreover, in Russia, Poland, and East Germany the blood toll was proportionally higher, decimating an entire generation of men, which pushed much of the burden of recovery onto the shoulders of women. Since Stalin rejected the U.S. offer of help in order to avoid its influence, the Soviet Union had to reconstruct the economy without outside assistance, scraping together from within its borders the resources needed to restore the burnt cities and razed factories. With the fields fallow, farm animals dead, and machinery wrecked, famine swept the Soviet Union in the postwar years, and people lived in earthen dugouts while houses were being rebuilt. Though externally Moscow acted as a mighty conqueror, internally many Russians struggled for bare survival.[7]

Because of these problems, the Soviets firmly insisted on receiving reparations, partly from new production, but partly also from the dismantling of German factories. The original list comprised about 1,600 plants in order to reduce Germany's industrial output to about three-fifths of the prewar level. The Russian share of $10 billion worth of materials was supposed to come partly from their own occupation zone and partly also from the Ruhr Basin, but the West stopped its deliveries once it started to rebuild. Nonetheless, the Russians did remove about 760 factories from East Germany, especially anything of potential military value such as machine production, even stripping the second track from many railroad lines. This ruthless exploitation of the defeated enemy reduced the Soviet zone's industrial capacity to two-thirds of the prewar level, taking away the livelihood of the very proletariat that the Communist Party was trying to court ideologically. While some of the material helped rebuild Russian production facilities, much of the equipment was left to rust at railroad sidings because no one knew how to use it.[8]

Military victory also made Soviet rule rather Byzantine, because it enhanced Stalin's reputation, increased his power, and fed his paranoia. In countless paintings, statues, poems, and songs a burgeoning cult of personality portrayed him as the wise leader, the *vozhd*, who had saved the fatherland from aggression, disregarding his mistakes and murders along the way. Getting older and more inflexible, Stalin distrusted his close associates ever more strongly, making Old Bolsheviks like Vyacheslav Molotov fawn over him lest they lose his favor and thereby their lives. His chief lieutenant Andrei Zhdanov, who had successfully defended Leningrad during the long siege, was especially hostile to cultural innovation, forbidding the experimental works of poets like Anna Akhmatova. During his last years Stalin also invented a "doctors' plot," accusing mostly Jewish physicians of a conspiracy to kill Soviet officials and triggering an anti-Semitic, anti-cosmopolitan campaign that declared all international ties suspect.[9] The triumph over Hitler therefore reinforced the negative sides of Stalinism, making Soviet communism even more dictatorial.

The joy of liberation was short-lived, since this fear of foreign contamination rendered Soviet authorities increasingly intolerant. Instead of being reunited with their loved ones, hundreds of thousands of returning prisoners were shipped off to the gulag because they might have seen a better life in Central Europe and were potentially subversive. In the universities the pseudoscientific teachings of the biologist Trofim Lysenko held sway, claiming that genes could be environmentally altered to improve yields of grain. In the cultural realm, the works of writers such as the deeply patriotic Boris Pasternak were banned, while Aleksandr Solzhenitsyn was sent to a labor camp for criticizing Stalin. In architecture, a blend of neotraditional styles celebrated Soviet power through the construction of gingerbread-style skyscrapers in Moscow, Warsaw, and East Berlin. Because victory had not brought the hoped-for freedom, Pasternak formulated the widespread disappointment of intellectuals: "If, in a bad dream, we had seen all of the horrors in store for us after the war, we should have been sorry not to see Stalin go down together with Hitler."[10] The elation of victory and Stalin's security mania contributed to the militarizing of Russia in spite of its incessant peace propaganda.

The military was the most prestigious institution in the Soviet Union, tying up three to five million men and devouring enormous economic resources. Initially serving for three years, conscripts were harshly trained and stationed all over Eastern Europe from Poland to East Germany, from Czechoslovakia to Hungary. Conceiving of the next conflict as a repetition of the war against the Wehrmacht, the Russian force was primarily a land army with tanks and artillery, although the air force developed MiG jet fighters and the navy expanded its fleet of submarines. Helped by captured German scientists and by effective espionage, the Soviet military strove to develop rockets and acquire first the A- and then the H-bomb in order to catch up to the technically more advanced U.S. arsenal.[11] In the belief that power rested on military might, the Soviet Union built up the largest army in the world, supported by a huge military-industrial complex, thereby impairing the improvement of living standards.

The establishment of Russian hegemony over Eastern Europe therefore proceeded by force in an almost mirror-reversed repetition of Nazi practices. First, a series of direct annexations from Finland to Romania cemented the gains of the Ribbentrop-Molotov Pact, enlarging Soviet territory considerably. With ruthless ethnic cleansing the victors expelled local inhabitants and moved Russian nationals in, while at the same time imposing one-party communist dictatorships. Second, the brutal occupation of areas like East Germany, whose fate was to be decided in a peace treaty, created a military administration that secured Russian dominance. This presence also started the process of Sovietization through denazification according to social class, eliminating large landowners and industrialists, and support of local communists in their project to seize political power and transform the occupied nations' social and economic structure. Third, even in nominally independent satellite states like Poland, the Soviet Union acted as a repressive hegemon through the stationing of troops, the activities of the secret service, and so-called advice to fraternal parties that had to do Moscow's bidding.[12]

Disappointing hopes in communist modernity, Eastern Europe's liberation from Nazi repression merely brought Soviet domination, exchanging one dictatorship for another. In part, the personal paranoia of the aging dictator Stalin was to blame because he no longer respected any restraints on his power. In part, the structure of the Bolshevik system was at fault, since its one-party rule eliminated all competitors and limited policy discussions to a small party elite that was always afraid of being accused of deviations. Moreover, the victory over Hitler greatly strengthened the influence of the Soviet military, a hierarchical institution that was used to employing force in order to get what it wanted. At the same time the expansion of Russian rule over Eastern and Central Europe also reinforced the authority of an imperial bureaucratic apparatus inherited from tsarist precedents. This postwar incarnation of Soviet communism was therefore a far cry from the utopian visions of liberty, equality, and fraternity stemming from the Enlightenment. Because of its many defects, the reality of the Soviet version ultimately discredited the ideals of socialism.[13]

PEOPLE'S DEMOCRACIES

During its march toward Berlin, the Red Army was greeted with much rejoicing, since its arrival heralded the end of the Nazi nightmare. Most East Europeans were grateful that Russian troops "brought ultimate liberation," because they "finally got rid of those Germans." Conservative patriots were especially delighted with the defeat of the Wehrmacht since they hoped now to be able to regain a measure of independence. At the same time local socialists praised their good fortune of coming under Soviet rule, because that "helped in implementing a number of changes" toward establishing socialism, which would have been impossible without Red Army support. Aware that the majority of the population preferred the return of democracy, Polish Marxists like Jakub Berman were glad that the Russian presence allowed them to dispense with the nicety of free elections, "because we'd lose." Shielded from German revanchism by Soviet tanks and relying on Russian support against their own citizens, East European communists now embarked on creating their kind of "people's democracy."[14]

For the Germans and their allies, defeat turned into a traumatic experience, deeply etched into collective memory, which inhibited support for communism. Thoughtful Russian officers like Lev Kopelev worried that the fierceness of the Red Army's vengeance resembled the brutality of Nazi atrocities. Inspired by antifascist propaganda and encouraged by liberal doses of vodka, the victorious troops often killed indiscriminately and burned buildings, paying back with interest what had been done to their own families. Women were especially victimized by gang rapes, amounting according to some estimates to over two million cases in Germany alone. Moreover, units coming from the poorer regions of the Soviet Union engaged in much plunder, taking wristwatches with cries of "Uri, Uri," bicycles, or anything else of value and vandalizing the rest. Encouraged by the Red Army command, this train of destruction created a visceral hatred that protestations of "people's friendship" could never completely erase. As a result "liberation" gained a double meaning, inspiring not just support of socialism but also vigorous anticommunism.[15]

The East-Central Europeans therefore reacted ambivalently to the arrival of Soviet communism, withholding their final judgment until its actual performance became clear. About one-third, largely composed of workers and intellectuals, welcomed the chance to reform their societies by abolishing class distinctions and creating planned economies. Disappointed in the West and hoping for help from their Slavic brethren, the Czechs were particularly eager to embrace the Soviet model. Another third, consisting of farmers, craftsmen, and traders, were impressed by the thoroughness of the Red Army victory and therefore willing to give communism a chance to prove itself as more peaceful and stable than the failed democracies. Only the final third, including mostly nationalist businessmen, professionals, and the clergy were either skeptical or openly opposed. Since they had experienced not just Nazi but also Bolshevik atrocities, sizable segments of the Polish elite were, for instance, unwilling to collaborate with the Soviets, with some parts of the Home Army waging a guerrilla campaign against Russian dominance.[16]

As a result of western pressure, politics in the satellite states initially followed the mixed approach of a "people's democracy," which retained parliamentary forms but gradually tipped toward one-party communist rule. In order to outmaneuver the moderate parties, the

Soviets sponsored the creation of "national fronts" that included bourgeois representatives and peasant deputies but allowed communists to wield power indirectly by controlling strategic positions in the police and the military. In order to prevent electoral defeats like the one in Hungary in November 1945, the small communist parties also merged with the larger social democratic parties in one united party, thereby overcoming the historic split between socialists and communists within the labor movement. These pseudocoalitions were held together by an understandable hatred of Nazism, widespread fear of German revenge, and sincere commitment to postwar rebuilding. With surprising candor, the East German dictator Walter Ulbricht formulated the general rationale of this transitional course: "It should look democratic, but we must control everything."[17]

The Soviet zone of occupation in Germany was a special case, since it only gradually became clear that it would develop into a second German state. In the beginning Stalin wavered between using his conquest as a bargaining chip for neutralizing a demilitarized but united Germany or as an attractive showcase in order to spread socialism to the rest of the country. In selecting the latter path, the Soviet zone had to overcome more severe obstacles than its neighbors: it was part of a defeated and divided nation, which had lost its eastern territories, was forced to accept millions of refugees, and had to pay enormous reparations. The returning exiles who rallied around Ulbricht and the internal survivors around Erich Honecker nevertheless set out to create a "better Germany" than in the capitalist West. But their failure to win a sufficient majority in the local and state elections of 1946 made them erode the parliamentary system by creating a "national bloc" in which the distribution of seats was determined beforehand. In typical fashion, the German Democratic Republic reinterpreted the concept of democracy to mean government *for* the people by the Socialist Unity Party (SED).[18]

Already during the rebuilding from war damage, the East German communists began to lay the foundations for the future construction of socialism. Often Marxist zealots, counting on Red Army support, would push radical measures on a reluctant populace under the cover of denazification. In contrast to the western practice of punishing individual guilt, in the East the removal of Nazi perpetrators or collaborators sought to eliminate their underlying class basis, echoing Georgi Dimitrov's 1935 definition of fascism as "the open terrorist dictatorship of the most reactionary, most chauvinistic and most imperialist elements of finance capital." Concretely, that approach meant expropriating the *Junkers* (i.e., large landowners) as a group and redistributing their holdings to landless laborers. At the same time it also required taking factories away from capitalists and nationalizing industries so as to put the means of production under workers' control. These measures culminated in the introduction of economic planning on the Soviet model, which gradually replaced market competition with production targets decided in government plans.[19]

Many intellectuals on both sides of the Iron Curtain waxed enthusiastic about this new beginning that promised to realize the socialist dream. From their U.S. exile writers such as Bertolt Brecht and Stefan Heym returned to East Germany, while Holocaust survivors like Tadeusz Borowski and Marcel Reich-Ranicki volunteered to help revolutionize Poland. Three aspects proved particularly seductive: Since communists had offered the most resolute resistance against fascism, their ascendancy promised to prevent any relapses into racism. At the same time, the noble experiment of creating an egalitarian society entrusted intellectuals with a special mission of guiding the transformation. Finally, the opening of access to education aspired to create a truly popular culture that would bridge the gap between the elite and the masses. However, some clairvoyant observers like the Polish writer Czesław Miłosz quickly realized the deceptive nature of socialist modernization: "What is happening in Russia and the countries dependent upon her bespeaks of a new kind of insanity."[20]

In the first postwar years the Soviets slowly tightened their grip on their sphere of influence, since they were increasingly willing to disregard western objections. Red Army liberation morphed successively into military occupation, material rebuilding, and social transformation. In the satellite states, a broad coalition of socialists, opportunists, and nationalists supported the establishment of communist dominance because it promised a better life in the future. Even bourgeois democrats such as Victor Klemperer, who had barely survived the Third Reich, were convinced to join the SED so as to support the fresh start. The Soviet use of force and the communist regime's disregard for human rights were rationalized away as necessary means of overcoming the resistance of unregenerate traditionalists. A personal conversion, provided it looked sincere enough, as in the case of the youthful Christa Wolf, sufficed to erase the Nazi blemish and let one participate in the heroic project of building a new society. Only a few critics like Arthur Koestler realized that the communist "god that failed" was bringing a new form of bondage.[21]

SOVIETIZING THE BLOC

Russian dominance over Eastern Europe led to the partly compulsory imposition and partly voluntary adoption of Soviet modernity, effectively ending national roads to socialism. Stalin himself admitted: "In this war nothing is as it was before. Whoever has occupied a territory installs his system where his army has advanced." The visible presence of the Red Army and the invisible activities of the NKVD established unquestionable control, supplemented by Cominform dictates to fraternal parties and orders by political advisers in the Russian embassies. At the same time many East Europeans also began to imitate Soviet styles of food, dress, behavior, and outlook, redirecting their social and cultural gaze away from London or Paris to Moscow. For instance, most transnational contacts took place between delegations, cementing their friendship in sumptuous banquets with endless toasts of vodka. This counterpart to Americanization transformed both the substance and the appearance of eastern politics as well as daily life in a strange mixture of communist modernization and Stalinist repression.[22]

The first step in imposing the Soviet model was the open establishment of a "dictatorship of the proletariat" after the coup of the Czechoslovak communists in February 1948. Since the Cold War made concessions to the West irrelevant, the united communist and social democratic parties like the Polish ZPR, the German SED, and the Hungarian Working Peoples' Party now formally seized power in their respective countries. Their general secretaries Klement Gottwald, Boleslaw Bierut, Walter Ulbricht, and Matyas Rakosi thereby became sole dictators, controlling the government apparatus through their parties. To compensate for their lack of charisma, they muzzled all opposition, reduced other parties to ciphers, and hollowed out parliamentary forms. At the same time, they violated constitutionally guaranteed civil rights by imposing censorship, forbidding debate, and outlawing public assemblies. The remaining discussion within the newly enlarged communist parties was limited through the prohibition of factionalism and the strict execution of dictates from Moscow.[23] By the early 1950s East European politics was reduced to the conformity of mature Stalinism.

The second move was the systematic suppression of civil society so as to leave communist associations in sole control of the field. In the German Democratic Republic (GDR), for instance, the trade unions were unified in a single organization, the Free German Trade Union (FDGB), which metamorphosed from a representation of labor interests into a transmission belt of orders to the proletariat, moderated only by the dispensing of small favors such as bonus pay or vacation reservations. Similarly the variety of youth groups, ranging from scouts to sailing clubs, was reduced to a single-party youth association, the Free German Youth (FDJ), which combined ideological indoctrination with the provision of leisure activities. Numerous other organizations like the party-dominated Democratic Women's League of Germany (DFD) sought to appeal to a specific clientele, while making sure that its demands would not contradict communist policy.[24] This coordination of social activities and indoctrination created endless conflicts with the Protestant and Catholic churches, who insisted on more autonomy. As a result, citizens were forced to channel their activities solely through party organizations.

The introduction of a planned economy that was supposed to assure workers' control and repeat the Russian miracle of industrialization was yet another aspect of Sovietization. In order to create larger, machine-assisted farming units, agriculture was collectivized everywhere except in Poland, where small holdings survived. The transposition of the industrial model to the countryside did facilitate the mass production of grain and meat, but at the expense of personal initiative. Similarly the nationalization of industry and trade created a large state-owned sector of companies but failed to liberate workers, putting them under the new control of union, party, and government bureaucrats. The introduction of Five Year Plans in Eastern Europe sought to create a heavy industrial base in coal mining and steel production, essential for postwar rebuilding, but it neglected the manufacture of consumer goods. Moreover, the elimination of market competition, ignoring of costs in pricing, and lack of incentives left allocation decisions to the planners, who often failed to anticipate the desires of the public.[25]

The Soviet model came to dominate even in the less tangible realm of culture, thereby stifling intellectual debate and artistic creativity. Studying the great Russian writers or musicians was certainly justified, but the support of ideological stultification by poets like Johannes R. Becher and philosophers like György Lukacs was reprehensible. The dogma of Marxism-Leninism not only pervaded all schools but also severely constricted freedom of research and teaching in the universities and academies.[26] Moreover, the petit bourgeois style of socialist realism rejected modernist experimentation, and the injunction to "pick up the pen, comrade" in order to create a working-class literature largely produced literary drivel. The warping of thought and the twisting of language due to the ubiquitous insistence on citing the classics of Marxist-Leninism as the sole font of wisdom was similarly insidious. Associations like the Writers' League and the Culture League kept creative intellectuals in line by offering privileges such as access to publication or travel. This process of reorientation culminated in the cultivation of cultural ties by Soviet friendship societies.[27]

Sovietization was not just imposed from above but also supported by a vocal minority from below. The surviving communists liberated from the Nazi concentration camps, emerging from the anti-Nazi underground, or returning from exile in the Soviet Union and the West were the most determined advocates of social revolution. They could count on many members of the labor movement who hoped finally to realize their egalitarian aims with the help of the big brother in Moscow. Of course, those new farmers who had received land from the dissolved estates of the nobility also had a considerable stake in the socialist regime. Moreover, quite a few intellectuals embraced Marxism-Leninism as an ideology, since they could interpret the communist classics for the masses. While some opportunists also sought to advance their careers by emulating the victorious Soviet example, the bulk of the East European population withdrew from politics in order to get their personal life in order.[28] As a result, the remaining anticommunist opponents in the churches, older parties, and nationalist circles found ever less support.

The outward expression of bloc solidarity was the economic cooperation of the Comecon and the military alliance of the Warsaw Pact. Communist party leaders from various countries customarily met for bilateral talks and multilateral consultations during congresses of the Bolshevik Party in Moscow. But in response to the creation of the western Organization of European Economic Cooperation in 1949, Stalin decided to go further, founding a Council for Mutual Economic Assistance with his satellite states that shared the same planned economy in order to intensify mutual trade. When West Germany entered NATO, Moscow also formalized its military cooperation with seven other East European countries, ranging from Albania to Romania. The mutual defense treaty was named the Warsaw Pact after the site of signing, which took place in the Polish capital.[29] Creating a formidable image of united strength, these organizations were nevertheless dominated by the Soviet Union as the biggest member and therefore served to institutionalize Russian hegemony, even if some tensions over goals and methods continued with mavericks like Yugoslavia.

During the postwar decade, a combination of compulsion and imitation transformed Eastern and Central Europe according to the Soviet model of modernity. Marxism-Leninism, as interpreted by the Soviet Union, provided the ideological bond and the legitimation for Moscow's dominance. Because the eastern currencies were not freely convertible on the world market, trade with the West withered, and was redirected toward bilateral exchanges with the Soviet Union and barter with other Comecon countries. Moreover, the Warsaw Pact justified the continued stationing of Soviet army troops in most satellite states and provided an integrated defense doctrine, practiced in annual maneuvers that tested the military coordination between the members. The propaganda glue holding the Soviet Bloc together was fear of a revanchist West Germany, which lurid posters depicted as dominated by ex-Nazi NATO generals and financed by evil U.S. capitalists. Just when Moscow's ascendancy seemed secure, the Chinese began to challenge its orthodoxy with a new version of agrarian communism, better suited to Korea and Vietnam.[30]

DE-STALINIZATION

After Stalin's death in 1953, the temperamental Nikita Khrushchev finally won the successor struggle by promising to soften repression without losing control. The early favorite, secret police chief Lavrenti Beria, was shot by the army on treason charges, while the second competitor, Prime Minister Georgy Malenkov, was gradually pushed aside since he was blamed for mismanaging the economy. Trained as a metalworker, the fifty-nine-year-old Khrushchev, who had risen as a political commissar in the Ukraine where he fought against nationalists, proved to be more adroit in getting the party to appoint him as first secretary. Though he had participated in the purges, he cultivated a populist down-to-earth image and understood the need to distance himself from Stalin's excesses in order to preserve communist power by making it less repressive. This contradictory policy demanded an extraordinary balancing act between, on the one hand, admitting some of his predecessor's crimes so as to respond to resentment of the gulag and, on the other, setting clear limits to public criticism in order to maintain Communist Party control.[31]

During Stalin's last years, popular discontent had been building in the Soviet Bloc without finding an appropriate outlet. In the Soviet Union the slow economic recovery from wartime devastation and the high costs of the Cold War arms race frustrated citizens, while the arbitrariness of the purges left a trail of fear, substantiated by tales of suffering from returning camp inmates. Moreover, the censorship of culture turned many intellectuals against the system, even if they supported socialism in principle. Among the citizenry of defeated Nazi allies like Hungary there was much nationalist anger over Russian domination, since Sovietization appeared as the imposition of an alien model. At the same time the open establishment of dictatorship and the construction of socialism, with its collectivization and industrialization, victimized numerous opponents in Poland and Czechoslovakia, many of whom fled to the West. Moreover, the persecution of the churches created martyrs like Cardinal Jozsef Mindszenty and alienated faithful Christians from the communist regime. Only western media like Radio Free Europe in Munich and RIAS in Berlin were able to voice such discontent.[32]

Surprisingly enough, the first explosion occurred on June 17, 1953, in East Berlin when workers dared to revolt against the SED dictatorship. The attempt of an "accelerated transition" to socialism encountered special problems in the GDR such as food shortages, repression of dissent, and persecution of the Protestant church. When the government raised work quotas, thereby lowering pay, construction workers went out on strike and began marching down the Stalinallee, a wide boulevard, calling for the pay cuts to be taken back. During their demonstration the crowd grew to twenty-five thousand, and demands escalated to political reforms like "free elections" and "German unification." Broadcast by western media, the unrest quickly spread to about five hundred East German cities and towns, with angry citizens beating up party functionaries and freeing prisoners. Fearing for its rule, the GDR Politburo appealed to the Soviets, who authorized the use of Red Army tanks to put the uprising down. About seventy-five people were killed and another sixteen hundred imprisoned as punishment for the "counterrevolutionary coup attempt." Thereafter the SED remained traumatized, since the revolt showed the illegitimacy of its rule.[33]

During the Twentieth Party Congress on February 25, 1956, Khrushchev finally decided to risk denouncing the excesses of Stalin's rule so as to rehabilitate the communist project. For four hours he harangued the stunned delegates with an impassioned speech, accusing his predecessor of "intolerance ... brutality, and ... abuse of power." He began his litany of Stalin's "repression and physical anni-

hilation" with the purge of Old Bolsheviks and continued with Stalin's deportation of entire nationalities, only to conclude with details
on the exaggeration of Stalin's role in the war and the propagandistic
elevation of Stalin as a monumental hero. Though a committee had
prepared these charges, functionaries were shocked because Khrushchev tore the veil of silence from a whole series of transgressions in
which many of them had participated.[34] This spirited attack on the
cult of personality toppled Stalin from the pedestal of a guiding saint
in the quasi-religious belief system of Marxism-Leninism. Though the
"secret speech" was intended to reinvigorate communism by distancing it from its prior crimes, internal dissidents and external critics
now found their worst fears officially proven.

By encouraging such a de-Stalinization, Khrushchev initiated a
cultural liberalization in the Soviet Union that inspired hopes for
a more open form of socialism in the satellites as well. Named after a
1954 novel by Ilya Ehrenburg, this "thaw" not only toppled Stalin's
statues, renamed places named after Stalin, and released prisoners
from the gulag; it also allowed more experimentation in the arts by
lessening censorship. Now the innovative compositions of Dmitri
Shostakovich and Sergei Prokofiev could be played in public concerts. Though Pasternak's *Dr. Zhivago*, printed in Italy, remained
prohibited, Aleksandr Solzhenitsyn's *One Day in the Life of Ivan Denisovich* was allowed to appear. Suddenly movie directors were able to
show the horrors of war in films like *The Cranes are Flying*, which
won the Golden Palm at the Cannes Festival in 1958. Bands were
permitted to play U.S.-style music, youth festivals brought in foreign
visitors, and more eastern athletes were able to compete in world
championships and Olympic Games.[35] Among sympathetic intellectuals the thaw once again revived hope that it might be possible for
Soviet communism to develop in a liberal direction.

When testing the new freedom at the end of June 1956, Polish
workers in the city of Poznań quickly learned that communists were
still ready to repress any real challenge to their power. While intellectuals grumbled about ideological controls, laborers at the Stalin
Metal Plant went out on strike to demand better food and higher
wages. The general resentment against political repression and poor

living conditions drove about one hundred thousand sympathizers into the central square. They sacked the headquarters of the Polish United Workers' Party, disarmed the police, and opened prison gates. To keep things from spiraling out of control General Konstantin Rokossovsky sent four hundred Soviet tanks and about ten thousand troops into the city to fight, ostensibly against "German provocateurs." At least 57 people were killed, 600 wounded, and 250 arrested. In order to keep the unrest from spreading, the Soviets subsequently permitted the appointment of Władysław Gomułka as first secretary of the Workers' Party, and he initiated some limited reforms.[36] Nonetheless, the Poznań protests were a warning that de-Stalinization should not be carried too far.

The subsequent Hungarian uprising of October 1956 was an even more dramatic challenge to Soviet domination because it involved an entire nation. Associated with the Dual Monarchy's and independent Hungary's defeat and the loss of ethnic territories, communism had never been especially popular in Budapest. When students demonstrating in front of the parliament building were stopped from broadcasting their demands by radio, violence broke out in the Hungarian capital. Rebellious crowds formed workers' councils and militias to battle the secret police and chase away party functionaries, inducing the government to fall. As new prime minister, the reform communist Imre Nagy promised free elections and announced that Hungary might leave the Warsaw Pact. Afraid of losing power, orthodox Politburo members eventually called for help from the Red Army, which on November 4 invaded the country, setting off a week of desperate but unequal fighting. About twenty-five hundred Hungarians and seven hundred Russian soldiers were killed, but the West did not come to the aid of the revolution, afraid that intervention would trigger World War III. Some two hundred thousand people fled during the harsh repression, which again revealed Soviet communism's dictatorial face.[37]

Khrushchev's effort at a limited de-Stalinization therefore produced a paradoxical mixture of hope and disappointment in the Soviet Union and its satellites. In some ways, the attempt to distance communism from the use of force in collectivization and industrialization and to end the murderous repression of the Great Purges and the gulag was an overdue course correction, designed to make the system more palatable to East Europeans and Soviet citizens. Moreover, the creativity unleashed by the thaw was truly impressive, since it produced cultural works of lasting merit, appreciated by international audiences. But even in Moscow, Khrushchev used the denunciation of Stalin to reassert his dictatorial control, and the party squelched all efforts at public debate. Moreover, in East Berlin, Poznań, and Budapest the brutal repression of the successive revolts indicated that any dissent would be snuffed out by the Soviet military, intent on defending its empire by force. Because granting freedom remained at the discretion of the party rather than being a fundamental right, the idea of a liberal communism remained a contradiction in terms.[38]

CONSUMER COMMUNISM

Afraid of making political concessions, communist dictators turned instead to raising living standards in order to gain public approval for their unpopular regimes. After brutally suppressing all dissent, the new Hungarian leader János Kádár began to promote a compromise, called "goulash communism" after a popular stew of meat, noodles, and paprika. In the economic realm this policy implied a gradual shift away from the heavy-industry emphasis of "smokestack socialism" to the production of consumer goods such as television sets and cars, even if they were more modest than their western counterparts. In the cultural arena, this course meant the grudging acceptance of international modernism as a style of architecture, such as prefabricated concrete apartment buildings similar to housing developments in the West. The underlying bargain, promoted all over the Soviet Bloc, was public toleration of the system in exchange for a slow improvement in living standards.[39] While the people were grateful for every step toward a better life, communism thereby entered a dangerous competition with the West.

In some areas related to defense expenditures, the Soviet Union was surprisingly successful, exceeding western expectations. On

October 4, 1957, Russia launched a satellite into earth orbit from Baikonur, thereby winning the first leg of the "space race" with the United States. Called Sputnik, the shiny one-hundred-kilogram globe with two antennas was of simple design, containing a radio transmitter that sent back scientific data for three weeks. A propaganda success, the launch nonetheless proved that Soviet development had increased the range of the R-7 rocket to such an extent that it could reach the North American continent. Understandably the Soviet government used Sputnik to tout communist science, while the U.S. public went into a "Sputnik shock" because its faith in the superiority of western research was severely shaken.[40] Another arena was sports competition, in which Soviet athletes claiming to be "state amateurs," supported by the armed forces, scored an increasing number of successes against westerners who were still trying to compete as genuine amateurs. Winning against capitalists in space and athletic contests was therefore an important source of pride.

The communists were less adept in the consumer competition of "peaceful coexistence" since they remained wedded to a production ideology. Ebulliently optimistic, Nikita Khrushchev promised that the Soviet Union would soon achieve a higher living standard than that of the United States, but this claim proved more difficult to realize than he anticipated. During the American National Exhibition in Moscow in 1959, the Soviet first secretary and Vice President Richard Nixon jousted in the "kitchen debate" over which system provided better appliances, a contest won hands-down by the typical American home. Trying to ease women's frustration, the Soviet regime sought to go beyond providing basic necessities by offering more attractive clothes, shoes, and furniture, even allowing a touch of fashion in modern design. This campaign also attempted to make other consumer goods more appealing and to transform the drab state-run shopping outlets of the local Konsum into something approaching a department store. To forestall future revolts, the leaders of the Eastern Bloc realized that they had to make greater efforts to satisfy popular wishes for consumption.[41]

The goal of improving living standards seemed within reach, since the communists achieved a modest Economic Miracle of their own, albeit later and at a lower level than in the reconstruction of West Germany. For postwar rebuilding of industrial plants and infrastructure, which required coal and steel as well as much labor, smokestack socialism was actually quite appropriate. Collectivization did gradually produce enough food to overcome shortages, and nationalized industries could offer sufficient products to end rationing. But owing to the emphasis on fixed quantitative targets, meeting the more flexible challenge of making consumer goods proved difficult for the planned economy, since satisfaction also depended on quality and style. With a delay of a decade or more, the Eastern Bloc also started to produce refrigerators, television sets, and cars, but their prices were high, deliveries slow, and design often outdated when they arrived. Since lack of supplies, production shortfalls, distribution bottlenecks, and political interference hindered creative designers, the East was always playing catch-up to the more dynamic West.[42]

The communist failure in the consumer competition was ultimately due to the structure of the planned economy, which proved too rigid to meet shifting demand. It did not help that the arms race, secret service, and party bureaucracy devoured enormous sums. The price controls, which ignored production costs by subsidizing food, housing, and transportation, contributed to the misallocation of resources. The guarantee of job security, regardless of performance, also undercut work morale, since frequent bonuses or preferred vacation destinations provided only modest incentives. The nonconvertibility of eastern currencies shielded local production from the stiff competition of the world market, leading to a series of Comecon barter agreements. As a result, the dollar and deutsche mark functioned as second currencies with which western goods could be bought at privileged Intershops. In spite of gradual improvement, the economy remained full of bottlenecks, requiring barter in services and standing in line. Various efforts to reintroduce elements of market competition foundered on the rigidity of planning ideology.[43]

The lessening of ideological fervor also deepened the Sino-Soviet split, since it suggested that Moscow had abandoned its commitment to revolution. Initially Mao Zedong had been quite grateful for Russian support in the Chinese Civil War and for subsequent help in rebuilding his ravaged country. But Khrushchev's de-Stalinization shocked the Chinese leadership, which also rejected the policy of "coexistence" as a revisionist sellout. Instead, Mao developed an independent form of agrarian communism that inspired the Great Leap Forward and attracted North Korea and North Vietnam, which were fighting anti-imperialist struggles against their southern cousins. In contrast to the pragmatic policies advocated by a satiated Soviet Union, the radical Chinese path appealed to national-liberation movements that had yet to seize power and wanted to modernize their countries. Behind Beijing's refusal to follow Moscow's dictates also lay divergent national interests, which eventually surfaced in the border clashes in the Amur region. Because of its relative moderation, Moscow slowly lost ideological control over the communist camp.[44]

After eleven years of leading the Soviet Union, Khrushchev was suddenly overthrown by a coup of his own associates who claimed that he had lost his touch. On October 14, 1964, the Presidium of the Central Committee of the Communist Party voted to oust him but allowed the fallen dictator to retire and write his memoirs. There were many reasons for the party's dissatisfaction with him. Khrushchev's mercurial personality, his rudeness to subordinates, and his authoritarian leadership style did not exactly endear him to his colleagues. At the same time the failure of the agricultural reforms to deliver more food also disappointed his erstwhile supporters. Moreover, Khrushchev's attempts to restructure the party bureaucracy threatened many functionaries, who feared losing their positions. Finally, his erratic foreign-policy record of suppressing rebellions in the bloc, crises over Berlin and Cuba, as well as disagreements with China raised doubts about the correctness of his course. Repudiating this "adventurism," the party leadership chose the war hero Leonid Brezhnev, who returned to a more orthodox neo-Stalinist policy.[45]

Shifting from outright oppression to economic competition therefore turned out to be both frustrating and dangerous for the Soviet Bloc. In Walter Ulbricht's dialectical image, the East needed to "overtake [the West] without catching up" to it—an impossible task in physical terms. Because of their materialist ideology, communists could not resist the trap of wanting to outproduce the West in consumer goods, even if their starting position was rather unfavorable. No doubt the citizens of the Soviet Bloc were grateful for every improvement in their living standard that eased the burden of coping with a shortage economy and lightened their daily routine of standing in line for special goods like bananas or coffee. But those privileged cadres who were allowed to travel to the West soon realized that the race was unwinnable, because market competition created more economic dynamism. As a result of entering this economic contest of consumption, the eastern leadership discredited itself and fueled that popular discontent with communism which eventually precipitated its overthrow.[46]

REAL EXISTING SOCIALISM

Contrary to some western charges that communism was merely trying to catch up, the Soviet project was an effort to create an alternate, postcapitalist form of modernization. The planned economy was supposed to avoid the cyclical crises of the market and the exploitation of wage labor; the egalitarian abolition of class privilege was intended to enable political participation beyond the squabbling of democracy; and the scientific worldview of Marxism-Leninism was expected to overtake bourgeois scholarship in discoveries and technical innovation.[47] Flush with victory over the fascist enemy, Moscow set out to impose this vision of progress on its newly conquered territories and satellite states in Eastern Europe. Many workers and intellectuals, even in the West, hoped that this party-dominated approach would offer a shortcut to economic development, yielding the benefits of modernity without its attendant insecurities. While state socialism worked fairly well during postwar reconstruction and for creating a smokestack industry, it ultimately turned out to be a reform-resistant dead end.

Because of the failure of interwar democracy, the Soviet Union initially had more success in transforming Eastern Europe than is acknowledged in retrospect. In some countries like Bulgaria, Moscow could rely on Slavic ethnic ties and hopes for development; in other nations like Poland it could claim credit for having defeated Hitler and keeping the Germans at bay; in yet other places like Czechoslovakia it could count on sizable sympathies for the project of revolutionizing society; and in defeated states like Hungary it could rely on the intimidating presence of the Soviet army. Moreover, after several years of control, the communist regimes were able to point to some notable achievements: In all eastern countries Stalinist policies created a heavy industrial base needed for further development. The massive use of labor succeeded in rebuilding most of the wartime damage in infrastructure and housing. The mechanization of agriculture finally overcame food shortages. Careful planning also produced an ample supply of basic goods.[48] In contrast to the prewar crisis, communist leaders were therefore quite certain that they were now much better off.

After economic security had been achieved, the limitations of the communist road to modernity became more and more apparent. The biggest handicap in the East European countries was the imposition of the Soviet model by force from the outside, which ran counter to the wishes of the majority of East Europeans. While catch-up industrialization offered progress to Bulgaria and Romania, it was actually a step backward in the more highly developed economies of Czechoslovakia, East Germany, Hungary, and Poland. At the same time, the reduction of political participation to mere membership in mass organizations and to public acclamation of the communist dictators seemed a hollow ritual to citizens who had experienced a taste of democracy during the interwar period. Moreover, the inculcation of the Marxist-Leninist dogma as method and result of inquiry constrained scientific and artistic innovation among intellectuals who recalled the excitement of free debate and inquiry. By suppressing civil society and ignoring human rights, the dictatorial communist approach robbed modernization of its self-correcting dynamism.[49]

Instead of suggesting a road to social progress, "Sovietization" became a term of derision during the Cold War, pointing to Eastern Europe's subjection to Stalinist terror. From the outset the rapes, plunder, and wanton killing of the liberation saddled the Soviet project with negative associations difficult to overcome. The ruthless class warfare in the name of denazification that expropriated land-owners and industrialists revealed the callousness of Marxist social engineering in creating a more egalitarian social order. The brutal suppression of political alternatives, the systematic persecution of opponents by the secret police, and the muzzling of public discussion also showed a fundamental disregard for the people. Finally the imposition of ideological conformity by obligatory training in Marxism-Leninism and systematic censorship demonstrated the inhumane character of the regimes. Only a minority of supporters praised the positive aspects of communism, while the majority of the public resented its massive repression. In the end, both the excessive goals and brutal methods discredited the socialist project.[50]

For the Soviet Bloc, the communist path toward modernity therefore turned into a "civilisational mirage" in which self-destructive traits smothered the progressive potential. Conceived as an alternative developmental path for avoiding the "crisis of western modernity," the Soviet model consisted of a curious mixture of Marxist ideology, antifascism, and Russian imperialism. The proposed solutions such as the planned economy, the single-party dictatorship, and the inculcation of socialist ideology created internal contradictions that proved impossible to resolve. At the same time the presence of the Soviet army, the activities of the secret police, and the role of Russian advisers exported a repressive version of socialism that was never able to shed its Stalinist deformation entirely.[51] As a result, efforts of liberalization from above in de-Stalinization and in protests from below during 1953 and 1956 could not alter the dictatorial character of the system sufficiently to make it bearable. Though appreciating the victory over fascism, most East Europeans experienced the communist project as a frightful dystopia.

Chapter 17

COLD WAR CRISES

Peter Fechter, Berlin Wall victim, 1962. *Source*: bpk, Berlin / Art Resource, NY.

On June 24, 1948, the Soviet Military Administration cut all rail, road, and water access to West Berlin and turned off the power. With this measure the Russians retaliated against the western currency reform that threatened their economic control of the city by making the old reichsmark worthless. Suddenly not only the Allied garrisons but about 2.2 million civilian Berliners found themselves without supplies, at the mercy of East German deliveries. But General Lucius D. Clay, military governor of the U.S. zone, was determined to hold out, and, instead of mounting a tank attack, which might have started World War III, organized an airlift, using planes to supply the beleaguered city and thereby shifting the onus of opening hostilities to the Soviets. The ensuing "air bridge" was a masterpiece of improvisation, delivering five thousand tons of fuel and food in about fifteen hundred flights daily through three air corridors. Though fog and snow cost eighty-three pilots and ground personnel their lives, one plane after another landed about every three minutes. Defeated by this technical feat, the Soviets lifted the blockade after eleven months on May 12, 1949.[1]

The first Berlin crisis was a test of western resolve that initiated the open Cold War confrontation for the control of Europe. Though primarily intent on defending its World War II gains, the Soviet Union was tempted to expand its influence westward by taking advantage of economic disruption and political chaos. American policy makers like Clay understood that they needed to rise to the challenge: "We are convinced that our remaining in Berlin is essential to our prestige in Germany and in Europe. Whether for good or bad, it has become a symbol of the American intent." Since West Berlin mayor Ernst Reuter also saw the blockade as a test of western resolve, he appealed to the world in front of half a million demonstrators: "Look at this city and realize that you shall not and cannot abandon this city and these people!" Splitting even the Berlin government, this ideological conflict signaled the division of Europe into two hostile camps vying for control of the continent. At the same time, the American and British commitment also created a symbolic bond with West Germany that would not be broken.[2]

The disappointment of hopes for genuine peace after the defeat of fascism has led to a fierce debate about responsibility for the breakdown of cooperation between communism and democracy. During the Cold War itself, anticommunists were convinced that the threat of yet another major war emanated from Stalin's personality and socialist dreams of world revolution. But disenchantment with western claims to superior morality during the Vietnam War motivated a generation of "revisionists" to criticize U.S. policies as imperialist apologetics, driven by capitalist interests. After the fall of the Soviet Union, traditionalists found their suspicions of Russian expansionism borne out in newly accessible documents, but gradually less-partisan observers succeeded in differentiating this black-and-white picture by showing the disagreements within the Eastern Bloc. No longer just focusing on the bilateral confrontation between Washington and Moscow, they also paid more attention to Europe and the global extent of the Cold War.[3] By going beyond casting blame, such approaches interpret the conflict as an interactive process driven by a mixture of clashing interests and misperceptions on both sides.

Divergent personal recollections have also created conflicting collective memories and public commemorations of the Cold War. On the one hand, many contemporaries recall acute fears of nuclear Armageddon that would incinerate the world, fueled by government calls to build bomb shelters and civil defense exercises of hiding under desks in schools. On the other hand, nostalgic political retrospectives often portray the East-West conflict as a period of extraordinary stability, in which the superpowers exercised a condominium over the polarized world, keeping their respective satellites in line. A closer look reveals instead a confusing pattern of multiple conflicts, crises, and coexistence, waxing and waning unpredictably, which defies linear representation. The very adjective "cold" that designates this ideological confrontation suggests that there were also "hot" wars, and indeed there were, primarily in Asia, as well as numerous insurrections and counterinsurgencies in Africa and Latin America. Far from being simply a grand game of the superpowers, the Cold War was a ceaseless struggle with many participants in multiple arenas.[4]

From the perspective of modernity the Cold War was essentially a conflict between the communist and democratic blueprints for shaping the future. Growing out of the East-West conflict since 1917, the postwar struggle intensified the competition between the Marxist and liberal versions of economic development, since both sides wanted to make their vision prevail, leaving little space for intellectuals searching for a third way.[5] The rival alternatives involved fundamentally different forms of development: collective versus individualistic, party-dominated versus pluralistic, and state-planned versus market-competitive modernity. Their competition enhanced technological innovation through the arms race of rockets, jets, and nuclear warheads; it speeded economic development through expenditures for infrastructure and design of consumer goods; it fostered cultural experimentation with (non)representational styles of painting and functionalist architecture.[6] In this light, the Cold War appears as a global race for modernization with humankind teetering on the brink of either humane progress or nuclear self-destruction.

MUTUAL MISPERCEPTIONS

Both conflicting priorities and mistaken perceptions combined to disappoint hopes for peaceful postwar cooperation. Once the common aim of defeating fascist aggression in Europe and Asia had been achieved, the shotgun marriage of the Grand Alliance was bound to result in divorce, allowing prior divergences to reappear. The underlying ideologies of communism and democracy were too dissimilar and the political aims of both sides too antagonistic to allow for collaboration in the long run. Individual policy disputes did not necessarily have to result in a global confrontation, if they remained subordinate to the antifascist consensus. Instead, mistaken perceptions of largely defensive intentions led to aggressive overreactions that then served as proof of increasing threats, which in turn required tough countermeasures. Since diplomatic efforts to resolve various postwar issues continued after Allied victory, it was this corrosive spread of suspicion that ultimately inhibited compromise.[7] The Cold

War was not just an inevitable result of clashing interests but also a product of mutual mistrust.

Proud of having defeated the Wehrmacht's invasion, Stalin above all wanted security to heal the wounds of war and to consolidate the newly won Soviet empire. Ideologically he was suspicious of the bourgeois West and hoped for a crisis of capitalism that would pit the United States and the United Kingdom against each other. As a result of Russia's immense human and material sacrifices, the dictator also firmly believed that he had a moral claim to those territories liberated by the Red Army. But in contrast to the indirect methods of western rule, Stalin was determined to govern the "sphere of influence" conceded to him at Yalta and Potsdam with an iron fist, disregarding the niceties of parliamentarianism and free elections. Beyond controlling the conquered lands and satellite states, he was also willing to help local communists seize power, provided they could do so without endangering the security of the Soviet Union. The basic Soviet mind-set was therefore defensive—but Russian actions were often brutal and offensive, leading western politicians to interpret them as expansionist.[8]

As leaders of the western Allies, the Americans also desired security for themselves and their client states, albeit in a capitalist and democratic form. Having suffered much less, since except for Pearl Harbor fighting did not take place on its own soil, the United States had on the contrary prospered: its economy had grown into the largest in the world during the conflict. But Presidents Roosevelt and Truman were well aware of the depth of isolationist sentiment among Americans, who demanded a quick drawdown of troops in order "to bring the boys home." The detonation of the two nuclear bombs over Hiroshima and Nagasaki not only knocked Tokyo out of the war, denying Russia a share of the occupation of Japan, but also set the United States apart because it alone controlled the most powerful weapon that had ever existed. Instead of wielding this power to intimidate other countries through "atomic diplomacy," New Deal liberals preferred to persuade them by positive incentives and by employing the United Nations as a global forum of debate and negotiation.[9] Washington's consistent effort to open doors to trade and secure self-determination nevertheless sent mixed messages to Moscow, which saw U.S. aims as threatening its own control and therefore hardened its stance.

Great Britain and to a lesser degree France followed the American lead but also insisted on pursuing their own special interests. Economically weakened by the lengthy fighting, London wanted the continent to remain stable so it could focus instead on retaining its colonial empire, which was beginning to break away in India. In general, the British sought to play the role of sophisticated Greeks to the naive Americans who were supposed to be the new Roman Empire. Toward Germany they were willing to engage in reconstruction in order to integrate it in the postwar world. Preoccupied with rebuilding their country materially and psychologically, the French wanted to see their Rhenish neighbors permanently weakened by division into separate states. Paris was continually tempted to follow Moscow's hard line in the Allied Control Council and had to be pressured by Washington to allow the unification of the three western zones into the Federal Republic. Moreover, the French were also busy reasserting their hold on North Africa and Indochina. The western camp therefore had to cope not only with threats from without but also division from within.[10]

Caught between the rival blocs, the Central European nations had little choice but to accommodate themselves to their respective superpowers. Aside from the western withdrawal from Leipzig in exchange for a share of the Berlin occupation, countries found themselves under the political control of whichever army had liberated their territory. Eastern hopes for some latitude during the people's democracy phase were disappointed by the open establishment of "dictatorships of the proletariat" on Stalin's orders in the late 1940s. Western expectations of reconstruction fared somewhat better owing to the material assistance of the Marshall Plan and the indirect nature of the American "empire by invitation," which left more room for local initiative. The growing rift between the victors affected the defeated Germans most, because the breakdown of the Allied Control Council divided their country according to the existing occupation boundaries. The emergence of two rival successor states such as the western Federal Republic and the eastern German Democratic Republic was the logical result.[11]

As the failures of cooperation proliferated, perceptive analysts began to recognize the growing antagonism between East and West and to warn policy makers to prepare for the inevitable conflict. In February 1946 George Kennan, an American diplomat in Moscow, sent a secret "long telegram" to Washington that attributed the "Kremlin's neurotic view of world affairs" to the "traditional and instinctive Russian sense of insecurity." Trying to dispel illusions of cooperation, he cautioned: "We have here a political force committed fanatically to the belief that with [the] U.S. there can be no permanent *modus vivendi*." Hence he called for a concerted policy of "long-term, patient but firm and vigilant *containment* of Russian expansive tendencies." In turn, the Soviet ambassador to the United States, Nikolai Novikov, similarly described U.S. foreign policy as reflecting "the imperialistic tendencies of American monopoly capitalism" and accused Washington of "striving for world supremacy." Andrei Zhdanov, Stalin's chief lieutenant, formulated this Soviet view as "the two-camps policy."[12] These complementary statements recognized that East-West disputes had grown into a global confrontation between the superpowers.

The concept that came to describe this fundamental conflict that nonetheless stopped short of an armed struggle was "the cold war." A few months after the end of World War II British novelist George Orwell used the term in an article about the implications of the atomic bomb to describe "a state which was at once unconquerable and in a permanent state of 'cold war' with its neighbors." The U.S. financier Bernard Baruch then picked up the notion to describe the growing tension between the Soviet Union and the United States. But it was the liberal columnist Walter Lippmann who publicized the concept in a series of articles, printed as a book with the title *The Cold War* in 1947. While agreeing with Kennan's analysis of the Soviet threat, this New Deal intellectual rejected the effort to stop Soviet expansion by forming military alliances. Instead he proposed "a policy of settlement" with Russia, aiming "to redress the balance of power" by getting the Red Army and U.S. forces out of Europe.[13] This dispute between advocates of the hard and soft views on how to respond to Russia thereafter dominated the western debate.

The awareness of a new confrontation, called the Cold War, emerged gradually out of efforts to explain the inability of the Americans and the Russians to compromise, which was turning the prior allies into mutual enemies. The underlying East-West conflict between the capitalist and socialist paths to modernity since 1917 had only been temporarily suspended by the need to cooperate against the fascist enemies. While the Grand Alliance did attempt to lay an institutional basis for postwar collaboration, the wartime summits and expert negotiations were unable to agree on specific details, leaving room for subsequent disputes. Moreover, some of the central concepts, such as "democracy," had a completely different meaning on each side, referring to the rule of the proletariat in the Soviet Union and to free elections in the United States. Diverging interests and contending ideologies created increasing suspicion that interpreted the moves of a former partner in a sinister light, leading to overreactions that in turn hardened mistrust. During the first postwar years, this slow shift of perceptions and attitudes plunged the world into decades of superpower confrontation.

DISPUTED ISSUES

A series of concrete policy disputes hastened the alienation of the former partners because both sides interpreted them as a pattern of dangerous expansionism. In themselves, the issues were not particularly grave, but when seen as related moves in a systematic effort to win the upper hand, they appeared rather threatening. Most of the conflicts arose in border areas where local forces struggled over their orientation to Moscow or Washington, appealing to their hoped-for protectors and thereby drawing them into the contest. Surprisingly enough, the disputes centered on control of Europe, because both Soviet and American policy makers considered the Old Continent, in spite of its destruction, crucial for future ascendancy in their competition. As a result, the Chinese Civil War between the communists led by Mao Zedong and the Kuomintang government under Chiang

Kai-shek was treated as a regional Asian issue rather than a question of global importance.[14] Because of their ideological nature, each of these conflicts involved both a struggle for domestic control and confrontation over international hegemony, which made them rather difficult to resolve.

One disputed area was the Near Eastern periphery of Europe, in which Stalin wanted to improve the Soviet position since the Red Army had conquered a part of the Balkans. Threatening to support Armenian claims against Turkey, Moscow demanded control of the Straits of Constantinople, pursuing a tsarist dream of free access to warm-water ports. Similarly, the Soviets refused to withdraw their forces from Iran, where they had been stationed in order to deny Persian oil to the Nazis, and supported local efforts to install a communist regime. An even more dangerous conflict involved the future allegiance of Greece. Due to British naval supremacy in the Mediterranean, Stalin and Churchill had assigned Athens to the western orbit in their spheres-of-influence agreement. But emboldened by the Red Army presence in Bulgaria, Greek Communists started an armed insurrection against the pro-western royalist regime, which asked the United States for help since Britain felt unable to afford the cost.[15] By bearing out suspicions of communist subversion, these Soviet-supported moves began to alarm western public opinion.

True to his reputation as a feisty politician from Missouri, President Harry Truman decided on a rather tough anticommunist response. Born in 1884, he had grown up on a farm, served as an artillery officer in France during World War I, and briefly run a clothing store. The Pendergast machine had helped him to be elected to the U.S. Senate in 1934 and named vice president ten years later in order to keep the radical Henry Wallace off the Democratic ticket. When FDR died in April 1945, Truman suddenly had to make foreign-policy decisions for which he was hardly prepared. But taking an increasingly dim view of Soviet expansionism, he offered a program of military and economic assistance to Greece and Turkey on March 12, 1947. Using the occasion for a statement of principle, he announced that it "must be the policy of the U.S. to support free peoples who are resisting attempted subjugation by armed minorities

Map 9. Cold War Europe, 1961. Adapted from German Historical Institute, Washington, DC.

and outside pressures." Inspired by Kennan's containment theory, this American promise that "[w]e must assist free peoples to work out their own destinies in their own way" became known as the Truman Doctrine.[16]

The Marshall Plan was another U.S. initiative "to prevent the complete breakdown of Western Europe" so as to keep it from falling into Soviet hands. Unrelieved hunger, cold, and disease were bolstering the appeal of the sizable French and Italian communist parties, both of which could hope to gain power peacefully with a popular-front strategy and thereby put the entire continent under Soviet control. In a signal speech at Harvard University, the new secretary of state George Marshall in June 1947 therefore promised that the Truman administration would financially assist "the revival of a working economy in the world so as to permit the emergence of political and social conditions in which free institutions can exist." Instead of combating communism rhetorically, this strategy sought to reduce its appeal by improving the living conditions of the European masses. Although the offer was open to all European nations, Stalin rejected it out of hand for Russia and the satellites, afraid of becoming economically dependent on the United States. By helping to buy American machines and foodstuffs, the generous Marshall Plan credits sped the Western European recovery, reinforcing its commitment to the anticommunist camp.[17]

Frustrated in his hopes for further expansion, Stalin ruthlessly consolidated the socialist empire already under his military and political control. At home he tightened his grip through mobilizing for reconstruction, putting the army leadership in its place by retiring some popular generals and campaigning against cosmopolitan influences creeping into the culture. In his satellites he condoned ethnic cleansing, such as the expulsion of millions of German speakers from Eastern Europe and the displacement of Poles from the eastern part of their country annexed by Russia to the new western provinces detached from Germany. At the same time, the Soviet secret service persecuted the anticommunist opposition in the occupied nations, arresting thousands of critics who disappeared into Siberia without a trace. Moreover, the very presence of the Red Army as occupation force served to intimidate bourgeois nationalists, making them willing to collaborate with local communists. In short, Stalin was not content to exert a prevailing influence over Eastern Europe and the Balkans but rather stamped his own ideology, social system, political institutions, and cultural styles upon his satellites. When hearing about the brutality of his methods, western leaders were appalled and resolved to resist where they could.[18]

The crucial contest revolved around the future of Germany, because both sides saw it as key to the control of the entire continent. During the Potsdam Conference, Stalin, Truman, and Attlee had been able to agree on the principles of "demilitarization, denazification and decartelization" as the mandate for the Allied Control Council, a joint military administration of the four Allied powers that would govern the defeated country. Except for the territorial losses in the East, all deliberations still referred to Germany as a whole—but differing occupation practices in the four occupation zones encouraged a divergent development. In the beginning, Stalin apparently wanted to keep his options open. Optimally he hoped to have all of Germany under socialism; second best would be a neutralized country between the two European blocs; and failing that the Soviet zone could be transformed into a communist showcase.[19] When western statesmen finally realized the extent of Soviet aims, U.S. secretary of state Byrnes in September 1946 called for the United States, Britain, and France to rebuild their own zones by joining them together and extending help for recovery. The result was a fierce competition for the allegiance of the Germans in all four zones.

In the struggle between socialist antifascism and capitalist democracy, the Soviets held the weaker cards, even though they controlled the heart of Germany. The brutality of the Red Army frightened hapless civilians, and Germany's loss of East Prussia, Pomerania, Silesia, and part of Brandenburg to Poland made the Russians unpopular. The willful arrogance of the Soviet Military Administration also fed resentment, while the economic exploitation through reparations, dismantling of factories, and joint Soviet-German companies angered especially the proletariat.[20] In contrast, American administrators like General Clay understood that material aid for rebuilding would convince more citizens of the attractiveness of democracy than would lengthy lectures during reeducation programs. Hence Washington shifted from a punitive to a reconstructive policy and, after some hesitation, decided to include the three western zones in the European

Recovery Program of the Marshall Plan. For the cowed Germans, the contrast was stark: conditions in the Soviet zone remained difficult, while in "trizonesia" life was beginning to get noticeably better. Whenever they had a choice, most East Germans opted for the western side.[21]

These policy disputes hastened a polarization that by the late 1940s divided the entire European continent into two hostile blocs. The victors were unable to assure their cooperation by concluding a peace treaty with Germany, since they were unwilling to maintain the essential precondition of an open dialogue between their competing ideologies. In order to control his empire, Stalin resorted to force and repression because propaganda was not sufficient to make communism prevail in the satellites and beyond. Alarmed by the extent and methods of Soviet expansion, the United States and United Kingdom did not, as predicted, withdraw from Europe but rather remained engaged, changing their policy from passive cooperation to active resistance. As a result of compulsion in the East and persuasion in the West, each side was able to consolidate its own sphere of influence, while Germany, lying between the blocs, became divided. Already on March 5, 1946, Winston Churchill had warned against the imposition of Soviet control: "From Stettin in the Baltic to Trieste in the Adriatic an 'iron curtain' has descended across the continent."[22]

GROWING CONFRONTATION

Once the contest had been joined, both sides tried to build up their own strength while probing their enemy's weaknesses in order to tip the precarious balance. In the East, Stalin therefore authorized Klement Gottwald's communist coup in Prague in February of 1948. But in Italy he counseled in no uncertain terms the restive activists of the Communist Party who wanted to stage an armed uprising to back off, since Rome clearly lay in the U.S. sphere. On the western side, seven countries tried to reinforce their defenses in 1948 by creating the Western Union Defense Organization to coordinate their efforts. Moreover, in Germany the western occupying powers speeded up the fusion of their three zones into one area, administered by a German economic council, in order to facilitate the recovery. The Cold War therefore developed in a ping-pong pattern in which one side would undertake an act deemed dangerous by the other, which would then resort to countermeasures of its own that produced further hostile actions. This vicious cycle led to a series of crises that brought the European continent repeatedly to the brink of war.[23]

The first flash point of the Cold War was the Berlin blockade, since it was a symbolic test of western commitment. Angered by head of the Economic Council Ludwig Erhard's currency reform in the western Allies' zones in the spring of 1948, which made the Soviet zone's printing presses worthless in financing the occupation, Stalin cut off all access routes to the German capital in the hope that "maybe we shall succeed in kicking [the western Allies] out." Clearly, his strategic position favored such a power play, since Berlin lay in the middle of the Soviet zone. Moreover, the western part of the city had only a small garrison of American, British, and French forces, insufficient for effective defense. Finally, over two million West Berliners were dependent for all their food and fuel on shipments through three land routes, and on receiving most of their electricity from power stations in the East. Since the western Allies' position was militarily untenable, they would either have to mount a tank attack against superior Soviet army forces and thereby provoke another war, or be compelled to withdraw ignominiously from Berlin, admitting their weakness. In either case the Soviets would win.[24]

The daring technological solution of an airlift foiled Stalin's plans by supplying West Berlin for eleven months with cargo planes. General Clay, military governor of the American zone, chose this risky method because the three air corridors were legally guaranteed, therefore shifting the onus of interdicting the flights and starting another war onto the Soviets. The entire operation was a logistic masterpiece, organized by General William H. Tunner, who used military versions of the Douglas DC-4 flying around the clock in ladder formations. They were supported by German ground crews who speedily unloaded the supplies in Tempelhof, Gatow, and the newly built Tegel airport. The children of Berlin now cheered as "raisin bombers" the same U.S. Air Force and RAF planes they had feared before. Since

West Berliners were holding out in spite of severe privations, the western press suddenly transformed them from evil Nazi perpetrators into "freedom loving Berliners."[25] Instead of forcing the western Allies out of the former capital, the blockade backfired and created a transatlantic emotional bond by proving that West Germans could rely on American support.

Revealing the polarization between East and West, the first Berlin crisis hastened the establishment of two German states embedded in the respective blocs. In the western two-thirds of the country local elections had already produced state governments, which offered West German citizens a chance for renewed participation. The fusion of the three western occupation zones also created a joint Economic Council that reformed the currency and reintroduced a competitive market so as to jump-start the recovery in the spring of 1948. In the summer, delegates met at the Herrenchiemsee in order to draft a provisional constitution, called Basic Law, which tried to avoid the mistakes of the Weimar Republic by weakening the powers of the presidency, reviving a federal structure, requiring political parties to win at least 5 percent of the votes to be represented in Parliament, and insisting on a constructive vote of no-confidence when toppling a government. The Christian Democratic Union won the first federal election a year later, making Konrad Adenauer chancellor.[26] While it deepened the division of the country, supporters justified the establishment of the Federal Republic (FRG) in 1949 as preparation for reuniting a free Germany in the future.

Thwarted in his desire to control all of the defeated country, Stalin had no choice but to authorize the creation of a socialist satellite state in the East. Already during the last of the wartime fighting in 1945, party functionaries led by Walter Ulbricht were flown in from Moscow in order to revive the underground Communist Party (KPD). Its merger with the larger Social Democratic Party in the spring of 1946, forming the Socialist Unity Party (SED), was supposed to broaden the electoral base, while measures such as the expropriation of big landowners and the nationalization of industry appealed to many farmers and workers. In order to gain legitimacy for founding a separate state, a massive propaganda campaign, called the People's Congress Movement, accused the FRG of being a neo-Nazi state and claimed that socialism and democracy could only be realized in the East. The constitution of this German Democratic Republic (GDR) was remarkably liberal and eschewed any direct references to communism, but the practice of persecuting political opponents and other social classes was typically Stalinist. Unable to stop the establishment of the FRG, the SED created its own state in October 1949.[27]

In 1950 the Korean War heightened Cold War tensions by sending shock waves of fear around the globe. Since the establishment of the North Atlantic Treaty Organization in 1949 had blocked Stalin in Europe, he saw new opportunities in Asia due to the victory of the Chinese Communists. By allowing North Korean leader Kim Il-Sung to attack South Korea, he hoped to draw the United States into a local conflict. But he failed to anticipate that when his delegation boycotted the UN Security Council to protest Red China's exclusion, the United Nations, no longer restrained by a Soviet veto, would condemn the North Korean aggression and mobilize an international force that stopped its advance. On the European continent, the invasion created a war scare, spreading fear by analogy that the massive tank forces of the Soviet army might rush to the Channel coast at any time. The Korean War also produced a boom in the Federal Republic, proving the superiority of the market economy, since German coal and steel—the material basis of two world wars—were once again in great demand. While the escalating Cold War tensions enhanced the strategic importance of East Germany as a Soviet staging area, they also hardened the anticommunist conviction among West Germans that all danger emanated from the East.[28]

The Asian wars accelerated the militarization of the European continent, since both sides began to rearm their Germans as potential allies. U.S. surveys of German opinion showed a deep aversion against the military, born of fear of another war, because World War II had turned out to be truly disastrous. But Soviet advisers to East Germany ignored the Potsdam prohibition, and the GDR began to create a "garrisoned people's police" (KVP) with heavy weapons as core for a National People's Army (NVA) within the Warsaw Pact, capable of putting down domestic risings and helping the Soviet army. At the same time Chancellor Adenauer began to plan an FRG contribution to western defense, as he believed that regaining sovereignty required possession of an armed force. To calm fears of a re-armed Germany in the allied capitals, he favored integrating FRG soldiers into the supranational units of a proposed European Defense Community, but after France rejected that proposal he pushed successfully against strong opposition for the inclusion of the Bundeswehr into NATO in 1955.[29] With rearmament, both sides assembled a huge concentration of conventional forces and nuclear weapons, making Germany a likely battlefield.

Though taking place a world apart, the Berlin crisis and the Korean War intensified the Cold War by suggesting that it might turn hot not just in Asia but also in Europe. Only five years after their joint effort to defeat the Nazis, Moscow and Washington were engaged in an ideological confrontation which assumed a depth and extent that was truly global. In Korea the conflict led to actual fighting because it remained somewhat of a proxy war, with the United States participating only within a multinational UN force and the Soviet Union acting mostly through its North Korean and Chinese auxiliaries. In Europe the confrontation fortunately remained below the threshold of bloodshed, since both sides were more directly engaged and feared the outbreak of another world war, with deterrence resting on Soviet conventional armor and American nuclear-strike capacity. Instead, with a mixture of compulsion and persuasion the superpowers created two hostile blocs that were locked in a fierce propaganda battle, extolling the virtues of peace and freedom respectively. By sparking frightening crises, the Cold War made both sides more insecure.[30]

ARENAS OF COMPETITION

The popular memory of the Cold War as a military confrontation between the two blocs is correct but incomplete, since it was a multi-dimensional struggle that left hardly any area untouched. The physical remnants of missile silos, tank tracks, command bunkers, and troop barracks in the Central European countryside support the reality of the arms race. A whole genre of spy fiction, epitomized by John le Carré and amplified by espionage films like the early James Bond series, recalls the efforts at mutual subversion. But the East-West conflict was also an ideological competition between socialist and democratic versions of modernization, pitting antifascism against antitotalitarianism. Moreover, it was an economic race for public improvement as well as individual prosperity, which played out in welfare provisions and consumer expectations. Ultimately, the Cold War was a competition for allegiance to a communist utopia or western values that dominated domestic politics as well as international relations. A more comprehensive understanding has to take the interaction of all of these dimensions into account.[31]

The arms race was the most dangerous part of the Cold War, because the nuclear buildup was large enough to blow up the entire world. In conventional forces the Soviet Union had a clear advantage in Europe, only partly compensated by NATO superiority in naval and air forces. For four years the United States also enjoyed a nuclear monopoly and was the first to test a hydrogen bomb in 1954. But through spying and a crash program, the Soviets acquired nuclear capability in 1949 and caught up with the H-bomb in 1955. Initially, the preferred delivery vehicle was the strategic bomber, because the new jets could fly across oceans. Building on the German V-2, scientists on both sides developed intercontinental ballistic missiles that could be armed with nuclear warheads. These ICBMs were no longer battlefield weapons but, rather, "total war" devices, able to threaten the entire enemy country by killing its civilians. Bombers and missiles offered a "second strike" capacity, creating a "mutually assured destruction" of both camps.[32] Ironically, it was the fear of their deadliness that kept these arms from being used, since no practical advantage could be gained from them.

Another weapon of the Cold War was espionage, because it could provide access to military secrets and spread disinformation. Drawing on communist sympathies among intellectuals, the Soviet KGB recruited Klaus Fuchs and Julius Rosenberg, who delivered crucial information on the U.S. nuclear program. In return the CIA drew on the expertise of former Nazi specialists on the Soviet Union as well as anticommunist resisters in order to gain knowledge about Soviet army activities in Central Europe. Since the Americans shared information with British intelligence, the recruitment of the Cambridge Five as Soviet agents was another coup, only gradually discovered by the decryption efforts of the Venona project. Aside from prominent defectors like Oleg Penkovsky, the United States relied on technical reconnaissance gathered, for example, by U-2 spy planes and satellites equipped with cameras, which played a crucial role in the Cuban missile crisis. West Germany was especially vulnerable, since Stasi spymaster Markus Wolf could easily infiltrate his agents from the East.[33] While cloak-and-dagger activities had a certain conspiratorial appeal, the exploits of both sides largely neutralized each other.

Equally important, but less obvious, was the ideological competition between both camps in vying for cultural dominance. The Soviets relied on a series of propaganda arguments involving themes such as antifascism, world peace, and social equality. In likely venues, be they disarmament congresses or international youth festivals, the communists sought to mobilize fellow travelers among the intellectuals (e.g., Jean-Paul Sartre), the labor movement, and the clergy. In its America Houses—information centers with free lending libraries—the United States countered by emphasizing freedom, human rights, and Western civilization, confident that its prosperous lifestyle would look more attractive than drab Russian egalitarianism. Especially in the airwaves with Radio in the American Sector (in Berlin) and Radio Free Europe and Radio Liberty (Munich), the United States catered to the rock 'n' roll tastes of the young in order to spread the political message of market democracy. Led by journalists like Melvyn Lasky, the Congress of Cultural Freedom sought to counteract socialist appeals to equality with democratic promises of liberty in highbrow journals like *Encounter*.[34] This culture war tried to make converts by portraying its own cause as an idealist quest.

Economic rivalry was also a central aspect of the East-West conflict, since ordinary Europeans used actual living standards as a test of political systems. In the first three years after the war, the differences were marginal, but after the reintroduction of competition in the West, aided by the Marshall Plan, the market economies visibly outperformed state planning in the East. Spreading from the Federal Republic to neighboring states, the western Economic Miracle offered higher wages, lower prices, and better quality than smokestack socialism. While communist governments sought to satisfy their citizens through public projects and subsidized basics, the unfettering of market competition in the West created higher rates of growth, evident in the rebuilding of infrastructure and housing. In the consumer-goods competition, the market won hands down over the plan because it provided a broader array of attractive products, catering to a variety of tastes. Across the open border of Berlin, the East tried to compete with social services, but the glamour of the western Kurfürstendamm proved ultimately irresistible.[35]

Essentially the Cold War was a political struggle that was fought between the radical Left and the democratic middle and Right within each country. Since the communists tended to lose free elections, they resorted to the "dictatorship of the proletariat" within their own bloc, adopting popular-front tactics only in the West. Their utopian promise was an egalitarian revolution to uplift the masses by providing better education, health care, job security, welfare, and entertainment. In contrast, western democrats offered a parliamentary government in which political parties would formulate policies according to the wishes of citizens, expressed in civil associations. The democrats envisaged a pluralistic society, guaranteeing human rights as well as offering cultural freedom and secured against economic crises through an extended welfare state.[36] Both sides tried to force ideological conformity on their own camp while at the same time subverting the other. Though the ideological witch hunt of American McCarthyism hampered the credibility of the West, the outright repression of dissent and persecution of opponents in the East discredited socialism more strongly.

To counteract the polarizing pull of the Cold War, a movement of nonaligned nations developed around the principles of nonaggression and noninterference in the 1950s. Yugoslavia, Indonesia, India, Egypt, and Ghana refused to be drawn into the ideological confrontation between hostile camps composed of a superpower, its allies, and dependent client states. In order to escape this pressure, their leaders—Tito, Sukarno, Nehru, Nasser, and Nkrumah—decided to form a third bloc large enough to make its own voice heard. In 1956 in Bandung and five years later in Belgrade, representatives of anti-imperialist nations met to proclaim a policy of nonalignment, hoping to remain free to take economic aid and military assistance from the East or the West without being forced to become a member of one side or the other. Though playing an important role in the United Nations due to the increasing number of independent states, the nonaligned countries were, like India and Pakistan, often deeply divided in ideology and interests. Hence they could only reduce but not bridge the cleavage of the Cold War.[37]

The pervasiveness of the confrontation created a distinctive Cold War mentality not just among policy makers but in the general public as well. The East-West conflict polarized allegiances within and between countries by focusing on military security and promoting rampant fear. This mind-set led to thinking in black-and-white terms, classifying everything as being for or against one's cause, and thereby eliminated the possibility of compromise. Within the Eastern Bloc the Cold War outlook led to outright persecution and suppression of opponents, while within the West this attitude produced self-censorship and illiberal reactions to dissent. Between the two sides this cast of mind fostered unrelenting suspicion that construed even harmless activities as devious forms of subversion. This paranoid perception saw the world as a ceaseless struggle in which no one could be trusted and nothing was quite what it seemed to be.[38] Ultimately this security mania became a self-fulfilling prophecy that made domestic politics rigid and international affairs confrontational.

RENEWED CRISIS

During most of the 1950s, the Cold War seesawed unpredictably between dangerous confrontations and efforts at coexistence. The success of the UN counteroffensive against North Korea sparked discussions in Washington about a "rollback" of communism in Eastern Europe as long as the United States enjoyed a nuclear monopoly. Secretary of State John Foster Dulles, especially, advocated an aggressive stance, making it clear that the "eventual liberation" of nations under communist control was "an essential and enduring part" of American foreign policy. However, President Eisenhower refused to come to the aid of East German demonstrators during the June 17, 1953, uprising, thereby respecting the Soviet realm.[39] As a result of American restraint, the Austrian State Treaty reestablishing Austria as a neutral, unaligned state was signed in May 1955, and the subsequent Geneva summit produced an atmosphere of peace. Nikita Khrushchev provided a theoretical rationale for this relaxation of tension, calling it "peaceful coexistence." Often misunderstood, the concept did not mean an end of ideological conflict but rather emphasized its limitation to nonmilitary forms.[40]

Just when it seemed that hostility was subsiding, the Hungarian crisis once again threatened peace in Europe. In spite of pacific rhetoric, both camps continued trying to destabilize each other with propaganda efforts, such as international peace rallies and cross-border broadcasts of Radio Free Europe. When the Poles did revolt and the Hungarians called for western help with their revolution in the fall of 1956, Washington was once again forced to decide whether to live up to its rollback oratory or limit itself to cheering from the sidelines. But news of the Soviet acquisition of the A- and also the H-bomb and the fear that these devastating weapons might be dropped on American soil forced even anticommunist hawks like Dulles to desist from intervention. This reluctant restraint created an informal understanding between the superpowers to respect each other's spheres of influence in Europe and to compete thereafter in other fields like economics and athletics. The subsequent meeting of Khrushchev and Eisenhower at Camp David expressed this willingness to treat one another as equals, even if it failed to produce any concrete disarmament steps.[41]

By initiating the second Berlin crisis in November 1958, Khrushchev returned to brinkmanship, confident of his nuclear and missile parity with the West. Since prior conferences and initiatives such as the Eden Plan had failed to resolve the German problem, the western part of the former capital remained a thorn in the side of the Soviet empire by being a showcase of free politics and attractive consumer culture. In an undiplomatic ultimatum, the Soviet leader demanded that Allied troops withdraw and West Berlin become a "free city" within six months or he would abrogate Russian responsibility and turn all controls over to the GDR. Surprised by this attack on the four-power status of the city, western leaders were worried that Khrushchev might be serious about his threat. But West Berliners rallied behind Mayor Willy Brandt, and Washington, which was actually in possession of more nuclear warheads than Moscow, persuaded Britain and France to refuse any concessions. Even concurrent Soviet overtures toward deep disarmament, directed at international opinion, could not shake the negative impression of a one-sided power play.[42]

The crisis deepened when East German dictator Walter Ulbricht pressed for a closing of the Berlin border to keep his population from running away. From 1952 on the GDR had fortified the inner German frontier between East and West Germany—a border fourteen hundred kilometers long from the Baltic Sea to Czechoslovakia—rendering it impossible to escape across the barbed wire and land mines, past watchtowers and guard dogs. But in the city of Berlin, citizens could cross from one sector to the other on trains, subways, buses, streetcars, bicycles, or on foot. Owing to the collectivization of agriculture, nationalization of factories, discrimination against the church, and persecution of political opponents in East Germany, about three and one-half million people in search of a better life fled to the West through the Berlin escape hatch in the fifteen years after the end of the war, while only half a million followed the socialist promise to the East. Though the exodus got rid of malcontents and critics, it cost the GDR farmers, engineers, doctors, and skilled workers—a desperately needed labor force. The FRG welcomed these valuable refugees by immediately granting them citizenship and welfare benefits. To keep the GDR alive, Khrushchev finally agreed to close the last hole in the Iron Curtain.[43]

During the night of August 12–13, 1961, GDR work battalions and border guards started to string barbed wire across streets, cutting off all traffic between East and West. Justified as an "antifascist protection barrier," the new Berlin Wall gradually grew into an elaborate system of concrete slabs, electrified fences, guard towers, search-lights, and patrols to make it impenetrable. Nonetheless, several thousand daring easterners managed to jump out of windows, crawl through tunnels, swim through canals, or burst through road blocks to get out. To stop these desperate flights, the SED authorized the border police to shoot escapees, which they did—killing about 138 and imprisoning hundreds of others. Tension reached a climax when U.S. and Soviet tanks faced each other at Checkpoint Charlie in Oc-tober 1961 over who could administer border controls. Ironically, the division of the city stabilized the GDR by cutting off escape and forcing the East Germans to cope with their unloved SED system.[44] But the Wall also undermined the legitimacy of the East German state by becoming a symbol of communist repression reviled around the world.

The Cuban missile crisis was even more dangerous, since it brought the world to the brink of thermonuclear war. Castro's revo-lution pleased Moscow by apparently proving the viability of its anti-imperialist strategy, especially after the ill-conceived Bay of Pigs in-vasion by CIA-trained Cuban exiles had failed. Underestimating the resolve of the young U.S. president Jack Kennedy after their Vienna meeting, Khrushchev gambled on stationing intermediate-range missiles with nuclear warheads on the island in order to "equalize what the West likes to call 'the balance of power'" and protect Castro. The discovery by U-2 reconnaissance of the Soviet missiles in Cuba created panic in Washington by threatening the United States di-rectly with a nuclear strike. After some hesitation Kennedy alerted the international public to the danger, forcing Khrushchev to back down. Contrary to public perception, the crisis was resolved by a compromise, with the Soviets withdrawing their missiles while the U.S. pulled back its own missiles from Turkey and guaranteed the inviolability of Cuba. Europeans could only watch impotently when the world teetered on the verge of nuclear annihilation.[45]

Through the sheer terror of facing Armageddon, the Cuban mis-sile crisis ironically had the salutary effect of making both sides back away from nuclear brinkmanship. Khrushchev stopped his generals from making plans for space stations or artificial islands from which to attack the United States, and Kennedy abandoned Robert Mc-Namara's scenarios that envisaged a limited nuclear war. While each claimed to have won the showdown, Moscow and Washington began a slow and difficult effort to negotiate arms-control measures, since military costs were spiraling out of control and scientists advised against further weapons buildup. In 1963 both sides signed a Limited Test Ban Treaty, which abolished testing in the atmosphere; in 1968 they concluded a Nuclear Non-Proliferation Treaty, promising not to help other nations to acquire atomic weapons; and in 1972 they achieved a Strategic Arms Limitation Interim Agreement that capped the number of ballistic missiles and provided for verification.[46] The realization of how dangerous the Berlin Wall and Cuban missile crises had been ultimately inspired efforts to reduce future threats.

This unpredictable cycle of crises and coexistence deepened the division of Europe and made the Old Continent aware of its impotence. By dropping the Iron Curtain, the Cold War created a physical border, cutting off the East from western developments. It also produced a military confrontation between highly armed conventional forces, backed by nuclear arsenals controlled by the superpowers. At the same time it inspired an ideological demarcation between hostile worldviews using different vocabularies and often misunderstanding each other. Finally, it led to the emergence of distinctive socioeconomic systems with competing production regimes and patterns of consumption. With travel, trade, and communication between the camps drastically reduced, the polarization of Europe into competing blocs created divergent trajectories, impoverishing both sides by cutting established ties.[47] Even if life in the western part of the continent was more agreeable than in the East, the first two decades of the Cold War demonstrated to the divided Europeans that they had largely lost control of their own affairs.

EAST-WEST CONFLICT

The concept of competing modernities that has been suggested for contrasting American with German development offers a new reading of the Cold War by transcending the sterility of the traditional blame game. No doubt the East-West conflict was a global super-power confrontation, characterized by ideological hostility as well as a nuclear-arms race that polarized the world into rival camps. But at the same time the Cold War was also an effort to learn lessons from the defeat of the organic modernity of fascism and apply them to building a more benign future without aggressive war or racist imperialism. In many ways it was therefore a search for alternate ways to get out of the murderous first half of the century and restore the benign potential of modernity. If modernization is seen not as a single homogenous process but as a competition between different blueprints of progress, then the Cold War appears as the result of the elimination of the National Socialist competitor, leaving communism and democracy to vie with each other for hegemony.[48]

As "a comprehensive counter-model to capitalist modernity," the "socialist modernity" of the Soviet Bloc promised to overtake its competitors by ushering in a social revolution. Communists hoped to dry up the sources of fascism and to blunt the temptations of democracy by eliminating their socioeconomic bases through collectivization of land and nationalization of industry. Beyond the radicalized traditions of the labor movement, the Soviet model stressed its uncompromising antifascism and its continuing anti-imperialism. Socialist modernizers could claim that the breathtaking speed of Russian industrialization and the technological innovations of the missile program that put the Sputnik into orbit offered an accelerated form of development.[49] However, even Soviet leaders knew that their march toward progress was hampered by the massive destruction of the war, the backwardness of many Sovietized regions, and the repressive legacy of Stalinism. But by controlling the eastern half of the continent, Moscow could impose its form of modernity on its satellites and hope that other developing countries would follow its path.

In contrast, western "democratic modernity" offered personal prosperity and political liberty by improving the existing capitalist economy and parliamentary system. Its evolutionary approach hoped to build on the dynamism of competition and on the freedom of self-government while at the same time reforming their abuses. Western democrats promised a better life by improving individual living standards, as well as participation in public affairs by safeguarding human rights. To help their cause they tried to limit the effects of capitalist excesses by broadening the social safety net of the welfare state, and they tried to counteract the sense of political anomie by supporting associations of civil society. In foreign policy and defense, the American system of "empire by invitation" appealed to allies as a form of voluntary cooperation for the advancement of shared values of Western civilization.[50] Yet the West's high-flown rhetoric was marred by class conflict, labor exploitation, lingering racism, and involvement in imperialism. Since both camps had attractions and deficits, the outcome of their competition remained in doubt.

The military rivalry of the Cold War perpetuated the frightful face of modernity by bringing humanity closer than ever before to the verge of self-destruction. The frantic effort to gain an advantage over the other side triggered a technological race for developing ever more effective weapons systems, ranging from powerful tanks to supersonic jet fighters that still crowd the halls of war museums. Most lethal was the creation of atomic and hydrogen bombs, because their destructiveness exceeded the expectations of engineers and even the fallout from their tests killed observers in the vicinity. Moreover, the development of missiles on which nuclear warheads could be mounted abolished any distinction between combatants and civilians, since they mostly targeted large population centers. The logic of deterrence rested on sufficient second-strike capability that would create the "mutually assured destruction" of the telling acronym MAD. The shocking images of the ashes of Hiroshima and Nagasaki inspired a passionate peace movement, while the uncertainty about whether even an attacker would suffer such destruction ultimately restrained decision makers on both sides of the Iron Curtain.[51]

Fortunately, the deadliness of the weapons proved therefore self-limiting and turned the Cold War into a peaceful competition between modernization alternatives. In Europe the nuclear standoff stabilized frontiers, leading to a mutual recognition of spheres of influence that excluded the resort to arms in advancing social revolution or rolling back communism. With coexistence the contest shifted to less-violent arenas such as consumer goods, popular culture, social services, and sports. Even the space race remained peaceful, with the Soviets launching the first satellite and the Americans accomplishing the initial moon landing. Ironically the very intensity of the competition between "alternative visions of modernity" ultimately led to a certain convergence in a style that has been called "Cold War modern." In its architecture, design of consumer products, and clothing fashions as well as in popular music western modernism gradually conquered the East so that high-rise buildings and television towers on both sides of the divide began to look almost identical.[52] The new dangers therefore would come from unresolved conflicts on the colonial periphery.

Chapter 18

DISAPPOINTING DECOLONIZATION

Algerian independence, 1962. *Source*: Marc Riboud / Magnum Photos.

I n order to grant his restless Congolese colony independence, the Belgian king Baudouin I landed in steamy Leopoldville on June 30, 1960. After the ruthless paternalism of his colonial administration, the local population was hardly prepared to assume the reins of self-government. But encouraged by the retreat of the other empires, a loose coalition of intellectuals and tribal leaders had clamored for national liberation, leading to anticolonial riots. In order to prevent a lengthy guerrilla war, the panicked government in Brussels abandoned its plans for a gradual transition and decided to transfer power immediately. Unfortunately the king insisted on praising the colonizing achievements of his great uncle, provoking the charismatic prime minister Patrice Lumumba to denounce his rule as a "regime of injustice, oppression and exploitation." Nonetheless the withdrawal of the colonialists was eagerly anticipated: "It was simply beyond words. 'Independence' was wrapped in an atmosphere of religious, almost mystical joy, and apocalyptic expectation but at the same time of the most tragicomic misunderstanding and fears."[1]

Such high hopes were quickly dashed when the Congo dissolved into chaos. In July the army mutinied against its white officers, prompting Belgian troops to return in order to rescue European settlers. At the same time Moishe Tschombe seceded with the province of Katanga so as to exploit its rich copper, gold, and uranium deposits. To preserve Congolese unity, the United Nations intervened, leading to Secretary General Dag Hammarskjöld's death in a plane crash. As support for his leftist agenda, Lumumba called for Soviet help, which triggered American fears of another Cuba in Africa. In 1961 the radical leader was murdered in Katanga, becoming a martyr to independence. When conservative elites relied on brutal South African mercenaries, a grassroots rebellion developed, helped by none other than Che Guevara. After more than five years of regional disintegration, social conflict, and tribal hostilities Joseph Mobuto seized power in a military coup, supported by the United States.[2] In a nutshell the Congo crisis illustrates the difficulties of decolonization due to internal inexperience and external intervention.

Disappointment in the results of independence has created a fierce controversy between postcolonial critics who blame the legacy of imperialism and imperial apologists who point to the ineptitude of the new elites. Inspired by the moral outrage of activists like Franz Fanon, the anti-imperialist rhetoric reflects the ideology of the national liberation movements that threw off the imperial yoke. Similarly, the project of "subaltern studies" rejects Eurocentrism by emphasizing the suffering of the suppressed, ignored in the narratives of the colonial masters.[3] Appalled by the chaos following national independence, the defenders of colonialism have sought to rescue the reputation of empire by emphasizing its civilizing achievements and the largely peaceful withdrawal of the imperialists. In contrast to Marxist accusations of exploitation, they portray imperial rule as basically benign, benefiting the colonies as well as the mother country.[4] Neither the postcolonial perspective that celebrates the anti-imperialist struggle nor the apologetic argument that stresses the acquiescence of the metropole provides a complete picture of decolonization.

Instead, the rapid collapse of the European empires was a complex process that assumed a wide variety of local forms, ranging from bloody fighting to reluctant retreat. The concept of decolonization describes "the emancipation of Asia and Africa from European control" in political, economic, and cultural terms, all of which took place during roughly one generation after World War II. In part, European hegemony over the rest of the world was terminated by pressure from below, as the suppressed peoples sought to end colonial rule by protest or insurrection. In part, the imperialists lost their own determination to maintain their domination as a result of their internecine struggles during the world wars. Finally, the mounting criticism of international opinion and the role of organizations like the United Nations also hastened their retreat. Unfortunately, the result of decolonization has often been disappointing to the people involved. While independence has brought self-determination at last, the new states have remained unstable, economic development has lagged, and Europe has experienced a blowback of unexpected consequences such as new immigration of its former subjects.[5]

The relationship of decolonization to the process of modernization has therefore been rather ambivalent. In some ways, the liberation struggle was an attempt to reject the imposition of European modernity because of its deleterious consequences. But the methods used by the anticolonial movements such as military weapons, political organization, and nationalist ideology were, nonetheless, distinctly modern. Independence activists like Agostinho Neto of Angola knew that they confronted a double challenge: "We are trying to free and modernize our people by a dual revolution: against their traditional structures which can no longer serve them and against colonial rule." Even after the withdrawal of European imperialists, their languages, state boundaries, governmental systems, and institutions such as businesses, schools. and hospitals persisted as necessary basis for further progress.[6] The process of decolonization therefore involved a selective rejection *and* retention of the European legacy, which led to the creation of a new hybrid of postcolonial modernity.

WORLD WARS AS CATALYST

The internecine warfare on the continent during the first half of the twentieth century initiated the collapse of the European empires on land and overseas. The Japanese naval victory over imperial Russia in the war of 1905 had already tarnished the nimbus of white invincibility. During the First World War the colonies themselves became a battleground, most notably in East Africa, where German General Paul Emil von Lettow-Vorbeck waged a lengthy guerrilla war against the British.[7] The United Kingdom drew on volunteers from the dominions of Canada, Australia, New Zealand, and South Africa, especially in the ill-fated Gallipoli campaign. Strapped for manpower, the French used hundreds of thousands of colonial troops from North Africa in their defense of Verdun, as Arabic names in the military cemeteries indicate. As a result of defeat, the grand land empires of Russia, Austria-Hungary, Germany, and the Ottomans crumbled, dissolving into newly founded national states. World War I not only destroyed continental imperialism but also damaged overseas colonialism by eroding the sense of European superiority.

The interwar period was, nonetheless, an Indian summer of imperialism, since the maritime empires were ostensibly restored, though their foundations continued to weaken. While Japan annexed

Germany's Asian colonies, the League of Nations created a mandate system for Berlin's African possessions that was supposed to prepare them for independence. Trying to retain its indirect influence, Britain let Egypt become formally independent in 1922, and Iraq followed a decade later. The other new Near Eastern states, formerly under Ottoman control, remained in an ambivalent relationship of semi-independence within the British or French spheres of influence. When Mussolini attempted to capture Ethiopia, the international public was outraged not only because of the brutality of his methods but also since acquiring colonies seemed no longer to be appropriate. In contrast, the United Kingdom tried to reward the white dominions with greater independence by creating the Commonwealth of Nations during the mid-1930s, which permitted more self-rule while retaining the tie to the crown.[8]

The Second World War struck so devastating a blow against European overseas colonies that they were never able to recover. The surprisingly rapid fall of France in the summer of 1940 shook its control over its African and Asian possessions, since local administrators had to choose whether to adhere to Vichy or join the Free French. The German-Italian desert war threatened French domination of the Maghreb and the lifeline of the British Empire, but the Allied landing restored their imperial domination and ended the Italian possession of Libya. More lasting were the effects of the Japanese advance into Southeast Asia, which conquered numerous colonies from the British, French, or Dutch. In contrast to the fighting among Europeans and Americans, the military triumphs of Tojo's armies showed conclusively that white men could be defeated by men of other races, since captured soldiers and civilians looked pitiful in POW or internment camps. Although with American help the Japanese aggressors were eventually driven out, the prestige of the European imperialists was damaged beyond repair.[9]

The temporary loss of colonial control boosted indigenous movements for independence because it made self-rule seem like a goal that could actually be achieved. In order to save manpower, the British and French had educated local subalterns in missionary schools and even sent the sons of the elite to their universities, teaching them

European techniques and ideologies. Moreover, the United Kingdom had mobilized 2.5 million Indians and 150,000 Africans to fight against the Axis powers, training them in the use of weapons and related technology, military discipline, and tactics of warfare. Nazi and Japanese propagandists also appealed to the subject peoples to rise up against their European masters even if their own racist practices belied their promises. No longer content with subaltern roles or limited autonomy, westernized intellectuals who were drawn into the global conflict formed various kinds of independence movements that turned European methods against the colonizers. The struggle showed the vulnerability of the imperialists, which made the project of national liberation appear to be feasible.[10]

After the end of the Second World War, the process of decolonization gathered speed due to the creation of the United Nations. This international organization not only facilitated national independence by enshrining the principle of "equal rights and self-determination of peoples" in its charter but also provided a mechanism for recognizing new states and accepting them as members into the international community. The advent of the United Nations therefore added a third player to the bilateral negotiations between colonies and the metropole, which helped facilitate the contested process of transition. While the African mandates were transformed into trusts and continued as dependents, the Near Eastern states like Lebanon, Syria, and Jordan were quickly recognized as independent. As these new members joined the United Nations, they became a significant pressure group that pushed European governments to let go of additional possessions. In cases of border disputes the United Nations mediated, and where there was civil unrest, as in the Congo, it eventually developed a new instrument of sending soldiers as "peacekeepers."[11]

The first to take advantage of this opportunity was Mohandas Gandhi, the leader of the independence movement of the Indian subcontinent. "Mahatma," as he was reverently called, was born into a Hindu merchant family in 1869 and trained at the Inner Temple in London. As an expatriate lawyer in South Africa he developed a strategy of nonviolent civil disobedience in order to protest social inequalities of the colonial class system. Back in his home country, he was elected leader of the Indian National Congress in 1921, campaigning for national independence in his famous march against the salt tax in 1930. Though he supported the war effort against the Axis, Gandhi continued to push for self-rule, calling on Britain to "Quit India" in 1942. His simple lifestyle, vegetarianism, disregard of the cast system, and advocacy of women's equality made him appear charismatic and saintlike. In order to retain their influence, the British Raj decided to let their "jewel in the crown" become peacefully independent in 1947, partitioning the subcontinent into two states. Tragically, India descended into a civil war between Hindus and Muslims, leading to Gandhi's assassination.[12]

In contrast, Indonesia was liberated after Japan's defeat in a four-year-long bloody struggle against the Dutch colonizers. Taking advantage of the vacuum after Tokyo's surrender, the nationalist leaders Sukarno and Hatta proclaimed independence in August 1945, setting off celebrations and outbursts of violence. Though British troops tried to restore order, the republicans began to create their own government structures. When the Dutch returned in force in 1946 they encountered fierce resistance while recapturing the cities and found it impossible to control the countryside. The United Nations condemned the bloodshed, and the United States also supported the independence movement, once it was clear that it would remain anticommunist. Having just escaped Nazi occupation themselves, the Dutch had neither the military capacity nor the political will to fight a protracted guerrilla war in the jungle. As a result the Hague government finally agreed to the creation of a United States of Indonesia in the fall of 1949. However, the liberated country was soon torn asunder by new social, ethnic, and religious conflicts.[13]

The surprising onset of decolonization therefore reflected not just the rise of anticolonial aspirations but also the weakening of European resolve. The decline of military and economic power inspired administrators in London and Paris to move from the practice of "indirect rule" toward a more inclusive conception of empire. By creating umbrellas like the Commonwealth and the French Union, these weary imperialists offered their subjects a partial citizenship, plans for economic development, and even some access to the mother country. But the atrocities of the fighting and racial killing associated with European colonization discredited the civilizing values on which Europeans based their claims to superiority. Frustrated by the discrepancy between promises of equality and practices of discrimination, many intellectuals mobilized in order to throw off colonial control and create their own nation-states. Ironically, in that process they adopted many European values and methods in defense of local traditions, creating paradoxical blends of indigenous and Western societies. Ultimately, the cooperation between European reformers, seeking to cede some power, and colonial activists, intent on liberating their own societies, spelled the end of overseas empires.[14]

NATIONAL LIBERATION STRUGGLES

Since most colonizers were not about to leave on their own accord, it took massive pressure from national liberation movements to push them out. The Allies' victory in the Second World War made it possible for Great Britain, France, and other imperialist countries to attempt to reassert their control. But the United States supported a gradual transfer of power to moderate members of native elites so as to keep the transition orderly and safeguard the interests of multinational corporations. Moreover, the concurrent advance of the Soviet Union into Central Europe and the victory of the Chinese Communists offered a more radical blueprint for anti-imperialist mobilization. It was therefore not only European weakness but also American pressure and communist ideology that emboldened anti-imperialist intellectuals to create popular movements clamoring for independence and social revolution.[15] Hastened by the Cold War, most anti-colonial movements were broad coalitions of nationalists and Marxists, united in overthrowing colonial control but at loggerheads over the postindependence course.

The most successful advocate of violent liberation was Ho Chi Minh, the leader of the Vietnamese independence movement. Born into a Confucian family in 1890, he went to a French school in Vietnam and lived in Europe and the United States as a young adult, subsisting on menial jobs. Later, in Paris, he joined a group of Vietnamese nationalists. When their petition for independence was ignored by the Allied powers at Versailles he joined the Communist Party, moved to Moscow, and participated in the communist uprising against the nationalist government in China. During World War II he organized a guerrilla force in Vietnam, supported by the United States, to expel the Japanese invaders. Believing that "the white man is finished in Asia," he pushed for the declaration of an independent Democratic Republic of Vietnam on December 2, 1945. When the French restored their control, he led the Viet Minh forces in a bloody revolt, using surprise attacks on communication routes and outposts. Helped by heavy weapons from the Chinese, he inflicted a disastrous defeat on the French at Dien Bien Phu.[16] As a result, the Geneva Conference in 1954 recognized Vietnamese independence but divided the country along the 17th parallel, since the South rejected communist control.

The successive withdrawals of the British, Dutch, and French from Southeast Asia facilitated the drive for independence in North Africa. Libya had already become independent in 1951, since resistance to the return of Italian control motivated the United Nations to push for the creation of a separate state. Although the French had attempted to create an indissoluble union with their colonies in their postwar constitution, in 1956 Paris allowed Tunisia and Morocco to assume independence as well. In the same year the British also decided to end their condominium with Egypt over the vast Sudanese territory in order to avoid a military confrontation from which they expected little profit.[17] These concessions were less the result of anti-imperialist militancy than of prescient policy, intent on restoring states that had only briefly been under European control and possessed neither crucial economic resources (oil was not yet an issue) nor great strategic importance. In contrast, white settlers in Algeria, Rhodesia, and South Africa clamored for the continuation of imperial control.

The Suez crisis in the fall of 1956, the last military hurrah of European imperialism, demonstrated that Britain and France could no longer police their empires against international pressure. Resenting the western refusal to finance the building of the Aswan Dam, Egyptian president Abdel Nasser had asked for Soviet aid and announced the nationalization of the Suez Canal. In retaliation against Palestinian raids, Israel attacked Egypt across the Sinai Peninsula, while Anglo-French naval forces and paratroopers seized control of the strategic canal, decisively defeating Egyptian defenders. But in typical Cold War fashion, Soviet president Nikolai Bulganin warned the western powers that Russia would not let its newfound client state down. Fearing the outbreak of World War III, President Eisenhower, who had opposed the invasion, threatened London and Paris with economic sanctions if they persevered. Eventually the outcry of international opinion forced the invaders to withdraw and let the United Nations patrol the Sinai border. Though a military success, the Suez adventure was a diplomatic humiliation for London and Paris that hastened decolonization.[18]

In spite of this setback, France refused to grant Algeria independence, waging a prolonged war that was both imperialist and civil at the same time. The 2.5 million European settlers considered Algeria an integral part of France, while traditional Maghreb society refused to give up the veil as symbol of resistance against western modernity. In 1954 the Arab National Liberation Front (FLN) started a revolutionary insurgency, using terrorist methods. Paris declared the conflict a "police action" and employed counterterrorist violence to break the resistance. The country quickly descended into a civil war, since French troops and their Harki auxiliaries controlled the new parts of the cities and settled countryside, while the insurgents were based in the old quarters and inaccessible mountains. When the undeclared war dragged on, the French military staged a 1958 coup in France, installing World War II hero Charles de Gaulle in power who then created a presidentially governed Fifth Republic. But much to the chagrin of the *pieds-noirs* (white settlers) he considered the Algerian struggle unwinnable and assented to independence in the Evian Accords of 1962. The result was a mass exodus of the settlers and of collaborators to the metropole.[19]

Failure to be content with the autonomy-within-Commonwealth schemes put forth by London and Paris triggered a cascade of independence declarations in sub-Saharan Africa from the late fifties to the early sixties. The British had tried to prepare their colonies for "responsible self-government" through elections and economic development, while the French clung to assimilation and integration. But the strength of the African nationalist movement led by Kwame Nkrumah forced Ghana to become independent in 1957, followed by Nigeria in 1960 and Sierra Leone in 1961. The United Nations simultaneously released the trustee territories of the Cameroons, Togo, and Somalia. After Guinea in 1960, the other French colonies followed quickly as well. In East and Central Africa the British withdrawal took more time, since London first wanted to put down the bloody Mau-Mau uprising before relinquishing control of Kenya and its neighbors like Tanzania and Zambia.[20] The purpose of these partly forced and partly voluntary retreats from empire was the preservation of economic property, cultural ties, and political influence.

Alarmed by the fall of colonial dominoes, the Portuguese dictatorship in Lisbon and white settlers in Africa tried to stave off the inevitable but were ultimately unable to stop the process. For instance, even Botswana gained independence in 1966. But it required a revolution in Lisbon, born of military frustration with an unwinnable and costly colonial war, in order to free its colonies in Guinea, Angola, and Mozambique in 1974–75. Unfortunately, these ill-prepared territories quickly sank into civil strife between pro-communist and pro-western factions. In Rhodesia, white settlers under Ian Smith demanded independence for themselves, ignoring the wishes of the more numerous blacks. Only after much international pressure did the whites agree to black majority rule and allow Zimbabwe to become independent in 1980. A decade later Namibia was finally able to escape Pretoria's trusteeship. Already independent since 1910, the beleaguered Afrikaners of South Africa continued to reinforce their racist apartheid regime before finally accepting the victory of Nelson Mandela's African National Congress in 1994.[21]

The rapid end of European empire comprised both an overthrow from below and a collapse from above. Led by inspiring leaders like Sekou Touré and Léopold Senghor, liberation movements containing nationalists and socialists pushed for independence through mass mobilization, civil disobedience, and, if need be, guerrilla warfare. At the same time criticism from the labor movement, liberal clergymen, and progressive intellectuals undercut the imperialist consensus in the metropoles, making it difficult to justify holding on to colonies by force of arms. Moreover, the Cold War created a competition between capitalist and socialist roads to independence, with both camps vying for the allegiance of emerging countries through propaganda, economic help, and military assistance. Finally, the increasing number of independent states in the United Nations provided a pressure group in favor of advancing self-government. While the particular interaction of these factors differed according to the imperial power and the local context, it was their mutual reinforcement that made decolonization such a swift and irresistible process.[22]

CHALLENGES OF INDEPENDENCE

Independence provided formidable challenges, since it proved easier to kick the European colonizers out than to establish a functioning self-rule. No doubt much of the imperial legacy was toxic and left colonial populations ill prepared for assuming the reins of government. After accomplishing the transfer of power, the liberated elites had to engage in state-building quasi overnight, forging nations, creating administrations, and instituting the rule of law. To respond to popular hopes for a better life, they also needed to jump-start economic development, improve the terms of trade for raw materials, and seek to escape their dependence on foreign aid. At the same time, they were required to find their way between the ideologically hostile blocs of the Cold War in order not to get drawn into internal and international conflicts.[23] The process of developing their own postcolonial identities out of European imports and native traditions therefore turned out to be more difficult than expected by the overjoyed populace. In many cases the rapidity and extent of the necessary changes proved overwhelming.

Managing the transition to independence raised the question of how to replace European administrators while acquiring the expertise necessary for self-government. The symbolic act of assuming control and moving into vacated colonial offices confronted the new rulers with the task of actually administering their territories. It became clear that this required experience not just in wielding power but also in solving practical problems. National liberation movements that had waged the anti-imperial struggle were not well prepared to assume such responsibilities, feeling deeply ambivalent about the future role of Europeans: on the one hand they wanted nothing more than to throw their erstwhile oppressors out, but on the other they also needed the colonizers' technical expertise in order to render their independence secure. Wherever the liberation struggle had been bloody, as in Indonesia, the impulse to clean house prevailed, and wherever withdrawal was more voluntary, as in Senegal, Europeans advisers and ties to the colonizing country remained. As a result, postcolonial networks developed between the new elites and the old masters.[24]

Once in power, the rulers of the independent countries faced the challenge of nation-building, turning disparate territories created by the colonizers into political communities. Owing to tribal, religious, regional, and social fragmentation, just maintaining the unity and integrity of a country like the Congo could prove exceedingly difficult. At the same time the independent states had to guarantee domestic security in order to protect their own business and foreign investment. Moreover, they needed to create a sense of citizenship among disparate peoples, bonding them emotionally to a larger whole, thereby inventing nationhood in territories that lacked cohesion because they were the result of colonial rivalries. This process also involved creating competent public administrations that could address a myriad of problems from schooling to health. Finally, as a crowning achievement, the mobilized population expected to gain more participation in self-government.[25] Since structures that had taken Europeans decades to develop had to be improvised within weeks, it was only natural that the process turned out to be difficult.

Another crucial task was economic development in order to fulfill popular hopes for a visible improvement in living standards. Escaping "underdevelopment" meant abandoning the colonial structure of plantation agriculture and raw-material extraction, which benefited Europe through the use of cheap local labor. Chief obstacles to change were external ownership of crucial sectors, the power of multinational corporations, as well as unfavorable terms of trade that kept prices low. Lack of education, insufficient infrastructure, and civil strife did not help either. Supported by loans from the International Monetary Fund and the World Bank, the postcolonial countries embarked on ambitious development schemes, often neglecting their agricultural roots and investing in prestige projects that relied on inexpensive labor. In Africa the peasant economies had some success in market adaptation, whereas the settler colonies proved more adept at industrializing. The Ivory Coast was initially successful, and subsequently Ghana advanced even more rapidly. But only Botswana has managed to grow consistently since achieving independence.[26]

The newly independent states faced a difficult choice of which modernizing model to follow. The advantages of the Marxist path of developmental dictatorship attracted much interest among the radical intelligentsia and the labor unions in states like Guinea. Its revolutionary rhetoric promised an egalitarian society with free access to education and health care for all. Moreover, it offered a blueprint for industrialization by labor-intensive projects. The material support of the Soviet Union generated a sense of anti-imperialist solidarity in the heady experiment of building socialism. But its practice soon revealed considerable disadvantages. Once European colonizers were chased out, local elites were also dispossessed. To overcome their resistance, the new system became quite dictatorial, instituting censorship, relying on a secret police, and militarizing society. And because of the official penchant for grand projects, the majority of the population tended to remain grindingly poor. Many countries, such as Benin, that started on the revolutionary track with great enthusiasm were utterly disappointed by its result.[27]

In spite of its advocacy by economists like W. W. Rostow, the capitalist alternative of a right-wing developmental dictatorship hardly fared any better in improving ordinary lives. To be sure, the continuity of elites and of European advisers retained a greater degree of competence. Moreover, there was more extensive investment by western banks and multinational corporations like Nestlé and Royal Dutch Shell, which created some pockets of development. And the appearance of governmental processes remained democratic. But the fear of communism allowed scoundrels like Idi Amin to use the military in order to establish a personal dictatorship and to amass great fortunes for the ruling clan. If anything, social disparities between the profiteers of aid and the masses, crowding into urban slums, tended to increase with independence. Free speech was also repressed, and the majority of the population remained in poverty and was often illiterate to boot. The rhetoric of belonging to the free world therefore rang rather hollow.[28] Neither variant was particularly successful in delivering visible improvements to the majority.

The polarizing logic of the Cold War pushed decolonizing countries toward choosing one of those paths and thereby becoming a client state of one of the blocs. The reward was the provision of foreign aid and of expert advisers who promised to help solve practical problems like digging wells or improving crops. The sale of arms to the new nations so that they could suppress domestic dissent and fend off foreign attacks was an especially nefarious business. On the one hand, the acquisition of modern tanks, artillery and airplanes was a powerful demonstration of national sovereignty; but on the other, it was a costly game of one-upmanship with neighboring countries that drove developing nations ever deeper into debt. Moscow and Washington vied with each other to provide military technology to dictators and insurgencies, thereby triggering devastating proxy wars.[29] Only a few states, for instance Egypt, managed to switch sides, playing the Americans and the Soviets off against each other. Many developing countries therefore tried to escape this dilemma and join the bloc of nonaligned nations.

The enormity of the postcolonial challenges only became clear once the festivities during the transfer of power were over. Kept in check by the halfway house of colonialism, modernization set in with force after independence, producing a full-fledged crisis. Ancient beliefs, customs, and traditions that had hitherto regulated life now began to fade quite rapidly, turning into superstitions. The new demands of scientific rationality, personal discipline, economic efficiency, and individual assertiveness rapidly replaced them, making life more hectic and stressful. The result was a deep sense of cultural uncertainty, with youths seeking orientation from pop-culture stars like Miriam Makeba in music or Didier Drogba in soccer. Since only a minority of officeholders and businesspeople directly profited from the changes, expectations of sharing the benefits of independence rose much faster than governments could possibly fulfill them. Especially in Africa a younger generation felt stymied in their aspirations, making many youths turn to Islamic fundamentalism or seek a better life through a dangerous emigration to Europe.[30]

DISAPPOINTING RESULTS

In spite of some promising exceptions, the performance of the newly independent states has been rather disappointing. Jomo Kenyatta had been sure: "If we respect ourselves and our independence, foreign investment will pour in and we will prosper." But a myriad of ethnic, religious, regional, and ideological conflicts made the consolidation of statehood quite difficult. The human-rights record of the dictatorships has been abysmal, including civil wars, ethnic cleansing, and even full-scale genocide. Hindered by dependence on foreign aid and a parasitical bureaucracy, economic development has generally stagnated, enriching a new class of businessmen and functionaries but leaving the rest behind. The social upheaval has been dramatic with unchecked population growth pushing people into urban slums, eking out a marginal living. Moreover, cultural uncertainty has left many stranded between traditional ways and western practices. On top of all of these problems have come natural catastrophes like flooding in Bangladesh and drought in Saharan Africa, not to forget the medical scourge of AIDS.[31]

One recurring obstacle to progress has been political instability, with most countries oscillating between authoritarian regimes and civil strife. While the outward trappings of democracy have remained, elections have often been rigged as acclamatory plebiscites, since power has been construed as something to be exploited rather than as temporary trust. In consequence, popular insurrections and military coups have become the preferred means to turn the rulers out. Opposition has tended to be proscribed, free expression circumscribed, and rivals persecuted. In such states politics was considered a way to advance one's clan, tribe, or ethnic group at the expense of others by milking the community. Moreover, in Nigeria, Somalia, and the Sudan there have been periodic attempts at secession in order to provide minorities with their own government. Even well-meaning leaders have therefore instituted dictatorial regimes in order hold their nation-states together, but their draconian measures have sparked militant subversion in turn. Only a few fortunate places like Botswana and Singapore have escaped this cycle of upheavals.[32]

It almost seems as if there has been more bloodshed after independence than during the heyday of imperialism. Aggrieved groups like radical Muslims have resorted to terrorizing their Christian neighbors or western businessmen. In Angola, Marxist-sponsored revolutionaries like the MPLA and capitalist-supported factions like the UNITA have waged interminable civil war, killing half a million people and displacing a million more. In such conflicts pillage, rape, and murder have uprooted masses of refugees and thereby effectively engaged the perpetrators in ethnic cleansing of ideological, religious, or tribal opponents. More deadly yet were the full-scale genocides by the Khmer Rouge in Cambodia during the 1970s, murdering about two million people, and the Hutu slaughter of the Tutsis in Rwanda in the 1990s, killing between half a million and one million citizens, and the recent repression in Darfur.[33] Hamstrung by great-power rivalries, the United Nations has not stopped such killings, merely mediating when the worst of the conflict was over. Similarly the Red Cross and other relief agencies have only been able to help refugees without preventing their flight.

As a result of bad governance, postindependence economies have often stagnated, since they failed to overcome the colonial division of labor that extracted crops and raw materials for the benefit of Europe. If they possessed a commodity such as cocoa or oil that could bring a good price on the world market, some countries like Ghana or Gabon were able to prosper. Others could, like South Africa, use their income from mining diamonds to generate a regional manufacturing sector, relying on low wages. But many new states lacked such attractive resources or were unable to exploit them, being able to export only their labor. Instead of taking off, they became increasingly reliant on international aid payments, corrupting their elites without improving the lot of the masses. Countless agricultural or industrial development schemes also foundered on ignorance of local conditions and misunderstandings of indigenous customs.[34] As a result, a deep cleavage has developed between an internationally competitive export sector with good wages for a few and a marginal subsistence of those limited to the local economy for the many.

One of the key problems that hampered political and economic development was the rapid population growth in postcolonial countries. Repeating the European experience of the "demographic transition," the greater availability of food and medicine has lengthened life expectancy, while the lack of birth control continues to produce a high number of children. In Africa alone, the population has been growing between 3 and 5 percent annually, producing a fivefold rise from two hundred million to one billion within the last sixty years! India, Indonesia, and other Southeast Asian countries already have huge populations, which are still increasing. In contrast to aging Europe, the great number of young people is straining the capacity to educate them and find sufficient jobs. When a country like Benin grows economically at a modest rate, the entire increase is eaten up by demographic growth—keeping the population in exactly the same degree of poverty. The result has been an urban explosion in which government buildings and the villas of the rich contrast with the endless shantytowns of the poor.[35]

Coping with overpopulation was made more difficult by a series of natural disasters and medical emergencies. Some problems were due to the intensification of grazing and clear-cutting of the jungle, which created adverse changes in the microclimate. Other difficulties stemmed from cyclical weather variations, as when the Sahel region between the Sahara and the tropical rain forest experienced a severe drought from 1970 to 1990 that threatened fifty million people with famine. Perhaps linked to global warming, a series of unusually severe cyclones created immense flooding in the low-lying Ganges delta of Bangladesh in 1998, which claimed many victims. Similarly tsunamis of enormous strength devastated the rim of the Indian Ocean in 2004 and the coast of Japan a few years later.[36] Owing to a lack of condoms and of sexual restraint Africa also became the chief victim of the AIDS epidemic, condemning many HIV-infected patients to death because of the high cost of drugs. Difficult enough in developed countries, such disasters were particularly hard on states with insufficient resources, compounding their other problems.

Hopeful signs, however, suggest that some postcolonial countries are starting to overcome these problems and to enter sustained growth that will stabilize their politics. The by now classic case consists of the Asian "tiger" states like Singapore, Korea, and Taiwan, which succeeded during the last two generations in pulling themselves up by the bootstraps. Copied from Japan, their recipe started with low-wage manufacturing through license agreements, producing labor-intensive goods like textiles but then moving on to more technical areas like consumer electronics and cameras, and finally pushing into high-technology sectors like computer chips. Optimistic journalists are therefore beginning to speak of an "African miracle," since a select group of seven states has achieved growth rates of 6 percent during the past years. One trade association concluded: "After emerging Asia, Africa is the fastest-growing region in today's world." While some countries such as Ghana and Nigeria have oil and South Africa minerals, Kenya and Côte d'Ivoire are moving in spite of disturbances, and Tanzania and Zambia are just starting out.[37]

The disappointment of independence has largely been a result of political failure of the postcolonial elite. While the imperial legacy presented enormous challenges, fifty years after the transfer of power it is no longer credible to blame all problems on colonial rule. Many founding statesmen like Nkrumah and Senghor were inspiring spokesmen for independence, but all too few succeeded in governing democratically like Jawaharlal Nehru in India. The litany of "corruption, genocide, refugees, civil wars, military coups, and ethnic conflicts" suggests that there was indeed a "dismal record of post-colonial African leadership, whether revolutionary or accommodationist." Being suddenly thrust into having to decide their own fate also overtaxed the maturity of the citizens of the new national states who looked to paternalistic authority and sought advantages for their own group rather than caring for the whole. Finally, the Cold War meddling of the Soviet Union and the United States proved destabilizing, because the superpowers exploited local conflicts for their own ends.[38] As a result, the number of false starts has been depressingly high.

IMPERIAL BLOWBACK

Decolonization not only liberated the former colonies but also had profound effects on the metropolitan countries in Europe that are rarely discussed. One term that highlights the "unintended consequences of policies" is the notion of a "blowback," coined by the U.S. intelligence community.[39] If applied to the end of imperialism, this concept draws attention to the unplanned impact of the retreat from empire on the former colonizers, highlighting its ambivalent interpretation: From the nostalgic perspective of the apologists involved in maintaining and profiting from colonies, decolonization involved a decided loss of prestige, possession, and privilege, an ignominious abandonment of a grand mission in the world. From the point of view of the critics of imperialist exploitation, long frustrated by the moral duplicity of the enterprise, the granting of independence seemed like liberation from a heavy burden of enormous costs and far-flung responsibilities, which finally opened the way for domestic reform. The blowback from imperial collapse had rather contradictory effects on Europe.

In European perception during the 1950s the process of decolonization inspired fear, based on horror stories recounted by newspapers. Eyewitnesses told frightening tales of revenge killings of white settlers, rape of their women, and enslavement of their children. Less-sensationalist accounts focused on the likely expropriation and expulsion of European settlers, construing such acts as showing a lack of gratitude for the colonizers' civilizing efforts. These lurid tales were in part inspired by descriptions of native uprisings, like that of the Mau-Mau in Kenya, which were portrayed as the barbarism of atavistic tribal killers rather than as independence movements,[40] or by reports of spontaneous antiwhite massacres such as in the Congo after independence. On the whole such fears were exaggerated because imperial governments and liberated regimes strove to suppress racial violence as counterproductive. Instead the alarmist accounts revealed a guilty conscience among the colonizers who expected revenge for their misdeeds. Nonetheless, the official story of peaceful liberation was contradicted by a counternarrative of postimperial anxiety.

The withdrawal from empire triggered a large-scale, partly voluntary, partly forced exodus of Europeans back to their home countries. When the transfer of power made administrators, soldiers, and policemen redundant, they were simply recalled. Many businessmen and settlers were also compelled to leave, since independence often led to nationalization and confiscation of land for redistribution to indigenous peoples as in Zimbabwe. Most acrimonious was the flight of the *pieds-noirs*, French colonists in Algeria whose ancestors had lived in North Africa for generations. When it became clear that France would relinquish the colony, almost one million precipitously left, overwhelming the receiving bureaucracy, which had expected one-third that number. Most of them settled in the southern *départements* of France, where the climate and the soil were familiar, but many had difficulty integrating themselves into metropolitan life. Resentment against being abandoned has turned the *pieds-noirs* into a reservoir for the right-wing politics of the National Front. Altogether about three to four million Europeans were repatriated during decolonization.[41]

Added to this number should be 2.5 million nonwhite immigrants from the former colonies, whose arrival at their doorstep surprised the former colonial powers. Many of them were, like the Algerian Harkis, administrative or military subalterns who had collaborated with the colonizers and feared for their lives after independence. Others were merely energetic migrants who bought into the attractive picture purveyed in colonial schools and sought a better life in the metropole. Coming from Asia, like Indonesians to Holland; from Africa, like Kenyans to Britain; or from the Maghreb, like North Africans to France, they also brought different foods, social customs, and especially religions like Islam, adding a sizable Muslim population to the continent. In contrast to the repatriated whites, these colored immigrants often had difficulty obtaining citizenship, struggled to find jobs, and were confined to urban ghettos while their children had trouble coping with schools. As a result this post-colonial immigration has created minorities who have been discriminated against and have proven hard to integrate.[42]

This double migration has triggered an anti-immigration backlash against "Islamization" in European countries, not all of which even participated in imperialism. While the repatriates tended to the right, supporting the National Front of Le Pen in France, the presence of nonassimilated Muslim immigrants set off a wave of protests even in paragons of social liberalism like Denmark. From the British Conservatives to the Lega Nord in Italy, political parties of the Right have campaigned for stronger legal and physical barriers against immigration, trying to stop the influx of refugees from across the Mediterranean. Populist politicians like Jörg Haider in Austria and Geert Wilders in Holland scored surprising electoral successes, complicating domestic politics even in tolerant societies. Apparently the fear of international terrorism fed into a widespread resentment against the building of mosques and the wearing of head scarves and burkas as outward signs of cultural difference.[43] Ironically, the poison of racist and religious prejudice therefore followed the collapse of empires into Europe proper.

In spite of the transfer of power and flight of colonizers, many ties between the former colonies and the European metropoles have continued. Especially where decolonization was negotiated peacefully, a series of bilateral economic and cultural agreements has sought to maintain the previous relationship. Supported by education and media contacts, the instruments of *francophonie* and Anglophonie sustained cultural influence through the retention of European languages so as to communicate between different tribal idioms.[44] Even after European businessmen and settlers left, economic relations remained profitable via privileged trade and investment in new enterprises. In North Africa, the French also continued to intervene militarily in order to uphold political stability. British relations with colonies were somewhat looser, since the United States was always in the background as a more potent partner. As a result of the influence of multinational corporations, leftist critics soon raised the specter of "neocolonialism." Nonetheless this continuing dependency has become somewhat pluralized and competitive, allowing for more choice.[45]

In the guise of helping the independent states to modernize, some idealists have also continued to be involved in the former colonies, now no longer in the name of Europe but of the West. A new generation has rediscovered Africa and Southeast Asia, learning the languages and customs of former colonies. Younger academically trained advisers went out to the developing countries in order to manage international projects of aid in contact with local administrators. By digging wells, checking teeth, or dispensing birth-control information, various NGOs, such as the French-inspired Médecins Sans Frontières, or members of the Peace Corps became a new actor in the postcolonial transition. On a more political level Amnesty International has kept a close watch on the human-rights record of the new states, while activists of Greenpeace have tried to prevent environmental catastrophes. Sometimes this involvement was resented as a neoliberal fig leaf because it was ineffective and had a tutelary tone.[46] But on the whole such efforts were well intentioned, trying to solve current problems rather than to reestablish western hegemony.

The sobering experience of this imperial blowback shows that both colonizers and colonized are still trying to cope with the after-effects of imperialism. The shadow of empire has not yet lifted completely after half a century of independence, because the ties were not as easily dissolved as expected during the handover of power. The former colonies are facing immense challenges of population control, economic development, and good governance in order to satisfy the desires of their citizens. The erstwhile colonizers are also retaining some responsibility for helping their earlier possessions on their feet, while at the same time having to deal with the new multiethnic and religious minorities in their midst in order to assure them a better life. Fortunately, both partners are no longer just dependent on each other but can resort to a complex multinational network of organizations such as the United Nations, International Monetary Fund, World Bank, International Health Organization, and the like. The central challenge remains for them accept the burden of their violent past in order to craft a new, more equal relationship and strive for a peaceful future together.

POSTCOLONIAL LEGACIES

In retrospect, decolonization looks like a surprisingly swift process, propelled by an anti-imperialist search for an independent version of modernity. Within one generation after the Second World War, which eroded European hegemony, the overseas empires dissolved. Only rarely were the Europeans defeated in open battle like the French in Vietnam, but the national liberation revolts were bothersome enough to make the metropolitan governments, preoccupied with rebuilding their own countries, decide that the defense of their possessions was not worth the cost and manpower needed. Because of the speed of the colonizers' retreat, the newly independent countries faced enormous challenges of political stability and economic development. The UN declaration of 1960 provided support for independence, but the meddling of Cold War competitors aggravated the transition, while inexperience produced disasters that cast a pall over the achievement of independence. Decolonization was therefore driven by a complex mix of metropolitan, colonial, and contextual factors that left an ambivalent legacy for postcolonial independence.[47]

Imposed from the outside for the benefit of European colonizers, the modernization of the colonies appeared as a destructive force to the colonized. Taking advantage of existing enmities, the imposition of colonial rule abolished tribal structures of self-government, subjecting the locals to the dictates of a colonial office far away. By rationalizing plantation agriculture and mineral extraction, the economic exploitation of colonial resources pushed local competitors to the wall and degraded the population into a cheap labor force. The impact of European lifestyles dissolved the collective living patterns of villages, introducing a competitive individualism that strove for personal advancement rather than the common good. The introduction of compulsory schooling promoted a rationalism that declared ancient traditions to be superstition, leaving people stranded between their prior beliefs and the redemptive message of Christianity that clashed with imperial practice.[48] The importation of European patterns triggered a modernization shock that destroyed cultural orientation without putting new guidelines into place.

Yet in contrast to earlier nativist revolts, the postwar national liberation movements succeeded only because they were willing to adopt ideologies and techniques introduced by the European colonizers. None of the anticolonial leaders wanted to dispense with the new infrastructure of cities, ports, railroads, airfields, hospitals, and schools. While Nkrumah's Pan-African movement hoped to overcome the arbitrary boundaries left by the imperialists, this effort failed to stop the transformation of territories into nation-states on the western pattern. Moreover, the guerrilla warfare waged to push the imperialists out used weapons and tactics learned from the European occupiers during the world wars. Both market liberals and Marxist revolutionaries resorted to ideologies and mobilizing techniques learned from western intellectuals during university study in the metropole. Finally, the creation of trade unions and political parties followed the organizational pattern developed on the Old Continent. Though vigorously anti-imperialist, the national liberation movements were at the same time also ardent domestic modernizers.[49]

Achieving a self-sustaining form of development after independence proved to be more difficult than expected, since the antiimperialists repeated many of the mistakes of the colonizers. Statebuilding alone has been a vexing process because of the prevailing ethnic, religious, and regional fragmentation of the citizenry. Establishing viable forms of self-government has also been elusive, since many of the leaders of liberation turned into authoritarian patriarchs or outright dictators. Keeping domestic and international peace has been equally trying, since multiple conflicts, aggravated by outside economic interests and fought by mercenaries, have torn the new states apart. The task of economic development has turned out to be especially trying due to the involvement of multinational corporations and the corruption of local bureaucracies. Finally, controlling population growth and urbanization has proven well-nigh impossible.[50] Since the transplantation of institutions has turned out to be difficult, the experience of independence has been rather discouraging, with the good life promised by modernity receding like a mirage.

Yet there are promising signs that the positive potential of modernization is also gradually being realized through the development of a hybrid postcolonial modernity. Even if living standards continue to lag, other indicators such as infant health and life expectancy have been rising steadily. Compulsory schooling has also raised levels of literacy everywhere. New technological gadgets like radios, portable phones, and even computers are spreading rapidly, and urban streets in developing countries are clogged with bicycles and mopeds. The young generation is flocking into the cities to share in the consumption and popular culture offered by globalization, while building institutions of civil society from below. No longer constrained by traditions, it is striving for a new blend of identities, accepting modern technology and western lifestyle while searching for its own form of democracy. With the rise of China, Europe has receded, serving as a resource for potential help but as merely one player among others in a global system.[51] If this progress continues, this growing confidence might finally lead to a more equal relationship.

Chapter 19

ECONOMIC INTEGRATION

Founding of the Common Market with the signing of the Treaty of Rome, 1957.
Source: bpk, Berlin / Campidoglio, Rome / Art Resource, NY.

Despite a steady drizzle, the leaders of six West European nations were overjoyed when they concluded the Treaties of Rome on March 25, 1957. In a televised ceremony on Capitoline Hill German chancellor Konrad Adenauer and the foreign ministers of France, Belgium, Holland, Luxembourg, and Italy signed two documents establishing a customs union, the European Economic Community, and a convention for the peaceful use of nuclear energy, titled Euratom. After the failure of ambitious plans for a European Defense Community in 1954, this was a more modest approach, using economic instruments for political ends. By including "a Court of Justice, a rudimentary Parliament and the embryo of a future European Cabinet," these treaties created structures "designed to serve as central organs of what could in time develop into a government of a European federation." The mayor of Rome underlined the importance of the signing by claiming that it prepared Europe for "a century of union in peace, freedom and prosperity." The church bells rang, the holiday crowd cheered. Only the communists grumbled.[1]

The founding of the Common Market was a concerted attempt to prevent a repetition of the disasters of the first half of the twentieth century. Its central purpose of laying "the foundations of an ever-closer union among the peoples of Europe" intended to achieve multiple aims: By linking the economies of France, Germany, Italy, Belgium, the Netherlands, and Luxembourg, the treaty sought to make future war impossible by eliminating "the barriers which divide Europe." At the same time the agreement tried to ban the specter of another depression by striving for "the constant improvement of the living and working conditions" of European citizens. Through ensuring "economic and social progress" the customs union attempted to strengthen the transition to democracy in the two postfascist member states. The preamble even expressed the pious wish of confirming "the solidarity which binds Europe and the overseas countries" during decolonization. Conscious of the Cold War, the signatories hoped to "preserve and strengthen peace and liberty" even for those East Europeans who might want to join them in the future.[2]

Enthusiastic Europhiles have created an optimistic narrative of European integration that celebrates the development from the Common

Market to the European Union as a straightforward success story. In optimistic speeches, leading politicians like former German foreign minister Joschka Fischer have been competing with public intellectuals like Timothy Garton Ash in proposing appealing visions of present benefits and future harmony. Many political scientists involved in European studies have been fascinated by an emerging continental polity, eager to offer advice to Brussels bureaucrats on how to take the next step. Even some historians have become involved in hailing the development of a common European society and public sphere, as if it had already taken place. This advocacy of a normative Europeanism risks falling into the Treitschke trap of intellectual partisanship, thereby repeating the failings of nineteenth-century nationalism on a larger geographic scale. The problem of this involvement in promoting integration is the lack of critical distance and exaggeration of its achievements.[3]

An equally determined minority of Euroskeptics contradicts this positive view by opposing the European Union and rejecting any increase of its power. In Western Europe right-wing populists like the UK Independence Party and the Alliance for Germany (AfD) voice such opposition, calling for a withdrawal from the EU for reasons of nationalism, whereas in East Europe the "postaccession" disappointments have led to vocal opposition. A softer version objects to further advances of integration or to specific aspects like the common agricultural policy, shading thereby into legitimate criticism for improving the EU. In free-trading countries like Britain, many commentators complain about invasive regulations of the Brussels bureaucracy or its presumed protectionism. In the United States prominent neoconservatives tend to dismiss the EU as militarily impotent and politically divided. Critics who express open skepticism about European identity prefer instead to argue for greater Eurorealism. Though often exaggerated, this resentment indicates the need for more detachment that also admits the many setbacks and failures of the process.[4]

By recognizing both achievements and shortcomings, the perspective of modernization offers a fresh way to deal with the integration of "Europe without illusions."[5] Traumatized by the triple disaster of the world wars, the Great Depression, and the collapse of democracy, the founders of the EEC essentially attempted to recapture the benign aspects of liberal modernity: overcoming the hostility between France and Germany would guarantee continental peace; economic cooperation based on market competition and free trade would ensure future prosperity; and the establishment of supranational self-governing institutions would cement democracy. The benefits of closer cooperation in the West European core would eventually also help the Mediterranean, East European, and Balkan countries to modernize. Finally the approaching loss of empire also demanded that attention should shift toward reforming the metropole. While agreeing on the need to reverse the trajectory of self-destruction, European leaders in subsequent decades struggled over how actually to put these guiding principles into practice.

BEGINNINGS OF COOPERATION

In broad historical terms, the project of European integration was inspired by the evident failure of prior attempts to dominate the entire continent. As a dim memory, the legacy of the Greek culture, the Roman Empire, and the spread of Christianity demonstrated that cooperation was possible and had many benefits. But the subsequent aspirations of Charlemagne, Philip II, and Louis XIV to establish hegemony over the continent precipitated dynastic wars rather than creating unity. The impact of Napoleon was also deeply ambivalent, ushering in a liberal legal code, continentwide trade, and enlightened administration but also imposing French rule and initiating an endless series of military conflicts. Finally, even Hitler's racist Reich tried to mobilize wider support by claiming to fight for Europe in its campaign to eradicate Jewry and Bolshevism. These negative experiences with military efforts to gain domination over Europe made thinkers from the Abbé de Sieyès to Jürgen Habermas look for a more peaceful and constructive form of unity.[6]

More directly, the integrationist impulse was an effort to continue the interwar initiatives at cooperation on a broader scale. In spite of all conflicts, transportation, communication, sports, and tourism had been creating a shared sense of Europeanness.[7] Impressed by the collapse of the Habsburg Empire, the Austrian philosopher Count Coudenhove-Kalergi in 1923 penned an appeal, called *Pan-Europa*, that advocated European unification. Some clairvoyant youths also participated in Franco-German exchanges in order to break out of nationalism and foster mutual understanding. Trying to build on the spirit of Locarno, the French premier Aristide Briand and the German foreign minister Gustav Stresemann talked about closer cooperation, but their efforts were cut short by the latter's death and the Great Depression. Instead, it was Nazi conquest that united the entire continent in a war-driven, resource-extracting, and slave-labor-exploiting *Großraumwirtschaft*. Realizing that transnational cooperation was needed to throw off this fascist yoke, the resistance movement developed ideas of European federalism that inspired the Italian theoretician Altiero Spinelli to propose a voluntary cooperation of liberated nations.[8]

Allied victory provided a chance to integrate Europe rather than just to reconstitute national states. Realizing that their countries were too small to compete, representatives of Belgium, the Netherlands, and Luxemburg had already signed a Benelux customs union in 1944. After the war, integration idealists began to meet in order to formulate their program, founding a Union of European Federalists in the fall of 1946. Out of office, Winston Churchill proposed "to re-create the European family, or as much of it as we can, and to provide it with a structure under which it can dwell in peace, in safety and in freedom. We must build a kind of United States of Europe." Since Britain was tied to the Commonwealth, he suggested "a partnership between France and Germany." Meeting at The Hague in 1948, advocates of integration created the Council of Europe as an intergovernmental institution, disappointing the federalists. This institution became a debating club without real power, but it sponsored the creation of the Court of Human Rights at Strasbourg, whose decisions have contributed to strengthening civil rights among its forty-seven member states.[9]

Jean Monnet, the chief of French postwar planning, advocated modernization through a form of integration that went beyond the mere cooperation of national states. As a successful businessman and diplomat with connections to Dean Acheson and John McCloy, he understood that the increasing tensions of the Cold War were shifting American priorities from punishing the Nazis toward rebuilding western Germany. Though he welcomed the foundation of the Organization for European Economic Cooperation (OEEC) in April 1948, he considered this intergovernmental body of eighteen members too big to do more than distribute Marshall Plan aid. Since France was not strong enough alone to contain a resurgent West Germany, Monnet hit upon the fortuitous idea of Europeanizing coal and steel production as the key power source and the crucial material for economic reconstruction. Supranational supervision of this strategic sector of industry would facilitate the continuation of Allied control over the Ruhr Basin and prevent the forging of new weapons of war: "To pool them across frontiers would reduce their malign prestige and turn them instead into a guarantee of peace."[10]

With wartime hostilities still running high, the establishment of the European Coal and Steel Community (ECSC) was a political feat of the first magnitude. French foreign minister Robert Schuman was happy to seize upon Monnet's idea and give it his own name, since the proposal provided security through cooperation rather than confrontation. Happy to be included in the Marshall Plan, West German chancellor Adenauer was eager to take the outstretched hand, because it allowed him to lift the Allies' exclusive control over the Ruhr and thereby claim equality for the Federal Republic through a conciliatory policy of western integration. Italian prime minister Alcide de Gasperi was delighted just to be included. But, clinging to insularity, the British government refused to join. Intent on fostering continental cooperation, U.S. diplomats like John Foster Dulles, however, welcomed the Franco-German rapprochement. In economic terms, the Schuman Plan was attractive since it formalized a long-standing cooperation between French iron-ore producers and German coal-mine owners.[11] After overcoming communist and nationalist opposition, the Treaty of Paris was signed on April 18, 1951.

The ECSC was the first practical step toward the supranational integration of Western Europe. While the preamble argued that "Europe can be built only by concrete actions which create a real solidarity," the text announced that its purpose was "to contribute to economic expansion, the development of employment and the improvement of the standard of living." Its central instrument was the High Authority under Monnet, which controlled the production and pricing of coal and steel. But its real innovation was the creation of accompanying institutions such as a Council of Ministers that had ultimate authority, a rudimentary parliament with the right to discuss policies, and a court to adjudicate disputes. These were embryonic governmental structures that went far beyond the limited task of supervising a strategic economic sector. As a result of the burgeoning demand for weapons materials during the Korean War, the ECSC was initially successful in raising production. But the progressive shift to oil as energy base and the post-Korean steel glut diminished its importance.[12] Ultimately, the ECSC's significance was therefore political rather than economic.

The plan of a European Defense Community (EDC) was even more ambitious, since it dared to address military power, the core of national sovereignty. Creating fears in Europe of a Soviet invasion, the North Korean attack of the South on June 25, 1950, raised the question of German rearmament to strengthen western defense. Prodded once again by Monnet, in 1952 French defense minister René Pleven proposed the creation of a supranational European army that would draw on German manpower without full German rearmament. Designed to square the circle, the EDC plan proposed basic units that would remain national but command structures that would be integrated, while German soldiers were to be concentrated in infantry without access to advanced weapons systems. As one cartoon had it, the EDC was supposed to be a fierce wolf toward the East to repel the Red Army but a tame lapdog toward the West to reassure its allies. In a heated debate the French parliament defeated the treaty's ratification in 1954 by a vote of 319 to 264, with both extremes, the nationalist Gaullists and pro-Soviet Communists, against it.[13]

After a decade of trying to modernize Europe through integration, the result remained rather disappointing, having produced more rhetoric than substance. In the beginning, European leaders concentrated on rebuilding their own immediate surroundings, from cities to states. The rising fear of communist attack and the consistent prodding by Washington sufficed only to establish various forms of cooperation between existing states in the Council of Europe and the OEEC. The pressure of European federalists, the appeals of intellectuals, and the initiatives of visionaries like Monnet merely succeeded in creating a single supranational institution controlling one key sector of the economy, needed both for reconstruction and rearmament. A more ambitious plan, the EDC failed because integrating the military also required creating a European Political Community, a common government to command its forces, which no longer seemed necessary with the end of the Korean War. Since its failure inspired other solutions like German membership in NATO, the project of forging European unity appeared stalled by the midfifties.[14]

THE COMMON MARKET

Surprisingly enough European integration did not die, but rather acquired a different form. When idealists failed to realize their grand vision, pragmatists took up the issue and pursued a more modest approach, in the hope that the logic of cooperative problem solving would require further integrative steps. Having built up enough momentum, the project shifted from federalism to functionalism, from one great leap to a succession of small steps.[15] The incremental course had the advantage of convincing skeptics of the benefits of each limited advance, rather than having to sell them on the ultimate goal. In this way the integration built on the achievement of the ECSC but sought to broaden it from one sector to the entire economy. A customs union could appeal both to free traders who would appreciate the enlargement of the market and to protectionists who insisted on shielding continental production against outside competition. The result of the rethinking after the defeat of the EDC therefore inspired a broadening of the push for modernization by establishing a comprehensive common market.

Undeterred by their setback, advocates of integration sought a way to "relaunch Europe" during the mid-1950s. Even after resigning as head of the ECSC, Jean Monnet was still influential enough to suggest a joint effort to develop nuclear power as an energy source capable of supplanting coal and oil. Already during the debates about the EDC, Dutch foreign minister J. Willem Beyens had proposed going beyond sectoral integration to establish a customs union and common market in order to speed economic development on the continent. Belgian foreign minister Paul-Henri Spaak picked up both ideas during the brainstorming at the Messina Conference in June 1955. After lengthy deliberation his committee produced a report for the foreign minister meeting in Venice in May 1956 recommending the creation of two separate but politically linked communities for a common market and nuclear cooperation. Subsequent negotiations between the six ECSC members France, West Germany, Italy, and the Benelux countries developed two agreements, the Treaty of Rome and the Euratom Treaty, signed a year later.[16]

Multiple compromises between member countries and economic interest groups were needed to achieve agreement and ratification. While French protectionists hoped to shield their companies through shared external tariffs, German free traders welcomed the removal of the internal barriers to trade. Whereas Paris was excited about the potential of nuclear energy, Bonn was more interested in the advantages of a common market for its competitive industries. Entrepreneurs looked forward to greater business opportunities, but labor leaders insisted on the inclusion of a European Social Fund. To convince his hesitant compatriots, French negotiator Robert Marjolin demanded "the adoption of a common policy in the sphere of agriculture" as help for his farmers. Worried about weakening connections to its colonial empire, Paris also called for association agreements with its overseas territories. In order to overcome the skepticism of German economics minister Ludwig Erhard, Chancellor Adenauer stressed the abolition of restraints on continental trade within the common market.[17]

The Treaty of Rome was infused with the modernizing language of economic liberalism, stressing competition. Internally, creating a common market required the "free movement" of goods, persons, services, and capital by tearing down all barriers to trade, including indirect obstacles and subsidies. It also necessitated outlawing the

European Economic Community 1956
Joined in 1973
Joined in 1981
Joined in 1986
COMECON countries
Nonaligned countries

Map 10. European integration: the European Economic Community / European Community, 1956–86. Adapted from German Historical Institute, Washington, DC.

"prevention, restriction or distortion of competition" through dumping or taxation. Externally, the establishment of a customs union demanded removal of separate duties and imposition of a common tariff, with receipts shared between the governments. As a compromise between free traders and protectionists, the level of outside duties was set at the arithmetical average of the current tariffs of the members. The concurrent but separate Euratom treaty sought to "create the conditions required for the development of a powerful nuclear industry," spreading the costs to all member states and giving Germans access to research without letting them develop their own weapons. But with oil rapidly replacing coal as energy, atomic cooperation became less relevant.[18]

Resembling the ECSC, the institutions of the Common Market (EEC) were basically intergovernmental with some supranational elements. The Commission of the European Economic Community, led by a president, was so to speak the executive, guiding the functioning of the market, recommending measures, and assuring their implementation. But its policies depended on the Council of Ministers, instructed by the member states, which retained ultimate control through deciding by majority vote. At the same time there was also a European Parliament composed of elected representatives, which had merely "advisory and supervisory powers." Finally, a Court of Justice whose decisions were binding watched over the correct application of the treaty. This mixed system was both the nucleus of a European government and a formalized cooperation between sovereign states, which functioned well when in agreement but stalled when France and Germany were at loggerheads.[19] Symbolic of the tensions within the EEC was the dispersal of its institutions, leaving the nascent bureaucracy and commission in Brussels, the court in Luxembourg, and the parliament in Strasbourg.

In economic terms the Common Market turned out to be highly successful, since its introduction coincided with the postwar boom of the *trente glorieuses*. Under the forceful leadership of the German lawyer Walter Hallstein, the commission rapidly removed internal trade barriers, completing the customs union within nine years, much faster than planned. Although the abolition of other distortions of trade would take decades, the six member countries enjoyed vigorous growth, averaging around 5 percent annually. For producers, the Common Market had the advantage of larger scale, which allowed them to establish factories and retail outlets beyond national limits, leading slowly to the emergence of Europewide corporations and marketing chains. For consumers, the increased competition brought improved products at lower prices, ranging from luxury cars to reliable washing machines. While economists argue about whether these developments would not have taken place without the Common Market, it undeniably had a strong psychological impact, which added to the impetus of economic growth.[20]

The Common Agricultural Policy (CAP) was both the showcase and Achilles' heel of European integration, since it represented a triumph of bureaucratic interest-group politics. Under the able advocacy of the Dutch commissioner Sicco Mansholt, the regulation and support of agricultural production consumed 80 percent of the common budget in the first several decades. On the one hand, the CAP was a spectacular success in increasing production, banishing the specter of hunger and agrarian extremism. It mostly aided rural regions in France and Italy as well as market producers in Holland. For shoppers it provided a more variegated offering of fruits and vegetables. On the other hand, its price supports led to overproduction, the infamous "milk lakes" and "butter mountains" that had to be dumped below cost on the world market. By raising consumer prices in Europe, it increased living costs and indirectly hurt industrial exports. While touting the protection of the family farm, the CAP effectively benefited large producers and helped transform agriculture from small-scale operations to mass-market production.[21]

Two decades after the end of the war, the balance sheet of European integration remained decidedly mixed, showing some real progress but also continuing deficits. The establishment of the Common Market created a successful institution for one crucial policy field that modernized European production and consumption by orienting the economy to a larger continental arena. But by refusing to limit the EEC to a pure free-trade area, the founding members in effect divided Western Europe, since the British founded a rival free-trade organization, called EFTA, which consisted of countries of the European periphery. Without direct taxation the EEC Commission remained "a pensioner of the member states," incapable of influencing core issues such as defense, diplomacy, or the welfare state. Walter Hallstein's more encompassing vision of increased budget powers that was supposed lead to the creation of a European federal state was rejected by French president Charles de Gaulle, who forced Hallstein's resignation in 1967.[22] Since supranationalism remained elusive, Europeans turned to pragmatic functionalism as an integrating strategy.

EUROPE OF THE FATHERLANDS

Ironically, the economic success of the Common Market actually helped rescue the nation-state in postwar Europe. Though it may seem counterintuitive, "without the process of integration the West European nation-state might well not have retained the allegiance and support of its citizens the way it has." Indeed, it was the Common Market that provided the economic foundation for the "security and prosperity" that saved national independence from extinction. Instead of being antithetical, integration and nation-states were actually interdependent, since by partial delegation of sovereignty over trade and agriculture policy the national governments were able to retain the rest. In the postwar division of labor NATO took care of defense, the European Community of the economy, and the nations of the welfare state.[23] But the new lease on life, produced by the positive impact of the Common Market, subsequently stood in the way of further progress with integration.

Calling for a "Europe of the fatherlands," French president Charles de Gaulle demonstrated this national turn by provoking the empty-chair crisis of 1965. When the EEC Commission tried to use negotiations over the CAP to increase its power and the European Economic Community's budget, de Gaulle withdrew the French representative from the Council of Ministers. The crucial issue was his objection to the introduction of majority voting, which might override French interests. This move was also part of a more general assertion of power by withdrawing from active NATO membership and developing the *force de frappe* as an independent nuclear deterrent in order to demonstrate France's *grandeur*. The crisis was finally resolved by the Luxembourg compromise of 1966, which required "unanimous agreement" on "very important issues," instituting in effect a national veto. Though merely amending the rules, this agreement halted further progress with integration for well over a decade. In order to defend its interests, Paris eventually resumed working in

Brussels, but Gaullism reasserted the power of the member states over the European Community.[24]

Intent on preserving political dominance, de Gaulle also prevented the expansion of the EEC by twice vetoing the accession of Britain. When it became clear that the Common Market was growing faster than EFTA, Prime Minister Harold Macmillan decided to apply for membership in 1961. But the general said "*non!*" to the British entry in 1963 and again in 1967 because he feared losing control over a diffident Germany, which was bending over backward not to offend the French, signing the Elysée Treaty of Franco-German cooperation in 1963. Only when de Gaulle left office in 1969 did the pro-European Conservative Party leader Edward Heath renew the British bid for membership, which succeeded in 1973. But this time it was the Labour Party that objected, as it feared a diminution of sovereignty. After Harold Wilson won the next election, he held a referendum in 1975, promising to renegotiate the terms of membership, in which a substantial margin of 67.2 voted for remaining in the European Community, renamed EC in 1967. The Danes and Irish also entered in 1973, though the oil-rich and fishing-focused Norway refused to go along.[25]

While columnists were complaining about a "Eurosclerosis," the collapse of the Bretton Woods system inspired a renewal of integration efforts. The disappearance of fixed exchange rates after 1971 and the Oil Shock of 1973 confronted the Council of Ministers with difficult decisions regarding the relationship of monetary and economic policies. To restore a semblance of stability, they created a "snake," in which the value of member currencies could vary no more than 2.25 percent against one another. But only the Benelux states were able to follow the lead of the strong German mark (DM), acting as reserve currency. To fix this problem, French president Giscard d'Estaing and German chancellor Helmut Schmidt worked out an improved version, the European Monetary System (EMS). It created a European Exchange Rate Mechanism that returned to the snake in a more flexible manner and established a joint accounting currency, the ECU, which became the basis of all transactions. While subject to frequent adjustment, the EMS succeeded in giving the EC members control over their own currencies by creating a common monetary instrument.[26]

The next crisis was precipitated by another ardent nationalist, the combative prime minister of the United Kingdom Margaret Thatcher. She had already attacked the EC in her maiden speech as Conservative opposition leader of the House in 1975, calling the British contribution unfair. Since the United Kingdom imported more industrial and agricultural products than any other EC member, it also paid higher import duties. However, owing to its small and efficient agricultural sector, London received less support from the CAP than the others. When Thatcher entered 10 Downing Street in 1979 she peremptorily demanded a renegotiation of the European Community's finances to ease the British burden. Because of her aggressive style, she alienated even those colleagues who admitted that she had a sound case. After five years of strife in which the British budget question inhibited the work of the EC Commission, French president François Mitterrand finally succeeded in brokering a compromise at the Fontainebleau summit. The British contribution was reduced by 66 percent, the CAP finally reigned in, and revenues for the EC generally increased.[27]

In spite of these heated conflicts, the European Community's aura of economic and democratic modernity attracted Greece, Spain, and Portugal to apply for membership. As long as they remained under dictatorships, had underdeveloped economies, and exported labor, they had not been invited to become candidates. But when the colonels were overthrown in 1974, Greece asked to join, followed by Spain after the death of General Franco (1975) and Portugal after the demise of Antonio Salazar's successors (1974). To make membership possible, the candidates had to modernize by becoming functioning democracies and by liberalizing their economies. Moreover, they had to accept European Community law, implementing all those regulations which the existing member states had developed in the meantime. The EC was willing to help by creating a regional fund to assist their development. Ultimately the decision was a political one. Although the per capita GNP of the candidates was only about half of the EC average and their civil societies remained weak, they were allowed to join in 1981 and 1986 so as to facilitate their postdictatorial transition.[28]

Even though the intergovernmental phase of the midsixties to the early eighties disappointed many federalist hopes, some incremental progress in European integration continued. While ambitious EC Commission proposals were often blocked, the newly created European Council cooperated through regular summit meetings, while the rapport between French president Giscard d'Estaing and German chancellor Helmut Schmidt facilitated the resolution of problems. Though member states reasserted their power, the bureaucracy in Brussels expanded considerably, becoming a regular infrastructure for the implementation of common policies. It sought to establish fair competition by regulating community standards in everything from the size of imported bananas to the pasteurization of French cheeses and the contents of German beer. Slowly the European Parliament acquired more powers over the EC budget through direct election of its deputies, reducing the democracy deficit. Finally the European Court also regularly issued decisions that overrode national legislation in strengthening freedom of trade and competition.[29]

Far from proceeding in a straight line, modernizing integration therefore moved in fits and starts, even backsliding or lying dormant for a time and then gathering momentum again. In a stylized fashion it can be described as a cycle: Committed Europeans in the EC Commission would draw up visionary plans, but the Council of Ministers would block them, issuing vague communiqués instead. Clashing national interests, dramatized in provocative statements for domestic news-media consumption, would result in confrontations, leading to a veritable crisis. The ensuing negotiations between national representatives and European bureaucrats would sometimes drag on for years, with the Commission making various proposals. Finally a dramatic summit meeting going on into the wee hours would strike a political bargain, sometimes finding a suitable compromise or in other times simply postponing a resolution to a later date.[30] The modernizing push of integration was therefore not an automatic spillover effect from prior decisions but rather the result of reconciling conflicts of interests, expressed in rival visions of the European future.

THE EUROPEAN UNION

Ending a period of prolonged stagnation, the creation of the European Union (EU) was the result of a second relaunching of integration. It took an unlikely combination of national and European leaders to resume progress after the failure of plans such as the Tindemans Report of 1976, which had already sketched the goal of a closer union. On the European side, the appointment of the French socialist Jacques Delors as president of the European Commission in 1985 put a visionary who was exceptionally committed to reviving the integrationist agenda into a key position. On the national side, Prime Minister Margaret Thatcher's effort to gain a better deal for Britain and to extend her neoliberal domestic reforms to the European level provided an agenda that demanded further steps toward completing the single market. Moreover, the concurrent chancellorship of the Christian Democrat Helmut Kohl meant that Germany would welcome steps to strengthen integration as long as these agreed with its interests.[31] This constellation produced a set of agreements that transformed the Common Market into a nascent union of Europe.

The Single European Act (SEA) of 1986 was a crucial step forward because it linked the completion of the market to the strengthening of the European Community's powers. It originated in a Commission White Paper that proposed to create an area "in which the free movement of goods, persons, services and capital is ensured." Approved by the European Council in February 1986, the SEA sought to complete the single market by 1992, develop the EMS further, and coordinate social, scientific, and environmental policy. Superseding national vetoes, it also expanded qualified majority voting and increased the power of the European Parliament through a "cooperation procedure." Finally, it outlined a constitutional basis for what might become a European Political Community. Approved by referendum in Denmark and Ireland and by parliament elsewhere, the SEA was the first major revision of the Rome Treaties. It revived the integration process so as to establish a single market by removing the remaining barriers and at the same time strengthening the political institutions and decision-making processes of the European Community.[32]

One demonstration of the benefits of free movement was the Schengen Agreement, which liberalized the movement of persons within the signatory states. Starting in 1985, France, Germany, and the Benelux countries agreed to end their border controls, simplifying land and air travel considerably. But when abandoning frontier policing raised fears that criminal activities like drug trafficking would spread, implementation was postponed until a second convention was negotiated to clarify internal security measures. The most difficult problem was the influx of asylum seekers into the European Community, especially from the global South, which was resolved in Dublin in 1994 by the principle of "first handling," making the country where an applicant had initially entered the EU responsible for determining an immigrant's status. Starting with a trial period, the Schengen Agreement was put into practice in 1995 among the original five, joined thereafter by Italy, Spain, Portugal, Greece, and Austria. For vacation and business travelers the lifting of controls in "Schengenland" proved a great boon, illustrating the advantages of integration.[33]

The next, even more important step was the Treaty of the European Union, signed at the Dutch border town of Maastricht in February 1992. It was propelled by the effort to contain a stronger Germany after its reunification and by a demonstration of European impotence during the first Iraq War. Difficult negotiations between François Mitterrand of France, Helmut Kohl of Germany, and John Major of Britain led to agreement on the consolidation of existing structures into a new body, called the European Union. Expanding the Common Market, it created a political union with a common citizenship, governed by the principle of subsidiarity in making decisions on the lowest level possible. A second pillar was a common foreign and security policy, complemented by a third pillar of cooperation in justice and police affairs. The European Parliament received more budgetary powers and new competences in consumer protection and support of culture were added, though Britain opted out of a shared social policy. Because of the supranational tone of the document, ratification proved difficult in Denmark and France but succeeded in the end.[34]

The most visible aspect of the Maastricht Treaty was the introduction of a common currency, since it affected the daily lives of European citizens directly. The coordination of the European Monetary System was upgraded into an agreement on fixed exchange rates, which in 1999 transformed the ECU into a new currency, called euro. Put into circulation in 2002, the new bills used symbolic designs derived from famous buildings, while the coins had one common side and another with national images. To supervise the new exchange medium, a European Central Bank (ECB) was created and located in Frankfurt, the financial heart of the leading economic power in the EU. Stringent convergence criteria were supposed to guarantee the stability of the new currency, limiting annual inflation to less than 2 percent, government deficits to below 3 percent of GNP, and public debt to no more than 60 percent of GNP. Though these were fairly rigorous demands in order to reassure the German public, the French and Italians actually switched from a soft to a hard money policy.[35] Businessmen and vacation travelers were delighted with the common currency.

After some initial difficulties, the euro performed reasonably well, soon rivaling the U.S. dollar as a reserve currency for international monetary transactions. Starting with the six original EEC members, it was eventually adopted by seventeen nations, with other currencies in Africa pegged to it. By abolishing currency conversion costs, it facilitated internal trade and made external exchanges more predictable. Initially there was some speculation against it, starting out with a rate of 0.82 euro to the dollar, but after 2002 it exceeded the U.S. currency in value, and more recently it has been traded above $1.25 to one euro. By introducing the euro, the member states have turned over control of monetary policy to the European Central Bank, which has favored financial stability over growth. Especially during the recession caused by the dot-com bubble, its decisions have been controversial, since even France and Germany violated the convergence criteria, making it difficult to insist on their observance by the weaker economies.[36] In order to function more smoothly, the euro therefore required a harmonization of economic policies.

Another arena of modernization was EU support for innovation and cooperation in higher education and scientific research. Starting in the mid-1970s, the European Science Foundation sought to pool some of the resources of about thirty countries in order to fund transnational research, while the European Space Agency prepared to send satellites into orbit. Beginning in the mid-1980s, the EU financed technological and scientific research directly through a series of increasingly ambitious "framework programs" so as to keep Europe competitive on the world market. From 1987 on the Erasmus Program supported exchanging several million students and hundreds of thousands of teachers among countries to learn other languages and cultures. Constituted by a declaration at Bologna in 1999, the European Higher Education Area also tried to improve the compatibility of national degree programs by introducing the Anglo-American sequence of BA, MA, and PhD in order to make their diplomas more comparable.[37] Though creating initial chaos, the homogenization of curricula ultimately facilitated student exchanges.

Propelled by modernizing pressures of globalization, the new impetus for integration in the 1980s and 1990s created a complex structure of multilevel governance that has baffled political analysts. The European Union gained numerous features that were clearly supranational such as the common currency of the euro, suggesting the gradual emergence of a common polity. But the retention of ultimate decision-making power by the Council of Ministers of the member states, and within it by the Franco-German axis, also demonstrated the continued importance of intergovernmentalism. Moreover, the introduction of regional policies by funding those areas that had lagged in economic development added an element of subsidiarity to the mix, in which some powers were actually devolved from the national level to the regions concerned. The result was an exceedingly complicated structure of competing competences, taxing the ingenuity of citizens trying to make sense of the system. Even if the comparison with the arcane Holy Roman Empire seems a bit far-fetched, it does suggest the difficulty of creating "unity out of diversity."[38]

WIDENING OR DEEPENING?

The overthrow of communism confronted the emerging European Union with an unforeseen dilemma of whether to welcome new eastern members or to pursue further integration. In part, the peaceful revolutions showed that western-style consumer democracy was more attractive than eastern-style welfare dictatorship. The "socialist economic integration" of the Comecon had remained rather limited, because planning was inflexible and the division of labor privileged bilateral barter.[39] Propelled by popular resentment, the Soviet retreat from Central Europe lifted the Iron Curtain that had long divided the continent, thereby posing the question of how to deal with former satellite countries such as Poland, Czechoslovakia, and Hungary. Since their dissident counterelite was intent on a "return to Europe," it clamored for admission to the emerging EU. But at the same time the original Western European members were attempting to integrate even further, shifting more powers to the European Commission. In practice, these divergent goals of widening and deepening proved difficult to reconcile.

The first round of post–Cold War enlargement was rather unproblematic, since it involved several neutrals who now felt free to formalize their ties to the EU. During German reunification in 1990 the five eastern *Länder* that had formerly been the German Democratic Republic became EU members by joining the Federal Republic. With the end of the Cold War and the collapse of the Soviet Union, Finland and Austria reinterpreted their neutrality obligations so as to allow them to enter, while Sweden did not want to be excluded from participating in the continental market. In order to deal with these new applicants, the EU in its Copenhagen meeting in 1993 established clear membership criteria, calling for full democracy, a free market, and the acceptance of the existing body of European Community law. Since there was no doubt that all three countries fulfilled these demands, they were welcomed in 1995 as strong economies that would help augment the shared budget.[40] Only the idiosyncratic Swiss and the oil-rich Norwegians refused to join, but they negotiated special agreements providing them with market access.

The second widening of the EU concerning the former Soviet Bloc countries (plus Cyprus and Malta) was more difficult, since these were less ready owing to their communist legacy. Not only were they still attempting to catch up economically and transition into a new political system, but the economic disparity was enormous, with some applicants averaging only one-quarter of the members' per capita GNP. But the argument that inclusion would be "a historic opportunity" to heal the continent's division and strengthen the drive to democracy proved irresistible. As a result, negotiators agreed on a lengthy transition period with a gradual phase-in of economic support so as not to push the EU budget beyond its agreed limit. One sticky issue was the question of labor, since German and Austrian unions feared a flood of low-wage workers from the East and insisted on postponing full mobility. The first group of countries consisting of the Baltic states, Poland, the Czech Republic, Slovakia, Hungary, and Slovenia was admitted in 2004, and Bulgaria and Romania were added three years later.[41] Thereby the EU expanded to twenty-seven countries with about five hundred million citizens.

To streamline decision making in the enlarged union, supporters of further integration pushed for a new constitution that would consolidate and accelerate EU development. In 2001 the Laeken meeting created a constitutional convention, chaired by Giscard, which was charged with drafting a text that would combine the various treaties into one document. To create "a Union that is more cohesive and more understandable to the general public," the eventual draft proposed "to promote peace, its values and the well-being of its peoples." Reaffirming the human rights of European citizens, the constitution differentiated between exclusive, shared, and reserved competences, starting with the common market but expanding into new areas such as energy. The text also clarified the institutional structure, strengthened qualified majority voting, and moved explicitly toward a common foreign and security policy while giving the European Parliament powers of codecision. Signed in 2004, the document tried to affirm current practices while moving further in selected areas toward a European superstate.[42]

The surprising rejection of the draft during the subsequent ratification process exposed flaws in the top-down approach to European integration. Though eighteen states had already endorsed the constitution by parliamentary vote or plebiscite, referenda in France and Denmark on May 29 and June 2, 2005, repudiated the constitution by a vote of 55 to 45 percent and 61 to 39 percent respectively. While the turnout was modest, the media cried doomsday and pronounced the entire integration project dead on arrival. More differentiated analyses pointed out that the constitutional convention had been an elite project that failed to ignite public interest and therefore did not create a groundswell of support. The referenda also gave Euroskeptics a chance to vent their resentment of their own governments as well as the "Brussels bureaucrats" for unpopular policies. Moreover, for most Europeans the current version of the EU with its shared currency, open borders, student exchanges, and wider offerings of fruits and vegetables worked well enough already. A largely symbolic constitution therefore seemed unnecessary.[43]

Instead of giving up, the proponents of integration succeeded in salvaging the core of the constitution through an intergovernmental agreement called the Lisbon Treaty. The more modest approach of amending prior treaties with a shorter document had the advantage of being ratified more easily, though it took two tries to do so in Ireland. The most important provisions aimed at strengthening the internal functioning of the EU by giving greater powers to the European Parliament and expanding qualified majority voting in the European Commission. At the same time the treaty sought to enhance the external influence of the EU through the creation of a European Council president, serving for two and one-half years, and the addition of a commissioner for foreign affairs and security issues. Moreover, the citizenry gained the right to initiative, if signed by one million voters, and protection for human rights by making them legally binding.[44] Coming into force in 2009, the Lisbon Treaty put the EU onto a more solid footing and recovered a sense of momentum for the integration process.

Almost immediately, the sovereign debt crisis in peripheral European countries severely tested the EU's cohesion and ability to react.

When the U.S. rating agencies downgraded Greek, Irish, Portuguese, and eventually also Spanish government bonds because of those countries' large budget deficits, interest rates went through the roof. Easy credit and transfer of funds from Brussels had led to excessive spending and fed a real-estate boom that now threatened to collapse. Egged on by hysterical commentators, the EU had to find a way to bail out the debtors in order to defend the euro. As the largest economy of the euro zone, Germany was loath to support undisciplined overspenders but eventually understood that its exports depended on saving the common currency and helping its neighbors. Chancellor Angela Merkel reluctantly agreed to a series of rescue packages, provided that the debtors reduced their expenditures and undertook structural reforms. With the help of ECB refinancing, the EU succeeded in calming the markets. But the crisis showed that monetary union required stronger controls and a shared fiscal policy.[45]

In spite of annoying setbacks, many indicators point to the growth of a common European identity at the beginning of the twenty-first century. In the stores appliances from Germany, fashions from France, wines from Italy, oranges from Spain, whiskey from Ireland are all paid for in the same currency. On the superhighways trucks from Ukraine pass Danish campers heading for vacations in Portugal, while repair vans from Poland drive to work sites in Holland, mixing license plates and destinations as never before. In the airports travelers with European passports pass through special fast-track lanes, while tourists from the United States and the rest of the world have their papers more carefully scrutinized. On university campuses, Erasmus (ESN) students from within-EU countries mingle with local youths and other exchange students from all over the world, discussing the latest rock bands in accented English. While some of their elders still marvel at the disappearance of borders, denizens of the younger generation take such blending of backgrounds and cultures for granted, developing into an emergent European elite, thinking in continental or global terms.[46]

EUROPEAN DREAM

After the catastrophic first half of the twentieth century, many European intellectuals dreamed of recovering a benign version of modernity that would bestow bountiful benefits instead of wreaking death and destruction. From classical antiquity to Christianity, from the Renaissance to the Enlightenment, leading thinkers had formulated visions of "universal peace" in order to pacify the continent. The terrible suffering produced by the world wars, the Great Depression, and the dictatorships turned the realization of such pious wishes into a necessity of practical politics, if Europeans wanted a better future. During the darkest hours, resistance leaders clung to their faith in the possibility of resuming progress through scientific discovery, market competition, individualistic lifestyles, and rule of law. In the midst of the ruins left by World War II and the Holocaust, survivors searched for new political arrangements that would constrain the dangers of nationalism, militarism, authoritarianism, and international strife.[47] The quest for integration was one answer to the question of how to shape a better future.

Though these hopes were only partly realized, the modernizing achievements of the EU have nonetheless been impressive. To begin with, European integration has made war unthinkable among its members, because it has eliminated barriers between them and bound them together in a shared enterprise. No doubt bilateral reconciliation attempts such as the Elysée Treaty between France and Germany and the more recent effort to reduce tensions between Warsaw and Berlin have also made a contribution. While the transatlantic anchoring of the NATO alliance has provided a crucial nuclear umbrella, the Europeans were instrumental in moderating the renewal of Cold War confrontation. The only exception, the wars of Yugoslav secession during the 1990s in the Balkans, took place outside the EU, serving as a drastic reminder of what could go wrong. At the same time a basic change of attitudes toward war extinguished the fires of militarism to such a degree that U.S. neoconservatives attacked Europeans as having become too reluctant to fight.[48] Compared to the bellicose past, this pacification has been astounding.

The spread of prosperity has been an equally impressive gain in modernity, even if it has slowed noticeably during the past decades. Remarkable efforts of reconstruction have produced a "new Europe" out of the rubble with an intriguing mixture of restored historical buildings and gleaming modern designs. The return to the market was largely responsible for this economic miracle, since it unfettered individual initiative and competition, weeded out the inefficient structures. But neoliberal commentators tend to forget that the *trente glorieuses* were also a product of the systematic expansion of the welfare state that made it possible for the underprivileged parts of the population to participate in consumption. After the Oil Shocks of the 1970s this "social market economy" had considerable difficulties adjusting to the pressures of globalization, but its social protections proved more crisis-resistant than during the late 1920s. Though some pockets of poverty remain at the periphery, some European countries have in the meantime achieved a higher standard of living than the United States, which serves as a barrier against radicalism.[49]

In spite of critiques of a "democracy deficit," European integration has also contributed considerably to stabilizing a renewed form of democracy on the continent. Already in the first postwar years, the beginnings of cooperation reaffirmed self-government in those West European countries where it had been under pressure before. More importantly, in the postfascist states of Germany and Italy integration speeded westernization by making democracy the expected standard for recovering international respectability. Several decades later the EC took an active role in the Greek, Spanish, and Portuguese transition to parliamentary rule by providing economic aid to facilitate development and assisting with the rebuilding of democratic structures from the ground up. In the postcommunist transition in Eastern Europe the EU served as magnet for the fledgling governments by welcoming them into the European community with material help and political advice. Even if European censure was unable to prevent the rise of populists like Jörg Haider, the principle of "conditionality" as prerequisite to membership reinforced the turn to democracy.[50]

In spite of much progress, "an ever closer union" remains elusive, since the contest between federalists and skeptics over the meaning of European modernity continues to be undecided. Proponents of further integration like the German philosopher Jürgen Habermas argue that a "deepening of the federative aspect of the European Union" is necessary to prepare the continent for global citizenship. Neoliberal opponents of additional steps like the UK Independence Party see Brussels as the root of all evil, accuse it of overregulation, and demand that Britain leave the EU. Between these extremes commentators take a range of positions, from advocating a moderate strengthening of common institutions to calling for a halt with no further advancement. Through this debate "Europe" has become a signifier for conflicting views of modernization, be it embraced as progress or rejected as danger. Brussels can be applauded as a guarantor of free movement and gender equality, or it can be damned as an incarnation of technocracy and bureaucracy.[51] Though populist critics of integration are getting more vociferous, the process of integration is likely to continue.

Chapter 20

POP AND PROSPERITY

Advertising consumer society, 1957. *Source*: bpk, Berlin / Germin / Art Resource, NY.

W hen the hot rhythms of rock 'n' roll reached the European shores during the 1950s, traditionalists feared that "American cultural barbarism threatens our youth." Alarmist press reports described riotous scenes during Bill Haley concerts in which venues were vandalized and dozens of spectators injured. Other stories pictured teenage girls swooning over the hip gyrations of idols like Elvis Presley, who served in the U.S. Army in Germany. The East German communist (SED) newspaper claimed that "the de-humanizing effect of anti-music" was systematically destroying the inhibitions of young men in order to make them tools of NATO aggression.[1] Similarly, in West Germany spokesmen of the churches warned against the licentiousness of the Teddy Boys or *Halbstarken*, working-class youths in leather jackets, cruising around on mopeds, and pressured conservative politicians to pass a law for youth protection. While the SED continued to denounce this rebellious subculture, western Cold War liberals eventually learned to live with unruly youth behavior, even using pop music as a wedge to destabilize the East.[2]

The heated debate about rock music and movie fandom was part of a larger conflict over the basic direction of society and culture. Trying to restore order and stability, cultural pessimists deplored many of the postwar changes as a decline of Western civilization. The interwar laments of Oswald Spengler and Arnold Toynbee became popular after 1945 because they provided a larger explanation for the physical destruction and moral disintegration. Members of the old elite decried the loss of social distinctions and the disappearance of style and decorum. Moreover, they regretted the replacement of Latin by English in the secondary schools, the questioning of the literary canon, and the shift from reading books to listening to the radio or watching TV as an erosion of cultural norms. Feeling overwhelmed by developments they could no longer control, they tried to revive religious observance or at least restore humanistic values among the educated. One of their favorite thinkers was the French Catholic philosopher Jacques Maritain, since his message of "integral humanism" sought to reconcile reason with belief.[3]

Buoyed by the general rise in prosperity, cultural optimists, however, endorsed the changes as progress toward a more democratic version of modernity. Western advertisers had little difficulty persuading the public to buy new products, since their messages appealed to pent-up consumption desires and touted technological advances. Social commentators celebrated the reduction of class distinctions as a step toward what Helmut Schelsky called "a leveled middle class" society. Decrying "socialist realism" as dictatorial, the leaders of the high-cultural avant-garde such as Pablo Picasso similarly claimed that their experimental styles were an expression of human freedom and creativity. Purveyors of popular culture ridiculed the exclusivity and stiffness of high culture, arguing that their own mass entertainment was more socially inclusive, even if it catered to simpler tastes. Finally, sociologists justified such changes by elaborating a "modernization theory" that made its constituent developments seem inevitable.[4] While many pessimists remained ambivalent about modernity, the optimists endorsed it wholeheartedly.

Since restoration efforts still dominated the cultural scene in the 1950s, it was by no means a foregone conclusion that the self-styled innovators would ultimately prevail. All over Europe, it took a series of heated battles in which an international avant-garde network defeated local resistance to create space for new initiatives. In circles of visual artists it was the provocative Biennale exhibition of Venice, resumed in 1955, that shattered convention and made modern art popular.[5] In music the crucial impulses emanated from events like the Donaueschingen Festival of Contemporary Music, which celebrated twelve-tone and other experimental approaches. In architecture competitions like the international building exhibition in Berlin in 1957 allowed Le Corbusier, Oscar Niemeyer, and Walter Gropius to show off their modernist architectural designs. Unlike in the interwar period, the proponents of change ultimately won a series of fierce social conflicts and cultural controversies because they managed to portray such innovation as a positive and progressive force, capable of solving rather than of creating problems.

The reasons for the gradual acceptance of cultural modernity after the Second World War consisted of a complex mixture of material gains, technical advances, social changes, and intellectual reorientations.[6] In contrast to the interwar crises, the noticeable rise in living standards during the postwar boom made modernization look like a source of material progress. By lowering prices, technological innovation provided ever wider circles with access to luxury products previously reserved for the elite, triggering a growth of mass consumption. These visible improvements in daily lives led to a blending of clothing styles and speech patterns that leveled social distinctions, thereby reducing class barriers. Avant-garde criticism also convinced the public that modern art and experimental fiction represented artistic freedom by accusing realist painting and writing of being totalitarian since it was the style misused by dictators like Hitler and Stalin for propaganda. Finally, the explosion of popular culture on radio, TV, and in the cinema associated mass entertainment positively with being modern.[7] Against this multilevel onslaught, traditionalists were unable to resist.

RISING PROSPERITY

One major reason for the acceptance of modernity after the Second World War was the economic boom, which visibly improved people's lives. Initially the recovery lagged because of the postwar chaos, destruction of transportation, idling of manufacturing capacities, dislocation of labor, and administrative restrictions. But with the West German currency reform of 1948, a quarter century of rapid growth began that has not been paralleled before or since. During this period average annual gains in GDP for Western Europe exceeded 5 percent, more than twice the rate at which the U.S. economy expanded concurrently. Already in 1970 a French historian was amazed at the speed and extent of the transformation: "In only a few years, this devastated, decimated, famished continent achieved a prosperity it had never known before, its material and intellectual forces regained their strength." Within one generation Europe had risen like the proverbial phoenix out of the ashes of self-destruction, making the postwar period seem like the three glorious decades of continual advance.[8]

Promising "prosperity for all," German economics minister Ludwig Erhard promoted a "social market economy" that became the key to the European revival after the war. Born in Franconia in 1897, he was a disciple of a small group of ordoliberals who sought to restore competition within a state framework. His gamble on currency reform and market liberalization in 1948 set off the Economic Miracle in the Federal Republic, which spread to the rest of Western Europe. Because of the public preference for nationalization and industrial cartels, overcoming corporatist habits proved difficult, but ultimately the power of competition prevailed, since the free-market approach was also supported by the United States. In contrast to the frequent conflicts and strikes in Britain and France, Germany's Rhenish capitalism strove for a social partnership in which management and labor sat down to negotiate pay and benefits in a constructive atmosphere, aided by formal codetermination in the larger enterprises.[9] This model was so successful that even the Social Democrats came around to accepting it in the Godesberg Program of 1959. Although actual practices varied considerably between French technocracy and Scandinavian socialism, the West European consensus combined market competition with state supervision and social welfare.

In some ways, the postwar boom was merely the process of catching up to the level of development that the Old Continent would have reached without the Great Depression and World War II. During the initial decade, the chief engine for growth was the reconstruction of the transportation grid, production facilities, and housing stock. But after the midfifties development continued through innovation and emulation of the best practices of the U.S. economy, which increased the GDP per capita from 54 percent to 77 percent of the American level for Western Europe as a whole and from 49 percent to 87 percent for West Germany. This notable narrowing of the gap was the product of an impressive increase in productivity that drew on traditional European strengths such as a highly skilled workforce and on U.S. modes of mass manufacturing and merchandising. The process was helped by international support from the Marshall Plan, loans from the International Monetary Fund, and the effect of liberalization in the Common Market. By repairing war damage and adopting technological innovation, West Europeans achieved sustained growth.[10]

After the initial postwar stasis was overcome, a virtuous cycle developed in which the expansion largely fed on itself because expectations and actions favored further advancement. The reluctant lifting of wartime controls such as rationing allowed the market to function again as an allocation mechanism and permitted competition to reward individual initiative. The result was the emergence of a new generation of entrepreneurs, like Heinz Nordhoff, who were willing to pursue risky business strategies such as producing, in his case, just one simple but durable car: the Volkswagen "Beetle." Much of the growth was financed through self-investment, plowing profits back into increasing production rather than distributing them to shareholders. Moreover, the expansion was driven by the manufacturing sector, which was actually making goods that were in demand, such as textiles, using Fordist mass-production techniques that were labor intensive.[11] As a result of venturing into new areas, entrepreneurs like Werner Otto of mail-order business and Max Grundig of radio and TV production managed to make enormous fortunes.

The expansion was also propelled by gains in real wages, which increased buying power in the working class and thereby avoided the interwar problem of underconsumption. Initially, returning soldiers were just happy to have a job at all and restrained their wishes for pay raises in return for social benefits, ignoring communist agitation. But by the 1950s the arrival of full employment strengthened the bargaining power of the trade unions to compel employers to grant wage increases. Coupled with the need to replace damaged or worn-out clothes and furniture as well as the desire for new household appliances or entertainment gadgets, the increase in take-home pay directly augmented demand for industrial goods. Since competition was holding down prices, the rise in real wages also increased buying power, allowing workers to purchase goods previously out of their reach. The dearth of skilled labor made it possible for unions to force a reduction of the working day to eight hours, the abolition of work on Saturday, and the extension of vacation time. Living standards therefore improved dramatically even for the working class.[12]

The extension of the welfare state also contributed to the increase of demand by providing socially disadvantaged groups with the means to purchase consumer goods. The growing prosperity increased national tax receipts, which in turn enabled governments to strengthen the social safety net and spread it to new kinds of recipients. Beyond increasing disbursements for the classic purpose of retirement pensions, health insurance, and unemployment benefits, the welfare bureaucracy discovered the needs of the many victims of World War II such as widows, veterans, and refugees. In the Federal Republic of Germany the Christian Democratic Union government passed an "equalization of burdens law" that authorized massive transfers from people unscathed by the fighting to expellees, bombing casualties, and other victims. As long as tax receipts allowed it, this social policy created increasing numbers of clients who depended on public assistance. In economic terms, welfare checks allowed numerous disadvantaged people to participate in some fashion in prosperity, thereby reinforcing its continuation.[13]

Though communist statistics are unreliable, Eastern Europe also experienced some economic growth, albeit on a more modest scale. While central planning managed to accomplish reconstruction with public direction, the nationalization of industry and collectivization of agriculture virtually eliminated the private sector, stifling initiative. Fulfilling plan targets became the mantra, since allocation decisions were based not on pricing but on bureaucratic decisions, which could ignore production costs. Because supplies were unreliable, large industrial combines called *Kombinate* developed, which manufactured everything from tiny screws to finished automobiles under one roof. Party control of industry inhibited technological innovation since ideological conformity trumped engineering ingenuity. With trade unions transformed into transmission belts, labor had to be mobilized with campaigns and premiums. The economic development of the Soviet Bloc remained mired in smokestack industrialism because it was shielded from world-market competition and therefore failed to generate sufficient advances in technology.[14]

The unparalleled growth during almost an entire generation fundamentally transformed the mental outlook of most Europeans from residual fear to confidence in the future. In western and northern Europe the positive effects of the Economic Miracle were felt in every pocketbook, workplace, and home. In contrast to counting each penny, laboring with worn-out machinery, and living in dilapidated buildings, more and more Europeans had money to spare, used new equipment, and lived in recently built housing blocks with modern conveniences. These encouraging experiences generated a sense of security in the population, transforming change from a potential threat into a positive force. No doubt the advances came slowly enough and reached the southern and eastern nations last—but during the 1950s and 1960s ever more people experienced their blessings or could at least hope to do so in the near future. While the older generation still tended to worry about the recurrence of war and depression, the young grew confident that progress would further improve their lives.[15] Modernity thereby turned from a threat into a boon.

EXPANDING CONSUMPTION

Rising incomes and technological advances transformed the elite's buying of luxury goods into mass consumption of affordable products, making some elements of the good life available to the majority of Europeans. For the first time in history, the spread of affluence allowed people to think beyond subsistence and dream about sharing those items previously reserved for the rich, thereby fulfilling long-held wishes. During the postwar decades, this possibility gradually changed shopping from obtaining food and clothing for physical survival to expressing a lifestyle, opening a seductive world of new experiences that transcended the drudgery of daily routines. Part of this shift was due to the decline of prices through technical inventions in mass production, which made durables more affordable. Part of it was also a response to advances in advertising and merchandising, which awakened new desires that had to be gratified. This transition to a consumer society began to create a new kind of "consumer democracy" that legitimated self-government through mass consumption more successfully than in the interwar period.[16]

One factor reinforcing the desire to consume was technological innovation, which created attractive products and reduced the prices of existing devices. While many appliances such as electric stoves, refrigerators, water heaters, and vacuum cleaners had already been invented around the turn of the century, their refinement made them more convenient for housewives, their chief customers, to use. Other electronic products like television sets and portable record players were newcomers that quickly attracted buyers because they offered unparalleled entertainment possibilities. In contrast to women-oriented household appliances, men bought technical devices like still or movie cameras to inflict slide shows or home movies of the last vacation on family and friends. Through mass production and further development, new products such as pocket calculators got continually cheaper, coming within reach of the lower classes, whose purchases increased the volume of production and thereby further reduced prices. Trade shows and magazines hyped these products, accelerating the introduction of novelties.[17]

Another impulse behind mass consumption was a new, more aggressive form of advertising and marketing. Copying American styles, continental ads no longer just informed about products but sought to stimulate desires by the use of appealing images, colors, and layouts. Creating a fantasy world, they promised to fulfill wishes for beauty or happiness through the purchase of otherwise mundane items loaded with symbolic meaning. Department stores, once limited to the elite, like the Galeries Lafayette, now began to cater to mass tastes; the French chain Carrefour, for example, became a world leader in offering a wide range of merchandise. Another U.S. import was franchising; chains like the German discounter Aldi successively replaced corner grocery stores because of their larger assortments and cheaper prices, based on purchasing volume. When desires exceeded a shopper's means, stores also began offering layaway plans to save up for a big-ticket item or installment credit to pay for it afterward. These merchandising innovations made it easier for consumers to desire, find, and buy products.[18]

One of the most dramatic developments was the increase in individual mobility due to the spread of automobiles and airplane travel. Since in Europe cars were more expensive than in the United States, they had remained a prerogative of the elite, being owned by roughly one-tenth of the population. Most people used bicycles, streetcars, buses, or trains. But after the war motorization took off with a vengeance, first in motorcycles and then also automobiles. By the late 1960s costs had fallen and wages risen sufficiently to allow more than half of the West European households to own a car. Cheap gas prices and public subsidies for the construction of local roads and superhighways made driving automobiles an everyday convenience. At the same time long-distance travel was transformed through the introduction of cheaper and faster jet planes that made far-away destinations suddenly accessible. The impact of motorization on the ground and in the air was profound, since ever more people commuted to work by car while vacations at the shore or in the mountains now became a mass pursuit.[19]

In the countries devastated by the war, the spread of consumption occurred in several successive waves. At first, purchasers sought to satisfy the craving for food, which led men to gorge on meat and potatoes and women to splurge on chocolates or cakes. Then shoppers sought new clothing, advancing from utilitarian garments to fashion statements. Next, many West Europeans turned to shelter, trying to get into an apartment with modern conveniences or even saving up to build their own houses. These new homes needed to be furnished, providing an occasion to throw out the turn-of-the-century stuff and buy functional "modern" Scandinavian furniture, marketed by stores like IKEA. Then the wish to see distant places triggered a travel boom to Mediterranean beaches and Alpine mountains in order to rest up from the pressures of work. This was the chance for package tours in buses, trains, and eventually also airplanes to cart masses of vacationers into concrete silos in the name of leisure.[20] Only after these elemental desires were satisfied came culture, with opera tickets or art vernissages showing one's superior taste.

The crucial agents in these transformations were women as price-conscious consumers, since they determined many of the choices of how money was spent. Men might control technological expenses like the acquisition of a car or a TV set, but housewives purchased the daily food, exerting their preferences over what came to the dinner table. Moreover, women bought and maintained clothing in accordance with their notions of fashion, picking a style appropriate to their social position. Finally, female customers were also instrumental in lobbying for and ultimately choosing the major household appliances, since they were the ones who were actually using them in order to make cooking, cleaning, or sewing easier for themselves. While women were still discriminated against in the workplace, this gendered division of labor gave them consumer power through which they could decide what products and styles would be successful and which ones would languish on the shelves.[21] Their purchasing choices among competing products ultimately created an attractive western lifestyle.

In the Eastern Bloc an alternative communist version of consumer society developed in competition with the western model. Official Soviet influence could be seen in delegations fraternizing with vodka toasts among the nomenklatura; this clashed with the pull of a youth subculture that welcomed Americanization. Initially an economy characterized by scarcity, state socialism did eventually succeed in providing basic necessities, periodic bottlenecks notwithstanding. Rejecting Stalinist curlicues, product designers of plastic dishes joined the international modernist style, producing quite attractive forms. There was even a modest fashion industry catering to the party elite, media personalities, and sports stars. In order to dry up the black market, some countries authorized hard-currency stores, called Intershops in the GDR, where one could buy nonsocialist products with western money. For a while, the bargain between party and population—the granting of modest gains in living standards in exchange for political loyalty—succeeded. But in the long run, the glitzier consumer culture of capitalism destabilized its communist rival.[22]

The visible expression of the emerging consumer society was the construction of pedestrian zones in city centers, which created a distinctly European urbanism. Beginning in the 1950s, the restoration of damaged historical buildings coupled with new glass-and-steel construction produced a unique blend of tradition and modernity that characterized continental cities. The banning of automobile traffic from the centers by building underground garages and maintaining trolleys or buses reduced noise, exhaust fumes, and congestion, allowing people to stroll or bike at their leisure. The diversity of small specialty shops offered an enticing variety of goods that were more expensive than the products of big-box stores but made the shopping experience more interesting. From Copenhagen to Zurich, from Leipzig to Barcelona, crowds would gather in the car-free streets, sit in cafes at squares, listen to street musicians, or admire break-dancers. Without the blight of huge parking lots and the sterility of American shopping malls, European downtowns prospered by offering the pleasures of a livelier and greener urbanity.[23]

LEVELING CLASS DISTINCTIONS

Beyond the rise in prosperity and the spread of consumerism, a fundamental transformation of economic structure tended to decrease social-class differences both in reality and in perception. Growing incomes as well as welfare-state redistribution reduced class distinctions owing to the general improvement of living standards. Moreover, the mass consumption of similar products flattened hierarchies by erasing discrepancies in dress and appearance, shifting clues about one's social status to more subtle variances in style. More important yet was the change in employment patterns in which agriculture declined precipitously, industry peaked, and the service sector expanded considerably. This transformation enhanced individual social mobility and eroded long-standing socioeconomic milieus, blending their members with the rest of society. The concurrent increase in access to education also gave more women a chance for gainful employment. Because of the resulting narrowing of differences, some sociologists began to talk about a convergence on middle-class patterns.[24] Communist critics, however, dismissed this claim as western propaganda.

In a dramatic development, the reduction of labor needed in agriculture sparked a mass exodus to urban jobs. Whereas at the end of the war about two-fifths of the workforce had still been employed on farms, by 1990 only about one-tenth worked on the land. The introduction of better machinery, application of fertilizers and pesticides, use of higher yield crop varieties, and intensive animal husbandry increased the productivity of agriculture impressively. Moreover, the shift from comprehensive subsistence to specialized market production also required fewer hands. Those no longer needed on the land moved to the cities or at least commuted to urban employment. Therefore individual family farms came under great pressure either to increase their scale of production by acquiring more land as well as animals or to give up.[25] More and more farmsteads were deserted, and entire villages began to die out until the counterculture movement of the 1960s brought young ecologists back or wealthy urbanities bought up old farmhouses as weekend homes.

While the working class remained numerous, it ceased to advance further, belying Marx's prediction that it would become ever more dominant. Comprising almost one-half of the workforce by 1970, industrial labor reached the peak of its numbers, cohesion, and influence during the postwar decades. In West European countries most of the workers holding long-term jobs were unionized and also belonged to other voluntary associations such as sports clubs. As a result they succeeded in getting better pay and electing social democratic governments, thereby expanding welfare-state provisions. But especially among younger workers, greater access to education and more participation in consumption such as buying motorcycles, rock records, and hip clothes reduced their visible differences from middle-class youths. Moreover, the shifting of mass production to industrializing countries in Asia also meant that the absolute number of factory workers began to decline, decreasing their share of the workforce to approximately one-third.[26] Together such developments reduced the cohesion of the working-class subculture as well as its political power.

In contrast, the middle class grew in size and importance in the postwar period to over half the workforce while transforming its composition and outlook. The economic recovery especially benefited the propertied bourgeoisie because it revived business opportunities and restored property values, savings, and investments. An increasing number of educated professionals also profited from the rise in prosperity, since it improved their salaries or fees. As a result, the lifestyle and social mores of the middle class became the example to be emulated. The structural growth of the tertiary sector also swelled its numbers, since government and business hired ever more white-collar employees so as to provide essential services. The increasing ranks began to augment the petite bourgeoisie (i.e., lower middle class) and change its character from small independent producers and shopkeepers to dependent but more highly trained salaried employees.[27] With the recovery of its prior advantages and addition of new recruits, the middle class became the dominant stratum in postwar society.

With traditional ruling circles often discredited by Nazi collaboration, a postwar elite also emerged that blended various incompatible ingredients. The landed aristocracy had lost its influence with World War I, while many entrepreneurs and some professionals were discredited by their involvement with fascism. But the redemocratization of the West and the Sovietization of the East created a new group of political leaders, including untainted members of the old elite. Public demand for guidance by experts also propelled some academics and scientists into the limelight. At the same time, the tycoons like Rupert Murdoch who had made great fortunes after the war claimed leading roles and adopted upper-class lifestyles. Finally, the stars of the movies like Gina Lollobrigida, pop music like Charles Aznavour, and professional sports like Eddy Merckx also clamored for attention in glossy magazines. These heterogeneous groups met during public occasions and social functions, gradually coalescing into a new elite.[28] Since there was no agreement on membership criteria, this postwar upper class lacked the traditional cohesion and sense of noblesse oblige.

The loosening in the structure of West European society contributed to decreasing social inequality, although it failed to overcome it completely. Until the mid-1970s, comparative data show a clear reduction of income disparities in the West, since the share gained by top earners declined and the share of the bottom group increased notably. According to most measures, the economic boom and welfare transfers reduced outright poverty, even if its core proved remarkably irreducible. The upheavals of depression, war, and recovery also increased social mobility, since failing members of the elite vacated top positions in the hierarchy, allowing newcomers to move into them. The broadening of educational access created modest gains for working-class children who managed to get secondary education, which enabled their offspring to go to college. Women profited most from the white-collar opportunities, occupying many of the newly created jobs.[29] The broadening of the top and the middle of the social pyramid created an optimistic climate that made class barriers feel less insuperable.

In contrast, the Soviet Bloc tried to reduce inequality through a rigorous egalitarianism that toppled traditional elites, sponsored mobility, and inhibited new distinctions. Nationalization of industry and collectivization of the land did indeed get rid of capitalists and landowners. Moreover, the communist takeover chased bourgeois politicians out and installed a new party elite that controlled political life. Less flamboyant than its predecessor, this nomenklatura nonetheless enjoyed privileges like access to hard-currency stores, special vacation spots, and hunting preserves. Though ideologically out of favor, some remnants of the middle class whose trained services could not be dispensed with survived as technical specialists, medical professionals, or clergymen. For the first generation, the replacement of the old elite created a good deal of mobility, but eventually the nomenklatura became self-perpetuating through educational preferences and career favoritism. This blockage betrayed the egalitarian promise and restratified "real existing socialism" according to political connections or access to western currency.[30]

Complementing the rise in prosperity and turn toward consumer culture, the leveling of social differences also contributed to making modernity seem more welcome. In contrast to the privations of the first postwar years, the return to so-called normalcy proved rather reassuring, because it once again made life patterns predictable. The structural changes of the European economy such as the decline of agriculture, the topping out of industrial labor, and the growth of services also helped reduce tension between the proletariat and the capitalists, since white-collar workers generally embraced middle-class standards. Moreover, easier access to consumer goods and education also reduced mutual hostility, especially in the younger generation. Even if it did not completely eradicate poverty or erase all class distinctions, the reduction of income inequality and the increase in mobility created a more optimistic mood, gradually restoring faith in progress.[31] Unlike the interwar period, when change was disruptive, in the first three decades after World War II modernity began once more to look promising.

TRIUMPH OF MODERNISM

In high culture, the promoters of modernism struggled hard to overcome the determined resistance of the defenders of traditional styles and conservative values. Appalled by the inhumanity and primitivism of the dictatorships, conservative intellectuals sought to salvage elements of the grand European tradition that had not been damaged by collaboration with the Nazis or threatened by communist leveling. During the first postwar decade, cultural institutions like museums were busy recovering their collections while opinion leaders like the German historian Friedrich Meinecke promoted a return to classicism—in his case, through the establishment of Goethe societies. Searching for transcendent values and explanations of their suffering, many people also flocked to the churches for religious consolation. In the schools, leading educators stressed the need to retain Latin and Greek instruction in order to remain conversant with the humanistic heritage. Though they railed against tasteless mass-culture and ideological-indoctrination threats from America and Russia, these pessimistic defenders of European taste and tradition were ultimately unable to keep the onslaught of cultural modernity at bay.[32]

A growing enthusiasm for science and technology that captured the public imagination nonetheless propelled the transition to cultural modernism. Ignoring the danger of unrestricted experimentation, popular magazines, museums of technology, medicine, or natural history, automobile salons, airplane shows, and other purveyors of culture-cum-entertainment portrayed research and development as beneficial. In science, important discoveries like the structure of the DNA molecule in 1953 suggested that with further efforts the very secrets of life could be unlocked and disease combated more effectively. In technology, the development of airplanes from small propeller-driven machines to big transcontinental jets illustrated the blessings of innovation by revolutionizing long-distance travel. As a result, the public welcomed big projects such as the harnessing of atomic energy for peaceful purposes, which created dozens of nuclear power plants all over France. Although Europeans were not directly involved themselves, they were in awe of Soviet and American space exploration, which dramatized the benevolent potential of technology.[33]

An existentialist skepticism also helped to undercut the authority of traditional philosophy by claiming that human beings had to determine the purpose of life themselves. Inspired by Søren Kierkegaard and Martin Heidegger, this outlook captured the loss of faith in traditional authorities in the wake of mass murder and utter destruction. In essays like "Existentialism Is a Humanism" and his novel *Nausea* the French philosopher Jean-Paul Sartre wrestled with concepts such as authenticity, the absurd, and existential despair, suggesting that each person had to find his own way to reaffirm life. The Algerian-born novelist Albert Camus likened this task to the myth of Sisyphus, whose effort to roll a stone uphill remained forever futile but could nonetheless prove meaningful. The Irish playwright Samuel Beckett dramatized this stance in his absurdist play *Waiting for Godot*, in which two characters wait for someone who never comes. Without fully understanding its implications, Parisian Left Bank intellectuals flocked to this philosophy, creating an existentialist style of ennui that was widely imitated.[34] Its biting critique of tradition seemed to clear the path for the radical departures of modernity.

In painting and sculpting, partisans of "modern art" denounced the simplistic realism of the dictators in order to identify their transnational styles with democracy, making them dominant in galleries and museums. Some of the nonrepresentational pioneers like Pablo Picasso and Joan Miró resumed painting in a freer atmosphere. Moreover, aided by European exiles as representatives of "degenerate art," abstract expressionism, invented by New York artists like Jackson

Pollock, radiated back to the continent after the war, inspiring a wave of imitation. This style rejected conventions of representation in order to liberate color and line and to express thought and emotion more freely. Self-consciously experimental, these painters and sculptors kept pushing the boundaries of what could be shown, claiming to represent the discordance of modern life. Initially most of the public was puzzled by the freer forms, but art critics celebrated this new work as liberation from tradition, thereby furthering its acceptance.[35] Through the support of leading galleries the avant-garde artists eventually prevailed, ironically canonizing the stance of protest in turn.

In a similar vein, modern architecture became the leading building style during the postwar decades because its bold forms represented the self-image of a technological age. The credo of "form follows function," which had inspired the angular simplicity of the Bauhaus during the 1920s, was internationalized through the exile to America of its leaders such as Walter Gropius. Rejecting nineteenth-century historicism, architectural modernism no longer sought to hide the new industrial materials like steel, reinforced concrete, and plate glass behind decorative facades but rather to expose or use them as the building's outer surface, making them interesting in their own right. The proponents of this style such as Mies van der Rohe, Le Corbusier, and Oscar Niemeyer designed soaring skyscrapers, factory complexes, and public buildings that were both functional and artistic, achieving an almost classical simplicity. In Tel Aviv these innovators built private residences as "machines for living" with a Mediterranean look: white cubes with huge windows and flat rooftops. Although modernism subdivided into competing movements, it dominated European architecture after World War II.[36]

Modern music was less successful as a version of cultural innovation, since audiences remained somewhat resistant to its dissonant experiments. Rejecting the constraints of late Romanticism, favored by the dictators in Berlin and Leningrad, musicians like Pierre Boulez began experimenting with twelve-tone scales or atonal techniques and pushed toward electronic production or incorporation of other sounds. However, many concertgoers failed to appreciate the discordance, lack of melody, and bewildering rhythms of experimental compositions because they were looking for harmony, melodic line, and rhythmic order. As a result, composers like Paul Hindemith, Sergei Prokofiev, and Benjamin Britten, who returned to an expanded but neoclassical language, were more popular than radical innovators like Karlheinz Stockhausen and Luigi Nono. Justification of dissonance by music critics failed to sway a public looking for pleasure rather than shock. As a result, only a small number of enthusiasts embraced modern music, while the general public only slowly abandoned its skepticism.[37]

The Soviet Bloc struggled to develop its own form of modernity, since accepting the modernist style required overcoming Stalinist prohibitions. There was much enthusiasm for science because Marxism itself claimed to be a scientific ideology, and the Soviet Union managed to send the first satellite into orbit. Also the atheist agitation within the party gave communism an antireligious bias. Many Marxists wanted to dispense with religion as the "opium of the people," though in some countries such as Poland the church retained popular support by allying with nationalism. Stylistically, the majority of the functionaries had a petit-bourgeois taste, oblivious of the close connection between political and artistic radicalism evident in the interwar period. The party's initial preference for "socialist realism" made it difficult for artists to use abstract styles and for writers to dissolve narrative forms. Eventually the pressure of competition prevailed in architecture and consumer design, allowing the use of prefabricated construction methods for apartment blocks and the production of plastic items or furniture for international export. The tension between popular taste and artistic ambition created endless conflicts with an uncertain outcome.[38]

Against stiff opposition, the modernizers gradually prevailed in the West and even the East of Europe because they identified themselves with the future. The defenders of cultured taste and tradition in the churches, conservative circles, and communist parties still controlled many institutions. But the proponents of modernism appealed to the younger generation, which was tired of established conventions and wanted to experiment with creativity. In spite of transatlantic support, it took a series of local confrontations in museums, theaters, and exhibition juries to establish the legitimacy of innovation against the guardians of the canon and to erect daring buildings like the New National Gallery and the Philharmonie concert hall in Berlin.[39] In the Second Vatican Council of 1962–65 even the venerable Catholic Church under the leadership of Pope John XXIII tried to reconcile its teaching to the modern world by switching from Latin to the vernacular language for masses and making other reforms.[40] Ultimately, the arguments of the modernizers proved irresistible, since they portrayed themselves as progressive, fusing artistic experimentation with political democracy.

EXPLOSION OF POPULAR CULTURE

The proliferation of popular culture also contributed to generating positive attitudes toward modernity, because it provided new forms of entertainment for the masses. After suffering depression, war, and reconstruction, the public had an enormous desire for distraction so as to forget the terrible past and the difficult present. The development of new electronic gadgets like the transistor radio and the tape recorder provided access to popular music for people who had not gone to the trouble of learning an instrument. Moreover, the mass production of technical innovations made them affordable for consumers with limited means, augmenting the potential market and creating a huge audience. Since adults were slower to embrace the new equipment, the change was largely driven by the development of a youth subculture, centered on film stars and rock music, which were popularized by fan magazines like *Bravo*.[41] While traditionalists deplored the loss of taste and decorum, young people enjoyed popular culture as newfound freedom, considering themselves more modern than their elders.

One medium was the glossy magazine for sale in newsstands and printed in millions of copies. During the postwar period the paper improved, print became sharper, pictures gained color, and layouts grew bolder. Lavishly illustrated big-format magazines like *Stern* and *Paris Match* offered content ranging from political information to society gossip. Other, more specialized publications like *L'Express* dealt primarily with news, often in a muckraking tone that sought to expose real or imagined scandals. When *Der Spiegel* was suppressed for divulging secrets of a NATO maneuver, the ensuing storm of criticism hastened Adenauer's retirement in 1963.[42] Other publications, like *Brigitte* and *Marie Claire*, targeted specific audiences such as women, while magazines about sports, such as soccer and skiing, or technology, such as cameras and cars, appealed to men. Every hobby generated its own publication, ranging from stamp collecting to beekeeping. In photo essays these magazines offered glimpses into the world of the rich and famous, creating movie or sports stars while exploiting their sexual affairs. Often passed from hand to hand, these magazines purveyed a mixture of information and amusement.[43]

Another popular source of entertainment was the radio, which experienced its golden age during the 1950s. After the war receivers became more powerful and elaborate, including FM, offering stereo sound and incorporating record players in big wooden consoles. In most countries broadcasting was government controlled, financed by mandatory fees rather than advertisements. Initially the family and even neighbors listened together to a single program in the evening, available only regionally. But eventually broadcasting covered the entire day and night, targeting specific daytime audiences such as housewives or schoolchildren and switching to men after work. Surveys revealed that classical music and academic lectures, designed to uplift and edify the public, were quickly overshadowed by dance tunes and variety shows, especially popular among women. In contrast, men were attracted mainly by news and sports, while the young demanded jazz or rock. By the 1960s, the introduction of transistor radios and commercial stations further fragmented programming by addressing ever smaller audiences.[44]

Movies remained the dominant form of entertainment outside the home, setting new records in attendance and box-office receipts. Technical innovations like closer sound and picture synchronization, color film, and wider screens made the experience of viewing ever more lifelike. After the war many European production facilities lay in ruin, offering Hollywood a chance to conquer the continental market, previously dominated by UFA. Talented directors like Roberto Rossellini, Robert Bresson, and Ingmar Bergman nonetheless created modernist films in experimental styles such as neorealism, minimalism, and symbolism, exploring the complications of social deprivation or psychological suffering. Some filmmakers on the left dared confront the terrors of war and genocide directly, but the bulk of movie production continued to provide escapist fare such as the German *Heimatfilm*, which tried to project a comforting sense of home in the midst of the rubble. Partly directed by European émigrés, Hollywood movies were even more successful in creating the illusion of a righteous, if sometimes violent, world through simplistic morality plays such as the Western genre.[45]

During the first half of the 1960s television became the dominant medium in European households, overtaking both radio and film. The increasing quality of picture tubes and diversity of programs attracted millions of viewers, because TV news reports provided the illusion of direct participation in major events like the British queen's coronation or the Olympic Games. Initially TV sets were placed in public gathering or viewing places like bars and shop windows, but steeply dropping prices turned the luxury item into a household necessity. Like radio, TV was originally government controlled, fee financed, and limited to just one channel, but it gradually expanded to multiple channels. Offerings rapidly diversified, supplementing the nightly news with such items as quiz shows, murder mysteries, made-for-television movies, sitcoms, documentaries, and sports events. With their slick production, U.S. serials like *Bonanza* captured a good deal of the market, because language differences made Eurovision efforts difficult. Encouraging domesticity, television quickly became the leading mass medium, widening horizons but also stultifying audiences.[46]

The conquest of popular music by rock 'n' roll also appeared as an element of modernity, since it was part of a youth rebellion against traditional adult taste. French *chansons* and German *Schlager* maintained their appeal to the older generation, but young workers flocked to James Dean films, Bill Haley concerts, and Elvis Presley records during the second half of the 1950s. Heard on the American Forces Network, rock and jazz were popularized by the transnational Radio

Television Luxembourg and broadcast by regular national stations. Despite French radio quotas intended to stem the Anglophone invasion, the exciting rock beat spread irresistibly all over Europe through hit parades, 45 rpm records, portable radios, and tape decks. By abandoning conventional restraint, the amplified volume and primitive lyrics turned rock 'n' roll into a generational style, taking grown-ups' dislike as proof of its rebellious message. The simple melodies and hammering rhythms were easy enough to copy, inspiring garage bands to imitate them.[47] Without understanding the complex American background, continental youths embraced such popular music, since it seemed to be modern and cool.

The most successful European adaptation of American rock was achieved by the British band named the Beatles, whose softer-sounding hits swept the charts during the 1960s. The working-class teenagers John Lennon, Paul McCartney, and George Harrison on guitar, accompanied by the drummer Ringo Starr, started playing rock in local pubs until they got an engagement in Hamburg, where they performed for several years. In 1963 they broke through with the album *Please Please Me*, following up with hits like "A Hard Day's Night" and "Sgt. Pepper's Lonely Hearts Club Band" and movies like *Help*. Their music blended rock influences with folk ballads and psychedelic sound in a pleasing fashion that even included classic elements. With their mop haircuts, fresh faces, drug use, and informal dress, they set off a veritable "Beatlemania," inspiring thousands of female fans to swoon at their concerts. Until breaking up in 1970, they captured the imagination of an entire generation around the globe, selling more records than any other group.[48] The Beatles phenomenon became emblematic of the commercialized youth-protest strand of western modernity.

Communist leaders attempted to develop their own popular culture that would be both entertaining and ideologically reliable. While print products could be kept out by border controls, broadcasts of Radio Free Europe and some West German TV transmissions as well as rock records penetrated the Iron Curtain. This media competition forced the East to follow western patterns of technical developments and program initiatives with some time delay. But radio receivers and

TV sets remained more expensive in relative terms. While the news was highly biased, there were also many entertainment programs and East European films, coupled with didactic documentaries showing antifascist resistance, capitalist repression, and anti-imperialist freedom struggles. Some GDR programs like the children's show *Sandmann* were popular enough to survive the overthrow of communism. But especially in commentary, cabaret, and youth music, programming conflicts continued.[49] Where both could be received, state media lost the competition with commercial western products, since these were more entertaining and credible at the same time.

IMPACT OF AMERICANIZATION

The key concept with which Europeans debated the advance of modernism was Americanization, since they saw many of the new developments as coming from the United States. Quite correctly, they believed that the techniques of scientific management that helped continental business to prosper had been developed in the New World. They also attributed the restless spirit of individual initiative and social mobility to the freedom of America. Moreover commentators thought that U.S. subsidiaries imported more effective forms of merchandising that transformed bourgeois buying into mass consumption. Even in high culture, they assumed that the return of the exiled avant-garde contributed to the victory of modernist styles through stylistic copying or actual remigration. Finally, in popular culture, they used the slogan "coca-colonization" to indicate the transformative power of Hollywood films and rock 'n' roll in reshaping popular lifestyles. Most observers believed that modernization inevitably meant Americanization, making Europe part of the informal U.S. "market empire."[50]

This perceived Americanization of Europe triggered a visceral anti-Americanism among the pessimistic enemies of modernity. Continental elites had a long history of criticizing U.S. egalitarianism, fearing the rule of the masses as a dangerous form of populism. European competitors complained about the aggressive business practices of American companies, while trade unions deplored the antilabor bias of U.S. market capitalism. Defenders of high culture railed against the lack of tradition and refinement in the New World, seeing a cultural wasteland characterized as "barbarism." Some of these strictures contained elements of racism, decrying "miscegenation" between whites and blacks or spreading a conspiratorial version of anti-Semitism. During the Cold War, the European Left also accused the United States of capitalist exploitation and of pursuing neoimperialist designs of world domination. Though such charges at best exaggerated some negative aspects of the American record, they found a credulous audience among those Europeans who resented their own political impotence and inability to stop the advance of popular culture.[51]

Overriding such objections, Americanization nonetheless proved seductive, because it represented a renewed and confident version of liberal democratic modernity. Beyond the appeal of Marxism-Leninism to intellectuals, Sovietization required force, wielded by the Soviet army, the local communist party, and the secret service. In contrast, the American "empire by invitation" promised security during the Cold War and relied more on its clients' voluntary cooperation. In the displays, lectures, and films of America Houses, the United States appeared as a land of peace, prosperity, and freedom—an attractive utopia to which Europeans might aspire as well, if they put their murderous past behind them. Moreover, the American version of modernity proceeded less by central plan than by the multiple efforts of diplomats, business managers, academic scholars, film directors, and recording artists, proving much harder to repel.[52] Finally, most of the representative Americans, like the friendly GIs, seemed more likable than Soviet functionaries. As a result, many Europeans such as the young found modernity in its American guise quite irresistible.

The popular equation between Americanization and modernization was nonetheless misleading since it exaggerated the modernity of the United States and overlooked European innovation. Large parts of the United States, such as rural areas and the old South, remained rather traditional, as the strength of religious observance, the creationist anti-intellectualism, and the lingering racism showed.

At the same time, many of the innovative developments in industry, society, and culture had originated in Europe, being reintroduced or revived after the Second World War on their own accord. The defeated countries especially, whose traditions had been destroyed along with their buildings, welcomed American imports as a short-cut toward democratic modernity. But among the proud victors, resistance was stronger. In France, for example, not only the Gaullists but also the Left tried to defend their own *civilisation* by means of a quota system for broadcast content. Within the broader rubric of Western civilization, a contest developed between the pressure of market-driven Americanization and the preservation of a distinctive European version of liberal modernity favoring the welfare state.[53]

Modernity ultimately prevailed in the postwar decades because it blended American and European elements in a transatlantic hybrid, containing elements of both. Cultural influence was no one-way street, as the Europeanization of American high cuisine, the spread of youth soccer, and the popularity of the Beatles indicated. Of course, Europeans also picked up many ideas from the United States, ranging from the controversial BA degree of the Bologna process to the golden arches of McDonald's "gracing" historic buildings. Much of this hybridization was promoted by the travel of thousands of American backpacking tourists riding European trains each summer and hordes of pale Europeans invading Florida beaches during the winter. In high and popular culture well-known music performers, movie stars, and even public intellectuals started to function in an international hyperspace, jetting from their shows and condos on one continent to the other. Overcoming the legacy of depression, war, and genocide, this blended modernity became attractive because it promised access to an exciting world of transatlantic interchange.[54]

Chapter 21

PLANNING SOCIAL REFORM

Satellite city Sarcelles, 1963. *Source*: Getty Images.

Ten miles outside Paris the high-rise apartments of Sarcelles jut into the sky, punctuating the once bucolic landscape with concrete towers as a "true city of the future." Built in three phases from the mid-1950s to the mid-1970s, this *grand ensemble* began as a solution to the postwar housing crisis but subsequently developed into a showcase of architectural modernism. Its promoters were both social reformers seeking to restore the health of the family and architects trying to develop an urban design that would "constitute *a harbor of peace and tranquility for modern man.*" The resulting mix of 12,331 apartments, shops, parking areas, streets, and green spaces was carefully laid out to create the feeling of a community, offering a leisure space in which to regenerate for work. Tired of the cramped and decrepit apartments of older cities, renters flocked to the development in hopes of a better life, defined by modern conveniences such as indoor plumbing and electric stoves.[1] Even if they differed in details, similar satellite towns sprang up all over Europe during the 1960s, epitomizing the optimism of social engineering.

In 1965 the jurist Joseph H. Kaiser articulated this renewed confidence in the possibility of progress by scientific design: "Planning is the great tendency of our times.... Planning is the systematic blueprint of a rational order on the basis of all available knowledge." While cultural pessimists considered the future unknowable and economic liberals objected to regimentation, many scientists, journalists, and politicians began to believe that it was possible to predict what was going to happen and to make decisions accordingly. Overwhelmed by what they considered to be the rapid pace of economic growth, social change, and cultural experimentation, observers felt that piecemeal reactions did not suffice any longer. Instead, systematic plans were needed in order to guide such development. Ignoring philosophical objections, the public was willing to endorse transportation planning in order to accommodate the increasing numbers of automobiles clogging urban streets. At the same time, behavioral scientists claimed to offer research-based solutions to social problems, shifting policy arguments from opinions to evidence.[2]

This turn toward social planning responded to the widespread preoccupation with shaping the future as a method of anticipating and directing coming developments. In literature and film, the genre of science fiction gained popularity in the 1960s by appealing to the public as speculation about the potential consequences of space exploration. Its attraction derived from a peculiar blend of technological fantasies with dreams of social alternatives, alternating between utopia and dystopia.[3] Only slightly more respectable was the academic discipline of "futurology," promoted by Bertrand de Jouvenel and Robert Jungk, which aspired to finding a systematic, scientific method of making prognoses about what was to come. The establishment of think tanks and professorships concerned with the future resulted from the desire of governments and corporations to predict developments in order to minimize the risks of erroneous decisions. Reinforced by the emergence of mainframe computers, the new interdisciplinary science of cybernetics promised to handle the complexities of advanced industrial society in both the East and West, leading to hopes for a convergence of market with plan.[4]

This optimistic outlook was based on shared assumptions about modernization that transcended the Iron Curtain but possessed limitations that became visible only in retrospect. One common belief was that technological innovation was benign and would provide ever more ingenious ways of reducing the need for labor. Another conviction, due to the postwar boom, was the presupposition that economic growth would automatically continue as long as there were no new wars. Perhaps even more important was the notion that society was basically plastic, amenable to being shaped by political decisions. Yet another premise implied that scientific research, institutionalized in various advisory bodies, could provide empirical data as well as objective interpretations that ought to guide actual decisions. As a result, politics would become more rational and efficient, no longer consisting of struggles over ideology but rather turning into an effort to implement scientific recommendations. Propelled by experts, this enthusiasm for social planning was the high point of classical modernity, since it recovered the lost faith in progress through human rationality.[5]

This planning effort modernized the face of Europe during the postwar decades but fell short of achieving a perfect society. While all levels of planning played a crucial role in organizing reconstruction, the direction of that effort remained highly contested. During the postwar boom, the revival of western growth was largely a consequence of the return to market competition, moderated by a neo-Keynesian approach to government direction that encouraged corporatist cooperation between management and labor.[6] Planning cities for automobile traffic, designing satellite towns, and building commercial space created an urban landscape of concrete, steel, and glass—comprising not only buildings but also much of the space between them—whose technocratic inhumanity provoked a counterimpulse of restoring and reviving older neighborhoods. Similarly the drastic expansion of secondary and tertiary education, which broadened social mobility, also alienated many of the new graduates. Finally, the expansion of welfare benefits created greater equality but also involved costs that triggered resentment. Ironically, the very success of modern planning eventually limited its further advance.

ORGANIZING RECONSTRUCTION

In contrast to the Anglo-American credo of free trade, continental Europeans had a long history of state involvement in the economy. Memories of the mercantilism pursued by absolutist rulers facilitated government guidance during catch-up industrialization, even in the liberal nineteenth-century interlude that favored market competition. After the Second World War, the deep trauma of the Great Depression predisposed the public toward statist measures to prevent its recurrence, while socialist agitation called for nationalization of key sectors of industry and redistribution of land. Moreover, the experience of wartime coordination of the economy also militated in favor of public coordination of rebuilding efforts. While everyone agreed that the most onerous controls such as rationing cards for food and clothing ought to be lifted, opinions were divided over the course to be followed in the future. Socialist supporters of government organization of the economy so as to create a more egalitarian society clashed with liberal advocates of the free play of the market in order to ignite growth.[7]

One extreme was the communist course of economic planning in the hope of duplicating the success of Soviet industrialization in Eastern Europe. In part, Marxist-Leninists wanted to fulfill the aspirations of the labor movement to end capitalist exploitation by nationalizing industry and breaking up landed estates. In part, they sincerely believed in eliminating pricing as a method of allocating resources and replacing the individual profit motive with a collective sense of social responsibility. The mechanism for achieving such a lofty aim was the plan. In the most general sense, the party set economic priorities that functioned as an overall framework. In a more specific application, industrial managers formulated targets for their factories such as raw-material needs, labor requirements, and production goals, based on prior performance. These competing individual plans were then coordinated by a central planning bureaucracy, which aggregated their goals into an overall design for the next three to five years. For rebuilding the war damage and forced industrialization this system functioned reasonably well.[8]

In contrast, the Scandinavian model, promoted by progressive scholars like the economist Gunnar Myrdal, rested on a compromise between market freedom and welfare support. When the Swedish Social Democrats were elected in 1932, they had agreed with business leaders on a compromise that established a broad array of social protections but preserved free trade and private property. Following the vision of a people's home (*folkhemmet*), they created a safety net with high unemployment and pension benefits, authorizing as well sizable transfer payments that drastically reduced the number of the poor. Since this approach had proven successful in fighting the effects of the Great Depression, the Nordic states extended it further after the war, creating the most extensive welfare states in the West. Of course, such social supports required high public spending and some of the steepest income taxes in Europe, averaging around 50 percent. But in most international comparisons of well-being the Scandinavian countries ranked at the top of the scale, while surveys of life satisfaction inevitably also showed them in the lead.[9]

The French planning for postwar reconstruction was less generous but animated by a similar spirit. Convinced that France "must modernize," Jean Monnet sent "Proposals for a Modernization and Investment Plan" to President Charles de Gaulle in December 1945, which led to the establishment of a Commissariat Général du Plan. This planning commission set goals to be achieved and requested the necessary resources for twenty-four key industries. Starting as a response to the postwar crisis, the Monnet Plan tried to renew the basic infrastructure so as to make France more competitive with its eastern neighbor. In many ways this approach was a product of Parisian centralization promoted by the elite graduates of the *hautes écoles*, who wanted to direct economic affairs in the provinces from the capital. Based on a large nationalized sector of the economy, the French plan proposed a strategy of investment helped by American loans and intended to put the country back on its feet. Since it thereby reenergized private business, this plan generally succeeded in launching postwar recovery and modernizing the French economy.[10]

Though forced to cope with austerity, Britain's key effort focused on the introduction of a modern welfare state as compensation for the wartime effort of the lower classes. The victorious Labour government did nationalize some industries like the railroads but gave more attention to implementation of the Beveridge Report, which proposed minimum standards of social protection. With breathtaking boldness, the Attlee cabinet introduced a series of measures such as the National Insurance Act of 1946, which provided sickness, unemployment, retirement, maternity, orphan, and death benefits through one comprehensive payment by most working citizens, deducted from their wages or salaries. Moreover, this initiative was complemented by family allowances, accident insurance, and national assistance for the poor. The most ambitious legislation, championed by Aneurin Bevan, was the controversial introduction of the National Health Service, which socialized the provision of medical care to be paid out of tax receipts.[11] While leaving private business largely untouched, this impressive package of welfare measures vastly expanded the scope of government action for important sectors of society.

In contrast, defeated and devastated West Germany tried to escape from an excess of state control in order to revive the largest economy on the continent. While Nazi measures were quickly repudiated, the underlying cartel structures proved more difficult to undo. Concerned with preventing a revival of German military power, the victorious occupiers moreover insisted on large-scale dismantling of factories and lowering industrial production levels in order to pastoralize the country. Since these Allied plans were only gradually revised upward, the reemerging German authorities were forced to administer aid to a population facing severe deprivation: they had to provide a minimum of food (twelve hundred calories per day), assign cramped emergency housing, and distribute scarce heating materials. In this dire situation, calls for nationalization of industry and for distribution of estate land to farmers found a receptive audience even in bourgeois Christian Democratic Union circles. Only a small minority of liberal economists followed Friedrich von Hayek's call in *The Road to Serfdom* and argued vigorously for a lifting of restrictions in order to have the dynamism of the free market spark a recovery.[12]

American pressure and assistance, however, kept Western Europe from experimenting further with socialist planning and led to a return to the free market. While some New Dealers sympathized with welfare reforms, on balance U.S. elites were rather inclined to favor capitalist competition. In occupied Germany the American veto stopped nationalization drives in Hesse and North-Rhine Westphalia, limiting the socializing impulse to codetermination between management and labor. In Western Europe direct U.S. loans as well as the Marshall Plan and indirect financial assistance through the OEEC helped revive private enterprise and allowed competition to recover. Moreover, the dynamic growth of the American economy was an attractive example of what an unrestricted market at home and free trade between nations could accomplish. Encouraged by exchange programs and service clubs like Rotary and Lions, European business leaders therefore strove to emulate this example and positioned themselves in domestic debates in favor of reducing the role of the state and returning to competition.[13]

Ultimately the superior performance of the market over the plan tipped the balance in favor of free enterprise, albeit within the framework of welfare-state expansion. Once the initial balance-of-payments crisis was solved, the western market economies outperformed the East European planned competitors, even if one were to believe the inflated socialist statistics. The fastest-growing economies were those of the FRG, led by Ludwig Erhard, as well as Austria and the Netherlands. They profited from the abolition of restrictions, low unit costs, a favorable mix of basic and consumer industries, sizable reinvestment of earnings, an export-oriented structure, and a cooperative workforce supported by welfare-state measures. Helped by flexible planning and coordination, France and Italy grew somewhat more slowly, since their labor relations were more contentious. Great Britain, Belgium, and Ireland were the laggards, partly because they started at a higher level, partly because their productivity gains remained lower.[14] Though the mix differed between various countries, postwar modernization was propelled by the compromise of a social market economy.

ECONOMIC PLANNING

After the return to the free market during the 1950s, the new "planning fervor" of the 1960s in Western Europe was all the more surprising. In many ways the turn toward thinking ahead was a response to the pace of technological innovation, which required public investments in such areas as the building of transmission towers for television signals. While a piecemeal approach of local rebuilding sufficed to repair most of the housing damage, a more coordinated effort was needed to move ahead and find new ways to meet the demand for better habitation. Moreover, both conservative and labor parties agreed on the need to find a way to sustain growth so as to increase prosperity and reap the blessings of consumer society. At the same time engineers and scientists also offered solutions like nuclear power to satisfy the growing demand for electricity and statistical methods to evaluate the performance of the economy.[15] This constellation produced a euphoric sense of possibility that promised to reap the rewards of a benign modernization, if only the necessary changes were planned systematically.

Ironically some pioneers of planning in Eastern Europe were concurrently seeking to modify their bureaucratic system by reintroducing market incentives. It had been easier to gain control of the commanding heights of the economy than to administer the details of business exchanges as long as pricing reflected political decisions rather than actual costs as well as supply and demand. Moreover, the amount of information needed by the planning commission exceeded the capacity to process it, since mainframe computers were just beginning to come on line. At the same time the administrative choices proved too cumbersome. If forecasts for a warm summer, for which bathing suits were needed, turned out to be wrong, it was impossible to switch quickly enough to umbrellas to fend off the rain. East German planners like Erich Apel and Czech economists like Ota Šik therefore advocated a return to some market mechanisms in order to motivate workers, exchange goods efficiently, and meet consumer desires. But ultimately their efforts to modify the command economy foundered on the communist parties' resolution to maintain political control.[16]

Undeterred by these negative experiences, the Commission of the European Economic Community in October 1962 initiated a western discussion about economic planning. Its memorandum for the second stage of European integration called for "an overview over its future development for several years." Inspired by the French example of *planification*, it differed from communist control by offering only "a framework" for coordinating the measures of the governments and community institutions in order to develop a stability-oriented growth policy. The purpose of this initiative was to harmonize the divergent national policies with the strategy of the European Commission. Liberals like German economics minister Ludwig Erhard were appalled and rejected this "economic fashion," since it reeked of state interference. But the Left was rather delighted, since the proposal agreed with its inclination to extend the welfare state. Moreover, most economists, organized in councils of economic advisers since the late 1950s, were only too happy to assist governments with recommendations, based on macroeconomic statistics.[17]

The French model of dirigisme was a moderately successful form of planning the modernization of the economy by setting goals, providing investment, and creating incentives. Paris controlled an extensive state sector in railroads (SNCF), communication (PTT), power (EDF), and airlines (Air France) while at the same time investing in key sectors like automobile production. The Planning Commission defined general targets, directed investment, and used inducements rather than micromanaging, thereby guiding rather than replacing private business. The definition of priorities and the consolidation of companies into national champions that would be internationally competitive scored some remarkable successes such as the development of high-speed trains (TGV) and the proliferation of nuclear power plants. But government direction also produced spectacular failures that were not commercially viable such as the Minitel telephone-computer hybrid as well as the supersonic Concorde airplane. Moreover, the fragmented trade unions exacted wage concessions that made large companies like Renault uncompetitive.[18]

Reluctantly Britain also turned to state planning in order to compensate for its disappointing growth rate, which was only half the European average. To modernize industry and increase productivity, even the Conservative government in 1961, prodded by Selwyn Lloyd, set up a National Economic Development Committee in order to recommend measures to achieve better results. But Prime Minister Harold Macmillan's effort to get the Trade Union Congress (TUC) and the employers' associations to agree to moderate wage increases failed because of deep-seated mutual suspicion. After the Labour victory in 1964, the Wilson cabinet created an entirely new Department of Economic Affairs under George Brown to draft a comprehensive National Plan in the hope of greater TUC cooperation. Based on inadequate statistical data, the targeted growth rate of 4 percent per annum turned out to be too ambitious, since the British economy proved to be too complex to be directed from above and the underlying structures were too fragmented to be coerced into cooperation. As a result, the public grew disenchanted, dooming the effort to failure.[19]

Deterred by these problematic examples, the Federal Republic of Germany moved toward economic planning only in response to the first postwar recession in 1966–67. The pause in growth and small rise in unemployment were so shocking that they cost Ludwig Erhard his chancellorship, initiating a Grand Coalition between the Christian Democrats (CDU) and the Social Democrats (SPD) in Bonn. By endangering the fruits of the Economic Miracle, this unexpected downturn gave the Social Democratic economist Karl Schiller the chance to argue for a countercyclical growth program and a rational plan for future economic development, while the conservative Bavarian (CSU) politician Franz Josef Strauß attempted to rebalance the budget. Enshrined in the Stability Law of June 1967, Schiller's program was in effect a neo-Keynesian effort to surmount the recession and to prevent future setbacks through a "global direction of the economy." Inspired by the concurrent American discussions of a "new economics," this effort tried to balance the competing goals of currency stability with a resumption of economic growth.[20]

In practice Schiller's approach relied on the "concerted action" of management and labor, moderated by government, in pursuit of stable growth. Presented with convincing rhetoric, this concept pursued a "magic quadrangle" of aims. The top priority was price stability in order to assuage inflation fears; almost equally important was full employment so as to prevent a recurrence of the Great Depression; another goal was a balanced international trade for the sake of keeping exports flowing; and its capstone was an appropriate level of economic expansion for financing the welfare state. Since this vision was supported by the Council of Economic Advisers, created in 1962, both management and labor were persuaded to cooperate, with the former willing to invest and the latter restraining its wage demands. When growth quickly resumed because of greater liquidity and a revival of exports, it seemed that the countercyclical approach had been successful. For the next half decade this soft version of indicator-driven planning dominated German economic policy, since it was clothed in "an aura of progressiveness."[21]

Encouraged by the return of expansion, the planning consensus was ready to tackle a number of other reforms. In the Federal Republic the victory of the social-liberal coalition under Willy Brandt in the 1969 election installed Horst Ehmke in the chancellor's office in order to undertake systematic policy planning. One big challenge was the modernization of the bureaucracy to streamline organization, eliminate redundant personnel, and make it more efficient. Another task was the dissolution of small administrative districts and their recombination into larger units better capable of providing necessary service. With the slogan "dare more democracy," the coalition undertook a whole raft of reforms to modernize the Federal Republic.[22] However, since planning the development of an entire society was too complex to be realized in practice, planners subsequently focused on more specific areas like housing, education, and welfare. But until the fixed exchange rates of Bretton Woods collapsed and the Oil Shocks eroded the economic basis for additional initiatives, European elites faced the future with renewed optimism, confident that rational analysis could solve any problems that might arise.

URBAN DESIGN

One particular area in which planning played a central role was the resolution of the postwar housing crisis in those regions in Europe that had been subjected to bombing or ground combat. Photographs of Rotterdam, Coventry, Warsaw, Cologne, and Dresden, just to mention some of the most affected cities, show a moonscape of devastation with hardly a wall left standing. Not only was no new housing built during the Second World War; about half the available units were destroyed or damaged. While DPs and POWs hoped to go home or emigrate, millions of refugees poured into Central Europe, compounding the scarcity. People crowded into bunkers, basements, barracks, or barns—anywhere they could find some shelter from the elements. As a result municipal authorities had to redistribute the scarce housing, assigning strangers to families living in dwellings that had survived more or less intact.[23] The resulting overcrowding and unsanitary conditions required public investment, since piecemeal private reconstruction remained clearly inadequate.

European governments responded to the housing shortage by financing the rapid construction of low-rent apartment blocks in order to get the people off the streets. Continuing the social experiments of the 1920s, the British Labour cabinet set out to replace four million damaged units through "council houses" sponsored by local authorities. In Germany an even more ambitious program was called *sozialer Wohnungsbau*, since it provided subsidies to municipalities or cooperatives for the erection of unpretentious apartments in the gaps between the remaining buildings. Spurred by the uncommonly cold winter of 1946–47, this public effort attempted to create basic housing that would allow families to reconstitute themselves and daily life to return to a semblance of normalcy. The buildings tended to be simple multistory affairs and the individual units relatively small, but they at least had indoor plumbing. State subsidies kept rents low enough to be affordable for workers or impoverished middle-class occupants who could not afford to pay the rapidly rising prices of the commercial market.[24]

Once the immediate emergency had passed, urban planners were confronted with rising expectations for better accommodations. The demand for new housing continued to increase, since the decline of agriculture pushed former farm laborers into cities, while the fragmentation of families augmented the number of independent households. At the same time the old dwellings deteriorated, and many would never meet higher standards for comfort. The public started to demand more space per individual occupant, insisting on the privacy of separate bedrooms for each child, and at the same time also expected modern conveniences such as a shower-bath, central heating, or an electric kitchen. Moreover, the progress of motorization required the construction of new streets, highways, garages, and parking lots. The pressure to build additional units forced planners to rethink the entire layout of cities, figuring out where to construct clusters of apartment buildings, cut thoroughfares, and locate centers for shopping, even including some new churches.[25]

Aided by increasing prosperity, the continuing demand for housing provided architects and construction companies with an unprecedented opportunity to design novel high-rise cities. In international building exhibitions such as the Berlin IBA of 1957 the stars of the architecture scene—Le Corbusier, Eero Saarinen, Oscar Niemeyer, Walter Gropius—vied with each other in proposing futuristic visions of urban space. Disregarding the weight of tradition and the context of existing buildings, their modernist style emphasized steel, glass, and concrete slabs, creating skyscrapers situated in parklike green spaces connected by roads and supplied with clusters of shopping infrastructure. The leading construction firms embraced such designs because building large-scale high-rise apartments with prefabricated materials was easier than erecting detached single-family homes. Politicians endorsed the architects' exciting blueprints, since they promised a cheap way of creating entire new quarters of cities, thereby rapidly providing housing for the masses.[26]

The cooperation between ambitious architects, construction companies, and political leaders produced new satellite cities like Sarcelles, entirely determined at the designer's table. In 1956 Hans Werner Reichow used four hundred hectares outside the West German manufacturing center Bielefeld to create a novel suburb called Sennestadt. In order to accommodate expellees and refugees from Eastern Europe, he developed a plan for a mixture of high-rises, regular apartments, and row houses along curving streets and under pine trees. Accessible by tram, bus, and road, this satellite town had a friendly feeling. In contrast, the East German project of Halle-Neustadt, a.k.a. "Chemical Workers' City," set out to accommodate workers for the nearby "chemical triangle" of industrial sites. Approved in 1963 and designed by Richard Paulinck, it used only prefabricated high-rise buildings, separated by some green spaces, in order to establish a socialist model city. But from the beginning it was plagued by shortages, had an insufficient commercial infrastructure, and therefore developed into a sterile bedroom community.[27] During the 1960s similar peripheral settlements sprang up all over Europe.

With only minor alterations, the methods used for building satellite towns could also be applied to renewal of the declining inner cities or special problem areas. Neglected by the new construction boom, older urban districts and unused areas like abandoned waterfronts had become decrepit and unattractive. As a result migrants and the new poor congregated there, often using drugs and attracting crime. Since refurbishing seemed too expensive, communist leaders in the East simply called in bulldozers and built new prefab apartment complexes in the cleared space regardless of the architectural value being lost. In the West the more innocuous term "urban redevelopment" through public subsidies or private tax incentives also implied evicting tenants, tearing down dilapidated buildings, and replacing them with faceless concrete structures. In some cities like Manchester, in the United Kingdom, the "slum clearance" approach resulted in impressive but lifeless central districts, whereas in the London dockyards the new investment sparked a colorful mixed-use economy that later proved attractive to tourists.[28]

Not surprisingly, responses to this kind of urban modernization varied considerably. For the promoters of urban reform like the architect of Sarcelles, such towns were model suburban islands that followed Le Corbusier's injunction to live, work, relax, and circulate, marking "a lifestyle evolution" for humanity. Having escaped from their run-down firetraps, many of the new buildings' inhabitants also appreciated the larger size and technical conveniences of their apartments, which were a definite step up in comfort. But one critical psychiatrist diagnosed, in these faceless high-rise apartment blocks, a new disease he called *sarcellite*, that affected especially women through "menstrual irregularities, gastrointestinal hypermotility, false cardiac-arrest, tachycardia, extra systoles, anxiety," and so on. Similarly a socialist journalist was appalled by the sterility of the modernist design. Hyperbolically, he claimed that in contrast to the men, whose lives gained variety through work, the women staying behind were afflicted by a "kind of stupor," feeling as if they were "living in a dead city, placed in a space without real location, almost the same as purgatory."[29]

As a result of such criticism, the pendulum of planning fashions eventually swung away from satellite towns and urban renewal toward an incremental reclamation of older city districts, sometimes helped by public funds. From the 1970s on citizens' initiatives opposed the construction of superhighways through their neighborhoods as well as the tearing down of buildings, rejecting the logic of architectural modernism. At the same time younger professionals rediscovered the charm of Victorian apartments with parquet floors, high ceilings, and stucco trim, deciding to renovate historic structures while adding new kitchens or bathrooms. Such conversion of older buildings was called gentrification because it was typically accompanied by the influx of wealthier residents, the new in-town "gentry," who brought with them an upscale and countercultural lifestyle. The successive transformation of neighborhoods like Prenzlauer Berg in Berlin thus created new conflicts, since increasing rents and condo conversions displaced older and poorer residents.[30] But on the whole, this revival has been benign, since it preserved more complex and humane living spaces.

EDUCATIONAL EXPANSION

Another field of planned reform was the expansion of European education, which seemed increasingly inadequate for the demands of modern life. Though producing distinguished scholarship, the traditional system consisted of a pyramid with a broad primary base, followed by a much narrower pillar of secondary schools and ending in a thin column of universities for the elite. Access was socially stratified, with working-class children getting only elementary instruction, the middle class completing a longer course while acquiring some foreign languages, and only the future professionals being exposed to higher learning and academic research. The great majority of youths were funneled into apprenticeships where they were prepared for practical occupations. Moreover, the secondary school curriculum was still dominated by the classics rather than modern subjects, and technical training was considered socially inferior. With the Sputnik shock in 1957 it became obvious that such a structure was incapable of coping with the challenges of technological innovation in an emerging service economy.[31]

Although expansion had already begun, in various countries a chorus of critics vehemently demanded a reform of education during the 1960s. For instance, in the Federal Republic, the publicist Georg Picht created a stir with a series of articles on the "crisis of education" in 1964, charging that there were too few graduates and that the conditions in the schools were deplorable. The liberal sociologist Ralf

Dahrendorf went even further, claiming that education was "a general citizenship right," pointing out that children from the working class, rural and Catholic homes, as well as girls were drastically underrepresented in secondary and tertiary institutions. Calling for "investment in education," industrialists also criticized the traditional content of the curriculum, demanding more instruction in science and mathematics as well as modern languages. The conservative defenders of the stratified system responded that any changes would water down quality and endanger the transmission of cultural heritage.[32] Yet buoyed by reform euphoria, the demand for greater "equality of opportunity" ultimately prevailed.

The communists in Eastern Europe implemented the most radical reform of education by largely transferring the Soviet system. Considering the schools as a seedbed of reaction, the party demanded a purge of teachers and an antifascist revision of instructional content. Intent on realizing the labor movement's call for "breaking the educational privilege" of the bourgeoisie, the communists made strenuous efforts to advance children of workers and farmers, often formally excluding the offspring of professionals. Considering the classical curriculum irrelevant, the functionaries insisted on "polytechnic training," sending classes into the factories for one day each week in order to get acquainted with the working world. The introduction of comprehensive secondary schools was a progressive move, but the requirement of political loyalty showed that education was instrumentalized for the maintenance of party power. While such reforms increased attendance in secondary schools, strict manpower management constrained individual choice and limited university study to about one-fifth of the age group, half of the western average.[33]

In Western Europe, the modernization of the educational system proceeded more incrementally, favoring expansion over reformation of content. The first task was the enforcement of actual school attendance through the primary grades to erase illiteracy in the Mediterranean and Balkan countries. A second effort concerned the raising of the length of schooling from age ten to sixteen, accomplished in Britain by 1972. Another step forward was the abolition of separate religious schools in Germany, so that all children attended secular institutions, though confessional instruction continued in Catholic states like Italy. At the same time rural minischools with one or two classes were consolidated into larger institutions with a full complement of age grades. Especially in Scandinavia and France, preschool offerings and kindergartens were expanded in order to make it possible for mothers to work. Finally, teacher training was upgraded in most countries and made part of higher education. Together these efforts noticeably improved learning outcomes, although they were unable to eliminate all peculiarities like half-day instruction in the FRG.[34]

Pedagogical planners also promoted the expansion of secondary education in order to widen social access by producing more graduates. Reformers campaigned especially among skeptical working-class parents to send their gifted children on to high school so as to give them a chance to move up into white-collar occupations. To facilitate access, existing institutions were expanded and many new schools built in industrial districts and small towns. At the same time the curriculum was updated, jettisoning Greek and reducing Latin in favor of modern languages like English, with additional emphasis placed on the natural sciences and mathematics. In many countries the old divisions between different types of secondary institutions were abolished and the higher age grades included in comprehensive schools, even if some traditionalists tried to defend the classical *Gymnasium*. These efforts made continuing schooling more attractive to girls and Catholics. But raising the proportion of graduates in an age cohort from 10 percent to over two-thirds by the end of the century also devalued the diploma and broke the link with the "entitlement system" that had hitherto guaranteed attractive government jobs.[35]

Higher education experienced an equally dramatic construction boom in existing institutions as well as new foundations. The growth in high school graduates led to a steep increase in the number of university students from about 4 percent to 30 percent of an age cohort by 1990, which threatened to overwhelm traditional instruction. Education planners responded to this overcrowding with four strategies: they tried to raise the capacity of older campuses through adding classroom space; they upgraded pedagogical academies and technical schools to university status; they founded a spate of new institutions; and they tried to transform technical colleges into universities by adding humanities and social sciences. For instance, during the 1960s Britain created twenty new "plate-glass" universities (as opposed to the older "red brick" civic universities and the prestigious "ancient" Cambridge and Oxford). In France the Parisian Sorbonne swelled to several hundred thousand students, forcing it to divide into thirteen campuses. In Germany, several dozen industrial-looking universities were built in Bochum, Bielefeld, Konstanz, and the like. The resulting transition to mass higher education relieved some of the pressure but created new feelings of alienation in turn that would inspire the student revolt.[36]

The last beneficiary of the educational expansion of the 1960s was research in independent centers and institutes outside the universities. The rapidity of technological development and the rise of the social sciences rendered the traditional academy model of a learned society inadequate. In the Eastern Bloc, the academy name was kept, but the institution vastly expanded, following the Soviet model, to house research institutes for basic and applied science with thousands of employees. Similarly ambitious was the huge French Centre des Recherches Scientifiques (CNRS), which also focused on the natural sciences and on technology, with just a nod to the social sciences. In contrast, the Federal Republic chose a decentralized model of several hundred independent institutes, loosely coordinated in the Max Planck, Fraunhofer, Helmholtz and Leibnitz societies. Britain retained more advanced research in its leading universities, supported by grants from the Research Council. These institutions kept Europe competitive in Nobel prizes by greatly increasing the amount and quality of extrauniversity research.[37]

Public responses to the modernization of all levels of education remained nonetheless ambivalent, since the new opportunities also created unforeseen problems. Unquestionably, the numerical growth raised levels of literacy, improved citizens' understanding of complex issues, and widened social access for underprivileged groups such as women and working-class children. Moreover, the doubling or tripling of staff provided career opportunities for an entire generation of teachers, professors, and researchers who now became part of a self-sustaining academic enterprise. But the unparalleled enlargement soon reached its limits, since costs of maintaining a bigger system rose to unsustainable levels and the increase in size also made managing the system more complicated. Many of the new pupils and students who came from educationally disadvantaged backgrounds felt alienated from their less-educated parents and strange in a system that had been designed for the cultivated taste of the *Bildungsbürgertum*.[38] The very success of the expansion therefore posed new challenges of having to alter pedagogical methods, change curriculum content, and liberalize authority relations.

WELFARE STATE

The most popular project of reformist planners was the expansion of the welfare state, which reached its high point in the early 1970s. Ironically, it was the conservative statesman Otto von Bismarck who had a century before introduced social insurance so as to stop the spread of Marxism by giving workers "a stake in society" with protection against old age, illness, and unemployment. Britain moved toward a similar scheme under the Liberal Asquith cabinet before the First World War, while in France it took the Popular Front reforms under Léon Blum in the mid-1930s to establish a comparable system. But it was in the Scandinavian countries, controlled by the social democratic parties, that the welfare state achieved its greatest coverage in the West, while the Soviet model of Marxist egalitarianism prevailed in the East. As a result several different approaches to providing social protection emerged—the East European communist variant of basic provision; the social democratic Scandinavian comprehensive model; the Christian Democratic French, German, and Italian variant of subsidiarity; and the liberal British and Swiss market version.[39]

Driven by the aspirations of the labor movement, the communists' effort to eliminate exploitation, inequality, and illness was rather ambitious, because it attempted to restructure the entire economy and society. Its primary method was to guarantee everyone a job, since that would avert unemployment, the greatest of the capitalist dangers. Another element was subsidizing the price of basic food, housing, and transportation so that nobody would go hungry, live on the street, or be unable to get to work. A final dimension was the free provision of education and health care in order to allow all children to be educated and the entire population to receive medical attention. Because of the enormous cost of this comprehensive effort, wages remained relatively low and pensions meager. During the initial postwar decades communist leaders argued that a social policy was unnecessary, since socialism was already taking care of all needs. As a result the classic western welfare instruments remained underdeveloped until the party realized during the 1970s that "real existing socialism" had not solved all social problems.[40]

Promoted by social democrats, the Nordic model represented the most extensive welfare system in the West by trying to provide a high level of social services within a capitalist framework. In contrast to the Soviet Bloc, the Scandinavian countries maintained individual initiative and monetary rewards as engines of economic growth. Moreover, they supported market competition and free trade and therefore imposed few regulations on products and labor mobility while supporting technological innovation. But the strong trade unions pushed through a social pact regulating collective bargaining with business that was mediated by the government. Perfected in subsequent decades, this approach offered comprehensive insurance against the vagaries of life plus free education and universal health care. Trying to escape the polarity of the Cold War, the Nordic model strove for a third way between capitalism and communism. Leading to public expenditures of over 50 percent of the GDP, this generous redistribution of wealth required a high rate of taxation, about half of personal income. While celebrities like the children's writer Astrid Lindgren grumbled, voters supported this system since it brought them social peace and security.[41]

Still extensive, but less comprehensive, was the Christian Democratic model exemplified by the Federal Republic. Its Basic Law defined the purpose of the state as the "social rule of law," which promised security and equality. While Erhard believed that the market was the best guarantee of welfare, the strong trade unions clamored not only for alleviating the consequences of the war but also for improving the lot of the working class. To be able to win elections, the Adenauer cabinet gradually expanded coverage but retained individual achievement as the basis for insurance premiums, which yielded graduated benefits. Since war and inflation had wiped out savings, the pension system was financed by current taxes—unproblematic as long as there were enough wage earners to keep up with the costs after their indexing in 1957. The social-liberal coalition under Willy Brandt expanded the *Sozialstaat* further by increasing benefits and including new clients based on the assumption of continued growth. Since health insurance remained privatized, German income taxes and public expenditures also remained lower at about one-third.[42]

The system of French social protection also started out with insurance but then systematically expanded its coverage in the direction of a universal guarantee of a minimum standard of living. Established immediately after the war, Social Security grew to cover lack of income due to illness, maternity, disability, death, and accident as well as provide for old age and offer family supports. Owing to this broad coverage, the funding gradually changed from payroll deductions to general taxes. In order to make up for a stagnating population size, both the Catholic Church and secular nationalists agreed on establishing extensive maternity benefits and family support. From crèches to kindergarten, most mothers had a system of infant care available that allowed them to have children and continue to work at the same time, since these institutions were open the entire day. As a result of such support, the French birthrate became one of the highest in Europe. The downside of this broad *protection sociale* was a high rate of deductions and taxes and a large amount of public expenditure, which slowed economic growth.[43]

Growing out of the Beveridge Report in 1942, the British welfare state was an effort to combat the evils of "want, disease, ignorance, squalor and idleness." Its implementation by the Labour government was nonetheless based on a "welfare capitalism" that tried to combine full employment, housing, food, and health care with a market economy. The subsequent Conservative cabinet under Macmillan tried to rein in expenses and limit claims. But the Wilson government returned to expanding welfare provisions in order to attack inequality, and added wage-related unemployment benefits to the guaranteed minimum. Other programs like child benefits followed, and social-service departments were created, while the National Health Service began to devour ever larger funds. The basic problem was, however, that the underperformance of the British economy drastically limited which services the state could actually sustain in the long run. Though social policy became an entitlement for the poor, its extent remained an ideological and practical battleground between the Labour and the Conservative parties.[44]

The results of this welfare-state expansion were somewhat contradictory. As a consequence of extensive support the absolute number of the poor sank below 10 percent of the population between 1960 and 1991 in all European OECD member states except Italy. While not completely eradicated, poverty therefore declined notably. Moreover, the consistent effort at the redistribution of earnings reduced the income disparity between rich and poor considerably, creating not complete equality but narrowing the gap between the top and bottom deciles sufficiently so that it remained socially acceptable. Of course such efforts at diminishing inequality required substantial marginal tax rates, approximating or even occasionally exceeding 50 percent. Moreover, the funding of the expansion of welfare programs also increased the share of public expenditures as percentage of GDP to well over two-fifths in the Scandinavian countries, somewhat less so among the Christian Democratic states, and one-quarter in Britain.[45] No wonder that this growing burden eventually created resentment among those who had to shoulder it.

On balance most European voters were, however, willing to pay the price during the postwar years, because they were convinced that they had a moral obligation to practice social solidarity. Of course, the direct beneficiaries in the various client groups appreciated their support, even if their lobbyists could never quite get enough. The churches were glad that they no longer had to carry the load of charity alone and that the state was ready to step in. The vocal trade unions also congratulated themselves for having a central plank of their socialist agenda put into practice so that they could prove their continuing relevance to their members. Moreover, social scientists were happy to have convinced the public that their recommendations increased social peace by solving specific problems. Finally, the social politicians of various parties were able to argue that these welfare expenditures broadened citizenship and put postwar democracy on a more solid footing by limiting the appeal of extremist parties. Based on higher public expenditures than in the United States (16.8 percent versus 10.6 percent of GNP in 1990), the provision of a generous welfare state became characteristic of European modernity.[46]

RISE OF EXPERTS

During the seemingly long 1960s, the sense of rapid change ushered in a technocratic attempt to guide the process of modernization through a corps of experts capable of planning the future. Confronted with unprecedented complexity, European governments felt in need of scientific knowledge in order to make the right decisions.[47] Designing highways, airports, nuclear reactors, or computer systems appeared to demand informed choices so as to develop responsible policies. Transcending the calculus of partisanship, promoters of a technical logic argued that the structure of problems required "objective" solutions. Since the legally trained civil service often proved incapable of dealing with complicated issues of technology or society, governments turned to researchers in the universities or independent centers for assistance, thereby creating a group of academic advisers. Flush with confidence in their professional authority, these consultants produced plans for the economy, urban design, education reform, and the welfare state. In many ways, the emergence of these experts represented the culmination of modernist politics.[48]

Rivaling technical experts, social scientists also grew confident of being able to solve societal problems through social reforms. One prerequisite was the ever more extensive collection of social indicators and their publication in various statistical series, which allowed detailed quantitative studies of economic and social trends. Another impulse was the growing sophistication of survey research, both as political-opinion polling and as the study of consumer preferences, which provided governments with a firmer sense of public wishes. Reinforced by behaviorism, an empirical approach to psychology imported from the United States, these improvements led to a shift from normative argumentation to generalizations derived from empirical research. This methodological revolution made economics, sociology, and political science the new lead disciplines for government planning of economic and social policies in contested areas such as reforming family policy or liberalizing the labor market. Such experts convinced the public that they possessed sufficient knowledge to forecast the economy, regulate society, and manage politics scientifically.[49]

The Swedish economist Gunnar Myrdal was one such socially engaged expert who combined research with politics. Born around the turn of the century into modest circumstances, he forsook law for economics, anticipating in his early work some of the Keynesian theories. Together with his spirited wife Alva, he undertook a study of Swedish population policy in the early 1930s that shocked the public because it uncovered a declining birthrate. Elected as a Social Democrat to the Senate, Myrdal helped lay the foundations of the Swedish welfare state by instituting social supports for families in order to help reduce the birth deficit. During the war he studied the discrepancy between the U.S. rhetoric of opportunity and the reality of racial discrimination, laying through his book, *An American Dilemma*, the foundation for desegregation. Subsequently he served as minister of trade in the Swedish government and then chaired the UN Economic Commission for Europe that aided postwar reconstruction. Also getting involved in decolonization and peace research, Myrdal was a reformer who used his academic expertise to advocate progressive changes.[50]

The growing influence of experts changed the nature of political debate, because they employed research reports, policy analyses, and statistical predictions rather than partisan rhetoric. Prominent natural and social scientists like the historian A.J.P. Taylor became media personalities, giving the public advice on controversial questions. At the same time interest groups began to recruit scholars who might support their causes, trying to insert them into the deliberations of political parties. Governments created a series of standing commissions, such as the councils of economic advisers, in order to obtain forecasts and work out planning projections. They also convened ad hoc commissions charged with reporting on topics like making public administration more efficient, and they sponsored research projects on controversial issues such as the new poverty, right-wing radicalism, youth unemployment, and gender equality. Their recommendations claimed to depoliticize politics by following only scientific evidence. But it soon became evident that experts themselves had distinct value preferences and therefore did not speak with a united voice.[51]

The rise of the experts therefore turned out to be a mixed blessing for the modernization of democracy. No doubt the effort to base political decisions on scientific evidence brought gains in information and reflection about technical, economic, and social problems. But implementation was another matter. In communist countries the party retained the ultimate authority, while in the West many recommendations were shelved because they were too costly, impractical, or unwelcome. And correctness was yet another issue. More often than not predictions like economists' forecasts of continued growth were simply wrong because unanticipated events changed the parameters, thereby tarnishing the planners' credibility. Moreover, experts liked to proceed without consulting the concerned public sufficiently, for instance producing angry grassroots rebellions against their plans to install nuclear power plants in the German countryside. Measured by their claims, even many well-conceived plans failed, because politics could not be reduced to a clear scientific choice. At best, expert interventions added another voice to the multivocal debate in modern democracy.[52]

Part IV

CONFRONTING
GLOBALIZATION, 1973–2000

Chapter 22

REVOLT AGAINST MODERNITY

French student revolt, 1968. *Source*: Jean-Pierre Rey / Gamma-Rapho / Getty Images.

On February 18, 1973, three hundred demonstrators assembled near the village of Wyhl in southwestern Germany to protest against the construction of a nuclear reactor. The press conference they had called to explain their anger at having their objections ignored by the government quickly escalated into a heated exchange with the head of the building crew. Appalled that century-old trees were cut down, "the protestors broke through the fence and surged onto the site" of the future power plant. By climbing into bulldozers and jumping onto the shovels of excavators, the unruly crowd blocked further work and started arguing with the construction workers. But, having learned their techniques in a previous protest against the establishment of a lead factory in Marckolsheim on the French side of the Rhine, the demonstrators eventually calmed down, pitched tents, and got out the food and sleeping bags they had brought along for an extended vigil. Misrepresented by the press as nothing more than illegal interference, the site occupation was a spontaneous response to a growing confrontation that turned into a peaceful, well-disciplined protest using nonviolent methods of civil disobedience to stop the erection of a nuclear reactor promoted by a big power company.[1]

Such antinuclear protests were a delayed product of the grassroots mobilization inspired by the generational rebellion of 1968. This surprising youth revolt rejected the compromises of the older generation, which was willing to trade acquiescence in parliamentary politics for rising prosperity and personal comfort. A whole cluster of perceived injustices such as authoritarian paternalism, academic overcrowding, sexual repression, and imperialist war triggered the transnational protest wave. In strictly political terms the leftist attempt to incite a "new class" revolution of students and white-collar workers failed wherever it was attempted, but in cultural terms of changing lifestyles and values it was a smashing success.[2] Ironically, in Eastern Europe the revolts in Poznań and the Prague Spring simultaneously sought to liberalize the one-party communist system with even less chance of victory. These efforts to create a more participatory democracy ironically proceeded at cross-purposes, since western protesters criticized the injustices of liberal modernity, while eastern dissidents rejected the repressiveness of its communist alternative.

Though these rebellions did not succeed politically, they triggered a series of new social movements during the early 1970s that eventually spread from the West to the East. In contrast to traditional labor-union agitation, these civil-society actions pursued a post–material prosperity agenda that tried to improve "the quality of life" rather than gain additional money. Growing out of local opposition to urban renewal, highway construction, or various intrusions on natural habitat, one such current was environmentalism, which campaigned for green spaces and ecological balance. Inspired by frustration with the insensitivity of male activists, another strand was the new feminism, which agitated for women's rights and gender equality. Prompted by the nuclear-arms race and proliferation of intercontinental missiles, a final cause was the peace movement, which weaved religious, secular, and socialist threads into a pacifism that opposed the stationing of additional NATO rockets.[3] Interestingly, this overlapping grassroots mobilization became increasingly critical of the negative consequences of industrial society and began to search for ways of transcending the constraints of high modernity.

The impact of the protest movements of the 1960s and 1970s is still disputed, because identity politics thereafter revolved around taking positions toward their aims and methods. Traumatized by Nazi excesses, conservatives and traditional liberals feared that the irrationalism of a mass movement would once again lead youths in a totalitarian direction. The Marxist rhetoric of some protests also suggested communist subversion, while the antiauthoritarian posturing implied a loss of civility and standards of achievement. In contrast, the youthful demonstrators of the New Left saw their revolt as Jürgen Habermas has described it: a "fundamental liberalization" of western society, a long-overdue effort to democratize parliamentary government. At the same time, they celebrated sexual liberation and changing values as necessary steps toward throwing off bourgeois constraints and embracing more permissive lifestyles. In the East the revival of civil society fed into dissident movements that eventually overthrew the communist regimes. Amplified and memorialized by media retrospectives during various anniversaries, the massive uprising of 1968 continues to cast a large shadow, since its aspirations and actions have been thoroughly mythologized by both opponents and supporters.[4]

By criticizing its practices and rejecting its values, the concurrent western and eastern revolts in effect repudiated the precepts of both democratic and socialist modernity. While the youth rebellion initially aimed to make life more humane, socially just, and peaceful, its neo-Marxist rhetoric, Maoist fashion, and turn toward violence signaled a rejection of liberal modernity by seeking to impose an unorthodox socialism on Western Europe. Ironically, the simultaneous unrest within the Soviet Bloc tried to humanize real existing socialism by recovering the bourgeois human rights and market incentives of that very rival version of modernity the western youth were rejecting. More successful in changing public priorities in the West were the new social movements that sought to escape the logic of the machine, male sexism, and the arms race. Finally, the reflections of postmodern theoreticians revealed a rising discontent with the rationalism, formalism, and inhumanity of mature industrial society. Taken together these diverse cultural currents expressed a search for a more humane form of politics beyond high modernity, a search that was to dominate the last quarter of the twentieth century.[5]

SOURCES OF PROTEST

In spite of rising prosperity and political freedom, some intellectuals had begun criticizing capitalist democracy, providing inspiration for the generational revolt of the late 1960s. One important impulse emanated from the British New Left, a loose cluster of intellectuals that sought to create a humane and liberal form of socialism, more radical than western social democracy and less Stalinist than Soviet communism. In their essays in the *New Left Review*, critics such as Perry Anderson and Edward P. Thomson strove for an unorthodox form of Marxism that probed cultural sources of alienation in consumer society according to the ideas of Antonio Gramsci. Revising the traditional concept of class conflict, they stressed that the shift to a service society made a new class of white collar workers and students the revolutionary vanguard of the future. Theoreticians of the Frankfurt School like Herbert Marcuse also attempted to incorporate Sigmund Freud's insights about the sexual repressiveness of bourgeois society.[6] These debates produced an exciting mix of critiques that rejected the postwar restoration of liberal capitalism.

More colorful yet was the antiauthoritarian counterculture of various bohemian movements that also sought to reject the compromises inherent in bourgeois society. Inspired by Guy Debord, artists in France formed a group called Situationist International, which was intent on critically analyzing the situations of daily life in order to fulfill authentic individual desires. Vaguely Marxist in outlook, these situationists rejected modernist functionalism à la satellite city Sarcelles and strove to blend artistic creativity with personal freedom. The Dutch Provos followed similar impulses, seeking to provoke the established order by turning to drugs, sex, and rock 'n' roll. Their manifesto attacked "capitalism, communism, fascism, bureaucracy, militarism, professionalism, dogmatism, and authoritarianism," calling for "resistance wherever possible." A motley collection of beatniks, vegetarians, pacifists, and artists, these antiauthoritarians often used humor to discredit the rules and norms they considered repressive. In contrast to the Marxist theoreticians of the New Left, the supporters of the counterculture represented a more anarchistic strain of rebellion.[7]

A final inspiration paradoxically came from the United States, since activists generally opposed its policy while adopting its protest methods. Popular culture styles such as wearing jeans and listening to rock music had already annoyed straitlaced bourgeois adults during the 1950s. More importantly, the nonviolent protest forms of the U.S. civil rights movement served as inspiration to European campus radicals trying to mobilize university students. Transmitted by a few key individuals, the provocations of the Free Speech Movement in Berkeley, California, quickly made their way to Berlin, while the cultural critique of the Frankfurt School was eagerly received in San Francisco. Joint opposition to the Vietnam War intensified this transatlantic exchange, since prominent antiwar songwriter/singers like Joan Baez performed at mass rallies on the continent. Photogenic icons of the Black Power movement such as Angela Davis were popular on both sides of the Iron Curtain. Borrowing protest methods and popular culture from the United States, student radicals rejected the Vietnam War and called for a "second front" of anti-imperialist solidarity.[8]

Beyond such inspirations, the youth revolt also stemmed from a series of concrete irritations such as the prevailing authoritarianism that complicated the passage through adolescence. In most families fathers were still firmly in control, and superiors in institutions set rules that were expected to be observed, while youths craved more personal freedom. This paternalistic order enforced middle-class virtues such as punctuality, cleanliness, and hard work—much of which seemed increasingly onerous to rebellious adolescents. Still subject to memories of deprivation during the war, most adults were proud of visible signs of material prosperity such as houses, cars, and washing machines, while the young who had grown up in increasing affluence took such possessions for granted and sought other, postmaterial meanings in life. In Germany, Italy, and their former allies and occupied countries, authority figures were discredited by having collaborated with Nazis, provoking awkward silences to the question "Daddy, what did you do during the war?" The young therefore embraced the slogan "Trust no one over thirty."[9]

Frustration with overcrowding in schools and personal alienation from mass universities were additional motives of protest. The enormous expansion of secondary education had produced a tidal wave of graduates that made university lecture halls and seminars overflow with students, since construction and personnel had not been able to keep up. Many new institutions like Nanterre and Bielefeld were built in modernist styles of glass, steel, and concrete, resembling factory halls in their sterile impersonality. An increasing number of students also stemmed from underprivileged backgrounds without experience of academic culture and therefore felt intellectually overtaxed and socially foreign in their unaccustomed surroundings. At the same time, the traditional teaching practices of the universities were slow to adapt, with the chaired professors remaining all-powerful and their didactic styles rooted in monotone lectures. Denouncing the "musty smell of a thousand years under the academic gowns," radical students therefore had ample reason to feel like an academic proletariat.[10]

Yet another impulse was the attempt to end the sexual repression that characterized the moralism of restored bourgeois society. Youths resented the fraudulence of the "double standard," which allowed successful men to have mistresses while demanding absolute fidelity of their wives. At the same time they opposed the lack of information about birth control, the prohibition of abortion, and the legal prosecution of homosexuals as outmoded. For the first time in history, the introduction of the "pill" made it possible to have intercourse without having to fear the consequences of unwanted pregnancy. The availability of effective oral contraception fundamentally shifted the alleged purpose of sex away from procreation and toward recreation. Gradually, religious teachings lost their force among a generation eager to explore their bodies and to experiment freely with sexual pleasure—a shift of attitudes also supported by progressive media. The new practice of living in communes or just sharing apartments also provided more opportunities for having sex. As a result, sexual liberation became part of the generational revolt, politicizing private desire.[11]

Mounting opposition to the U.S. intervention in the civil war between North and South Vietnam was a final spur to rebellion. Since most youths were ignorant of the complexities of national liberation struggles against European colonialism, the presence of international students from the Third World created anti-imperialist solidarity on European campuses. This was the first war to be carried live on TV, in which the evening news tended to show shocking images of devastation from U.S. bombing and chemical warfare that killed civilians and destroyed farms and villages. It did not help that the South Vietnamese regime was considered a military dictatorship, mired in corruption—hardly a beacon of the so-called free world. Moreover, none of the brutality of the communist-supported Vietcong appeared on the screens, since journalists were reluctant to navigate booby-trapped trails or crawl through supply tunnels in order to report on the violence of these presumed liberators of the nation. By seeming to betray its own ideals through the "slaughter of the civilian population," American policy discredited itself and broke the Cold War framing of the moral superiority of the West.[12]

Inspired by a mix of neo-Marxist, anarchist, and civil rights examples, the charismatic German student leader Rudi Dutschke embodied many central facets of the protest movement. Born in East Germany, he left the GDR just before the Berlin escape route was closed because he found the repression of "real existing socialism" unbearable. Married to Gretchen Klotz, a devoutly religious American exchange student, he was in touch with radical currents in the United States. Chafing at western duplicity, he was drawn to anarchistic forms of lifestyle rebellion. But as a graduate student of sociology, he tried to construct a new social theory that might explain the contradictions of mature capitalism. Ideologically, he was looking for a truly democratic form of socialism that would provide peace, freedom, and equality. In mass rallies this combination of theoretical grounding and emotional commitment made him an inspiring speaker, adored by youthful crowds. As symbolic leader of the German student movement he rejected both communist modernization and liberal consumer modernity, looking for a revolution that would create a more just form of progressive politics.[13]

PATTERNS OF REVOLT

The protest movements spread quickly in part because their novel methods confused the authorities and intrigued potential followers. Unlike conventional street demonstrations of the labor movement, sit-ins blocked the normal functioning of educational and governmental institutions, sometimes for weeks, while teach-ins subverted regular instruction by spreading radical messages. This civil disobedience worked with calculated rule violations, designed to incense the establishment by making it difficult to counter them with legal means since they remained nonviolent. It was especially the irreverence of slogans like "by day they are cops, at night they are flops" as well as the innovative design of placards, such as one with the picture of the Shah of Iran on a wanted poster for murder, that drew attention.[14] These tactics baffled the authorities because public officials would look repressive if they retaliated but might appear incompetent if they just let the protests pass. Many activists considered poking fun at the professoriate or the police as an exciting game in which they gained new adherents by outwitting their opponents.

In due course the protesters learned to evoke sympathy from bystanders and intellectuals through appearing as victims of clumsy repression. They carefully planned their provocations so as to achieve notoriety and unmask the oppressive nature of state power. When frustrated policemen beat peaceful students with billy clubs, dragging them bodily into paddy wagons, it looked as if the state were initiating violence to suppress dissent. Even if their headlines condemned the demonstrators, the media descriptions and photographs of police actions seemed to bear out accusations of the political intolerance of parliamentary democracy. The activists became quite adept at not only establishing a public sphere of their own through leaflets, counterculture newspapers, and so on, but also at using the TV images and newspaper editorials of the establishment for their cause. Reported in dramatic detail, each official repression created new converts to the cause. By the spring of 1968, the growing following on campuses inspired leaders like Daniel Cohn-Bendit and Rudi Dutschke to think about the feasibility of a "revolutionary seizure of power."[15]

In West Germany, two reactionary acts of violence speeded the gradual buildup of protest by arousing mass support. The initial campus confrontations over free-speech issues gained only local notice, though the campaign against the controversial emergency laws, which reduced citizens' rights during natural or civil emergencies, drew church and union support. But when the police officer Karl-Heinz Kurras shot bystander Benno Ohnesorg on June 2, 1967, during an antishah demonstration, shocked students organized sympathy demonstrations in other cities, while intellectuals like Heinrich Böll denounced the repressiveness of the state. Claiming that "the post-fascist system in the Federal Government has become a pre-fascist one," the Socialist German Student League (SDS) called for attacks on the capitalist oligarchy. The international Vietnam Congress in February 1968 radicalized its message to fighting "imperialism in its metropolitan centers." When on April 11 the neo-Nazi Josef Bachmann shot Rudi Dutschke, students stormed the offices of the right-wing Springer tabloid *Bild*, which had incited antistudent violence. But just when activists thought that the movement was becoming irresistible, it started to fizzle.[16]

In France student activists came closer to seizing power when they resumed the tradition of nineteenth-century revolutions by erecting barricades in the Quartier Latin. In the early 1960s the national student union UNEF had begun to criticize the war in Algeria, while half a decade later it protested against the technocratic restructuring of the universities. Led by "Danny the Red" Cohn-Bendit, activists gathered in Nanterre in March 1968 and moved on to the Sorbonne in late April. When the police brutally evicted them in early May, the students, encouraged by public sympathy, defended the university with cobblestone barricades, following the ironic slogan: "The beach lies under the pavement." For several days the students and the police fought pitched battles. On May 13 about ten million laborers staged a wildcat general strike, demanding *autogestion* (workers' control of the factories). The government seemed ready to fall when the frightened president Charles de Gaulle flew to a military base in Germany. But after Prime Minister Georges Pompidou offered Renault laborers wage increases, the excitement passed.[17]

Only in Italy did the confrontation assume a similar intensity, while in Britain and the smaller West European countries the conflict remained more moderate. Starting with the occupation of universities in 1967, Italian students became quite radical in denouncing academic authoritarianism, calling for *potere studentesco*. In May 1968 the revolt turned violent when the police brutally repressed protests at the Villa Giulia in Rome. The activists were supported by leftist workers who were clamoring for control of their industries, initiating a decade of violence that culminated in the terrorism of the Red Brigades. In contrast, the demonstrations in British universities remained generally peaceful, even though the activists were making similar demands for liberalizing the academy and opposing the war in Vietnam. While Belgian students polarized into Flemish and French speakers, in the Netherlands they followed the German example of creating "critical universities" that attacked capitalist democracy intellectually rather than physically. The fervor infected even Scandinavia, but here the debates also remained relatively civil.[18]

Much to the surprise of the activists, the generational revolt collapsed almost as rapidly as it had begun. One key reason was the weakness of neo-Marxist class-struggle theory, since white-collar employees and university graduates, supposedly the new proletariat, were ultimately more interested in achieving a bourgeois lifestyle than in overthrowing the social order. In spite of the popularity of iconic revolutionary heroes like the ubiquitously placarded Che Guevara, it proved quite difficult to transfer Maoist-inspired urban guerrilla tactics to the European metropole. The majority of the continental working class refused to join forces with the disgruntled intellectuals because it already had too much to lose as a result of rising prosperity. Moreover, the accusation of neofascism that radical protesters hurled against the elite was clearly an exaggeration, since parliamentary democracy responded by not just reelecting President de Gaulle in France but also creating a progressive social-liberal coalition led by Willy Brandt in Germany. When their revolutionary fervor cooled, most youths were willing to embark instead on "the long march through the institutions" in order to reform them from within.[19]

The failure to seize power fragmented and radicalized the student movement. Much protest energy focused on making the existing system more responsive by democratizing it from below. During the struggle many activists also figured out that in order to transform the world, "we had to change ourselves" by embracing an antiauthoritarian lifestyle of informal dress and libertine sex. But an incorrigible minority of Marxist theoreticians splintered into competing Trotskyite, Maoist, or Stalinist sects, combating each other rather than fighting capitalism. A few hard-core radicals in the German Red Army Faction and the Italian Red Brigades progressed from "violence against things" to violence against persons, waging a terrorist war against government and business that cost dozens of lives. Dispelling the protest movement's initial romantic appeal, the collateral damage of innocent blood shed for "the revolution" turned even supportive intellectuals against this ideological crusade. The militant self-defense of democracy in Italy and the resolute German response to an airplane hijacking in the autumn of 1977 reduced terrorism to irrelevance.[20]

By narrowing into Maoist dogmatism, the splinter groups' search for a socialist humanism led to a dead end that sought to substitute the Marxist alternative for liberal modernity. Rejecting technocratic modernization, one former activist recalled that he "would not want to lead a life anymore where you would just function for the machine, and the machine would be so heinous that you would decide this machine had to be stopped."[21] This understandable critique led many activists to choose a cure that turned out worse than the disease—the Maoist prescription for modernizing the Third World. The "little red book" of *Quotations from Chairman Mao Tse-Tung* could only become popular among some western intellectuals because of their profound ignorance of the Cultural Revolution taking place in China at the same time. Killing millions of innocent citizens, this campaign to speed the ideological transformation of China and enforce a Chairman Mao–approved lifestyle abused youthful idealism so as to destroy many ancient cultural traditions. No wonder the effort to replace liberal democracy with its Maoist alternative was doomed to failure: its prescriptions were inappropriate for Western Europe.

SOCIALISM WITH A HUMAN FACE

While the protest movement gathered steam in the West, popular discontent was also building up in the Eastern Bloc under the surface of dictatorial control, hoping to reform socialism. With the help of Soviet army and secret service intimidation, the local communist parties had generally succeeded in stamping out any open anticommunist opposition by the late 1950s. But workers were becoming increasingly disgruntled when they realized that the planned economy was causing their living standards to fall behind those of their cousins on the other side of the Iron Curtain. Writers and painters too, frustrated by the simplemindedness of the proletarian literary and artistic styles mandated by the leadership, chafed at the heavy hand of censorship, wanting more freedom to experiment. Even genuine supporters of Marxism among the intellectuals resented the Stalinist remnants of communist politics and longed for a more democratic form of socialism.[22] While the Soviet military interventions in 1953 and 1956 served as a deterrent against open dissent, pressures were building in Eastern Europe that sought a sudden release.

The first rumblings of protest occurred in Poland, directed against the regime of Władysław Gomułka, who steered a zigzag course between Soviet control and national independence. In contrast to its subjugation in other East European countries, the Catholic Church in Poland remained a public force, as did dissidents like oft-imprisoned Jacek Kuroń, who courageously published his criticism abroad. Moreover, the failing economy, concentrated in heavy industry, disappointed the workers, who demanded better living conditions. After the banning of a patriotic play by Adam Mickiewicz, students protested in Warsaw in March 1968. The brutal repression of the demonstration by riot police spread their strike to other universities where it was again harshly subdued, with 2,725 participants, including the dissident Adam Michnik, arrested. Shifting the blame, Minister of Interior Mieczysław Moczar accused "hidden Zionists" of being responsible for the unrest. Moreover, he created a card file of Jews and expelled them from the party, subsequently prompting more than fifteen thousand members of the Jewish community to emigrate.[23] Though the regime reasserted control with this campaign of hate, new waves of protests broke out in Poland during the following years.

The rise of dissatisfaction in Czechoslovakia was more surprising, because that country had welcomed liberation by the Red Army and possessed a large Communist Party. Nonetheless the slowness of de-Stalinization irritated many citizens who remembered Stalin's anticosmopolitan trials. The stalling of the already highly developed economy due to inappropriate smokestack-industrialization plans also frustrated consumers, who had hoped that the reintroduction of incentives by Ota Šik during the mid-1960s would restore growth.

At the same time talented writers like Václav Havel, Ivan Klima, and Milan Kundera rebelled against the tightness of censorship that stifled their creativity. Moreover, tensions between the Czech and the Slovak halves of the state were rising, since the latter felt neglected in economic planning. As a result of these pressures, the flexible Slovak party chief Alexander Dubček replaced the orthodox Antonin Novotny in January 1968. Hinting at his willingness to initiate changes, the new leader proposed building "a socialism that corresponds to the historical democratic traditions of Czechoslovakia."[24]

In April Dubček announced an even more extensive Action Program of reforms that became known by its symbolic name as "socialism with a human face." Arguing that the period of forceful class struggle was over, it promised a reorientation to a consumer economy, directed by capable experts, as well as freedom of speech and the press, and of individual movement in order to support the revitalization. Though the Communist Party (KPC) intended to lead the reforms, they quickly developed an unstoppable momentum of their own. When censorship was lifted, the author Ludvík Vaculík published a manifesto titled "The Two Thousand Words," which called on the people to take the initiative in pushing for further changes. As a result of the increasing freedom, the media also started to expose the corruption of the Communist Party. At the same time, some moderate socialists revived an independent Social Democratic Party. In the heady spring days of Prague, anything seemed possible—even the democratization of communism from within.[25]

Increasingly concerned about the KPC's loss of control, Soviet leader Leonid Brezhnev finally decided to stop the liberalization with military intervention by Warsaw Pact troops. During a March meeting in Dresden, Dubček still managed to reassure his colleagues that he was just trying to put communism on a firmer foundation. But the unpopular leaders Walter Ulbricht of the GDR, Władysław Gomułka of Poland, and Janós Kádár of Hungary were afraid that demands for liberalization would spill across their borders. During the August Warsaw Pact conference in Bratislava, the Czech reformers no longer succeeded in dispelling such worries. When a conservative minority in the Prague Politburo called for Soviet assistance against an alleged counterrevolution, Brezhnev ordered an invasion to halt the dismantling of communism. On the night of August 20, 1968, two hundred thousand Warsaw Pact troops with two thousand tanks invaded Czechoslovakia, encountering only token opposition. Seventy-two Czechs were killed and seven hundred others wounded in the struggle.[26] Passive resistance was unable to prevent this suppression of the daring experiment.

Gradually, but all the more effectively, orthodox communism regained control over Czechoslovakia, condemning it to torpor for another twenty-one years. Verbal protests by western countries and some neutrals were of little avail, and a critical UN resolution was blocked by a Soviet veto. Even the dramatic self-immolation of Jan Palach on Wenceslas Square could not halt the ouster of Dubček and the appointment of Gustav Husák. The new Czech leader pursued a "normalization policy" that rolled back the economic reforms, tightened party control, and reinstituted a harsh form of censorship. Outwardly the cowed citizenry had no choice but to comply, but inwardly many continued to resent the Soviet-led invasion. Husák tried to stifle the criticism by improving living standards, that is, providing more consumer goods and more distracting TV entertainment. But the heavy hand of the censor drove dissident intellectuals underground, forcing them to engage in a form of "antipolitics" that refrained from open challenge and yet tried to reconstitute an independent civil society.[27]

The suppression of the Prague Spring had a profound effect, since it ended the utopian appeal of communism for intellectuals on both sides of the Iron Curtain. Within the Soviet Bloc, the Soviet army's invasion dashed hopes for a communist self-reform that would shed at least its Stalinist if not Leninist guise to arrive at a more democratic version. The armed intervention of the Warsaw Pact powers revealed that Soviet rule over Eastern Europe was a form of Russian imperialism, propping up minority dictatorships in the client states. Moreover, the use of force to squash dissent also shocked members of the West European communist parties who had seen the Soviet Union as a beacon of progress, strengthening their Eurocommunist impulses to find a more moderate and independent path toward socialism. At the same time the failure of the Czech experiment also disillusioned myopic western fellow travelers of communism like Jean-Paul Sartre by pointing out that Moscow's rhetoric of peace and equality was a sham. In global terms, the Soviets suddenly looked conservative in contrast to revolutionary Maoism.[28]

Another result of the invasion of Czechoslovakia was the discrediting of the Soviet version of modernization, since it rested on compulsion rather than voluntary cooperation. Especially for those countries that possessed a developed consumer economy, the heavy industrialization mandated by the Soviet Union proved counterproductive, since it did not lead them forward. The communist claim of superior social welfare lost its luster in a dictatorship where basic freedoms did not exist. Political repression made western human rights once again relevant for intellectuals and citizens in the East, although such bourgeois liberties were supposed to have been superseded by the building of socialism. In 1968 European intellectuals therefore pursued two rather contradictory agendas for transcending high modernity: while western radicals dreamed of some kind of socialist revolution to end capitalist exploitation and imperialist aggression, eastern dissidents rediscovered civil rights as a necessary guarantee of their freedom of expression.[29] These cross-purposes inhibited communication across the Iron Curtain, creating an unresolved tension until 1989.

NEW SOCIAL MOVEMENTS

The new social movements that arose from the debris left behind by the generational revolt moved away from high modernity, since they pursued a fundamentally different vision. Dispirited and disorganized, the European Left gradually distanced itself from the dead end of neo-Marxist sectarianism and the counterproductive cult of terrorist violence. Surprised by the intensity of local protests against urban renewal, highway construction, and nuclear power, various activists quickly recognized their mobilizing potential. Civic conflict offered a new brand of open-ended grassroots politics, addressing single issues like environmental protection, gender equality, or international peace that created a movement identity for participants. In contrast to the tight organization and material aims of the labor movement, these contestations were loosely organized and pursued a postmaterialistic quality-of-life agenda, which reflected the value shift of the generational revolt. Their young and well-educated members wanted to regain control of their lives, rejecting the domination of the machine, the corporation, and the state.[30]

The novel form of "citizens' initiatives" arose spontaneously as a result of local confrontations over often mundane issues affecting urban neighborhoods. For instance, when city planners wanted to build a feeder road through Hamburg's working-class district of Ottensen, its inhabitants rebelled because the highway would cut their quarter in two. They protested vociferously against the decision of their elected officials, signing petitions, holding rallies, drawing up posters, and distributing leaflets. To coordinate the plethora of initiatives, the protesters eventually formed an Action Community network in order to negotiate with the city authorities. Expecting passive acquiescence to their efforts to make Hamburg more car friendly, officials were eventually forced to abandon their plans and instead find ways to renovate the dilapidated buildings of the quarter.[31] Multiplied dozens of times in different European cities, such instances of mobilization from below created a new kind of politics outside parliamentary channels that proved surprisingly successful.

A key issue that inspired widespread protests was the deterioration of the environment due to unchecked economic growth. In industrial areas like the Ruhr Basin, uncontrolled factory effluents had made the water undrinkable, while in the chemical triangle of East Germany the air had grown so foul as to cause allergic coughs in children. In Czech forests acid rain was killing woods on exposed hillsides, initiating a *Waldsterben* (forest dieback) that left spindly skeletons of trees, ruining forestry. At the same time the factory-farming of animals and the use of pesticides in fields contaminated Dutch soil, killing all manner of birds and small animals. Moreover, accidents in nuclear plants like the Ukrainian Chernobyl explosion in 1986 threatened to poison whole areas for generations. Responding to personal concerns and dramatic media reports, traditional nature groups transformed themselves into organizations for environmental protection. Their constant warnings gradually changed the political climate from pro–industrial expansion to ecological sensitivity, making political parties adopt this issue in their platforms.[32]

Another important cause was gender equality, which inspired a new feminism that sought to overthrow patriarchy and lighten the double burden of managing a household and career work. As a result of socialist egalitarianism and communist planning that increased the need for labor, East European women had many formal rights, though obtaining daily provisions remained difficult. In the West it was resentment of male activists' insensitivity that in 1968 inspired Helke Sander to fight against "the social oppression of women" by calling on them "to emancipate themselves." Concretely that meant legalizing abortion, a demand voiced by several hundred French women who confessed publicly that they had ignored its prohibition. Another related issue was the easing of divorce laws to allow the dissolution of broken marriages without attributing legal fault to either party. Female professionals also chafed at the "glass ceiling" that kept pay unequal and denied chances for promotion. As a result of such frustration a new women's movement evolved that campaigned for turning the abstract principle of equality into equal chances of social citizenship.[33]

A final problem that mobilized a broad-based following was the preservation of peace during the nuclear confrontation of the Cold War. Pacifist engagement was complicated by communist propaganda that styled the Soviet Bloc as the "camp of peace" in spite of its militarization. Moreover, earlier campaign of the 1950s against West German rearmament and the Campaign for Nuclear Disarmament in Britain, spearheaded by Bertrand Russell, had failed. But the Soviet invasion of Afghanistan and the NATO dual-track decision in 1979, which pursued, simultaneously, nuclear-arms reduction talks and a buildup of nuclear-armed missiles, gave the issue a renewed urgency. Supported by churches, trade unions, and prominent intellectuals, a widespread protest movement "reject[ed] the arms buildup that would turn Central Europe into a nuclear weapons platform for the United States" and demanded that no intermediate-range missiles be stationed there. In London, Bonn, and all over Western Europe three million people demonstrated between 1981 and 1983 for "a nuclear-free Europe." But after the FRG parliament voted for the missiles and they were deployed, the movement collapsed.[34]

By the late 1970s some of these different groups—environmentalists, feminists, antiwar activists, and so on—started to combine their political efforts under the banner of new parliamentary parties, known according to the dominant issue as the Greens. Ecology parties scored the first successes in Britain and Belgium. In West Germany it took until 1979 for a loose alliance, led by the charismatic Petra Kelly, to win 3.2 percent of the vote in an election for the European Parliament, enough to give it public funding. Its founding program of 1980 declared the West German Greens to be an "alternative to the traditional parties" aiming at "four principles, which can be described as: ecological, social, grassroots democratic, and nonviolent." In the election of 1983 the party won 5.6 percent and thereby entered the Bundestag, and two years later Joschka Fischer became the first Green Hessian cabinet member, wearing jeans and sneakers in symbolic protest against the establishment. Split between fundamentalists who wanted radical change and realists who were willing to work within parliament, the Greens offered a different style as "antiparty" and attracted a young and educated clientele. Eventually Green parties also formed in other countries but had less electoral success.[35]

Owing to the dictatorial control of public space, new social movements developed in Eastern Europe somewhat later and with greater difficulty. But some of the concerns about the environment, sexism, and militarism were similar, because western media penetration of the Iron Curtain provided information on issues and examples of organization, while visits offered direct personal encouragement. The gradual reemergence of civil society and underground publication allowed the formation of an ecology club in Poland that dared criticize the government's industrial policy. In the GDR it was the peace movement that appropriated official propaganda for its own ends, coining the slogan "swords into plowshares" to protest the militarization of East German society. The Protestant Church offered a quasi-public sphere in which critical groups could meet, discuss women's issues, and exchange ideas in homemade publications like the *Umweltblätter*. As a result of secret service repression, these groups realized the importance of human rights and became part of the civil opposition to communism.[36]

Though the new social movements were an outgrowth of modernity, they increasingly came to reject some of its central tenets. Their often inchoate protest opposed the unlimited extension of highly industrial society, since they considered the environmental, gendered, and military consequences deleterious. Ever since the Club of Rome's alarming study of *The Limits to Growth* in 1972, western critics denounced the gospel of economic expansion shared by both employers and employees. In the East, dissidents also rejected the productivist ideology of planning that ignored the social and ecological impacts of exploiting natural resources. In order to make their voices heard, these activists engaged in grassroots organization, demanding more participatory democracy. Their counterimage was of an ecologically sensitive, gender-equal, and peaceful world in harmony with itself and therefore sustainable for the future. The German sociologist Claus Offe claimed that this was "a 'modern' critique of further modernization."[37] But by trying to correct the mistakes of industrialization, the new social movements sought to leave both capitalist and communist modernity behind.

POSTMODERN CRITIQUE

Ironically, the most radical opposition to modernism arose from within modernity itself as a set of multiple discontents with its cultural forms and scientific worldview. In architecture it referred to a rejection of the bland functionalism of the International Style, dominant in city planning and urban renewal. In literary criticism it represented an appreciation of creative works beyond the classic modernism of T. S. Eliot as well as an opening to the study of popular culture. In the social sciences it consisted of a turn away from the grand modernization narratives and an acknowledgement of the negative aspects of development. And in philosophy it involved a subjectivist critique of traditional rationalism by exploring the implications of the "linguistic turn." When trying to leave modernism behind, artists and thinkers increasingly embraced Arnold Toynbee's concept of the "postmodern age" during the 1970s.[38] As a relational term, designating an era after high industrialism, the label postmodernism represented a diffuse mood rather than a coherent program, raising the question of whether the historic era of modernity might not have come to an end.

One impetus of the assault on high modernity came from architects who rejected the rationalist functionalism of the Bauhaus style. Since glass, steel, and concrete skyscrapers looked alike everywhere, architecture critics like Robert Venturi began to denounce them as boring, essentially a repetition of the same pattern irrespective of climate or landscape. Moreover, the negative results of city planning in traffic noise, air pollution, and individual anomie led to a disenchantment with the architectural pretension of curing social problems through building design or urban renewal. Breaking the modernist mold led to a liberating sense of experimentation, which allowed a plurality of styles, recovered the delight in decoration, and borrowed freely from preceding epochs. The transition from the industrial shape of the Centre Pompidou in Paris via James Stirling's playful use of technology in the Neue Staatsgalerie in Stuttgart to the soaring vision of Frank Gehring's Guggenheim Museum in Bilbao exemplifies this trajectory. The resulting newfound freedom of design made architecture interesting again.[39]

Another attack on the modernist synthesis came from the linguistic turn, which emphasized the centrality of language for human understanding. Going beyond structuralist semiotics, the French philosopher Jacques Derrida developed a method of "deconstruction" that implied a close reading of the text for its ideological underpinnings, hidden subtexts, and covert messages, not accessible on the surface. This approach contrasted sharply with literary history, which focused on the intention of an author, and with Marxist probing of the social context of a work. Instead, a deconstructive reading focused on a given text itself, analyzing its stylistic traits and multiple layers of meaning. Moreover, Derrida also proclaimed the axiom that "there is no such thing as outside-of-the-text," denying that texts could refer to something called "reality," because all references to an outside world had to be expressed by words. This radical questioning opened the way to a multiplicity of imaginative readings but at the same time undercut the possibility of objective cognition, a central tenet of scientific modernity.[40]

Yet another French theorist, Jean-Francois Lyotard, attempted to spell out the implications of this linguistic approach in his reflections on the "postmodern condition," published as a book bearing that title in 1979. Disillusioned with Marxist politics and with Freudian psychoanalysis, he also rejected the Enlightenment heritage of faith in human progress. Afraid of the reduction of human knowledge to mere "data" as a result of the introduction of computers, he counseled a fundamental incredulity against "meta-narratives," which attempt to explain and justify human development, because he believed these usually justified some kind of suppression of others. Such a radical critique only left "language games," though even these were to be treated with suspicion.[41] But instead of despairing, Lyotard enjoyed the newfound freedom of the artistic avant-garde, supporting experimentation with appreciative reviews. This deconstruction of grand narratives came to be especially important for historians, because it provided them with a tool to dispute the claims of nationalist, proletarian, or religious mythologizing.

Michel Foucault, whose colorful life inspired a set of eclectic political commitments and philosophical stances, was an even more controversial critic of modernity. Like his contemporaries, he gradually emancipated himself from the rationalist legacy of Marxism though he remained active in various leftist causes such as decolonization and the antipsychiatry movement. In his sprawling works, he attempted nothing less than an "archaeology of knowledge," wrestling with the development of the whole philosophical tradition from Kant onward. Owing to the medical background of his parents, his first books dealt with disease, madness, and civilization, revealing the social construction of illness and sanity. Since being gay was still looked down upon in France, he fearlessly explored the history of sexuality. Moreover, as a moralist he reflected on the importance of power, through "governmentality" and routines of discipline and punishment. But his most important contribution was the concept of "discourse" as an interrelated rhetorical system of talking about certain topics and as a way of justifying certain policies.[42]

In part, this postmodern onslaught, amplified by the media, had a liberating effect, since it created space for innovation. In architecture, painting, and music artists felt free to ignore the conventions of high modernism, experimenting with even more radical styles. In literature the emphasis on deconstruction encouraged a proliferation of close readings that were no longer limited by canonic authority. In the media the postmodern eye recovered a multitude of photographic and filmic images regardless of their provenance or temporality. In philosophy this perspective undercut claims to objective knowledge, allowing for greater play of subjectivities. In the social sciences such a critique helped undermine linear notions of modernization as a progressive development according to the liberal capitalist or Marxist model. In history the attack on the grand narratives allowed the emergence of counterstories of previously suppressed minorities.[43] Especially feminist, black, and postcolonial thinkers in cultural studies embraced postmodernism in order to overthrow the hegemony of dead, white, European males.

Postmodernism, nonetheless, evoked widespread criticism that denounced it as a mere intellectual fashion, incapable of making a substantial contribution to illuminating the human condition. Especially conservative and religious thinkers castigated the moral relativism of a perspective in which "anything goes." At the same time Marxists in the East and West attacked the postmoderns as representatives of a decadent "late capitalism" who were unwilling to engage the massive injustices of the world. While natural scientists simply ignored the "pomo" talk, most social scientists also rejected its culturalist epistemology in favor of generalizations derived from quantitative data and rational-choice theory. The most serious challenge came, however, from liberal theorists like the sociologist Jürgen Habermas who attempted to rescue the emancipatory potential of the Enlightenment by establishing a method of discursive rationality.[44] While in France and the United States postmodern theories held sway, German intellectuals continued to cling to modernity as a progressive and democratic antidote to the reactionary spirit of National Socialism.

The postmodern attack on high modernity was therefore stronger in signaling that an epoch was coming to an end than in defining the character of what might come thereafter. What the self-proclaimed rebels rejected was quite clear—they disliked rationality, functionalism, objectivity, Marxism, and capitalism. In spite of distancing themselves from the ideology of modernization, they remained largely committed to causes of the Left. But the theoreticians were too confused, their philosophical arguments too arcane, and their claims too exaggerated to be entirely convincing. If human rights were not universally valid, what were the grounds on which opposition to patriarchy, racism, or imperialism could be based? Yet postmodernism spread rapidly through intellectual circles not just because it was hyped by the media, forever in search of novelty. In many ways the linguistic theorists touched a cultural nerve, signaling that something was ending without really knowing what that implied for the future. In that sense, postmodernism was both the end of high modernity and a prologue for things to come.

AFTER MODERNITY?

In many ways the postmodern provocation, proclaiming the end of modernity, seemed as preposterous to contemporary progressives as to cultural traditionalists. Skeptics could adduce many arguments that the term modernity, according to its various meanings, continued to be a valid description of the last quarter of the twentieth century. Certainly as a grand epoch, modern history, starting at the Renaissance and the Reformation, had not ended just because some French theorists and American literary critics were making such a grandiose pronouncement. At the same time the adjectival usage of the concept modern as continually new suggested an eternal present that would go on forever, though always changing its content. Finally, optimistic interpretations of modernization as a process that brought progress could be sustained for Europe by pointing to the improvement of numerous indicators such as personal wealth or life expectancy.[45] Although there were ample reasons not to believe that the present had entered an era "after modernity," the claim to postmodernity, nonetheless, enjoyed widespread resonance.

One source of postmodernism's popularity was the undoubted existence of a cultural movement that described itself as such. Dominant in the new playfulness of architecture, it extended to other fields like music and literature as well. Moreover, the impact of the linguistic and later iconic turns created a new form of literary and artistic criticism, interpreting these works for the general public. Of course, in many ways the postmoderns simply carried the experimentation of the avant-garde further, selectively advancing or leaving behind modernist forms. Since what was continued or rejected depended on the definition of high modernity in each respective field, no unified postmodern style did emerge. Instead postmodernism became defined as repudiation of the existing canon, giving voice and image to a plurality of approaches, freely mixing present with past, and ignoring the distinction between high and popular culture. This fragmentation proved at the same time advantageous and limiting, but it was justified by a cultural politics that rebelled against standards by stressing the creative power of diversity.[46]

Another cause of the rapid spread of the term was the "value change" to postmaterialism resulting from the generational rebellion of the 1960s. Almost immediately survey researchers like Ronald Inglehart discovered a shift from the postwar generation's pursuit of prosperity and security to their children's emphasis on quality of life and self-realization. Well-educated urban professionals, especially, set priorities that differed from those of the labor-union struggles over wages and working conditions by campaigning against environmental degradation, male patriarchy, or the arms race. Interestingly enough, their critique turned against both capitalist exploitation and socialist regimentation, since it rejected the continuation of economic growth and emphasized sustainability instead. In contrast to large-scale industry, big organizations, and government bureaucracy, the new social movements preferred small crafts, informal networks, and grassroots mobilization.[47] No doubt there was a romantic element in the rejection of high modernity, but the search for alternatives was also a constructive corrective to its shortcomings.

A final source of the postmodern rhetoric was the erosion of the modernization paradigm, both as a macro-sociological theory of human evolution and as a strategy of economic development. Since the benefits of modernity seemed self-evident because of improving living standards during the postwar boom, the social-science debate had revolved around how to advance the process more quickly and spread it to the so-called developing countries. But modernization lost its luster for theoretical as well as practical reasons: To begin with, the philosophical assault of the postmodern theorists undercut the epistemological foundations on which its social-science generalizations were based. Moreover, the results of capitalist and communist strategies of development in the decolonizing countries turned out to be rather disappointing. While the West successfully shifted to a consumer economy, the Soviet Bloc fell behind, discrediting its socialist alternative in the eyes of its own citizens. Finally, the growing sensitivity toward genocide, triggered by the growing awareness of the Holocaust, also robbed modernity of its emancipatory nimbus by revealing its dark underside.[48]

The question of whether modernity has passed has yet to find a definitive answer. Many arguments speak for a continuation of high modernity, since science and technology, industrial production, bureaucratic government, and urban living seem to be persisting. Yet there are other indicators such as the emergence of a service economy, the quantum jump in high technology, and the intensification of globalization that suggest something new might, indeed, be emerging. The cultural changes such as the shift in styles, the change in values, and the linguistic turn could be the cutting edge of a larger transformation not yet completely clear to the contemporaries caught up in it. Various attempts at labeling this perplexing situation have not yielded any convincing consensus, since the suggestion of a second or "reflexive modernity," advanced by Ulrich Beck and Anthony Giddens, has yet to catch on. A more ironic response to this conceptual uncertainty would be to call the last quarter of the twentieth century, provisionally, an era of "postmodern modernity."[49]

Chapter 23

POSTINDUSTRIAL TRANSITION

British deindustrialization, 1983. *Source*: Magnum Images.

O n October 16, 1973, the six largest oil-producing countries on the Persian Gulf suddenly announced a 70 percent increase in the price of their crude. By using "oil as an Arab weapon" they sought to pressure the supporters of Israel in the Yom Kippur War into forcing Israel to withdraw from the Sinai Peninsula and the Golan Heights. Moreover, the Organization of Petroleum Exporting Countries (OPEC), which controlled 40 percent of the global supply, also issued an embargo against the United States, Japan, and Western Europe "by monthly 5 percent cut-backs in the flow of oil." Quadrupling from around three U.S. dollars to twelve dollars per barrel, the subsequent price increase stunned the industrial countries, since not only their heating and transportation systems but also a good part of their industrial production depended on Near Eastern oil. Recalling World War II shortages, the public panicked, lining up at filling stations, while governments frantically proposed rationing, lower speed limits, and prohibitions on Sunday driving to conserve gasoline. Even after a pro-Arab statement by the EC had restored supply, the Arab embargo shattered western confidence.[1]

This "oil price shock," or Oil Shock, disrupted European economies and threw politics into confusion, since there was no quick way to substitute other energy sources. The Arabs were able to use oil to exert political pressure because the European Community depended on their crude for 80 percent of its supplies, since North Sea oil had not yet begun to flow. The price increase shifted the balance of power, for once, from the industrialized states to the raw-material countries, acting as a surtax that transferred profits to the Near East and allowed the producers to amass untold fortunes. By making everything that required petroleum more expensive, the steep rise in oil prices also triggered inflation because demand proved inelastic in the short run. Exaggerated by media alarmism, popular fears of lower living standards also contributed to a deep recession, which in effect ended the postwar boom that had lasted an entire generation.[2] Misunderstood as a problem of the business cycle, the Oil Shock distracted attention from a more fundamental problem—the transition to a postindustrial economy.

Since leftist politicians failed to find effective solutions, the rise in oil prices, redoubled again in 1979, helped discredit Keynesian policies and encouraged a surprising revival of neoliberalism. Opposed to fascist and communist regulation, a small group of economists following Friedrich von Hayek had persistently advocated a reduction of government control of the economy. Going back to the liberal theoreticians of the eighteenth century like Adam Smith, these monetarists of what was called the Chicago school argued in favor of individual autonomy, free-market competition, deregulation, and privatization in order to restore entrepreneurial initiative. When countercyclical spending failed to stimulate robust growth and bring down the high inflation, such neoliberal prescriptions suddenly began to seem more attractive. One of their key converts was Margaret Thatcher, who weaned the Conservative Party from corporatism and then won the election of 1979, getting a chance to implement the neoliberal agenda as prime minister.[3] The result of her tough policies speeded up and deepened the structural transition in Britain.

The turn to neoliberalism led to widespread attacks on the welfare state, seeking to cut back its excesses and to reverse direction toward self-reliance. Both objective pressures and subjective preferences combined in the call for lowering public expenditures. During the oil-induced recessions of 1974–75 and 1981–82 unemployment in the United Kingdom soared to over 10 percent, imposing huge costs on the exchequer. Moreover, the decline in tax receipts made it more difficult to keep funding extensive social programs. At the same time a growing number of middle-class voters, first in the United Kingdom but then also on the continent, revolted against the high marginal tax rates, approaching 90 percent in Scandinavia. Conservative parties profited from this resentment, demanding a reduction of welfare benefits, a decrease in unemployment payments, and a lowering of public assistance. While moderates wanted only to prune its proliferation, radical neoliberals intended to abolish the welfare state altogether. Psychologically understandable, this overreaction threatened to abolish social services just when they were most needed because of the restructuring.[4]

The dispute about how to respond to the Oil Shocks blocked the realization that the slowdown's underlying cause was the transition to the postindustrial phase of modernity. The recession resulted not just from the business cycle but also from the shift of Fordist mass production to the Asian "tiger states." Trying to stop the process of deindustrialization, which blighted entire areas and disrupted working-class lives, did soften its human impact but provided little hope for a resumption of growth. Gradually the failure of Keynesian countercyclical policies to overcome the stubborn combination of economic stagnation and high inflation shifted public sentiment toward neoliberal policies. The subsequent cutbacks of welfare-state expenditures helped make European industries somewhat more competitive. But it was ultimately the rise of the digital economy, fueled by computers and communication devices, that created new chances for the young and well educated.[5] Together with the cultural revolt, this postindustrial transition ushered in a new phase of global modernity, creating both insecurity and opportunity.

OIL SHOCKS

Even before the Arab-Israeli war, the international economy showed signs of growing strains. The chief cause was the high cost of the U.S. involvement in the Vietnam War, which rendered President Johnson's policy of having both "guns and butter" too costly in the long run. To relieve balance-of-payment problems, the Nixon administration in August 1971 decided to abandon the Bretton Woods system of fixed exchange rates that had made international trade predictable. Once the weakening dollar was allowed to float freely, other currencies like the DM and the yen followed suit, gaining in value, which reduced the export advantages of Germany and Japan.[6] Since oil revenues were denominated in U.S. dollars, the depreciation of the American currency eroded the profits of the producing countries, giving OPEC an economic motive to raise prices. The oil cartel was able to charge more, since the United States had just appeared to reach "peak oil" production, while the Europeans had no real source of crude of their own before the North Sea oil started to flow in the second half of the 1970s.

European countries were particularly vulnerable, as they had shifted their prime energy source from coal to oil during the 1960s. Most of the rebuilding after World War II and the Economic Miracle of the 1950s had still been fueled by anthracite coal, extracted from deep mine shafts in Wales, the Ruhr Basin, and Silesia. But oil won the energy competition not only because it was cheaper to produce and easier to transport but also because it offered additional advantages: For heating purposes, an automated oil burner could run continuously and cleanly, while a coal furnace required restoking and emitted noxious fumes. In transportation, petroleum drove the shift from public transport in coal-powered trains to individual mobility in automobiles since the latter was more flexible, allowing individual movement independent of fixed routes and timetables. And in industry, hydrogenation of coal was expensive, while petroleum derivatives opened up a whole new field of plastics for construction and consumer goods. Though coal-fired power plants persisted, the shift to oil was slowed only by the lack of European fields.[7]

The western governments responded to OPEC's "oil blackmail" with a confused mixture of short-range actions and long-range rethinking. To calm public fears, they hit upon a series of measures that looked as if they were doing something but ultimately had little effect. In West Germany the social-liberal coalition instituted a driving ban for four consecutive Sundays, which created an eerie picture of not-quite-empty superhighways, since they were reappropriated by pleased pedestrians and bicyclists. Some countries like France drastically lowered speed limits in order to save fuel, but the problem was enforcement, since too often drivers simply ignored them. Other efforts such as rationing fuel created confrontations at the filling stations with owners not knowing how to deal with the reduced supplies and angry customers fighting over scarce gasoline. Journalist Sebastian Haffner therefore concluded: "We have to free ourselves from oil, even if the withdrawal is hard to cope with."[8] Only gradually did it become clear that, along with conservation, a more constructive reaction would be the development of alternate sources of energy.

As a result of OPEC's reduction of oil production by about 7.5 percent, the West European economies fell into a recession that was both deep and long lasting. Though the precise figures differed in various countries, GNPs declined over 3 percent between November 1973 and the middle of 1975. In part, exaggerated fears were to blame, because they reduced consumer willingness to buy. In part, the recession was a result of government policies that reduced energy allotments to factories and private homes, for instance decreasing the workweek to three days in Britain in order to avoid blackouts. Finally, the recession was also induced by business decisions, such as anticipating dropping demand by reducing car production, which set a downward spiral in motion. As a result, unemployment inexorably rose to over 12 percent in the United Kingdom and Holland, aggravating the drop in purchasing power. Finally, the increase in energy costs also pushed up European inflation to 9.4 percent by 1983, which dampened business activity. The consequence of the downturn was the first major recession, which ended almost three decades of the postwar boom.[9]

Resuming economic growth was difficult because of the nasty "stagflation" that beset European economies after the rise in energy costs. This term was a combination of stagnation, indicating little growth, and inflation, suggesting a loss of buying power. Owing to the oil price increase, the expansion of the European economy did stall, accompanied by high unemployment and rising inflation. This unexpected predicament baffled Keynesian policy makers, since attempts to stimulate growth by government spending would drive up inflation, whereas efforts to stop currency depreciation would increase the number of unemployed. While Britain remained caught in a vicious cycle due to high wage demands and excessive government spending, West German chancellor Helmut Schmidt succeeded in decreasing inflation and joblessness by reducing some expenditures and applying limited stimulation.[10] Ultimately only the strategy of "recycling petrodollars," by getting the nouveau riche Arab elites to buy luxury goods and invest their gains, retransferred some of their earnings to Europe and revived some semblance of growth.

Unfortunately a second oil crisis from 1979 to 1981 nipped the weak recovery in the bud and triggered yet another recession. The overthrow of the shah of Iran by the Islamic revolution of Ayatollah

Khomeini reduced the oil supply by 7 percent, and then the ensuing war between Iran and Iraq cut output by another 6 percent. This renewed drop in production pushed the price per barrel up to over forty dollars, once again doubling energy costs in real terms. The predictable result was another, even more severe recession. Unemployment grew to about 8 percent in France and Germany, private consumption stagnated, and inflation reached a new postwar high. Hence trade between advanced industrial countries declined by one-fifth, and industrial output shrank by over 10 percent. After three decades of growth, this second recession came as an even greater shock because it indicated that the difficulties were not just temporary in nature.[11] Since the new crisis made incumbents look bad, Margaret Thatcher was elected in Britain in 1979, François Mitterrand assumed power in France in 1981, and Helmut Kohl became German chancellor in 1982.

The subsequent collapse of oil prices to twelve dollars a barrel by 1986 revealed that the anemic performance of the European economies actually had deeper causes. During the period of perpetual growth business had overinvested, generating idle capacity, while labor had become accustomed to high wages and long vacations. The subsequent curtailment of investment led to low productivity gains, miring European companies in mediocre performance. At the same time insistent union demands created a wage-price spiral that negated pay gains in real terms by pushing up commodity prices, perpetuating substantial rates of inflation. Many governments reacted with "defensive investments" to the growing worldwide competition, and the EC raised its external tariffs to protect native producers. The pressure of rationalization led to weak job creation, while rising expenditures for unemployment compensation limited funds for research and development. As a result external observers and internal critics increasingly talked about a "Eurosclerosis" that was rendering the Old Continent incapable of shaking off its lethargy.[12]

Though Eastern Europe appeared to have escaped the oil crisis, this impression turned out to be deceptive, since its consequences were ultimately even more deleterious. Shielded from world-market competition by the nonconvertibility of their currencies, communist leaders could gloat about the problems of "late capitalism" and predict its imminent demise. Members of the Comecon felt secure, since their oil was being supplied by the large fields of the Soviet Union and some smaller Marxist countries in the Third World. As a result of this protection, Soviet Bloc countries had even fewer incentives to modernize their smokestack, labor-intensive industries. With domestic growth practically stalled, however, they were forced to borrow from the West in order to supply those attractive consumer goods which they were unable to manufacture themselves. Eventually the Soviet Union raised its own oil price with a five-year moving average that slowed down the increase but kept costs high after prices once again declined on the world market. The postponed reckoning, when it finally came in 1989, turned out to be all the more severe.[13]

SCOURGE OF DEINDUSTRIALIZATION

Overshadowed by the oil crisis, the underlying process of deindustrialization proved even more challenging, since it destroyed the economic basis of high industrial society. Describing the closing of individual plants, the disappearance of whole branches of industry, and the general decline of manufacturing, this neologism was itself a product of the structural changes triggered by globalization in the 1970s. Its cause was the intensification of international competition, since developing countries in Asia were able to produce many consumer items more cheaply than mature economies, eventually putting their competitors out of business. The relocation of production was hastened by declining transport costs as well as technological innovations that automated production, reducing the advantage of a trained workforce. While consumers profited from lower prices, western producers lost their factories, creating structural unemployment and blighting old industrial regions. Unprepared for deindustrialization, the political elites misunderstood it as a problem of the business cycle and tended to defend the ailing industries rather than to invest in innovation.[14]

One key element was the decline of Fordist mass production of consumer goods such as textiles, which had already started in the

1950s. Once consumers had outfitted themselves with clothing after the war, overproduction intensified competition between firms. Many factories sought to survive through automation, borrowing in order to install new spinning and weaving machinery that needed fewer workers. Since this strategy did not return enough profit, energetic entrepreneurs tried outsourcing, shifting production to the European periphery in the South and East where wages were lower, while still designing clothes at home. When that did not work any longer, the bigger firms went to Asia, where wages were even lower. But these licensed manufacturers in Asia soon emancipated themselves and started to produce their own labels. As the making of items like T-shirts moved to the Far East, only a few firms such as Bennetton could hang on by combining European design with Asian manufacture.[15] Quietly, one factory after another had to close, and its displaced workers, often women, struggled to find new jobs.

Another, more devastating factor was the coal and steel crisis that had been gradually eroding the industrial core of European countries since the late 1950s. The conversion from coal to oil as the dominant fuel and competition from open-pit mining in the United States and Australia made much of the continental coal too expensive, since it had to be extracted deep underground from narrow seams that rendered using machines difficult. Over union protests, one coal mine after another had to be closed during the 1960s and 1970s, putting hundreds of thousands of miners out of work. Even British and French nationalization and the concentration of German coal production in one Ruhr Basin company could not stave off the closures. The end of rebuilding war-ravaged cities and the conclusion of the Korean War also created a glut in steel, since one of the biggest consumers, the shipbuilding industry in Belfast and Hamburg, was also failing. Owing to its cheaper coal and lower labor cost, basic steelmaking shifted to Asia, with only specialty steel surviving. The EC sought to salvage production by dividing the market in a cartel-like fashion and encouraging the fusion of competitors like Krupp and Thyssen.[16]

Often overlooked, a third dimension of technological change pushed deindustrialization even into more advanced sectors of manufacturing. Initially the catch-up industrialization of the Asian tiger states had concentrated on taking over cheap mass production, but gradually higher-quality manufacturing developed as well in countries like Japan. Traditional European companies such as Zeiss in optics, Leica in cameras, AEG in appliances, and Grundig in electronics relied on their superior design, craft-trained workforce, and prestigious names in order to sell expensive items. But their Asian competitors were quicker in making use of innovations like computer chips and robotic production, first capturing the market for inexpensive mass products. Gradually engineering advances and stylistic redesign shifted the frontier of innovation to Asia, leaving many well-known European brands scrambling to compete. Soon the combination of technical sophistication and reasonable price made Sony, Canon, and Samsung household words in Europe, while one traditional name after another like the film producer Agfa disappeared.[17]

The chief consequence of these deindustrialization processes was the emergence of structural unemployment that proved resistant to political countermeasures. Simply put, only some of the jobs lost during the recession of 1973–75 returned with the recovery, creating a new plateau from which further jobs were lost in 1979–81, consistently increasing the jobless rate to over 7.5 percent. In Britain alone, about two million jobs vanished with deindustrialization during the 1970s, much more than were gained with the shift to financial services and high-tech employment. Skilled or semiskilled male workers over forty years of age were reluctant to move elsewhere and quite difficult to retrain for new careers. Miners, steelmakers, ship welders—workers such as these, once part of a labor aristocracy, were extremely bitter about losing not only their employment but also a major source of their pride and self-identity to a macroeconomic process they did not fully understand. In contrast, women and the young adapted more easily, albeit landing often in low-paying positions. The effect of prolonged joblessness was much political resentment and enormous cost increases for social services, called *Sozialpläne*, that tried to cushion the loss.[18]

The struggle over the closure of the Krupp steelworks in Rheinhausen, once the biggest in Europe, was a dramatic example of globalization logic and labor impotence. Situated on the Rhine River across from the Ruhr, the factory had been founded in 1897 because the local coal was used to transform iron ore shipped from abroad into high-grade steel. Though the works had just been renovated at great cost, manager Gerhard Cromme decided to close the plant because of the world-market glut of rolled steel. When he announced his decision on November 26, 1987, six thousand shocked steelworkers suddenly faced unemployment. The strong union waged a spirited resistance, occupying the bridge across the Rhine, mobilizing the prime minister of North Rhine-Westphalia, and appealing to public sympathy. Trying to preserve an entire way of life, the strikers intoned an emotional song: "Rheinhausen, you must not die." Though the workers fought for 164 days, the factory was closed in 1993, the equipment partly sold to China, and the buildings torn down to make space for a trucking center, employing one-third of the previous workforce.[19]

The result of such profit-oriented decisions was the blighting of entire regions that had once been the industrial heartland of Western Europe. From the Midlands to Lorraine, from Lancashire to the Ruhr, abandoned factories stood with machines idled, windows broken, and grass growing through cracks in the parking lots. In working-class neighborhoods many apartments were empty and small stores boarded up. Men loitered in the street or congregated in pubs, while women scraped their meager cash together to buy a few victuals. The young were conspicuously absent, having moved away to more promising places. An air of depression and neglect hung over the afflicted communities, since hope had disappeared. Only in a few exceptional cases did new plants like Opel in Bochum pick up some of the slack, but even then they employed fewer workers than before. A few fortunate mines and steel plants were converted into industrial museums.[20] But the examples of turning factories into condominiums or artists' lofts were rare, since they required an affluent clientele. It was small comfort that the air became once again breathable and the water swimmable.

Shielded behind the Iron Curtain, Eastern Europe initially escaped the turmoil of deindustrialization, only to be overwhelmed by it after 1989. Even without its Stalinist distortions, Marxism-Leninism remained a high-industrial ideology based on factory production and the working class. Determined to prevent a repetition of the unemployment during the Great Depression, the communist leadership took pride in a policy of full employment that guaranteed everyone a job, even if much working time was spent on political indoctrination and on getting the shopping done. As a result of lack of investment, the basic industrial infrastructure crumbled, with much machinery decades old and in dire need of replacement. Moreover, the widespread desire for consumer goods drove communist governments into the trap of borrowing from the West, thereby becoming dependent on the class enemy.[21] Western visitors no longer marveled but stared in wonderment: some of the most important industrial plants, from Nowa Huta to Eisenhüttenstadt, had already began to look like museums—while the workers were still using their machines!

NEOLIBERAL TURN

Unable to overcome stagflation and structural unemployment, the Keynesian consensus gradually eroded, making way for a resurgence of free-market approaches. Social democratic efforts at stimulating the economy through countercyclical government spending were only raising inflation, which was approaching 20 percent in Britain during the late 1970s. Moreover, labor-union demands for sharing the remaining jobs by cutting the workweek down to thirty hours would have made European goods even more expensive. Hence a growing group of managers and economists pleaded for more "courage for competition." Arguing that government meddling in the economy, with the resulting high taxes and welfare costs, had priced European countries out of the market, these neoliberals called for drastic cutbacks in order to restore competitiveness and thus revive economic dynamism. In short, they proposed to fix the problem by not trying to fix it—that is, by letting the process of deindustrialization take its course. In the fierce policy controversy over whether to redistribute work or to let unrestrained competition revive the market, the latter position ultimately prevailed in the media and among the public.[22]

The controversial British prime minister Margaret Thatcher was the unlikely leader who spearheaded the neoliberal turn. Born in

Lincolnshire in 1925 as daughter of a Methodist greengrocer, she studied chemistry at Oxford and later became a barrister. Joining the Conservative Party, she quickly rose through the ranks because of her outspokenness, moralism, and political shrewdness, becoming secretary of education in 1970 and succeeding the ill-starred Edward Heath as opposition leader after the Conservatives' loss of the 1975 election. Influenced by neoliberal thinkers like Keith Joseph and the Institute of Economic Affairs, she gradually became a fervent free-market advocate, blaming Labour's "culture of dependency" for the decline of Britain. Her international views were firmly anticommunist, leading her to denounce the Soviet Union. When James Callaghan's Labour government failed to reduce inflation, unemployment, and strikes during the "winter of discontent" in 1979, she seized the chance to win the general election.[23] As the first female prime minister, she set out to restore entrepreneurship so as to put Britain back on its feet.

The combative "Iron Lady," as she was called, pursued monetarist policies aiming at nothing less than a fundamental transformation of British society. Upon assuming office, she cut government spending and lowered income taxes, shifting to indirect value-added taxation instead. To wean the country from socialism, she broke the back of the thirteen-million-strong trade unions by riding out the miner's strike called in 1984 to prevent the closing of twenty mines. Getting the state out of the economy, she launched an ambitious privatization program, selling off utilities, nationalized industries like British Steel, and public housing (the council houses). The program was a mixed success, since monopolies in private hands remained inefficient and the later privatization of the railroads turned out to be a disaster. But by reviving the spirit of individual responsibility, she managed to push ownership of stock-market shares up from 7 percent to 25 percent and of homes up to two-thirds of the public. Her neoliberal restructuring polarized British society, accelerating regional deindustrialization but also sparking new prosperity by deregulating financial services.[24]

Initially François Mitterrand's victory in the 1981 French presidential election bucked the neoliberal tide, as he was a committed socialist supported also by the Communist Party. He was born in 1916 in the Charente into a Catholic and nationalist family with his father being a vinegar producer. Studying law at the prestigious Ecole des Sciences Politiques, Mitterrand was active in right-wing causes, and after fleeing German captivity he became a minor official in the Vichy government until he joined the resistance in 1943. In the postwar period he served as minister in several cabinets and opposed the establishment of the Fifth Republic because a coup had put de Gaulle into power. As both a Socialist and a Machiavellian, he became a consensus challenger of the Left, attacking de Gaulle and his successors. During their twenty-three-year reign, the Gaullists had actually pursued centrist policies in the tradition of *étatisme* that were nationalist abroad and welfare-oriented at home, but they ultimately failed to end the second oil recession. Propelled by Giscard d'Estaing's scandals as well as the economic woes, Mitterand managed to enter the Elysée Palace.[25]

The rapid failure of his socialist program, however, forced Mitterrand to join the neoliberal camp, albeit rather reluctantly. His initial reform program, a leftist Keynesianism had envisaged further nationalizations of industry, workers' control over factories, and additional planning. Moreover, his government had also raised the minimum wage, lowered the retirement age, increased family allowances, and extended housing support, thereby pushing social transfer costs from 4.5 percent to 7.6 percent of GDP within one year. The creation of two hundred thousand new government jobs could not have come at a worse time, since it increased the budget deficit while neither inflation nor unemployment budged. In July 1983 a contrite Mitterrand had to admit the failure of his socialist experiment, because economic growth had refused to follow ideology. He was compelled to announce a harsh austerity plan that reduced government spending, froze wages, and decreased business taxes. Also, in order to stay in the European Monetary System, a humiliated France had to devalue the franc.[26] The failure of Mitterrand's Keynesianism reinforced the appeal of neoliberal Thatcherism, promoted in France by a neoconservative group of *nouvelles philosophes*.

The last of the new leaders, German chancellor Helmut Kohl, also sought to reenergize his country by turning away from unsuccessful social democratic policies. He similarly came to power as a result of the second oil crisis, which made the small, liberal Free Democratic Party (FDP) switch coalition partners to the CDU, overthrowing Helmut Schmidt. Born in 1930 in the Rhenish city of Ludwigshafen into a Catholic civil-service family, Kohl had lost his older brother at the end of the war. He studied political science and history at Heidelberg and joined the Christian Democratic Party as a teenager. Because of his openness to new approaches and his ability to network with people he rose within its regional ranks, becoming minister-president of Rhineland-Palatinate at the tender age of thirty-nine. Although his party won 48.6 percent of the popular vote in the 1976 election, the social-liberal coalition headed by Schmidt retained a bare majority. The disappointed Kohl remained opposition leader but became chancellor by winning a constructive vote of no confidence in October 1982, approved by a general election a few months later.[27]

Underestimated by intellectuals, Kohl firmly believed in the "social market economy" and therefore proclaimed a "spiritual-moral turnaround" of his own. As representative of business interests, the FDP, his coalition partner, had already called for "a policy to overcome the weakness of growth." Ideologically opposed to the legacy of 1968, Kohl similarly demanded moving "away from the state, toward the market" by breaking up entrenched special interests and rehabilitating individual initiative. This change of course was supported by the Council of Economic Advisers, which also called for an improvement in competitiveness "by accepting the structural transformation." In order to stimulate the economy, Kohl reduced public expenditures, rebalanced the budget, privatized assets like Deutsche Telekom, and deregulated business. Although the unions and the Social Democrats blocked more radical measures in the Bundesrat, this moderate neoliberalism reignited growth, raised incomes, and generated new jobs. Without abandoning social solidarity, the CDU/FDP reforms managed to overcome stagnation and restore a sense of progress.[28]

As a result of these experiences, neoliberalism spread through Western and Central Europe, becoming the new policy consensus. The reputation of Thatcherism improved when, after several years of turmoil, the British economy finally started to revive, raising the value of the pound, resuming growth, and adding jobs by the early to mid-1980s.[29] Moreover, in the United States the "Reagan revolution" conjured growth out of similar monetary policies, making Milton Friedman's economics the new orthodoxy. Neoliberalism therefore proliferated from Italy to Scandinavia, allowing bourgeois parties that had been in opposition for decades to take power in unlikely countries like Sweden and Denmark. Moreover, with the help of regional EU funds, new Mediterranean members were also at last liberalizing their economies. Though the Soviet Bloc remained firmly opposed, even behind the Iron Curtain some daring economists in Budapest and Prague dreamt of market incentives, while restive Polish workers demanded increased benefits. Reinforced by globalization, the neoliberal wave swept all objections before it.

WELFARE-STATE CUTBACKS

The neoliberals' favorite target was the proliferation of the welfare state, because its financial costs and extensive safety net seemed to stifle economic creativity. Critics such as businessmen, economists, and middle-class taxpayers used both economic and moral arguments to attack social policies, claiming that they made European products too expensive and created a mentality of dependency. But defenders of the welfare state in the trade unions, among client groups, and in the social sciences argued for the importance of solidarity in order to decrease tensions within society. The ensuing debate about the future of the welfare state therefore involved fundamentally different interpretations of capitalism and democracy, pitting individual initiative against collective security. During the postwar boom, economic growth allowed both views to be reconciled, but after the Oil Shocks their prescriptions started to diverge, triggering an intensive public discussion in which the anemic performance of the economy appeared to support neoliberal arguments.[30]

The chief impetus for cutting back the welfare state came from a widespread "tax revolt" against the high levels of taxation necessary for supporting its benefits. Inspired by the California Proposition 13 movement, European antitax activists emphasized that the top rate of income taxes of over 50 percent reduced incentives for high achievers. Inheritance taxes also tended to devour between one-third and one-half of the amounts bequeathed, making it difficult to pass a small firm on to the next generation. The high business taxes of around 50 percent on annual profits drove corporations to move their headquarters to so-called tax havens like Liechtenstein, Luxembourg, or the Channel Islands, where the rates were much lower. Finally, the antitax movement also had a moralistic undertone, claiming that the poor should simply work harder, and appealed to xenophobic resentment by refusing to pay for the support of penniless immigrants. Though its intensity varied regionally, tax resentment fueled the electoral success of rightist parties like the British Conservatives.[31]

Economists and columnists held the welfare state responsible for the growing loss of competitiveness of European businesses, due to its generous welfare provisions. They pointed out that in the EC people generally worked about one-third fewer hours per year than Americans since they enjoyed more holidays and longer vacations. Continental workers also tended to retire several years earlier than their U.S. counterparts, thereby adding to the cost of pensions. Each salary in Europe was burdened with a governmental component of about 50 percent, consisting of tax bites and social-security payments, compared to only about one-third for salaries in the United States. These burdens pushed the cost to businesses of the average hourly wage in Europe about one-quarter higher than in America—creating a sizable disadvantage for labor-intensive industries. As a result of considerably higher benefits, government social expenditures in 1980 averaged around 20 percent on the continent, compared with only 13 percent in the United States. Neoliberal commentators could claim with considerable justification that owing to such levies, the generosity of the European welfare state made its businesses less competitive.[32]

Defenders of the welfare state refused, however, to give up without a fight, claiming vigorously that "the Keynesian social democratic state has not failed." Leftist politicians, trade union leaders, and social scientists formulated a series of counterarguments. They claimed that there existed a "moral responsibility" for strangers in need, requiring a civilized society to show its empathy. Moreover, they pointed out that during the crisis of deindustrialization support payments were more important than ever in order to keep the affected workers from utter destitution. At the same time, they emphasized the considerable achievements of social policies in expanding access to education, improving public health, making better housing available, increasing social security, and providing personal services.[33] Moreover, left-wing economists stressed the importance of assuring sufficient demand for goods and services by income transfers to the poor. Finally, proponents of solidarity also claimed that a social safety net was essential for the functioning of democracy. Instead of being abolished, the welfare state should merely be reformed.

Judging by its rhetoric, Margaret Thatcher's attempt to reverse the "dependence upon the state" was a radical approach, since she demanded a "new ethics of welfare policy." One priority was to encourage self-help and charity, that is, voluntary solutions to social problems rather than government entitlements. Though she was loath to abandon the National Health Service altogether, she encouraged market elements such as the cooperation of physicians in groups and the introduction of private insurance. In contrast to prior Labour cabinets, she quickly stopped the futile effort of an incomes policy that tried to keep pay disparities from rising and, rather, encouraged monetary rewards for superior performance, which increased inequality. While not abandoning the network of various support payments, she changed the rhetoric, making it seem indecent to rely on the dole. Consequently the British system provided merely basic security rather than higher income replacement for the unemployed. Surprisingly enough, in spite of all of her attempts, tax rates and public expenditures declined only slowly, leaving the core of the welfare state untouched.[34]

The continental pattern, exemplified by the FRG, proceeded more cautiously in implementing cost containment to keep the *Sozialstaat* solvent. The German system was based on the principle of a male wage earner in a long-term industrial job, insuring him against misfortunes but leaving those without stable jobs to social assistance. The pension system, funded by "pay as you go" contributions of workers, and the generous medical coverage, consisting of a statutory health insurance, rendered change difficult. Already during the mid-1970s the social-liberal coalition started to make selective benefit cuts, limited pension increases, and demanded copayments while raising some contributions. During his chancellorship Kohl continued the focus on cost abatement via targeted reductions, fee increases, and a change in pension indexing, saving sufficient funds to permit modest increases in coverage. The French system was even more generous in supporting child care and family assistance. On the whole these modest adjustments kept the system functioning, although they failed to reduce its drag on competitiveness.[35]

The Scandinavian model's invention of an "activating welfare state" provided a better solution, since upgrading skills rather than cushioning unemployment kept people in the workforce. From the 1970s on this high-taxation and big-benefit system had also come under increasing strain, forcing some cutbacks. But ultimately the pressures led to the constructive response of human investment so as to help workers to adjust to globalization. One secret of its success was the active-labor policy, which qualified the jobless for new tasks through retraining schemes and compelled their relocation, if need be. Another element was the flexibility of the employment market, with few protections but more support during periods of joblessness that made getting a new position easier. Finally there was also an exemplary gender dimension of care for children and the aged, allowing women to remain in the workplace instead of being hamstrung by family obligations. Keeping people working rather than supporting their idleness seemed not just more humane but also more cost-efficient, since it allowed taxes to be reduced.[36]

The reform efforts of the European welfare state therefore steered a middle course between radical Reaganomics and Soviet immobilism. In its rhetoric the Anglo-American program was an ambitious attempt to reduce the welfare state as much as possible in order to restore the dynamism of the free market. In contrast, the Soviet Bloc under Brezhnev counted on the collapse of capitalism and, given its limited foreign trade, saw little need to adjust to globalization pressures. The French and the Germans pruned the continental model of the welfare state just enough in order to keep it solvent, but their halfhearted efforts did not do enough to make it competitive again. The Scandinavian approach had greater success, because the new concept of an "enabling welfare state" invested in human resources and thereby kept both social protections extensive and living standards high. As a result of these moderate corrections, also undertaken in other continental countries like the Netherlands and Austria, the welfare state not only survived but shed much of its apathy and regained some of its competitiveness.[37]

HIGH-TECH OPPORTUNITIES

In contrast to leftists who lamented industrial decline, neoliberals welcomed the postindustrial transition as a series of exciting opportunities for growth and social change. They viewed the dissolution of the high industrial order not just as a loss of security but also as a chance to break the stranglehold of entrenched interests by creating space for innovation that would bring individual rewards and make society as a whole more dynamic. The very same technology that social democrats tended to castigate as a "job killer" appeared to conservatives as a stimulus for resuming growth, shaking up an all-too-complacent corporatism. Especially the younger generation was quick to respond to the introduction of information technology in the workplace and in private life, experimenting with new uses and developing software for novel applications. In order not to fall behind the United States and Japan, European governments increased investment in research and development, looking to fund national-prestige projects. Rejecting intellectual predictions of doom, neoliberals hailed high technology as a potential savior.[38]

This technology enthusiasm was a product of positive experiences with the introduction of new machines that revolutionized many aspects of daily life. For instance, the development of passenger jets shortened international travel during the 1960s, making transatlantic flights feasible for a mass public. Similarly the development of color television during the second half of the 1960s and the addition of video recorders, which could play rented movies, transformed entertainment habits. Also, the creation of pocket calculators in the early 1970s facilitated computation for accountants, replaced the slide rule for engineers, and made individual purchases easier when built into cash registers. Moreover, the gradual introduction of electronically enabled credit cards not only rendered checks superfluous but radically altered spending habits.[39] The proliferation of such innovations changed personal lives and transformed economic relationships. The arrival of ever new gadgets like digital watches and the progressive decrease in their price endowed technological invention with a magic promise of facilitating a better life.

To stay at the cutting edge, European governments initiated a series of prestige projects, only some of which succeeded in the marketplace. The joint Franco-British development of a supersonic passenger plane, an engineering marvel named the Concorde that reduced flight times by half, did not prove commercially viable in the long run. Similarly the minitel, an ingenious combination of a TV screen, telephone, and computer, caught on only in France and was eventually displaced by the Internet. The German fast monorail train Transrapid also seemed promising, but only one line was eventually built, in Shanghai, since it proved too expensive. Other large-scale rapid-transit projects did become profitable, however, such as the French TGV and the even more extensive German ICE, which made flying for medium-range distances unnecessary by pushing rail speeds up to two hundred miles per hour. Another success was the Franco-German consortium called Airbus, which rivaled Boeing in producing efficient passenger airplanes.[40] While not all planning bets were practical, some large projects did keep European expertise at the forefront.

The most revolutionary new technology was the computer, as both a supercalculator and an essential communication link. While research sponsored by the U.S. military got it started, the privatization of computer development through IBM was more important in producing innovative mainframes in the 1960s and 1970s. Western

European states made efforts to support their own industries with Britain founding ICL, the French helping Bull, and the Germans underwriting Nixdorf and Siemens. But these "national champions" were unable to compete with the speed of American hardware and software development, since IBM cleverly shifted part of its research and manufacturing to the continent. Moreover, this large computational machinery was eventually outflanked by the invention of chip-based personal computers, coming first from Silicon Valley and then manufactured in Asia, exceptions like Nokia notwithstanding. Most software development also occurred in the United States, though in some areas such as business applications European firms like SAP could hold their own. However, the rapid adoption of computing in public and private use did bring Europe into the information age.[41]

Financial services became the new lead sector by profiting from information technology that made its transactions easier. Only computers could keep track of stock trading, exchange-rate fluctuations, and the like in real time, linking marketplaces around the world in split seconds. The deregulation of banking, authorized in Britain in 1986, encouraged trading by abolishing the distinction between retail and investment services, allowing traditional banks to speculate in a wide range of markets. Moreover, insurance companies and pension funds were also no longer content with the meager gains from traditional interest-bearing assets but began looking instead for larger returns in stocks, bonds, and currency transactions. Rising middle-class participation in these markets called for a new cadre of financial advisers to tell clients where to invest their money. Finally, the formerly forbidding banks began issuing credit cards and installing automatic teller machines for withdrawals, becoming a bit more consumer friendly. As a result, some financial centers like London and Frankfurt prospered, with hordes of young and well-paid investment bankers who acted like "masters of the universe" when speculating with other people's money.[42]

Another service area propelled by technology was private broadcasting, introduced on the continent in response to political and commercial pressures. Since public monopolies like the BBC sought to educate as well as entertain, producing programming was rather expensive, requiring mandatory user fees. Considering public-radio and TV journalists to be more liberal than the "silent majority" of the population, conservative parties urged the establishment of competing commercial networks. Italy was the first to deregulate in 1976, which led to the establishment of twenty-five hundred local stations—and to the rise of the Berlusconi empire. Advertisers also pushed for privatization, since they stood to make much money in the electronic media. Reluctantly the major European countries allowed commercial competitors like SKY TV and SAT.1 access to the airwaves in the early 1980s, though setting firm regulatory limits. Aided by cable and satellite TV, an advertising-driven media industry emerged that catered to soft porn and violence while spreading conservative political messages.[43] Ironically, the political project of the right undercut its own moral posturing.

Not all industries succumbed to global competition, since automobile production for instance reemerged stronger by adapting to innovation. The oil-price increase and Japanese competition pushed European manufacturers into a severe crisis by the mid-1970s, with some brands losing as much as one-quarter of their sales. Especially the mass producers of inexpensive cars like Opel, Fiat, and Renault were in trouble, since their small profit margins provided little cushion. These pressures revealed the inefficiency of British manufacturers like Vauxhall and Morris, and when Margaret Thatcher refused to bail them out with government money, they gradually went under or were bought up by the Japanese. On the continent, the French automakers were rescued through public funds, but German firms like VW, Mercedes, BMW, and Audi reinvented themselves through introducing industrial robots as well as adopting Japanese "just in time" methods. Moreover they also pushed into a higher market segment, making "German engineering" a code word for speed, luxury, and durability.[44] In contrast Soviet Bloc car producers became even more outdated, largely collapsing after 1989.

The arrival of high technology in Europe therefore did create a series of new opportunities, but it was not the panacea that its proponents claimed. Airplane production, the writing of computer software, financial services, and the creation of media programs added new careers to the surviving jobs in older sectors like the automobile or machine-tool industries. Whole new regions like the Southwest of the United Kingdom, the South of France, the German Southwest, and northern Italy prospered. But the old industrial heartlands like the Midlands, the French Northeast, and the Ruhr were largely left out.[45] In spite of their own efforts to develop a computer industry, most countries of Eastern Europe fell behind completely, because the Soviet Union directed its advanced research-and-development capacity toward weapons design and did not allow independent innovation in its satellites. While the risk takers in financial services could make enormous profits, many of the other service jobs, such as those in the call centers and big-box stores, were poorly paid. Rewarding the young and flexible, the emerging high-tech economy also introduced a new norm of high job insecurity.

POSTINDUSTRIAL SOCIETY

The disappointing performance of European economies after the Oil Shocks was not just a downturn of the business cycle but indicated a deeper transformation of modernity. While hardly realized by contemporaries, the 1970s revealed a fundamental "crisis of industrial society," ending Fordist production in Western and Eastern Europe.[46] Sparked by global competition, the process of deindustrialization pushed unemployment from virtually nothing during the three postwar decades to over 10 percent in 1985 and raised inflation rates to unprecedented levels. Only gradually becoming aware that this was a structural problem, social democrats like Helmut Schmidt tried to defend established industries, subsidizing their production in order to save domestic jobs. Demanded by labor unions, this strategy devoured much public money and only slowed rather than prevented the decline. In contrast, neoliberals like Margaret Thatcher let the market take its course, betting instead on the creation of new jobs through high technology and services. Sociologist Daniel Bell anticipated this development in the 1970s, predicting the emergence of a postindustrial society.[47]

Much of this transformation was driven by new information technologies that made old devices obsolete and stimulated fresh desires, creating novel products and services. Europeans continued to excel at incrementally perfecting existing consumer goods like washing machines and automobiles. But they lacked the Cold War complex of defense industries that sparked the development of computers, airplanes, and rockets in the United States and created civilian by-products. Moreover, their bureaucratic approach did not inspire individual inventiveness or provide start-up financing for chip-based miniaturization processes essential to hardware like personal computers, software like Microsoft, search engines like Google, and so on. European governments did increase their investments in research and development, producing their share of new patents that made it possible for them to participate in the digital revolution, which came largely from across the Atlantic.[48] Therefore they were able to absorb the new technologies rapidly, combine them with traditional manufacturing, and thereby join the information age.

Along with the technological quantum leap, the intensification of globalization led to a relocation of much industrial production away from Europe. During the 1970s international trade, financial transactions, and cultural communication grew rapidly, thereby raising global economic exchanges to a new level. Because the so-called developing countries offered lower wage costs while shipping grew cheaper with containers, their competition with the highly industrialized regions in Europe increased, forcing firms to close their factories and outsource much of their production to Asia. When these licensed producers developed products of their own and improved their quality, Europeans could no longer compete, losing entire industries such as textiles, steelmaking, shipbuilding, and the like. In some areas continental companies succeeded in keeping design in their home offices so as to cater to continental tastes, and in other branches a shift from mass to luxury production kept them in business. But when coupled with high technology, this increasing globalization largely ended the era of Fordist production on the continent.[49]

The shift from Keynesianism to neoliberalism accelerated the transition to post-Fordism in Europe, since it allowed technological advances and global market forces to wreak "creative destruction." The consensus on countercyclical policies frayed when public stimuli failed to break the stranglehold of stagflation in the wake of the Oil Shocks, thereby opening the door for monetarist advocates of the free market. Margaret Thatcher's refusal to rescue moribund industries, her campaign for privatization, and her effort to balance budgets through cutting welfare expenses removed a long-standing barrier to market competition behind which unions tried to rally to defend their industrial jobs. Since it facilitated the transformation from a manufacturing to a service economy, this policy was successful in generating many new white-collar jobs in finance, the media, and cultural pursuits. But it came at a tremendous cost of regional deindustrialization and personal unemployment for redundant blue-collar labor. The alternative approach of an activating welfare state in Scandinavia was more successful in combining competitiveness with solidarity.[50]

As a result of leaving high industrialism behind, Europe entered a new phase of modernity in a transformation that had all the hallmarks of a third industrial revolution. If the first stage consisted of the pioneering development of textiles, coal, steel, and railroads from the 1750s on in Britain, the second stage from the 1890s on was characterized by science-induced growth in chemicals, electronics, automobiles, and airplanes, typical of Germany. That configuration gradually came to an end during the last quarter of the twentieth century because of another leap involving information technology, globalized competition, and neoliberal policies. Therefore the continent was no longer dominated by the shaft towers of coal mines, the glow of the steel furnaces, or the dry docks of shipbuilders but rather by the gleaming skyscrapers of banks, the soaring headquarters of media companies, and the daring designs of museums. In some sense they were still modern, having been built with the methods of high industry. But in another way their eclectic styles, patchwork jobs, and software-dependent products signaled a different kind of post-industrial modernity.[51]

Chapter 24

RETURN TO DÉTENTE

East-West détente, 1986: Ronald Reagan and Mikhail Gorbachev. *Source*: Ronald Reagan Presidential Library.

O n August 1, 1975, the leaders of thirty-three European states, the United States, and Canada assembled in the Finnish capital to conclude the Helsinki Final Act. After more than two years of negotiations, President Gerald Ford, General Secretary Leonid Brezhnev, and their colleagues signed "a document the size of a telephone directory" in a modest ceremony in front of whirring TV cameras. Their host, President Urho Kekkonen, expressed the hope that the agreement would be "the foundation of and guideline for our future relations and their further development," finally ending the East-West confrontation. The core of the declaration consisted of ten principles such as the "inviolability of frontiers" and "nonintervention in internal affairs" and contained three general topics, or "baskets," calling for political-military cooperation, economic-environmental collaboration, and respect for human rights. The Soviets were delighted with the guarantee of their wartime conquests, but western critics underestimated the power of the reaffirmation of human rights. By reducing fear, this Helsinki Declaration marked the high point of détente.[1]

Barely four years later a second Cold War had broken out, renewing the ideological, political, and military confrontation between the West and the Soviet Bloc. Tensions between the superpowers had gradually increased through proxy conflicts in the Middle East, Chile, Ethiopia, and Angola in which pro-communist and pro-western movements struggled for superiority. When the Soviet Union actually sent its own army to support a minority communist dictatorship in Afghanistan, President Jimmy Carter condemned the invasion and the United States began to supply the mujahedin uprising with arms through Pakistan. At the same time, the basing of medium-range SS-20 missiles in Russia prompted Chancellor Helmut Schmidt to propose a "dual track" approach of stationing U.S. Pershing missiles in the West while simultaneously negotiating for the general elimination of all intermediate-range missiles. The subsequent election of President Ronald Reagan increased the East-West antagonism, since he denounced the Soviet Union as an "evil empire" while Brezhnev retaliated by decrying American imperialism.[2]

The surprising end of the Cold War in 1989–90 has sparked a heated ideological debate over who deserves the chief credit. All through the superpower confrontation some statesmen and many spokesmen of civil society had tried to promote détente, but virtually no one foresaw the speed and extent of the East-West reconciliation. A triumphalist group of anticommunists argued that the West's power-political realism, massive rearmament, and President Reagan's "Star Wars" initiative to build a new antimissile system forced the Soviet Union to back down, because Moscow was falling behind technologically and its economy could no longer bear the cost of the arms buildup. In contrast, supporters of détente asserted that the subtle use of "soft power" undermined communism by awakening consumerist dreams, stressing human rights, and increasing political communication, all of which alienated the silent majority in the client states from communism, created a growing opposition movement, and even persuaded party leaders of the need to reform.[3] Since both camps exaggerate their own contribution, the answer is likely to lie in the unwitting combination of armament and negotiation.

Focused on the bilateral superpower confrontation, the conventional views of the Cold War tend to neglect the constructive role of the Europeans during its final phase. Military planners in the East and West viewed the Old Continent primarily as a difficult battlefield that required a mixture of nuclear and conventional strategies so as to prevail in an armed conflict. Political leaders in Washington and Moscow considered their European partners recalcitrant auxiliaries, augmenting the power of their respective side but needing to be cajoled and kept in line. This bipolar perspective understated the agency of Europeans like de Gaulle and Brandt in the West and Tito and Ceaușescu in the East, who were no longer content to be ordered about and tried to steer a more independent course. Especially in the later stages of the Cold War, continental leaders like Helmut Schmidt and Erich Honecker developed a shared interest in maintaining détente, becoming increasingly insistent on reining in the bellicose superpowers. This European contribution to restraining and overcoming the second Cold War therefore needs to be more openly acknowledged.[4]

Paradoxically, it was the scientific advance of modernity that helped prevent the outbreak of a third world war by producing weapons that were too lethal to use. The development of hydrogen-bomb warheads and intercontinental ballistic missiles was a technological quantum leap that provided mankind with the power to annihilate itself. Thermonuclear war could no longer be fought, because it would involve the instant killing of millions of people, the additional death from radiation of untold numbers of civilians, and the devastation of the entire globe, rendering much of it uninhabitable for generations. Though they came close in the Berlin Wall conflict and the Cuban missile crisis, decision makers in Moscow and Washington pulled back from the brink when they realized that such a war was not winnable in a conventional sense, because the victor was as likely to be destroyed as the loser. This predicament pointed to the logical necessity to prevent such an inferno through diplomacy and disarmament.[5] It was the realization of the unprecedented lethality of modern arms that compelled the ideologically hostile blocs to end their confrontation.

NUCLEAR DETERRENCE

The immense destructiveness of the atomic bomb dropped on Hiroshima on August 6, 1945, fundamentally transformed the nature of warfare. Six years earlier Albert Einstein had alerted President Roosevelt to the potential of a "uranium bomb," hoping to forestall its use by unscrupulous Nazi leaders. In August 1942 the Army Corps of Engineers began building research and production facilities in the desert near Los Alamos, New Mexico, for an endeavor called the Manhattan Project. The organizational competence of Brigadier General Leslie Groves and the scientific brilliance of Robert J. Oppenheimer overcame various obstacles, and produced three operational bombs. Rather than just demonstrating their use, President Harry Truman decided to drop two of them, euphemistically called "Little Boy" and "Fat Man," on actual urban targets in order to force the Japanese to surrender. The unprecedented loss of life and physical destruction of the Hiroshima and Nagasaki bombs achieved their purpose, ending the war in the Pacific. But the double strike crossed a moral threshold, both making the atomic bomb an ultimate weapon and inhibiting its use.[6]

Since nuclear bombs could, in theory, make their possessors invincible, both superpowers strove to perfect their technical capacities and build up a superior arsenal. When Truman hinted at the success of the first test during the Potsdam Conference, Stalin feigned to be unimpressed but ordered the immediate development of a Russian A-bomb as well. Shocked by the destructiveness of their brainchild, some nuclear physicists around Oppenheimer were beginning to have second thoughts, but efforts to curb the spread of nuclear weapons via the Baruch Plan failed because of the intransigence of both sides. Although the United States expanded its arsenal, the Soviets caught up surprisingly quickly with a crash program and the help of spies like Klaus Fuchs, detonating their own nuclear bomb in 1949. Intent on maintaining their superiority, by 1954 the Americans developed the H-bomb, which surpassed fission weapons by using thermonuclear fusion that released even more energy. Not to be outdone, the Russians produced one of their own a year later, initiating a technological stalemate that lasted for the subsequent decades.[7]

As a result of the superpower rivalry, a nuclear-arms race developed in which each side tried to overtake the other. Since the number of warheads remained a closely guarded secret, the intelligence services tended to exaggerate enemy capabilities in order to spur their politicians into authorizing greater production. As an experienced commander and strategist, President Dwight D. Eisenhower was basically skeptical of nuclear weapons, worrying about their irresponsible use, but the anticommunist fervor of advisers like Secretary of State John Foster Dulles and the McCarthyist witch hunt for domestic communists and "fellow travelers" forced him on occasion to talk tough. Unfortunately his initiative to create an International Atomic Energy Agency for the peaceful use of atomic energy under the UN umbrella did little to halt the proliferation of nuclear weapons. By 1960, the United States had accumulated about twenty thousand warheads compared to the Soviet Union's sixteen hundred. But Nikita Khrushchev and his successors were bent on parity and eventually overtook the United States in 1978.[8] Not content with watching anxiously, the British and French built up their own more limited nuclear deterrents.

The growing stockpiles of nuclear weapons created a pervasive climate of fear that came to be typical of the Cold War hysteria. The Americans suffered from a Pearl Harbor complex, dreading a surprise attack, the Soviets distrusted their capitalist adversaries, and the Europeans resented being caught in between. In order to maintain a second-strike capacity, Washington created a Strategic Air Command with dozens of nuclear-capable bombers like the B-52 constantly in the air, ready to attack the Soviet Union even after the United States might have suffered a first strike by the Red air force. Such nuclear readiness was accompanied by propaganda campaigns, teaching schoolchildren to "duck and cover," that is, hide under their desks and put their arms over their heads. At the same time a vigorous civil defense campaign advocated the building of concrete bomb shelters in the backyard as well as the stockpiling of emergency rations, initiating a survivalist mind-set. Novels like *On the Beach* and movies such as *Dr. Strangelove* and *Failsafe* fed this atomic angst by dramatizing the lethal consequences of an accidental launch.[9]

The arms race accelerated further with the introduction of ballistic missiles capable of delivering H-bombs to any location within their range. Building initially on German V-2 blueprints but eventually far surpassing them, the formidable intercontinental ballistic missiles (ICBMs) were equipped with electronic guidance systems and matching warheads, and could span the distance between the two superpowers. The Soviet launch of the first earth-orbiting satellite in 1957, called Sputnik, shocked the western public because it demonstrated that Russia had a rocket capable of sending nuclear weapons not just to Europe but also across the Atlantic or Pacific, reaching the United States. Concerned Washington politicians invented a "missile gap," pressuring President Eisenhower to authorize a major buildup. The Americans sped up their development of ICBMs so as to outdo the Soviets in space by landing on the moon but also, more importantly, to be able to deliver their warheads to the Soviet Union and thereby deter any aggression. Although Eisenhower refused to deploy nuclear weapons in Korea or Vietnam, Kennedy's advisers made contingency plans to use them during the Berlin conflict and Cuban missile crisis, "the most dangerous moment in all of human history."[10]

The Europeans feared the nuclear stalemate because it illustrated their dependence on the superpowers, whose ultimate decisions they could not control. The Soviet satellite states were welcome as auxiliaries for augmenting the reputed 175 tank divisions ready to roll through the Fulda Gap, but they had no input into Moscow's nuclear decisions. The NATO allies Britain and France developed small nuclear deterrents of their own, but these were not big enough to ward off a Soviet attack, making them rely on the U.S. umbrella, while the FRG had forsworn nuclear weapons of its own. The smaller size of NATO's land forces compelled the West to compensate for this inferiority with sea and air power such as nuclear submarines and ICBMs. Uncertainty over whether Washington would actually defend Western Europe with nuclear strikes, risking its own annihilation, led to the development of battlefield nuclear weapons, downsizing the warheads for infantry-support use, while technological advances produced multiple warheads (MIRVs) mounted on a single missile. Moreover West Germany, as the likely battlefield, insisted on a "forward defense."[11]

Thinking about nuclear war was complicated because its unprecedented destructiveness rendered "the modern conception of war," in Churchill's words, "completely out of date." Since a likely massive retaliation by the enemy made fighting such a conflict impossible, the purpose of armament had to be to deter its outbreak. Avoiding it, however, required an unmistakable signal that an antagonist was able and resolved to fight such a war—something about which political leaders could never be sure. In the 1960s the key phrase was "mutually assured destruction," which would make a nuclear conflict unwinnable since the attacker would also be destroyed. But the uncertainty of transatlantic linkage led the Nuclear Planning Group of NATO to gradually embrace the doctrine of a "flexible response" that would resort to nuclear weapons only when losing a conventional war "as late as possible, and as early as necessary."[12] Entire think tanks tried to figure out ways to plan a first strike, but the risk of self-destruction due to uncertainty about the potential response fortunately kept the militaries from carrying out any such experiment.

The inherent irrationality of the nuclear-arms race finally inspired intermittent efforts at arms control, even if these fell short of real disarmament. The European peace movements periodically pushed for limitations, whereas Kennedy and Khrushchev realized how close they had come to nuclear Armageddon in the Cuban missile crisis. The Nuclear Test Ban Treaty of 1963 took a first step by prohibiting aboveground testing in order to reduce radioactive fallout. The Non-Proliferation Treaty of 1968, in which 183 nations pledged not to develop their own nuclear weapons, was more comprehensive, although India and Pakistan overtly failed to comply while Israel and North Korea did so secretly. Such confidence-building measures allowed the conclusion of a Strategic Arms Limitation Treaty (SALT I) and of an Anti-Ballistic Missile Treaty (ABM) in 1972. These agreements froze the number of strategic weapons but not the number of warheads, which continued to multiply. By somewhat reining in the threat of technological self-destruction, these arms-limitation efforts, nonetheless, helped to further détente.[13]

REASSERTION OF EUROPE

Caught in the superpower confrontation, European leaders on both sides of the Iron Curtain grew increasingly restless about their lack of control over ultimate nuclear decisions. Since the recovery of prosperity had put postwar shortages behind them, memories of the suffering during and after World War II had gradually faded away. Moreover the ongoing process of decolonization was lifting the imperial burden and shifting the focus of foreign policy back to the continent. Finally, the progress of West European integration made it possible to speak with a more united voice, articulating European desires. Even if they were not ready to leave their respective Cold War camps altogether, continental leaders became impatient with just being informed about decisions made in Moscow or Washington and demanded a greater say in the affairs of their respective alliances. During the 1960s a rather diverse group of statesmen started to test the boundaries of the Cold War order, using the growing space provided by détente in order to assert their heterodox views.

French president Charles de Gaulle issued the first challenge to the bipolar system by calling for a "Europe from the Atlantic to the Urals," independent of the United States. The successful general, liberator from Nazi domination, and postwar leader of France believed above all in the mission of his own country: "France cannot be France without greatness." Assuming that other countries also pursued their own mystical destiny, he promoted a "Europe of the fatherlands" in which independent nations would cooperate voluntarily. Since he considered the bipolar division of the continent a historical aberration, he set out to restore the concert of Europe in which France would conduct the West and Russia the East, with Germany safely contained between them. Still resenting the lack of recognition of the Free French movement during the Second World War, he distrusted the British and wanted the Americans to get out of Europe. As a result, France officially left the NATO military structure in 1966, forcing it to relocate its headquarters to Brussels, and started building his own nuclear deterrent, the *force de frappe*.[14]

The Federal Republic of Germany presented the opposite problem of excessive compliance, since it still suffered from a "star pupil syndrome." Although Chancellor Konrad Adenauer did not really understand the United States, he recognized that political cooperation and economic trade with Washington were essential for securing American defense protection. But with the Bundeswehr supplying most of the infantry for the Western Alliance, German defense planners wanted to increase their influence on NATO's strategic planning. Some politicians like the mercurial Bavarian Franz Joseph Strauß even flirted with the idea of gaining access to nuclear weapons, but Bonn ultimately signed the nonproliferation treaty, trusting in the U.S. nuclear umbrella. Other conservatives had high hopes for Franco-German friendship after the conclusion of the Elysée Treaty in 1963, but German Gaullism remained a pipe dream, since the French deterrent was not strong enough to provide sufficient protection.[15] Adenauer's successors Erhard, Kiesinger, and Brandt firmly believed in the Western Alliance, though they claimed a larger voice within it.

In spite of rising criticism of the Vietnam War, the United States succeeded in reconciling its own leadership aspiration with the European desire for greater consultation in the alliance. As a result of their comradeship in World War II, the British firmly believed in a "special relationship" with Washington, based on common interests and similar outlooks. The smaller West European nations were also grateful for the U.S. nuclear umbrella even if some, like Sweden and Austria, remained formally neutral. But critical reporting of the U.S. counterinsurgency war in Southeast Asia increasingly alienated European intellectuals and fed a widespread protest movement among the younger generation, since not only news reports but also drastic pictures of brutality showed violations of proclaimed Western ideals. Recognizing the importance of the Old Continent and promoting a transition from bipolarity to polycentrism, the realist Henry Kissinger consulted European governments often enough to make them feel in the loop.[16] Based on shared values and voluntary ties, the transatlantic relationship therefore proved sufficiently strong to withstand periodic strains.

Ironically enough, the Soviet Union had more problems with its allies, since it insisted on ideological uniformity and asserted its dominance more crudely. Titoism was a special irritant, denounced by Stalin as a dangerous deviation from orthodoxy because Yugoslavia tried to pursue its own road toward socialism. This "ism" was named after Josip Broz, nicknamed Tito, the charismatic partisan leader who managed to seize power in Belgrade at the end of World War II and bring the disparate provinces of Yugoslavia together into one country with the slogan of "brotherhood and unity." Under his dictatorial rule, Yugoslavia allowed workers' "self-management" of factories, permitted small-scale privately owned businesses, and encouraged western tourism, essential for gaining hard currency. Stalin and his successors considered Titoism a threat not because of its ideological innovations but because its independence threatened Russian control over the international communist movement. After being expelled from the Cominform in 1948, Tito became one of the key leaders of the "nonaligned nations movement," which tried to escape the pull of bipolarity.[17]

Another maverick in the Eastern Bloc was Nicolae Ceaușescu, the brutal dictator of Romania who pursued an independent nationalist foreign policy. In power from 1965 on, he not only suppressed his pro-Russian competitors but also instituted a severe censorship over artists and intellectuals. As party leader and president Ceaușescu built an extensive cult of personality around himself and his wife, styling himself as a populist modernizer. The West came to admire his independence from Moscow, since he withdrew Romania from active participation in the Warsaw Pact and condemned the Soviet invasion of Czechoslovakia in 1968. After receiving more than $13 billion in western credits, he felt compelled to make a drastic effort to repay them, thereby lowering the Romanian standard of living to a struggle for bare survival in the 1980s. To gain support against Russia, he also sought closer ties with China and North Korea, and imitated their revolutionary radicalism. Nonetheless, the West courted him in the hope of creating differences within the Soviet Bloc, thereby vastly overestimating his importance.[18]

The growing Sino-Soviet rift shattered the ideological unity of the communist movement and transformed geopolitical alignments. During the Civil War in China the Soviet Communist Party liberally helped its Chinese comrades with weapons and advisers, although Mao was expanding Marxism-Leninism into a theory of "peasant revolution." During the Korean War economic and military cooperation deepened further, with some sharing of military secrets. Though resenting Russian insensitivity to their own achievements, Chinese leaders still recognized Moscow's leadership. But by the late 1950s a split developed, since the Soviets became interested in stabilizing relations with the West, while Mao grew more radical, initiating the disastrous policies of the Great Leap Forward and the Cultural Revolution. In the early 1960s this disagreement turned into an open break when the Chinese accused the Russians of being "revisionist traitors," while the Soviets denounced Maoism as left-wing sectarianism. By the late sixties hostility between Moscow and Beijing had reached such a level as to trigger an undeclared border war along the Ussuri River.[19]

The initial attempts of European leaders to assert their independence during the 1960s therefore failed to break the bipolar structure of superpower confrontation during the Cold War. For all his rhetorical anti-Americanism, de Gaulle was careful not to sever relations with the Western Alliance completely, since he ultimately depended on the U.S. nuclear umbrella. Also the vociferous criticism of Vietnam as an imperialist war by the Left and the young did not change government policy, because continental elites were firmly committed to NATO and the EC. Similarly, the Soviet Union was ultimately more concerned with internal dissidents in Poland, Czechoslovakia, and Hungary than with the annoying antics of Tito or Ceauşescu. Only the breakdown of the Sino-Soviet alliance created a new geopolitical situation of multipolarity, which produced more diplomatic room for maneuver, an opportunity that was quickly recognized by President Richard Nixon.[20] While the Europeans' efforts to reassert a degree of independence remained unsuccessful, they showed that the polarized nations continued trying to regain control of their own destiny.

GERMAN OSTPOLITIK

The reversal of West German policy toward the East from revisionism to reconciliation was a major help in decreasing East-West tensions in Europe. Since the superpowers and direct neighbors shared an interest in keeping Germany divided, it was only logical that the initiative to end the continent's division should come from Bonn. Abandoning the visceral anticommunism of the Hallstein Doctrine was not easy for the Federal Republic, since it meant that millions of ethnic refugees from Eastern Europe had to give up all hope of returning to their erstwhile homes by reclaiming the borders of 1937. Though the attempt to reduce hostilities by accepting the loss of Germany's eastern provinces fit in with the general effort to create détente with the Soviet Bloc, Washington remained suspicious, because for the first time Bonn was pursuing an independent foreign policy.[21] The strategy of working toward the long-term aim of ending German and European division by stabilizing continental borders in the short run gave Ostpolitik a paradoxical character that made it quite difficult to understand.

As foreign minister of the Grand Coalition, the charismatic Willy Brandt pushed for a change of approach toward Eastern Europe. Born as an illegitimate child in 1913, he grew up as a socialist in the Weimar Republic, fled to Scandinavia in order to fight as a journalist against Hitler, and returned in 1946 to the destroyed capital to help democratize the defeated country. More than a generation younger than Adenauer, he rejected the Catholic conservatism of the FRG founder who tried to make West Germany part of an occidental bulwark against the onslaught of the Bolshevik hordes. As mayor of democratic Berlin between 1957 and 1966, Brandt had ample day-to-day experience with communists, understanding both the possibilities and problems of dealing with the Soviets and East Germans. His defining moment was his disappointment in the lack of a vigorous American and West German response to the building of the Berlin Wall in 1961. The inability to prevent the closing of the last escape hatch through the Iron Curtain convinced him of the futility of anti-communist rhetoric and made him cast about for a more constructive solution.[22]

Elected chancellor in 1969, the Social Democratic leader initiated a new Eastern Europe policy that pursued several complementary aims: First, he would continue to take "small steps" like the border-crossing agreements with the eastern authorities, an arrangement intended to improve the daily lives of West Berlin citizens by allowing them to visit their eastern friends and relatives. Second, the shift from denouncing the very existence of the GDR (which was the Hallstein Doctrine) to dealing with its representatives pursued "change through rapprochement," hoping to soften up eastern leaders by making them feel less threatened so that they would allow western media into their country and permit their citizens greater freedom. The ruling East German communists (SED) recognized the deviousness of this ostensibly harmless strategy by calling it an "aggression in slippers," but their insistence on sharper demarcation (*Abgrenzung*) vis-à-vis the West failed to neutralize the attractiveness of consumer society. Third, the admission of responsibility for Nazi crimes and recognition of the loss of former territories as their logical consequence sought to reassure the eastern neighbors by repudiating refugee revanchism. Persuasively supported by Egon Bahr as Brandt's adviser and emissary, this Ostpolitik struck a new chord by courageously accepting postwar realities.[23]

The process of reconciliation began with the signing of a nonaggression treaty with the Soviet Union on August 12, 1970. Since Moscow had blocked all earlier attempts to improve the Federal Republic's relations with its satellites, Brandt entered into direct negotiations with the Soviet Union. Using Bahr as a back channel, the FRG distanced itself from revisionism by repudiating the use of force in order to normalize the situation in Europe. The most important concession was the promise of accepting the Oder-Neisse line as the eastern border of Germany by undertaking "to respect without restriction the territorial integrity of all states in Europe within their present frontiers." Six months later, the Treaty of Warsaw repeated this declaration, although it maintained a reservation about final determination in a future peace treaty. In a surprising symbolic gesture of contrition, Willy Brandt then knelt at the memorial of the Warsaw ghetto uprising during his state visit on December 7, 1970, expressing German shame.[24] Although the "letter on German unity" kept the door open to peaceful reunification, these reassurances removed the fear of German aggression in Eastern Europe that had tied nationalists to communism.

The next step was the four-power agreement on Berlin, signed on September 3, 1971, which eliminated the city's status as a source of international crises. The text was a compromise between the western desire to secure the future of West Berlin and the eastern wish to have its sector serve as capital of the GDR. To prevent further disputes, the document essentially restated the existing rights and responsibilities of the World War II victors. Promising to refrain from another blockade, Russia assured that "transit traffic" would be "unimpeded" in the future. Moreover, "ties between the Western Sectors of Berlin and the Federal Republic of Germany" would be "maintained and developed," allowing more integration into the West. Finally, travel between West Berlin and the surrounding GDR would be somewhat increased. The western quid pro quo was recognition of the de facto merger of East Berlin with the GDR, allowing East Germany to be governed from there. Ending the 1948 and 1958 confrontations over the German capital, this legal reaffirmation of the status quo guaranteed the continued existence of the western island in a communist sea.[25]

The most controversial aspect of Ostpolitik was the conclusion of the Basic Treaty, which recognized the GDR de facto while keeping the door open for future unification. After lengthy negotiations East and West Germany agreed on December 21, 1972, to "develop normal, good-neighborly relations with each other on the basis of equal rights." Repeating the language of the nonaggression treaties, the document reaffirmed the inviolability of frontiers and the repudiation of the use of force. Eastern assurances of the regulation of "humanitarian questions" were accompanied by a western promise of closer "cooperation in the fields of economics, science and technology, transport ... culture, sport and environmental protection." Instead of full embassies, only permanent missions would be established in the respective capitals. In return for such quasi recognition, the FRG insisted in a separate letter that the treaty did not conflict with the aim of "a state of peace in Europe in which the German nation will regain its unity through free self-determination." Over incensed CDU protests against making division permanent, the treaty barely passed the Bundestag by two votes, apparently bought by the East German secret police (Stasi).[26]

This relaxation of tensions culminated in the Helsinki Conference on Security and Cooperation in Europe (CSCE), which institutionalized détente despite unresolved ideological disagreements. Moscow wanted to have the postwar borders recognized and East-West trade intensified. The FRG was willing to make these concessions so as to preserve the chance for peaceful reunification with the GDR in the future. Washington and London were skeptical that anything good could come from such a parley but felt compelled to go along lest they be left behind. The smaller European countries favored the CSCE negotiations so as to enhance their security by concurrent arms-limitation talks in Vienna. The result of these multiple interests was a complex set of compromises that seemed to offer Brezhnev everything he wanted—an objection that Cold Warriors immediately raised in the West. But anticommunists underestimated the explosive power of the human rights stipulation, which provided a platform for dissident protest in the East.[27] Hence the Helsinki Declaration helped turn acrimonious confrontation into cooperative competition.

The positive impact of Ostpolitik is easy to overlook, since it relied on soft power rather than on harsh rhetoric. Made in Europe's name, some of Bonn's painful concessions proved immediately beneficial: Apologies for Nazi crimes demonstrated the success of recivilizing Germans. Acceptance of the postwar borders reassured their neighbors' new residents that they needed no longer fear a territorial revanchism. De facto recognition of communist control made it possible to reach a pragmatic modus vivendi that improved the lives of people caught behind the Iron Curtain. The long-term benefits of reconciliation with the East turned out to be even greater. The sincerity of German contrition robbed communism of the argument of Bonn's revanchism. The increase of trade and communication made western consumer society appear more attractive. Finally, the insistence on individual human rights created space for an internal opposition to develop against the state socialist regimes.[28] By demonstrating a peaceful western modernity, the shift from confrontation to détente speeded the erosion of the Soviet dictatorships.

SECOND COLD WAR

Unfortunately the euphoria of CSCE cooperation quickly evaporated in the heat of a renewed ideological confrontation stemming from multiple conflicts in the Third World. During the first stage of the Cold War, the United States and the Soviet Union had realized that fighting a hot war in Europe would be too dangerous for them, since Russia was contiguous to the potential battlefield and America remained committed to maintaining its nuclear umbrella. But in the postcolonial countries both states were "locked in conflict over the very concept of European modernity," wanting to prove that either democratic capitalism or egalitarian communism was the correct path of modernization. Since the regimes of the developing states tended to be weak and in need of foreign aid, both sides tried to outflank each other in the Third World, using ideological appeals, material support, and military assistance.[29] These local insurrections, counter-insurgencies, and proxy wars undermined détente between the superpowers and drew some Europeans back into the conflict as former colonial powers or as revolutionary advisers.

Though East-West relations had been deteriorating before, the Soviet invasion of Afghanistan ultimately sealed the fate of détente. Jimmy Carter and Leonid Brezhnev were already sparring over African conflicts and human-rights issues. But the Russian decision to use its own troops to shore up a weak communist regime that had seized power in Kabul and was divided by personal intrigues turned growing tension into open hostility. In December 1979 the Soviet army quickly occupied the capital, other major cities and communication routes, and installed a puppet regime, but this action aroused a storm of international criticism and failed to gain sufficient support from the Afghan population. Instead, the Soviets were confronted by stubborn guerrilla resistance, which soon grew into a full-fledged Islamist uprising. Shocked by the direct Russian intervention, President Carter, pushed by his security adviser Zbigniew Brzezinski, decided on a massive covert operation to aid the mujahedin with weapons funneled through Pakistan. Though the superpowers did not fight directly, the unwinnable insurgency became the Soviets' Vietnam.[30]

The NATO dual-track decision further heightened East-West tensions because it extended the arms race to intermediate-range missiles equipped with nuclear warheads. West European leaders worried that the increasing deployment of Russia's mobile and accurate SS-20 rockets would create a communist advantage in a category not covered by the SALT agreement. German chancellor Helmut Schmidt was troubled by a break in "the continuum of deterrence," since any level of Russian attack could be countered only by launching U.S. intercontinental missiles. While he preferred a "zero solution" of abolishing such missiles altogether, he proposed to modernize western intermediary forces. Concerned about "Soviet superiority in theater nuclear systems," the NATO ministers decided in December 1979 to station 108 Pershing II missiles as well as 464 ground-launched cruise missiles in Europe. But recognizing Soviet worries, they offered at the same time to negotiate about the complete elimination of such weapon systems.[31] When Moscow refused to talk, a war of nerves ensued in which each side accused the other of further escalation.

Rampant nuclear fear mobilized a huge peace movement in Europe that denounced the NATO decision as "a fateful mistake" and called for a return to "the original intention of détente." Taking the Soviet stationing of SS-20s for granted, western activists tried instead to stop the NATO deployment of intermediate-range missiles, calling for an immediate beginning of serious arms-reduction negotiations. Growing spontaneously from below, the German branch of the movement was a colorful collection of intellectuals like Heinrich Böll, clergymen like Heinz Gollwitzer, Green politicians like Petra Kelly, leftist trade-union leaders, and various communist front organizations, paid by the East. Culminating between 1981 and 1983, the protests inspired a "women's peace camp" at Greenham Common in Britain and mass demonstrations with between 300,000 and 500,000 participants in Amsterdam, Bonn, Brussels, and Rome. Though the United Kingdom and the Federal Republic nonetheless went ahead with the missile deployment, this huge mobilization for peace helped limit the second Cold War by dramatizing popular European anxieties.[32]

Instead of inspiring negotiations, the renewed confrontation once again pushed the world to the brink of nuclear war. In Washington the election of Ronald Reagan bestowed the office of U.S. president on a former movie actor who had scant knowledge of foreign affairs and was more interested in making anticommunist speeches than in working on policy details. Some of his chief aides such as Caspar Weinberger and Richard Perle were hard-liners who hated the very word détente as Kissinger's legacy. In Moscow the aging alcoholic Leonid Brezhnev was increasingly incapacitated, followed in short order by the equally ailing Yuri Andropov and Konstantin Chernenko, making Russia unwilling to compromise. The Soviets' unprovoked downing of Korean Air flight 007 provoked outrage in Washington, while Moscow misread the provocative NATO maneuver "Able Archer" as preparation for a nuclear first strike and put its forces on highest alert.[33] But when Soviet radar erroneously reported an American missile attack, Lieutenant Colonel Stanislav Petrov fortunately refused to launch a counterstrike, saving the globe from incineration.

Owing to the failure of limitation efforts, the arms race intensified further with a new generation of weapons systems such as the ill-considered "Star Wars" initiative. As the Soviets kept adding warheads and developing new missiles, the hard-liners in the Reagan administration, only somewhat restrained by Secretary of State George Shultz, insisted on a massive rearmament program, including the MX missiles and the B-1 bomber. But the problem with the MX was that its silos could be attacked unless they were defended from incoming rockets. When Reagan heard the phrase that it might be better "to protect our people, not just avenge them" during a briefing, he seized upon building an antimissile defense system that would destroy incoming warheads with laser beams from space satellites (hence the initiative's graphic nickname, "Star Wars"). West European leaders were appalled by the Strategic Defense Initiative (SDI), since the prospect of an antimissile system rejected decades of deterrence theory by reviving a first-strike possibility and also decoupled American security from their own. Feeling threatened and angry, the East European leader, General Secretary Andropov, warned: "Washington's actions are putting the entire world in jeopardy."[34]

Intent on preserving the achievements of détente, European leaders grew increasingly frustrated with American bellicosity. Members of the peace movement tended to blame U.S. recalcitrance for lack of substantial progress in the Strategic Arms Reduction Talks (START). French president François Mitterrand, especially, considered Reagan's anticommunist rhetoric counterproductive, since he needed the domestic support of his own Eurocommunist party. Doubting the project's technical feasibility, British prime minister Margaret Thatcher also intensely disliked the costs of SDI and sought to rein in its excessive expectations. And finally German chancellors from Willy Brandt to Helmut Kohl believed in "a community of responsibility" that included their eastern cousins, as they were seeking to maintain a dialogue with East European leaders like Erich Honecker. Having to live in close proximity to their communist neighbors, continental statesmen rediscovered a sense of common fate across the Iron Curtain that made them intent on moderating the rising hostility between the superpowers.[35]

During the second Cold War the Europeans therefore played a restraining role in the strategic triangle between their own continent and the two superpowers. Since the Helsinki Declaration had lessened most continental conflicts, the renewal of confrontation clearly resulted from the rivalry between the United States and the USSR in the Third World and in the arms race. After the Europeans' withdrawal from empire had freed them from such responsibilities, the former imperialists were no longer directly involved in the ideological conflicts of the postcolonial countries. But fearing that they would have to bear the brunt of a third world war, European governments and the public were highly interested in the progress of arms-control negotiations. While the ultimate decisions were made in Moscow and Washington, continental leaders exerted considerable pressure on the superpowers, making the case for the benefits of peaceful modernity. Though the precise impact of their entreaties is hard to measure, European moderation did contribute to keeping the second Cold War from spinning out of control.[36]

RETURN TO DÉTENTE

Ultimately the failure of efforts to win the East-West confrontation prompted a return to détente in the second half of the 1980s, ending the Cold War once and for all. Slowly Moscow and Washington became disenchanted with the Third World strategy of trying to change the power balance by installing friendly regimes in developing countries, because that effort turned out to be costly and unreliable when clients like Egypt switched sides. Moreover, the futility of the arms race gradually dawned on American and Soviet leaders, since the implicit goal of nuclear superiority was receding while the number of their own nationals likely to be killed in a nuclear exchange steadily increased to encompass most of their population. At the same time the impressive size of the peace movement on the continent showed the public's mounting revulsion against the East-West conflict, encouraging the European leaders to exert restraining pressure on the superpowers. Nonetheless it took almost half a decade to overcome the ingrained hostility and suspicion between two ideological blocs.[37]

Instead of Reagan's belligerence, it was actually his relative moderation that laid the basis for peaceful accommodation with the Soviet Union. While hawks dominated the public rhetoric during his first term, the U.S. president deeply abhorred nuclear weapons and sought to escape from the trap of mutually assured destruction. Arms-control advisers like Paul Nitze and George Shultz gradually gained influence with the argument that once there were enough warheads and missiles to blow up the globe, further stockpiling became pointless. On January 16, 1984, Reagan proclaimed programmatically: "We want more than deterrence; we seek genuine cooperation; we seek progress for peace." This was a clarion call to move from hostility to realistic reengagement with Moscow—to reinvigorate arms-reduction talks, change the tone of the relationship with the Kremlin, and resolve the remaining regional conflicts in the Third World. Though the media paid insufficient attention to this message, since it contrasted with his previous hard-line image, this conciliatory agenda dominated Reagan's second term.[38]

At the same time Mikhail Gorbachev's assumption of leadership brought to power in the Kremlin a younger generation that was willing to engage in "new political thinking" at home and abroad. While the ailing Brezhnev, Andropov, and Chernenko had been averse to change, their successor understood the need to overcome the widespread stagnation. The new general secretary was an orthodox Leninist who wanted to rescue socialism by resuming Khrushchev's legacy of innovation so that it could reach its full potential. Domestically that meant shaking the party functionaries and state bureaucracy out of their lethargy and abolishing corruption. In particular the economy, strained by the arms race, needed reenergizing through more competition, through opening up to international trade, and through importing new technology—not to produce more weapons, but to fulfill popular dreams of consumption. The key concepts of this program were the "restructuring" (*perestroika*) of socioeconomic relations to make them more flexible as well as "openness" (*glasnost'*) in public discussions so as to correct mistakes.[39] This sweeping agenda brought a fresh spirit to Russia.

Part of this program involved a changed attitude toward international politics, with a view toward ending Soviet isolation by abandoning traditional Stalinist precepts such as the "two camps" theory. Improved relations with the West would facilitate economic recovery as well, which Gorbachev knew was sorely needed. But the hawks in the Reagan administration made reconciliation difficult, since they did not trust the new Russian leader and continued with their provocative rhetoric. As a result the Soviets refused to withdraw from Afghanistan, even increasing their military efforts in 1985 and 1986. But remembering the suffering of the Second World War, Gorbachev hated nuclear weapons, since he worried that the globe would be utterly devastated by fighting a nuclear war. Hence Russia announced a unilateral moratorium on weapons testing and even went so far as to propose general disarmament, abolishing all nuclear weapons, although this suggestion was not taken seriously in Washington. At the 1985 Geneva summit, Reagan and Gorbachev could only concur that "a nuclear war could not be won and must never be fought," but they disagreed on everything else.[40]

Disappointed in the lack of progress, West European leaders pushed for a return to détente while East European dissidents tried to reunite Europe from below. Getting on well with Gorbachev in spite of her pronounced anticommunism, Prime Minister Thatcher encouraged his agenda for domestic reform and his arms-control efforts. President Mitterrand tried to mediate between Moscow and Washington, pointing out that Reagan was less bellicose than some members of his entourage. Moreover, West German chancellor Kohl succeeded in hosting the East German SED secretary Honecker for a state visit in order to strengthen ties between the two Germanys, while Willy Brandt and SPD leaders made unofficial contacts with other East European politicians. Finally, intellectuals in Hungary, Czechoslovakia, and Poland began to revive the concept of *Mitteleuropa*, claiming that their countries at the heart of the continent were more Central than Eastern European, politically and culturally, since they wanted to escape Soviet domination through civil-society contacts.[41] Reinforcing one another, these efforts improved the East-West climate.

Although it was a diplomatic failure, the 1986 Reykjavik summit initiated the thaw in Cold War mind-sets that made subsequent agreements possible. Deeply disturbed by the horrible consequences of the Chernobyl nuclear power plant disaster, Gorbachev made a series of radical unilateral proposals such as scrapping the Soviet Union's controversial SS-20 missiles. Meanwhile, Reagan had gotten the impression that he could persuade the Soviet leader to abolish nuclear weapons altogether while maintaining SDI development. In fifteen hours of negotiations in the Icelandic capital, both leaders competed with each other, with Reagan offering to eliminate intercontinental missiles and Gorbachev to abolish all nuclear warheads. "All nuclear weapons? Well Mikhail, that's exactly what I've been talking about all along," the U.S. president queried. "Then why don't we agree on it?" the Soviet leader replied. This stunning agreement came quickly undone, however, when Reagan insisted on his pet project of developing Star Wars. According to Shultz, "Reykjavik was too bold for the world," but it did start the crucial shift toward the second détente.[42]

The improvement of the international atmosphere led to the conclusion of several crucial arms-limitation agreements. Increasing trust between Washington and Moscow scuttled hard-line efforts to reinterpret the Anti-Ballistic Missile Treaty in a way that would allow SDI development. More importantly, negotiators at Geneva succeeded in signing an Intermediate-Range Nuclear Forces Treaty following the "zero option" of eliminating all nuclear-armed missiles with a range between three hundred and three thousand miles. Although these ballistic weapons amounted only to about 4 percent of the nuclear arsenals, this agreement was nonetheless "a great success," since it reassured the Europeans on whom such missiles were targeted.

More importantly, such progress also revived the Strategic Arms Reduction Talks, which included the entire missile and warhead defense systems. In a preliminary agreement, both sides consented to deep cuts of 50 percent of their arsenals, limiting warheads to six thousand and delivery systems to sixteen hundred, including land-, sea-, and air-based missiles. Since new issues such as submarine-launched cruise missiles complicated the talks, they were concluded only in 1991.[43]

The credit for ending the second Cold War must therefore go to a combination of unlikely leaders and policies. Even if the U.S. buildup was responsible for raising the costs of the arms race, Reagan's change of tone from belligerence to cooperation was essential for lessening superpower tension. While they had no power over ultimate decisions, European leaders from Thatcher to Kohl kept lobbying for an accommodation with the Soviet Union, calling for arms reduction. But ultimately it was the arrival of the post-Brezhnev generation of Russian leaders represented by Gorbachev that was crucial in sending positive signals such as the long-sought withdrawal from Afghanistan. Though Gorbachev's reference to a "common European home" in several speeches was designed to soften NATO, it suggested a shared interest in disarmament on both sides of the Iron Curtain. Made possible by the improving East-West climate, the gradual abandonment of the Brezhnev doctrine also created space for satellite regimes to experiment with reforms, encouraging dissidents to speak up.[44] As a result the second détente not only limited but actually ended the Cold War.

NUCLEAR PEACE

By threatening the very survival of humanity, the development of nuclear bombs and intercontinental missiles compounded the negative dynamic of modernity. The construction of fission and fusion bombs made it possible to unleash unprecedented amounts of destructive energy from which neither combatants nor civilians could really be protected. At the same time the design of intercontinental ballistic missiles offered a delivery system reaching all corners of the globe, leaving no place to hide. Moreover, this arms race between the superpowers was a self-propelling process, since engineers sought to outdo each other with clever innovations while the military strategists wanted to create a bigger stockpile so as to gain first-strike capability or at least assure second-strike retaliation. Horrified by this growing arsenal, members of the scientific community argued that the use of these weapons would inevitably create a "nuclear winter," rendering the earth uninhabitable for generations to come.[45] Thereby the optimistic technological utopias of the 1950s turned into the frightening dystopias of the 1970s.

Fortunately, the common interest in survival across the Iron Curtain strengthened the incentive for cooperation at the same time, reinforcing the benign potential of modernity. Communist peace propaganda appealed only to leftist minorities in the West because it clashed with the militarization of eastern society. More constructive was the western emphasis on human rights, which provided some cover for eastern dissidents in dealing with political repression. But the main voice for peace was the grassroots movement against nuclear weapons, which campaigned for disarmament so as to keep the superpowers from destroying humanity. Led by intellectuals like Alva Myrdal, the campaign spilled over into the eastern satellite states. The increase in civil-society connections through academic exchanges, trade contacts, city partnerships, and athletic competitions, which allowed people to meet and exchange ideas, created a growing sense of commonality in facing the same predicament and inspired them to argue in favor of lessening hostilities. Though its impact is difficult to measure, this dialogue also contributed to restraint.[46]

During the second part of the Cold War after 1961, repeated cycles of conciliation and confrontation rendered it unclear which face of modernity would ultimately prevail. Though the Cuban missile crisis shocked the leaders in both Moscow and Washington by showing how close they had come to destroying the globe, the arms race continued, since neither side was content with nuclear parity. In Europe the nuclear stalemate created a strange stability by enforcing strict spheres of influence that kept the West from supporting the Prague Spring or the Polish Solidarity movement while restraining the East from intervening during the Portuguese Revolution. After the Helsinki agreement, the confrontation shifted to the decolonizing countries in a series of revolutions and counterinsurgencies that led to bloody proxy wars in Asia, Africa, and Latin America and contributed to the unraveling of détente. But once again both sides were disappointed because these local struggles in places like Nicaragua or Afghanistan proved costly and uncontrollable. Only after it became evident that neither outbuilding nor outflanking worked, was it possible to end the second Cold War.[47]

Ultimately both dimensions of modernity contributed to the peaceful outcome to the East-West conflict by offering a combination of fear and hope. On the negative side, the unwinnability of a nuclear war finally convinced leaders in Moscow and Washington that their shared interest in survival outweighed the potential gains from a first strike, since an aggressor might not be able to enjoy the fruits of victory. At the same time, the inconclusive results of local conflicts in the Third World, which resisted being pressed into a Cold War schema, made it clear that neither superpower would succeed in shifting the global balance of power permanently to its advantage. On the positive side, the increasing dialogue across the Iron Curtain after Helsinki provided a check on the rising tension, since it let politicians and citizens discover that the common interest in survival outweighed hostile propaganda stereotypes. Regardless of ideological affiliation, European leaders finally understood that they needed to work together in order to revive détente lest their countries become the battlefield of World War III.[48]

In his testimony before the U.S. Senate Foreign Relations Committee in April 1989, the old Russian hand George Kennan announced that the Cold War had finally ended. Worried by the weapons buildup, he pointed out that the nuclear arsenals were vastly redundant: "Owing to their overdestructiveness and their suicidal implications, these weapons are essentially useless from the standpoint of actual commitment to military combat." Commenting on the momentous changes initiated by Gorbachev, he added that the Soviet Union was no longer a military opponent: "That country should now be regarded essentially as another great power" with its own history and aspirations, which "are not so seriously in conflict with ours as to justify the assumption that the outstanding differences could not be adjusted by the normal means of compromise and accommodation." To end the dangers of accident and proliferation, a substantial arms reduction agreement should be signed as soon as possible.[49] This sage advice represented one of the voices of reason that helped conclude the conflict and open the door to a more peaceful future.

Chapter 25

PEACEFUL REVOLUTION

Fall of the Berlin Wall, 1989. *Source*: bpk, Berlin / Brandenburg Gate, Berlin / Dietmar Katz / Art Resource, NY.

On the evening of November 9, 1989, journalists assembled in East Berlin, eager to listen to the latest SED Central Committee plans for liberalizing travel and emigration. Asked when the new regulations would take effect, press spokesman Günter Schabowski, who had not been sufficiently informed, erroneously replied "immediately." Hearing this welcome news on TV, incredulous East German citizens rushed to border-crossing points such as the Bornholmer Strasse, demanding to be allowed to go to West Berlin. The frantic frontier guards could not reach any higher officers, who had already retired for the night, to instruct them on how to react. They therefore eventually decided to yield to the growing crowd and simply opened the gates. Hearing of the first breach, "hundreds of thousands of East Berliners romped through the newly porous Wall in an unending celebration" to express their joy. Chancellor Helmut Kohl reassured the elated newcomers: "We are on your side; we are and remain one nation. We belong together." Lifted by accident and popular pressure, the Iron Curtain could never be closed again.[1]

The fall of the Wall was the product of a democratic awakening that swept over Eastern Europe much like the Springtime of the Peoples in 1848. It started in Poland, the least repressive satellite, when in 1979 Gdańsk dockworkers led by Lech Wałęsa formed an independent trade union called Solidarność, which martial law proved unable to suppress. The unrest subsequently spread to Hungary with hundreds of thousands of Budapest citizens turning out for the reburial of the heroes of the 1956 uprising, thereby protesting anew against communist repression. Thereupon a crisis of mass flight to the West and mass demonstrations against the regime engulfed East Germany, challenging the SED dictatorship and demanding unification with the West. Next the popular rebellion, encouraged by Soviet passivity, confronted the orthodox Husák regime in Prague, and from there moved to Bulgaria and Romania, attacking Zhivkov and Ceaușescu. Finally the movement reached the Soviet Union itself when nationalists in the former Baltic states and Ukraine demanded independence, and Russians themselves began to repudiate communism.[2] It was a stunning grassroots revolt that fundamentally redefined Europe.

For Central and Eastern Europeans, the surprising events of 1989–90 mark a caesura that overturned the Potsdam system of Soviet domination that had governed their lives for almost half a century. The democratic awakening concluded the Cold War, since the dissolution of the Soviet Union in 1991 meant that the eastern protagonist had collapsed while the western antagonist triumphed. Moreover, the fall of the Wall marked the overthrow of communist dictatorships that had suppressed the "captive nations" since 1945. The lifting of the Iron Curtain finally ended the division of Europe along the lines of military occupation at the end of the Second World War. At the same time, the crumbling of the Soviet Bloc initiated the recovery of national independence, previously submerged by Russian hegemony. Moreover, the uprising of East Europeans gave their countries another chance to revive their democratic institutions as well as to restore market economies, permitting them to live freer and more prosperous lives. Finally, the removal of the barbed wire barrier allowed the continent to overcome its division and gradually grow together again.[3]

Overwhelmed by the speed and extent of the changes, many observers are still wondering what exactly happened during the tumultuous year of 1989. Leftist conspiracy theorists blame a secret deal between the superpowers for selling out the socialist experiment so as to profit from privatization. Rightist analysts who look down from above stress that communism simply imploded because of its poor performance, internal self-doubt, and inept leadership, exemplified by Gorbachev's illusions. Liberals instead emphasize that a civil contestation from below overthrew the Soviet-style dictatorships, calling it a real revolution. Dissidents who actually participated in the uprising are loath to use that term, because they associate it with Jacobin or Bolshevik bloodshed, ignoring that revolution means, by definition, "an effort to transform the political institutions" of a state by mass mobilization. What set the revolutionary process of 1989 apart from other rebellions was, however, its nonviolent character, which made for a negotiated transition rather than a bloody struggle. As a result, most commentators have gradually accepted the designation of a "peaceful revolution."[4]

The overthrow of communism marked the defeat of the socialist modernization project in the ideological competition with its liberal democratic rival. In the long run the dictatorship of "real existing socialism" proved less attractive than the "open society" of democracy and capitalism because the latter satisfied citizens' desires more successfully. Initially communism seemed to have a good chance of prevailing, since it could contrast the exploitation of crisis-ridden capitalism with the utopia of a more just and stable socialist order. But the practice of Marxism-Leninism ultimately disappointed most of its supporters in Eastern Europe and in the Soviet Union, since it turned out to be more repressive and less productive than its western rival. Capitalism and democracy also became more attractive after liberals had remedied some of the glaring deficits of their own system by introducing a comprehensive welfare state and by integrating Western Europe. Since comparisons between the systems through travel generally came out in favor of the West, most East Europeans ultimately chose the more enticing democratic version of modernity.[5]

EROSION OF COMMUNISM

The overthrow of communism came as quite a surprise, because for decades the Soviet system had looked utterly impregnable. Convinced that history was on their side, the eastern dictators were confident, in Erich Honecker's children's rhyme, that "neither ox nor ass will stop socialism's advance." When looking at the massive military parades that celebrated the Russian victory over the Nazis, foreign journalists were also sure that Soviet military might was ready to put down any challenge. Moreover, western intellectuals like Günter Grass reluctantly believed that the division of Europe was the price to be paid for the Second World War and that the maintenance of peace depended on its perpetuation. A handful of Kremlinologists who were able to read between the propaganda lines pointed to signs of trouble: the stagnation of the planned economy, the demographic decline, and youthful dissatisfaction. But virtually all social scientists were certain that the Soviet Union and its empire would endure, hoping at best for a softening of repression through the functional logic of advanced industrial society.[6]

Behind the impressive facade, a series of unresolved problems, nonetheless, gradually eroded the solidity of the Soviet edifice. Chief among them was the loss of ideological certainty in the moral superiority and practical feasibility of the socialist quest. Ideology played a central role in Marxism-Leninism because the social-engineering project of creating a revolutionary modernity depended on firm belief in its ethical authority, scientific rationality, and historical inevitability. But the repeated military interventions in 1953, 1956, 1968, and 1981 showed that the system was incapable of self-renewal, because each time efforts to democratize socialism were brutally suppressed with force. While the use of tanks in East Germany and Hungary could still be justified as prevention of counterrevolution, the subsequent repression of "socialism with a human face" in Prague and of the independent trade union in Warsaw violated the claim that the communists were acting on behalf of the working class.[7] As a result of such shocking experiences, intellectuals became disenchanted, and socialism lost its utopian appeal.

Ironically, the spread of détente actually helped destabilize the communist dictatorships by removing the essential foreign adversary. In order to justify its continued militancy, socialism needed a "class enemy" as a threat against which it was necessary to preserve the unity and momentum of the movement. Soviet rhetoric was replete with references to foes that had to be vanquished, since it rested on an image of valiant revolutionaries struggling against internal and external antagonists. The gradual shift to détente made capitalism seem less menacing, transforming the West from a mortal enemy into a potential partner in trade, athletic competitions, and science. Moreover, the admission that both camps of the Cold War shared a common interest in preserving peace meant that the East-West dialogue might develop into real cooperation in arms limitation and other areas. Dissident appeals to the human rights provisions of the Helsinki Declaration also created more space for internal discussion. Facilitated by German Ostpolitik, the increasing communication across the Iron Curtain confused the secret service, because it dissolved the clear-cut image of an external enemy.[8]

Another underlying problem was the stalling of the centrally planned economies, because their disappointing performance falsified the claim of socialism's material superiority. The propaganda machine continued to churn out statistics pointing to vigorous growth achieved by exceeding planned targets and employing innovative technology. But the reality was starkly different, since infrastructure was deteriorating, machines were outdated, and many workers just went through the motions. Part of the problem was the priority of basic investment goods over the consumer products that the public really wanted. Another part was the structural inefficiency of planning due to its fixation on production figures and artificial pricing. Yet another cause of stagnation was the protection of inefficient producers from international competition through the lack of convertibility of eastern currencies, which reduced international trade to cumbersome bartering. For a while members of the Soviet Bloc like Poland and the GDR compensated for these shortcomings by borrowing from the West, but soon they ran into trouble servicing their external debt.[9] Even a fleeting glance, such as comparing a cramped Trabi car with a comfortable VW Golf automobile, revealed how much the East was falling behind.

These unresolved issues led to the increasing disaffection of several groups that were crucial for the stability of "real existing socialism." Of central importance was the disenchantment of the working class, since it was supposed to be the chief beneficiary of communism. As survey research remained taboo and secret service reports were "improved" on their way up, it is difficult to know what the proletariat was actually thinking. Nonetheless, it appears that the political bargain of the 1970s, which offered an increase in the standard of living in exchange for loyalty to the system, was fraying precisely because the plan was not delivering enough consumer goods. In contrast to the rhetoric of equality, daily encounters demonstrated that socialism had produced a stratified society of its own, with the party nomenklatura and western currency holders on the top, workers and peasants in the middle, and members of the former bourgeoisie as well as practicing Christians on the bottom. The result was a growing cynicism about the regime, which expressed itself in caustic jokes claiming that everything was better under communism: "The party congresses are larger, the shopping lines are longer, there are ten times as many secret policemen and instead of one country there are two Germanys."[10]

The reluctant liberalization in the wake of détente allowed an internal dissident movement to emerge, which gradually coalesced into a veritable opposition. Spurred by fears of nuclear annihilation, dissenters like the H-bomb designer Andrei Sakharov began to raise their voice in the Soviet Union, urging disarmament. In order to reconstitute a public space free of party censorship, they developed an underground press, called samizdat, consisting of mimeographed copies of news sheets and homemade periodicals. The dissident challenge spread to Poland, where the Catholic Church provided some protection while intellectuals like Jacek Kuroń and Adam Michnik also founded secular groups, such as KOR, supporting restive workers. In Czechoslovakia it was Charta 77, a group of intellectuals around Václav Havel, that developed an antipolitical agenda of reconstituting civil society, while in East Germany disappointed communists like Robert Havemann and Wolfgang Biermann criticized the SED dictatorship.[11] Police repression did not silence these dissidents but rather hastened their progression from critiquing individual policies to questioning the entire socialist system.

The final factor that undermined the legitimacy of Soviet rule was the ruling parties' loss of confidence in the mission that entitled them to hold power. In the bureaucracies, factories, and universities, communist functionaries played a central role in keeping the system going, since they controlled all decisions and supervised their implementation. Many younger party members were increasingly frustrated with the stagnation, called *zastoi* in Russian, which they blamed on the entrenched gerontocracy that was unwilling to make any changes. Through international travel even reliable cadres became gradually convinced that they were losing the competition with the West in technology and living standards. Therefore many party members were enthusiastic about Gorbachev's attempts to revitalize the system, only to find themselves blocked by their orthodox elders in the bureaucracy who denounced any reform as counterrevolution. For the party, the challenge was therefore to find a way to liberalize socialism in order to enable its survival without having the process get out of hand.[12]

During the 1980s the discrepancy between the formidable outward appearance and the internal weakening of the Eastern Bloc increased surreptitiously. On the one hand, the military power of the Soviet Union and the Warsaw Pact was never greater in terms of nuclear warheads and troop strength. If the East German Stasi is any indication, the secret police had also gotten larger and more sophisticated in combating foreign subversion and internal dissent. Moreover, the communist parties controlled the mass organizations such as the trade unions, had a media monopoly, and dominated the economy. But on the other hand, the self-will (*Eigensinn*) of the workers increased at the same time, since they no longer feared physical retribution for their noncompliance. Moreover, youth subcultures, literary circles, and dissident groups slowly revived a civil society independent of control and capable of formulating its own opinions about political issues.[13] Finally, the ruling parties began to fragment as hard-liners clashed with reformers. Owing to all these sources of creeping erosion, the alternative of communist modernity gradually lost its stability.

GROWING UNREST

A concatenation of unforeseen events was nonetheless necessary to expose this structural weakness and bring communism crashing down in Eastern Europe. In early October 1989 the German Democratic Republic could still celebrate the fortieth anniversary of its founding with the heads of the Warsaw Pact reviewing a huge parade of communist armed forces, party faithful, union workers, and youth-group members cheering the leaders. Yet behind the scenes the rift between an immobile Erich Honecker and an impatient Mikhail Gorbachev became obvious when the Soviet guest warned his host to embrace change with the perhaps apocryphal comment that "whoever comes too late, will be punished by life." None of Eastern Europe's specific problems—its economic underperformance, labor unrest, nationalist sentiment, or intellectual dissent—was in itself unsolvable, but their accumulation proved too much for the aging leaders of the communist parties. Ultimately, it was the surprising mass flight of East German citizens in the summer of 1989 that provided the push which shattered the Soviet Bloc.[14]

Civil resistance from below began in Poland with the organization of an independent trade union called Solidarność (Solidarity). Under the intrepid leadership of Lech Wałęsa, the workers of the Gdańsk shipyards banded together to protest the rise of food prices, which consumed too much of their already meager wages. The popular movement ignored the retaliation of the security organs because it was supported by the Polish pope John Paul II from abroad and by parts of the Catholic Church within. Although the creation of a nonparty trade union was a clear rejection of the communist claim to represent the interests of the proletariat, the government was forced to recognize Solidarity in August 1980 because it had mobilized about ten million members, one-third of the entire workforce! The Soviet Bloc leaders were outraged, but Brezhnev decided to let the Poles suppress the unrest themselves, having General Wojciech Jaruzelski proclaim martial law in order to use the army to arrest the union leadership. Forced to go underground, Solidarity nonetheless continued its agitation for constitutional reform, while a resurgent civil society insisted on free elections.[15]

The Soviet Union no longer intervened to suppress dissent when Gorbachev's "new thinking" in Moscow allowed the satellites greater latitude in coping with their problems. Frustrated by the resistance of the old party cadres, the Russian leader gradually radicalized his attempts at reform so as to save communism by modernizing it. Concretely that meant revitalizing the economy by introducing market incentives, building public support by lifting censorship, and changing the power balance within the party by holding competitive elections. In foreign policy Gorbachev initially moved carefully, only suggesting that he was more reluctant than his predecessors to interfere in the internal issues of the client states. Expecting that the leaders of the satellites would follow the reformist example of their big brother, he grew impatient with the old hard-liners, hoping that generational change would take care of the problem. In February of 1988 he went a step further when he proclaimed each country's "freedom to choose" its political system, thereby in effect repudiating the Brezhnev doctrine of Soviet intervention to maintain communist regimes.[16]

In Hungary a flexible communist leadership followed the call to reform and even went beyond Moscow's example. Budapest had always chosen a slightly more liberal course in allowing some economic and intellectual latitude, but only the arrival of new leaders such as Karoly Grosz and Miklós Németh in 1988 opened the door for major change. Trying to head off the pressure from below, the Hungarian parliament passed a "democracy package" in January 1989 offering civil rights, constitutional reform, and trade-union pluralism, which led to the emergence of noncommunist groups. The government also admitted that the 1956 rebellion was a popular uprising instead of a counterrevolution and permitted the reburial of Imre Nagy, which attracted hundreds of thousands of demonstrators in a reaffirmation of national pride. At the same time the party leadership reoriented its foreign policy, intensifying its relations with Western Europe.[17] During the summer of 1989 Hungary's dismantling of the 150-mile-long fence on its frontier with Austria and the suspension of border policing literally cut a hole in the Iron Curtain.

Fearing that reform would become uncontrollable, the orthodox communist regimes in the GDR, Czechoslovakia, Romania, and Bulgaria vigorously resisted making any changes. Since they were sure they could suppress internal dissent, Erich Honecker, Gustav Husák, Nicolae Ceaușescu, and Todor Zhivkov rejected Gorbachev's liberalization course as a misguided effort and called for joint Warsaw Pact action to maintain the Iron Curtain. But supported by the Poles and Hungarians, the Soviet Union refused to intervene, lest it endanger its own reform process and jeopardize détente. The hard-liners were encouraged by China's bloody repression of student protests at Tiananmen Square on June 4, 1989, which demonstrated that a resolute leadership in command of the armed forces could reassert control if it was willing to pay the human price.[18] Instead, Gorbachev reaffirmed his renunciation of force in a speech to the Council of Europe, calling interference in the domestic affairs of another socialist state "inadmissible." This unequivocal repudiation of the Chinese bloodbath further encouraged the restive dissidents and dissatisfied workers in Eastern Europe.

Ironically, the antireform front caved in where it was least expected—the German Democratic Republic. A key bastion of Soviet power, East Germany, occupied by about four hundred thousand Soviet army troops, was Russia's victory prize for its horrendous suffering in World War II. The dictatorship of the Socialist Unity Party (SED) was also one of the most repressive, though the standard of living in the GDR was the highest in the communist world, generously supported by West German transit fees and loans. The internal opposition was relatively weak, consisting of a peace and environmental movement operating in the shadow of the Protestant Church, hamstrung by the Stasi tactic of expelling dissidents to West Germany. But in spite of all efforts at interdicting western influence, the electronic media penetrated the Iron Curtain, allowing GDR citizens to emigrate figuratively each evening in front of their TV sets and restive youths to record rock music from the air waves. Cooped up behind the Wall, many East Germans wanted to leave for a better life in the West, shouting in demonstrations "We want to get out." Suddenly the cutting of the fence during a pan-European picnic at the Austro-Hungarian frontier in July of 1989 opened an escape route.[19]

The ensuing East German mass exodus transformed the gradual erosion of communism into an acute crisis with which the system proved unable to cope. Afraid that its citizens would not return, the SED leadership had restricted vacations even to other countries in the Soviet Bloc, offering only loyal party members and retirees the privilege of travel to the West. East Germans vacationing at Lake Balaton in Hungary therefore considered the removal of the barbed wire at the Hungarian border with Austria a once-in-a-lifetime opportunity to cross the weakly policed frontier. Western media rushed to the scene, broadcasting emotional pictures of overjoyed refugees arriving in freedom, creating a panic among those who remained behind, afraid of missing their chance. When the GDR tried to stop the human hemorrhage by forbidding travel, desperate would-be emigrants crowded into the FRG embassies in Prague and Warsaw, drawing other states into the humanitarian drama and forcing their release to the West. Incapacitated by Honecker's gall-bladder surgery and slow recovery, East Berlin called for Warsaw Pact solidarity. But the Communist comrades failed to respond and the mass flight continued apace.[20]

Amplifying the prior Polish and Hungarian challenges, the East German exodus threatened Soviet control over Eastern Europe. The flight of tens of thousands of ordinary citizens from the GDR was a symbolic rejection of the Leninist version of modernity. The spontaneous escapes undermined the Iron Curtain and showed that the SED had lost its control over its citizenry. At the same time, the humanitarian emergency of the mass movement evoked a wave of international sympathy, which made measures to restrict the flow look arbitrary and repressive. The stampede from East to West also created a diplomatic crisis by forcing countries to choose sides: Aided by West German credits, the Hungarians maintained the border opening, while the Czechs tried to crack down at the risk of alienating their own people. TV images of East German refugees in overcrowded trains, tearfully celebrating their arrival in the West, also reopened the national question for FRG politicians who had become all too comfortable with division. Finally, the mass flight was the moment of truth for Gorbachev, forcing him to decide whether to live up to his own promises.[21]

FALL OF THE WALL

Among the many joyful moments of 1989–90, the fall of the Berlin Wall stands out because of its practical and symbolic importance for the overthrow of communist dictatorship. The opening of the border in Berlin and along the whole frontier between East and West Germany allowed GDR citizens to witness the reality of everyday life in the West firsthand. Their shocking experience of the FRG's superior standard of living and political pluralism derailed the project of the reform communists and civic-movement dissidents who wanted to democratize East Germany but maintain its independence as an alternative to liberal capitalism. Moreover, the free movement of West Germans to the East also endangered the Soviet military presence by exposing the numerous Soviet army bases, creating pressure for their withdrawal from amidst a largely hostile population. At the same time, forcing open the Brandenburg Gate was also a highly symbolic event that signaled the breach of the Iron Curtain at a central barrier of the Cold War. Other satellite regimes could liberalize without endangering Russian hegemony, but toppling communism in East Germany threatened the survival of the entire Soviet empire.[22]

The drama of the mass flight from East Germany mobilized the previously docile population to risk mass demonstrations, demanding internal reform with the slogan "we're staying here." The protests began with Monday night peace vigils at St. Nikolai Church in Leipzig during which Pastor Christoph Wonneberger criticized the SED and dissidents met to encourage each other. Brutal police repression attracted increasing numbers of sympathizers who responded by intoning "we are the people," thereby disputing the legitimacy of the so-called people's government. The decisive moment came on October 9, when about seventy thousand demonstrators marched peacefully around the inner city, forcing the local SED and Stasi leaders, without clear orders from Berlin, to decide between ordering a massive bloodbath and permitting protests against the regime. Owing to a joint civic and party appeal against violence, led by the orchestra conductor Kurt Masur, they decided to allow the demonstration to proceed, thereby conceding the recovery of free speech. Broadcast by western and increasingly open eastern TV, the protests spread to hundreds of towns in the GDR. As a result, opposition groups like the New Forum formed, demanding a public dialogue and insisting on reform.[23]

The ruling Socialist Unity Party responded to the challenge of mounting criticism in a confused fashion, because it was divided over which course to pursue. The aging dictator Honecker denounced the popular movement as "counterrevolution" and insisted on using force to put it down. Younger and more flexible leaders wanted instead to follow Gorbachev's example and offer controlled reforms in order to keep the party in power. Sure of Moscow's support, the pragmatists deposed Honecker on October 18, choosing the younger head of the Free German Youth and of the national defense council Egon Krenz as his successor. Though he offered to initiate an open dialogue, the restive public distrusted his sincerity, since he had endorsed the bloody repression in China just a few months before. Disappointed in the failure of the socialist experiment and afraid of being attacked by angry citizens, tens of thousands of SED members left the party, weakening its resolve.[24] Unimpressed by reform promises, the dissidents and workers kept demonstrating, with half a million protesters assembling at Berlin's Alexanderplatz to demand democracy.

On November 9, 1989, the distinctive strands of mass exodus, public protest, and regime reform combined to precipitate the fall of the Wall. Free travel was one of the key demands on the placards and slogans of the demonstrations all through the GDR. The SED was in a bind, since it feared that allowing unconditional emigration and tourist travel would lead to an even greater loss of population, ready to take up the FRG offer of immediate citizenship. Nonetheless, the Central Committee decided on liberalizing travel, dropping most preconditions and making the process less cumbersome. Schabowski's mistaken announcement that the change would take place immediately surprised the border guards and emboldened the citizens to test the change of policy on the spot. Western news reporters like Tom Brokaw of NBC captured the resulting opening of the transit gates on TV, broadcasting the spontaneous joy of Berliners around the globe. Already asleep in the Kremlin because of the two hour-time difference, the leaders of the Soviet Union woke up to a changed world, unable to close the border again by force without risking a major international crisis.[25]

In spite of the pent-up anger, the democratic awakening remained peaceful because the Round Table provided a way to negotiate a gradual transfer of power. Spreading to the entire Eastern Bloc, the idea had originated in Poland when Solidarity leaders met with representatives of the ruling Polish Workers Party to discuss necessary changes. It proved attractive in East Germany because the SED controlled the levers of power but lacked legitimacy, while the opposition groups of the civic movement had legitimacy but lacked resources and organization. Mediated by the churches, the debates of the central and local round tables turned out to be constructive, since both the regime and its opponents agreed on the need to democratize the state in order to preserve a freer version of socialism. The Round Table worked as an organ for controlling the SED government, now led by the more flexible Dresden party chief Hans Modrow, by insisting on the revitalization of parliamentary institutions, the dissolution of the secret police (Stasi), and invigoration of the economy through competition. The most important Round Table decision was the agreement on constitutional reform and free elections.[26]

The attempt to find a "third way" between the blocs failed, however, as public sentiment in the GDR shifted decisively in favor of reunification with the FRG. After the fall of the Wall the protesters began to shout "we are *one* people," modifying the previous slogan in one crucial detail. Though West German politicians had initially demanded only the democratization of the East, on November 28 Chancellor Helmut Kohl boldly proposed a Ten Point Plan, outlining a progression of steps from confederation to federation in order to regain popular-opinion leadership. This surprising suggestion created a storm of international criticism, because it moved the "German question" from pious platitudes to the level of actual politics. When tens of thousands of Dresden citizens shouted enthusiastically "Helmut! Helmut!" and "Deutschland! Deutschland!" during his visit in December, an emotional Kohl resolved to push for immediate unification in spite of Gorbachev's opposition, Thatcher's criticism, and Mitterrand's vacillations. Unlike the skeptical political elites, most ordinary people in the neighboring countries favored German self-determination.[27]

In the election of March 18, 1990, the East Germans decisively rejected communism and clearly endorsed German unification. The campaign was heated, because this time it involved not just a ritual of "folding ballots" but rather a decision about the future of the GDR. Drawing on western campaigners, finances, and polling, some eastern parties joined forces with their larger FRG counterparts. The Christian Democratic Union (CDU) relied on Kohl's support of unity, but the Social Democratic Party (SPD) was handicapped by the warnings of its leader Oskar Lafontaine about the potential cost. The outcome vindicated the Christian Democrats and their allies, who gained more than two-fifths of the votes, while the disappointing Social Democrats came in second with a quarter. The communists (former SED), renamed as the Party of Democratic Socialism (PDS), survived with one-fifth, and the Liberals got one-tenth. The fragmented civic movement, which had been the spearhead of the demonstrations, was the loser, receiving less than one-twentieth of the ballots due to its rejection of unification. The clear winner overall, CDU chief Lothar de Maizière, formed a coalition government so as to prepare the GDR for accession to the FRG according to Article 23 of the Basic Law, prepared by a customs union and codified in a unification treaty during the summer.[28]

The complicated two-plus-four negotiations (between the two Germanies seeking unification and the four Allied powers of the postwar occupation) translated this election mandate into an accepted international order for a postcommunist Europe. Seeing a chance to win the Cold War, President George H. W. Bush and Secretary of State James Baker supported German unification from the beginning. But a disappointed Gorbachev refused to give up the GDR until it became clear in January 1990 that his satellite was bankrupt and discredited. Talks between representatives of the two German states and foreign ministers of the four victor powers succeeded in producing an agreement accepted by all parties. International pressure forced Chancellor Kohl, who did not want to offend his refugee constituency, to accept the Oder-Neisse line as Germany's eastern frontier in exchange for keeping the issue of reparations off the table. Similarly, American arguments and sizable West German aid payments persuaded Secretary General Gorbachev to permit a united Germany to remain in the NATO alliance. The final settlement of the German question tied up the loose ends of World War II, dissolved the GDR as a separate state, and removed the Russians from Central Europe.[29]

SOVIET COLLAPSE

In a reverse scenario of American fears during the Vietnam War, one East European domino fell after another, dissolving the empire and eventually the Soviet Union as well. The Polish and Hungarian protests were the beginning, the fall of the Wall in the GDR removed the keystone, Czechoslovakia and the Balkans followed suit, the Baltic states and Ukraine shattered the USSR, and finally communism imploded in Russia. Amplified by the media, a process of contagion drove this astounding sequence, with each successful challenge in one country inspiring another elsewhere. Instead of saving communism by modernizing it, Gorbachev's strategy of reform from above unleashed popular forces that the party dictatorship was unable to control. Each time, a temporary alliance between dissidents calling for human rights and workers demanding a better life used the recovered freedom of speech and assembly to discredit the tired apparatchiks, setting an irresistible process of change in motion.[30] The crucial factor was Gorbachev's decision not to use force, since it gave away the one instrument that might have reasserted control.

Although the outcomes were similar, each path toward ending communist rule was somewhat different, depending on the particular situation of a country. In Poland the confrontation began with pressure from below such as the strikes in favor of relegalizing Solidarity. In April 1989 Jaruzelski agreed at the Round Table to opposition demands to permit free elections. The result of the June 4 balloting was a complete repudiation of the Polish Workers Party candidates, since in the lower house Solidarity won all seats for which it could compete and in the Senate it gained ninety-nine out of one hundred. As a result of the landslide the Catholic editor Tadeusz Mazowiecki became prime minister in mid-August, creating the first noncommunist government of Poland since 1945. The country then changed its name to the Republic of Poland and elected Lech Wałęsa as president in December 1990.[31] Since this transition proceeded by incremental steps, was based on overwhelming popular support, and took place peacefully, Gorbachev refused hard-line calls for intervention and agreed to withdraw Soviet troops.

In Hungary a similar mixture of popular demands from below and party concessions from above spelled the end of communism. The demonstrations began with environmental protests against damming up the Danube, forcing the government to abandon the project. Seeking to avoid a confrontation, reformist leaders of the Communist Party initiated a process of constitutional reform in order to control the outcome. The public kept the pressure on during the March 15, 1989, holiday, demanding civil and national rights, freedom of speech, media independence, withdrawal of Soviet troops, and economic reforms. Moreover, during the reburial of the leaders of the 1956 uprising the student Victor Orban called on the huge crowd to take matters into its own hands. As a result of such civic mobilization, the Round Table agreed in September to overhaul the constitution, legalize opposition parties, and hold free elections. Though the Communists reinvented themselves as the Socialist Party, the May 1990 ballot was a clear victory for the center-right parties, allowing the historian József Antall to form a noncommunist government.[32]

Encouraged by the fall of the Wall, the Velvet Revolution in Czechoslovakia emulated the successful example of its neighbors and overthrew communism in a mere six weeks. The dissident appeals of Charta 77 had already begun to resonate because of popular dissatisfaction with economic and political stagnation. But the spark that set off mass protests was the brutal repression of a student demonstration on November 17, 1989, by riot police in which one participant was rumored to have been killed. In subsequent days intellectuals in the media and in theaters, where public discussions took place, called for strikes, while hundreds of thousands of citizens turned out on Wenceslas Square to demonstrate against the Husák regime. A two-hour general strike on November 27, supported by three-quarters of the population, showed overwhelming support for the opposition Civic Forum, forced the unpopular president to resign, and enabled a noncommunist government to be appointed. On December 29, dissident writer Václav Havel was chosen president, and the free elections in June 1990 completed the transfer of power to the anticommunist parties.[33]

While Bulgaria followed the Czech pattern, the Romanian revolution resulted in eleven hundred dead because Ceauşescu was not willing to relinquish his rule. The Timisoara protests against the arrest of László Tökés, a Hungarian Protestant pastor who had made critical remarks in a TV interview, were brutally suppressed by Securitate, the secret police, and the army. When Ceauşescu condemned the uprising in a speech in front of about one hundred thousand people in Bucharest, he was booed, to his utter astonishment, then shots were fired and a riot broke out. The dictator ordered force to be used to quell the unrest, leading to the killing and wounding of many civilians. After the purported suicide of the minister of defense, many soldiers switched sides. Tanks joined the crowd and battled secret police and communist loyalists. When the commander in chief also abandoned the dictator, Ceauşescu fled with his wife by helicopter but was captured, tried for treason, and shot on December 25, 1989. As a result, a surprising combination of popular upheaval and regime opportunism brought Ion Iliescu and the reform communists into power.[34]

The crumbling of its East European empire ultimately led to the dissolution of the Soviet Union itself, since the liberalization of debate allowed nationalist sentiment to resurface. Sensing that the federal structure with fifteen separate republics was held together more by compulsion than by consent, the peripheral states with non-Russian ethnic majorities seized the opportunity to reclaim their independence. Resenting their annexation during World War II as illegal, Lithuania, Latvia, and Estonia were the first to opt out, declaring their sovereignty in the spring of 1990. This desire was initially suppressed by force but was granted in the fall of 1991 by a weakening Soviet center. The larger Ukraine and Belarus followed this example, seceding from the Soviet Union by popular referendum, which was recognized in the Belavezha Accords, that dissolved the Soviet Union. In mid-December the Alma Ata Protocol created a new voluntary association of the remaining republics, called Commonwealth of Independent States.[35] The Soviet Union's legal successor was the Russian Republic, largely reduced to its ethnic core and shorn of its imperial pretensions.

The loss of empire hastened the collapse of communism in Russia, since Communists-turned-democrats under Boris Yeltsin won the struggle for postimperial power. The fragmentation of the Soviet Union and its empire aggravated long-standing dissatisfaction with disappointing economic performance and the continued lack of political freedom. Communist hard-liners wanted to defend their federation and ideology by force; centrists around Gorbachev were ready to let the disaffected provinces go and liberalize the system; and reformers around Yeltsin intended to create a democratic Russia out of the wreckage. Owing to his popularity Yeltsin, the former mayor of Moscow, succeeded in resisting efforts to oust him as president of Russia, declaring it sovereign—that is, no longer subject to the Soviet Union. When on August 19, 1991, Communist plotters, including the chairman of the KGB Vladimir Kryuchkov, attempted a military coup, Yeltsin beat the putsch back by courageously defending the parliament building.[36] But as a result Gorbachev lost power, communism was discredited, and the Russian Republic embarked on the difficult road to independence, capitalism, and democracy.

Owing to their surprising lack of violence, the East European upheavals between 1989 and 1991 constituted a new type of "peaceful revolution." The basic pattern of civil contestation was similar everywhere, with dissident protests against the communist regime finding increasing resonance in the general population. While the challengers from below lacked weapons for a violent struggle, the authorities above were restrained by international opinion that would have abhorred any repetition of the "Chinese solution." The crucial innovation of the revolutionary process was the Round Table, which brought the opposition and the rulers together in order to discuss the necessary steps toward an orderly transition. Agreements on the restoration of human rights such as free speech and reform of the constitution to allow political pluralism prepared the ground for holding free elections as a way of deciding the issue of power. This "negotiated transition" offered a nonviolent way of consulting the population about the future shape of the political and social system. In spite of its gradualism, the impact of this process was quite revolutionary.[37]

AMBIVALENT CONSEQUENCES

The stunning events of the peaceful revolution marked the most important caesura since 1945, because they fundamentally transformed the structure of Central and Eastern Europe. Within the short period of three years, the communist dictatorships that controlled half of the continent were overthrown by their own citizens. Unlike the violent ruptures of 1918 and 1945, the process of regime change remained remarkably peaceful, requiring neither another world war nor outside intervention. Instead, a popular movement from below used the space generated by reforms from above and by international détente to reclaim human rights and force a transition to democracy. Dissatisfaction with the material performance of the planned economy inspired the return to capitalist competition in order to obtain a greater share of prosperity. The disintegration of the Soviet empire and the subsequent dissolution of the Soviet Union reconfigured international relations by freeing the satellites from Russian domination and ending the Cold War between the superpowers. Thereby Eastern Europe gained another chance for self-determination and a better life.[38]

The end of the Cold War concluded the ideological rivalry of the Soviet Union and the United States, which had divided Europe and polarized the globe for the second half of the twentieth century. As a result of the strengthening of détente, George H. W. Bush and Mikhail Gorbachev declared the Cold War over at their summit meeting on Malta in December 1989. During the subsequent months NATO changed its military doctrine to remove any trace of offensive intent in order to make it easier for the Soviet Union to allow Germany to remain in the Atlantic alliance as a safeguard against neutralist temptations. At the summit of July 1991 the offer of a strategic partnership facilitated the withdrawal of the Soviet army from Eastern Europe by reassuring Moscow that the United States harbored no offensive designs. Though still somewhat suspicious of each other, both countries finally signed the Strategic Arms Reduction Treaty at the same meeting and concluded a second START agreement in January 1993.[39] Since Russia was preoccupied with its own transformation, the United States remained the only superpower during the 1990s.

The lifting of the Iron Curtain provided an opportunity for healing the division of Europe by reconnecting the East to the West. The abolition of the reinforced border suddenly made the ancient capitals of Warsaw, Prague, and Budapest accessible, triggering a new tourism. The restoration of train connections and building of superhighways facilitated travel and trade, putting truckers into the forefront of reintegration. At the same time neighbors like Hungary and Austria rediscovered their historic connections, while former enemies like Poland and Germany launched efforts at reconciliation. In order to improve their security vis-à-vis Russia, Poland, the Czech Republic, and Hungary joined NATO in 1999, and the Baltic countries, Slovenia, Slovakia, Bulgaria, and Romania followed suit in 2004. The eastward expansion of the European Union was more complicated because of the enormous disparity between East and West in economic potential, western workers' fears of an influx of cheap labor, and the need of eastern economies to catch up to the prior level of western integration. After a considerable preparation period, eight East European states entered the EU in 2004 and two more in 2007, increasing its membership to twenty-seven.[40]

Unfortunately, the withdrawal of the Soviet army and collapse of the Soviet Union opened the door not only to human rights and democracy but also to the revival of nationalism as an ideological replacement for discredited communism. Finding itself reduced to the borders of the 1918 Brest-Litovsk Treaty, the Russian Republic looked back to tsarist times to find new sources of pride in its national heritage and used nationalist appeals in order to recover remnants of its former empire in the Caucasus, Crimea, and Ukraine. Russia's retreat and Germany's diminution revived the independence of a whole series of states such as the Ukraine, Belarus, and Moldova that had barely, if at all, existed before. Within the newly sovereign countries, the wish for consolidation and self-assertion fostered an intolerant nationalism, which reignited old minority problems that had escaped ethnic cleansing, for instance between Hungarians and Romanians. Nationalist fervor also led to the disintegration of two post–World War I barrier states, triggering a peaceful divorce between the Czech Republic and Slovakia but resulting in a series of

Map 11. NATO expansion, 2004. Adapted from German Historical Institute, Washington, DC.

bloody successor wars with the breakup of Yugoslavia.[41] As a result, the new countries vacillated between asserting their independence and cooperating with Europe.

The democratic awakening and the two-plus-four agreement also solved the long-standing "German problem" in Europe by restoring a chastened national state. International approval extended only to the accession of the bankrupt GDR to the flourishing FRG, since the latter had proven to be peaceful in the postwar decades. The price for unification was the unified Germany's confirmation of the permanent loss of the previously German provinces farther east, facilitated by an official acceptance of responsibility for the Second World War and the Holocaust. Though returning to the old capital of Berlin in 1999, the enlarged FRG remained a civilian power, firmly embedded in a web of multilateral obligations in NATO and the EU while sacrificing its hard DM currency to European integration by the creation of the euro. Nonetheless, Germany had the largest population on the continent with about eighty-two million people and also possessed the biggest economy, still relying to a considerable degree on manufacturing of high-end products. With unification the FRG regained its central position in Europe, serving as a bridge between East and West and becoming a leader by default.[42]

For the independent East European states the overthrow of communism brought great opportunities combined with difficult challenges, because they largely had to reinvent themselves. It was not enough to restore the formal structures of self-government; parliamentary life and democratic behavior had to be learned by representatives as well as citizens. After decades of planned scarcity, the economy had to be restructured for market competition, while the public had to figure out how to deal with the temptations of consumer society. At the same time the change from living in a collective to acting as a separate individual was a great shock, since much of the social-security apparatus evaporated and people had to make their own decisions. The problem of coming to terms with the legacy of communist dictatorship was especially taxing, since sweeping crimes under the rug seemed initially easier but poisoned societal relationships in the long run.[43] In the transition the Baltic countries and Central European states, which had some tradition of democracy, had more success than their less-experienced cousins.

Since the transformation involved Central and Eastern Europe, the West Europeans were only indirectly affected by it. Many westerners watched the spectacle of the peaceful revolution with amazement, incredulous that the Soviet Union was willing to relinquish its gains. But even those distant from the democratic awakening were soon drawn into some participation: Members of democratic parties worked as consultants in creating parliamentary institutions and running election campaigns. Businessmen and managers helped in the privatization of state-run companies and in procuring investments for start-up companies. Bureaucrats assisted in setting up public administration independent of party favors and in disbursing funds from aid organizations. Academics gave guest lectures and provided their expertise for introducing international standards of scholarship. Especially when they had to pay a surcharge as in West Germany, taxpayers grumbled about the steep costs of refurbishing the East.[44] But these complainers tended to forget the multiple benefits of a growing market, improved security, and enhanced community.

Experiences of the new reality after communism were therefore somewhat mixed, since not all sanguine hopes could be realized. Confronted with the contrast between the empowering elation during the democratic awakening and the labors of daily life thereafter, many East Europeans felt frustrated with the emerging postcommunist order.[45] During anniversaries of the peaceful revolution most editorial writers agreed that there had been substantial advances in international peace, political freedom, and individual prosperity for many citizens. But leftist critics could also point to important losses in economic security, predictable routine, and social services like free public child care. Unexpectedly, new problems arose, such as high unemployment, widespread corruption, and ugly xenophobia. Yet there were also unprecedented chances for intellectual debate, foreign travel, and the purchase of attractive consumer goods. Since the postcommunist transition to capitalist democracy remains a work in progress, East Europeans continue to hope that the gains will ultimately prove more important than its attendant aggravations.

TRIUMPH OF DEMOCRACY?

Essentially, the overthrow of communism ended the century-long competition between the socialist and democratic alternatives of modernity in Europe. The American theorist Francis Fukuyama therefore concluded that history, understood as ideological confrontation, had come to an end: "The twin crises of authoritarianism and social-ist central planning have left only one competitor standing in the ring as an ideology of potentially universal validity: liberal democracy, the doctrine of individual freedom and popular sovereignty." The Right was therefore rather triumphant, celebrating liberal democracy as the "final form of human government," and promoted a further lib-eration of capitalism from its remaining restraints. In contrast, the Left was not relieved that the defeat of Leninism opened the way for a more moderate version of social democracy. Dejected intellectuals like Eric Hobsbawm instead saw their entire project of social equal-ity discredited.[46] Even if understandable, both responses contained dangerous oversimplifications: the neoconservative gloating fed uni-lateral hubris, while the Left's despondence deprived capitalism of its critics.

The antithetical reading of the struggle between communism and democracy has tended to obscure their common roots and similari-ties as modernization blueprints. Both philosophies stemmed from the Enlightenment, with socialism harking back to Rousseau's *vol-onté générale* and liberalism deriving from Montesquieu's balance of power. Both ideologies also shared a belief in science and technology, relied on industrialized economies, promoted social organization, and followed elaborate rule systems. In practice both systems also produced nation-states, established huge bureaucracies, developed powerful militaries, and sought to shape international affairs ac-cording to their own interests. No wonder that in the lengthy com-petition both sides were forced to adopt rhetorical references as well as actual policies from each other, leading to a degree of functional convergence as advanced industrial societies: The Soviet Bloc main-tained the trappings of democratic institutions in order to claim pop-ular legitimacy, while the free world introduced welfare-state provi-sions in order to moderate class conflict.[47]

Following the conventions of propaganda, commentators have instead stressed the differences between socialism and liberalism in order to establish the superiority of their own camp. In the East scien-tific research was directed from above, the economy planned, society collectivized, and law instrumentalized to serve the grand project of establishing socialism. In the West technology was free to develop, market competition drove economic growth, individualism characterized social relations, and the legal system remained independent because liberals assumed that personal initiative would contribute more to the collective good. To achieve their political aims the communists stressed internationalism, subordinated the bureaucracy to the party, built an ideological fighting force, and ruled their empire by compulsion from above, because they believed in the necessity of struggle to overturn the bourgeois system. The democrats instead favored national self-determination, relied on an impartial civil service, preferred a professional military, and developed an "empire by invitation," since they thought voluntary cooperation more effective.[48]

To a large degree the failure of communism as a modernization strategy from above stemmed from a disappointment in the realization of its promises. For the exploited working class, faced with unemployment, the prospect of social security and an egalitarian society appeared attractive. For the intellectuals the social-engineering project of creating a new order was inspiring, since they would play a central role in it. And for leaders of developing countries the example of Stalinist (and later Maoist) industrialization provided hope, since it promised to jump over stages of development so as to catch up to or surpass the advanced West. In "real existing socialist" practice, however, the performance of the planned economy left much to be desired, since it proved inadequate in producing coveted consumer goods. At the same time the intellectuals found themselves subordinated to the party, limited in their artistic styles and censored in their criticism of the system. Finally, for the more developed satellites, smokestack industrialization was a step backward that inhibited the transition to a high-tech economy.[49]

To many East Europeans, unfamiliar with the problems of the other system, the western version of modernity therefore seemed superior enough to make them want to join it. Used to propaganda exaggerations, they tended to discount the party's stereotypical warnings against drugs, crime, unemployment, and inequality. Reinforced by travel impressions, the East Europeans' exposure to Western films, TV series, and Radio Free Europe broadcasts conveyed an enticing picture of popular affluence, intellectual debate, and technical sophistication. Though perhaps not perfect, the combination of market competition and individual freedom appeared to have produced a consumer democracy, supported by a social safety net, that was more colorful and satisfying than the drab existence under communist rule. Knowing what they disliked and hoping to get what they wanted, East Europeans repudiated Marxism-Leninism and chose liberal democratic modernity instead. In taking this leap, many assumed that they would retain socialist safeguards while adding the blessings of western competition. Little did they realize that they would be in for a difficult transition.[50]

Chapter 26

TRANSFORMING THE EAST

New Polish shopping center, 1990s. *Source*: 123RF.

In January 2005 the Indian magnate Lakshmi Mittal announced that he had just acquired the Tadeusz Sendzimir Steelworks in Poland. Opened in 1954 and initially named after Lenin, the plant was once the largest steel factory in Poland with forty thousand workers producing seven million tons of steel per year. As a Stalinist showcase at the edge of Kraków, the district of Nowa Huta (literally New Steel Mill), with a quarter million people in high-rise apartments, had been a beacon of communist modernity like its sister cities Magnitogorsk in Russia and Eisenhüttenstadt in the GDR. Ironically, during the 1980s the district became a hotbed of the Solidarity opposition, with two-thirds of the workers joining the union. Renamed after 1990 to commemorate a Polish engineer, the plant struggled to survive with state subsidies, since it was saddled with too many workers, antiquated machinery, primitive products, and huge debts of 1.5 billion zlotys. Though the aging complex needed to downsize, shed four-fifths of its workforce, and invest in new machines, Mittal took a chance on it, since labor costs were low and Eastern Europe's economic recovery needed steel to undergird it.[1]

The complications of the postcommunist transition to democracy and the market turned the heady excitement of the peaceful revolution into widespread disenchantment. During the democratic awakening, many East Europeans had dreamt of political freedom to participate in politics, material prosperity to enjoy consumption, individualism to realize different lifestyles, pluralism to make artistic experiments, and international peace to end the Cold War. However, in subsequent decades they all too often experienced political instability, economic collapse and personal unemployment, increasing crime and social coldness, shallow commercialism in the popular media, and new kinds of ethnic warfare. No wonder that a heated controversy developed in which anticommunist commentators blamed the disastrous legacy of communism for the problems, while the postcommunists held the mistakes of the transformation and the ruthlessness of the capitalist system responsible for such disappointments.[2]

Both sides were able to bolster their competing claims with considerable evidence, since the transformation was a contradictory process. Anticommunist critics could point to the prevalence of dilapidated apartment buildings, abandoned military bases, polluted industrial sites, and crumbling infrastructure. They tended to attribute the lingering authoritarianism, opportunist conformity, habits of corruption, and mindless collectivism to the socialist regime and stressed that state-owned industries were antiquated, overstaffed, overpriced, and noncompetitive. But postcommunist apologists, appalled by the new disparities of wealth, could retort that instability resulted from a media-driven populism and the undue influence of interest groups. They also attacked the destructiveness of economic "shock therapy," railed against the excesses of casino capitalism, and deplored the naked greed evident in privatization.[3] Since judgments depended on one's ideological outlook and personal experience, prior regime opponents praised the chances for a better life, while defenders of communism deplored the shortcomings of capitalism.

In actual fact, the terrible legacy of communism *and* the errors of an uncharted transformation complicated the postcommunist transition to democracy and capitalism. The "dilemma of simultaneity," involving a multiple transition from dictatorship to democracy, from a planned to a market economy, and from a multiethnic empire to a national state, was bound to create enormous difficulties. Moreover, the newly independent states revealed a surprising "path dependency," inspiring a revival of older, often problematic patterns. As a result countries closer to the West with traditions of civil society such as in the Baltic states, Poland, the Czech Republic, and Hungary succeeded in establishing liberal systems with parliamentary rule and market competition. States further distant with less democratic experience like Slovakia, Bulgaria, and Romania retained more authoritarian governments and economic controls, while countries in the Yugoslav and Russian orbit lagged further behind.[4] A quarter century after the peaceful revolution, the results of adopting western patterns turned out to be rather more mixed than expected.

Essentially, the postcommunist transformation was a transition from the communist to the liberal democratic version of modernity. The switch from a closed dictatorship to an "open society" was more than a "a catch-up revolution" because the revival of civil society, mediation of the Round Table, and legitimation by free elections constituted a novel type of system change—namely a peaceful revolution.[5] The process was so complicated because Eastern Europe was not just "backward" but had rather taken a different path of development, which its citizens subsequently rejected because they preferred the western way of life. In switching systems, the postcommunist countries had to democratize their political order, make their economies competitive, individualize their societies, pluralize their cultures, and find a place in the international order. In contrast to the ambitious social-engineering projects of the totalitarian dictatorships, the challenge of liberalization was managing a piecemeal transition from one modernity to another for which no blueprint existed, because it was unprecedented.[6]

POLITICAL DEMOCRATIZATION

The process of democratization depended largely on prior historical experiences, the vigor of the revolutionary movement, and the strength of communist elites. Wherever there had been some partial experience with self-government, the opposition was strong, and the nomenklatura had been evicted from power, the construction of a functioning democracy largely succeeded. This was generally the case in the Baltic countries, Poland, the Czech Republic, and initially also Hungary. Wherever civil society and protests were less vigorous and the party was stronger, the transformation took longer and often remained incomplete. Slovakia, Bulgaria, and Romania were examples of such a slow transition. Finally, wherever there had been little previous self-rule, the popular movement was weak, and the former elite retained its power, democratization made little headway. Belarus and Ukraine therefore remained quasi dictatorships, while in Yugoslavia the establishment of postcommunist populism triggered a civil war.[7] In contrast to the heady expectations of 1989, the establishment of democratic rule turned out to be full of difficulties and disappointments.

In drafting new constitutions, the reformers combined earlier precedents with imported examples from Western Europe and the United States. The first step was the revitalization of the existing parliamentary framework under communism in order to reintroduce debate and political choice. In the East European states with the strongest dissident groups, the combined opposition movements won the first electoral contest against the postcommunist parties. Except in Poland, which made a second effort in 1997, new constitutions were approved between 1990 and 1992 in order to provide a stable order for political competition. Most of the smaller states adopted a unicameral system, but some of the larger ones like Poland and Romania selected two chambers; about one-third of the countries picked a parliamentary format, while two-thirds allowed the election of the president by popular vote; most also chose a mixture of single-member district and proportional representation; and all stipulated a minimum threshold of between 3 and 5 percent of the votes for parties to win seats.[8] The formal arrangements tried to draw on the best practices of the West.

The new political parties only gradually managed to stabilize their programs and electoral support, since allegiances were fluid and strong personalities transcended ideology. Surprisingly, some precommunist groups such as the Smallholders Party in Hungary reemerged after 1990. However, the united opposition movements like the Civic Forum in Czechoslovakia swept the first election, and popular leaders such as Lech Wałęsa of Solidarity were chosen as first presidents. But after vanquishing the former regime supporters, these umbrella organizations tended to splinter, for example when the supporters of Václav Klaus in Prague became neoliberal champions of a radical transition to market economics. Various Catholic and nationalist groups also founded conservative parties like Vladimir Meciar's populist Movement for a Democratic Slovakia that pushed for independence.[9] In the Baltic states the nationalities' conflict with the Russian minority was the key issue. But after much initial fluctuation the party system began to stabilize, and a left-right spectrum similar to that in Western Europe emerged.

Ironically enough, the postcommunist parties also played a crucial role in the democratization of politics after 1990, because they represented a significant section of previous elites. Since Soviet-style communism was discredited, the former ruling parties reinvented themselves everywhere as parties of democratic socialism, as they were called in East Germany. Wherever they won the first election, as in Bulgaria and Romania, the subsequent transition was slow and incomplete, since their victory perpetuated communist dominance and prevented a fundamental exchange of elites. But when they lost, as in Hungary, Poland, and Czechoslovakia, the transformation was more rapid and successful, because the opposition groups that assumed power insisted on a more thorough regime change and conversion to a market economy. Responding to the difficulties of transition, the restructured postcommunists often won the second round of elections, thereby introducing a robust competition between political parties that kept up the pace of reform and limited the predatory exploitation of the state.[10]

The attraction of the European Union was another important factor that advanced the democratization of the postcommunist states. Basically, "the West" served as example of a free and prosperous life—the chief goal to which transforming countries aspired. Neighbors like Germany and Austria also helped with exchange programs for retraining eastern elites, contacts between political parties for creating networks, and economic investment for spreading international business practices. Moreover, the EU exerted a considerable passive pressure through the presumed benefits of its membership, because the East Europeans could hope to be accepted only if they had stable democracies and their economic performance caught up to western levels. Once local elites had decided that they wanted to join, an active leverage came into play, since applicants were required to accept and implement the explicit EU standards, the so-called *acquis communautaire*.[11] This preaccession conditionality powerfully influenced domestic politics by providing reform-minded groups with irrefutable arguments.

In the transition, the East-Central European countries succeeded in creating liberal democracies by making decisions that reinforced pluralist solutions. According to indicators such as the observance of human rights, the Baltic countries as well as Poland, Hungary, and the Czech Republic established open societies. They all had strong anticommunist opposition movements that could negotiate a peaceful transition of power and insist on decisive reform measures, in part inspired by the collapse of their economies. The result was an institutional structure that allowed vigorous competition, even from the postcommunist rivals; moreover in these states elites largely resisted the temptation of nationalist intolerance against minorities; and the new governments undertook vigorous economic reforms by risking the free play of the market. This resolute course did not shy away from conflicts but carried out the inevitable changes in such a manner that the population understood them to be necessary. This bold approach was internationally rewarded by praise, help, and foreign investment.[12]

When these factors were absent or even reversed, the transformation remained incomplete, producing an illiberal democracy that observed the form without the substance. In Romania, Bulgaria, and Slovakia as well as in the rest of the Balkans, the opposition was too weak to take over so that the relabeled communists could stay in power or populists take their place. Officially the communist dictatorship ended, there were elections, and new parties emerged, but the previous elites continued to extract profits from controlling the government with leaders like Ion Iliescu in Bucharest or parties like the Socialists in Sofia. Moreover, populists like Meciar in Bratislava fanned nationalist passions against minorities. No doubt the transition was a disaster in Yugoslavia, while Alexander Lukashenko established a dictatorial rule in Belarus, and after 2000 Vladimir Putin's Russia became an authoritarian and nationalist regime. But in Eastern Europe the development of Slovenia, the transformation of Slovakia, and the rehabilitation of Croatia showed that delayed progress was possible even in the Balkans.[13]

The leader who best symbolized the East European commitment to democratic values was the Czech intellectual Václav Havel. Born in 1936 in Prague into a wealthy entrepreneurial family, he initially turned to the theater, writing successful absurdist plays. But when his dramas were banned after 1968, he became a dissident, criticized the "living in a lie" of communism, and served several prison sentences. As one of the founders of Charta 77, he encapsulated the struggle for human rights in moving essays like "The Power of the

Powerless." As a result of his civic courage he was elected president of Czechoslovakia during the Velvet Revolution in order to guide its transformation into a republic. Due to his international fame he was instrumental in dissolving the Warsaw Pact, but he could not prevent the secession of the Slovaks from Prague. Reelected as Czech president, he continued to serve until 2003, when he was beaten by the neoliberal rival Václav Klaus. Even advocating reconciliation with the Sudeten Germans, Havel greatly contributed to consolidating Czech democracy with his moral integrity.[14]

ECONOMIC TRANSFORMATION

Reintroducing modern capitalism proved even more difficult than the political transition, since it involved the double challenge of transformation from plan to market and from protection to global competition. The conversion from a planning to a marketplace system ended the political allocation decisions to subsidize items like food by taking their actual production costs into account. This shift revolutionized the entire price structure of the economy by privileging comparative efficiency rather than ideological conformity, freeing companies to pursue profits while abandoning social services. At the same time, the end of protectionism through convertibility of eastern currencies exposed lumbering state-owned companies to tough global competition, which revealed their inefficiency. Often Asian producers were able to offer cheaper and better products through low wage costs and technological innovation that the East European countries could not match. While some individual companies managed to compete on price and quality, most of the industrial giants of the East quickly faltered, relying on state subsidies to survive.[15]

Lack of competitiveness created a liberalization shock that led to a decline in GDPs of more than one-quarter, triggering a severe drop in living standards. Though communists had prided themselves on creating an advanced industrial society, they had preserved an older structure of industrial and agricultural labor that the West had left behind by shifting to a service economy. On the micro level of individual companies, much of the machinery was outdated, labor productivity remained low, technological innovation lagged, and products were unattractive. On the macro level of states, many countries like Poland and Hungary had been carrying excessive external debt, while extensive social services, price supports, and the military as well as secret police costs strained their budgets. When consumers clamored for western products, the native goods went unsold, hurting numerous local producers. Moreover, the entire Comecon trading system collapsed when buyers imported products from the world market. As a result roughly half of the companies went bankrupt, and unemployment soared to about 20 percent.[16]

Privatization was an especially difficult task, since the lack of a precedent made it hard to know how to proceed. Neoliberal doctrine demanded the sale of state-owned assets in order to render companies more competitive, excluding the perpetuation of a mixed economy. Small-scale conversion was easiest because collectivized farmers, craftsmen, and shopkeepers had the know-how to resume an independent business. More complicated was the public distribution of shares of public stock, attempted in Poland and Czechoslovakia, since it failed to provide funds for modernization and deterred investors. Most challenging was the large-scale sale of public companies to investors, overseen in East Germany by a Trusteeship Agency, since where successful it generated capital and attracted know-how for making businesses competitive again. In many cases privatization was tarnished by insider deals in which members of the party or the secret police managed to obtain state property, getting a head start as capitalists. Nonetheless, this gigantic transformation of economic structure from public to private enterprise was a precondition for recovery.[17]

Another crucial factor was foreign investment, because outside capital was needed to sustain the economic transformation. While the International Monetary Fund (IMF) and the World Bank refinanced some loans and offered considerable credits, foreign direct investment in business was even more important. Some international investors like the Italian company Benetton were interested primarily in market access in order to be able to establish beachheads for selling their products in a developing economy. Other companies like

Adidas sought to take advantage of the East's relatively low labor costs and physical proximity to Western Europe by outsourcing labor-intensive production of textiles or other athletic accessories. Relatively rare was the funding of East European production for its own sake, since the future development of the market seemed uncertain. With U.S. and West European financiers largely uninterested, most investment came from Germany, with Volkswagen for instance buying up the foundering carmaker Škoda and returning it to profitability.[18] Much of this involvement came as a reward for reforms already underway.

One prominent method of conversion was "shock therapy," advocated by American neoliberal economists like Jeffrey Sachs. Such a radical approach used deregulation, privatization, and balancing budgets for a rapid transformation in order to jump-start economic recovery rather than to drag the process out. Facing industrial collapse and high inflation, the Polish and Czech governments initially tried such a policy, but the resulting lowering of living standards was so drastic that the reformers were forced to return to a more moderate course. Led by Estonia, the Baltic states embarked on drastic restructuring somewhat later but also made a radical break in liberalizing markets, limiting welfare expenditures, introducing low flat-tax rates, and other supportive policies. Part of their effort was also designed to end Russian dominance. Helped by investment from their Scandinavian neighbors across the sea, and having workers with high levels of education and technical expertise, the Baltic states succeeded in revitalizing their economies with such a tough approach.[19]

Another, ultimately successful path was a more moderate form of economic transformation that maintained a larger amount of social services. In contrast to the Balkans, most of East-Central Europe had the advantage of being more highly industrialized and having maintained more market remnants in agriculture and small business under communism. At the same time the creation of pluralist politics prevented the exploitation of revenue by a "rent-seeking" bureaucracy. Even if privatization proceeded more gradually and favored management buyouts, it was nonetheless resolutely carried out. Owing to their closeness to the West, these states also attracted most of the direct foreign investment in the former Soviet Bloc, turning the industrial zones of cities like Poznań into a haven for western industrial giants like GlaxoSmithKline, Bridgestone, or VW. As a result, they started to stop the brain drain of energetic young people and narrowed the gap in living standards with the West to two-thirds.[20] Hence Poland, the Czech Republic, Hungary, and Slovakia earned a reputation as cases of successful transition.

Unfortunately other postcommunist states largely faltered in their economic restructuring, because they were too irresolute to take the necessary steps. The Balkan countries had the disadvantage of starting out on a lower level of development and of functioning as an extended workbench for the West. In Romania and Bulgaria the incomplete political transition preserved a postcommunist culture of rent seeking and social subsidies. In the former Yugoslavian states it was the series of wars during the 1990s that prevented internal development and discouraged foreign investment. Moreover, the lack of legal security and the prevalence of insider privatization encouraged corruption, which hindered international aid. As a result, the recovery lagged, personal income remained low, and the gap with the West remained large. Only Slovenia managed to extricate itself through a corporatist strategy of internal investment, while Croatia began to catch up as well. However, Romania and Bulgaria appeared to have stalled while Serbia, Bosnia, and Kosovo first had to heal the wounds of war.[21]

A quarter century after the overthrow of communism the results of the economic transformation seem to be mixed, with some countries having made progress and others having fallen behind. The initial deindustrialization, the rise of inflation, and the widespread unemployment during the conversion from plan to market produced much "creative destruction." But the pessimistic thesis of a "detour from the periphery to the periphery" is also an oversimplification that fits only the unsuccessful countries.[22] In contrast, the Baltics, the East-Central European states, and a few Balkan countries have grown more rapidly than Western Europe, narrowing the gap in living standards. Of course, there were also some setbacks and crises, but on the whole progress has continued. The appearance of Poland, Czechoslovakia, and Hungary has dramatically improved: The ancient capitals of Warsaw, Prague, and Budapest are experiencing a second spring. New factories are being built, houses have a fresh coat of paint, and shiny cars stand at the curb. The dynamic impact of capitalist competition is visible everywhere.

SOCIAL RESTRATIFICATION

In the wake of political and economic transformation, the postcommunist societies also experienced a fundamental reorientation from collectivism to individualism. From early childhood on, life in the Soviet Bloc had been dominated by a progression of collectives, starting with a nursery, passing through a party youth group, going on to a trade union, and the like. This system had exerted pressure to maintain conformity through severe sanctions against outsiders such as observing Christians, creative artists, or gays. But the sudden shift to pluralism and economic competition put a premium on developing individuality and originality, liberating people from group constraints to realize personal dreams. Collectivist survival mechanisms such as not sticking out became useless, and new habits of self-assertion had to be learned. The increase in freedom therefore came at a high price of losing social cohesion, since the economic transformation also reduced a number of earlier welfare supports.[23] Though individualists were happy to be free, many East Europeans felt insecure in the competitive environment.

One immediate consequence of the transition to the market was the drastic shrinkage of the East European welfare states just when their assistance was most needed. The initial drop in industrial production of over one-third also curtailed government revenues, especially when the tax system was simplified at the same time. Moreover international lenders like the IMF exerted pressure to limit budget deficits. As a result, all postcommunist states were forced to reduce welfare benefits by limiting the length of unemployment compensation, lowering the amount of pensions, cutting health services, and curtailing free child care. At the same time the struggling factories eliminated their social and cultural programs, which were often not picked up by market providers. Facing rampant inflation and a loss of subsidies, many previously free services now charged fees, making them unaffordable. In effect the reform governments were forced to shrink the extensive communist welfare state back to the level that economic capacity could sustain.[24] These changes were not experienced as liberation but as loss.

Evaluations of the transformation were often dominated by complaints from the losers of the social restructuring, who decried their downward mobility. Chief among them were some members of the communist nomenklatura such as the party cadres and officers of the secret police as well as the military, who lost their cushy jobs or were sent into premature retirement. Many of the dismissed intellectual and academic apologists loudly criticized the injustice of the transformation for the postcommunist parties. Equally difficult was the adjustment for unemployed workers of the smokestack industries and the laborers on the collective farms whose workplaces had disappeared and whose skills were no longer in demand. Similarly the elderly, mostly women living on fixed pensions that eroded with inflation, had a hard time making ends meet. As a result poverty spread among the bottom quarter of the population which found itself left out of the subsequent recovery, forcing many to emigrate. The chief indicator of social inequality, the Gini coefficient, therefore rose in all transition countries.[25]

Nonetheless there were also sufficient winners who profited from the transformation and were interested in keeping the reforms going. Many victims of the regime now had a chance to resume their careers and receive compensation, while prominent dissidents could run for political office. Especially those businessmen who seized the opportunities offered by capitalism managed to amass large fortunes and become a group of nouveaux riches who flaunted their success by driving new Mercedes sedans. Moreover, dynamic white-collar workers employed by international companies at higher wages profited from the economic conversion. Similarly, those of the younger generation who managed to obtain foreign training had better chances for advancement upon returning home, since they understood global standards. Eventually the general population also benefited, as the rapid increase in the numbers of TV sets, dishwashers, and automobiles showed.[26] Even if the process of adjustment was difficult, the sizable electoral support for neoliberal parties suggested that the transformation process created a self-reinforcing constituency.

Women were in an especially paradoxical situation, since they both lost and gained from the transition to western social patterns. On the one hand, communists had introduced legal equality between the sexes in order to augment the labor force, drawing almost nine-tenths of women into paid work. But then many companies, desperate to become competitive, shed their female employees, since women were primarily in service jobs that were considered nonessential. At the same time the social support structure of free child care collapsed, forcing young mothers back into the home. On the other hand, daily life improved greatly with shopping no longer requiring standing in line and efficient household appliances easing the double burden. Moreover, western feminists introduced theoretical justifications for gender equality that went beyond socialist egalitarianism. Finally, the regulations of the European Union and the rulings of the European Court presented an international agenda of equalizing life chances that went beyond the practical equality experienced under communist dictatorship.[27]

Influential groups that favored the preservation of socialist gains retarded the economic transition. Marxist intellectuals defended social equality by painting a repulsive picture of unfettered capitalism's rapaciousness, pointing out shocking examples of tycoon greed in the "Wild East." Administrators of the various welfare policies as well as professionals who were implementing them feared for their jobs and lobbied strongly to retain their programs. Of course, clients who benefited from the transfer payments also insisted on their preservation, often demonstrating for their cause. These constituencies provided an electoral base for the postcommunist parties who wanted to salvage what they could from the collapse of their system.[28] Wherever they had transformed into western-style social democrats, they succeeded in moderating the harshness of the transition, thereby indirectly contributing to its popular acceptance. But wherever they had retained their penchant for exploiting the state, the merely re-named ex-communists actually prolonged the pain and hindered the conversion.

A growing chorus nonetheless advocated a thorough liberalization in order to make the postcommunist states competitive and capable of joining the EU. Even communist managers themselves admitted the need for reforming their enterprises so as to withstand international competition, while scientists knew that they had to catch up to the "world standard" in their disciplines. The informal groups in Prague, Budapest, and Warsaw that had begun discussing the necessary liberalization of their politics and economics during the second half of the 1980s assumed the opinion leadership during the reform process. Moreover, remigrants returning from abroad and advisers from the IMF or World Bank found an increasing audience for their insistence on neoliberal policies among the new capitalists and professionals who accepted the need for change. These groups formed the constituency of the liberal or conservative parties that urged a rigorous reconstruction, even if it inflicted some initial pain. Wherever they won elections, as in the Baltics and the East-Central European states, the transition moved ahead.[29]

The social transition to western modernity therefore led to a restratification of society, justified by a general improvement in the quality of life. The reintroduction of financial incentives for exceptional achievements rewarded energetic individuals while hurting persons less able to compete. The polarization between the new capitalists who were able to make fortunes and the poor whose welfare benefits did not keep pace with inflation introduced a new form of inequality. But the growing disparity between incomes was tolerated as long as most members of society also benefited from the return of economic growth, an impression supported by the spread of consumer goods, the increase of international travel, and the rise in life expectancy.[30] In spite of considerable suffering during the transformation, the social fabric did not rupture, because most people were convinced that "the valley of tears" was only temporary and needed to be crossed in order to reach a better future. Breaking with the nominal egalitarianism of the past, the social transformation restored a class system, moderated by rising consumption for the majority.

CULTURAL PLURALIZATION

Though the recovery of human rights created a pluralized public sphere free of party censorship, the shift to western cultural modernity also entailed partisanship and commercialization. During the 1980s, a growing but subcutaneous westernization had already prepared the transition within Eastern Europe. Especially the young had been fascinated by the loud beat of rock 'n' -roll and by informal clothing such as jeans, because these were associated with protest against authority. But many adults also coveted western consumer goods such as coffee, cigarettes, and liquor, sold as luxury items in special currency stores, since they not only tasted better but also possessed a special cachet of cosmopolitanism due to their scarcity. Moreover, the affluent lifestyles shown in Hollywood movies, symbolized by grilling steaks while lounging next to a swimming pool, created an exaggerated image of ease that was imitated in the Soviet Bloc. Finally, the accuracy and reliability of reporting on Voice of America and Radio Free Europe also convinced the eastern audience of the superiority of a free media.[31]

The peaceful revolution gave leading dissidents the opportunity to step out of the shadows of underground opposition into the limelight. It was only logical that courageous intellectuals like Adam Michnik, Václav Havel, György Konrád, and Bärbel Bohley, who had prepared the overthrow of communism with their trenchant critique of dictatorship, should become spokespeople for the transition. After all, their samizdat columns and manifestos had helped mobilize civil society by dramatizing the repressive nature of "real existing socialism," recalling the importance of human rights, and showing the possibility of apolitical resistance in daily life. But many of them were uncomfortable with switching from small-group opposition to assuming larger political responsibility. Those who merely wanted to reform socialism so as to make it more democratic were disappointed when the majority of the public rejected the "third way" and chose the liberal and capitalist version of democracy. While their moral credibility remained high, most were quickly shunted aside as leaders by new postcommunist politicians.[32]

Writers found themselves in an especially precarious position because they lost their role as advisers to the party and as substitutes for public debate. All over the Soviet Bloc, intellectuals had been privileged as allies of the proletariat, supported financially, given special vacations, allowed travel to the West, and honored with prizes. Since they were supposed to help build socialism, their writings were censored by the party as well as by themselves so as not to lose their paradoxical role of loyal opposition. The sudden overthrow of the dictatorship not only removed their material privileges but also destroyed their essential function of promoting the construction of communism. Now they were just one voice among many in a pluralized public sphere and were no longer courted from abroad as potential dissidents. Deprived of their state salaries, they had to sell their products on the open market in order to survive. At last they could say what they wanted and experiment with new literary forms—but would anybody listen? Like Christa Wolf in *City of Angels*, many authors were now reduced to reflecting on the reasons for the failure of their antifascist dream.[33]

Liberated from censorship constraints, the media and popular culture reflected the turmoil of the transition while trying to guide the process in a democratic direction. Underground news sheets and foreign broadcasts had played an important role in undermining communism, while the liberalization of eastern radio, TV, and the press had materially propelled the peaceful revolution. But amid the newfound freedoms the media fragmented along partisan lines, since journalists lacked professionalism and other outlets needed commercial backing by party or business sponsors. At the same time a tidal wave of western popular culture swept over eastern audiences, since these products were more colorful and entertaining than the drab local fare. In contrast to the implied educational purpose of socialist cultural production, the crass commercialism of the new publications like *Super Illu* shamelessly appealed to the lowest common denominator.[34] The freed media therefore provided a welcome link to global pop culture but at the same time added to the confusion of the transformation by their sensationalism.

A key challenge facing transition societies was dealing with the communist past, since "transitional justice" was essential for creating democratic legitimacy. Based on the experience of other transitions from dictatorship, this process involved the cleansing of government personnel to weed out partisans of the prior regime, the preservation of records so as to document oppression, and legal trials in order to punish human rights abuses. Since the victims were clamoring for restitution and compensation while the oppressors tended to deny their responsibility, the effort became inevitably political. Moreover, lustration of personnel was complicated by the task of dealing with the legacy of the secret police apparatus such as the Stasi, which had been the most ruthless arm of repression and had been veiled in a cloak of secrecy. In all transition countries a heated debate developed between advocates of "forgiving and forgetting," who argued that the fresh start demanded leniency, and supporters of "prosecuting and punishing," who insisted that the public needed to know about crimes and their perpetrators should be held accountable.[35]

The transition countries implemented different degrees of decommunization, depending on the repressiveness of the regime, the strength of the opposition, and the form of transition. In vetting personnel to exclude party and secret police members from highly placed jobs, East Germany, the Czech Republic, and the Baltics were most rigorous, while Hungary and Poland were more forgiving and the rest made no serious attempt. In the preservation of records, the Germans were also the first when they set up an elaborate Stasi archive, with the Czechs and Baltics coming immediately thereafter and the Poles and Bulgarians following later. The legal retribution proved rather disappointing, since Romania, Germany, and Poland as well as the Baltics made valiant efforts but brought few cases to trial and gained even fewer convictions. As a result, the East Germans, Czechs, and Baltic countries were most committed, Poland and Hungary somewhat engaged, but Slovakia, Slovenia, and other Balkan states largely stonewalled the process.[36] This uneven pattern of self-cleansing reflected the speed of the democratization in general.

Instead of debunking communist myths, the scandalmongering about regime repression often had the opposite effect, feeding nostalgia for socialism by making it look better in retrospect. The media revelations about informal collaboration with the secret police, which discredited not just politicians like Lothar de Maizière but also athletes like Katarina Witt, ultimately provoked incredulity. The revival of totalitarianism theory with its condemnatory equation of fascism and communism also clashed with the memories of ordinary East Europeans, who not only recalled hardships but also positive experiences. Moreover, the difficulties of the transformation made the prior regime seem like a place of warm solidarity rather than a society of scarcity, of standing in line for necessities. The disappearance of eastern material culture inspired the revival of popular brands, the return of rock bands like the Puhdys, and the foundation of "East shops" where such nostalgic items could be purchased.[37] Although hardly anyone wanted to go back to socialism, a strange disconnect emerged between improved living conditions in the present and longing for a mythical socialist past.

The pluralist modernity of cultural life after communism proved to be confusing, since it contained a whole range of positions. At the left end of the spectrum were the postcommunists who were defending their record, questioning what had gone wrong, and hoping for a second chance in the future. Then there were the erstwhile dissidents, who celebrated their heroism in defying repression but seemed somewhat at a loss as to where to engage in the transition societies. In the middle one could find the energetic westernizers, embracing capitalist opportunity with a vengeance and berating their conationals for not welcoming change with sufficient alacrity. Then there were the traditionalists, who were busy excavating a heritage that had been obscured under communism and often also sought to revive religious belief. And on the right extreme, reborn nationalists touted their superiority and spouted xenophobic slogans.[38] Instead of being harmonious, this cacophony of voices proved both energizing and disorienting, because different appeals to the past and analyses of the present struggled for control of the future.

NEW BALKAN WARS

Initiated by the collapse of Marxism-Leninism in Eastern Europe, the disintegration of Yugoslavia was the most drastic result of a failed transition. The breakup of the multiethnic South Slav state in a series of disastrous civil wars has created a heated controversy about its causes, course, and consequences. In order to explain the resulting ethnic cleansing and horrible crimes against humanity, some observers point to the "ancient hatreds" of the Balkan Peninsula stemming from Ottoman rule or from Nazi collaboration and resistance in World War II. Other analysts emphasize the revival of nationalism as a postcommunist ideology in the entire former Soviet Bloc, which inflamed the religious and ethnic tensions in the Balkans, turning cooperation into conflict. Yet other commentators blame the collapse of federal Yugoslavism on outside interference such as the German recognition of Slovenia and Croatia or ineffective western mediation.[39] Caught up in partisanship, these explanations tend to overlook that the conflict also involved "the outbreak of a deep-seated crisis of modernity and modernization" that eroded the economic basis of the common state.[40]

The fragmentation of Yugoslavia had already begun by the time communism collapsed in Eastern Europe. It started with the death of Marshal Tito in 1980, since he had held the diverse federation together by dint of his charismatic personality. His eventual successor, Slobodan Milošević, the Communist Party boss of Belgrade, whipped up a new ethnonationalism in the Serbian republic in order to gain control of the entire Yugoslav federation. However, his vow to protect the small Serbian minority in Kosovo fueled nationalist countermovements in Slovenia and, more problematically, also in Croatia under Franjo Tudjman, clamoring for greater economic and political autonomy. In this atmosphere of rising passions, the attempts to transform Yugoslavia into a looser confederation foundered when Serbia insisted on strengthening central authority instead of allowing

Map 12. Breakup of Yugoslavia, 2008. The dark gray color represents the area of the former Yugoslavia. Adapted from Institute for European History, Mainz, Germany.

the postcommunist governments of the other republics more room for autonomy. When the common institutions ceased to function, the Slovenes and Croats began to opt for independence while Milošević shifted his aims toward the establishment of a greater Serbian state.[41] Preoccupied with other issues, the West stood idly by, since it favored Yugoslav unity as guarantee of order.

The declarations of independence by Slovenia and Croatia triggered the first war in the summer of 1991 because Belgrade was unwilling to relinquish control over the other republics. Dominated by Serbs, the Yugoslav army made only halfhearted efforts to reconquer Slovenia on the northern border toward Austria, since there were no Serbs living there. But it mounted a full-scale assault on Croatia because a sizable Serbian minority inhabited the former Habsburg border region, called Krajina. Since Croatian settlements blocked its access to the Adriatic, the Yugoslav army shelled picturesque Dubrovnik. Serbian propaganda also incited the army and local militia to retaliate against Croatia for the atrocities committed by the Ustasha while fighting on the Nazi side in World War II. Though lacking heavy weapons, the Croats defended themselves tenaciously enough to reach a stalemate. While the EU sought to mediate, the Dutch and German governments pushed for recognition of Slovene and Croat secession. By early 1992 the conflict ended with the Serbs occupying the Krajina but the Croats gaining independence.[42]

The second war, centering on Bosnia and Herzegovina, turned out to be more devastating yet, since Serbia systematically used ethnic cleansing to remake the nationalities map. The composition of Bosnia was hopelessly mixed up, with almost half the population consisting of Muslims, about one-third of Serbs, and the remainder of Croats, settled partly contiguously and partly mixed together. When President Bakir Izetbegović also sought Bosnian independence, alternating secular appeals to toleration with Muslim calls for secession, the local Serbs, led by Radovan Karadžić and Radko Mladić, proclaimed a Republika Srbska of their own. In order to connect its territory with Belgrade, the Yugoslav army and local militias set out to create a land bridge to Serbia proper. Since the mediation of U.S. secretary of state Cyrus Vance and British foreign minister David Owen made no headway, the United Nations set up six towns as "safe havens" for Bosnian refugees. When pusillanimous Dutch peacekeepers failed to resist, Serbian forces overran the enclave of Srebrenica and executed between seven thousand and eight thousand Bosnian males of all ages.[43]

Media images of the shelling of Sarajevo and evidence of massacres during ethnic cleansing ultimately compelled the international community to intervene. Ignoring the UN arms embargo, other Muslim countries surreptitiously delivered arms to the Bosnians, increasing their capacity to resist. The Croatian reconquest of the Krajina region helped turn the military tide. Punishing the capital of Serbia itself, NATO air strikes against the Serbian army forced Milošević to the negotiating table. After lengthy talks in Dayton, Ohio, directed by Richard Holbrooke, a halfhearted compromise emerged in November

1995. Formally, the fiction of Bosnian unity was preserved with a rotating presidency; 51 percent of the land area remained with the multiethnic Bosnian and Croatian part of the country, but the rest was turned over to the Serbs, preserving most of their conquests. Basically the accords froze the results of the fighting in place, leaving none of the warring parties satisfied.[44] Bosnia was internally so divided as to require permanent UN supervision, becoming a ward of the international community. Hence the expellees' right to return remained a dead letter.

The third Balkan war revolved around Kosovo, a mountainous region of about two million people between Yugoslavia and Albania. Though about 90 percent of its inhabitants were Muslims, Milošević vowed to hang on to this province, since the decisive battle that cemented the Ottoman rule over the Balkans had taken place there in 1389. Physical intimidation by Serbian gangs sent about nine hundred thousand refugees fleeing, documented in moving TV coverage. Having learned from the embarrassment in Bosnia, the international community reacted more swiftly the second time around. Over Russian objections, NATO flew numerous air strikes against Belgrade, forcing Milošević to give in after seventy-eight days of pounding. Ground forces of the Atlantic Alliance therefore occupied the territory without being able to prevent some ethnic revenge by the Kosovo Liberation Army. Legitimized by elections, the Kosovo parliament declared its independence in 2008, splitting off another Yugoslav republic.[45] In contrast, Macedonia succeeded peacefully by declaring its independence in 1991, due to its lack of Serbs and grinding poverty.

The failure of Milošević's nationalistic dream of Greater Serbia finally opened the door to a democratic transition in Belgrade itself. The various wars worsened a deteriorating economy, making it difficult to repair the destruction wrought by NATO air strikes. As a result, an internal opposition grew within Serbia and overthrew Milošević in 2000 through street demonstrations, even turning the disgraced leader over to the International Criminal Tribunal in The Hague. In the subsequent free elections Serbia vacillated between embarking on the way to western-style democracy and retaining a xenophobic authoritarianism. While the EU tried to create incentives for democratization through aid, Russia under President Putin also made efforts to retain the former client state in its camp. Eventually, the prodemocratic forces won out, delivering Karadžić and Mladić to prosecution as well. Hence the province of Montenegro, situated on the Adriatic coast, was allowed to declare its independence peacefully through a referendum in 2006. Within a decade and a half, Yugoslavia had blown apart.[46]

The late-twentieth-century Balkan wars were a grim reminder that even the peaceful overthrow of an ideological dictatorship like communism could go awry. The multiple causes of the conflict also involved the clash between the Slovenian, Croatian, and Bosnian efforts to adopt the liberal democratic version of modernity and the Serbian project of substituting a populist nationalism for the discredited Marxist ideology. The brutal course of the wars wreaked atrocities on all sides, but Serbian forces killed roughly five times as many civilians as their antagonists. Moreover, the systematic project of national homogenization through ethnic cleansing was a relapse into the barbaric methods of Hitler and Stalin, suggesting a refusal to learn from the disasters of the first half of the century.[47] The failure of transition to a democratic Yugoslav confederation fragmented the western part of the Balkans into a series of ministates that could only hope to prosper by overcoming their hostility and joining the EU. As a result the development of a functioning democracy was set back a generation, leaving the region self-marginalized.

POSTCOMMUNIST TRANSITION

The conversion from communist to democratic modernity turned out to be quite difficult since the competing versions had diverged more drastically than anyone had realized. While both competitors were products of high industrialism, their methods of further development were fundamentally different. Communists actually believed that they had moved ahead of bourgeois capitalists by ending economic exploitation, instituting social equality, and implementing technocratic planning. Since the Soviet experiment took place in the most backward of the great powers, it did succeed in transforming Russia through industrialization, collectivization, urbanization, and education. But the communist path was flawed by its Stalinist repression and its transfer to some of the Central European satellites that were already more highly developed. Moreover, the democratic West did not stand still but rather reinvented itself by expanding the welfare state, introducing consumer democracy, and generating high technology. No wonder that Eastern Europeans chose to switch to this more dynamic and participatory system.[48]

Since the transformation from communism to democracy was unprecedented, there were no blueprints that could be followed. Some of the reformers, such as Leszek Balcerowicz in Poland, expected considerable difficulties that would follow a J-curve, with things first getting worse before finally improving. But in practice the trough turned out to be deeper than anticipated because the command economy was further behind its western rival and was experiencing a more dramatic crisis than even specialists realized. Moreover, the upward slope of improvement also remained flatter than hoped for because popular pressure insisted on cushioning the shock of transition, therefore drawing out the process.[49] During the four and a half decades of Soviet control, the communists had had a more powerful impact than people under their control perceived, requiring not just a reorientation of politics and economy but also a refashioning of social structures and cultural value systems. Even if the transition to western modernity could build on the revival of prior civil society, it required an enormous effort to return to a liberal path of development.

Except for the debacle in the former Yugoslavia, the criteria of transition showed considerable progress toward a revival of Eastern Europe. In spite of the huge stresses of the transformation, politics generally remained stable, elections were free, and changes of power became routine. While a considerable gap between East and West in living standards persisted, inflation was overcome, growth resumed, and prosperity was gradually spreading, creating a new middle class. Though benefits had to be drastically reduced, the welfare state was not abandoned but rather scaled back in order to make it sustainable in the long run, while some services rebounded with improving revenues. Even if there were fierce debates about the relative importance of suffering under the Nazis versus the Soviets, a sense of postcommunist identity gradually emerged as a result of greater freedom of debate. Finally, integration into NATO and the EU overcame the Cold War divide and reinforced peace.[50] Though under Viktor Orbán Hungary slid back into an authoritarian nationalism, on the whole Eastern Europe was freer and better off than a quarter century before.

East Germany was a special case since its transformation took place through unification with the democratic and wealthy Federal Republic. The citizens of the former GDR went to bed on October 2, 1990, and woke up the next morning in a successful western state without ever having left their home. As a result, they benefited from being integrated into a functioning democracy with a rule of law, as well as being included in an elaborate welfare state with an extensive safety net. But they paid for this effortless transition with the collapse of most of their industry, the necessity of changing their behavior overnight, and their lack of influence in the larger whole. While they became materially better off than before, they remained dependent on large transfer payments, since only parts of their economy recovered enough to become self-sustaining. Though older intellectuals groused about being second-class citizens, the younger generation was able to grow up in the united country, making use of the new opportunities.[51] Compared to the experience of their neighbors, the East German transformation was therefore privileged and problematic at the same time.

In the other East European countries, the balance of the transformation was rather mixed, ranging from impressive achievements to disappointing failures. The outcome of the shift to western modernity depended on a complex mix of older legacies, the manner of communist ouster, and transition decisions. Because of their prior democratic experience and economic development, the Baltic and Central European states, which had strong opposition movements and undertook resolute reforms, made much progress toward a liberal democracy and market economy. The Balkan countries with less prior development, and where the postcommunists retained power and undertook only halfhearted measures, continued to lag behind. Finally, the states that were involved in the wars of Yugoslav secession or followed the Russian example had a much harder time shedding the communist legacy and remained stalled between the communist and democratic systems, in illiberal rule and predatory capitalism.[52] As the travails of Ukraine show, the switch from communist to democratic modernity required such a fundamental reorientation that the outcome of the transition will likely remain undecided for some time to come.

Chapter 27

GLOBAL CHALLENGES

African refugees, 2011. *Source*: Magnum Photos.

B rutal police repression of antiglobalization protests turned the Genoa summit of the eight chief industrial nations in July 2001 into a veritable nightmare. When the leaders of the G-8 gathered in the Renaissance city to discuss aid for Africa, they encountered demonstrations of an unprecedented size and intensity. About seven hundred organizations had rallied activists to protest "against the present form of capitalist globalization," which they criticized for exploiting the developing countries, damaging the environment, and lacking democratic control. Since as host, the populist prime minister Silvio Berlusconi wanted to show Italy from its best side, he cordoned off the heads of state in the citadel and ordered the security forces to stop the tens of thousands of partly peaceful, partly obstructionist, and partly violent protesters by using tear gas, water cannons, and truncheons. In the ensuing melee, one twenty-three-year-old Italian was killed, hundreds hurt, and 329 arrested.[1] This overreaction of the authorities appeared to prove the charges against a repressive globalization from above leveled by a global protest movement from below.

The concept of "globalization" was itself a neologism to express the perception of a shrinking world due to the seeming compression of distances by instant communication and a multiplication of exchanges. According to the British sociologist Anthony Giddens, globalization can "be defined as the intensification of worldwide social relations which link distant localities in such a way that local happenings are shaped by events occurring many miles away and vice versa."[2] Although international trade, communication, and travel had already increasingly connected the globe before 1914, the world wars reversed this development, so that it took until the 1960s to regain the earlier intensity of exchanges. In the last third of the twentieth century a series of economic changes such as the relocation of mass production to Asia, technological innovations such as the Internet, and cultural trends such as the Americanization of popular culture brought countries, businesses, and people closer together than ever before. When the media began to use the term globalization in the second half of the 1980s, politicians quickly adopted the buzzword in order to promote a neoliberal agenda.

Globalization advocates like the Indian economist Jagdish Bhagwati rather optimistically claimed that the closer connection of the world was producing multiple benefits. The "Washington consensus" of the financial lenders asserted that fiscal austerity, privatization, and market liberalization would hasten economic development by fostering global trade. Publicist defenders argued that globalization reduced poverty by raising wages, ended child labor by international oversight, helped women by providing them with incomes, enriched culture by pluralizing offerings, protected the environment by raising standards, and aided corporations by encouraging self-policing codes.[3] Other apologists stressed the incentive to technological innovation, the benefit to consumers through reduced prices, and the positive effects of stimulating growth. Such arguments in favor of globalization appealed especially to the beneficiaries of the changes in the multinational corporations, the high-tech firms, and the popular-culture industry. Moreover, they provided conservative politicians like Margaret Thatcher with a future-oriented message.

In contrast, critics like the Italian theorist Antonio Negri pessimistically pointed out that many side effects of globalization were increasing hardships for people in the developing countries. A growing number of activists stressed the loss of jobs due to deindustrialization in Europe and the exploitation of natural resources, the intolerable working conditions and low wages in outsourced factories, the unprotected labor of women and children, the widespread destruction of the environment, and the lack of democratic accountability in the Third World. Other authors also exposed a "dark side of globalization" in increased arms trafficking that fueled civil wars, international crime that traded drugs and women, as well as transnational terrorism that hurt innocent civilians.[4] Protesters rejected the anti-globalization label as a misnomer by insisting that they were only demanding a more humane form of globalization and were themselves organizing their countermovement on a worldwide basis. On the continent intellectuals, trade-union members, and politicians of the Left like Oskar Lafontaine echoed such a critique.

The globalization of modernity remained quite controversial because it brought both opportunities and dangers for Europe. Some observers suggested that "globalization [was], *au fond*, a continuation, albeit in an intensified and accelerated form, of the perduring challenge of modernization."[5] Indeed, this development resulted from the spread of many European traits such as technological innovation, market capitalism, social individualism, and the rule of law to the rest of the world. But the intensification of exchanges and the triumph of democratic capitalism, which created a new, globalized stage of modernity, also produced unanticipated challenges for Europeans. During its latest phase, increasingly powerful competitors developed in Asia, the Near East, and Latin America that often made the Old Continent look sluggish by comparison. Having lost their initial monopoly on development, Europeans now faced strong pressures of competitiveness, raising the question whether their high-wage and welfare-state model could survive in an increasingly global environment.

ECONOMIC IMPETUS

The chief motor of globalization was economic, most notably the intensification of worldwide trade. Supported by agreements like General Agreement on Tariffs and Trade and agencies like the World Trade Organization, international commerce increased almost twice as fast as production since 1970. A key factor was the roughly tenfold reduction of shipping costs due to the development of container ships and supertankers. Fordist mass production could therefore be relocated in distant countries with low labor costs and willing workforces, often found in Asia. Since the external tariffs of the EU were not high enough to stop imports, European consumers profited from an array of affordable goods, ranging from textiles to electronics. Though deindustrialization took a heavy toll on jobs, firms fought back by specializing in higher-price sectors, raising the value of their exports from under 1.5 to over 2.5 trillion dollars between 1973 and 2000. Europe therefore remained the single largest trading bloc, leading both China and the United States in exports and imports.[6] As a result, containers bringing in Korean TV sets could be reloaded in Rotterdam with German luxury cars.

Accompanying this breathtaking increase in commerce was the construction of a global financial system, needed to fund the intensified exchanges. The deregulation of banking, beginning in the United States and then spreading to Europe, facilitated the worldwide movement of capital. Partly replacing the dollar, the introduction of the euro in 2002 helped simplify currency exchanges, which reached an unprecedented volume. Much of the financial transaction was foreign direct investment, which grew almost twice as fast as trade and helped large corporations establish a market presence in other countries. Another part of the money flow was, however, highly speculative, involving leveraged funds, derivatives, and currency options that contributed to a great deal of market volatility. Though the United States had led in foreign direct investment in the postwar period, the Europeans accounted for two-fifths of it by 2000, surpassing America both as place of origin and as destination.[7] As a result of its imperial connections and Thatcherite policies, London again became the center of finance, overshadowing Frankfurt and the European Central Bank.

Another aspect of globalization was the intensification of communication, made possible by the development of computer hardware and software. While the original applications were in the military and accounting, the technological innovation from mainframes to personal computers and beyond made it possible to store and process the burgeoning mass of data produced by trade and finance. Moreover, the introduction of the World Wide Web was essential in offering instantaneous communication across borders, necessary for the expanded scope of transactions, while the arrival of smartphones allowed individual consumers access to incredible amounts of information. The media were quick to take advantage of the potential of this new communication technology in spreading news services as well as advertisements for American popular-culture products to audiences around the world. Though contributing to some of the innovations, the Europeans, handicapped by their linguistic diversity, were overwhelmed by the Anglophone information society but gradually adapted with forms of hybrid manufacturing.[8]

In responding to these pressures Europe developed a paradoxical love-hate relationship to globalization, both supporting and opposing the process at the same time. Creating the largest market in the world with a GDP equivalent to that of the United States, European integration pioneered many aspects of trade and communication. While surveys showed that two-thirds of Europeans generally supported globalization, many were wary of its neoliberal form because of negative experiences with deindustrialization and casino capitalism. Even if influential minorities, especially in the United Kingdom, endorsed the Washington consensus, the majority on the continent preferred the mixed model of a social market economy, and was willing to support solidarity with a higher share of social expenditures than the individual-gain-oriented United States (at 25 percent to 15 percent of GDP). Intent on maintaining their high living standards, Europeans favored an alternate model of globalization, centered on regional integration, that avoided speculative excesses and allowed more diversity.[9] As a result, Europeans sought to develop their own strategies to cope with global challenges.

One successful form of adaptation was the development of transnational companies, which kept their headquarters in Europe but moved their production facilities overseas. This outsourcing was driven by the wish to lower labor costs and get access to markets by circumventing protectionism. Operating in more than one country made it possible to buffer currency fluctuations and to evade high taxes by sheltering foreign gains. Such transnationalization created "webs of enterprise" in which products were designed in one place and manufactured elsewhere out of components made somewhere else yet, optimizing the process. While big American corporations like Ford had led the way with investing on the continent, the Europeans, aided by the process of integration, subsequently held their own, with twenty-four of the top fifty multinationals listed by Forbes in 2008 headquartered there. These giant companies ranged from banks (HSBC, Paribas, Deutsche Bank) and oil (Shell, BP, Total), to insurance (ING, Allianz), cars (VW, Mercedes), equipment (Alstom, Siemens), utilities (EDF, E.ON), and food (Nestlé).[10]

Another coping strategy was a limited reform of the labor market in order to create greater flexibility, contain wages, and rein in social costs. Compared to the United States, European workers had enjoyed more security through tight regulations on hiring, longer vacations, and substantial welfare benefits. While globalization provided opportunities for the educated and also generated low-level service jobs, it directly threatened industrial labor. The pressure of international competition weakened trade-union efforts because employers could counter wage demands with the threat to relocate elsewhere. Shocked by such outsourcing to Eastern Europe as the Audi decision to produce new cars in Hungary, even social democratic leaders agreed to cut back on welfare protections by reducing unemployment benefits, lowering subsistence support, facilitating part-time jobs, and raising the age of retirement to sixty-seven. While British Labour led the way, the German SPD passed a similar Agenda 2010, and even the Scandinavians followed suit. Though such reductions created short-range outrage, they improved competitiveness in the long run.[11]

A final response to globalization was investment in education in order to make workers fit for competition in a "knowledge society." Since maintaining their technological edge required an educated workforce, European states increased their expenditures on technical training. Crash programs brought computers into the schools in order to overcome antitechnology prejudices and improve the employability of graduates by providing them with flexible IT skills. On the national level, governments increased their R&D expenditures to over 2.5 percent of GNP, pushing corporations to contribute a greater share as well. The EU sponsored a series of science and technology programs, investing billions of euros into cutting-edge research in sectors such as microelectronics, gene technology, and renewable energy. This effort culminated in the Lisbon Strategy of 2000, which called for making Europe "the most competitive and dynamic knowledge-based economy in the world" so as to resume economic growth and provide better jobs.[12] Similarly, the Bologna Process tried to stream line European higher education by making degree programs more compatible.

The results of Europe's encounter with global modernity were rather mixed, since the competitive pressures increased polarization between winners and losers of the restructuring. Some transnational and even midsize companies profited, while labor-intensive firms continued to fail. Some high-tech areas like the Southwest of England, the Île de France, and Southwest Germany were prospering, while old industrial regions like the Midlands, the Ruhr, and Wallonia as well as many areas in Eastern Europe fell further behind. Some high-skilled technical and financial employees were making big salaries and shareholders reaped large profits, while many industrial workers lost their jobs. Especially youths had a difficult time turning internships into permanent positions, while women were often consigned to part-time jobs, forming an insecure *Prekariat* that was forced to live from hand to mouth. As a result of moderate neoliberal reforms the core of Europe regained much of its competitiveness, but the challenge of reconciling cost-effective production with social protection still had to be met more convincingly.[13]

ENVIRONMENTAL CONCERN

The economic growth sparked by globalization raised widespread concerns about the concomitant deterioration of the environment. Ironically, deindustrialization helped the old industrial areas to overcome the worst effects of air and water pollution, so that the sky over the Ruhr turned blue again—but it merely shifted the problem to the developing countries, where there were fewer restraints. The continuing motorization of the continent led to a proliferation of superhighways, which disfigured the landscape, clogged inner cities, and raised small-particle emissions. At the same time the steep increase of air travel polluted the atmosphere and added airplane noise as an additional aggravation to urban life. While more restricted than in the United States, the suburbanization of European cities also paved over vast stretches of rural land with new housing and shopping malls. Confronted with an increase in smog, noise, and concrete, Europeans slowly changed their priorities from economic growth to quality of life, shifting their attention from exploitation to conservation.[14]

Since all environmental problems were ultimately local, it took time to realize that their sources were so widespread as to have transnational causes and effects. Excessive use of pesticides or intensive animal husbandry might contaminate only the direct surroundings in Holland, but the affected foods were sold all over the continent. Similarly, coal-fired power plants might directly pollute only the air in Poland, but acid rain derived from the same emissions killed trees on ridges downwind in the Czech and German mountains. Chemicals dumped by big pharmaceutical firms might poison only the water in Switzerland, but they rendered the few surviving fish downstream in the Rhine inedible. Even if activists succeeded in saving a few trees in their neighborhood, concerned citizens gradually came to understand that the more general environmental problems were interconnected, cutting across political jurisdictions and national frontiers. Scientific experts who measured the negative impact of pollution on health and journalists who exposed cases of food poisoning, air pollution, and water contamination helped to increase public awareness of their dangers.[15]

The reactor catastrophe at Chernobyl in the Ukraine dramatized the environmental dangers of reliance on nuclear energy even to unconcerned citizens. During a test in the night of April 26, 1986, block four of a plutonium reactor lost its cooling, melted down, and spewed a plume of radiation high into the atmosphere. Thirty-one courageous engineers and firemen sacrificed their lives to keep the chain reaction from igniting the neighboring blocks as well. Since Soviet leaders initially failed to admit the accident, it was Swedish nuclear observers who alerted the world to an unusual radiation spike. In Scandinavia, Austria, and Germany fragmentary reports set off a wave of hysteria about the likely contamination of the water, soil, crops, and animals from fallout rain. Although the Soviet authorities finally began to evacuate about half a million people and sealed the reactor, a mixture of ignorance and fear exaggerated the panic in Central Europe, leading to accusations against politicians dramatized in the poetic charge "They Have Failed."[16] As a consequence of its devastating impact on Ukraine and Belarus that forced 350,000 inhabitants to be resettled, Chernobyl became a powerful symbol of the fallibility of technological modernity in general.

The spread of such skepticism made Europeans receptive to warnings of climate change through global warming as a result of CO_2

emissions. Local observations of the dramatic shrinkage of Alpine ice fields reinforced the credibility of scientific studies documenting a gradual increase of temperatures. For instance the Morteratsch glacier in Switzerland has retreated 2,231 meters since 1878! Claiming that reliable measurements went back only a little over a century, those responsible for the release of noxious gases in the power companies, automobile manufacturers, big agriculture, and the like vigorously disputed the significance of these findings. But evidence from studies of tree growth and glacier cores convinced an increasing number of citizens of the truth of these warnings, especially since incidents of violent weather such as flooding, cyclones, and droughts increased as well. Located in the temperate zone, Europe was likely to be affected less than other continents except for the rise in sea levels or the drying up of water resources in the Mediterranean. Nonetheless, Europeans took the challenge of climate change more seriously than most others.[17]

Citizens concerned about the environment responded with a range of initiatives to force a reversal of policy on reluctant politicians and business managers. Ordinary individuals complied with recycling programs in order to reduce waste and either bicycled or took public transportation so as to reduce CO_2 emissions. Whenever they felt threatened by a large-scale building project such as the third runway of the Heathrow airport, they engaged in local protests, creating a coalition of ecologists and NIMBY citizens. In order to make their voices heard beyond their locality, they joined NGOs like Greenpeace and generously donated funding to their projects. At the same time the Green parties agitated for restrictions on nuclear power, calling for the shutdown of older reactors and protesting the storing of waste at sites like the French La Hague. Eventually, public pressure compelled national governments to require complicated environmental impact statements and public hearings that deterred undesirable projects by involving them in costly approval processes and litigation.[18] The result has been more energy conservation than in the United States or China.

Though it was not included in the Treaties of Rome, environmental protection eventually became an important EU policy area, organized by a special directorate. Growing out of an original concern with the leveling of the competitive playing field, this policy area has expanded considerably since the 1970s. One bone of contention was the Common Fisheries Policy, since the maritime countries like Ireland and Denmark, intent on protecting their stocks, resented giving other countries access. Initially the Common Agricultural Policy was a subsidy for big farmers, but it was refocused in 2004 to support more biodiversity as well as ecological farming. The Natura directive attempted also to preserve bird habitat in all EU member countries. Similarly a water directive stipulated quality standards and insisted on the management of river systems. Finally the REACH program aimed to register hazardous chemicals and protect the public and the environment from contamination. As a regulatory agency the European Union therefore sought to create a set of uniform minimum standards for all member countries.[19]

The EU also tried to be a leader in the global negotiations for protection of the ozone layer and the reduction of carbon emissions, even if it sometimes failed to live up to its own rhetoric. Though the notion of "sustainable development" only crystallized as a goal in the 1980s, national governments and the European Commission consistently supported international efforts from Stockholm via Tokyo to negotiate firm targets for a reduction of greenhouse gasses such as the Kyoto Protocol in 1997. The ambitious goals of an 8 percent reduction by 2013 and another 20 percent decrease by 2020 were partly met by deindustrialization, partly by switching to renewable energies, and partly by more efficient use of power. Not all initiatives were successful, since the originally popular EU emissions-trading scheme has all but collapsed. Moreover the developing countries, in order to grow further, have largely refused to be bound by such agreements, requesting aid for not polluting or not cutting down rain forests.[20] But on other issues like the admission of gene-modified foods into the EU, Europeans have been more skeptical than Americans.

As a result of such concerns, Europeans have developed a more careful use of their natural resources during the last decades. Many environmental improvements such as establishing national parks and imposing emissions standards for cars originated in the United

States. But having been forced to live on the same land for several thousand years, Europeans have developed a greater sense of stewardship that takes the coming generations into account, and they have imposed more stringent controls like zoning regulations. Moreover, they have been willing to finance the expensive switch to renewable energies by tax subsidies for solar and wind-driven power generation. Through the propagation of green technology, they have also been able to develop new jobs in manufacturing solar cells and wind turbines. Not all countries have been willing to go as far as Germany, which decided to abandon nuclear power altogether by 2020 in the wake of the Fukushima reactor catastrophe in Japan. But on the whole, Europeans developed a modern lifestyle that depended less on gas guzzlers and left a smaller carbon footprint than Americans.[21]

MIGRATION PRESSURE

The increasing pressure for immigration in the wake of globalization caught Europeans unprepared, because they continued to think of themselves as emigrants. Since the Old Continent had produced more hungry people than it could feed, migrants from the British Isles, the German lands, the Mediterranean, and Eastern Europe had left for centuries, populating distant shores from the United States to Australia. The last wave of emigrants departed from Europe after the Second World War, consisting of displaced persons, Jewish survivors, and even some fascist perpetrators. The Germans had therefore interpreted the ethnic remigration of twelve million refugees expelled from their lost eastern homes in 1945 as the arrival of fellow nationals who had a moral claim to be helped. Similarly, the French had accepted the return of former colonizers such as the *pieds-noirs* from Algeria after 1962 as a duty, since they were considered citizens.[22] But with fertility declining below replacement and longevity increasing substantially, an aging Europe turned from an emigration to an immigration continent, needing foreign migrants to survive.

In spite of the return of peace and prosperity, this demographic transition surprised European leaders and forced a reluctant change of attitudes toward immigration. After the arrival of the pill, the number of births per woman decreased steadily to about 1.4, with only France, the United Kingdom, Sweden, and Ireland bucking the trend. At the same time, the increase in longevity from the midsixties to the mideighties, which initially kept populations growing, led to a drastic extension of the number of retired people, with the over-eighty-year-olds expanding faster than any younger segment of the population in most countries. Among the young, this dual shift led to the shutting down of kindergartens and schools that no longer had sufficient pupils. Simultaneously the decrease below a four-to-one ratio of working adults to pensioners compelled the raising of the retirement age to beyond sixty-five and increased health costs. Since government policies failed to stop the creeping depopulation, there remained only the importation of labor to fill the necessary jobs.[23]

During the postwar boom, northern and Western Europeans therefore recruited migrants from southern Europe in order to sustain the industrial expansion. By the mid-1970s about eight million foreigners provided manual labor in France, Germany, and Britain, keeping the factories rolling. While these often rural newcomers spoke Mediterranean languages, they were Christians and considered to be temporary help that would eventually return to their home countries. Moreover, the establishment of the Common Market legalized this migration beyond bilateral treaties, since the free movement of workers was part of the EC's purpose. Problems arose, however, when the migrants came from non-European countries like Turkey and from North Africa and Asia, since they were different in skin color, social customs, food preferences, and especially in religion. Ignoring repatriation programs at the end of the boom in the 1970s, many of the so-called guest workers decided to stay and actually brought their families to join them. This temporary labor migration therefore turned into a permanent foreign presence, creating new ethnic minorities.[24]

The rapid increase of asylum applications from developing countries in the 1980s posed another dilemma of humanitarian openness versus self-interested restriction. As long as refugees came from Eastern Europe during the Cold War they were politically welcomed, and even during the Balkan wars there was a sense of responsibility to fellow Europeans. But when the origins of applicants shifted to global crisis regions marred by civil wars or climate catastrophes and their number grew into hundreds of thousands, attitudes became more restrictive, since many asylum seekers appeared to be motivated by economic reasons. When their papers were lost and claims of persecution could not be verified, applicants remained in legal limbo, depending on public support until their cases were decided, which often took years. In order to keep them from melting into the general population, they were generally held in detention centers so that they could be repatriated if rejected.[25] Complicated by the allegation of "asylum fraud," the treatment of non-European refugees revealed a discouraging discrepancy between charitable rhetoric and egotistic practice.

The overthrow of communism and the increase of globalization made the balancing act between cosmopolitan openness and social protectiveness even more difficult. On the one hand, economic success depended on attracting professionals to supplement the declining populations of aging European societies with highly skilled immigrants who could be attracted through special permits. On the other hand, desperation born from poverty increased the influx of undocumented illegals ready to do hard labor but lacking official recognition and denied access to the benefits of the welfare state. West European fears of being swamped by East European migrants after the EU accession of their countries opened the door turned out to be highly exaggerated, since the economic recovery of their eastern homelands induced many to return voluntarily. But the frequent drowning of African illegals who paid guides their life savings to be taken by overcrowded and unseaworthy boats across the Mediterranean remained a scandal, since the EU failed to create a policy liberal enough to provide orderly entrance. Europe therefore remained a reluctant immigration continent.[26]

In European cities, many of the visually and culturally distinctive arrivals clustered in defensive ghettos, re-creating a semblance of their home societies. Unable to afford more rent, immigrants gathered in low-cost districts, gradually displacing prior inhabitants. There they created their own grocery stores, cafes, and storefront mosques, retreating from their difficult encounters with the majority society. The availability of newspapers and electronic media, the founding of associations, and the formation of sports clubs provided a protective cocoon but also kept them from having to immerse themselves fully into their new surroundings. Especially the children often had difficulties learning enough of the host language to succeed in school or get decent jobs, therefore developing more resentment than their parents, who were usually content with their modest success. The confusion over where they belonged made young men vulnerable to the message of fundamentalist imams, whereas young women often tried to escape their families' control.[27] While ghettos provided short-run comfort, they postponed integration in the long run.

In response to growing immigration and economic downturn, an ugly nativist backlash formed in many European countries, somewhat irrespective of the actual size of the problem. Much of the motivation stemmed from irrational fear of losing one's job to the newcomers, envy of their purported welfare benefits, or ignorance of their different customs. About one-third of the Europeans surveyed favored deporting the immigrants to their countries of origin in 2003. Various rightist groups like the Freedom Party in Austria, the Front National in France, and the Republicans (REPs), in Germany and populist leaders such as Geert Wilders in the Netherlands capitalized on this widespread resentment to score surprising electoral victories even in Denmark. Their propaganda encouraged outbursts of xenophobic violence among skinheads such as assaulting blacks or burning down asylum dormitories. While civil society groups of the Left rallied for tolerance, schools encouraged acceptance of strangers, and sports clubs tried to celebrate difference, established conservative parties profited from popular anger by proposing restrictive legislation.[28]

The conflicting pressures of fear of foreigners and need for skilled immigration engendered a contradictory set of immigration policies. On the one hand, nativist backlash forced a tightening of ethnic remigration, family immigration, and recognition of asylum, decreasing the yearly influx. To stop the flow of illegal immigrants the EU agreed on a joint border regime, which sent asylum seekers back to "safe countries" through which they had come and increased policing via the Frontex agency. On the other hand, business lobbying forced the initiation of various "blue card" programs permitting university graduates to remain or professionals to enter if they earned sufficient salaries or created jobs. EU members also invented an in-between status of legal toleration for illegal immigrants, accepting their presence de facto. Finally Germany, with about seven million foreigners, liberalized its citizenship laws, allowing children born in the country the citizenship option at age eighteen and creating a path toward naturalization for older immigrants.[29] The perplexing mixture of multiculturalism and xenophobia rendered the task of integrating immigrants of non-European backgrounds into a cosmopolitan modernity incomplete.

TERRORIST THREAT

The rise of Islamic terrorism was another unforeseen development, which posed difficult problems for an advanced European society that considered itself liberal. Pioneered by anarchists, the "propaganda of the deed" had always been the weapon of those too weak to effect political change by democratic or even revolutionary means. Most Europeans thought that the threat had ended when the post-1968 attacks of the Italian Red Brigades and the German Red Army Faction began to abate. While irredentist violence of the Irish Republican Army, Basques, Corsicans, and South Tyroleans flared up intermittently, the efficient and ruthless security services seemed to have it under control. But the assault by a faction of the Palestine Liberation Organization on Israeli athletes during the Olympic Games in Munich in 1972 signaled a new quality because it brought the Arab-Israeli conflict to the European continent, and the media broadcast the PLO message around the globe.[30] Even though the subsequent cooperation between European and Near Eastern terrorists produced no further attacks, it was a harbinger of a threat to come by combining domestic with international terrorism.

Compared to nationalist or anarchist violence, religious inspiration created an even stronger dedication to terrorism since it endowed the use of force with transcendental legitimacy. The rise of fundamentalist Islam, which opposed the permissiveness of western modernity, combined a sense of sacred duty with concrete political projects such as the transformation of Iran into a Muslim state and the liberation of Palestine from Israeli control. In Europe radical imams promoted this program as teachers of the Quran, preaching a literalist and backward-looking version of their faith in the mosques. This message resonated especially among young men in the immigrant ghettos and the *banlieues*, stranded between their ethnic background and secular European culture. Their experience of setbacks in school, social hostility, or job discrimination created an unfocused but powerful sense of grievance against a society that did not respect them. The very rigidity of radical Islam offered the missing focus and identity to confused youths by rewarding them in the hereafter for the potential sacrifice of their lives. The new quality of suicidal terrorism also exploited media attention by dramatizing an assassin's cause.[31]

Horrified by the shocking news videos of hijacked passenger jets crashing into the World Trade Center, Europeans responded to Islamic terrorist attacks on the United States with a genuine wave of sympathy. After the eleventh of September 2001, individual Europeans reassured American acquaintances of their solidarity in transatlantic telephone calls. Even the leftist French paper *Le Monde* declared "we are all Americans," while German chancellor Gerhard Schröder, embarrassed that some of the terrorists had trained in his country, called the strike "a declaration of war against the civilized world." NATO immediately convened an emergency meeting and took the unprecedented step of defining the assault as a *casus foederis* requiring military intervention by the members of the alliance. The European public therefore sympathized with President George W. Bush's "declaration of war on international terrorism" in order to punish Osama bin Laden and destroy his Al Qaeda organization. Without hesitation, the European allies decided to participate in "Operation Enduring Freedom," sending troops into battle against the Taliban in Afghanistan.[32]

The preventive U.S. war against Iraq in 2003, however, deeply split Europe between countries ready to embrace its neoconservative justification and those distrusting its rationale. The continental public was less bellicose than the American populace because it neither wanted to secure oil nor believed the dubious claims that the dictator Saddam Hussein possessed weapons of mass destruction. France and Germany opposed Washington's unilateralism as did Russia and China, refusing to join the attack, which lacked sanction by the United Nations. Only Britain, intent on restoring its special relationship to the United States, as well as Italy, Spain, Poland, and some smaller states joined the "coalition of the willing." The leading continental countries were appalled by the condescending tone of U.S. secretary of defense Rumsfeld's chastisement of moribund "old Europe," while the general public engaged in mass demonstrations with the slogan "no blood for oil." In spite of the quick U.S. victory on the battlefield, French president Jacques Chirac and Chancellor Schröder felt justified by the subsequent failure to win the peace and the lack of proof regarding Iraq's weapons of mass destruction or links to Al Qaeda.[33]

A series of well-publicized critiques of Islamic fundamentalism nonetheless aroused Muslim anger and directed it against Europe. The publication of Salman Rushdie's satire *Satanic Verses* had already set off a furor among British Muslims who considered it blasphemous, rousing them to support Ayatollah Khomeini's fatwa, which the author survived in hiding. In 2004 the production of a film exposing the brutal treatment of women under Islamic law led a young Moroccan to kill its director, Theo van Gogh, triggering anti-Muslim violence in Holland. In the same year, the prohibition of wearing religious symbols in French schools, thereby outlawing Islamic head scarves, also angered the large North African community. The publication of a dozen cartoons of Mohammed in a Danish newspaper a year later shocked millions of the faithful around the world, triggering violent protests against the denigration of the Prophet.[34] A chasm therefore opened between secular Europeans pointing to human rights abuses in fundamentalist versions of Islam and Muslim youths feeling alienated and insulted in western society.

The heated atmosphere prompted several large-scale terrorist attacks in Europe as retaliation for the participation of U.S. allies in the Iraq War. On March 11, 2004, ten bombs exploded in the Madrid commuter train system, killing 191 people and wounding another eighteen hundred. Inspired by Al Qaeda's *jihad*, a loose group of Moroccan suicide terrorists was apparently responsible. One surprising casualty was the conservative Spanish government, defeated in a national election only four days later for wrongly blaming domestic Basque separatists and for supporting the U.S. war in Iraq. On July 7, 2005, four Islamic radicals exploded bombs in London subway cars and in a double-decker bus, killing fifty-two civilians and wounding over seven hundred others. One of the Islamist terrorists argued that the killings were justified as retaliation: "Your democratically-elected governments continuously perpetuate atrocities against my people all over the world." On October 27, 2005, alienated North African youths in Clichy-sur-Bois started burning cars, looting stores, and battling security forces. Fueled by resentment against French racism, the rioting spread to other urban areas, continuing for weeks.[35] This wave of violence brought terrorism home to Europe, excepting only Germany.

The rising threat of terrorist attacks led the reluctant governments to strengthen domestic measures against political violence. Based on their prior experiences in combating unrest, Britain, France, and Germany passed new antiterrorist laws that expanded their police capacities. Trying to reassure the French public, Minister of the Interior Nicolas Sarkozy talked tough, promising "active intolerance" against terrorists. In practice, the antiterrorist laws extended surveillance mechanisms, installed security cameras more widely, and facilitated electronic eavesdropping. But defenders of civil liberties protested that these measures seemed to violate the very rights that they claimed to protect. Since the EU lacked formal authority in this area, Brussels worked on strengthening police coordination and easing information exchanges, creating a Europewide file of terrorists. While individual member states were reluctant to give up their sovereignty, the EU eventually agreed to appoint an antiterrorism coordinator in order to prod countries into stronger joint efforts.[36]

The moderate European response to Islamic terrorism turned out to be more successful than the military interventionism of the United States. Since radical Islamists rejected Euro-American liberal values, they regarded both partners as the common enemy of the West. But the continent was less hysterical and bellicose than the Bush and Blair duo, trying to rely more on the UN and on reaching out to Palestinians to decrease hostilities. Along with expanding domestic police powers went a greater effort to understand the internal causes of terrorism, both in the lack of perspective within Islamic countries and in the multiple frustrations of ghettoized immigrants. Beyond trying to alleviate their material concerns, European governments made an effort to strengthen the forces of liberal Islam through engaging clerics in a dialogue that suggested respect for their religion while insisting on the observance of human rights.[37] Distinguishing between security threats and religious difference was more promising than the use of force, since it addressed the causes of discontent and refused to retaliate against antimodernism with the same kind of violence.

PARTICIPATORY DEMOCRACY

A final challenge revolved around the broadening of participation so as to enable democracy to cope with the transnational processes of globalization. Ironically, at the very moment when East Europeans were choosing representative government, West Europeans, having long enjoyed its blessings, began to lose faith in parliamentary institutions. Tired of the tedious compromises of *cohabitation* and grand coalitions, citizens stopped participating in the ritual battles between parties. As a result, voter turnout during elections dropped in almost all countries, allowing determined minorities a disproportionate voice in shaping policy. At the same time the large people's parties of the postwar era frayed at the edges, losing members because of the dissolution of the social milieus on which they were based. In continental systems of proportional representation smaller, issue-oriented parties made gains, fragmenting the spectrum and rendering the formation of coalitions more difficult. Citing such developments, commentators began to talk about growing *Demokratiemüdigkeit*, a widespread discontent with formal democracy.[38]

Lack of trust in the processes of parliamentary decision making inspired growing numbers of local protests against government projects opposed by engaged activists. One classic case was the movement against the building of a new underground train station in Stuttgart, which was supposed to replace the old turnaround terminal with through tracks, speeding up travel and offering better access to shopping. Formally the Federal Railway and the state government had observed all planning requirements. But when construction workers started to cut down ancient trees in the adjacent park, angry demonstrators gathered to stop the project. Ranging from older burghers to college students, the protesters were led by environmental activists who sought to discredit the technical claims of the railroad engineers. When the conservative government used water cannons and police truncheons to clear the way, the outcry grew so large that the CDU lost the following election and the Greens took control of the statehouse.[39] Though the subsequent referendum failed, the conflict added the new word *Wutbürger* to the vocabulary, designating enraged citizens.

Another criticism was the charge of a "democracy deficit" that reproached the European Union for its bureaucratic style of decision making. Young federalists had coined the term in the late 1970s in order to warn that public support for European integration was declining because of the distance of administrative rule-making bodies from ordinary citizens. As the German Constitutional Court pointed out, this deficit was structural, a result of the intergovernmental character of the EU institutions, in which the European Commission as the executive along with the heads of the member states tended to have the last word. The directly elected European Parliament was only gradually able to obtain greater powers of codecision but still lacked classic parliamentary attributes like ministerial responsibility and the authority to elect a government. As a result of its seeming irrelevance, voter turnout fell to 43 percent in the election of 2009. This discontent also motivated some of the negative votes during the French and Danish referenda against the draft constitution. At best the EU was an indirect form of democracy, based on delegation of power from nation-states.[40]

The protests against the G-8 summits similarly expressed the feeling that capitalist globalization had gotten out of hand and needed to be curbed by a worldwide countermovement, which some called alter-globalization because they viewed it as an alternative form of global cooperation. One of its more colorful local figures was the French activist cum sheep farmer José Bove from the Larzac, who led the dismantling of a McDonald's franchise under construction, protested against gene-modified food, and opposed the international agroindustry. The larger Global Justice Movement that organized the anti-G-8 demonstrations consisted of a grassroots network ranging from communists to NGOs like Attac, fighting "for the regulation of financial markets, the closure of tax havens," debt relief for the developing countries, and limitations on trade and capital flows. Though the demonstrations succeeded in getting their anticapitalist message into the international media, the protests foundered on their lack of organization and equivocation on the use of violence.[41] The very multiplicity of participants and the diversity of their ideological orientation also inhibited the success of global grassroots democracy.

One response to these frustrations was the emergence of media-savvy populists who suggested simple solutions to complex problems. In Austria the self-styled rebel Jörg Haider succeeded with his ultranationalist Freedom Party in breaking the stalemate between Catholic Conservatives and Social Democrats in 1986. In Italy the media tycoon Silvio Berlusconi rose to power in the mid-1990s by magnetizing middle-class followers of the scandal-ridden Democrazia Cristiana with his neoliberal program, macho behavior, and dispensing of material favors. In France the neo-Gaullist politician Nicolas Sarkozy won the presidential election in 2007 through his tough talk, frenetic activism, and hobnobbing with the rich and powerful. In the Netherlands the populist Pim Fortuyn launched a xenophobic movement, calling for decency and security, before he was assassinated in 2002. Everywhere the pattern was a similar combination of a forceful personality, media manipulation, and appeals to resentment against foreigners. But the prevalent insider favoritism inevitably led to scandals that discredited such populism.[42]

A more responsible alternative was the attempt to make the welfare state fit for global competition and thereby save its essential solidarity. In the United Kingdom the eloquent Labour prime minister Tony Blair, who succeeded the Conservative John Major in 1997, did not repudiate the neoliberal legacy but rather tried to make its competitive impulses more humane. His "new labour" program promised to take "Britain on a further stage of modernization" by combining "personal ambition with social compassion" and "equity with efficiency." In Germany the dynamic Gerhard Schröder, who defeated Kohl in 1998, first attempted to implement socialist and environmentalist policies but then recanted when realizing that the global recession rendered further redistribution impossible. The daring Agenda 2010 of the Social Democrats sought to energize workers while cutting back some welfare provisions and easing regulations for the sake of competitiveness. Unfortunately Blair tripped over his unnecessary support of the Iraq War, while Schröder was punished at the polls for his reforms.[43] But both leaders showed that democracy was capable of making resolute decisions.

Various attempts to render representative democracy more participatory were only partially successful because the suggested instruments had contradictory results. For instance, the campaign for open meetings and Wikileaks exposures of government documents revealed some scandalous secrets but often displaced decisive debates into other forums. The advocacy of quota systems for nominating women and minorities broadened representation at the cost of privileging gender or race. Similarly the mobilization of civil society in NGOs to lobby for a particular cause led to charges of influence peddling and campaign-financing violations. The Swiss experience showed that direct consultations of the electorate by referenda opened the door to plebiscitary politics that oversimplified issues by appealing more to emotions than to reason. Moreover the introduction of primary elections as instrument of candidate selection pushed politics to the extremes, with the party faithful choosing ideologues rather than nominees who represented the common good. The solution therefore did not seem to lie in a particular device but in rekindling the active involvement of citizens in general.[44]

The technological dream of cyber-democracy—suggested by the Pirate Parties International as a way to broaden participation—produced mixed results as well. Promoters claimed that already during its short existence the World Wide Web had fundamentally changed political discourse: its data provided information previously inaccessible; its interactivity encouraged debate on blogs; its reach mobilized adherents in campaigns; its speed spread news and commentary in real time; and its imaging power revitalized interest in current events. Advocates also credited the Internet with setting records in fundraising as well as with being an indispensable tool for organizing democracy-promoting rebellions such as the Arab Spring. But skeptics countered with justified warnings: Social media also facilitated the mobbing of unpopular views; rampant commercialism encouraged advertising exploitation; the storing of e-mails enhanced government surveillance; lack of vetting multiplied unconfirmed rumors; and hate messages whipped up violent movements and terrorism. In short, the Internet only had the capacity to extend beneficial democratic participation, if it was used responsibly.[45] The problem of getting more citizens to participate in a constructive form of democracy therefore remained unresolved.

GLOBAL MODERNITIES

In trying to theorize the experience of the past few decades, many observers have interpreted globalization as a continuation of modernization on a worldwide scale. Some emphasize the isomorphic spread of Western values, practices, and institutions around the globe. Others stress instead that the diffusion of technological innovation and the pervasiveness of capitalism has pulled ever more regions into a global trading network. Yet other commentators point to the proliferation of nation-states as the dominant model of political organization around the world, enshrined in the very name of the United Nations. Some analysts also draw attention to the strengthening of international law and the growth of international organizations such as the IMF and the WTO. Regardless of the specific indicator and the positive or negative value judgment attached to it, there seems to be a growing consensus that globalization has accelerated modernization processes in the Euro-American core and transferred them to other continents, making them a universal standard by reducing cultural differences.[46]

But increases in the volume, scale, and speed of interconnections also suggest that their intensification has created a different quality that sets the "global age" apart from previous epochs. For instance the accelerating pace of technological innovation has produced a high-tech economy that superseded classical industrialism. The concurrent financial flows and trade exchanges have penetrated the nation-states, providing big multinational corporations with more economic power than many national governments. At the same time, digital communication has reduced the globe to a village, in McLuhan's felicitous phrase, and led to a McDonaldization of popular culture, creating a veneer of uniformity. The theoretical suggestions of terms such as post-Fordism, postindustrialism, and postmodernism are efforts to understand some key aspects of this transformation without being able to find a convincing label for it. Since the process is still ongoing, it is perhaps too early to find a concept that would describe its character definitively.[47] But one way to reconcile the contradictory positions might be to speak of an emerging global phase of modernity.

Ironically, the victory of democracy in the struggle with fascist and communist alternatives has pluralized capitalist modernity by producing competing interpretations. Though it started the process of globalization by inventing its ideas, patterns, and institutions, Europe has viewed it with deep ambivalence, often stressing its dangers more than its opportunities. In contrast, elites in the United States have endorsed its further advancement by preaching self-government and market competition as universal truths, irrespective of their potentially negative consequences. Having adopted crucial technological and economic aspects of modernity, the East and Southeast Asians have also become ardent promoters of globalization because it has raised their living standards dramatically, even if some of them disagree on the question of democracy. As a result, Europe finds itself in a new triangular competition, lectured by its erstwhile offshoot across the Atlantic and overtaken by its former colonial possessions. The spread of capitalist democracy around the globe has therefore subdivided this model into a new set of rival modernities.[48]

Widespread criticism tends to obscure the reality that Europe has benefited considerably from globalization during the past generation.

Prepared by the sharpening of competition within its own market, the EU has remained the largest exporter in the world, accounting for more than 40 percent of exports in 2006, since well over half of the biggest multinational corporations were located there. European businesses have profited from the returns on their overseas direct investment, and the increase of research and development funding has kept the continent competitive at least in medium-high technology. Consumers have gained as well, because the intensification of trade and the falling prices of many goods have raised their relative buying power. No doubt the job losses due to off-shoring have been appalling, but in the service sectors new positions have continued to grow as well. During the past decades the North and Central European countries have improved their competitiveness, while the Mediterranean and East European countries began to catch up.[49] The European performance was therefore rather better than the media on both sides of the Atlantic admitted.

Europeans nonetheless face the task of bringing globalization under democratic control so as to minimize its disruptions and maximize its potential benefits. Since neither intellectual criticism nor labor-union resistance succeeded in preventing the shift of much basic industry to Asia, a purely defensive attitude turned out to be futile. More promising has been the EU attempt with the Lisbon Strategy of 2000–2010, because it aimed at "preparing the transition to a knowledge-based economy" and at "stepping up the process of structural reforms for competitiveness and innovation." Even if the implementation left something to be desired, the effort pointed in the right direction of improving the structural underpinnings of economic performance. Such an attempt means neither giving in to neoliberal ideology by abolishing all welfare-state protections nor abandoning cultural diversity to the uniformity of American "coca-colonization." The moderate left has understood that the challenge of global modernity consists of finding a balance between increasing economic competitiveness and preserving social solidarity.[50]

Chapter 28

PROSPECTS FOR THE TWENTY-FIRST CENTURY

High-speed TGV train, 2011. *Source*: 123RF.

By publishing a controversial essay titled "Power and Weakness" on June 1, 2002, American journalist Robert Kagan brought transatlantic tensions to a boiling point. Summing up growing policy differences, he argued that "on major strategic and international questions today, Americans are from Mars and Europeans are from Venus." Based on its predominant military power the United States tended toward unilateral use of force, while Europeans, holding a weaker hand, preferred "negotiation, diplomacy, and persuasion to coercion." Though intended to stimulate reflection about the structural sources of conflicts within NATO, the article ironically had the opposite effect of reinforcing stereotypes by stirring a passionate debate. The American attack on Iraq to overthrow Saddam Hussein made Kagan's subsequent book look like a power-political justification of neoconservative adventurism. While the actual argument pleaded for greater mutual understanding, its caricature-like simplification resonated with Washington pundits who were growing increasingly frustrated with the European refusal to share their agenda.[1]

Eleven months later German philosopher Jürgen Habermas issued a countermanifesto with his French colleague Jacques Derrida, calling for a European foreign policy. Putting aside their philosophical differences, the theoretician of communication and the dean of deconstruction voiced widespread continental protest against President George W. Bush's invasion of Iraq. Both called on the core of Europe to throw its "weight on the scale to counterbalance the hegemonic unilateralism of the United States," pleading for the creation of a common European identity by developing a shared public sphere. Through past wars and revolutions, Europe had been painfully forced to learn how to create "a form of 'governance beyond the nation state'" and to establish an elaborate "social welfare system." In contrast to the United States, Europeans had acquired a greater "reflexive distance from themselves" and more understanding of the violence involved in the "uprooting process of modernization." Europe therefore ought to take the lead toward developing "a global domestic policy" for a world that was coming closer together.[2]

In the United States a widespread culturalist turn away from Europe had reinforced this growing transatlantic divide about approaches to international politics. By exposing the brutality of imperialism, postcolonial critics discredited the universalism of European human-rights ideas as cover for imperial domination. Similarly subaltern thinkers rejected the "master narratives" of the colonizers in order to recover the voice of their victims' stories. In his seminal work on orientalism, the literary critic Edward Said argued that the Orient was a European cultural projection, justifying the continent's hegemony through the process of "othering" that camouflaged an underlying racism. Other non-Western intellectuals suggested "provincializing Europe" so as to create space for an appreciation of a plurality of transitions to modernity.[3] Overdue as recognition of minority suffering and as acknowledgment of the rich experiences of other cultures, this repudiation of "Eurocentrism" inspired a general decline of interest in Europe that threatened to turn a once-positive legacy into a negative stereotype.

As a corrective, defenders of ties to Europe pointed to the surprising extent of continental renewal during the past several decades. In his widely discussed *The European Dream*, the American economist Jeremy Rifkin sought to make a case for taking a fresh look at the European model. Going beyond Habermas and Derrida, he argued that European integration was an exciting development that promised to transcend the nation-state with a shared, continentwide sovereignty. Citing Europe's smaller degree of inequality than the United States' disparity between rich and poor, he also lauded its social market economy for finding a better balance between competition and solidarity. In many indexes of well-being such as life span, literacy rates, and educational performance the Europeans had moved ahead of the Americans, much to the latter's dismay. Moreover, in international relations the soft-power and multilateral approach of the continent seemed more humane than Washington's resort to force.[4] Though Rifkin sometimes overstated the case, he did point out that as a blueprint of democratic modernization Europe was becoming the only serious alternative to the United States.

These conflicting assessments raise a number of questions about the prospects of the European model in a globalized modernity. With postcolonial critics challenging the Western heritage, Europeans are seeking to redefine their legacy in universal terms. Within the broad outlines of liberal modernity, they have begun to evolve a distinctive version of democratic government and cultural lifestyle. The recurrence of transatlantic tensions suggests that the differences with the United States involve more fundamental issues than just repeated policy disputes. Moreover, the fierce economic competition with Asian newcomers is forcing Europeans to recover a measure of competitiveness in order to sustain their high-wage commitment to social solidarity. Finally, the project of integration faces numerous internal differences that are threatening to leave the promise of the EU unfulfilled. As a result of globalization Europeans are facing a series of challenges regarding their cultural identity, economic effectiveness, and political decisiveness that have yet to be met.[5] No longer capable of naive enthusiasm for progress and yet committed to further change, Europeans are struggling to develop a more humane sense of the modern.

VANISHING WEST

A growing retreat from the Western tradition has begun to obscure the European origins of liberal modernity, questioning their future relevance. The concept "Western" itself originally denoted the difference between Constantinople, signifying the East, and Rome, representing the West, which generated a diffuse yet powerful notion of a civilization that empowered its citizens and excluded the so-called barbarians. The Latin version of Christianity provided not just a *lingua franca* but also a set of values that contrasted the Occident with the Muslim Orient. Subsequently, the Renaissance and the Enlightenment produced traits like scientific research, market competition, individualist endeavor, and the rule of law that came to be defined as "modern" in the designation of the last half millennium as "Modern Europe." It is this combination of ideas, practices, and institutions that settlers brought along to new continents and imperialists imposed on conquered peoples.[6] Because of the enormous suffering meted out in its name, this entire tradition has recently come under fundamental attack.

For almost a century, the notion of Western civilization described an understanding of historical development that justified capitalist democracy as irresistible progress. This perspective grew out of Columbia University's turn-of-the-century decision to supplant the Latin requirement by a course in major writings that constituted the canon of a common heritage. During the First World War this concept of Western civilization was the ideological glue that held together the disparate coalition of the "Allied and Associated Powers," ignoring the anomaly of tsarist Russia. In the United States, its role was to "convince farm boys from Iowa why they had to die at Chateau-Thierry" in order to defend the foundations of a shared value system. A selective reading of the European past, it celebrated the advancement of liberty in Britain and France as well as the artistic genius of Italy, but remained ambivalent about German-speaking Central Europe and ignored the Slavic East altogether. Nonetheless courses called Western Civilization became a general requirement for college freshmen, providing them with a sense of cultural identity.[7]

During the Cold War the idea of the West functioned as a counterpoint to the communist East and as a transatlantic bridge between the United States and Europe. The propaganda trope of the "free world" suggested a shared set of values such as democracy and capitalism, which were threatened by Bolshevik egalitarianism and Soviet expansionism. As a result, the security partnership of NATO was a grand bargain for the defense of the western lifestyle that offered American military protection in exchange for European political support. On the continent, Catholic leaders such as Adenauer, Schuman, and de Gasperi appealed to the grand heritage of the "Occident" or *Abendland*, ironically fusing Christian morality with U.S. consumerism. The common underpinning was an agreement on self-governing institutions, market economies, and intellectual freedom that seemed to be in danger. But with the fall of the Wall, the East has disappeared, thereby rendering a contrasting West superfluous. Since internal disagreements within the democratic camp now came to the fore, political scientists debated whether this signified "the end of the West."[8]

In the postwar period the broader notion of westernization narrowed into Americanization, reflecting Europe's loss of importance on a global scale. Initially, Europeans had spread nationally distinctive versions of modernity according to their respective "civilizing missions," profoundly altering the lives of people around the world. But after World War II, the focus shifted to the contest of the superpowers, in which the democratic U.S. model competed with its dictatorial Soviet rival. Now American economic practice, consumption patterns, and popular culture reversed the tables and swept across the Old Continent by being more innovative in presentation, backed by superior power, and offering a more attractive lifestyle. Overshadowing the waning European influence during decolonization, it was Americanization that became the universal image of modernity around the world. Looking old-fashioned by comparison, Europe was shouldered aside, and compelled to decide which elements of the American way of life it would appropriate selectively in order not to fall behind.[9]

As a result of Washington's increasing power and influence, antiwestern criticism thereupon shifted from Europe to the United States as the primary target. According to global survey data assembled by the Pew Research Center in Washington, American exceptionalism was often misunderstood as arrogant ignorance abroad. With the Vietnam War, anti-imperialist protest shifted from Paris to Washington, opposing American support for military dictatorships. Owing to the prominence of U.S.-based multinational corporations it was all too easy for neo-Marxists to accuse America of economic exploitation. Among religious fundamentalists it was the secular and hedonistic lifestyle, propagated by Hollywood media that aroused most of the ire. The continued value gap between individual freedom and social solidarity as well as the difference between unilateralism and multilateralism spurred many European intellectuals to distance themselves from the United States.[10] Ironically the rise of popular anti-Americanism lifted the burden of anti-imperialist complaints from Europe.

The intensification of globalization also led to the emergence of more global perspectives that supplanted the westernization paradigm. During the 1970s social scientists had started to explore the intensification of worldwide exchanges, and historians followed suit two decades later by probing transnational developments. The emerging global history was a product of postcolonial criticism by Third World intellectuals as well as of a realization among scholars in the former metropoles that many problems transcended the boundaries of nation-states. The new movement also responded to the increasing diversity of student populations in the United States, which called for an exploration of heritages from beyond Europe, integrating material from the African, Hispanic, and Asian pasts. Much of the work had an anti-imperialist undertone, blaming the West in general and the United States in particular for the problems of developing countries.[11] Moreover, global studies self-consciously set out to reject the European modernization perspective in favor of the more equal approach of a circulation of ideas.

Although the cultural conflict with Islamic fundamentalism revived a bipolar view of the world, intellectual attempts to defend the Euro-American model of Western civilization have made only little headway. Conservative efforts to stem the tide of global history by retaining courses on Western Civilization or Great Books were merely able to persuade a few traditional liberal-arts colleges. Since Muslim extremists reviled a unified West as enemy, Samuel Huntington's suggestive synthesis in *The Clash of Civilizations* tried to revive a similar dichotomy as analysis of the fault lines of world politics. But his injunction that "the survival of the West depends on Americans reaffirming their Western identity and Westerners accepting their civilization as unique not universal and uniting to renew and preserve it against challenges from non-Western societies" has provoked more criticism than approval. Even if one were to accept the importance of cultural motives in many conflicts, this analysis elides the tensions between the United States and Europe, assigning the latter only a subordinate role.[12]

The erosion of the cultural dominance of Western civilization has both been liberating and marginalizing for understanding Europe's paradoxical impact. The distinction of a general process of modernization from a more particular westernization has opened up space for an appreciation of a plurality of modernities. The recognition of the power shift within the concept of the West from its European origin to its American adoption, propagation, and European reimportation has added a greater sense of complexity to the story. Moreover, the rejection of cultural Eurocentrism has made it possible to embed European developments in a broader global perspective. But these helpful changes have also created new problems: Some of the postcolonial authors reject the notion of modernization altogether without putting anything else in its place to explain the great transformation. In the debate about America's leadership role, Europe has all but disappeared as an independent actor. And finally, the broadening of horizons runs the danger of cultural relativism by obscuring the continent's crucial contributions to the Western heritage of universal values such as human rights.[13]

EUROPEAN MODEL

To many international visitors Europe may seem like a "cultural theme park," as one commentator has rather pessimistically suggested. No doubt tourists from Asia are crowding the museums in capitals like Paris and Berlin in order to admire artistic masterpieces. Newly rich Russians visit the Riviera at Cannes, the spas of Baden-Baden, or the ski slopes of St. Moritz. Each summer American college students ride high-speed trains, admiring picturesque towns like Bruges, Siena, Stratford, or Rothenburg, while Allied veterans return to their former battlefields....[14] But this selective perception is seriously misleading, since it misses the financial dynamism of London and Frankfurt, the gleaming car factories at Wolfsburg and Sochaux, the airplane plants at Toulouse and Hamburg, the container terminals of Rotterdam and Bremen. A broader perspective of Europe that includes the daring new buildings in Warsaw and Helsinki reveals that the flip side of the continent is strenuously modern, albeit in a different key. The distinctiveness of Europe consists therefore of its unique blend of tradition and modernity.

Though pressed by global competition, Europeans have developed a controlled version of the economy that is less speculative than American capitalism. While MBA-think has also made inroads, most European companies are less shareholder-value driven and are able to plan in longer time frames than U.S. corporations fixated on quarterly returns. Trade unions are stronger but labor discipline is high, as workers are often involved in management through codetermination arrangements. Companies tend to protect their skilled workforce in crises rather than continually downsizing for short-term gain. The establishment of the Common Market has helped firms like Siemens and Aventis to become global players, but the real innovation often comes from midsize companies, called *Mittelstand* in Germany, that take the lead in a particular product or application. Even in the IT sector some Europeans have been successful, like the Dutch giant Philips and the German software firm SAP.[15] Though continental companies are more regulated than American competitors, the image of a hidebound Europe is a self-serving misconception.

Another European peculiarity is the extensive welfare state, which levies high taxes but also provides the benefit of a superior safety net. In contrast to Americans, by and large, Europeans favor government help in order to achieve solidarity and equality rather than counting on individual enterprise. These basic values have produced a social model that provides a cradle-to-grave protection against the vicissitudes of life with generous unemployment benefits and state-guaranteed old-age pensions. Though its implementation differs somewhat in various countries, health coverage is mandatory, leaving nobody uncovered. While in Britain the National Health Service is in principle free of charge, on the continent a mixture of state provision and private insurance prevails. Moreover, there is much less poverty in Europe than in the United States thanks to liberal redistribution programs that reduce the income gap between poor and rich. No doubt the costs in sales taxes and income taxes are onerous, but the benefits are also considerable. While some grumble about their contribution, most Europeans accept this levy since they are sure they will get something out of it.[16]

In a remarkable transformation Europeans have generally left the waging of war behind and moved to the forefront of promoting peace around the world. The endless military cemeteries on the continent demonstrate the enormity of death and destruction which has convinced Europe that war is pointless, even for the victor. The desire to overcome traditional hostilities, a key goal of the founders of the EU, still motivated more recent efforts to pacify the bellicose Balkans. As a result of the painful experience of warfare, which has touched every family in some way, many Europeans have been happy to hide behind the American nuclear umbrella, guaranteed by the NATO alliance, and have reduced their military spending to half of the U.S. level per person. Instead, individual states like Germany and the EU collectively have turned to "soft power" in order to promote their interests through international institutions, multilateral cooperation, financial contributions, and cultural influence. Deeply disagreeing with Washington strategists of *Realpolitik*, they are willing to offer forces only for peacekeeping and reconstruction.[17]

Funding for public provision rather than market response has produced an exemplary network of transportation and transit in Europe that supports individual mobility. While the automobile has also transformed movement with superhighways, Europe's compact settlement pattern has prevented its complete ascendancy. Though railroads have reduced service to small towns, passenger-train travel has not only survived but prospered, with the fast TGVs and ICEs connecting cities more rapidly than car or airplane travel. At the same time European urban areas maintain a dense network of mass transit consisting of subways, regional rail, buses, and even streetcars, making almost any point accessible by public transportation. Of course, the costs have to be highly subsidized, with ticket prices reduced for students and pensioners, but the gain in environment-friendly mobility is considerable. In spite of the individual convenience of cars, their speed, emissions, and parking have been tightly restricted so as to keep the inner cities from choking.[18] As a result sufficient space remains for bicycle lanes and sidewalks.

Even after their manifold destructions, European cities have remained more livable than their urban counterparts in America or Asia. Legal and administrative control over entire metropolitan areas has kept the tax base unified, preventing the deterioration of downtowns. Preservation of inner cities with half-timbered houses, cobblestoned streets, and public squares has mostly prevented the building of skyscrapers and retained residents in the center. Moreover, suburbs were originally designed for factories and workers, keeping the well-to-do closer to the urban core, and the tighter zoning restrictions have held the building of single-family homes on the outskirts to more manageable proportions. From Rome to Oslo, continental cities tend to have many trees, parks, and other green areas as breathing spaces. The survival of buildings from different epochs has created an interesting mixture of styles in private and public dwellings, blending apartments with shops, cafes, and offices. As a result, it is pleasant to stroll through pedestrian-friendly streets, look at shop windows, and encounter other people, all of which contributes to an interesting atmosphere of urbanity.[19]

As a consequence of their traumatic experiences Europeans have also developed a self-critical memory that has propelled their efforts at integration. While U.S. citizens are overwhelmingly proud of their country and Asians tend to be even more chauvinistic, less than half of the respondents in a European poll evinced similar levels of pride. Of course having to bear responsibility for the world wars and the Holocaust has engendered a profound self-questioning among most Germans. But other Europeans have also had enough problematic recollections regarding Nazi collaboration, imperialist domination, or racist exploitation to fuel a critical attitude toward their own past as well. While Russians still glory in their victory in the Great Patriotic War, the East Europeans are trying to cope with memories of Soviet repression. Instead of fostering hate, these painful remembrances have encouraged binational efforts at reconciliation between the French and Germans as well as Poles and Germans.[20] In contrast to the visceral nationalism of many Americans, most Europeans have developed a critical attitude toward their own past that helps them get along in the present.

These characteristics suggest that Europe has generated a distinctive model of modernity that provides an alternative to the ascendant American and emerging Asian variants. Owing to their past experiences and resource constraints, Europeans are more optimistic about the role of the state, more concerned with social solidarity, and more supportive of ecological sustainability than their rivals. Prizing the intangible benefits from a public commitment, they are also more willing to fund culture by using taxes to support museums, symphony orchestras, and so on. Believing that there are tasks best not left to the vagaries of the market, they recognize education as a government responsibility that needs to be generally free of charge. Since only a minority tries to maximize individual gain, most Europeans are more concerned with improving the quality of life for the common good.[21] This is not backwardness but the result of a different interpretation of shared Western values. It remains to be seen whether the unrestrained market of the United States, the catch-up development of China, or the social responsibility of Europe offers the best path into the future.

TRANSATLANTIC TENSIONS

With the disappearance of the external communist threat, relations between Europe and the United States have loosened and tensions multiplied. Even in the best of times the self-congratulatory professions of friendship in after-dinner speeches masked irritating policy disputes, though they helped to facilitate compromise. But after 9/11 commentators began to speak openly about the transatlantic "crisis and conflict," predicting either the transformation or the breakup of the relationship. Public disagreements between George W. Bush and Jacques Chirac, and between Bush and Gerhard Schröder, reached such a level that they could no longer be seen as mere misunderstandings but were interpreted rather as an expression of more fundamental structural divergences.[22] Clearly, the passing of the postwar generation of Atlanticists who had a personal, emotional stake in maintaining close ties between the Old Continent and the New World was one important factor. But the mutual disdain that led to the open rupture had deeper causes in the shifting roles of both partners as well as in a divergence of fundamental attitudes.

The gradual erosion of the transatlantic community has widened the Atlantic, leading to a dangerous alienation between Europe and America. Since the United States was primarily a product of European immigrants, bringing with them basic values of Christianity and the Enlightenment, the relationship was originally quite close.

Moreover, the West Europeans were immensely grateful for twice being rescued from German domination by American troops, some of whom remained stationed on the continent, making the United States a "European power" after 1945. Ironically, Washington's program of European recovery was so successful in reviving economies and spurring political integration that many Europeans began to take their protection in the Cold War for granted. Emboldened by the overthrow of communism, they wanted instead to escape transatlantic tutelage, since they increasingly disagreed with American neoliberalism and unilateralism. When U.S. neoconservatives aimed for imperial hegemony, many continental leaders balked at following their lead and chose to assert their independence.[23]

Angered by such ingratitude, conservative U.S. politicians and journalists engaged in an ugly wave of Europe-bashing by appealing to nativist prejudices. This frustration brought out a deep-seated ambivalence toward the "old country" that consisted of both a nostalgic longing for a lost home and a patronizing belief in American superiority. Casting the second Iraq War as a moral crusade for democracy meant that the "unwilling Europeans" had to be chastised as irresponsible and ridiculed as incompetent. The media had a field day in predicting "The Decline and Fall of Europe," ignoring such homemade disasters as the savings-and-loan crisis, the dot-com bubble, and the financial meltdown. Secretary of Defense Rumsfeld's disparagement of the "old Europe" was woefully ignorant of the newness of European integration, while Robert Kagan's celebration of military might inspired debates about the rise of a new "American empire." Fortunately, populist calls for the boycott of French wines and cheeses were rather ineffective. But this outburst reinforced a stereotype of Europe "as weak, socialist, an object of pity" that infused Republican campaign propaganda.[24]

Predictably, continental politicians and journalists countered this anti-Europeanism with a similarly demagogic anti-Americanism. During the previous two centuries, Europeans had also held ambivalent feelings about the United States, admiring the New World as a land of freedom and opportunity while rejecting its capitalist greed and imperialist expansion. At the height of the Cold War older conservatives were grateful for Washington's military protection but loathed Hollywood's popular culture as crude and commercial. During the 1960s younger leftists adored the informality of the American lifestyle and the courage of the civil rights movement while rejecting the Vietnam War and the support of dictatorships. Especially among intellectuals, the invasion of Iraq brought out resentment against U.S. interventionism and unilateralism, inspiring Habermas' critical essay. The disclosure of atrocities turned admiration of America into disdain, with polls showing a precipitous drop in appreciation.[25] Going beyond criticism of a misguided policy, this wave of anti-American criticism fed permanent stereotypes that increased mutual distrust.

Behind this alienation lay an increasing divergence of orientations and values between political elites on both sides of the Atlantic that widened with the Reagan administration. Agreement persisted on most basic issues like support for democracy and human rights. But regarding their implementation differences increased between a U.S. libertarian, individualistic, market outlook and a more statist, collectivist, welfare mentality in Europe. In other indicators the contrast was even stronger. In the crucial area of the legitimacy of the use of force, continental countries abhorred war, since it had devastated their homes and families, while Americans considered it legitimate, as only a much smaller proportion had suffered and the twentieth-century conflicts had always taken place elsewhere. Moreover, the observance and influence of religion were much higher in the United States than in most European countries, which could be described as post-Christian societies. Differences in attitudes toward gun control, international institutions, gene-modified food, and climate change complicated the resolution of transatlantic disputes.[26]

Another reason was the European effort to develop a softer, but better, alternative to the American exercise of hard power. Since many Gaullists and leftists chafed under U.S. dominance of the international arena, they welcomed the Franco-German refusal to participate in the second Iraq War. Trying to provide an intellectual rationale, European commentators claimed that the Old Continent had developed a different approach to regional cooperation and international politics. Provocatively predicting that "Europe will run the

21st century," a British journalist and consultant argued in 2005 that American military power was "shallow and narrow," but European influence ran "broad and deep" because it did not rely on force but on persuasion. Such "transformative power" was more effective than force in spreading democratic institutions, human rights, and the market economy by leading through example. He forecast that a network approach would ultimately prevail in a globalized world of closer connections. Though overly sanguine about the end of military force, this perspective presented the EU as a more promising form of modernity.[27]

The recent retreat from claims of U.S. hegemony and European moral superiority has provided a chance for a more sober reassessment of the transatlantic relationship. The inconclusive war against terrorism suggested that simply substituting Islam for communism as the new threat did not provide sufficient motivation to hold the disparate sides together. Instead it would be more constructive to rediscover the commonality of basic values. Timothy Garton Ash correctly argued that "America and most of the diverse countries of Europe belong to a wider family of developed, liberal democracies. America is better in some ways, Europe in others."[28] At the same time it might be helpful to appreciate the strength of shared interests. In 2012 the United States and the EU, with about 10 percent of the world's population, accounted for 40 percent of GNP and one-third of global trade, and their bilateral exchanges amounted to $646 billion. The suggested Transatlantic Trade and Investment Partnership would strengthen this material basis further. Both cultural affinity and economic self-interest indicate that the EU and the United States complement each other quite well.

Ultimately the transatlantic partnership will only work if both sides treat one another somewhat more as equals. American difficulties with winning the peace and extricating themselves from Iraq and Afghanistan have inspired a partial reduction of neoconservative hubris. Its pivot toward Asia notwithstanding, the Obama administration has been more open to multilateral approaches and international organizations than its predecessor, even if the Tea Party has kept tooting the nationalist horn. Meanwhile, Europeans have realized that some conflicts, like those in Libya and Syria, do need force in order to be resolved. They have also begun to understand that if they want to emancipate themselves from transatlantic tutelage, they have to take more responsibility for their own defense, although they need not rival the inflated American military expenditures. Though it is unlikely that their cooperation will once again become as close as during the height of the Cold War, the new aggressiveness of Putin's Russia in Ukraine underscores the need for both partners to cease their bickering so as to rebalance the transatlantic relationship.[29]

GLOBAL ROLE

Owing to its bloody impact on the world, Europe continues to have a global responsibility for maintaining peace, nurturing democracy, and developing prosperity. While the appointment of Catherine Ashton as EU representative for foreign and security policy in 2009 has improved coordination, the national governments of the major states still make the key decisions. Within its own region, the EU's priority has primarily been to pacify the Balkans, decide about Turkey's membership, and establish friendly relations with its eastern neighbors such as Ukraine without alienating Russia. In regard to its former colonies, the lingering ties of language and expertise have created the challenge of contributing to their stability and economic development without perpetuating a pattern of dependency. Toward the Asian competitors, Europe has had to insist on fair trade, the observance of intellectual-property rights, and acceptable labor practices without using these concerns as instruments of protectionism. And toward the entire globe, the EU has needed to support international organizations and treaties so as to benefit the whole.[30]

After the end of the wars of Yugoslav secession, Brussels has used the leverage of prospective EU membership to help with the task of pacifying the Balkans. Since the entire region was considered to be part of Europe and many inhabitants wanted to join the West, the accession of Romania and Bulgaria went smoothly, even if they did not fully meet the criteria. Among the former Yugoslav states, Slovenia also rapidly democratized and developed, while it took Croatia longer to shed its authoritarian past and qualify for membership. The crucial country in the region is Serbia because of its size, economic power, and problematic past. After the victory of the democratic movement, Belgrade began negotiating for accession, reinforcing its positive transformation. The smaller countries such as Albania, Montenegro, and Macedonia appear viable only under the EU umbrella. The toughest problems continue to be Kosovo, since it needs Serbian recognition, and Bosnia-Herzegovina, because of ethnic irredentism.[31] Solutions seem hard to find, but one can hope that the wealth and influence of the EU will prevail in the long run.

In spite of American pressure for Turkish membership, entry into the EU looks more complicated for cultural, political, and strategic reasons. Becoming accepted as part of Europe has long been a goal of secular and democratic Turks, but although negotiations were started in 2005, the recent Islamicization of the state has dampened that wish. Led by France and Germany, the European public has become more skeptical, worried about the accession of about seventy-four million Muslims, the unsolved Cyprus issue, the internal conflict with the Kurds, and the return to authoritarian patterns under Recep Tayyip Erdogan. The geostrategic advantage of Near Eastern location now turns into a disadvantage due to Turkey's dangerous proximity to war-torn Syria, factionalized Iraq, and fundamentalist Iran. During the Arab Spring, Ankara has also started to find a new regional role as champion of a moderate Islamic modernization that promises to restore some of its Ottoman influence. As in the internally and externally contested case of Ukraine, a "privileged partnership" with the EU may turn out to be the best solution for both sides.[32]

Though competing with the United States and China, some European countries have maintained close relations to their former colonies. Often overlooked in the literature have been cultural ties based on the acceptance of English or French as the language of communication between indigenous groups speaking a welter of different tongues. While English has become the global *lingua franca*, appearing in diverse creoles through the addition of local idioms, the French have made strenuous efforts to maintain *francophonie* as a sphere of cultural influence. By subsidizing TV and radio broadcasts, distributing films and print media, and training journalists, Paris has maintained a bond of shared language and content. The educational connections also remained strong with African or Southeast Asian countries through fellowships in the metropoles, while Europeans received grants to do field research, which in turn created new networks.[33] Not tarnished as much by a colonial past, the German Academic Exchange Service has been quite active in this area as well. In NGOs like Médecins Sans Frontières Europeans also play a central role.

The structure of trade between Europe and the former colonies has been controversial, since it has had a direct bearing on the success of development and the reduction of poverty. The preferential regime of the Lomé Convention in 1975, which linked the EU with a large number of African, Caribbean, and Pacific (ACP) countries, was revised in Cotonou in 2000 in order to liberalize exchanges by signing Economic Partnership Agreements. While for the European countries imports and exports with the ACP states amounted only to a bit more than 5 percent, this trade was crucial for their partners, since the EU was their largest market and supplier. The developing countries complained about the restrictions on market access due to EU agricultural subsidies, while at the same time wanting to shelter their infant industries from competition. Moreover, their dependence on raw-material production made them subject to falling world-market prices. All efforts at subsequent renegotiations of the terms had little success, since the Europeans continue to dominate the asymmetrical arrangement.[34]

The economic relationships with Asian competitors such as China, Japan, India, or Korea were more contested because of the rapid rise in trade and the obstacles to fairness. China alone has become the EU's second-largest trading partner, while the EU is the biggest market for Chinese products. Europeans bought mostly mass-produced consumer goods, whereas China imported machinery, cars, and aircraft. With most Asian countries the EU ran a trade deficit, since those countries purchased few services from the outside and informal restrictions made access to their markets difficult. Foreign direct investment was much smaller than in the United States, though it was rising rapidly. One area of conflict was the lack of observance of intellectual-property rights, as Asian competitors copied European products and sold imitations more cheaply. A second complaint concerned state subsidies by Asian countries, for instance in the manufacturing of solar panels, which facilitated market domination and drove European producers to ruin.[35] But with wages rising and WTO rules hardening, there was some hope that trade would become more balanced in the future.

Behind the disagreements on trade lay a culture gap in the definition and importance of key values, which separated the EU from China and to a lesser degree from other Asian countries. While most political concepts had originated in Europe, the memory of colonial exploitation gave them a different meaning in Asia. In China national pride fed an emphasis on sovereignty and stability that the Europeans hoped they had overcome. Similarly, the European ideas of individual liberty and democracy have seemed disruptive of order and had at best to be introduced quite gradually. A special bone of contention was the European stress on human rights, which seemed to many Chinese a form of outside interference that violated their notions of collective consensus and party authority. These cultural differences also created an emphasis on national advancement instead of reciprocal partnership, and so justified an effort to catch up to the West by whatever means necessary. While the Japanese, Indians, and Koreans largely accepted liberal modernity, the Chinese were still searching for an authoritarian path to prosperity.[36]

After decolonization and the end of the Cold War, Europe was gradually developing a role in the world that sought to reconcile its own interests with common necessities. This approach differed from the hegemonic aspirations of the United States by putting a greater emphasis on soft rather than hard power, trusting international agreement rather than *Realpolitik*. It also diverged from the Asian project of national advancement by a decided preference for reciprocity, multilateralism, and international organization, with hope that reasoned discourse would eventually produce workable compromise. For instance, in combating global warming, Europeans were more ready than Americans or Asians to make binding agreements on CO_2 emission reductions, even if they impinged on their lifestyle and slowed economic growth.[37] With neither imperial designs nor nationalist objectives, they were relying less on military force than on leading by peaceful example.[38] Compared to the brutal imperialism of the 1900s, this moderation has been a truly dramatic change within the last century.

CLOSER UNION?

If Europe wants to play a constructive role in world affairs, it first needs to put its own house in order by resolving a series of problems that have so far limited its potential. One central dispute involves the very character of the EU. On the one hand, British, Swedish, and Danish free traders want a flexible interpretation of the Treaties of Rome with the possibility to opt out of policies from which they cannot see direct benefits. On the other, the German, Benelux, and EU federalists want to progress toward "an ever closer union of the peoples of Europe." While a withdrawal of Cyprus or even Greece would hardly be noticed, since they represent only a small fraction of EU GDP, a British exit would "be the most serious setback for the stability and security that the peoples of Western Europe have enjoyed since 1945." The rise of Euroskepticism in the United Kingdom, fed by the chauvinism of the popular media, is dangerous, because Prime Minister David Cameron has promised a referendum to settle the issue by 2017.[39] Given the increasing agitation of the UK Independence Party, the outcome of the vote remains in doubt.

A second area of concern has been the strengthening of the institutional structure of the EU so as to make it more efficient and democratic. After the French and Dutch referenda buried the constitutional project, the Treaty of Lisbon, in force since 2009, sought to provide moderate improvements while dropping the symbolic trappings of supranationalism. This agreement, ratified by all member countries, created a more visible president of the European Council of the heads of state, demonstrating the intergovernmental nature of the EU. Moreover it introduced qualified majority voting within the

Council of Ministers for most treaty areas, overcoming the problem of national obstruction at last. It also increased the power of the European Parliament by beefing up the codecision procedure with the EU Council, which would give each body a veto right. Finally, the treaty made the European Union's bill of rights legally binding. This effort succeeded in streamlining existing procedures and strengthening EU institutions, but it failed to provide the great leap forward that might have created a European superstate.[40]

Yet another serious problem has been the disagreement about a lasting solution to the sovereign debt crisis, which has threatened the euro as common currency. Emergency measures such as the promise of the European Central Bank to step in, if needed, have managed to calm the financial markets, reducing the inflated interest rates for the indebted countries to manageable levels. But the neoliberal austerity program has produced a stubborn recession that has pushed unemployment rates up to over 20 percent in some affected countries. Those Europeans who refuse to take responsibility for their own mistakes are blaming German chancellor Angela Merkel for their predicament, while some Euroskeptics call for the end of the euro as currency. In Ireland and Spain the reduction of unit labor costs and balancing the national budget have reignited growth, and even in Greece there are first signs of a recovery.[41] But a long-term solution to the predicament requires a compromise between a banking union that shields taxpayers from speculation risks, a strengthening of fiscal oversight mechanisms of the EU, and some stimulus spending to end the recession.

The common foreign and security policy of the EU is another unfinished work, because this is the area in which the national sovereignty of the member states remains most pronounced. The European Union has contributed greatly to the democratic transition in the Mediterranean region and in Eastern Europe as well as to the pacification of the entire continent. Moreover, the Lisbon Treaty has provided new tools with the introduction of the high representative and the establishment of an External Action Service, a kind of diplomatic corps. But in this field the EU plays only a coordinating role, maximizing agreement between members rather than having exclusive or joint jurisdiction. This limitation is most evident in the area of defense, in which joint action is possible only by unanimous agreement. Moreover, owing to the preponderance of NATO, military means such as the multinational Eurocorps are rather limited in size and capability. While the EU has tried to develop a strategy toward its African, Mediterranean, and Near Eastern neighbors, realist skeptics continue to consider it a weak actor in its own right.[42]

In contrast to such unresolved problems, there are other areas in which European unity has been making substantial progress that augurs well for the future. Ever since the Single European Act, the EU has been working to facilitate the free flow of goods, finances, people, and finally also of services. While the prospect of a market of twenty-eight states with about five hundred million inhabitants with a high standard of living has attracted much investment, regulatory decisions by the EU commissioner for competition in removing indirect restraints on trade have also made an important contribution to creating a level playing field. The commission has repeatedly struck down government support for industries such as automobile manufacturers and abolished other restraints such as exclusive professional degrees in order to allow a free play in services. The benefits of increased competition in making companies more effective and lowering prices have been considerable.[43] Moreover, the size of this trading bloc has enhanced its role in the IMF and WTO, leading the United States and Japan to try to conclude free-trade agreements with the EU.

Another positive development is the gradual emergence of a sense of European identity, especially among educated youths. Though citizenship is subsidiary to national affiliation, the EU has developed a common passport design. Moreover, the euro as common currency for currently nineteen nations has facilitated international travel by obviating the annoying need to exchange money. At the same time the Schengen Agreement has abolished internal borders among most European states, including Switzerland, eliminating lengthy delays while crossing frontiers. For the younger generation the Erasmus, Socrates, and Lifelong Learning programs have made it possible to study in another European country with financial support. Over twenty million students have taken advantage of this chance during the last two decades, widening their horizons to the entire continent in sometimes unpredictable ways, illustrated in the comedy *L'auberge espagnole*. The cumulative effect of individual and sponsored mobility has been the growth of a feeling of being Europeans, especially when traveling in the rest of the world.[44]

At the same time, there are indications that a European public sphere is gradually emerging, transcending the media's focus on national news. Though involving popular voting, the lame pop-song contest called "Eurovision" has not contributed much. More important have been the soccer games of the European Champions League, since all leading teams want to play "in Europe" so as to gain additional prestige and revenue. In spite of the limited scope of some publishing projects like *The European*, the European content of television news on the continent has been increasing, since EU decisions are often controversial. Moreover, not just political parties but also interest groups have started to organize on a European level in order to influence policy debates and regulatory decisions in Brussels. The funding opportunities of European science programs have also begun to reorient academic applications toward the EU Commission offerings.[45] Finally, as the joint initiative of Habermas and Derrida shows, a transnational conversation about European issues is slowly emerging among intellectuals.

In spite of a number of serious problems, the European project is therefore not moribund but rather very much alive. Neither the arrogant deprecations of "Euro wimps" by some Washington circles nor the federalist celebrations of the "superstate" of Europe are close to the mark. Well over half a century after the Treaties of Rome, the EU is still a work in progress, because it needs to find solutions for the pressing problems listed above. But doom-and-gloom predictions from neoliberal Anglo-Americans unwilling to understand the complexity of integration have also been proven wrong as often as they have been uttered. Though public enthusiasm has cooled considerably and corruption continues, Croatia has become the latest state to join the EU on July 1, 2013. Similarly, Latvia introduced the euro in January 2014, while Lithuania has followed at the beginning of 2015. These decisions are both a signal of the Baltic states' orientation to the West and their firm belief that the sovereign debt crisis will be mastered.[46] The project of a closer union moves frustratingly slowly, but it continues to make progress.

POSTMODERN POLITY

The institutional patchwork of the European Union frustrates analysts, politicians, and citizens who are striving for conceptual clarity. Jacques Delores, the prickly French president of the European Commission, therefore once quipped that the EU was "an unidentified political object." Neither the Europhobe stress on a free-trade area nor the Europhile hope for the emergence of a United States of Europe sufficiently characterizes the emerging polity. Similarly, both the defenders of the nation-state who reduce the EU to a device for facilitating economic growth and the idealist federalists who consider the European institutions as a future federation are equally off the mark in their evaluations. It would therefore be more sensible to leave behind such emotional oversimplifications and acknowledge the paradoxical combination of supranational elements and inter-governmental practices as a shifting balance without a predictable outcome.[47] In view of its inherent complexity and continuing evolution, the EU might, therefore, ironically be understood as a post-modern polity.

Undoubtedly the European Union is a postnational entity that has moved beyond the nation-state because of the limitations of that model in an age of postmodern globalization. The nation-state that developed in the nineteenth century was characterized by sovereignty over decisions, territoriality with well-defined borders, and military power for self-defense, while striving for linguistic as well as cultural homogeneity and gradually providing social services. Since the EU possesses hardly any of these attributes, realist expectations that it needs to develop into some kind of nation-state beyond the existing ones are likely to be disappointed. While the world wars have exposed the vulnerability of all but the largest countries, the economic, political, and cultural pressures of globalization are penetrating national borders. As a result of the postindustrial shift, the association between high industrialization and the nation-state has been broken, forcing leaders to find new ways to protect their citizens. In many ways the development of the EU has been a constructive reaction to the limitations of the nation-state by developing a new model beyond it.[48]

One way of explaining this complex structure might be the analogy of the medieval Holy Roman Empire, which offered a comprehensive umbrella above increasingly sovereign territorial states. Even if at first blush it might seem far-fetched, this perspective emphasizes the multitiered nature of authority, the multispeed commitment to further progress, and the multiethnic composition of the citizenry. Such an approach can deal with the subsidiarity of local, regional, national, and supranational power, explain the distinction between the eurozone of eighteen and the wider EU of twenty-eight members, and address the linguistic and cultural variety of constituencies that precludes uniformity. But such a premodern conceptualization also flies in the face of global postmodernity, and the EU possesses only sectoral sovereignty over the Common Market, having to share power in many crucial policy areas and playing only an advisory role in others. Seen from a more contemporary vantage point, the EU is therefore a novel hybrid, a contradictory mixture of modern and postmodern elements at the same time.[49]

In practice, the emerging Europe is a decentered but consensual community of states, regions, and citizens. Instead of a set of concentric circles with a fixed center and a periphery, the EU is a conglomeration of variable policy clusters. The Franco-German axis has been the core around which the Benelux and other countries such as Austria gather, although its balance has shifted from Paris to Berlin in recent years; the free traders around Britain form another cluster; the indebted Mediterranean states are another grouping; the East European newcomers such as Poland also share special concerns; and then there are the even more recent arrivals of the Balkan countries. The euro (or sovereign debt) crisis has revealed an elliptical structure, with decision foci in Berlin and Brussels that need to act in concert with each other while seeking to create consensus among the community's members. Though as the largest country Germany finds itself thrust into a reluctant leadership role, it can only lead if it convinces the others that it is acting in the common interest.[50] What is therefore emerging is a new intermediary level of domestic politics within Europe.

The postmodern nature of the EU as polity provides Europeans a chance to fashion unity from below, because its variable structure invites participation on different levels. Due to the diversity of languages and cultures, a common identity cannot be decreed from above; it rather has to emerge out of the strengthening of civil-society contacts. The sponsorship of youth exchanges creates a new horizon beyond the nation-state; city partnerships allow local politicians to understand the similarity of their problems; service-club contacts such as between the Lions Clubs of different countries create networks among business leaders; and finally transnational academic projects begin to address Europe as a whole. In short, the complicated institutional framework of the EU has created a space in which people can encounter one another and gradually develop a sense of being European. On the basis of such a lived experience institutional solutions are bound to follow. As German foreign minister Joschka Fischer said in his Berlin speech in 2000, the creation of the EU is a promising first step. Now Europeans must take the next one.[51]

A CHASTENED MODERNITY

Past and future wind energy, 2010. *Source*: 123RF.

The turbulent events of the twentieth century have disrupted the lives of many Europeans and twisted them in unforeseen directions. For instance, the Latvian fraternity student Victors Arajs formed an auxiliary police unit that collaborated in the Holocaust by killing hundreds of Jews and partisans. After going underground in West Germany, this anticommunist perpetrator was eventually caught and imprisoned. In contrast, the daughter of a prominent Jewish lawyer in Saxony, Irmgard Mueller, had to abandon her academic training, was forced into a labor battalion, and finally sent to Auschwitz. Having learned sewing and typing, she managed to survive by working in the camp laundry and administration, and eventually emigrated to the United States. Or take the Alsatian poet André Weckmann, who was dragooned into the Wehrmacht but deserted from the eastern front and joined the French resistance. As a high school teacher he nonetheless chose German as his subject and worked for European reconciliation after the war.[1] Each in its own way, these lives were profoundly shaped by the Second World War and the Holocaust.

The story of such European encounters with modernity has been told as either a cautionary tale or an encouraging narrative. On the one hand, painful memories highlight the brutality of the world wars, the repressiveness of the dictatorships, and the race- or class-based genocides during the first half of the century. Projecting the image of a "dark continent," this immense suffering and dying exhibits Europe as a giant cemetery, concentration camp, or pile of rubble. Its lesson is a grim warning against the evil potential of murderous modernity. On the other hand, satisfaction with the peacefulness, astounding prosperity, and growing integration during the second half of the century suggests a more positive picture. It focuses on the dynamic postwar renewal of the continent, creatively blending tradition with progress. Its message is the reaffirmation of faith in human recovery from catastrophe, showing the benign side of modernity.[2] Instead of debating which of these representations is correct, it might be more constructive to reflect on how such opposite sides came to be part of the same coin.

PERPLEXING CENTURY

The contrast of the public mood between 1900 and 2000 reflects some of the travails of the twentieth century that make it difficult to characterize the period in retrospect. In 1900, the London *Times* viewed the future with supreme confidence: "With such a [democratic] instrument of government, with our vast accumulations of wealth, widely diffused among the community, and, above all, with a people prosperous, contented, manly, intelligent and self-reliant we may look forward with good hope to the storms and conflicts that may await us." By the dawn of the third millennium the outlook had become much bleaker owing to the immensity of human suffering that had taken place in the interval. "How does one look at the twentieth century? It is not a tragedy or a comedy. It is not an epic. No political manifesto captures it. Only a bureaucratic document can mimic its impersonality, its reality." The Indian intellectual Shiv Visvanathan summed up his impression: "The twentieth century was the century of utopia, the utopia of plan, market and revolution. It was a century of nightmares."[3]

The past one hundred years need to be interpreted as a long rather than a short century so as to grasp their entire trajectory. Since the concept of a century is only an artifact of the calendar, its boundaries are not numerical but rather depend on the choice of caesuras. Eric Hobsbawm's thesis of a "short century" spanning from 1914 to 1991 has much to recommend it because it highlights the rise and fall of the socialist experiment, as manifested in Soviet communism. Nonetheless, this conception is too narrow, since it understates the impact of the rival fascist and democratic ideologies. Moreover, it surprisingly ignores the development of capitalism, which had already culminated in the 1890s with the second phase of the industrial revolution. It was not a coincidence that this was also the decade in which the notion of "modernity" became popular in artistic movements as a self-description of the revolt against tradition. Finally, whether to end the twentieth century with the terrorist attack on the World Trade Center on September 11, 2001, or the great recession of 2008 remains an open question because many of its developments are continuing into the present. With the period still lacking definitive closure, the full implications of the shift to a postindustrial and global modernity have yet to become clear.[4]

Most retrospectives characterize the twentieth century as an era of exceptional cruelty, perpetrated for largely ideological reasons. The atrocities began with the murderous practice of imperialism by its exploitation of labor and the suppression of native uprisings. The First World War continued the mass killing, since in terms of the chief losses it was an internecine conflict between European nation-states and empires that cost millions of lives. The casualties of the Soviet Revolution, the Civil War, the Holodomor in the Ukraine, the Great Purges, and other Stalinist projects undertaken in the name of a better future met or exceeded its toll. The Nazi-inspired Second World War was even more murderous, since it involved not just a war of annihilation but the systematic racial genocide of the Holocaust.[5] Preoccupied with mourning their many dead, most Europeans have distanced themselves from mass murder during the second half of the century, helping to contain the Cold War short of actual bloodshed. But the killing did not stop—mass murder merely migrated to China, Southeast Asia, Africa, and Latin America.

The surprising rebirth of Europe that restored democracy and civility after 1945 has received less attention, though this story is more encouraging. The prior suffering was so intense, affecting virtually every family, that many Europeans understood the necessity of changing course. The western countries had democratic traditions that could be renewed by being made more socially inclusive. Ironically, both American aid with the Marshall Plan and the threat of Soviet communism during the Cold War speeded the westernization of the former enemies. Moreover, the reluctant decolonization, which spawned several ugly wars but avoided universal conflagration, freed the continent from its colonial burdens so that it could concentrate on addressing its own social problems by extending the welfare state. The visionary initiatives of West European integration also helped to promote prosperity and stability and facilitated the Mediterranean transition. Finally, the overthrow of communism reunited the continent.[6] The story of this European recovery casts the outlook of the second half of the century in a much brighter light.

Because of the period's multiple ruptures, most Europeans experienced it as an era of accelerating change that reconfigured their basic sense of time. The increase in the speed of transportation from horse to car and the many technical advances from telegraph to smartphone allowed an escape from the past by accentuating the possibility of progress. Moreover, the experience of increasing social mobility, both vertical and horizontal, and the multiple regime changes made the future appear malleable, subject to human control, and society appear plastic, capable of being shaped according to ideological blueprints. This liberation from tradition and the emphasis on things to come fundamentally revised the notion of the present as escape from inherited bonds but not yet fulfilled promise, a suspended moment of choice between different trajectories. But disappointment in the results of social-engineering projects that tried to forge a better future ultimately produced a new cult of memory.[7] For Europeans the twentieth century's acceleration of time offered exciting possibilities as well as new insecurities.

MASTERING MODERNITY

The notion that described this transformation as a dynamic advance was the elusive concept of "modernity." Claiming to act as beneficiaries of mankind, a group of self-proclaimed innovators championed the modernization of their societies against the fierce resistance of the guardians of tradition. At the turn of the twentieth century, only some advanced members of the upper and middle classes in the leading cities considered themselves modern and set out to convert their backward neighbors. With scientific, economic, and moral arguments, they promoted modernity among the lower orders as an idea and set of practices, promising to improve their lives. In the name of progress, these modernizers preached the bourgeois values of rationality, hygiene, and discipline throughout the countryside, in the small towns and villages. Far from being inevitable, the unremittent propagation of change created countless conflicts and yielded unanticipated results.[8] The history of Europe in the twentieth century therefore offers an instructive record of the drive for modernization and the backlash against it.

Confident in progress, European elites while transforming their own countries simultaneously sought to spread the message of modernity around the globe so as to reshape the world in their own image. The prime conduit was imperialism, using science and technology for political control and economic exploitation rather than for improving the lives of indigenous people in different continents. Ironically, in the settlement colonies the process of transformation encountered fewer obstacles and could make more rapid progress, allowing the New World to overtake the Old Continent in size and efficiency of production. As a result, Americanization gradually replaced Europeanization as label for modernization, although both were often combined in the notion of westernization.[9] The successful adoption of this model brought nationalist ideology, business practices, communication networking, and popular culture to Asian countries, starting with Japan and then spreading to Korea, India, and China, creating another center of rapid development. The encounter with such high cultures has produced regional amalgams between tradition and change, ultimately spreading the contest over modernity to the entire globe.

In the heat of the First World War, however, the loose alliance of progressive movements fragmented into competing ideologies that promoted alternate visions of progress, pluralizing the notion of modernity. During much of the nineteenth century the liberal, democratic, and socialist movements had often cooperated in order to defeat the so-called forces of reaction. But due to the strains of World War I, Lenin's Bolsheviks broke away from the constitutionalism of the Provisional Government and proposed a revolutionary program of modernization for Russia and the world. Seeking to defend self-government and market competition, U.S. president Wilson countered with his democratic internationalism, centered on the creation of the League of Nations. Moreover, the disappointed Italian interventionists as well as the defeated German neoconservatives developed their own vision of an organic modernity, rejecting the Soviet and liberal versions. Many of the subsequent domestic and international conflicts revolved around the struggle between these ideological alternatives, with the fascists defeated by war and the Soviets by economic competition.[10] Surprisingly enough, democracy ultimately prevailed by reinventing itself and broadening its social appeal.

Both dictatorial modernities of communism and fascism experienced a similar cycle of development that characterized their rise, institutionalization, and eventual defeat. Emerging from the struggle between the liberal and authoritarian versions of modernity during the First World War, the totalitarian alternatives to democracy started out as opposition movements, full of hope, appealing to the newly enfranchised masses as blueprints for a better future. After their seizure of power in the Soviet Union, Mussolini's Italy, and Nazi Germany, they tried to create permanent institutional structures in order to realize their ideological aims. But the imperatives of stable government clashed with the need for acclamatory mass mobilization, leading to a series of internal conflicts like Lenin's suppression of the Kronstadt revolt and Hitler's decimation of the Brownshirts' (Sturmabteilung) leadership.[11] Ultimately the dictatorial versions of modernization failed in the task of reconciling administrative stability with dynamic self-renewal, while the major western democracies surprisingly succeeded in overcoming their crises by creating welfare states and evolving toward postindustrial modernity.[12]

Far from being a predictable process, the explosion of ever new facets of modernity during the past century produced a series of shock waves, whose impact ranged from peaceful progress to wartime destruction and back. The initial expectation of a better life was severely strained by the mechanized killing of the First World War, only to revive during the heyday of the 1920s. The communist effort at social revolution and the fascist project of racial genocide snuffed out this optimism, since Stalinist industrialization and the Holocaust showed the murderous consequences of social engineering. During the conservative Cold War recovery of stability, modernization once again gained a positive resonance due to the global competition for a better future between the communist "camp of peace" and the liberal democratic "free world." But just when it seemed that liberal modernity had triumphed and communism collapsed, a cultural revolt and the shock of globalization produced new uncertainties in the transition to a postmodern and postindustrial order.[13] The process of modernization in twentieth-century Europe was therefore full of ruptures and surprises, making it impossible to predict whether a benign or malignant version would win.

The inescapability of the modern condition suggests that the political challenge consists of finding a form for its dynamism that proves con- rather than destructive. Since science and technology are basically amoral, their innovations have to be harnessed to constructive purposes. The energizing force of market competition proves beneficial only if greed, speculation, and exploitation are sufficiently curbed. The creative impulse of individualism requires the counterweight of social solidarity so as not to shatter community with its egotism. Democratic institutions have to defend human rights lest they degenerate into populist props for dictatorship. Patriotism has to remain tolerant of foreigners so as not to turn into exclusivist chauvinism. Public administration needs to stay impartial in order not to become a deadening bureaucracy. Military preparedness has to focus on self-defense so as not to invite violent aggression. Finally, national pride and independence ought to be balanced by willingness for international cooperation.[14] As the Faustian legend suggests, only when controlled by humanist ethics can the dynamic power of modernity truly become a force for good.

EUROPEAN METAMORPHOSES

During the twentieth century Europe experienced breathtaking transformations that took the continent from global hegemony to utter self-destruction and back to a surprising recovery. Though divided into competing empires and emerging nation-states, around 1900 Europeans collectively controlled the rest of the world, exploiting and governing a vast array of colonies in Africa and Asia. Considering themselves as the carriers of a superior civilization, they were spreading their understanding of progress with force or persuasion across their dependent territories such as India, forcing potential rivals like China, Japan, or the Ottoman Empire to reform themselves by adopting European technologies, organizations, and standards. No wonder that imperialists like Cecil Rhodes were confident that the white race in the United Kingdom, Germany, and the United States had reached the top of human development and that future advancement was assured. Only some critics among the colonized, the labor movement, or nervous intellectuals worried that the splendor of the Victorian age rested on shaky foundations.[15]

As the "seminal catastrophe of the twentieth century," the First World War shattered the optimistic belief in the inevitability of progress and initiated the decline of European supremacy. The immense carnage of industrial warfare that killed a large proportion of male youths and maimed countless others depleted manpower in a literal sense. The concurrent destruction of entire regions that served as battlefields squandered wealth and obliterated their cultural heritage. The totalizing nature of the struggle that mobilized the home front burdened women working in factories, strained laborers, and impoverished middle-class families. While intellectuals volunteered for propaganda efforts, the horrendous descriptions of suffering by the "war poets" undercut the heroic image of combat and sowed doubt in the justice of one's national cause.[16] In order to end the struggle and prevent its recurrence, ideologues like Lenin, Wilson, and Mussolini developed competing blueprints of modernity with labels such as communism, democracy and fascism that competed for ascendancy during the subsequent decades.

The return of peace during the 1920s offered European powers a kind of Indian summer, suggesting that the prewar trajectory of liberal progress was about to be resumed. With the United States sulking in isolationism and the Soviet Union preoccupied with its own modernization, the traditional Great Power directory of the continent reasserted its control over the new institution of the League of Nations that strengthened international cooperation. Moreover, the principle of self-determination that broke up the ancient empires of the East heralded the advance of nation-states and democratic self-government over the entire continent. The revival of international trade and the recovery of economic growth promised to ease the burden of labor and restore prosperity to the middle class. At the same time modernist experimentation dominated high culture, while more popular styles of entertainment and consumption also made much headway.[17] Europe seemed once again to be moving forward until the Great Depression stopped this momentum, turning the direction of development toward another, yet more devastating conflict.

The second stage of what Charles de Gaulle called "a thirty years' war for or against world domination of Germandom" destroyed Europe physically and politically, ending its hegemony. This time there was no doubt that Hitler was the aggressor, seeking to reverse the prior defeat and intending to conquer living space for the Aryan race. Except for Britain, the Nazis succeeded in subduing the entire continent with lightning strikes, exploiting the defeated countries in the service of Greater Germany. Hitler's attack on Russia turned the conflict into a "war of annihilation" with ethnic cleansing and racial genocide, culminating in the anti-Semitic Holocaust that ruptured all bonds of civilization. The defeat of the Nazis' organic modernity required the unlikely cooperation of its communist and democratic rivals in a joint antifascist crusade that itself employed some morally questionable methods.[18] As a result of World War II liberated Europe lay prostrate and lost control of its affairs, allowing the United States and USSR to exercise an uneasy condominium over the destroyed continent.

Visible proof of the European decline was the loss of the colonies, which took place with surprising speed between 1945 and 1975. In part, the impetus came from protests or insurgencies of westernized elites in the colonies, which pushed for formal independence from their masters. In part, the Europeans' lack of resolve to prevent the end of empire was due to their war weariness and their vastly reduced means, which needed to be used for rebuilding their own cities. While the grudging and not always peaceful withdrawal of the colonizers was a triumph of anti-imperialist resistance, the challenges of economic development and political stability once again drew in Westerners, now in the role of advisers and financiers, thereby perpetuating unequal relationships in a different context. In the former metropoles, the blowback of native collaborators created a new problem of black or Islamic minorities. Ironically, the modernization imposed by the colonizers provided the slogans and weapons for independence.[19]

Instead of ushering in a peaceful modernity, the Cold War led to a bipolar division of Europe between the American and Soviet superpowers. With the National Socialist contender eliminated, the erstwhile allies now competed for control over the ruined continent, seeking to transform their respective parts according to their own ideological visions. Occupied Europe was forced to choose sides, gravitating in the end more toward the western model of liberal democracy than toward Soviet egalitarianism because the informal U.S. empire allowed more freedom than the Russian dictatorship. Fortunately the very lethality of nuclear weapons coupled with intercontinental missiles ultimately prevented their use. Spurred on by a massive peace movement, the European leaders sought to promote détente so that the continent would not become a nuclear or conventional battlefield.[20] The peaceful ending of the second Cold War showed that it was possible to escape the logic of the arms race and avoid nuclear annihilation through negotiation from above and protest from below.

The amazing rise of Europe from the ashes of self-destruction ultimately reconciled West Europeans with embattled liberal modernity. Led by the Scandinavian and British extension of the welfare state, the western countries reinvigorated democracy and spread it to the defeated enemies. Of course, the help of the United States was crucial, since Washington provided advice, material aid, and psychological support for a mixture of tradition and innovation. In Germany, Ludwig Erhard's promotion of a social market economy also contributed significantly to freeing economic competition while at the same time retaining a sense of societal solidarity. Under the heavier hand of the Soviets, the East European countries healed the wounds of the war and made some modest progress, but their drab smokestack industrialism eventually lost the competition with western consumer society. The glorious three postwar decades were a spectacular success in not only catching up to but exceeding prewar levels of prosperity until the challenge of globalization raised new concerns about the dangers of uncontrolled development.[21]

The final transformation of Europe, the construction of the European Union, ranked "among the most extraordinary achievements in modern world politics." Through a series of crises and subsequent political bargains, the Europeans created a unique, multilevel transnational political system. During the fifties the Treaties of Rome laid the foundation, during the sixties the creation of the Common Market stimulated economic growth, during the seventies the invention of the European Monetary System stabilized currencies, during the eighties the Single European Act expanded the areas of competition, during the nineties the Maastricht Treaty invented a common currency, and during the two thousands the Lisbon Treaty streamlined decision making. The growth from the original six to the present twenty-eight members was a sign of the model's attractiveness. Propelled by a mixture of idealism and economic interest and realized through intergovernmental bargaining, the partial pooling of sovereignty was an innovation that made unifying Europe into a powerful competitor in the global economy.[22]

LESSONS OF HISTORY

The bloody course of the twentieth century taught the Europeans a chastened outlook on modernity—a lesson some overconfident Americans have yet to learn. The world wars were so physically destructive, demographically murderous, and mentally devastating as to spur a fundamental reorientation of politics. While German military cemeteries in Normandy send a pacifist message, American war graves still extol national "competence, courage and sacrifice." Except when confronting dictators, Europeans consider peace preferable, since even a winner is likely to be grievously damaged. The result of this experience is a social demilitarization, not only of the defeated fascists, but also among the winning Allies, which has diminished respect for uniforms, decreased defense budgets, and rejected recourse to arms when other alternatives were left. This rethinking inspired a reconciliation between erstwhile enemies like the Germans, the French, and the Poles, and, in contrast to the United States, a strong preference for working through international organizations.[23] The development of the European Union, recognized by the Nobel Peace Prize in 2012, testified to the extent to which the poison of nationalism had been neutralized.

A second point, driven home by the terrible impact of the Great Depression, was the need to manage the dynamism of capitalism in such a way as to maintain political stability. The liberal countries' superior performance during the wars showed that the market was more productive than corporate cartels or state planning. But some European economists like John Maynard Keynes also realized that competition needed a framework of rules in order to prevent exploitation of labor and the recurrence of cyclical crises. In the West the reintroduction of free enterprise sparked the Economic Miracle, while in the East communist planning produced only a modest upswing. Since neither neoliberal deregulation nor socialist control seemed to offer the right answer, the continent eventually settled for the compromise of a social market economy, exemplified by Rhenish capitalism. In contrast to the American stress on unrestrained competition, this mixture of personal initiative and state guidance appeared preferable to Europeans, since they prized the common good as much as individual gain.[24]

Another imperative learned from the critique of the labor movement and the threat of communism was the need for social solidarity through public provision of welfare. At the beginning of the twentieth century most workers felt badly exploited, since their wages barely covered the minimum necessary for existence. As a result they organized powerful unions and created socialist parties that engaged in class warfare against the merciless capitalist bosses. When the Bolshevik Revolution scared the middle class while the moderate social democrats gained at the polls, the introduction of a welfare state became a necessary concession in order to pacify society. The moral critique of intellectuals and the experience of wartime solidarity also helped establish a sense of collective responsibility for those in need. Moreover, the Cold War competition with the Soviet Bloc hastened the postwar expansion of the welfare state.[25] In contrast to the strong American streak of individualism, Europeans internalized a commitment to solidarity that defined a more social vision of modernity.

The finiteness of continental resources also encouraged an attitude of environmental stewardship, of thinking in terms of sustainability rather than the quick-profit orientation of American business. Having lived in the same places for several thousand years, Europeans were forced to learn that wasting materials like Mediterranean timber had deleterious consequences in denuding the countryside. Except for British and Norwegian oil and recent natural gas discoveries, the older precious minerals and coal deposits had largely run out. Less driven by quarterly profits than Americans, Europeans usually thought of passing a firm on to their children and therefore developed a more long-range strategy. That frame of mind made continental businessmen more receptive to ecological critiques, and citizens more willing to recycle and take public transportation instead of throwing things away and burning fossil fuels. Hence many Europeans embraced green technology, and the Germans even tried to end their use of nuclear energy.[26] This ecological awareness proposed an alternate form of postindustrial modernity.

The repression by the left and right dictatorships finally illustrated the importance of reaffirming human rights and revitalizing democracy. The struggle for civil rights was part of the project of liberal modernization, but the failure of interwar democracy meant that participation remained circumscribed. Substituting acclamation, the communists privileged workers and intellectuals, persecuting their class enemies, while the fascists excluded Jews and blacks from the national community as racially unfit. Nazi oppression made the resistance realize that democracy had to broaden its social base and respond to demands for greater participation after the war. Moreover, the Soviet suppression of East European dissent helped create a new sensitivity to the importance of human rights as protection of individuals. While Americans and Europeans shared the goal of self-government, the continent's system of proportional representation provided greater responsiveness to minority views.[27] Both are now confronting the challenge of powerful transnational corporations and media empires that threatens the rise of a "postdemocracy."[28]

THE EUROPEAN ALTERNATIVE

Doomsday predictions of the Anglo-American media notwithstanding, the ghosts of Europe's bloody past are not returning and repeating previous catastrophes. On the one hand, ever since the outbreak of the euro crisis, with its excessive government debts and bank bailouts, even well-informed commentators have predicted the "collapse of the European economic and social model," criticized the cumbersome nature of EU decision making, and decried German-imposed austerity.[29] On the other, the impact of "casino capitalism," the growth of social inequality, and the rise of right-wing populism have inspired members of the continental Left to revive theories of a "delayed crisis of democratic capitalism," warning against its imminent demise.[30] Even though the 2014 elections returned many Euroskeptics, the eurozone has not fallen apart, the euro kept trading one-quarter to one-third higher than the almighty dollar on the currency markets, and the joint leadership of Berlin and Brussels succeeded in stabilizing the international financial markets. Such polemical oversimplifications of both ideological camps betray a fundamental lack of understanding of the European alternative.

A more nuanced approach to the continental experience during the past century recognizes that Europe has been developing its own distinctive model of democratic and social modernity. No doubt the continent is confronting serious problems of aging, immigration, fiscal control, institutional structure, and global competitiveness—but they are ultimately solvable. Instead of being an imperfect clone of American modernity, Europe has different ideas about the role of religion, gun control, capital punishment, welfare support, public transportation, and international organization, just to mention a few.[31] To many liberal Americans, these European solutions are more appealing than Tea Party prescriptions of military strength, unilateral intervention, unrestrained speculation, and social conservatism. In President Barack Obama's words, a global "struggle for freedom and security and human dignity" continues to unite Europe and the United States. Since both would profit from closer cooperation in addressing worldwide challenges, a renewed transatlantic dialogue is needed to foster greater appreciation of the European lesson of a chastened modernity.[32]

ACKNOWLEDGMENTS

Many individuals and institutions have helped to further my interest in European topics, though only a few can be acknowledged here. For instance, the political scientists Gary Marks, the late Ruth Pitts, and I cofounded the Center for European Studies at the University of North Carolina. A working group of the Zentrum für Zeithistorische Forschung, including Thomas Lindenberger and Martin Sabrow, helped inspire a critical approach to European development. Colleagues in the EURHISTXX-network such as Henry Rousso broadened my view of contemporary history, while Hannes Siegrist and Rüdiger Hohls invited me to participate in constructing of a Web portal of sources on modern European history and Bo Strath prodded me to confront issues of European memory culture. While Christoph Kleßmann stressed the importance of Eastern Europe, Michael Geyer and Matthias Middell kept insisting on the global embeddedness of European problems. Jürgen Kocka, director of the Wissenschaftszentrum Berlin, Paul Nolte of the Free University, and Christian Ostermann of the Woodrow Wilson International Center for Scholars in Washington provided precious writing time. Andreas Kunz made the maps of the Institut für Europäische Geschichte available, and Kelly McCullough helped with the search for images. Victoria Pardini and Kristen Dolan aided with the preparation of the manuscript, Michal Skalski prepared the index, while Brigitta van Rheinberg provided invaluable editorial guidance. Finally, Hannelore Louise Flessa proved to be a patient guide to the French difference.

I would like to dedicate this volume to my grandchildren Tyson and Charlotte Ober Jarausch as well as Anneliese and Johanna Tracey Jarausch. May its pages provide them with some sense of their European heritage.

NOTES

INTRODUCTION: THE EUROPEAN PARADOX

1. Alexander Geppert, *Fleeting Cities: Imperial Expositions in Fin-de-Siècle Europe* (Houndmills, 2010). For the sake of brevity the endnotes have been kept to a minimum, only indicating direct references and some suggestions for further reading.
2. "1900 Figures Forecast a Century's Dangers," *New York World*, December 30, 1900. Cf. Volker Drehsen and Walter Sparn, "Die Moderne: Kulturkrise und Konstruktionsgeist," in idem, eds., *Vom Weltbildwandel zur Weltanschauungsanalyse: Krisenwahrnehmung und Krisenbewältigung um 1900* (Berlin, 1996), 11–29.
3. Willibald Gutsche, "Jahrhunderterwartungen in Deutschland," in Fritz Klein and Karl Otmar von Aretin, eds., *Europa um 1900* (Berlin, 1989), 377–86.
4. Hans Ulrich Gumbrecht, "Modern, Modernität, Moderne," in Otto Brunner, Werner Conze, and Reinhart Koselleck, eds., *Geschichtliche Grundbegriffe* (Stuttgart, 1978), 4:93–131.
5. Paul Nolte, "Modernization and Modernity in History," *International Encyclopedia of the Social and Behavioral Sciences* (London, 2001), 9954–61.
6. Michael Latham, "Modernization," *International Encyclopedia of the Social Sciences*, 2nd ed. (Detroit, 2008), 232–34. Cf. Peter Wagner, *Modernity as Experience and Interpretation: A New Sociology of Modernity* (Cambridge, 2008).
7. Frederick Cooper, *Colonialism in Question: Theory, Knowledge, History* (Berkeley, 2005); Dipesh Chakrabarty, *Provincializing Europe: Postcolonial Thought and Historical Difference* (Princeton, 2000); and Zygmunt Bauman, *Modernity and the Holocaust* (Cambridge, 1989).
8. Jürgen Kocka, *Das lange 19. Jahrhundert: Arbeit, Nation und bürgerliche Gesellschaft* (Stuttgart, 2004); and Björn Wittrock, "One, None, or Many? European Origins and Modernity as a Global Condition," *Daedalus* 129 (2000), Nr. 1 on "Multiple Modernities."
9. Eugen Weber, *Peasants into Frenchmen: The Modernization of Rural France, 1870–1914* (Stanford, 1976). Cf. Siegfried Weichlein, *Nation und Region: Integrationsprozesse im Bismarckreich* (Düsseldorf, 2004).
10. Peter Fritzsche, *The Turbulent World of Franz Göll: An Ordinary Berliner Writes the Twentieth Century* (Cambridge, MA, 2011). Cf. Ulrich Herbert, *Geschichte Deutschlands im 20. Jahrhundert* (Munich, 2014), 42–65.
11. Florian Greiner, *Wege nach Europa: Deutungen eines imaginieren Kontinents in deutschen, britischen und amerikanischen Printmedien, 1914–1945* (Göttingen, 2014), 352–454.
12. Kenneth Pomeranz, *The Great Divergence: China, Europe, and the Making of the Modern World Economy* (Princeton, 2000).
13. Cheikh Hamidou Kane, *Ambiguous Adventure* (New York, 2012).
14. Walter Rüegg, ed., *Universities in the Nineteenth and Early Twentieth Centuries* (Cambridge, 2004).
15. David S. Landes, *The Unbound Prometheus: Technological Change and Industrial Development in Western Europe from 1750 to the Present*, 2nd ed. (Cambridge, 2003).

Cf. Peer Vries, *Ursprünge des modernen Wirtschaftswachstums: England, China und die Welt in der Frühen Neuzeit* (Göttingen, 2013).

16. Alain Renaut, *The Era of the Individual: A Contribution to a History of Subjectivity* (Princeton, 1997).

17. John Headley, *The Europeanization of the World: The Origins of Human Rights and Democracy* (Princeton, 2008).

18. Benedict Anderson, *Imagined Communities: Reflections on the Origin and Spread of Nationalism*, rev. ed (New York, 2006).

19. Hans Rosenberg, *Bureaucracy, Aristocracy and Autocracy: The Prussian Experiences, 1660–1815* (Boston, 1966).

20. Martin van Creveld, *Technology and War: From 2000 BC to the Present* (New York, 1991).

21. Paul Schroeder, *The Transformation of European Politics, 1763–1848* (Oxford, 1994).

22. Volker R. Berghahn, *Europe in the Era of Two World Wars: From Militarism and Genocide to Civil Society, 1900–1950* (Princeton, 2006).

23. Mark Mazower, *Dark Continent: Europe's Twentieth Century* (New York, 1999); Eric J. Hobsbawm, *Age of Extremes: The Short Twentieth Century, 1914–1991* (London, 1994); Richard Vinen, *A History in Fragments: Europe in the Twentieth Century* (London, 2000); and Tony Judt, *Postwar: A History of Europe Since 1945* (New York, 2005).

24. Eric Dorn Brose, *A History of Europe in the Twentieth Century* (New York, 2005); Robert O. Paxton and Julie Hessler, *Europe in the Twentieth Century*, 5th ed (New York, 2011); Spencer M. Di Scala, *Europe's Long Century: Society, Politics, and Culture 1900–Present* (New York, 2013); and Bernard Wasserstein, *Barbarism and Civilization: A History of Europe in Our Time* (Oxford, 2007).

25. John McCormick, *Europeanism* (Oxford Scholarship on Line, 2010); Winfried Eberhard and Christian Lübke, eds., *Die Vielfalt Europas: Identitäten und Räume* (Leipzig, 2009), 53–56; Rüdiger Hohls, Iris Schröder, and Hannes Siegrist, eds., *Europa und die Europäer: Quellen und Essays zur modernen europäischen Geschichte* (Wiesbaden, 2005).

26. Christoph Cornelißen, "Vom Schreiben einer Geschichte Europas im 20. Jahrhundert," in Martin Sabrow and Frank Bösch, eds., *Zeiträume: Potsdamer Almanach 2012/13* (Göttingen, 2013), 65–86.

27. Claus Leggewie, *Der Kampf um die europäische Erinnerung. Ein Schlachtfeld wird besichtigt* (Munich, 2011).

28. Donald McNeill, *The New Europe: Imagined Spaces* (London, 2004).

29. Norbert Frei, *Was heißt und zu welchem Ende studiert man Geschichte des 20. Jahrhunderts?* (Göttingen, 2006).

30. Lutz Raphael, "Ordnungsmuster der 'Hochmoderne'? Die Theorie der Moderne und die Geschichte der europäischen Gesellschaften im 20. Jahrhundert," in Ute Schneider and Lutz Raphael, eds., *Dimensionen der Moderne: Festschrift für Christoph Dipper* (Frankfurt, 2008), 73–91.

1. GLOBAL DOMINATION

1. R. W. Paul's 1897 film *Queen Victoria's Diamond Jubilee*, http://www.youtube.com/watch?v=HxohzRe9D6w. Cf. Herfried Münkler, "Imperium und Imperialismus," *Dokupedia Zeitgeschichte*, February 11, 2010.

2. Niall Ferguson, *Empire: The Rise and Demise of the British World Order and the Lessons for Global Power* (London, 2002), ix–xxvi, 303–17; Charles S. Maier, *Among Empires: American Ascendancy and Its Predecessors* (Cambridge, MA, 2006).

3. J. A. Hobson, *Imperialism: A Study*, 3rd. ed (London, 1988); Vladimir I. Lenin, *Imperialism, the Highest Stage of Capitalism: A Popular Outline* (London, 1996); Michael Hardt and Antonio Negri, *Empire* (Cambridge, MA, 2000).

4. Jane Burbank and Frederick Cooper, *Empires in World History: Power and Politics of Difference* (Princeton, 2010).

5. In contrast to Frederick Cooper, *Colonialism in Question: Theory, Knowledge, History* (Berkeley, 2005).

6. Jonathan Hart, *Comparing Empires: European Colonialism from Portugese Expansion to the Spanish-American War* (New York, 2003).

7. Harrison M. Wright, ed., *The "New Imperialism": Analysis of Late-Nineteenth-Century Expansion*, 2nd ed. (Lexington, 1976).

8. Parker T. Moon, *Imperialism and World Politics* (New York, 1926); Jörn Leonhard and Ulrike von Hirschhausen, eds., *Comparing Empires: Encounters and Transfers in the Long Nineteenth Century* (Göttingen, 2011), 12.

9. Maria Paula Diogo and Dirk van Laak, "Europeans Globalizing: Mapping, Exploiting, Exchanging," forthcoming in 2015.

10. H. Glenn Penny, *Objects of Culture: Ethnology and Ethnographic Museums in Imperial Germany* (Chapel Hill, 2002).

11. Erika D. Rapaport, *Shopping for Pleasure: Women in the Making of London's West End* (Princeton, 2000).

12. John M. MacKenzie, *Propaganda and Empire: The Manipulation of British Public Opinion, 1880–1960* (Manchester, 1984).

13. Rudyard Kipling, "The White Man's Burden," *McClure's Magazine*, February 1899; Boris Barth and Jürgen Osterhammel, eds., *Zivilisierungsmissionen* (Constance, 2005).

14. Alfred T. Mahan, *The Influence of Seapower upon History, 1660–1783* (New York, 2004); David K. Fieldhouse, *Colonialism, 1870–1945: An Introduction* (London, 1981).

15. Hans-Ulrich Wehler, *Bismarck und der Imperialismus* (Cologne, 1969).

16. David K. Pizzo, "To Devour the Land of the Mkwawa: Colonial Violence and the German-Hehe War in East Africa c. 1884–1914" (PhD dissertation, University of North Carolina, 2008).

17. Winston Churchill, *My Early Life: A Roving Commission* (New York, 1930); and Christian Methfessel, "Spreading the European Model by Military Means? The Legitimization of Colonial Wars and Imperialist Interventions in Great Britain and Germany around 1900," *Comparativ* 22 (2013), 42–60.

18. Dirk van Laak, *Über alles in der Welt: Deutscher Imperialismus im 19. und 20. Jahrhundert* (Munich, 2005).

19. Isak Dinesen, *Out of Africa* (London, 1937).

20. Catherine Coquery-Vidrovitch and Odile Goerg, eds., *La ville européenne outre mers: un modèle conquérant? (XVe–XXe siècles)* (Paris, 1996).

21. Ronald Edward Robinson, *Africa and the Victorians: The Climax of Imperialism on the Dark Continent* (New York, 1961).

22. Robert I. Rotberg and Miles F. Shore, *The Founder: Cecil Rhodes and the Pursuit of Power* (Oxford, 1988).

23. Jacques Fremeaux, "France: Empire and the Mère-Patrie," in Robert Aldrich, ed., *The Age of Empires* (London, 2007), 152–75. Cf. Alice Conklin, *A Mission to Civilize: The Republican Idea of Empire in France and West Africa, 1895–1930* (Stanford, 1995).

24. Eric Ames, Marcia Klotz, and Lora Wildenthal, eds., *Germany's Colonial Pasts* (Lincoln, 2005).
25. Nicholas Doumanis, "The Ottoman Empire: A Resilient Polity," in *Age of Empires*, 26–41.
26. Dominic Lieven, *Empire: The Russian Empire and Its Rivals* (London, 2000).
27. Alan Sked, *The Decline and Fall of the Austrian Empire, 1815–1918* (Harlow, 2001).
28. Marcus Reinkowski and Gregor Thum, eds., *Helpless Imperialists: Imperial Failure, Fear and Radicalization* (Göttingen, 2013).
29. The worst exploitation occurred in the Belgian Congo. Cf. Jean Luc Vellut, "Belgium: The Single-Colony Empire," in *Age of Empires*, 220–37.
30. Lora Wildenthal, *German Women for Empire, 1884–1945* (Durham, 2001). Cf. Anne McClintock, *Imperial Leather: Race, Gender and Sexuality in the Colonial Contest* (Ithaca, 1995).
31. Niels P. Petersson, "Markt, Zivilisierungsmission und Imperialismus," in *Zivilisierungsmissionen*, 33–54.
32. Joachim von Puttkamer, "Schooling, Religion and the Integration of Empire: Education in the Habsburg Monarchy and in Tsarist Russia," in *Comparing Empires*, 359–72.
33. Benedikt Stuchtey, "One Big Imperial Family? Religion and Missions in the Victorian Age," in *Comparing Empires*, 312–36.
34. Andreas Eckert and Michael Pesek, "Bürokratische Ordnung und koloniale Praxis," in Sebastian Conrad and Jürgen Osterhammel, eds., *Das Kaiserreich transnational: Deutschland in der Welt 1871–1914* (Göttingen, 2004), 87–106.
35. Jürgen Osterhammel, ed., *Europa um 1900: Auf der Suche nach einer Sicht "von außen"* (Bochum, 2008).
36. McKenzie, *Propaganda and Empire*, versus Bernard Porter, *The Absent-Minded Imperialists: Empire, Society, and Culture in Britain* (Oxford, 2004).
37. Andrew Zimmerman, *Anthropology and Antihumanism in Imperial Germany* (Chicago, 2001).
38. Jürgen Osterhammel, *Globalization: A Short History* (Princeton, 2005).
39. Andreas Eckert, "Die Verheißung der Bürokratie. Verwaltung als Zivilisierungsagentur im kolonialen Westafrika," in *Zivilisierungsmissionen*, 269–83.
40. Catherine Hall, *Civilizing Subjects: Colony and Metropole in the English Imagination, 1830–1867* (Chicago, 2002).
41. David Canadine, *Ornamentalism: How the British Saw Their Empire* (New York, 2001).
42. Susan D. Pennybacker, *From Scottboro to Munich: Race and Political Culture in 1930s Britain* (Princeton, 2009).
43. Mathew G. Stanard, *Selling the Congo: A History of European Pro-Empire Propaganda and the Making of Belgian Imperialism* (Lincoln, 2011).
44. Anne Godlewska and Neil Smith, eds., *Geography and Empire* (Oxford, 1994).
45. Jügen Osterhammel, *Die Verwandlung der Welt: Eine Geschichte des 19. Jahrhunderts* (Munich, 2009).
46. Dirk van Laak, "Kolonien als 'Laboratorien der Moderne'?" in *Kaiserreich transnational*, 256–79.
47. Felix Driver and David Gilbert, eds., *Imperial Cities: Landscape, Display and Identity* (Manchester, 1999).
48. Paul M. Kennedy, *The Rise and Fall of the Great Powers: Economic Change and Military Conflict from 1500 to 2000* (New York, 1987).

2. BREAKDOWN OF PEACE

1. Vladimir Dedijer, *The Road to Sarajevo* (New York, 1966).
2. Roger Chickering, *Imperial Germany and a World without War: The Peace Movement and German Society, 1892–1914* (Princeton, 1975).
3. Wayne C. Thompson, *In the Eye of the Storm: Kurt Riezler and the Crises of Modern Germany* (Iowa City, 1980).
4. Fritz Fischer, *Germany's Aims in the First World War* (New York, 1967).
5. Christopher Clark, *The Sleepwalkers: How Europe Went to War in 1914* (London, 2012), xxvii; and Herfried Münkler, *Der große Krieg: Die Welt von 1914–1918* (Berlin, 2013).
6. Martin H. Geyer and Johannes Paulmann, eds., *The Mechanics of Internationalism: Culture, Society and Politics from the 1840s to the First World War* (Oxford, 2001).
7. Johannes Paulmann, *Pomp und Politik: Monarchenbegegnungen in Europa zwischen Ançien Regime und Erstem Weltkrieg* (Paderborn, 2000).
8. Sidney Pollard, "Free Trade, Protectionism and the World Economy," in *Mechanics of Internationalism*, 27ff.
9. Niall Ferguson, *The House of Rothschild* (New York, 1998).
10. Madeline Herren, "Governmental Internationalism and the Beginning of a New World Order in the Late Nineteenth Century," in *Mechanics of Internationalism*, 121ff.
11. Peter Paret, *The Berlin Secession: Modernism and Its Enemies in Imperial Germany* (Cambridge, 1980).
12. Fritz Stern, *Einstein's German World* (Princeton, 1999).
13. Sandi E. Cooper, *Patriotic Pacifism: Waging War on War in Europe, 1815–1914* (New York, 1991).
14. Geoff Eley, *Forging Democracy: A History of the Left in Europe, 1850–2000* (New York, 2002).
15. Margaret MacMillan, *The War That Ended Peace: How Europe Abandoned Peace for the First World War* (London, 2013).
16. Hugh Strachan, *The Outbreak of the First World War* (Oxford, 2004).
17. John Breuilly, *Nationalism and the State*, 2nd ed. (Manchester, 1993).
18. James Joll and Gordon Martel, *The Origins of the First World War*, 3rd. ed. (Harlow, 2007).
19. Paul Kennedy, *The Rise of the Anglo-German Antagonism,1860–1914* (London, 1980), 291ff.
20. Hans-Ulrich Wehler, *The German Empire, 1871–1918* (Leamington Spa, 1987).
21. Erskine Childers, *The Riddle of the Sands: A Record of Secret Service Recently Achieved* (London, 1905).
22. Volker R. Berghahn, *Germany and the Approach of War in 1914*, 2nd. ed. (London, 1993).
23. David Stevenson, *Armaments and the Coming of War: Europe, 1904–1914* (Oxford, 1996).
24. Friedrich von Bernhardi, *Germany and the Next War* (New York, 1914).
25. E. Malcolm Carroll, *Germany and the Great Powers, 1866–1914: A Study in Public Opinion and Foreign Policy* (New York, 1938).
26. Klaus Hildebrand, *Deutsche Aussenpolitik, 1871–1918* (Munich, 1989).
27. William L. Langer, *The Franco-Russian Alliance* (New York, reissued 1967).
28. John A. White, *Transition to Global Rivalry: Alliance Diplomacy and the Quadruple Entente, 1895–1907* (Cambridge, 1995).
29. Eugene N. Anderson, *The First Moroccan Crisis, 1904–1906* (Hamden, reissued 1966).

30. Holger Afflerbach, *Der Dreibund: Europäische Großmacht- und Allianzpolitik vor dem Ersten Weltkrieg* (Vienna, 2002), 609ff.

31. Katharine Lerman, *The Chancellor as Courtier: Bernhard von Bülow and the Governance of Germany, 1900–1905* (New York, 1990).

32. Emily Oncken, *Panthersprung nach Agadir: Die Deutsche Politik während der zweiten Marokkokrise 1911* (Düsseldorf, 1981).

33. Richard Hall, *The Balkan Wars, 1912–13: Prelude to the First World War* (London, 2000).

34. Samuel R. Williamson, *The Politics of Grand Strategy: Britain and France Prepare for War, 1904–1914* (Cambridge, 1969).

35. Sean McMeekin, *July 1914: Countdown to War* (New York, 2013).

36. Clark, *Sleepwalkers*, 553–62; and Annika Mombauer, *The Origins of the First World War: Diplomatic and Military Documents* (Manchester, 2013).

37. David MacKenzie, *Black Hand On Trial: Salonika, 1917* (Boulder, 1995).

38. Samuel R. Williamson, *Austria-Hungary and the Origins of the First World War* (New York, 1991).

39. D.C.B. Lieven, *Russia and the Origin of the First World War* (New York, 1983).

40. Konrad H. Jarausch, *The Enigmatic Chancellor: Bethmann Hollweg and the Hubris of Imperial Germany* (New Haven, 1973).

41. Raymond Poidevin, *Les relations économiques et financières entre la France et l'Allemagne 1904–1914* (Paris, 1998).

42. Zara Steiner, *Britain and the Origins of the First World War* (London, 1977); and Niall Ferguson, *The Pity of War* (London, 1998).

43. Frederick A. Dickinson, *War and National Reinvention: Japan in the Great War, 1914–1919* (Cambridge, 1999).

44. Mustafa Aksakal, *The Ottoman Road to War in 1914: The Ottoman Empire and the First World War* (Cambridge, 2008).

45. Clark, *Sleepwalkers*, 555–62; Münkler, *Der große Krieg*, introduction.

46. Richard F. Hamilton and Holger Herwig, eds., *Decisions for War, 1914–1917* (Cambridge, 2004).

47. Konrad H. Jarausch, Daniel Morat, and Markus M. Payk, eds., "World War I and the Twentieth Century: A Roundtable," *Zeithistorische Forschungen*, 2014, No. 1.

48. Marti Koskenniemi, *The Gentle Civilizer of Nations: The Rise and Fall of International Law, 1870–1960* (Cambridge, 2002).

49. John J. Mearsheimer, *The Tragedy of Great Power Politics* (New York, 2001).

50. Jost Dülffer, *Regeln gegen den Krieg? Die Haager Friedenskonferenzen von 1899 und 1907 in der internationalen Politik* (Frankfurt, 1981).

51. Stephen van Evera, "Offense, Defense, and the Causes of War," *International Security* 22 (1998), 5–43.

52. Holger Afflerbach and David Stevenson, eds., *An Improbable War: The Outbreak of World War I and European Political Culture before 1914* (New York, 2007).

53. Hans Joas, *War and Modernity* (Cambridge, 2003).

3. WAGING TOTAL WAR

1. See the diaries and eyewitness accounts in firstworldwar.com/diaries. Cf. Jay Winter and Antoine Prost, *The Great War in History: Debates and Controversies* (Cambridge, 2005).

2. George Lachmann Mosse, *Fallen Soldiers: Reshaping the Memories of the World Wars* (New York, 1990).

3. Roger Chickering and Stig Förster, *Great War, Total War: Combat and Mobilization on the Western Front, 1914–1918* (Cambridge, 2000). Cf. Michael Epkenhans, "Totalisierung des Krieges" (MS, Potsdam, 2014).

4. Paul Fussell, *The Great War and Modern Memory* (New York, 2000).

5. Jennifer D. Keene and Michael S. Neiberg, eds., *Finding Common Ground: New Directions in First World War Studies* (Leiden, 2011).

6. Jeffrey Verhey, *The Spirit of 1914: Militarism, Myth and Mobilization in Imperial Germany* (Cambridge, 2000); and Lancelot L. Farrar, *The Short War Illusion: German Policy, Strategy and Domestic Affairs, August to December 1914* (Santa Barbara, 1973).

7. Niall Ferguson, *The Pity of War* (New York, 1999), 248ff.

8. Hew Strachan, *The First World War*, vol. 1: *To Arms* (Oxford, 2001), 163ff.

9. John Keegan, *The First World War* (New York, 1999), 71ff.

10. Gerhard P. Groß, ed., *Die vergessene Front: Der Osten 1914–1915* (Paderborn, 2006).

11. Keegan, *First World War*, 219ff.

12. David Stevenson, *Cataclysm: The First World War as Political Tragedy* (New York, 2004), 71ff.

13. Stephen Bull, *Trench: A History of Trench Warfare on the Western Front* (Oxford, 2014).

14. Stevenson, *Cataclysm*, 145ff.

15. Keegan, *First World War*, 175ff.

16. Strachan, *First World War*, 1:644ff.

17. Arthur J. Marder, *From Dreadnought to Scapa Flow: The Royal Navy in the Fisher Era, 1904–1919*, 3 vols. (London, 1961–78).

18. Alistair Horne, *The Price of Glory: Verdun, 1916* (New York, 1963).

19. Keegan, *First World War*, 257ff.

20. Stevenson, *Cataclysm*, 199 ff.

21. Bernd Ulrich and Benjamin Ziemann, eds., *German Soldiers in the Great War: Letters and Eyewitness Accounts* (Barnsley, 2010).

22. Marc van Hagen, *War in a European Borderland: Occupations and Occupation Plans in Galicia and the Ukraine* (Seattle, 2007).

23. Fritz Fischer, *Germany's Aims in the First World War* (New York, 1967).

24. Alexander Dallin, *Russian Diplomacy and Eastern Europe, 1914–1917* (New York, 1963).

25. David Stevenson, *French War Aims against Germany* (Oxford, 1982).

26. Victor Rothwell, *British War Aims and Peace Diplomacy, 1914–1918* (Oxford, 1971).

27. Wolfgang Steglich, *Die Friedenspolitik der Mittelmächte, 1917–1918* (Wiesbaden, 1964).

28. Jürgen Kocka, *Facing Total War: German Society, 1914–1918* (Cambridge, 1984).

29. Roger Chickering, *Imperial Germany and the Great War, 1914–1918* (Cambridge, 2004).

30. Jay Winter, ed., *Capital Cities at War: Paris, London, Berlin, 1914–1919*, 2 vols. (Cambridge, 1997, 2007).

31. John Horne, *German Atrocities, 1914: A History of Denial* (New Haven, 2001).

32. Fischer, *Germany's Aims*, 155–83.

33. Strachan, *First World War*, II:815ff, 993ff.

34. Roger Chickering, *The Great War and Urban Life in Germany: Freiburg, 1914–1918* (Cambridge, 2007).

35. Gerald D. Feldman, *Army, Industry and Labor in Imperial Germany, 1914–1918* (Princeton, 1966).

36. Belinda Davis, *Home Fires Burning: Food. Politics and Everyday Life in World War I Berlin* (Chapel Hill, 2000); and Susan R. Grayzel, *Women and the First World War* (Harlow, 2002).

37. Arndt Bauerkämper and Elise Julien, eds., *Durchhalten! Krieg und Gesellschaft im Vergleich, 1914–1918* (Göttingen, 2010).

38. Alfred F. Havinghurst, *Britain in Transition: The Twentieth Century*, 4th ed. (Chicago, 1985), 130–35.
39. Arthur S. Link, *Woodrow Wilson: Revolution, War and Peace* (Arlington Heights, IL, 1979).
40. Dirk Böhnker, "Ein German Way of War? Deutscher Militarismus und maritime Kriegsführung im Ersten Weltkrieg," in Sven Oliver Müller and Cornelius Thorp, eds., *Das Deutsche Kaiserreich in der Kontroverse* (Göttingen, 2009), 308ff.
41. Holger Herwig, *Luxury Fleet: The Imperial German Navy, 1888–1918* (London, 1980).
42. Konrad H. Jarausch, *The Enigmatic Chancellor: Bethmann Hollweg and the Hubris of Imperial Germany* (New Haven, 1973), 264ff.
43. Barbara Tuchman, *The Zimmermann Telegram* (New York, 1966). Cf. Elizabeth Sanders, "The War and Peace Election of 1916" (MS, Ithaca, 2014).
44. Keegan, *First World War*, 392ff.
45. Jörg Nagler, "Pandora's Box: Propaganda and War Hysteria in the US during World War I," in *Great War, Total War*, 485ff.
46. Text in War Poetry Website, http://www.warpoetry.co.uk/owen1.html. Cf. Alan Bishop and Mark Bostridge, eds., *Letters from a Lost Generation: The First World War Letters of Vera Brittain and Four Friends* (Boston, 1999).
47. Alan Kramer, *Dynamic of Destruction: Culture and Mass Killing in the First World War* (Oxford, 2007). Cf. John Horne, "War and Conflict in Contemporary European History," *Zeithistorische Forschungen* 3 (2004), Nr. 1.
48. Laurence Houseman, ed., *War Letters of Fallen Englishmen* (London, 1930); and Jay Winter, ed., *German Students' War Letters* (Philadelphia, 2002).
49. Dorothy Goldman, ed., *Women and World War One: The Written Response* (New York, 1993).
50. Wolfgang J. Mommsen, *Die Urkatastrophe Deutschlands: Der Erste Weltkrieg* (Stuttgart, 2002), vol. 17 of the 10th edition of the Gebhard handbook.

4. BOLSHEVIK REVOLUTION

1. Text in Wladislaw Hedeler, Horst Schützler, and Sonja Strignitz, eds., *Die Russische Revolution 1917: Wegweiser oder Sackgasse?* (Berlin, 1997), 231ff.
2. John Reed, *Ten Days That Shook the World* (New York, 1997); Leon Trotsky, *The History of the Russian Revolution* (Ann Arbor, 1961); and Sergei Eistenstein's films *Battleship Potemkin* and *October*.
3. Jörg Baberowski, "Was war die Oktoberrevolution?" *APuZ* 44–45 (2007); and Ian D. Thatcher, ed., *Reinterpreting Revolutionary Russia* (Houndmills, 2006).
4. Richard Pipes, *Die Russische Revolution*, vol. 2: *Die Macht der Bolschewiki* (Berlin, 1992), versus Sheila Fitzpatarick, *The Russian Revolution* (Oxford, 1982). Cf. Edward Hallett Carr, *The Bolshevik Revolution, 1917–1923*, 3 vols. (New York, 1951–53).
5. Steve Smith, "Writing the History of the Russian Revolution after the Fall of Communism," in Martin A. Miller, *The Russian Revolution: The Essential Readings* (Oxford, 2001), 261–81.
6. Vasilii O. Kliuchevskii, *A History of Russia*, vol. 5 (New York, 1960).
7. Orlando Figes, *Die Tragödie eines Volkes: Die Epoche der russischen Revolution, 1891 bis 1924* (Berlin, 1998), 23ff.
8. Theodore H. von Laue, *Sergei Witte and the Industrialization of Russia* (New York, 1963).
9. Manfred Hildermeier, *Geschichte der Sowjetunion, 1917–1991* (Munich, 1998), 32ff.

10. Helmut Altrichter, *Rußland 1917: Ein Land auf der Suche nach sich selbst* (Paderborn, 1997), 61ff.
11. Pipes, *Russische Revolution*, 2:44ff.
12. Victoria Bonnell, *Roots of Rebellion: Workers' Politics and Organizations in St. Petersburg and Moscow, 1905–1914* (Berkeley, 1983).
13. Benjamin Beuerle, "Westernization as the Way to Modernity—Western Europe in Russian Reform Discussions of the Late Tsarist Empire, 1905–1917," *Comparativ* 22 (2013), 21–41.
14. Karen Petrone, *The Great War in Russian Memory* (Bloomington, 2011).
15. Joshua A. Sanborn, *Drafting the Russian Nation: Military Conscription, Total War, and Mass Politics, 1905–1925* (DeKalb, 2003).
16. Figes, *Tragödie eines Volkes*, 275ff.
17. Altrichter, *Rußland 1917*, 101ff.
18. Figes, *Tragödie eines Volkes*, 313f.
19. Altrichter, *Rußland 1917*, 110ff.
20. Peter Gatrell, *Russia's First World War* (Harlow, 2005).
21. Mike Rapport, *1848: Year of Revolution* (New York, 2008).
22. Robert P. Browder, ed., *The Russian Provisional Government: Documents* (Stanford, 1961).
23. Altrichter, *Rußland 1917*, 132ff.
24. Martin McCauley, ed., *The Russian Revolution and the Soviet State, 1917–1921: Documents* (Basingstoke, 1991), 23–24; Figes, *Tragödie eines Volkes*, 349ff.
25. Hildermeier, *Geschichte der Sowjetunion*, 75ff.
26. Figes, *Tragödie eines Volkes*, 410ff.
27. Altrichter, *Rußland 1917*, 170ff.
28. Hildermeier, *Geschichte der Sowjetunion*, 86ff.
29. Matthew Rendle, *Defenders of the Motherland: The Tsarist Elites in Revolutionary Russia* (Oxford, 2010).
30. Frederick C. Corney, *Telling October: Memory and the Making of the Bolshevik Revolution* (Ithaca, 2004).
31. Robert T. Service, *Lenin: A Political Life*, vols. 2–3 (Basingstoke, 1991–95).
32. Hildermeier, *Geschichte der Sowjetunion*, 98ff. Cf. Donald F. Raleigh, *Revolution on the Volga: 1917 in Saratov* (Ithaca, 1986).
33. Figes, *Tragödie eines Volkes*, 446, 465ff.
34. McCauley, *Russian Revolution*, 113f, 115ff.
35. Altrichter, *Rußland 1917*, 215ff.
36. Hildermeier, *Geschichte der Sowjetunion*, 111ff.
37. Sheila Fitzpatrick, *The Russian Revolution*, 3rd rev. ed. (New York, 2008).
38. McCauley, *Russian Revolution*, 396, 402ff. Cf. Alexander Rabinowitch, *The Bolsheviks in Power: The First Year of Soviet Rule in Petrograd* (Bloomington, 2007).
39. Pipes, *Russische Revolution*, 2:387ff.
40. Hildermeier, *Geschichte der Sowjetunion*, 122ff.
41. Figes, *Tragödie eines Volkes*, 533ff.
42. Hildermeier, *Geschichte der Sowjetunion*, 134ff.
43. Figes, *Tragödie eines Volkes*, 638ff.
44. Hildermeier, *Geschichte der Sowjetunion*, 352.
45. Konrad H. Jarausch, "Kurt Riezler and the Failure of German Ostpolitik, 1918," *Slavic Review* 31 (1972), 381–98.
46. The concept of "defensive modernization" is borrowed from Hans-Ulrich Wehler, *Deutsche Gesellschaftsgeschichte, 1700–1815* (Munich, 1987), 531ff.

47. Altrichter, *Rußland*, 367ff.
48. Service, *Lenin*, 2:216ff.
49. Vladimir I. Lenin, *Collected Works* (Moscow, 1960–70), 30:335. Cf. Jonathan Copper-smith, *The Electrification of Russia, 1880–1926* (Ithaca, 1992).
50. Jörg Baberowski, ed., *Moderne Zeiten? Krieg, Revolution und Gewalt im 20. Jahrhundert* (Göttingen, 2006).

5. DEMOCRATIC HOPES

1. "Appeals to German People," *New York Times*, January 9, 1918; August Heckscher, *Woodrow Wilson* (New York, 1991), 468–74.
2. The multivolume biography by Arthur S. Link remains the best guide to the twenty-eighth American president.
3. Arno Mayer, *Wilson vs. Lenin: Political Origins of the New Diplomacy, 1917–1918* (Cleveland, 1963), 368–93.
4. Harold Nicolson, *Peacemaking 1919* (London, 1964), versus Leon Trotsky, *My Life: An Attempt at an Autobiography* (Mineola, NY, 2007), 362ff.
5. Manfred F. Boehmke, Gerald Feldman, and Elisabeth Glaser, eds., *The Treaty of Versailles: A Reassessment after 75 Years* (Cambridge, 1998); and Gerd Krumeich, *Versailles 1919: Ziele–Wirkung–Wahrnehmung* (Essen, 2001).
6. Amos Perlmutter, *Making the World Safe for Democracy: A Century of Wilsonianism and Its Totalitarian Challengers* (Chapel Hill, 1997).
7. Thorstein Veblen, *Imperial Germany and the Industrial Revolution* (New York, 1915); Hans-Ulrich Wehler, *The German Empire, 1871–1918* (Leamiangton Spa, 1985); and Herfried Münkler, *Der große Krieg: Die Welt von 1914–1918* (Berlin, 2013), introduction.
8. Erich Ludendorff, *Meine Kriegserinnerungen, 1914–1918* (Berlin, 1919), 430–546.
9. Hew Strachan, *The First World War* (New York 2004), 267ff.
10. John Keegan, *The First World War* (New York, 1999), 372ff.
11. Ludendorff, *Kriegserinnerungen*, 583ff.; and Jeffry R. Smith, *A People's War: Germany's Political Revolution, 1913–1918* (Lanham, 2007), 183ff.
12. Harry Rudin, *Armistice, 1918* (Hamden, 1967).
13. Robert Gerwarth and John Horne, eds., *War in Peace: Paramilitary Violence in Europe after the Great War* (Oxford, 2012).
14. Michael Clodfelter, *Warfare and Armed Conflicts—a Statistical Reference to Casualty and Other Figures, 1494–2007* (Jefferson, NC, 2008).
15. Adam Seipp, *The Ordeal of Peace: Demobilization and the Urban Experience in Britain and Germany, 1917–1921* (Farnham, UK, 2009).
16. Ferdinand Czernin, *Versailles 1919: The Forces, Events and Personalities That Shaped the Treaty* (New York, 1964); and Lawrence E. Gelfand, *The Inquiry: American Preparations for Peace, 1917–1919* (New Haven, 1963).
17. Gregor Dallas, *1918: War and Peace* (Woodstock, 2002), 169–522.
18. Alan Sharp, *The Versailles Settlement: Peacemaking after the First World War, 1919–1923* (Basingstoke, 2009), 109–38.
19. Ibid., 139–68.
20. Arno Mayer, *Politics and Diplomacy of Peacemaking: Containment and Counterrevolution at Versailles, 1918–1919* (New York, 1967).
21. Carolyn Kitching, *Britain and the Problem of International Disarmament, 1919–1934* (London, 1999).

22. John Maynard Keynes, *The Economic Consequences of the Peace* (New York, 1920); and Margaret McMillan, *Paris 1919: Six Months That Changed the World* (New York, 2002), 180–93.

23. Erez Manela, *The Wilsonian Moment: Self-determination and the International Origins of Anticolonial Nationalism* (Oxford, 2007).

24. Jonathan Schneer, *The Balfour Declaration: The Origins of the Arab-Israeli Conflict* (London, 2010).

25. John N. Snell, "Wilson on Germany and the Fourteen Points," *Journal of Modern History* 26 (1954), 364–69.

26. T. Ivan Berend, *Decades of Crisis: Central and Eastern Europe before World War II* (Berkeley, 1998).

27. Seipp, *Ordeal of Peace*, 203ff.

28. David A. Adelman, *A Shattered Peace: Versailles 1919 and the Price We Pay Today* (Hoboken, NJ, 2008), 84ff.

29. A. J. Ryder, *The German Revolution of 1918: A Study of German Socialism in War and Revolt* (Cambridge, 1967).

30. Arthur Rosenberg, *A History of the German Republic* (New York, 1965); and Detlev Peuckert, *The Weimar Republic: The Crisis of Classical Modernity* (New York, 1992).

31. Anton Pelinka, "Intentionen und Konsequenzen der Zerschlagung Österreich-Ungarns," in *Versailles 1919*, 202–10.

32. Jon Jacobson, "The Soviet Union and Versailles," in *Treaty of Versailles*, 451–68.

33. Carole Fink, *Defending the Rights of Others: The Great Powers, the Jews, and International Minority Protection, 1878–1938* (New York, 2004).

34. Hugh Seton-Watson, *Eastern Europe between the Wars, 1918–1941*, 3rd ed. (Hamden, 1962).

35. David Lloyd George, *Memoirs of the Peace Conference*, 2 vols. (New York, 1939). Cf. Alfred F. Havinghurst, *Britain in Transition: The Twentieth Century*, 4th ed. (Chicago, 1985), 158–78.

36. Patrik Renshaw, *The General Strike* (London, 1975).

37. Robert Fitzroy Foster, *Modern Ireland, 1600–1972* (London, 1988).

38. Christopher Fischer, *Alsace to the Alsatians: Visions and Divisions of Alsatian Regionalism, 1870–1939* (New York, 2010), 128ff.

39. John F. Keiger, *Raymond Poincaré* (Cambridge, 1997).

40. Conan Fischer, *The Ruhr Crisis, 1923–1924* (Oxford, 2003).

41. Wilfried Loth, *Geschichte Frankreichs im 20. Jahrhundert* (Stuttgart, 1987), 33–65.

42. Severine Ansart et al., "Mortality Burden of the 1918–1919 Influenza Pandemic in Europe," *Influenza and Other Respiratory Viruses* 3 (2009), 99–106.

43. Ruth B. Henig, *The League of Nations* (London, 2010). Cf. Susan Pedersen, "Back to the League of Nations: Review Essay," *American Historical Review* 112 (2007), 1091–1117.

44. F. S. Northedge, *The League of Nations: Its Life and Times, 1920–1946* (Leicester, 1986).

45. Carole Fink, Axel Frohn, and Jürgen Heideking, eds., *Genoa, Rapallo and European Reconstruction in 1922* (Cambridge, 1991).

46. Stephen Schuker, *The End of French Predominance in Europe: The Financial Crisis of 1924 and the Adoption of the Dawes Plan* (Chapel Hill, 1976). Cf. Mark Swartzburg, "The Call for America: German-American Relations and the European Crisis, 1921–1924" (PhD dissertation, University of North Carolina, 2005).

47. Gaynor Johnson, ed., *Locarno Revisited: European Diplomacy, 1920–1929* (London, 2004).

48. Sally Marks, *The Illusion of Peace: International Relations in Europe, 1918–1923* (New York, 2003).

49. Jon Jacobson, *Locarno Diplomacy: Germany and the West, 1925-1929* (Princeton, 1972).
50. Marc Trachtenberg, "Versailles after Sixty Years," *Journal of Contemporary History* 17 (1982), 487–506. Cf. Patrick O. Cohrs, *The Unfinished Peace after World War I: America, Britain and the Stabilization of Europe, 1919-1932* (Cambridge, 2006).
51. Arno Mayer, *The Persistence of the Old Regime: Europe to the Great War* (New York, 1981).
52. Joseph Rothschild, *East Central Europe between the Two World Wars* (Seattle, 1974).
53. Pieter M. Judson and Marsha L. Rozenblit, eds., *Constructing Nationalities in East Central Europe* (New York, 2005).
54. Alan Sharp, *Consequences of Peace: The Versailles Settlement: Aftermath and Legacy, 1920-2010* (London, 2010).
55. Wolfgang J. Mommsen, "Der Vertrag von Versailles. Eine Bilanz," in *Versailles: 1919*, 351–60. Cf. Norman Graebner and Edward M. Bennett, *The Versailles Treaty and Its Legacy: The Failure of the Wilsonian Vision* (New York, 2011).

6. FASCIST ALTERNATIVE

1. Benito Mussolini, *My Rise and Fall* (New York, 1998), 68ff.; Stanley Payne, *A History of Fascism, 1914-1945* (Madison, 1995), 89ff.
2. Zeev Sternhell, *The Birth of Fascist Ideology: From Cultural Rebellion to Political Revolution* (Princeton, 1994), 221ff.
3. David Roberts, "How Not to Think about Fascism and Ideology: Intellectual Antecedents and Historical Meaning," *Journal of Contemporary History* 35 (2000), 185–211.
4. Payne, *A History of Fascism*, 3–14, is more comprehensive than Ernst Nolte, *Three Faces of Fascism* (New York, 1966). Cf. Robert O. Paxton, *The Anatomy of Fascism* (New York, 2004), 206–20.
5. Roger Griffin and Matthew Feldman, eds., *Fascism: Critical Concepts in Political Science*, vols. 1–4 (London, 2004).
6. Mark Choate, *Emigrant Nation: The Making of Italy Abroad* (Cambridge, MA, 2008).
7. Denis Mack Smith, *Modern Italy: A Political History*, rev. ed. (Ann Arbor, 1997), 3–24.
8. Manfred Clark, *Modern Italy: 1871 to the Present*, 3rd ed. (Harlow, 2008), 54ff.
9. Ibid., 99ff.
10. Mack Smith, *Modern Italy*, 41–47.
11. Clark, *Modern Italy*, 84 ff., 133ff. Cf. also Paul Corner, "The Road to Fascism: An Italian *Sonderweg?*" *Contemporary European History* 11 (2002), 273–95.
12. Mack Smith, *Modern Italy*, 115ff., 163ff., 241ff.
13. Clark, *Modern Italy*, 217–43.
14. Michael Ledeen, *The First Duce: D'Annunzio at Fiume* (Baltimore, 1977).
15. Clark, *Modern Italy*, 247–53.
16. Nicholas Farrell, *Mussolini: A New Life* (London, 2003), 1–75.
17. Mussolini, *My Rise and Fall*, 1–56. The leading biography is the multi-volume work by Renzo de Felice, *Mussolini* (Torino, 1965–98).
18. Farrell, *Mussolini*, 75–105.
19. George Lachmann Mosse, *Nationalism and Sexuality* (New York, 1985), as the first in a long line of scholars.
20. Farrell, *Mussolini*, 95ff.
21. Mussolini, *My Rise and Fall*, 120; Clark, *Modern Italy*, 256–66.
22. Mack Smith, *Modern Italy*, 282–308.
23. William Brustein, "The 'Red Menace' and the Rise of Italian Fascism," *American Sociological Review* 56 (1991), 652–64; and E. Spencer Wellhofer, "Democracy and

Fascism: Class, Civil Society, and Rational Choice in Italy," *American Political Science Review* 97 (2003), 91–106.

24. Mussolini, *My Rise and Fall*, 169–88.
25. Clark, *Modern Italy*, 266ff.
26. Farrell, *Mussolini*, 135ff. Cf. Paul Corner, *The Fascist Party and Popular Opinion in Mussolini's Italy* (Oxford, 2012).
27. Christopher Duggan, *Fascist Voices: An Intimate History of Mussolini's Italy* (London, 2012).
28. Stuart Joseph Wolf, ed., *European Fascism* (New York, 1969).
29. Benito Mussolini, *Fascism: Doctrine and Institutions* (Rome, 1935), 14.
30. Ivone Kirkpatrick, *Mussolini: A Study in Power* (New York, 1964); Farrell, *Mussolini*, 161ff.
31. Mack Smith, *Modern Italy*, 337–47.
32. Clark, *Modern Italy*, 315–31.
33. Farrell, *Mussolini*, 199–213.
34. Clark, *Modern Italy*, 290–96.
35. Victoria de Grazia, *The Culture of Consent: Mass Organization of Leisure in Fascist Italy* (Cambridge, 1981).
36. Mack Smith, *Modern Italy*, 367–74.
37. Philip Morgan, *Italian Fascism, 1815–1945*, 2nd ed. (Basingstoke, 2004).
38. Konrad H. Jarausch, *The Four Power Pact, 1933* (Madison, 1965).
39. Farell, *Mussolini*, 254–80.
40. Hugh Thomas, *The Spanish Civil War*, anniv. ed. (New York, 2011).
41. Gerhard L. Weinberg, *Hitler's Foreign Policy: The Road to World War Two, 1933–1939*, comb. ed. (New York, 2005).
42. Emil Ludwig, *Mussolinis Gespräche mit Emil Ludwig* (Berlin, 1932); and Farrell, *Mussolini*, 157ff., 225ff.
43. Richard Griffiths, *An Intelligent Person's Guide to Fascism* (London, 2000), 72ff.; Payne, *History of Fascism*, 245ff.
44. Clark, *Modern Italy*, 301ff.
45. Barrington Moore, *Social Origins of Dictatorship and Democracy: Lord and Peasant in the Making of the Modern World* (Boston, 1966). Cf. also Renzo de Felice, *Interpretations of Fascism* (Cambridge, MA, 1977), 174–92.
46. Juan J. Linz, *Totalitarian and Authoritarian Regimes* (Boulder, 2000). Cf. Griffin and Feldman, *Fascism*, vol. 2.
47. A. James Gregor, "Fascism and Modernization: Some Addenda," *World Politics* 26 (1974), 370–84; and Jon S. Cohen, "Was Italian Fascism a Developmental Dictatorship? Some Evidence to the Contrary," *Economic History Review* 41 (1988), 95–113.
48. Andrew Hewitt, *Fascist Modernism: Aesthetics, Politics and the Avant-garde* (Stanford, 1993): Ruth Ben-Ghiat, *Fascist Modernities: Italy, 1922–1945* (Berkeley, 2001). Cf. Griffin and Feldman, *Fascism*, vol. 3.
49. Roger Griffin, "Modernity, Modernism, and Fascism. A 'Mazeway Resynthesis,'" *Modernism/modernity* 15 (2008), 9–24.

7. MODERNIST PROVOCATIONS

1. For Dada manifestos and images see http://www.dada-companion.com.
2. Eve M. Duffy, "Representing Science and Technology: Politics and Display in the Deutsches Museum, 1903–1945" (PhD dissertation, University of North Carolina, 2002).

3. Thomas Rohkrämer, *Eine andere Moderne? Zvilisationskritik, Natur und Technik in Deutschland 1880–1933* (Paderborn, 1999), 9–36.
4. Peter Gay, *Weimar Culture: The Outsider as Insider* (New York, 1968).
5. John A. Williams, ed., *Weimar Culture Revisited* (Basingstoke, 2011).
6. Carl E. Schorske, *Fin-de-siècle Vienna: Politics and Culture* (New York, 1981).
7. Peter Watson, *German Genius* (New York, 2010), 341–97; and Peter Gay, *Freud, Jews and Other Germans: Masters and Victims in Modernist Culture* (New York, 1978).
8. David S. Landes, *The Unbound Prometheus: Technological Change and Industrial Development in Western Europe from 1750 to the Present* (London, 1969), 231–358.
9. Peter Paret, *The Berlin Secession: Modernism and Its Enemies in Imperial Germany* (Cambridge, MA, 1980). Cf. Staatliche Museen zu Berlin, ed., *Das XX. Jahrhundert: Ein Jahrhundert Kunst in Deutschland* (Berlin, 1999).
10. Alex Ross, *The Rest Is Noise: Listening to the Twentieth Century* (New York, 2007), 3–73.
11. Neil Blackadder, *Performing Opposition: Modern Theater and the Scandalized Audience* (Westport, 2003).
12. Collections like Maynard Mack, ed., *The Norton Anthology of World Masterpieces*, 4th ed. (New York, 1979), have a strong Anglocentric bias.
13. Mary Ann Caws, *Pablo Picasso* (London, 2005). Cf. Werner Haftmann, *Painting in the Twentieth Century* (New York, 1965).
14. Paul Fussell, *The Great War and Modern Memory* (Oxford, 1975).
15. Modris Eksteins, *Rites of Spring: The Great War and the Birth of the Modern Age* (Boston, 1989), 139ff.
16. Jay Winter, *Remembering War: The Great War between Memory and History in the Twentieth Century* (New Haven, 2006).
17. Harvard H. Arnason and Elizabeth C. Mansfield, *A History of Modern Art: Painting, Sculpture, Architecture, Photography*, 6th ed. (Upper Saddle River, NJ, 2010).
18. Ross, *The Rest Is Noise*, 74–119, 178–212.
19. Kenneth Douglas and Sarah N. Lawall, "Masterpieces of the Modern World," in *The Norton Anthology of World Masterpieces*, 2:1231–1308.
20. Tom Gunning, *The Films of Fritz Lang: Allegories of Vision and Modernity* (London, 2000).
21. Fussell, *Great War*, 310ff.
22. Adelheid von Saldern, ed., *The Challenge of Modernity: German Social and Cultural Studies, 1890–1960* (Ann Arbor, 2002).
23. Peter Fritzsche, *Reading Berlin 1900* (Cambridge, MA, 1996).
24. David L. Morton, *Sound Recording: The Life Story of a Technology* (Westport, 2004).
25. Kristin Thompson and Richard Bordwell, *Film History: An Introduction* (Boston, 2003); and Siegfried Krakauer, *From Caligari to Hitler: A Psychological History of German Film* (Princeton, 2004).
26. Karl-Christian Führer and Corey Ross, eds., *Mass Media: Culture and Society in Twentieth Century Germany* (Basingstoke, 2006).
27. Arnd Krüger and Else Transbaek, eds., *The History of Physical Education and Sport from European Perspectives* (Copenhagen, 1999); and David Clay Large, *Nazi Games: The Olympics of 1936* (New York, 2007).
28. Bill Cormack, *A History of Holidays, 1812–2000* (London, 1998).
29. Elisabeth Otto and Vanessa Rocco, eds., *The New Woman International: Representations in Photography and Film from the 1870s through the 1960s* (Ann Arbor, 2011). Cf. Marie Louise Roberts, "Samson and Delilah Revisited: The Politics of Women's Fashions in 1920s France," *American Historical Review* 98 (1993), 657–84.
30. John Willett, *Art and Politics in the Weimar Period: The New Sobriety, 1917–1933* (New York. 1996).

31. Watson, *German Genius*, 480–84, 595–99.
32. Mary Nolan, *Visions of Modernity: American Business and the Modernization of Germany* (New York, 1994).
33. Frederic J. Schwartz, *The Werkbund: Design Theory and Mass Culture before the First World War* (New Haven, 1996); Michael Siebenbrodt and Lutz Schöbe, *Bauhaus, 1911–1933: Weimar-Dessau-Berlin* (New York, 2009).
34. Emile Langui, ed., *50 Jahre moderne Kunst* (Cologne, 1959).
35. Martin Esslin, *Bertolt Brecht* (New York, 1969).
36. Thoma Mann, "Autobiography," http://www.nobelprize.org/nobel_prizes/literature/laureates/1929/mann-bio.html; and Anthony Heilbut, *Thomas Mann: Eros and Literature* (New York, 1997).
37. Martin Jay, *The Dialectical Imagination: A History of the Frankfurt School and the Institute for Social Research, 1923–1950* (Berkeley, 1996).
38. Herbert Strauss, ed., *Hostages of Modernization: Studies on Modern Anti-Semitism, 1870–1933/39* (Berlin, 1993), pt. 1 on Germany, Great Britain, and France.
39. Michael Burleigh, *Earthly Powers: The Clash of Religion and Politics from the French Revolution to the Great War* (New York, 2005).
40. Konrad H. Jarausch, *Students, Society and Politics in Imperial Germany: The Rise of Academic Illiberalism* (Princeton, 1982), 348–56.
41. Fritz Stern, *The Politics of Cultural Despair: A Study in the Rise of the Germanic Ideology* (Berkeley, 1961); and George L. Mosse, *The Crisis of German Ideology: Intellectual Origins of the Third Reich* (New York, 1964).
42. John Carey, *The Intellectuals and the Masses: Pride and Prejudice among the Literary Intelligentsia, 1880–1939* (London, 1992).
43. Yvonne Sherrat, *Hitler's Philosophers* (New Haven, 2013).
44. Zeev Sternhell, *The Birth of Fascist Ideology: From Cultural Rebellion to Political Revolution* (Princeton, 1994). Thomas Höpel, "Die Abwehr 'artfremder' internationaler Kunst im Nationalsozialismus," at http://www.europa.clio-online.de/.
45. Eric D. Weitz, *Weimar Germany: Promise and Tragedy* (Princeton, 2007).
46. Anton Kaes, Martin Jay, and Edward Dimendberg, eds., *The Weimar Republic Sourcebook* (Berkeley, 1994).
47. Debbie Lewer, "Revolution and the Weimar Avant-Garde: Contesting the Politics of Art, 1919–1924," in *Weimar Culture Revisited*, 1–21.
48. Peter D. Stachura, *The German Youth Movement, 1900–1945: An Interpretative and Documentary History* (New York, 1981).
49. Wendy Perry, "Remembering Dreyfus: The Ligue des Droits de L'homme and the Making of the Modern French Human Rights Movement" (PhD dissertation, University of North Carolina, 1998).
50. Detlev J. K. Peukert, *The Weimar Republic: The Crisis of Classical Modernity* (New York, 1992).

8. DEVASTATING DEPRESSION

1. "World Bank's Aid Sought by Austria" and "Bankers Here Seek Means to Aid Berlin," *New York Times*, May 13 and July 14, 1931. Cf. Harold James, *The German Slump: Politics and Economics, 1926–1936* (Oxford, 1986).
2. Ivan T. Berend, *An Economic History of Twentieth Century Europe: Economic Regimes from Laissez-Faire to Globalization* (Cambridge, 2006), 61ff.

3. Carmen Reinhart and Kenneth S. Rogoff, *This Time Is Different: A Panoramic View of Eight Centuries of Financial Crisis* (Princeton, 2009). Cf. Barry Eichengreen and Peter Temin, "The Gold Standards and the Great Depression," *Contemporary European History* 9 (2000), 183–207.

4. Joseph Schumpeter, *Capitalism, Socialism and Democracy* (New York, 1942); and Konrad H. Jarausch, *The Unfree Professions: German Lawyers, Teachers and Engineers, 1900–1950* (New York, 1990), 80ff.

5. Barry Eichengreen, "Viewpoint: Understanding the Great Depression," *Canadian Journal of Economics* 37 (2004), 1–27; and Harold James, *The End of Globalization: Lessons from the Great Depression* (Cambridge, MA, 2001).

6. John Maynard Keynes, *The Economic Consequences of the Peace* (New York, 1920).

7. Berend, *Economic History*, 50ff.

8. Michael Clodfelter, *Warfare and Armed Conflicts: A Statistical Reference to Casualty and Other Figures, 1500–2000*, 2nd ed. (Jefferson, NC, 2002).

9. Berend, *Economic History*, 564f.

10. Patricia Clavin, *The Great Depression in Europe, 1929–1939* (New York, 2000), 26ff.

11. Adam Tooze, *The Deluge: The Great War and the Remaking of Global Order, 1916–1931* (London, 2014).

12. Jürgen Osterhammel, *Globalisation: A Short History* (Princeton, 2005).

13. Clavin, *Great Depression*, 30ff.

14. Gerald D. Feldman, *The Great Disorder: Politics, Economics and Society in the German Inflation, 1914–1924* (New York, 1993).

15. Carl-Ludwig Holtfrerich, *The German Inflation, 1914–1924: Causes and Effects in International Perspective* (New York, 1986).

16. Conan Fischer, *The Ruhr Crisis, 1923–1924* (Oxford, 2003).

17. Stephen A. Schuker, *The End of French Predominance in Europe: The Financial Crisis of 1924 and the Adoption of the Dawes Plan* (Chapel Hill, 1976).

18. Berend, *Economic History*, 56ff.

19. Peter Jelavich, *Berlin Alexanderplatz: Radio, Film, and the Death of Weimar Culture* (Berkeley, 2009).

20. Clavin, *Great Depression*, 68ff.

21. Michael Tracy, "Agriculture in the Great Depression: World Market Developments and European Protectionism," in Herman Van der Wee, ed., *The Great Depression Revisited* (The Hague, 1972), 91–119.

22. Christoph Buchheim, "The 'Crisis before the Crisis'—the Export Engine Out of Gear," in Harold James, ed., *The Interwar Depression in an International Context* (Munich, 2002), 113–22.

23. Mary Nolan, *Visions of Modernity: American Business and the Modernization of Germany* (New York, 1994).

24. Robert Beevers, *The Garden City Utopia: A Critical Biography of Ebenezer Howard* (New York, 1988).

25. Bärbel Schrader and Jürgen Schebera, eds., *The "Golden" Twenties: Art and Literature in the Weimar Republic* (New Haven, 1988).

26. Thomas E. Hall and J. David Ferguson, *The Great Depression: An International Disaster of Perverse Economic Policies* (Ann Arbor 1998), 57ff.; and John Kenneth Galbraith, *The Great Crash, 1929*, rev. ed. (Boston, 1988).

27. John A Garraty, *The Great Depression: An Inquiry into the Causes, Course and Consequences of the Worldwide Depression of the Nineteen-Thirties as Seen by Contemporaries and in the Light of History* (Garden City, 1987), 28–49.

28. Berend, *Economic History*, 61ff.

29. Herinrich August Winkler, *Weimar 1918–1933: Die Geschichte der ersten deutschen Demokratie* (Munich, 1993, 409–43.

30. Hans Jaeger, "Business in the Great Depression," in *Great Depression Revisited*, 134–42.

31. For contrasting figures see Berend, *Economic History*, 71, and Clavin, *Great Depression*, 132.

32. The German figure of 43.7% in 1932, cited by Clavin, *Great Depression*, 112, seems a bit high. Cf. Alfred F. Havinghurst, *Britain in Transition: The Twentieth Century*, 4th ed. (Chicago, 1985), 221–40.

33. Maria Jagoda, Paul Lazarsfeld, and Hans Zeisel, *Marienthal: The Sociography of an Unemployed Community* (Chicago, 1971); and Garraty, *Great Depression*, 100–113

34. Hans Fallada, *Kleiner Mann, was nun?* (Berlin, 1932); and George Orwell, *The Road to Wigan Pier* (London, 1937).

35. *Men Without Work: A Report Made to the Pilgrim Trust* (Cambridge, 1938), 144–49. Garraty, *Great Depression*, 113–26.

36. From "Our Poverty–Your Responsibility," *Labour Magazine* 9, No. 1 (May 1932), 29–31.

37. Winkler, *Weimar*, 477ff.

38. Paul Nolte, *Was ist Demokratie? Geschichte und Gegenwart* (Munich, 2012), 258–71.

39. Vincent Barnett, *John Maynard Keynes* (New York, 2013); and Garraty, *Great Depression*, 128ff.

40. Clavin, *Great Depression*, 127ff., 147ff.

41. Ibid., 130ff.; and Hall and Ferguson, *Great Depression*, 85ff.

42. Garraty, *Great Depression*, 220–35; and Wilfried Loth, *Geschichte Frankreichs im 20. Jahrhundert* (Stuttgart, 1987), 70–95.

43. Francis Sejersted, *The Age of Social Democracy: Norway and Sweden in the Twentieth Century* (Princeton, 2011).

44. Cf. Kiran Klaus Patel, *Soldiers of Labor: Labor Service in Nazi Germany and New Deal America, 1933–1945* (New York, 2005).

45. Richard Overy, *The Nazi Economic Recovery*, 2nd ed. (Cambridge, 1995); and Adam Tooze, *Wages of Destruction: The Making and Breaking of the Nazi Economy* (London, 2006).

46. Hall and Ferguson, *Great Depression*, 131ff.; and Garraty, *Great Depression*, 245ff.

47. Hall and Ferguson, *Great Depression*, 160.

48. Lutz Niethammer, ed., *Lebensgeschichte und Sozialkultur im Ruhrgebiet 1930 bis 1960*, 2 vols. (Berlin, 1983). Cf. also Studs Terkel, *Hard Times: An Oral History of the Great Depression* (New York, 1970).

49. Jarausch, *Unfree Professions*, 80ff.

50. David Caute, *The Fellow Travelers: Intellectual Friends of Communism*, rev. ed. (New Haven, 1988), 1–19.

51. Alastair Hamilton, *The Appeal of Fascism: A Study of Intellectuals and Fascism, 1919–1945* (New York, 1971); and Elliot Neaman, "Mutiny on Board Modernity: Heidegger, Sorel and other Fascist Intellectuals," *Critical Review* 9 (1995), 371–401.

9. STALINIST MODERNIZATION

1. "Huge Industries Planned by Soviet," *New York Times*, April 26, 1929; and Walter Duranty, "Stalin Dominates Fete of Revolution," ibid., November 8, 1929.

2. Hubert R. Knickerbocker, "The Soviet Five Year Plan," *International Affairs* 10 (1931), 433–59.

3. Jan Plamper, *The Stalin Cult: A Study in the Alchemy of Power* (New Haven, 2012).
4. Stephane Courtois et al., *The Black Book of Communism: Crimes, Terror, Repression* (Cambridge, 1999).
5. For instance Robert Conquest, *Lenin* (London, 1972).
6. Robert C. Tucker, ed., *Lenin Anthology* (New York, 1975); and George Brinkley, "Leninism: What It Was and What It Was Not," *Review of Politics* 60 (1998), 151–64.
7. Jörg Baberowski, *Verbrannte Erde: Stalins Herrschaft der Gewalt* (Munich, 2012).
8. Robert Service, *Stalin: A Biography* (New York, 2004), 96–100.
9. Robert Service, *A History of Modern Russia: From Tsarism to the Twenty-First Century*, 3rd ed. (Harvard, 2009), 123–49.
10. Service, *Stalin*, 209–18. Some scholars claim that the testament was forged.
11. Ibid., 219–22.
12. Adam Ulam, "Lenin: His Legacy," *Foreign Affairs* 48 (1970), 460–70.
13. This critical attitude still inspires most of the biographies such as Isaac Deutscher's classic *Stalin: A Political Biography*, 2nd rev. ed. (London, 1966).
14. Service, *Stalin*, 13–42.
15. Deutscher, *Stalin*, 27–128; Service, *Stalin*, 43–112.
16. Deutscher, *Stalin*, 129–72; Service, *Stalin*, 113–57.
17. Deutscher, *Stalin*, 173–227; Service, *Stalin*, 157–85.
18. Deutscher, *Stalin*, 228–73; Service, *Stalin*, 219–29.
19. Deutscher, *Stalin*, 273–93; Service, *Stalin*, 240–50.
20. Most of the explanations focus on concrete economic problems or on the rivalry with Bukharin rather than on the more fundamental reasons for the great change. Cf. Service, *History of Modern Russia*, 169ff.
21. R. W. Davies, *The Soviet Collective Farm, 1929–1930* (Cambridge, MA, 1980).
22. W. Ladejinsky, "Collectivization of Agriculture in the Soviet Union," *Political Science Quarterly* 49 (1934), 1–43.
23. Robert Conquest, *The Harvest of Sorrow: Soviet Collectivization and the Terror Famine* (Edmonton, 1986); and Timothy Snyder, *Bloodlands: Europe between Hitler and Stalin* (New York, 2010).
24. Sheila Fitzpatrick, *Stalin's Peasants: Resistance and Survival in the Russian Village after Collectivization* (Oxford, 1994).
25. Holland Hunter, "The Overambitious First Soviet Five-Year Plan," *Slavic Review* 32 (1973), 237–57.
26. Knickerbocker, "Soviet Five Year Plan," 437ff.
27. Samuel N. Harper, "Soviet Five-Year Plan," *American Academy of Political Science* 14 (1931), 422ff.
28. Hunter, "Overambitious," 241ff.
29. Service, *Stalin*, 264–75.
30. Stephen Kotkin, *Magnetic Mountain: Stalinism as Civilization* (Berkeley, 1995).
31. Robert Conquest, *The Great Terror: A Reassessment*, 40th anniv. ed. (New York, 2008), vii–xxvi.
32. Ibid., 341ff.; and Karl Schlögl, *Moscow 1937* (Cambridge, 2012).
33. Norman Naimark, *Stalin's Genocides* (Princeton, 2010), 99ff.
34. Jochen Hellbeck, *Revolution on My Mind: Writing a Diary under Stalin* (Cambridge, MA, 2006).
35. Anne Applebaum, *GULAG: A History* (New York, 2003), xv–xl.
36. Arthur Koestler, *Darkness at Noon* (London, 1941); Aleksandr Solzhenitzyn, *A Day in the Life of Ivan Denisovich* (New York, 1963); and idem, *The GULAG Archipelago, 1918–1956* (New York, 1973).

37. Henry Reichman, "Reconsidering 'Stalinism,'" *History and Theory* 17 (1988), 57–89.
38. Plamper, *Stalin Cult*, viii–xx.
39. Sheila Fitzpatrick, *Everyday Stalinism: Ordinary Life in Extraordinary Times: Soviet Russia in the 1930s* (New York, 1999).
40. Alexei Rybakov, "'Es wird ganz Deutschland einstmals Stalin danken.' Johanns R. Bechers, *Stalin-Oden* und die Strukturen der totalitären 'Kultur,'" *FORUM für osteuropäische Ideen- und Zeitgeschichte* (2004), Nr. 1.
41. Service, *Stalin*, 491–530.
42. Zhores Medvedev, "Riddles Surrounding Stalin's Death," in Roy and Zhores Medvedev, *The Unknown Stalin: His Life, Death, and Legacy* (Woodstock, 2004), 11–42.
43. Service, *Stalin*, 571–90.
44. Roy Medvedev, "The Twentieth Party Congress: Before and After," in *Unknown Stalin*, 102–18.
45. Vladislav M. Zubok, *A Failed Empire: The Soviet Union in the Cold War from Stalin to Gorbachev* (Chapel Hill, 2007).
46. Service, *Stalin*, 298–309. Even a critic like Deutscher still defends the project: *Stalin*, 627–30.
47. Alexander Chubarov, *Russia's Bitter Path to Modernity: A History of the Soviet and Post-Soviet Eras* (New York, 2001), 101–10.
48. Paul R. Gregory, ed., *Behind the Façade of Stalin's Command Economy* (Stanford, 2001), 11ff.
49. David Satter, *It Was a Long Time Ago, and It Never Happened Anyway: Russia and the Communist Past* (New Haven, 2012).

10. HITLER'S *VOLKSGEMEINSCHAFT*

1. "Berlin Reds Urge Strike," *New York Times*, January 31, 1933. Cf. Graf Harry Kessler, *Tagebücher 1918–1937: Politik, Kunst und Gesellschaft der Zwanziger Jahre* (Frankfurt, 1961), 704; and Victor Klemperer, *Ich will Zeugnis ablegen bis zum letzten: Tagebücher 1933–1941* (Berlin, 1995), 6.
2. Peter Fritzsche, *Germans into Nazis* (Cambridge, MA, 1998), 210ff.
3. Norbert Frei, "Wie modern war der Nationalsozialismus?" *Geschichte und Gesellschaft* 19 (1993), 367–87; and Günter Könke, "'Modernisierungsschub' oder relative Stagnation?" ibid., 20 (1994), 584–608.
4. Jeffrey Herf, *Reactionary Modernism: Technology, Culture and Politics in Weimar and the Third Reich* (Cambridge, MA, 1984); and Paul Betts, "The New Fascination with Fascism: The Case of Nazi Modernism," *Journal of Contemporary History* 37 (2002), 541–58.
5. Ian Kershaw, *The Nazi Dictatorship: Problems and Perspectives of Interpretation* (London, 1989).
6. Eric Weitz, *Weimar Germany: Promise and Tragedy* (Princeton, 2007).
7. Kessler, *Tagebücher*, 20; A. J. Ryder, *The German Revolution of 1918: A Study of German Socialism in War and Revolt* (Cambridge, 1967).
8. Hans Mommsen, *The Rise and Fall of Weimar Democracy* (Chapel Hill, 1996).
9. Eberhard Kolb, *Gustav Stresemann* (Munich, 2003); and Robert P. Grathwohl, *Stresemann and the DNVP: Reconciliation or Revenge in German Foreign Policy, 1924–1928* (Lawrence, 1990).
10. Peter Gay, *Weimar Culture: The Outsider as Insider* (New York, 1970); and Detlev Peukert, *The Weimar Republic: The Crisis of Classical Modernity* (New York, 1989).

11. Anna von der Goltz, *Hindenburg: Power, Myth, and the Rise of the Nazis* (New York, 2009).
12. Henry Ashby Turner, *Hitler's Thirty Days to Power, January 1933* (Reading, MA, 1996).
13. Dona Harsch, *German Social Democracy and the Rise of Nazism* (Chapel Hill, 1993).
14. Earlier studies by Alan Bullock and Joachim Fest have been superseded by Ian Kershaw, *Hitler: A Biography* (New York, 2008).
15. Kershaw, *Hitler*, 1–46. Cf. John Boyer, *Culture and Political Crisis in Vienna: Christian Socialism in Power, 1897–1918* (Chicago, 1996).
16. Thomas Weber, *Hitlers erster Krieg: Der Gefreite Hitler im Weltkrieg—Mythos und Wahrheit* (Berlin, 2011).
17. Adam Seipp, *The Ordeal of Peace: Demobilization and the Urban Experience in Britain and Germany, 1917–1921* (Farnham, UK, 2009): and Kershaw, *Hitler*, 66–104.
18. Harold J. Gordon, *Hitler and the Beer Hall Putsch* (Princeton, 1972).
19. Kershaw, *Hitler*, 160–235.
20. Hermann Beck, *The Fateful Alliance: German Conservatives and Nazis in 1933: The Machtergreifung in a New Light* (New York, 2008).
21. Kershaw, *Hitler*, 173ff.
22. Eberhard Jaeckel, *Hitlers Weltanschauung: A Blueprint for Power* (Middletown, CT, 1972).
23. Adolf Hitler, *Mein Kampf*, trans. Ralph Manheim (Boston, 1943), 302; and Gerhard Weinberg et al., eds., *Außenpolitische Standortbestimmung nach der Reichstagswahl Juni–Juli 1928* (Munich, 1995), 25, 32, 34, 65, 76.
24. Weinberg et al., *Außenpolitische Standortbestimmung*, 5ff.; Hitler, *Mein Kampf*, 284–329.
25. Habbo Knoch and Detlef Schmiechen-Ackermann, eds., *Nationalsozialistische "Volksgemeinschaft": Studien zur Konstruktion, gesellschaftlichen Wirkungsmacht und Erinnerung* (Paderborn, 2012).
26. Hitler, *Mein Kampf*, 87ff., 442ff.
27. Michael H. Kater, *The Nazi Party: A Social Profile of Members and Leaders, 1919–1945* (Cambridge, MA, 1983), 234–39.
28. Thomas Childers, *The Nazi Voter: The Social Foundations of Fascism in Germany, 1919–1933* (Chapel Hill, 1983); and Richard Hamilton, *Who Voted for Hitler* (Princeton, 1982).
29. Larry E. Jones, *German Liberalism and the Dissolution of the Weimar Party System, 1918–1933* (Chapel Hill, 1988).
30. Kessler, *Tagebücher*, 708; and Kershaw, *Hitler*, 260ff.
31. Kessler, *Tagebücher*, 709; Sven Felix Kellerhoff, *Der Reichstagsbrand: Karriere eines Kriminalfalls* (Berlin, 2008).
32. Klemperer, *Tagebücher*, 8, 14ff.; Kershaw, *Hitler*, 278ff.
33. Konrad H. Jarausch, *The Unfree Professions: German Lawyers, Teachers and Engineers, 1900–1950* (New York, 1990), 116ff.; and Werner Treß, *"Wider den undeutschen Geist!" Bücherverbrennung 1933*, 2nd ed. (Berlin, 2008).
34. Kershaw, *Hitler*, 301–19.
35. Robert Gellately, *Backing Hitler: Consent and Coercion in Nazi Germany* (New York, 2001).
36. Richard Overy, *The Nazi Economic Recovery, 1932–1938* (Atlantic Highlands, NJ, 1982); and Adam Tooze, *Wages of Destruction: The Making and Breaking of the Nazi Economy* (London, 2006).
37. Kershaw, *Hitler*, 391–400; Sebastian Haffner, *Defying Hitler: A Memoir* (New York, 2002).

38. David Welch, "Nazi Propaganda and the *Volksgemeinschaft*: Constructing a People's Community," *Journal of Contemporary History* 39 (2004), 213–38.

39. Richard Evans, *The Third Reich in Power, 1933–1939* (London, 2005).

40. Ronald Smelser, *Robert Ley: Hitler's Labor Front Leader* (Oxford, 1988); and Shelly Baranowski, *Strength Through Joy: Consumerism and Mass Tourism in the Third Reich* (Cambridge, 2004).

41. Michael Kater, *Hitler Youth* (Cambridge, MA, 2004).

42. Claudia Koonz, *Mothers in the Fatherland: Women, the Family and Nazi Politics* (New York, 1987); and Dagmar Herzog, *Sex after Fascism: Memory and Morality in Twentieth Century Germany* (Princeton, 2005).

43. Herwart Vorländer, "NS-Volkswohlfahrt und Winterhilfswerk des deutschen Volkes," *Vierteljahrshefte für Zeitgeschichte* 34 (1986), 341–80.

44. Klemperer, *Tagebücher*, 18ff.; Eric Johnson, *The Nazi Terror: Gestapo, Jews and Ordinary Germans* (New York, 1999).

45. David Clay Large, *Nazi Games: The Olympics of 1936* (New York, 2007).

46. Roger Griffin, "Modernity under the New Order: The Fascist Project for Managing the Future," Oxford Brookes School of Business Imprint 1994; Ulrich Herbert, *Deutsche Geschichte im 20. Jahrhundert* (Munich, 2014), 301.

47. See James Murphy's translation of *Mein Kampf* (London, 1939), https://archive.org/details/MeinKampf_483, 72, 203, 293, 488, 505.

48. Ibid., 214, 248, 314, 414, 437, 440. Cf. Hugh Trevor-Roper, ed., *Hitler's Table Talk, 1941–1944: His Private Conversations* (New York, 2000), 91, 129, 353, 445, 517, etc.

49. Thomas Zeller, *Driving Germany: The Landscape of the German Autobahn, 1930–1970* (New York, 2007).

50. Edward Ross Dickinson, "Biopolitics, Fascism and Democracy: Some Reflections on Our Discourse about 'Modernity,'" *Central European History* 37 (2004), 1–48.

51. Konrad H. Jarausch and Fitz Brundage, "Masses: Mobilization versus Manipulation," in Christof Mauch and Kiran Klaus Patel, eds. *The US and Germany in the Twentieth Century: Competition and Convergence* (New York, 2010).

11. UNLEASHING WORLD WAR II

1. Hoßbach Protocol, November 10, 1937, in *German Historical Institute Documents and Images*, vol. 7.

2. David Hoggan, *The Forced War: When Peaceful Revision Failed* (Costa Mesa, CA, 1989); and Gordon Martel, ed., *The Origins of the Second World War Reconsidered: The A.J.P. Taylor Debate After Twenty-Five Years* (Boston, 1986).

3. Andreas Hillgruber, *Germany and the Two World Wars* (Cambridge, 1981), versus Martin Broszat, *The Hitler State: The Foundation and Development of the Internal Structure of the Third Reich* (London, 1981).

4. Nick Smart, *Neville Chamberlain* (London, 2010).

5. Keith Robbins, *Appeasement* (Oxford, 1988), 78–82.

6. Eric D. Weitz, "From the Vienna to the Paris System: International Politics and the Entangled Histories of Human Rights, Forced Deportations, and Civilizing Missions," *American Historical Review* (December 2008), 1313–43.

7. Patricia Clavin, *Securing the World Economy: The Reinvention of the League of Nations, 1920–1946* (New York, 2013).

8. Zara Steiner, *The Lights That Failed: European International History, 1919–1933* (Oxford, 2005); and John Fischer Williams, "Recent Interpretations of the Briand-Kellogg Pact," *International Affairs* (1935), 346–68.

9. F. S. Northredge, *The League of Nations: Its Life and Times, 1920–1946* (New York, 1986).

10. Carole Fink, *Defending the Rights of Others: The Great Powers, the Jews, and International Minority Protection, 1878–1938* (New York, 2004), 257–74; and Philipp Ther, *Die dunkle Seite der Nationalstaaten: "Ethnische Säuberungen" im modernen Europa* (Göttingen, 2011).

11. Andrew Weber, "The Transnational Dream: Politicians, Diplomats and Soldiers in the League of Nations' Pursuit of International Disarmament, 1920–1938," *Contemporary European History* 14 (2005), 493–518.

12. Sir Herbert Samuel, "The World Economic Conference," *International Affairs* (July 1933), 458–49. Cf. Barry Eichengreen and Marc Uzan, "The World Economic Conference as an Instance of Failed International Cooperation," Berkeley Working Paper 90–149, 1990.

13. Philip Jowett, *Rays of the Rising Sun*, vol. 1: *Japan's Asian Allies 1931–1945, China and Manchukuo* (London, 2005).

14. Zara Steiner, *The Triumph of the Dark: European International History, 1933–1939* (New York, 2011).

15. "Hitler's Comments at a Dinner with the Chiefs of the Army and the Navy" (February 3, 1933), *German History in Documents and Images*, vol. 7. Cf. Klaus Hildebrand, *Das vergangene Reich: Deutsche Außenpolitik von Bismarck bis Hitler* (Stuttgart, 1995), 563–78.

16. Konrad H. Jarausch, *The Four Power Pact, 1933* (Madison, 1966).

17. Steiner, *Triumph of the Dark*, 9–61.

18. Wilhelm Deist, *The Wehrmacht and German Rearmament* (Toronto, 1981). Cf. Adam Tooze, *Ökonomie der Zerstörung. Die Geschichte der Wirtschaft im Nationalsozialismus* (Munich, 2007), 127–200.

19. Gerhard Weinberg, *The Foreign Policy of Hitler's Germany*, vol. 1: *Diplomatic Revolution in Europe, 1933–1936* (Chicago, 1970), 207–16.

20. Steiner, *Triumph of the Dark*, 136–80.

21. Tooze, *Ökonomie der Zerstörung*, 243–334; and Hildebrand, *Vergangenes Reich*, 618–32.

22. Hugh Thomas, *The Spanish Civil War*, rev. ed. (New York, 2001).

23. Ian Kershaw, *Hitler* (London, 2008).

24. Kevin Mason, "Building an Unwanted Nation: The Anglo-American Partnership and Austrian Proponents of a Separate Nation, 1918–1934" (PhD dissertation, University of North Carolina, 2007).

25. Ernst Hanisch, *Der lange Schatten des Staates: Österreichische Gesellschaftsgeschichte im 20. Jahrhundert* (Vienna, 1994).

26. Günter Bischof, Anton Pelinka, and Alexander Lassner, eds., *The Dollfuss/Schuschnigg Era in Austria: A Reassessment* (New Brunswick, 2003).

27. Hildebrand, *Vergangenes Reich*, 644–51.

28. Gerhard Botz, *Wien vom Anschluss zum Krieg* (Vienna, 1978).

29. Werner Welzig, *Anschluss: März–April 1938 in Österreich* (Vienna, 2010).

30. Evan Bukey, *Hitler's Austria: Popular Sentiment in the Anschluss Era, 1938–1945* (Chapel Hill, 2000).

31. Peter Judson, *Guardians of the Nation: Activists and the Language Frontiers of Imperial Austria* (Cambridge, 2006).

32. Ron Smelser, *The Sudeten Problem: Volkstumspolitik and the Formulation of Nazi Foreign Policy* (Middletown, CT, 1975). Cf. Gary B. Cohen, *The Politics of Ethnic Survival: Germans in Prague, 1861–1914* (Princeton, 1981).

33. Telford Taylor, *Munich: The Price of Peace* (Garden City, 1979).

34. Hildebrand, *Vergangenes Reich*, 651–66.

35. Steiner, *Triumph of the Dark*, 610–68. Cf. Alfred F. Havinghurst, *Britain in Transition: The Twentieth Century*, 4th ed. (Chicago, 1985), 266–77.

36. Chad Bryant, *Prague in Black: Nazi Rule and Czech Nationalism* (Cambridge, MA, 2007).

37. Gerhard L. Weinberg, *The Foreign Policy of Hitler's Germany: Starting World War II, 1937–1939* (Chicago, 1980), 465–534.

38. Jeffrey Record, *The Specter of Munich: Reconsidering the Lessons of Appeasing Hitler* (Washington, 2007).

39. Steiner, *Triumph of the Dark*, 832–44.

40. Weinberg, *Foreign Policy*, 497–504.

41. Hildebrand, *Vergangenes Reich*, 678ff.; and Tooze, *Ökonomie der Zerstörung*, 335–79.

42. Geoffrey Roberts, *Stalin's Wars: From World War to Cold War, 1939–1953* (New Haven, 2006).

43. Anna Kaminsky, Dietmar Müller, and Stefan Troebst, eds., *Der Hitler-Stalin Pakt 1939 in den Erinnerungskulturen der Europäer* (Göttingen, 2011), 49–84.

44. Steiner, *Triumph of the Dark*, 995–1035.

45. Weinberg, *Starting World War Two*, 628–55.

46. Ibid., 656–77.

47. Gordon A. Craig and Francis L. Loewenheim, eds., *The Diplomats, 1939–1979* (Princeton, 1994).

48. Akira Irye, *Cultural Internationalism and World Order* (Baltimore, 1997).

49. Geoff Eley, *Forging Democracy: The History of the Left in Europe, 1850–2000* (Oxford, 2002).

50. Richard Evans, *Das Dritte Reich*, vol. 2: *Diktatur* (Munich, 2006), 853–62.

12. AXIS CONQUEST

1. Guido Enderis, "Ceremony Is Brief: Keitel Reads Preamble to Demands in Presence of Hitler and Others," *New York Times*, June 22, 1940. Cf. William S. Shirer, *Berlin Diary: The Journal of a Foreign Correspondent, 1934–1941* (New York, 1941), 419–28.

2. Louis P. Lochner, "The Blitzkrieg in Belgium: A Newsman's Eyewitness Account," *Wisconsin Magazine of History* 50 (1967), 337–46. Cf. Robert M. Citino, *The Path to Blitzkrieg: Doctrine and Training in the German Army, 1920–1939* (Boulder, 1999).

3. Henry J. Reilly, "Blitzkrieg," *Foreign Affairs* 18 (1940), 254–65.

4. William J. Fanning, "The Origin of the Term 'Blitzkrieg': Another View," *Journal of Military History* 61 (1997), 283–302; Tobias Jersak, "Blitzkrieg Revisited: A New Look at Nazi War and Extermination Planning," *Historical Journal* 43 (2000), 565–82; and Richard Overy, "Hitler's War and the German Economy: A Reinterpretation," *Economic History Review* 35 (1982), 272–91.

5. Heinz Guderian, *Panzer Leader* (New York, 2001), reissue with foreword by Basil H. Liddell Hart.

6. Lochner, "Blitzkrieg," 339; and Ian Kershaw, "War and Political Violence in Twentieth Century Europe," *Contemporary European History* 14 (2005), 1007–1123.

7. Shirer, *Berlin Diary*, 191–201.

8. Jochen Böhler, *Der Überfall: Deutschlands Krieg gegen Polen* (Frankfurt, 2009).
9. Alexander Rossino, *Hitler Strikes Poland: Blitzkrieg: Ideology and Atrocity* (Lawrence, 2003).
10. Gerhard Weinberg, *A World at Arms: A Global History of World War Two* (Cambridge, 1995), 64–73; and Adam Tooze, *Ökonomie der Zerstörung: Die Geschichte der Wirtschaft im Nationalsozialismus* (Munich, 2007), 381–427.
11. Robert Edwards, *The Winter War: The Russian Invasion of Finland, 1939–1940* (New York, 2008).
12. Douglas C. Dildy, *Denmark and Norway, 1940: Hitler's Boldest Operation* (Oxford, 2007).
13. Shirer, *Berlin Diary*, 325–27; and Tooze, *Ökonomie der Zerstörung*, 380–427.
14. Shirer, *Berlin Diary*, 532; and Weinberg, *World at Arms*, 122ff.
15. Weinberg, *World at Arms*, 107–112.
16. Karl-Heinz Frieser, *Blitzkrieg-Legende: Der Westfeldzug, 1940*, 2nd ed. (Munich, 1996).
17. Alistair Horne, *To Lose a Battle: France, 1940* (Middlesex, 1969). Cf. MGFA., ed., *Das Deutsche Reich und der Zweite Weltkrieg* (Stuttgart, 1979), vol. 2.
18. Hugh Sebag-Montefiore, *Dunkirk: Fight to the Last Man* (Cambridge, MA, 2006).
19. Julian Jackson, *The Fall of France: the Nazi Invasion of 1940* (Oxford, 2003). Shirer, *Berlin Diary*, 412.
20. Robert O. Paxton, *Vichy France: Old Guard, New Order* (New York, 1972); and Henry Rousso, *Vichy: L'événement, la mémoire, l'histoire* (Paris, 2001).
21. Joel Blatt, ed., *The French Defeat of 1940: Reassessments* (Providence, 1998).
22. Martin Gilbert, *Churchill: A Life* (London, 1991); The Churchill Centre, http://www .winstonchurchill.org/learn/speeches/speeches-of-winston-churchill/128-we-shall -fight-on-the-beaches.
23. Martin Marix Evans, *Invasion! Operation Sealion, 1940* (Harlow, 2004). Cf. Alfred F. Havinghurst, *Britain in Transition: The Twentieth Century*, 4th ed. (Chicago, 1985); 298–308.
24. James Holland, *The Battle of Britain: Five Months That Changed History, May–October 1940* (New York, 2011).
25. Weinberg, *World at Arms*, 148–50; and Tooze, *Ökonomie der Zerstörung*, 459–71.
26. Franz Kurowski, *Das Afrika Korps: Erwin Rommel and the Germans in Africa, 1941–1943* (Mechanicsburg, PA, 2010).
27. Jozo Tomasevich, *War and Revolution in Yugoslavia, 1941–1945: Occupation and Collaboration* (Stanford, 2001).
28. MGFA, ed., *Das Deutsche Reich und der Zweite Weltkrieg* (Stuttgart, 1984), vol. 3.
29. Andrew Roberts, *Storm of War: A New History of the Second World War* (London, 2010), 119–35.
30. Tooze, *Ökonomie der Zerstörung*, 495–532.
31. Roberts, *Storm of War*, 136–73.
32. MGFA, ed., *Das Deutsche Reich und der Zweite Weltkrieg*, 2nd ed. (Stuttgart, 1987), vol. 3.
33. Klaus Reinhardt, *Die Wende vor Moskau: Das Scheitern der Strategie Hitlers im Winter 1941/42* (Stuttgart, 1972).
34. Christian Hartmann, *Unternehmen Barbarossa: Der deutsche Krieg im Osten 1941–1945* (Munich, 2011).
35. Konrad H. Jarausch, *Reluctant Accomplice: A Wehrmacht Soldier's Letters from the East, 1939–1941* (Princeton, 2011).
36. Roberts, *Storm of War*, 315ff.
37. Weinberg, *World at Arms*, 408–20.

38. Gerhard L. Weinberg, *Visions of Victory: The Hopes of Eight World War II Leaders* (Cambridge, 2007).

39. Christian Leitz, *Nazi Germany and Neutral Europe during the Second World War* (Manchester, 2000). Cf. Jean-François Bergier, ed., *Die Schweiz, der Nationalsozialismus und der Zweite Weltkrieg* (2002).

40. Bernd Martin, *Japan and Germany in the Modern World* (Providence, 1995); and Ricky Law, "Knowledge Is Power: The Interwar German and Japanese Media in the Making of the Axis" (PhD dissertation, University of North Carolina, 2012).

41. Weinberg, *World at Arms*, 153–61, 238–45.

42. Ernest R. May, "Nazi Germany and the United States," *Journal of Modern History* 41 (1969), 207–14; and Jochen Thies, *Hitler's Plans for Global Domination: Nazi Architecture and Ultimate War Aims* (New York, 2012).

43. Roberts, *Storm of War*, 185–95. Cf. Emily S. Rosenberg, *A Day Which Will Live: Pearl Harbor in American Memory* (Durham, 2003).

44. Saul Friedlander, *Prelude to Downfall: Hitler and the United States, 1939–1941* (New York, 1967).

45. Weinberg, *World at War*, 262–63; and Roberts, *Storm of War*, 193–97.

46. Hermann Foertsch, *The Art of Modern Warfare* (New York, 1940); and Cyril Falls, *The Nature of Modern Warfare* (New York, 1941).

47. Bevin Alexander, *Inside the Nazi War Machine: How Three Generals Unleashed Hitler's Blitzkrieg upon the World* (New York, 2010).

48. Roberts, *Storm of War*, 136–84.

49. Weinberg, *World at Arms*, 408–31; and Tooze, *Ökonomie der Zerstörung*: 560–90.

50. George Kassimiris and John Buckley, eds., *The Ashgate Research Companion to Modern Warfare* (Farnham, UK, 2010).

13. NAZI HOLOCAUST

1. Patrick Dempsey, *Babi Yar: A Jewish Catastrophe* (Measham, 2005).

2. Peter Novick, *The Holocaust and Collective Memory: The American Experience* (London, 2001). Cf. Christopher Browning, "The Personal Contexts of a Holocaust Historian: War, Politics, Trials and Professional Rivalry" (MS, Chapel Hill, 2014).

3. Norman Naimark, *Fires of Hatred: Ethnic Cleansing in Twentieth Century Europe* (Cambridge, MA, 2001).

4. Daniel J. Goldhagen, *Hitler's Willing Executioners: Ordinary Germans and the Holocaust* (New York, 1996). Cf. Geoff Eley, ed., *The "Goldhagen Effect": History, Memory, Nazism—Facing the German Past* (Ann Arbor, 2000).

5. Timothy Snyder, *Bloodlands: Europe between Hitler and Stalin* (London, 2010), 119–337.

6. Ian Kershaw, *Hitler: A Biography* (New York, 2008), 486, 498, 521, 573f. Cf. Norman Rich, *Hitler's War Aims*, 2 vols. (New York, 1973).

7. Vejas G. Lulevicius, *The German Myth of the East, 1800 to the Present* (New York, 2009).

8. Gustavo Corni, *Blut und Boden: Rassenideologie und Agrarpolitik im Staat Hitlers* (Idstein, 1994).

9. Jacob Katz, *Out of the Ghetto: The Social Background of Jewish Emancipation* (Syracuse, 1998).

10. Konrad H. Jarausch, *Students, Society and Politics in Imperial Germany: The Rise of Academic Illiberalism* (Princeton, 1982).

11. Peter Longerich, *Heinrich Himmler* (Oxford, 2012). Cf. Also Omer Bartov, "Defining Enemies, Making Victims: Germans, Jews, and the Holocaust," *American Historical Review* 103 (1998), 771–816.

12. Saul Friedländer, *Nazi Germany and the Jews*, vol. 1: *The Years of Persecution, 1933–1939* (New York, 1997).

13. Saul Friedländer, *Nazi Germany and the Jews*, vol. 2: *The Years of Extermination, 1939–1945* (New York, 2007).

14. Kershaw, *Hitler*, 597–603.

15. Snyder, *Bloodlands*, 379–408.

16. Richard Bessel, "Functionalists vs. Intentionalists: The Debate Twenty Years," *German Studies Review* 26 (2003), 15–20.

17. Gerhard Weinberg, *A World at Arms: A Global History of World War Two* (Cambridge, 1994), 509–32.

18. Ibid., 205ff., 245ff.

19. Joseph Rothschild, *Return to Diversity: A Political History of East Central Europe since World War II* (New York, 1989).

20. Robert O. Paxton, *Vichy France: Old Guard, New Order, 1940–1944*, 2nd. ed. (New York, 2001).

21. Philippe Burrin, *France under the Germans: Collaboration and Compromise* (New York, 1998).

22. T. Ivan Berend, *Decades of Crisis: Central and Eastern Europe before World War II* (Berkeley, 1998), 396ff.; and Adam Tooze, *Ökonomie der Zerstörung: Die Geschichte der Wirtschaft im Nationalsozialismus* (Munich, 2007), 591–633.

23. Istvan Deak, *Europe on Trial: The Story of Collaboration, Resistance, and Retribution during World War II* (Boulder, CO, 2015), 41–107.

24. *Report of the Commission of Experts Established Pursuant to United Nations Security Council Resolution 780* (1992), May 27, 1994.

25. Götz Aly and Susanne Heim, *Architects of Annihilation: Auschwitz and the Logic of Destruction* (Princeton, 2002).

26. Valdis O. Lumans, *Himmler's Auxiliaries: The Volksdeutsche Mittelstelle and the German National Minorities of Europe, 1939–1945* (Chapel Hill, 1993).

27. Snyder, *Bloodlands*, 119–54.

28. Christian Gerlach, *Kalkulierte Morde: Die deutsche Wirtschafts- und Vernichtungspolitik in Weißrussland, 1941–1944* (Hamburg, 1998). Cf. Konrad H. Jarausch, *Reluctant Accomplice: A Wehrmacht Soldier's Letters from the East, 1939–1941* (Princeton, 2011), 239–366.

29. Mark Spoerer, *Zwangsarbeit unter dem Hakenkreuz: Ausländische Zivilarbeiter, Kriegsgefangene und Häftlinge im Deutschen Reich und im besetzten Europa 1938–1945* (Stuttgart, 2001).

30. Robert Koehl, *RKFDV: German Resettlement and Population Policy, 1939–1945: A History of the Reich Commission for the Strengthening of Germandom* (Cambridge, MA, 1957).

31. Snyder, *Bloodlands*, 379–414.

32. Eric Weitz, *A Century of Genocide: Utopias of Race and Nation* (Princeton, 2003).

33. Henry Friedlander, *The Origins of Nazi Genocide: From Euthanasia to the Final Solution* (Chapel Hill, 1995).

34. Christopher R. Browning, *The Origins of the Final Solution: The Evolution of Nazi Jewish Policy 1939–1942* (Lincoln, 2004).

35. Christopher Browning, *Remembering Survival: Inside a Nazi Slave Labor Camp* (New York, 2010).

36. Eric Steinhart, "Creating Killers: The Nazification of the Black Sea Germans and the Holocaust in Southern Ukraine, 1941–1944" (PhD dissertation, University of North Carolina, 2010); and Waitman Beorn, *Marching into Darkness: The Wehrmacht and the Holocaust in Belarus* (Cambridge, MA, 2014).

37. Patrick Desbois, *The Holocaust by Bullets: A Priest's Journey to Uncover the Truth behind the Murder of 1.5 Million Jews in 2008* (New York, 2008).

38. Saul Friedländer, *The Years of Extermination: Nazi Germany and the Jews, 1939–1945* (New York, 2007).

39. Charles Katzengold to Henri and Paula, August 30, 1945, Paula Cassen, "Mes Mémoires de Guerre," http://cassen.weebly.com/documents.html. I would like to thank Flora Cassen for sharing this document.

40. Laurence Rees, *Auschwitz: A New History* (New York, 2005).

41. Elie Wiesel, *Night* (New York, 1982), 21–32. Cf. also Tadeuz Borowski, *This Way for the Gas, Ladies and Gentlemen* (New York, 1976), 20–49.

42. Paul J. Weindling, *Nazi Medicine and the Nuremberg Trials: From Medical War Crimes to Informed Consent* (Houndmills, 2004).

43. Oral testimony of Irmgard Mueller, Chapel Hill, 2004; and Ruth Klüger, *Still Alive: A Holocaust Girlhood Remembered* (New York, 2001).

44. Yehuda Bauer, *The Death of the Stetl* (New Haven, 2009).

45. Lucy S. Davidowicz, *The War on the Jews, 1933–1945* (New York, 1986).

46. Alon Confino, *Foundational Pasts: The Holocaust as Historical Understanding* (New York, 2012).

47. Peter Longerich, *"Davon haben wir nichts gewusst!" Die Deutschen und die Judenverfolgung, 1933–1945* (Munich, 2006). Cf. Eric A. Johnson and Karl-Heinz Reuband, *What We Knew: Terror, Mass Murder and Everyday Life in Nazi Germany* (Cambridge, MA, 2005).

48. Ulrich Herbert, *Best: Biographische Studien über Radikalismus, Weltanschauung und Vernunft, 1903–1989* (Bonn, 1996); and Michel Wildt, *An Uncompromising Generation: The Nazi Leadership of the Reich Security Main Office* (Madison, 2009).

49. Konrad H. Jarausch, "The Conundrum of Complicity: German Professionals and the Final Solution," in Alan E. Steinweis and Robert D. Rachlin, eds., *The Law in Nazi Germany: Ideology, Opportunism and the Perversion of Justice* (New York, 2013).

50. Gerhard Paul and Klaus-Michael Mallmann, *Milieus und Widerstand: Eine Verhaltensgeschichte im Nationalsozialismus* (Bonn, 1995).

51. Martin Broszat, *The Hitler State: The Foundation and Development of the Internal Structure of the Third Reich* (London, 1981). Cf. Joachim Hagenauer and Martin Pabst, *Anpassung, Unbotmäßigkeit und Widerstand* (Munich, 2014).

52. Norman Davies, *Rising '44. The Battle for Warsaw* (New York, 2004).

53. Peter Hoffmann, *The History of the German Resistance, 1933–1945*, 3rd ed. (Montreal, 1996).

54. Zygmunt Bauman, "Sociology after the Holocaust," *British Journal of Sociology* 39 (1988), 469–97.

55. Omer Bartov, *The Eastern Front, 1941 1945: Germany and the Barbarisation of Warfare*, 2nd ed. (New York, 2001).

56. Hans-Ulrich Wehler, *Deutsche Gesellschaftsgeschichte*, vol. 4: *Vom Beginn des Ersten Weltkriegs bis zur Gründung der beiden deutschen Staaten, 1914–1949* (Munich, 2003).

57. Michael Freeman, "Genocide, Civilization and Modernity," *British Journal of Sociology* 46 (1995), 207–3.

58. Dan Diner, "Einleitung," in idem, ed., *Zivilisationsbruch: Denken nach Auschwitz* (Frankfurt, 1988).

59. Eric Dunning and Stephen Mennell, "Elias on Germany, Nazism and the Holocaust: On the Balance between 'Civilizing' and 'Decivilizing' Trends in the Social Development of Western Europe," *British Journal of Sociology* 49 (1998), 339–57.

14. BITTER VICTORY

1. Andy Rooney, *My War* (New York, 2000).
2. Andrew Roberts, *The Storm of War: A New History of the Second World War* (London, 2009).
3. Gerhard Weinberg, *A World at Arms: A Global History of World War Two* (New York, 1994).
4. Kurt Vonnegut, *Slautherhouse-five, or, the Children's Crusade: A Duty-Dance with Death* (New York, 1969); and W. G. Sebald, *Luftkrieg und Literatur* (Munich, 1999).
5. William I. Hitchcock, *The Bitter Road to Freedom: A New History of the Liberation of Europe* (Glencoe, 2008).
6. Weinberg, *World at Arms*, 438–40.
7. Antony Beevor, *Stalingrad* (New York, 1998).
8. Wolfram Wette and Gerd R. Überschär, eds., *Stalingrad: Mythos und Wirklichkeit einer Schlacht* (Frankfurt, 2012).
9. Anthony Beevor and Luba Vinogradova, eds., *A Writer at War: Vasily Grossman with the Red Army, 1941–1945* (New York, 2007); and S.L.A. Marshall, ed., *Last Letters from Stalingrad* (New York, 1965).
10. Charles R. Anderson, *Algeria-French Morocco, 8 November 1942–11 November 1942* (Washington, 1993).
11. Roberts, *Storm of War*, 281–314. Cf. Robert M. Citino, *Death of the Wehrmacht: The German Campaigns of 1942* (Lawrence, 2007).
12. Randall L. Bytwerk, *Landmark Speeches of National Socialism* (College Station, 2008). Cf. Jay Baird, "The Myth of Stalingrad," *Journal of Contemporary History* 4 (1969), 187–204.
13. Albert Speer, *Inside the Third Reich* (London, 1970).
14. Adam Tooze, *Ökonomie der Zerstörung: Die Geschichte der Wirtschaft im National-sozialismus* (Munich, 2007), 734–35.
15. Roberts, *Storm of War*, 351–69.
16. Ibid., 369–374. Donald F. Bittner, *The Lion and the White Falcon: Britain and Iceland in the World War Two Era* (Hamden, 1983).
17. Jörg Friedrich, *The Fire: The Bombing of Germany, 1940–1945* (New York, 2006); and Randall Hansen, *Fire and Fury: The Allied Bombing of Germany, 1942–1945* (Toronto, 2008).
18. Alfred C. Mierzejewski, *The Collapse of the German War Economy, 1944–1945: Allied Air Power and the German National Railways* (Chapel Hill, 1988).
19. Francis Harry Hinsley and Alan Stripp, *Codebreakers: The Inside Story of Bletchly Park* (Oxford, 2001).
20. Jay Baird, *The Mythical World of Nazi War Propaganda, 1939–1945* (Minneapolis, 1973); and Susan A. Brewer, *Why America Fights: Patriotism and War Propaganda from the Philippines to Iraq* (New York, 2009).
21. Stephen Ambrose, *The Supreme Commander: The War Years of General Dwight D. Eisenhower* (New York, 2012).
22. Roberts, *Storm of War*, 375ff.
23. George F. Botjer, *Sideshow War: The Italian Campaign, 1943–1945* (College Station, 1996).

24. Michael Carver, *War in Italy, 1943-1945* (London, 2004).
25. Stephen D. Ambrose, *D-Day, June 6, 1944: The Climactic Battle of World War II* (New York, 1995). Cf. Jean Quellien, *Landing Beaches* (Bayeux, 2010).
26. Anthony Beevor, *D-Day: The Battle for Normandy* (London, 2009).
27. Werner T. Angress, *Witness to the Storm: A Jewish Journey from Nazi Berlin to the 82nd Airborne, 1920-1945* (Durham, 2012), 227ff.
28. Roberts, *Storm of War*, 461-519.
29. Ibid., 529ff. Cf. Robert M. Citino, *The Wehrmacht Retreats: Fighting a Lost War, 1943* (Lawrence, 2012).
30. Roland G. Foerster, ed., *Gezeitenwechsel im Zweiten Weltkrieg? Die Schlachten von Char'kov und Kursk in operativer Anlage, Verlauf und politischer Bedeutung* (Hamburg, 1996).
31. David M. Glantz and Jonathan House, *The Battle of Kursk* (Lawrence, 1999).
32. Earl F. Ziemke, *Stalingrad to Berlin: The German Defeat in the East* (Washington, 1968).
33. Gerhard Krapf, "Recollections" (MS, Calgary, 1990s), 550-779.
34. Norman Davies, *Rising '44: The Battle for Warsaw* (London, 2004).
35. Alexander Glantz, *When Titans Clashed: How the Red Army Stopped Hitler* (Lawrence, 1995).
36. Istvan Deak, *Europe on Trial: The Story of Collaboration, Resistance, and Retribution during World War II* (Boulder, CO, 2015), 179-89.
37. Ian Kershaw, *The End: Hitler's Germany, 1944-1945* (London, 2011).
38. Friedrich Georg, *Hitler's Miracle Weapons: Secret Nuclear Weapons and Their Carrier Systems in the Third Reich* (Solihull, 2003); vol. 1.
39. David K. Yelton, *Hitler's Volkssturm: The Nazi Militia and the Fall of Germany, 1944-1945* (Lawrence, 2002).
40. Stephen G. Fritz, *Endkampf: Soldiers, Civilians and the Death of the Third Reich* (Lexington, 2004).
41. Patrick Delaforce, *The Battle of the Bulge: Hitler's Final Gamble* (Harlow, 2004).
42. Max Hastings, *Armageddon: The Battle for Germany* (New York, 2004).
43. Richard J. Overy, *Russia's War* (New York, 1998).
44. Anthony Beevor, *The Fall of Berlin, 1945* (New York, 2002).
45. Earl F. Ziemke, *The US Army in the Occupation of Germany, 1944-1946* (Washington, 1975).
46. Roberts, *Storm of War*, 578-608; and Richard Overy, *Why the Allies Won* (New York, 1996).
47. Ian Kershaw, *Hitler: A Biography* (New York, 2008), 956-69.
48. Alexander Werth, *Russia at War, 1941-1945* (New York, 1964).
49. Weinberg, *World at Arms*, 894-920.
50. Hitchcock, *Bitter Road to Freedom*, 367ff. Cf. Michael Bess, *Choices Under Fire: Moral Dimensions of World War II* (New York, 2006); and Jörg Echternkamp and Stefan Matens, eds., *Der Zweite Weltkrieg in Europa: Erfahrung und Erinnerung* (Paderborn, 2007).

15. DEMOCRATIC RENEWAL

1. "Report of the Crimea Conference (Yalta), February 11, 1945," *Foreign Relations of the United States: Diplomatic Papers; The Conferences at Malta and Yalta, 1945* (Washington, 1955); and Charles E. Bohlen, *Witness to History, 1929-1969* (New York, 1973), 173-201.

2. Margaret Bourke-White, *"Dear Fatherland, Rest Quietly": A Report on the Collapse of Hitler's Thousand Years* (New York, 1946).

3. John Lewis Gaddis, *The United States and the Origins of the Cold War, 1941–1947* (New York, 1972).

4. Gerhard Weinberg, *Visions of Victory: The Hopes of Eight World War II Leaders* (Cambridge, 2007).

5. Axel Schildt and Arnold Sywottek, eds., *Modernisierung im Wiederaufbau. Die westdeutsche Gesellschaft der 50er Jahre* (Bonn, 1998).

6. "City's Celebration Chilled by Mayor," "Russia Emphasizes Triumph of Allies," "Paris Celebrates Resistance Birth," and "King Urges Britain to Work for Peace," *New York Times*, May 8, 11; June 19; August 16, 1945.

7. Drew Middleton, *The Struggle for Germany* (Indianapolis, 1949).

8. Rüdiger Overmans, *Deutsche militärische Verluste im Zweiten Weltkrieg* (Munich, 2000). Since casualty statistics are notoriously imprecise, the above figures are only rough estimates.

9. Anna M. Holihan, *Between National Socialism and Soviet Communism: Displaced Persons in Postwar Germany* (Ann Arbor, 2011); and R. M. Douglas, *Orderly and Humane: The Expulsion of the Germans after the Second World War* (New Haven, 2012).

10. Alan S. Milward, *The Reconstruction of Western Europe, 1945–1951* (London, 1984). Cf. Paul Steege, *Black Market: Everyday Life in Berlin, 1946–1949* (Cambridge, 2007).

11. Michaela Hönicke-Moore, *Know Your Enemy: The American Debate about Nazism, 1939–1945* (New York, 2010), 271–350.

12. Ulrich Herbert and Axel Schildt, eds., *Kriegsende in Europa: Vom Beginn des deutschen Machtzerfalls bis zur Stabilisierung der Nachkriegsordnung, 1944–1948* (Essen, 1998).

13. For instance the reportages of William Vandiver in *Life Magazine*, summer 1945.

14. Tony Judt, *Postwar: A History of Europe since 1945* (London, 2005) 100–128.

15. Geoffrey Roberts, *Stalin's Wars: From World War to Cold War, 1939–1953* (New Haven, 2006).

16. Gerhard L. Weinberg, *A World at Arms: A Global History of World War Two* (New York, 1994), 842–93.

17. "The Potsdam Decisions" and "Text of Communiqué Issued by Big Three after Conclusion of Berlin Conference," *New York Times*, August 3, 1945. Herbert Feis, *Between War and Peace: The Potsdam Conference* (Princeton, 1960).

18. Klaus-Dietmar Henke, *Die amerikanische Besetzung Deutschlands* (Munich, 1995).

19. Steven K. Pavlowitch, *A History of the Balkans, 1804–1945* (London, 1999).

20. James L. Gormly, *From Potsdam to the Cold War: Big Three Diplomacy, 1945–1947* (Washington, 1990).

21. Robert Cecil, "Potsdam Legends," *International Affairs* 46 (1970), 455–65.

22. Marcel Gauchet, *L'avènement de la démocratie*, 3 vols. (Paris, 2007–10).

23. Judt, *Postwar*, 41–62. Cf. Istvan Deak, *Europe on Trial: The Story of Collaboration, Resistance, and Retribution during World War II* (Boulder, CO, 2015), 211–23.

24. Melvyn P. Leffler, *A Preponderance of Power: National Security, the Truman Administration, and the Cold War* (Stanford, 1992).

25. Rodney Lowe, *The Welfare State in Britain since 1945*, 3rd ed. (Basingstoke, 2005); and Alfred F. Havinghurst, *Britain in Transition: The Twentieth Century*, 4th ed. (Chicago, 1985), 375–85.

26. Jean-Pierre Rioux, *The Fourth Republic, 1944–1958* (Cambridge, 1987).

27. Judt, *Postwar*, 63–99.

28. Jan-Werner Müller, *Contesting Democracy: Political Ideas in Twentieth Century Europe* (New Haven, 2011), 126ff.
29. Hönicke-Moore, *Know Your Enemy*, 177–269.
30. Henke, *Amerikanische Besetzung*, passim.
31. Konrad H. Jarausch, *After Hitler: Recivilizing Germany* (New York, 2005).
32. Anthony J. Nicholls, *Freedom with Responsibility: The Social Market Economy in Germany, 1918–1963* (Oxford, 1984).
33. Wolfgang Benz, *Auftrag Demokratie: Die Gründungsgeschichte der Bundesrepublik und die Entstehung der DDR, 1945–1949* (Berlin, 2009).
34. Hans–Peter Schwarz, *Konrad Adenauer: A German Politician and Statesman in a Period of War, Revolution, and Reconstruction*, 3 vols. (Providence, 1995ff.).
35. Norman Kogan, *A Political History of Italy: The Postwar Years* (New York, 1983).
36. Rolf Steininger, *Austria, Germany, and the Cold War: From the Anschluss to the State Treaty, 1938–1955* (New York, 2008).
37. Jeremi Suri, *Liberty's Surest Guardian: American Nation-Building from the Founders to Obama* (New York, 2011).
38. I. William Zartman and Saadia Touval, eds., *International Cooperation: The Extents and Limits of Multilateralism* (New York, 2010).
39. Daniel Chernilo, *A Social Theory of the Nation-State: The Political Forms of Modernity beyond Methodological Nationalism* (London, 2007).
40. United Nations, "History of the United Nations," http://www.un.org/en/aboutun/history/.
41. Mark Mazower, *No Enchanted Palace: The End of Empire and the Ideological Origins of the United Nations* (Princeton, 2009).
42. Alan S. Milward, *The Reconstruction of Western Europe, 1945–51* (London, 1984).
43. Gustav Schmidt, ed., *A History of NATO: The First Fifty Years*, 3 vols. (London, 2001).
44. Sergio Pistone, *The Union of European Federalists* (Milan, 2008).
45. Sherill Brown Wells, *Jean Monnet: Unconventional Statesman* (Boulder, 2011).
46. Lutz Niethammer, ed., *Lebensgeschichte und Sozialkultur im Ruhrgebiet, 1930–1960*, 2 vols. (Bonn, 1983).
47. Paul Nolte, *Was ist Demokratie? Geschichte und Gegenwart* (Munich, 2012), 284–340.
48. Ludger Helms, *Presidents, Prime Ministers and Chancellors: Executive Leadership in Western Democracies* (New York, 2005).
49. Peter Baldwin, *The Politics of Social Solidarity: Class Bases of the European Welfare State, 1875–1975* (Cambridge, 1991).
50. Charles S. Maier, "The Two Postwar Eras and the Conditions for Stability in Twentieth Century Western Europe," *American Historical Review* 86 (1981), 327–52.

16. DICTATING COMMUNISM

1. Robert Powell, "Jan Masaryk," *The Slavonic and East European Review* 28 (1950), 332–41; and Igor Lukes, "The Birth of a Police State: The Czechoslovak Ministry of the Interior, 1945–48," *National Security* 11 (1996), 78–88.
2. Voitech Mastny, *The Cold War and Soviet Insecurity: The Stalin Years* (New York, 1996).
3. Hannah Arendt, *The Origins of Totalitarianism* (New York, 1958, new ed., 1966); and Carl Friedrich and Z. K. Brzezinski, *Totalitarian Dictatorship and Autocracy* (Cambridge, 1956, 2nd ed., 1967). Cf. Anson Rabinbach, "Moments of Totalitarianism," *History and Theory* 45 (2006), 72–100.

4. Sheila Fitzpatrick and Michael Geyer, eds., *Beyond Totalitarianism: Stalinism and Nazism Compared* (Cambridge, 2009). Cf. Konrad H. Jarausch, ed., *Dictatorship as Experience: Towards a Socio-Cultural History of the GDR* (New York, 1999).
5. Konrad H. Jarausch and Hannes Siegrist, eds., *Amerikanisierung und Sowjetisierung in Deutschland 1945–1970* (Frankfurt, 1997). Cf. Balasz Apor, Peter Apor, and E. A. Rees, eds., *The Sovietization of Eastern Europe: New Perspectives on the Postwar Period* (Washington, 2008), 1–27.
6. Markku Kangaspuro, Jussi Lassila, and Tatiana Zhurzhenko, eds., *Renarrating Heroism, Making Sense of Suffering: Memories of WWII in Russia and Beyond* (New York, 2014).
7. Special exhibition on postwar Russia in the Deutsch-Russisches Museum in Berlin-Karlshorst, Germany.
8. Rainer Karlsch and Jochen Laufer, eds., *Sowjetische Demontagen in Deutschland, 1944–1949: Hintergründe und Wirkungen* (Berlin, 2002).
9. Milovan Djilas, *Conversations with Stalin* (New York, 1962).
10. Olga Ivinskaya, *A Captive of Time: My Years with Pasternak* (Garden City, 1978), 80.
11. Roger R. Reese, *The Soviet Military Experience: A History of the Soviet Army, 1917–1991* (New York, 2000).
12. Rothschild, *Return of Diversity*, 78–80; and the digitized SMAD database of David Pike.
13. Gale Stokes, ed., *From Stalinism to Pluralism: A Documentary History of Eastern Europe since 1945*, 2nd. ed. (New York, 1996).
14. Teresa Toranska, *"Them": Stalin's Polish Puppets* (New York, 1987), 256ff.
15. Norman Naimark, *The Russians in Germany: A History of the Soviet Zone of Occupation* (Cambridge, MA, 1995).
16. Gale Stokes, *The Walls Came Tumbling Down: Collapse and Rebirth in Eastern Europe*, rev. ed. (New York, 2012). Cf. I. Lukes, *On the Edge of the Cold War: American Diplomats and Spies in Postwar Prague* (New York, 2012).
17. Wolfgang Leonhard, *Die Revolution entlässt ihre Kinder* (Leipzig, 1990), 406.
18. Corey Ross, *The East German Dictatorship: Problems and Perspectives in the Interpretation of the GDR* (London, 2002).
19. Andre Steiner, *The Plans That Failed: An Economic History of the GDR* (New York, 2010).
20. Czesław Miłosz, *The Captive Mind* (New York, 1951), 57ff.
21. Richard Crossman, ed., *The God That Failed* (London, 1949).
22. Michael Lemke, ed., *Sowjetisierung und Eigenständigkeit in der SBZ/DDR, 1945–1953* (Cologne, 1999).
23. Joseph Rothschild, *Return to Diversity: A Political History of East Central Europe since World War II* (New York, 1989), 77–146. Cf. Mike Schmeitzner, "Auf dem Weg zur Diktatur des Proletariats: Die KPD/SED als Instrument der Diktaturdurchsetzung," in Jens Gieseke and Hermann Wentker; eds., *Die Geschichte der SED: Eine Bestandsaufnahme* (Berlin, 2011), 60–82.
24. Klaus Schroeder, *Der SED-Staat: Partei, Staat und Gesellschaft, 1949–1990* (Munich, 1998); and Donna Harsch, *Revenge of the Domestic: Women, the Family and Communism in the GDR* (Princeton, 2007).
25. T. Ivan Berend, *Central and Eastern Europe, 1944–1993: Detour from the Periphery to the Periphery* (Cambridge, 1996).
26. John Connelly, *Captive University: The Sovietization of East German, Czech, and Polish Higher Education, 1945–1956* (Chapel Hill, 2000).
27. David Pike, *The Politics of Culture in Soviet Occupied Germany, 1945–1949* (Stanford, 1992).

28. Andrew I. Port, *Conflict and Stability in the German Democratic Republic* (Cambridge, 2007).
29. Vojtech Mastny and Malcolm Byrne, eds., *A Cardboard Castle? An Inside History of The Warsaw Pact, 1955–1991* (Budapest, 2005).
30. Zbigniew K. Brzezinski, *The Soviet Bloc: Unity and Conflict* (Cambridge, MA, 1967).
31. Sergei Khrushchev, *Memoirs of Nikita Khrushchev*, 3 vols. (College Station, 2004–7). Cf. William Taubman, *Khrushchev: The Man and His Era* (New York, 2003).
32. Arch Puddington, *Broadcasting Freedom: The Cold War Triumph of Radio Free Europe and Radio Liberty* (Lexington, 2003).
33. Gary Bruce, *Resistance with the People: Repression and Resistance in Eastern Germany, 1945–1955* (Lanham, 2003).
34. "Text of Speech on Stalin by Khrushchev as released by the State Department," *New York Times*, May 6, 1956; and Taubman, *Khrushchev*.
35. Steven V. Bittner, *The Many Lives of Khrushchev's Thaw: Experience and Memory in Moscow's Arbat* (Ithaca, 2008).
36. Pawel Machcewicz, *Rebellious Satellite: Poland 1956* (Stanford, 2009). Cf. Carole Fink, Frank Hadler, and Thomas Schramm, eds., *1956: European and Global Perspectives* (Leipzig, 2006).
37. John P. C. Mathews, *Explosion: The Hungarian Revolution of 1956* (New York, 2006). Cf. Janos M. Rainer, *Imre Nagy: Vom Parteisoldaten zum Märtyrer des ungarischen Volksaufstands* (Paderborn, 2006).
38. Polly Jones, ed., *The Dilemmas of De-Stalinization: Negotiating Cultural and Social Change in the Khrushchev Era* (London, 2006).
39. Eli Rubin, *Synthetic Socialism: Plastics and Dictatorship in the German Democratic Republic* (Chapel Hill, 2008).
40. Matthew Brzezinski, *Red Moon Rising: Sputnik and the Hidden Rivalries That Ignited the Space Age* (New York, 2007).
41. Susan E. Reid, "Cold War in the Kitchen: Gender and the De-Stalinization of Consumer Taste in the Soviet Union under Khrushchev," *Slavic Review* 61 (2002), 211–52.
42. Judd Stitziel, *Fashioning Socialism: Clothing, Politics and Consumer Culture in East Germany* (Oxford, 2005).
43. Jonathan R. Zatlin, *The Currency of Socialism: Money and Political Culture in East Germany* (Cambridge, 2007).
44. Lorenz M. Lüthi, *The Sino-Soviet Split: The Cold War in the Communist World* (Princeton, 2008).
45. William J. Tompson, "The Fall of Nikita Khrushchev," *Soviet Studies* 43, 1101–21.
46. Malgorzata Mazurek and Matthew Hilton, "Consumerism, Solidarity and Communism: Consumer Protection and the Consumer Movement in Poland," *Journal of Contemporary History* 42 (2007), 315–43.
47. Johann P. Arnason, "Communism and Modernity," *Daedalus* 129 (2000), 61–90.
48. Rothschild, *Return to Diversity*, 145–90; and Mary Fulbrook, *The People's State: East German Society from Hitler to Honecker* (New Haven, 2005).
49. Jürgen Kocka, "The GDR: A Special Kind of Modern Dictatorship," and Detlef Pollack, "Modernization and Modernization Blockages in GDR Society," in *Dictatorship as Experience*, 17–45.
50. Ann Applebaum, *Iron Curtain: The Crushing of Eastern Europe, 1945–1956* (New York, 2012).
51. Arnason, "Communism and Modernity," 76–79. Cf. Rothschild, *Return to Diversity*, 191–225.

17. COLD WAR CRISES

1. Roger Gene Miller, *To Save a City: The Berlin Airlift, 1948–1949* (College Station, 2000).
2. Daniel F. Harrington, *Berlin on the Brink: The Blockade, the Airlift and the Early Cold War* (Lexington, 2012).
3. Michael F. Hopkins, "Continuing Debate and New Approaches in Cold War History," *Historical Journal* 50 (2007), 913–34. See also the Cold War International History Project of the Woodrow Wilson International Center for Scholars in Washington, headed by Christian Ostermann.
4. Melvyn P. Leffler and Odd Arne Westad, eds., *The Cambridge History of the Cold War*, 3 vols. (Cambridge, 2010).
5. Sean Forner, *German Intellectuals and the Challenge of Democratic Renewal: Culture and Politics after 1945* (Cambridge, 2015).
6. Richard H. Immerman and Petra Goedde, eds., *The Oxford Handbook of the Cold War* (Oxford, 2013); and Geoffrey Warner, "The Cold War in Retrospect," *International Affairs* 87 (2011), 173–84.
7. John Lewis Gaddis, *The Cold War: A New History* (London, 2005), 7ff.
8. Vladislav M. Zubok, *A Failed Empire: The Soviet Union in the Cold War from Stalin to Gorbachev*, rev. ed. (Chapel Hill, 2009), 16–36.
9. Melvyn Leffler, *For the Soul of Mankind: The United States, the Soviet Union and the Cold War* (New York, 2007).
10. J.P.B. Dunabin, *The Cold War: The Great Powers and Their Allies* (Harlow, 1994).
11. Gerhard Wettig, *Stalin and the Cold War in Europe: The Emergence and Development of the East-West Conflict, 1939–1953* (Lanham, 2008).
12. George Kennan, "The Long Telegram," February 22, 1946, http://www.ntanet.net/KENNAN.html; and Gaddis, *Cold War*, 29–30.
13. Walter Lippmann, *The Cold War: A Study in US Foreign Policy* (New York, 1947).
14. Zubok, *Failed Empire*, 35–36.
15. Ibid., 36–46.
16. Gaddis, *Cold War*, 30–31; Aida D. Donald, *Citizen Soldier: A Life of Harry S. Truman* (New York, 2012).
17. Günter Bischof and Dieter Stiefel, eds., *Images of the Marshall Plan in Europe: Films, Photographs, Exhibits, Posters* (Innsbruck, 2009).
18. J. F. Brown, *Eastern Europe and Communist Rule* (Durham, 1988).
19. Zubok, *Failed Empire*, 62–74.
20. Gerhard Wettig, ed., *Der Tjulpanov-Bericht: Sowjetische Besatzungspolitik in Deutschland nach dem Zweiten Weltkrieg* (Göttingen, 2012).
21. Klaus-Dietmar Henke, *Die amerikanische Besatzung Deutschlands* (Munich, 1995).
22. Winston Churchill, "The Sinews of Peace," in Robert Rhodes James, ed., *Winston S. Churchill: His Complete Speeches, 1897–1963* (New York, 1974), 7:7285–93.
23. Bernd Stöver, *Der Kalte Krieg, 1947–1991: Geschichte eines radikalen Zeitalters* (Munich, 2007).
24. William R. Smyser, *Yalta to Berlin: The Cold War Struggle over Germany* (New York, 1999), 75–76.
25. Andrei Cherny, *The Candy Bombers: The Untold Story of the Berlin Airlift and America's Finest Hour* (New York, 2008).
26. Henry Ashby Turner, *Germany from Partition to Reunification* (New Haven, 1992).
27. Peter Griedcr, *The German Democratic Republic* (Basingstoke, 2012).
28. Zubok, *Failed Empire*, 78–85.

29. David Clay Large, *Germans to the Front: West German Rearmament in the Adenauer Era* (Chapel Hill, 1996).
30. Gaddis, *Cold War*, 32–47.
31. Andreas Etges, Konrad H. Jarausch, and Christian Ostermann, eds., *The Cold War: History, Memory and Representation* (Stanford, 2015).
32. Gaddis, *Cold War*, 48–72.
33. Richard C. S. Trahair and Robert L. Miller, eds., *Encyclopedia of Cold War Espionage, Spies and Secret Operations*, rev. ed. (New York, 2012).
34. Volker R. Berghahn, *America and the Intellectual Cold Wars in Europe: Shepard Stone between Philanthropy, Academy, and Diplomacy* (Princeton, 2001).
35. Michael Lemke, *Vor der Mauer: Berlin in der Ost-West-Konkurrenz, 1948–1961* (Cologne, 2011), 29–418.
36. Siegfried Weichlein, "The Cultural Cold War and Cold War Culture: Interdisciplinary Perspectives," in *The Cold War: History, Memory and Representation.*
37. Chris Alden, Sally Morphet, and Marco Antonio Vieira, *The South in World Politics* (Basingstoke, 2010).
38. Charles E. Osgood, "An Analysis of the Cold War Mentality," *Journal of Social Issues* 17, No. 3 (1961), 12–17.
39. Bernd Stöver, *Die Befreiung vom Kommunismus: Amerikanische Liberation Policy im Kalten Krieg, 1947–1991* (Cologne, 2002).
40. Zubok, *Failed Empire*, 101–22.
41. Gaddis, *Cold War*, 66–72.
42. Zubok, *Failed Empire*, 129–37.
43. Hope Harrison, *Driving the Soviets up the Wall: Soviet-East German Relations, 1953–1961* (Princeton, 2003).
44. Pertti Ahonen, *Death at the Berlin Wall* (Oxford, 2011); and Hans-Hermann Hertle and Maria Nooke, eds., *The Victims at the Berlin Wall, 1961–1989: A Biographical Handbook* (Berlin, 2011).
45. Dan Munton, *The Cuban Missile Crisis: A Concise History* (New York, 2012).
46. Zubok, *Failed Empire*, 149–52; and Gaddis, *Cold War*, 79–82.
47. Edith Sheffer, *Burned Bridge: How East and West Germans Made the Iron Curtain* (New York, 2011).
48. Christof Mauch and Kiran Klaus Patel, eds., *The United States and Germany during the Twentieth Century: Competition and Convergence* (New York, 2010). Cf. Ulrich Herbert, *Geschichte Deutschlands im 20. Jahrhundert* (Munich, 2014), 616.
49. Marie-Janine Calic, Dietmar Neutatz, and Julia Obertreis, eds., *The Crisis of Socialist Modernity: The Soviet Union and Yugoslavia in the 1970s* (Göttingen, 2011), 9–14.
50. Geir Lundestad, *The United States and Western Europe since 1945: From "Empire by Invitation" to Transatlantic Drift* (New York, 2003), 1–3.
51. Holger Nehring, "National Internationalists: British and West German Protests against Nuclear Weapons, the Politics of Transnational Communications and the Social History of the Cold War, 1957–1964," *Contemporary European History* 14 (205), 559–82.
52. Victoria and Albert Museum catalogue, *Cold War Modern: Design 1945–1970* (London, 2008).

18. DISAPPOINTING DECOLONIZATION

1. Harry Gilroy, "Lumumba Assails Colonialism as Congo Is Freed," *New York Times*, July 1, 1960.

2. Ilunga Kabongo, "The Catastrophe of Belgian Decolonization," in Prosser Gifford and W. Roger Louis, eds., *Decolonization and African Independence* (New Haven, 1988), 381–400.

3. Gyan Prakash, " Subaltern Studies as Postcolonial Criticism," *American Historical Review* 99 (1994), 1475–90.

4. Niall Ferguson, *Empire: The Rise and Demise of the British World Order and the Lessons for Global Power* (New York, 2002).

5. Gifford and Louis, "Introduction," in idem, *Decolonization*, ix–xxix.

6. Ibid., xxvi, and Frederick Cooper, *Decolonization and African Society: The Labor Question in French and British Africa* (Cambridge, 1996).

7. Hew Strachan, *The First World War in Africa* (New York, 2004).

8. Krishnan Srinivasan, *The Rise, Decline and Future of the British Commonwealth* (Basingstoke, 2005).

9. Gerhard L. Weinberg, *World at Arms: A Global History of World War Two* (New York, 1994), 1142ff.

10. András Balogh and Zafar Imam, *A Political History of National Liberation Movement in Asia and Africa, 1914–1985* (New Dehli, 1988).

11. United Nations, "The United Nations and Decolonization," http://www.un.org/en/decolonization/charter.shtml.

12. Simone Panther-Brick, *Gandhi and Nationalism: The Path to Indian Independence* (London, 2012).

13. Adrian Vickers, *A History of Modern Indonesia* (New York, 2005).

14. Prasenjit Duara, *Decolonization: Rewriting Histories* (London, 2004), 2–18. Cf. Frederick Cooper, "Reconstructing Empire in British and French Africa," *Past and Present* 210, suppl. 6 (2011), 196–210.

15. Michael Burleigh, *Small Wars, Faraway Places: Global Insurrection and the Making of the Modern World, 1945–1965* (New York, 2013).

16. Pierre Brocheux, *Ho Chi Minh: A Biography* (New York, 2007); and Martin Winslow, *The Last Valley: The French Defeat at Dien Bien Phu* (London, 2004).

17. Anthony Low, "The End of British Empire in Africa," and Keith Panter-Brick, "Independence, French Style," in Gifford and Louis, *Decolonization*, 33–104.

18. Anthony Gorst and Lewis Johnman, *The Suez Crisis* (London, 1997).

19. Franz Fanon, "Algeria Unveiled," in idem, *A Dying Colonialism* (New York, 1967); and Benjamin Stora, *Algeria, 1830–2000: A Short History* (Ithaca, 2001), 29–116.

20. William R. Louis, *Ends of British Imperialism: The Scramble for Empire, Suez and Decolonization* (London, 2006).

21. Lindsey Michie Eades, *The End of Apartheid in South Africa* (Westport, 1999).

22. Duara, *Decolonization*, 2–18. Cf. Alfred F. Havinghurst, *Britain in Transition: The Twentieth Century*, 4th ed. (Chicago, 1985), 471–79.

23. Cooper, *Decolonization*, 455ff.

24. Timothy C. Weiskel, "Independence and the *Longue Dureé*: The Ivory Coast 'Miracle' Reconsidered," in Gifford and Louis, *Decolonization*, 347–80.

25. Crawford Young, "The Colonial State and Post-Colonial Crisis," in Gifford and Louis, *Decolonization*, 1–32.

26. Gareth Austin, "African Economic Development and Colonial Legacies," *International Development Policy* 1 (2010), 11–32.

27. Martin Thomas, Bob Moore, and L. J. Butler, *The Crises of Empire: Decolonization and Europe's Imperial States, 1918–1975* (London, 2008).

28. Walt W. Rostow, *The Stages of Economic Growth: A Non Communist Manifesto* (Cambridge, 1960).

29. Christopher E. Goscha and Christian F. Ostermann, eds., *Connecting Histories: Decolonization and the Cold War in Southeast Asia, 1945–1962* (Washington, 2009).
30. Michael Mann, "Post-Colonial Development in Africa," *Foreign Policy Journal*, June 3, 2012.
31. Edmond J. Keller, "Decolonization, Independence, and the Failure of Politics," in Phyllis Martin and Patrick O'Meara, eds., *Africa*, 3rd ed. (Bloomington, 1995), 156–71.
32. Albert Memmi, *Decolonization and the Decolonized* (Minneapolis, 2006), ix–xiv.
33. Ben Kiernan, *Blood and Soil: A World History of Genocide and Extermination from Sparta to Darfur* (New Haven, 2007).
34. Giuliani Garavini, *After Empires: Integration, Decolonization and Challenges from the Global South* (Oxford, 2012).
35. Massimo Livi-Bacci, *A Concise History of World Population*, 5th ed. (Chichester, 2012).
36. Leslie J. Favor, *Natural Disasters* (New York, 2011).
37. Simon Allison, "Africa's Economic Growth Miracle: 'It's the Real Thing,'" *Daily Maverick*, November 9, 2012.
38. Cheik Anta Babou, "Decolonization of National Liberation: Debating the End of British Colonial Rule in Africa," *The ANNALS of the AAPSS*, 632 (November 2010), 41–54.
39. Chalmers Johnson, *Blowback: The Costs and Consequences of American Empire* (New York, 2000).
40. Bethwell A. Ogot and Tiyambe Zezela, "Kenya: The Road to Independence and After," in Gifford and Louis, *Decolonization*, 401–26.
41. Andrea L. Smith, ed., *Europe's Invisible Migrants* (Amsterdam 2003).
42. Bouda Etemad, "Europe and Migration after Decolonization," *Journal of European Economic History* 27 (1998), 457–70.
43. Joan Scott, *The Politics of the Veil* (Princeton, 2010). Cf. Jytte Klausen, *The Islamic Challenge: Politics and Religion in Western Europe* (Oxford, 2005).
44. Tony Chater, "France and Senegal: The End of an Affair?" *SAIS Review* 23 (2003), 155–67.
45. Jewan-Philippe Peemans, "Imperial Hangovers: Belgium—the Economics of Decolonization," *Journal of Contemporary History* 15 (1980), 257–86.
46. Hans Holmen, *Snakes in Paradise: NGO's and the Aid Industry in Africa* (Sterling, VA, 2010).
47. David Strang, "From Dependency to Sovereignty: An Event History Analysis of Decolonization, 1870–1987," *American Sociological Review* 55 (1990), 846–60.
48. Alexander McCall Smith's novels, called *The No. 1 Ladies' Detective Agency* (New York, 2002), provide an imaginative description of the transition in Botswana.
49. Martin Shipway, *Decolonization and Its Impact: A Comparative Historical Approach to the End of the Colonial Empire* (Oxford, 2008).
50. Sabelo J. Ndlovu-Gatsheni, "Fiftieth Anniversary of Decolonization in Africa: A Moment of Celebration or Critical Reflection?" *Third Word Quarterly* 33 (2012), 71–89.
51. Steve McDonald, "Africa's Long Spring," *Wilson Quarterly*, Winter 2013.

19. ECONOMIC INTEGRATION

1. Arnaldo Cortesi, "West Europeans Sign Pacts Today," and "Europeans Unite in Customs Union and Atom Agency," *New York Times*, March 24 and 26, 1957.
2. Europa (European Union), "The Treaty of Rome," March 25, 1957, http://ec.europa.eu/economy_finance/emu_history/documents/treaties/rometreaty2.pdf.

3. Konrad H. Jarausch and Thomas Lindenberger, eds., *Conflicted Memories: Europeanizing Contemporary Histories* (New York, 2007).
4. Florian Hartleb, *A Thorn in the Side of European Elites: The New Euroscepticism* (Brussels, 2011).
5. Andrew Moravscik, ed., *Europe without Illusions: The Paul-Henry Spaak Lectures, 1994–1999* (Cambridge, 2005).
6. Marie-Louise von Plessen, ed., *Idee Europa—Entwürfe zum "Ewigen Frieden": Ordnungen und Utopien für die Gestaltung Europas von der pax romana zur Europäischen Union* (Berlin 2003).
7. Florian Greiner, *Wege nach Europa: Deutungen eines imaginierten Kontinents in deutschen, britischen und amerikanischen Printmedien, 1914–1945* (Göttingen, 2014), 352–453.
8. Walter Lipgens, *A History of European Integration, 1945–1947: The Formation of the European Unity Movement* (Oxford, 1982).
9. Council of Europe Parliamentary Assembly, "Speech of Sir Winston Churchill," Zurich, September 19, 1946, http://assembly.coe.int/Main.asp?link=/AboutUs/zurich_e.htm.
10. Sherrill Brown Wells, *Jean Monnet: Unconventional Statesman* (Boulder, 2011), 127–84.
11. John Gillingham, *Coal, Steel and the Rebirth of Europe, 1945–1955* (Cambridge, 1991).
12. Walter Lipgens and Wilfried Loth, eds., *Documents on the History of European Integration*, 4 vols. (Berlin, 1985–1991).
13. Pascaline Winand, *Eisenhower, Kennedy and the United States of Europe* (New York, 1993), 26–63. Cf. Wilfried Loth, *Geschichte Frankreichs im 20. Jahrhundert* (Stuttgart, 1987), 138–51.
14. Derek K. Urwin, *The Community of Europe: A History of European Integration since 1945* (London, 1995).
15. Ernest B. Haas, *The Uniting of Europe: Political, Social, and Economical Forces, 1950–1957* (London, 1958).
16. Desmond Dinan, *Ever Closer Union? An Introduction to the European Community* (Boulder, 1994).
17. John Gillingham, *European Integration, 1950–2003: Superstate or New Market Economy?* (Cambridge, 2003), 43–52.
18. Europa, "Treaty of Rome," see fn. 2. For the "Treaty Establishing the European Atomic Community," see Wikisource, http://en.wikisource.org/wiki/Treaty_establishing_the_European_Atomic_Energy_Community.
19. Europa, "Treaty of Rome." Cf. Urwin, *Community of Europe*, 78–84.
20. Barry Eichengreen, *The European Economy since 1945: Coordinated Capitalism and Beyond* (Princeton, 2007).
21. Kiran Klaus Patel, ed., *Fertile Ground for Europe? The History of European Integration and the Common Agricultural Policy since 1945* (Baden-Baden, 2009).
22. Gillingham, *European Integration*, 53–72.
23. Alan Milward, *The European Rescue of the Nation State*, 2nd ed. (London, 2000), 1–20.
24. N. Piers Ludlow, *The European Community and the Crises of the 1960s: Negotiating the Gaullist Challenge* (London, 2006).
25. Denise Dunne O'Hare, *Britain and the Process of European Integration: Continuity and Policy Change from Atlee to Heath* (London 2013).
26. Emmanuel Moulon-Druol, *A Europe Made of Money: The Emergence of the European Monetary System* (Ithaca, 2012).
27. Stephen George, *An Awkward Partner: Britain in the European Community*, 2nd ed. (Oxford, 1994).

28. Desmond Dinan, ed., *Encyclopedia of the European Union* (Boulder, 1998), 256ff., 430ff., and 389ff.
29. Michael Geary, *Enlarging the European Union: The Commission Seeking Influence, 1961–1973* (New York, 2013).
30. Jean-Marie Palayret, Helen Wallace, and Pascaline Winand, eds., *Visions, Votes and Vetoes: The Empty Chair Crisis and the Luxembourg Compromise Forty Years On* (Brussels, 2006).
31. Gillingham, *European Integration*, 149–227.
32. Andrew Moravcsik, "Negotiating the Single European Act: National Interests and Conventional Statecraft in the European Community," *International Organization* 45 (1991), 19–56.
33. Ruben Saiotti, *Cultures of Border Control: Schengen and the Evolution of European Frontiers* (Chicago, 2011).
34. Clive Church and D. Phinnemore, *European Union and European Community: A Handbook and Commentary on the 1992 Maastricht Treaties*, 2nd. ed. (London, 1995).
35. Kenneth Dyson and Kevin Featherstone, *The Road to Maastricht: Negotiating Economic and Monetary Union* (Oxford, 1999).
36. Thomas Mayer, *Europe's Unfinished Currency: The Political Economics of the Euro* (London, 2012).
37. Adrian Curaj, Peter Scott, Lazăr Vlasceanu, and Lesley Wilson, eds., *European Higher Education at the Crossroads: Between the Bologna Process and National Reforms* (Dordrecht, 2012).
38. Jan Zielonka, *Europe as Empire: The Nature of the Enlarged European Union* (Oxford, 2006).
39. Jenny J. Brine, *COMECON: The Rise and Fall of an International Socialist Organization* (New Brunswick, 1992).
40. Ian Bache and Stephen George, *Politics in the European Union*, 2nd ed. (Oxford, 2006), 543–47.
41. Geoffrey Pridham, *Designing Democracy: EU Enlargement and Regime Change in Post-Communist Europe* (Houndmills, 2005).
42. Andrew Moravcsik, "The European Constitutional Settlement," in Sophie Meunier and Kathleen McNamara, eds., *Making History: European Integration and Institutional Change at Fifty* (Oxford, 2007), 23–50; and Stephen Haseler, *Super-State: The New Europe and Its Challenge to America* (London, 2004).
43. Michael O'Neill, *The Struggle for the European Constitution: A Past and Future History* (London, 2009).
44. Loukas Tsoukalis and Janis A. Emmanouilidis, eds., *The Delphic Oracle on Europe: Is There a Future for the European Union?* (Oxford, 2011).
45. Carlo Bastian, *Saving Europe: How National Politics Nearly Destroyed the Euro* (Washington, 2012).
46. Rebecca Friedman and Markus Thiel, eds., *European Identity and Culture: Narratives of Transnational Belongings* (Farnham, UK, 2012).
47. Anthony Pagden, ed., *The Idea of Europe: From Antiquity to the European Union* (Washington, 2002).
48. James J. Sheehan, *Where Have All the Soldiers Gone? The Transformation of Modern Europe* (Boston, 2008).
49. Eichengreen, *European Economy since 1945*, 379ff.
50. Anette Jünemann and Michele Knodt, eds., *Externe Demokratieförderung durch die Europäische Union* (Baden-Baden, 2007).

51. Jürgen Habermas, *Time of Transitions* (Cambridge, 2006), 71–110; and Andrew Geddes, *Britain and the European Union* (Houndmills, 2013).

20. POP AND PROSPERITY

1. Alice Stettiner, "Amerikanische Kulturbarbarei bedroht unsere Jugend," *Neues Deutschland*, April 4, 1950; "Bill Haley und die NATO," ibid., October 31, 1958.
2. Uta Poiger, *Jazz, Rock and Rebels: Cold War Politics and American Culture in a Divided Germany* (Berkeley, 2000).
3. Jude P. Dougherty, *Jacques Maritain: An Intellectual Profile* (Washington, 2003).
4. Paul Nolte, *Die Ordnung der deutschen Gesellschaft: Selbstentwurf und Selbstbeschreibung im 20. Jahrhundert* (Munich, 2000).
5. Michael Glasmeier and Karin Stengel, eds., *50 Jahre documenta* (Göttingen, 2005).
6. Dirk Moses, *German Intellectuals and the Nazi Past* (Cambridge, 2007).
7. Hanna Schissler, ed., *The Miracle Years: A Cultural History of West Germany, 1949–1968* (Princeton, 2001).
8. Maurice Crouzet, *The European Renaissance since 1945* (New York, 1970), 7.
9. Anthony J. Nicholls, *Freedom with Responsibility: The Social Market Economy in Germany, 1918–1963* (Oxford, 1994).
10. Martin Neil Baily and Jacob Funk Kirkegaard, *Transforming the European Economy* (Washington, 2004), 33–46.
11. Barry Eichengreen, *Europe's Post-War Recovery* (Cambridge, 1995), 3–35.
12. Lutz Niethammer, ed., *Lebensgeschichte und Sozialkultur im Ruhrgebiet 1930 bis 1960*, 2 vols. (Berlin, 1983).
13. See the multivolume *Geschichte der Sozialpolitik in Deutschland seit 1945* (Baden-Baden, 2001ff.), edited by the Bundesministerium für Arbeit und Sozialordnung.
14. Ivan T. Berend, *An Economic History of Twentieth-Century Europe: Economic Regimes from Laissez-Faire to Globalization* (Cambridge, 2006), 142–82.
15. Tony Judt, *Postwar: A History of Europe Since 1945* (New York, 2005), 324–53.
16. Sharon Zukin and Jennifer Smith Maguiere, "Consumers and Consumption," *Annual Review of Sociology* 30 (2004), 173–97.
17. Wolfgang König, *Geschichte der Konsumgesellschaft* (Stuttgart, 2000).
18. Geoffrey Crossick and Serge Jaumain, eds., *Cathedrals of Consumption: The European Department Store, 1850–1939* (Aldershot, 1998).
19. König, *Konsumgesellschaft*, 305ff.
20. Michael Wildt, *Am Beginn der 'Konsumgesellschaft.' Mangelerfahrung, Lebenshaltung, Wohlstandshoffnung in Westdeutschland in den fünfziger Jahren* (Hamburg, 1994).
21. Erica Carter, *How German Is She? Postwar West German Reconstruction and the Consuming Woman* (Ann Arbor, 1997); and Rebecca J. Pulju, *Women and Mass Consumer Society in Postwar France* (New York, 2011).
22. Paulina Bren and Mary Neuburger, eds., *Communism Unwrapped: Consumption in Cold War Eastern Europe* (Oxford, 2012), 3–19.
23. Timothy Beatley, *Green Urbanism: Learning from European Cities* (Washington, 2000). Cf. Friedrich Lenger, *Metropolen der Moderne: Eine europäische Stadtgeschichte seit 1850* (Munich, 2013).
24. Peter N. Stearns, *European Society in Upheaval: Social History since 1750* (New York, 1992), 360–70.
25. Hartmut Kaelble, *A Social History of Europe, 1945–2000: Recovery and Transformation after Two World Wars* (New York, 2013), 41. Cf. George Gerolimatos, "Structural

Change and Democratization of Schleswig-Holstein's Agriculture, 1945–1973" (PhD dissertation, University of North Carolina, 2014).

26. Stefan Berger and Daniel Broughton, eds., *The Force of Labour: The Western European Labour Movement and the Working Class in the Twentieth Century* (Oxford, 1995).

27. Jürgen Kocka, ed., *Industrial Culture and Bourgeois Society: Business, Labor and Bureaucracy in Modern Germany* (New York, 1999).

28. Stefan Hradil and P. Imbusch, eds., *Oberschichten, Eliten, Herrschende Klassen* (Opladen, 2003).

29. Peter Flora et al., eds., *State, Economy, and Society in Western Europe, 1815–1975: A Data Handbook*, 2 vols. (Frankfurt, 1983).

30. Martin Diewald and Karl Ulrich Mayer, eds., *Zwischenbilanz der Wiedervereinigung: Strukturwandel und Mobilität im Transformationsprozess* (Opladen, 1996).

31. Hartmut Kaelble, *Auf dem Weg zu einer europäischen Gesellschaft: Eine Sozialgeschichte Westeuropas, 1880–1980* (Munich, 1987).

32. Marcus Payk, *Der Geist der Demokratie: Intellektuelle Orientierungsversuche im Feuilleton der frühen Bundesrepublik: Karl Korn und Peter de Mendelssohn* (Munich, 2008).

33. Peter J. Bowler, *Science for All: The Popularization of Science in Early Twentieth Century Britain* (Chicago, 2009), 264ff.

34. Steven Crowell, ed., *The Cambridge Companion to Existentialism* (Cambridge, 2012).

35. Hans Werner Holzwarth and Laszlo Taschen, eds., *Modern Art* (Los Angeles, 2011).

36. Kenneth Frampton, *Modern Architecture: A Critical History*, 4th ed. (London, 2007).

37. Paul Griffiths, *Modern Music and After*, 3rd ed. (New York, 2010).

38. Katherine Pence and Paul Betts, eds., *Socialist Modern: East German Everyday Culture and Politics* (Ann Arbor, 2008).

39. Tim Armstrong, *Modernism: A Cultural History* (Cambridge, 2005).

40. Gavin D'Costa and Emma Jane Harris, eds., *The Second Vatican Council: Celebrating Its Achievements and the Future* (London, 2013).

41. Kaspar Maase, *Das Recht auf Gewöhnlichkeit: Über populäre Kultur* (Tübingen, 2011).

42. David Schoenbaum, *The Spiegel Affair* (Garden City, 1968).

43. Margot Lindemann, *Geschichte der deutschen Presse*, 4 vols. (Berlin, 1966–1986).

44. Axel Schildt, *Moderne Zeiten: Freizeit, Massenmedien und "Zeitgeist" in der Bundesrepublik der 50er Jahre* (Hamburg, 1995), 208–61.

45. Johannes von Moltke, *No Place Like Home: Locations of Heimat in German Cinema* (Berkeley, 2005).

46. Knut Hickethier, *Geschichte des deutschen Fernsehens* (Stuttgart, 1998).

47. Annette Vowinckel, Marcus M. Payk, and Thomas Lindenberger, eds., *Cold War Cultures: Perspectives on Eastern and Western European Societies* (New York, 2012).

48. Hunter Davies, *The Beatles*, with a new introduction (New York, 2010).

49. Carl Christian Führer and Corey Ross, eds., *Mass Media, Culture and Society in Twentieth Century Germany* (Basingstoke 2006).

50. Victoria de Grazia, *Irresistible Empire: America's Advance through Twentieth-Century Europe* (Cambridge, 2005), 1–14.

51. Alexander Stephan, ed., *The Americanization of Europe: Culture, Diplomacy and Anti-Americanism after 1945* (New York, 2006); and Andrei S. Markovits, *Uncouth Nation: Why Europe Dislikes America* (Princeton, 2007).

52. Richard F. Kuisel, *Seducing the French: The Dilemma of Americanization* (Berkeley, 1993).

53. Hartmut Kaelble, *A Social History of Europe, 1945–2000: Recovery and Transformation after Two World Wars* (New York, 2013).

54. Heide Fehrenbach and Uta G. Poiger, eds., *Transactions, Transgressions, Transformations: American Culture in Western Europe and Japan* (New York, 2000), xiii–xl.

21. PLANNING SOCIAL REFORM

1. Michael Joseph Mulvey, "Sheltering French Families: Parisian Suburbia and the Politics of Housing" (PhD dissertation, University of North Carolina, 2011).
2. Michael Ruck, "Ein kurzer Sommer der konkreten Utopie: Zur westdeutschen Planungsgeschichte der langen 60er Jahre," in Axel Schildt, Detlef Siegfried, and Karl Christian Lammers, eds., *Dynamische Zeiten. Die 60er Jahre in den beiden deutschen Gesellschaften* (Hamburg, 2000), 362–423.
3. Hans-Edwin Friedrich, "'One Hundred Years from This Day …' Zur Semantik der Zukunft in den 1960er Jahren," in Heinz Gerhard Haupt und Jörg Requate, eds., *Aufbruch in die Zukunft: Die 1960er Jahre zwischen Planungseuphorie und kulturellem Wandel. DDR, CSSR, und Bundesrepublik Deutschland im Vergleich* (Weilerswist, 2004), 133–63.
4. Alexander Schmidt-Gernig, "'Futurologie': Zukunftsforschung und ihre Kritiker in der Bundesrepublik der 60er Jahre," in *Aufbruch in die Zukunft*, 109–31.
5. Gabriele Metzler, *Konzeptionen politischen Handelns von Adenauer bis Brandt: Politische Planung in der pluralistischen Gesellschaft* (Paderborn, 2005).
6. Mark Mazower, "Reconstruction: The Historiographical Issues," *Past and Present* 210, suppl. 6 (2011), 17–28.
7. Tony Judt, *Postwar: A History of Europe since 1945* (New York, 2005), 63–99.
8. Andre Steiner, *The Plans That Failed: An Economic History of the GDR* (New York, 2010).
9. Nik Brandal, Øivind Bratberg, and Dag Einar Thorsen, *The Nordic Model of Social Democracy* (Basingstoke, 2013).
10. Sherrill Brown Wells, *Jean Monnet: Unconventional Statesman* (Boulder, 2011), 95–126.
11. Keith Laybourn, *The Evolution of British Social Policy and the Welfare State c. 1800–1993* (Keele, 1995), 209–36.
12. Friedrich von Hayek, *The Road to Serfdom* (London, 1947).
13. Volker Berghahn, *The Americanization of West German Industry, 1945–1973* (Leamington Spa, 1986).
14. Barry Eichengreen, *The European Economy since 1945: Coordinated Capitalism and Beyond* (Princeton, 2007), 86–130; and James C. Van Hook, *Rebuilding Germany: The Creation of the Social Market Economy, 1945–1957* (Cambridge, 2004).
15. Glen O'Hara, *From Dreams to Disillusionment: Economic and Social Planning in 1960s Britain* (Basingstoke, 2007), 9–36.
16. Jeffrey Kopstein, *The Politics of Economic Decline in East Germany, 1945–1989* (Chapel Hill, 1997).
17. Ruck, "Ein kurzer Sommer der konkreten Utopie," 365–74.
18. Eichengreen, *European Economy*, 100–112.
19. O'Hara, *From Dreams to Disillusionment*, 37–71; and Alfred F. Havinghurst, *Britain in Transition: The Twentieth Century*, 4th ed. (Chicago, 1985), 513–15.
20. Alexander Nützenadel, *Stunde der Ökonomen: Wissenschaft, Politik und Expertenkultur in der Bundesrepublik, 1949–1974* (Göttingen, 2011).
21. Ruck, "Ein kurzer Sommer der konkreten Utopie," 380–86.
22. Metzler, *Konzeptionen politischen Handelns*, 315–82.

23. Clara Oberle, "Redistribution: Ruins, Housing, and the Politics of Order in Berlin, 1945–1949" (MS, San Diego, 2014). Cf. Frank Biess, *Homecomings: Returning POWs and the Legacies of Defeat in Postwar Germany* (Princeton, 2006).

24. Kerstin Dörhöfer, *Erscheinungen und Determinanten staatlich gelenkter Wohnungsversorgung in der Bundesrepublik Deutschland: Zur Planung und Durchführung des Wohnungsbau für die "breiten Schichten des Volkes"* (Berlin, 1978).

25. O'Hara, *From Dreams to Disillusionment*, 129–66.

26. Kenneth Frampton, *Modern Architecture: A Critical History*, 4th ed. (New York, 2007).

27. See the dissertation by Albrecht Wiesener on Sennestadt and Halle-Neustadt (Potsdam, 2015).

28. Examples in Hugh Clout, ed., *Europe's Cities in the Late Twentieth Century* (Utrecht, 1994), 44ff., 117ff.

29. Citations from Mulvey, "Sheltering French Families," passim.

30. Yuri Kazepov, *Cities of Europe: Changing Contexts, Local Arrangements, and the Challenge of Urban Cohesion* (Malden, 2005), 210–32.

31. Fritz K. Ringer, *Education and Society in Modern Europe* (Bloomington, 1979).

32. Alfons Kenkmann, "Von der bundesdeutschen 'Bildungsmisere' zur Bildungsreform in den 60er Jahren," in *Dynamische Zeiten*, 402–23.

33. John Connelly, *Captive University: The Sovietization of East German, Czech and Polish Higher Education, 1945–1956* (Chapel Hill, 2000). Figures in the subsequent discussion from Hartmut Kaelble, *A Social History of Europe, 1945–2000: Recovery and Transformation after Two World Wars* (New York, 2013), 290–300.

34. Karen Hagemann, Konrad H. Jarausch, and Cristina Allemann-Ghionda, eds., *Children, Families and States: Time-Policies of Childcare, Preschool, and Primary Education in Europe* (New York, 2011).

35. Margret Kraul, *Das deutsche Gymnasium, 1780–1980* (Frankfurt, 1984).

36. Walter Rüegg, ed., *A History of the University in Europe*, vol. 4: *Universities since 1945* (Cambridge, 2011), 31–69.

37. Axel C. Hüntelmann and Michael C. Schneider, eds., *Jenseits von Humboldt: Wissenschaft im Staat, 1850–1990* (Frankfurt, 2010).

38. Mitchell G. Ash, ed., *Mythos Humboldt: Vergangenheit und Zukunft der deutschen Universitäten* (Vienna, 1999).

39. Gosta Esping-Anderson, *The Three Worlds of Welfare Capitalism* (Princeton, 1990).

40. Christoph Klessmann, *Arbeiter im 'Arbeiterstaat' DDR: Deutsche Traditionen, Sowjetisches Modell, Westdeutsches Magnetfeld, 1945–1989* (Bonn, 2007).

41. Mary Hilson, *The Nordic Model: Scandinavia since 1945* (London, 2008).

42. Gabriele Metzler, *Der deutsche Sozialstaat: Vom Bismarckschen Erfolgsmodell zum Pflegefall* (Stuttgart, 2003).

43. Paul V. Dutton, *Origins of the French Welfare State: The Struggle for Social Reform in France, 1914–1947* (Cambridge, 2002).

44. Howard Glennerster, *British Social Policy 1945 to the Present*, 3rd ed. (Malden, 2007), 44–151.

45. L. Kenworth, "Do Social-Welfare Policies Reduce Poverty? A Cross-National Assessment," *Social Forces* 77 (1999), 1119–39; and N. Barr, *Economics of the Welfare State* (New York, 2004).

46. Winfried Süss, *Soziale Ungleichheit im Sozialstaat: Die Bundesrepublik Deutschland und Großbritannien im Vergleich* (Munich, 2010). Cf. Kaelble, *Social History of Europe*, 250–70.

47. Gabriele Metzler, "Demokratisierung durch Experten: Aspekte politischer Planung in der Bundesrepublik," in *Aufbruch in die Zukunft*, 267–87.

48. Thomas L. Haskell, ed., *The Authority of Experts: Studies in History and Theory* (Bloomington, 1984).
49. Konrad H. Jarausch and Peter A. Coclanis," Quantification in History," forthcoming in *International Encyclopedia of Social and Behavioral Sciences*, 2nd ed.
50. William J. Barber, *Gunnar Myrdal: An Intellectual Biography* (New York, 2008).
51. Nico Stehr and Reiner Grundmann, *Experts: The Knowledge and Power of Expertise* (Milton Park, 2011).
52. O'Hara, *From Dreams to Disillusionment*, 205–19. Cf. Tomas Etzemüller, ed., *Die Ordnung der Moderne: Social Engineering im 20. Jahrhundert* (Bielefeld, 2009).

22. REVOLT AGAINST MODERNITY

1. Stephen Milder, " 'Today the Fish, Tomorrow Us': Anti-Nuclear Activism in the Rhine Valley and Beyond, 1970–1979" (PhD dissertation, University of North Carolina, 2012), 193–200.
2. Arthur Marwick, *The Sixties: Cultural Revolution in Britain, France, Italy and the United States, c. 1958–c.1974* (New York, 1998).
3. Stephen M. Buechler, *Social Movements in Advanced Capitalism: The Political Economy and Cultural Construction of Social Activism* (New York, 2000).
4. Konrad H. Jarausch, "Protesting Authority," in idem, *After Hitler: Recivilizing Germans, 1945–1995* (New York, 2006), 156–81.
5. Tony Judt, *Postwar: A History of Europe since 1945* (New York, 2005), 390–449, and Carole Fink, Philipp Gassert, and Detlef Junker, eds., *1968: The World Transformed* (Cambridge, 1998), fail to address the issue of modernity.
6. Paul Blackledge, *Perry Anderson: Marxism and the New Left* (London, 2004).
7. Martin Klimke and Joachim Scharloth, eds., *1968 in Europe: A History of Protest and Activism, 1957–1977* (New York, 2008); and Timothy S. Brown, *West Germany in the Global Sixties: The Anti-Authoritarian Revolt, 1962–1978* (Cambridge, 2013).
8. Martin Klimke, *The Other Alliance: Student Protest in West Germany and the United States in the Global Sixties* (Princeton, 2010), 236–45.
9. Mark Roseman, ed., *Generations in Conflict: Youth Revolt and Generation Formation in Germany, 1770–1968* (Cambridge, 1995).
10. Louis Vos, "Student Movements and Political Activism," in Walter Rüegg, ed., *A History of the University in Europe*, vol. 4: *Universities since 1945* (Cambridge, 2011), 276–318.
11. Dagmar Herzog, *Sexuality in Europe: A Twentieth Century History* (Cambridge, 2011).
12. Mark Atwood Lawrence, *Assuming the Burden: Europe and the American Commitment to War in Vietnam* (Berkeley, 2005); Quinn Slobodian, *Foreign Front: Third World Politics in Sixties West Germany* (Durham, 2012).
13. Michaela Karl, *Rudi Dutschke: Revolutionär ohne Revolution* (Frankfurt, 2003).
14. Jürgen Mierenmeister and Jochen Staadt, eds., *Provokationen: Die Studenten- und Jugendrevolte in ihren Flugblättern, 1965–1971* (Darmstadt, 1980).
15. Rudi Dutschke, *Jeder hat sein Leben ganz zu leben: Die Tagebücher 1963–1979*, ed. Gretchen Klotz-Dutschke (Cologne, 2003), 53ff.
16. Ingrid Gilcher-Holthey, *Die 68-Bewegung: Deutschland, Westeuropa, USA* (Munich, 2001).
17. Jean-Pierre Le Goff, *Mai 68: L'heritage impossible* (Paris, 2002).
18. Vos, "Student Movements and Political Activism," 291–97.
19. Norbert Frei, *1968: Jugendrevolte und globaler Protest* (Munich, 2008).
20. Karrin Hanshew, *Terror and Democracy in West Germany* (New York, 2012).

21. Belinda Davis, Wilfried Mausbach, Martin Klimke, and Carla MacDougall, eds., *Changing the World, Changing Oneself: Political Protest and Collective Identities in West Germany and the U.S. in the 1960s and 1970s* (New York, 2010), 277–301.

22. Andrew I. Port, *Conflict and Stability in the German Democratic Republic* (Cambridge, 2007).

23. David Ost, *Solidarity and the Politics of Anti-Politics: Opposition and Reform in Poland since 1968* (Philadelphia, 1990). Cf. Dariusz Stola, "Anti-Zionism as a Multipurpose Policy Instrument: The Anti-Zionist Campaign in Poland, 1967–1968," *Journal of Israeli History* 25 (2006), 171–205.

24. Galia Golan, *The Czechoslovak Reform Movement: Communism in Crisis, 1962–1968* (Cambridge, 1971), 223–74. Cf. Joseph Rothschild, *Return to Diversity: A Political History of East Central Europe since World War II* (New York, 1989), 166–73.

25. Kieran Williams, *The Prague Spring and Its Aftermath: Czechoslovak Politics, 1968–1970* (Cambridge, 1997).

26. Günter Bischof, Stefan Karner, and Peter Ruggenthaler, eds., *The Prague Spring and the Warsaw Pact Invasion of Czechoslovakia in 1968* (Lexington, 2010).

27. Paulina Bren, *The Greengrocer and His TV: The Culture of Communism after the 1968 Prague Spring* (Ithaca, 2010).

28. M. Mark Stolarik, ed., *The Prague Spring and the Warsaw Pact Invasion of Czechoslovakia: Forty Years Later* (Mundelein, IL, 2010).

29. Edward Richardson-Little, "Human Rights, Pluralism and the Democratization in Post-War Germany," forthcoming in Karin Goihl, Konrad H. Jarausch, and Harald Wenzel, eds., *Different Germans: New Transatlantic Perspectives* (New York, 2015).

30. Paul D'Anieri, Claire Ernst, and Elizabeth Kier, "New Social Movements in Historical Perspective," *Comparative Politics* 22 (1990), 445–58; and Steven M. Buechler, "New Social Movement Theories," *Sociological Quarterly* 36 (1995), 442–64.

31. "Die Bürger wehren sich: Partizipation oder: Die einzige Alternative? Bürgerinitiative am Beispiel Hamburgs," *Frankfurter Allgemeine Zeitung*, October 27, 1973.

32. Sandra Chaney, *Nature of the Miracle Years: Conservation in West Germany, 1945–1975* (New York, 2008).

33. Anna Bull, Hanna Diamond, and Rosalie Marsh, eds., *Feminism and Women's Movements in Contemporary Europe* (New York, 2000).

34. Holger Nehring, *Politics of Security: British and West German Protest Movements and the Early Cold War, 1945–1970* (Oxford, 2013); and Philipp Gassert, Tim Geiger, and Hermann Wentker, eds., *Zweiter Kalter Krieg und Friedensbewegung: Der NATO-Doppelbeschluss in deutsch-deutscher und internationaler Perspektive* (Munich, 2011).

35. Andrei Markovits and Philip S. Gorski, *The German Left: Red, Green and Beyond* (New York, 1993). Cf. also the special issue of *German Politics and Society* on the Greens, edited by Konrad H. Jarausch and Stephen Milder, forthcoming in 2015.

36. Erhard Neubert, *Geschichte der Opposition in der DDR, 1949–1989* (Berlin, 1999).

37. Claus Offe, "New Social Movements: Challenging the Boundaries of Institutional Politics," *Social Research* 52 (1885), 817–68.

38. Robert B. Pippin, *Modernism as a Philosophical Problem*, 2nd ed. (Malden, 1999), 168–75.

39. Charles Jencks, *The Story of Postmodernism: Five Decades of the Ironic and Critical in Architecture* (Chichester, 2011).

40. Jonathan D. Culler, *On Deconstruction: Theory and Criticism after Structuralism* (Ithaca, 2007), 25th anniversary ed.

41. Jean-Francois Lyotard, *The Post-Modern Condition: A Report on Knowledge* (Minneapolis, 1984).

42. Clare O'Farrell, *Michel Foucault* (London, 2005).
43. Charles Jencks, ed., *The Post-Modern Reader*, 2nd ed. (Chichester, 2011).
44. Jürgen Habermas, *The Philosophical Discourse of Modernity* (Cambridge, 1987).
45. For a rejection of the term see Ulrich Herbert, *Geschichte Deutschlands im 20. Jahrhundert* (Munich, 2014).
46. Peter V. Zima, *Modern/Postmodern: Society, Philosophy, Literature* (London, 2010).
47. Ronald Inglehart, *Modernization and Postmodernization: Cultural, Economic and Political Change in 43 Countries* (Princeton, 1997).
48. Zygmunt Bauman, *Modernity and the Holocaust* (Ithaca, 1989); and idem, *Postmodernity and Its Discontents* (New York, 1997).
49. Ulrich Beck, Anthony Giddens, and Christopher Lash, *Reflexive Modernization: Politics, Tradition and Aesthetics in Modern Society* (Stanford, 1994); and Wolfgang Welsch, *Unsere postmoderne Moderne* (Weinheim, 1987).

23. POSTINDUSTRIAL TRANSITION

1. Clyde E. Farnsworth, "Oil as an Arab Weapon," *New York Times*, October 18, 1973.
2. Karen R. Merrill, *The Oil Crisis of 1973–1974: A Brief History with Documents* (Boston, 2007).
3. Hugo Young, *One of Us: A Biography of Margaret Thatcher* (London, 1989).
4. Brian Harrison, *Finding a Role? The United Kingdom, 1970–1990* (Oxford, 2010), 288–370.
5. Konrad H. Jarausch, ed., *Das Ende der Zuversicht? Die Siebziger Jahre als Geschichte* (Göttingen, 2008).
6. David M. Andrews, ed., *Orderly Change: International Monetary Relations since Bretton Woods* (Ithaca, 2008).
7. Vicky S. Birchfield and John S. Duffield, eds., *Toward a Common European Union Energy Policy: Progress, Problems, Prospects* (New York, 2011).
8. "Die Erdöl Erpressung," cover of *Der Spiegel*, November 12, 1973; and Sebastian Haffner, "Geht es nicht auch ohne Öl?" *Der Stern*, November 15, 1973.
9. James D. Hamilton, "Historical Oil Shocks," National Bureau of Economic Research working paper Nr. 16790 (Cambridge, MA, 2011).
10. Ivan T. Berend, *An Economic History of 20th Century Europe* (Cambridge, 2006), 280ff.
11. Barry Eichengreen, *The European Economy since 1945: Coordinated Capitalism and Beyond* (Princeton, 2007).
12. Martin Neil Baily and Jacob Funk Kirkegaard, *Transforming the European Economy* (Washington, 2004), 43ff.
13. Ivan T. Berend, *From the Soviet Bloc to the European Union: The Economic and Social Transformation of Central and Eastern Europe since 1973* (Cambridge, 2009), 6–37.
14. Lloyd Rodwin and Hidehiko Sazanami, eds., *Industrial Change and Regional Economic Transformation: The Experience of Western Europe* (London, 1991).
15. Rainer Wirtz, ed., *Industrialisierung–Ent-Industrialisierung–Musealisierung?* (Cologne, 1998), 98–126.
16. Christoph Nonn, *Die Ruhrbergbaukrise: Entindustrialisierung und Politik, 1958–1969* (Göttingen, 2001); and Yves Meny and Vincent Wright, eds., *The Politics of Steel: Western Europe and the Steel Industry in the Crisis Years 1974–1984* (New York, 1987).
17. Silke Fengler, *Entwickelt und Fixiert: Zur Unternehmens- und Technikgeschichte der deutschen Fotoindustrie, dargestellt am Beispiel der Agfa AG Leverkusen und der VEB Filmfabrik Wolfen, 1945—1995* (Essen, 2009).

18. Martin Werding, ed., *Structural Unemployment in Western Europe: Reasons and Remedies* (Cambridge, MA, 2006).

19. Klaus Werner Schatz and Frank Wolter, *Structural Adjustment in the Federal Republic of Germany* (Geneva, 1987); Werrner Bartels, "Vor 25 Jahren starb Krupp Rheinhausen," *Rheinische Post online*, November 18, 2013.

20. Rodwin and Sazanami, *Industrial Change*, 3–36.

21. Berend, *From the Soviet Bloc to the European Union*, 7–36.

22. Konrad H. Jarausch, "Zwischen 'Reformstau' und 'Sozialabbau': Anmerkungen zur Globalisierungsdebatte in Deutschland, 1973–2003," in *Ende der Zuversicht*, 330–49.

23. Margaret Thatcher, *The Path to Power* (New York, 1995). Cf. Kenneth O. Morgan, *Ages of Reform: Dawns and Downfalls of the British Left* (London, 2011).

24. Harrison, *Finding a Role*, 305–47.

25. David S. Bell, *François Mitterrand: A Political Biography* (Cambridge, 2005).

26. Ronald Tiersky, *François Mitterrand: A Very French President* (Lanham, 2003), 130–40; and Wilfried Loth, *Geschichte Frankreichs im 20. Jahrhundert* (Stuttgart, 1987), 237–49.

27. Helmut Kohl, *Erinnerungen* (Munich, 2004).

28. Hans-Peter Schwarz, *Helmut Kohl: Eine politische Biographie* (Bonn, 2012).

29. Ben Jackson and Robert Saunders, eds., *Making Thatcher's Britain* (Cambridge, 2012).

30. Anselm Doering-Manteuffel and Lutz Raphael, *Nach dem Boom: Perspektiven auf die Zeitgeschichte nach 1970* (Göttingen, 2008).

31. Jacobs and Saunders, *Making Thatcher's Britain*, 1–21.

32. Baily and Kirkegaard, *Transforming the European Economy*, 56–75.

33. Paul Wildling, ed., *In Defense of the Welfare State* (Manchester, 1986), 1–3.

34. Harrison, *Finding a Role*, 251–76.

35. Sabina Stiller, *Ideational Leadership in German Welfare State Reform: How Politicians and Policy Ideas Transform Resilient Institutions* (Amsterdam, 2010), 45–74.

36. Jon Kvist, "Activating Welfare States: Scandinavian Experiences in the 1990s," Working Paper of the Danish National Institute of Social Research, 2000, Nr. 7.

37. Stefan Svallfors, *Contested Welfare States: Welfare Attitudes in Europe and Beyond* (Stanford, 2012).

38. Jarausch, *Ende der Zuversicht*, 9–26.

39. Andreas Wirsching, *Abschied vom Provisorium, 1982–1990* (Munich, 2006).

40. Stephen Aris, *Close to the Sun: How Airbus Challenged America's Domination of the Skies* (London, 2002).

41. James W. Cortada, *The Digital Flood: The Diffusion of Information Technology across the U.S., Europe, and Asia* (Oxford, 2012).

42. Irene Finelk Honigman, *A Cultural History of Finance* (Abingdon, UK, 2010).

43. Frank Bösch, "Politische Macht und gesellschaftliche Gestaltung: Wege zur Einführung des privaten Rundfunks in den 1970/80er Jahren," *Archiv für Sozialgeschichte* 52 (2012), 191–210.

44. Reinhold Bauer, "Ölpreiskrisen und Industrieroboter: Die 1970er Jahre als Umbruchphase für die Automobilindustrie in beiden deutschen Staaten," in *Ende der Zuversicht*, 68–83.

45. Rodwin and Sazanami, *Industrial Change*, 39–167.

46. Niall Ferguson, Charles S. Maier, Erez Manuela, and Daniel J. Sargent, eds., *The Shock of the Global: The 1970s in Perspective* (Cambridge, MA, 2010), 25–48.

47. Daniel Bell, *The Coming of Post-Industrial Society: A Venture in Social Forecasting* (New York, 1973).

48. Cortada, *Digital Flood*, 91–145; and Eichengreen, *European Economy since 1945*, 414–26.

49. Max Koch, *Roads to Post-Fordism: Labor Markets and Social Structures in Europe* (Aldershot, 2006).
50. Jürgen Kocka, *Geschichte des Kapitalismus* (Munich, 2013).
51. Peter Marsh, *The New Industrial Revolution: Consumers, Globalization and the End of Mass Production* (New Haven, 2012).

24. RETURN TO DÉTENTE

1. Christopher Wren, "Curtain Falls Softly on Helsinki Parley," and Flora Lewis, "After Parley, a Long Way to Go," *New York Times*, August 2, 1975.
2. Olav Njolstad, "The Collapse of Superpower Détente, 1975–1980," in Melvyn P. Leffler and Odd Arne Westad, eds., *The Cambridge History of the Cold War* (Cambridge, 2010), 3:1135–55.
3. Frederic Bozo, Marie-Pierre Rey, N. Piers Ludlow, and Bernd Rother, eds., *Visions of the End of the Cold War in Europe, 1945–1990* (New York, 2012), 1–14.
4. Standard histories like John Lewis Gaddis, *The Cold War: A New History* (New York, 2005), suffer from this myopia.
5. Michael Quinlan, *Thinking about Nuclear Weapons: Principles, Problems, Prospects* (Oxford, 2009), 20–55.
6. Ibid., 5–12.
7. Joseph Cirincione, *Bomb Scare: The History and Future of Nuclear Weapons* (New York, 2007), 1–14.
8. John Newhouse, *War and Peace in the Nuclear Age* (New York, 1989), 53–116.
9. David D. Hoffman, *The Dead Hand: The Untold Story of the Cold War Arms Race and Its Dangerous Legacy* (New York, 2009).
10. Newhouse, *War and Peace*, 117–84.
11. Carl H. Amme, *NATO Strategy and Nuclear Defense* (New York, 1988).
12. Quinlan, *Thinking about Nuclear Weapons*, 20–45.
13. Richard Dean Burns, ed., *Encyclopedia of Arms Control and Disarmament* (New York, 1993), vol. 2.
14. Garret Martin, "Towards a New Concert of Europe: De Gaulle's Vision of a Post–Cold War Europe," in *Visions of the End of the Cold War*," 91–104. Cf. Wilfried Loth, *Geschichte Frankreichs im 20. Jahrhundert* (Stuttgart, 1987), 2008–221.
15. Roland J. Granieri, *The Ambivalent Alliance: Konrad Adenauer, the CDU/CSU and the West, 1949–1966* (New York, 2003).
16. Jeremi Suri, *Henry Kissinger and the American Century* (Cambridge, MA, 2007).
17. Geoffrey Swain, *Tito: A Biography* (London, 2011). Cf. Marie-Janine Calic, *Geschichte Jugoslawiens im 20. Jahrhundert* (Munich, 2010).
18. John Sweeney, *The Life and Evil Times of Nicolae Ceaucescu* (London, 1991).
19. Odd Arne Westad, *Brothers in Arms: The Rise and Fall of the Sino-Soviet Alliance, 1945–1963* (Washington, 1998), 1–46.
20. Newhouse, *War and Peace*, 185–265.
21. Timothy Garton Ash, *In Europe's Name: Germany and the Divided Continent* (New York, 1993).
22. Peter Merseburger, *Willy Brandt 1913–1992: Visionär und Realist* (Stuttgart, 2002).
23. Egon Bahr, *Zu meiner Zeit* (Munich, 1996).
24. Friedhelm Boll and Krystof Ruchniewicz, eds., *"Nie mehr eine Politik über Polen hinweg": Willy Brandt und Polen* (Bonn, 2010).

25. David M. Kiethly, *Breakthrough in the Ostpolitik: The 1971 Quadripartite Agreement* (Boulder, 1986).
26. Ernest D. Plock, *The Basic Treaty and the Evolution of East-West German Relations* (Boulder, 1986).
27. Michael Morgan, "The Seventies and the Rebirth of Human Rights," in Niall Ferguson, Charles S. Maier, Erez Manela, and Daniel J. Sargent, eds., *The Shock of the Global: The 1970s in Perspective* (Cambridge, MA, 2010), 237–50.
28. William E. Griffith, *The Ostpolitik of the Federal Republic of Germany* (Cambridge, MA, 1978), 228–34.
29. Odd Arne Westad, *The Global Cold War: Third World Interventions and the Making of Our Times* (Cambridge, 2005), 1–7.
30. Vladislav M. Zubok, "Soviet Foreign Policy from Detente to Gorbachev, 1975–1985," and Amin Saikal, "Islamism, the Iranian Revolution and the Soviet Invasion of Afghanistan," in *Cambridge History of the Cold War*, 89–134.
31. Jeffrey Herf, *War by Other Means: Soviet Power, West German Resistance and the Battle of the Euromissiles* (New York, 1991).
32. Lawrence S. Wittner, *The Struggle against the Bomb*, 3 vols. (Stanford, 1993); and Holger Nehring, *Politics of Security: British and West German Protest Movements and the Early Cold War, 1945–1970* (Oxford, 2013), passim.
33. Benjamin B. Fischer, "A Cold War Conundrum," Center for the Study of Intelligence (Washington, 1997).
34. Newhouse, *War and Peace*, 333–63. Cf. Mira Duric, *The Strategic Defense Initiative: US Policy and the Soviet Union* (Aldershot, 2003).
35. Bernd Rother, "Common Security as a Way to Overcome the (Second) Cold War? Willy Brandt's Strategy for Peace in the 1980s," in *Visions of the End of the Cold War*, 239–25.
36. John W. Young, "Western Europe and the End of the Cold War, 1979–1989," in *Cambridge History of the Cold War*, 3:289–310.
37. Michael I. Hogan, *The End of the Cold War: Its Meanings and Implications* (Cambridge, 1992).
38. Beth A. Fischer, "US Foreign Policy under Reagan and Bush," in *Cambridge History of the Cold War*, 3:267–88.
39. Vladislav M. Zubok, *A Failed Empire: The Soviet Union in the Cold War from Stalin to Gorbachev* (Chapel Hill, 2007), 277–94.
40. Archie Brown, "The Gorbachev Revolution and the End of the Cold War," in *Cambridge History of the Cold War*, 3:244–66.
41. John W. Young, "Western Europe and the End of the Cold War, 1979–1989," in *Cambridge History of the Cold War*, 3:289–310. Cf. Jose M. Faraldo, Paulina Gulinska-Jurgiel, and Christian Domnitz, eds., *Europa im Ostblock: Vorstellungen und Diskurse, 1945–1991* (Cologne, 2008).
42. Newhouse, *War and Peace*, 388–98.
43. Janne E. Nolan, "The INF Treaty: Eliminating Intermediate-Range Nuclear Missiles, 1987 to the Present," and Dan Caldwell, "From SALT to START: Limiting Strategic Nuclear Weapons," in *Encyclopedia of Arms Control*, 955–65 and 895–913.
44. Zubok, *Failed Empire*, 294–302.
45. Lawrence Badash, *A Nuclear Winter's Tale: Science and Politics in the 1980s* (Cambridge, MA 2009).
46. Alva Myrdal, *The Game of Disarmament: How the United States and Russia Run the Arms Race* (New York, 1976).

47. Westad, *Global Cold War*, 331–95; and Francis J. Gavin, "Wrestling with Parity: The Nuclear Revolution Revisited," in *Shock of the Global*, 189–204.
48. Adam Roberts, "An 'Incredibly Swift Transition': Reflections on the End of the Cold War," in *Cambridge History of the Cold War*, 3:513–34.
49. George Kennan, "Future of U.S.-Soviet Relations," transcript of testimony before the Senate Foreign Relations Committee, *Congressional Record* (Washington, 1989), April 4, 1989.

25. PEACEFUL REVOLUTION

1. Serge Schmemann, "A Jubilant Horde" as well as "Berlin, a Festival," *New York Times*, November 10, 1989. Cf. Hans-Hermann Hertle, *Der Fall der Mauer: Die unbeabsichtigte Selbstauflösung des SED-Staates* (Opladen, 1996).
2. Timothy Garton Ash, *Magic Lantern: The Revolution of '89 as Witnessed in Warsaw, Budapest, Berlin and Prague* (New York, 1990); and Adam Borowski, ed., *The Road to Independence: Solidarnosc, 1980–2005* (Warsaw, 2005).
3. Vladimir Tismaneanu, "The Revolutions of 1989: Causes, Meanings, Consequences," *Contemporary European History* 18 (2009), 272–88.
4. Konrad H. Jarausch, "Germany 1989: A New Type of Revolution?" in Marc Silberman, ed., *The German Wall: Fallout in Europe* (New York, 2011), 11–35; and "The Peaceful Revolution as Transnational Process: Global Dimensions of the Fall of the Wall," in Ulf Engel, Frank Hadler, and Matthias Middell, eds., *1989 in a Global Perspective* (Leipzig, 2015).
5. Ralf Dahrendorf, *Reflections on the Revolution in Europe: In a Letter Intended to Have Been Sent to a Gentleman in Warsaw* (New York, 1990).
6. Hans Joas and Martin Kohli, *Der Zusammenbruch der DDR: Soziologische Analysen* (Frankfurt, 1993).
7. Vladimir Tismaneanu, *The Devil in History: Communism, Fascism, and Some Lessons of the Twentieth Century* (Berkeley, 2012), 123–45.
8. Jens Gieseke, *Der Mielke Konzern: Die Geschichte der Stasi, 1945–1990*, 2nd. rev. ed. (Munich, 2006). Cf. Uwe Spiekermann, ed., "The Stasi at Home and Abroad," *Bulletin of the German Historical Institute*, supplement 9 (2014).
9. Barry Eichengreen, *Economy since 1945: Coordinated Capitalism and Beyond* (Princeton, 2007), 294–303.
10. Daniela Münkel and Jens Gieseke, eds., *Die DDR im Blick der Stasi: Die geheimen Berichte an die SED-Führung*, 6 vols. (Göttingen, 2009–12) Cf. arprin, "Das Beste vom Kommunismus," http://arprin.wordpress.com/2012/10/31/das-beste-vom-kommunismus/.
11. Gale Stokes, ed., *From Stalinism to Pluralism: A Documentary History of Eastern Europe since 1945*, 2nd rev. ed. (New York, 1996).
12. Archie Brown, *Seven Years That Changed the World: Perestroika in Perspective* (Oxford, 2007).
13. Joseph Rothschild, *Return to Diversity: A Political History of East Central Europe since World War II* (New York, 1989), 191–225; and Mary Fulbrook, *The People's State: East German Society from Hitler to Honecker* (New Haven, 2005).
14. Konrad H. Jarausch, *The Rush to German Unity* (New York, 1994).
15. Jan Kubik, *The Power of Symbols against the Symbols of Power: The Rise of Solidarity and the Failure of State Socialism in Poland* (College Park, 1994).

16. Jacques Levesque, *The Enigma of 1989: The USSR and the Liberation of Eastern Europe* (Berkeley, 1997), 52–90.
17. Patrick H. O'Neill, *Revolution from Within: The Hungarian Socialist Workers' Party and the Collapse of Communism* (Cheltenham, 1998).
18. Philip J. Cunningham, *Tiananmen Moon: Inside the Chinese Student Uprising of 1989* (Lanham, 2009).
19. Charles S. Maier, *Dissolution: The Crisis of Communism and the End of East Germany* (Princeton, 1997).
20. Stephen Pfaff, *Exit-Voice Dynamics and the Collapse of East Germany: The Crisis of Leninism and the Revolution of 1989* (Durham, 2006).
21. Konrad H. Jarausch, *Die unverhoffte Einheit* (Frankfurt, 1995); and Karel Vodicka, *Die Prager Botschaftsflüchtlinge: Geschichte und Dokumente* (Göttingen, 2014).
22. William F. Buckley, *The Fall of the Berlin Wall* (Hoboken, NJ, 2004).
23. Ilko-Sascha Kowalczuk, *Endspiel. Die Revolution von 1989 in der DDR* (Munich, 2009).
24. Stephen Kotkin, *Uncivil Society: 1989 and the Implosion of the Communist Establishment* (New York, 2009), 37–65.
25. Michael Meyer, *The Year That Changed the World: The Untold Story behind the Fall of the Berlin Wall* (New York, 2009).
26. Uwe Thaysen, *Der Runde Tisch, oder wo blieb das Volk? Der Weg der DDR in die Demokratie* (Opladen, 1990).
27. Helmut Kohl, *Erinnerungen 1982–1990* (Munich, 2005), 1020–28; and Andreas Rödder, *Deutschland, einig Vaterland. Die Geschichte der Wiedervereinigung* (Munich, 2009).
28. Wolfgang Jäger, *Geschichte der deutschen Vereinigung*, vol. 3: *Die Überwindung der Teilung. Der innerdeutsche Prozess der Vereinigung 1989/90* (Stuttgart, 1998).
29. Mary E. Sarotte, *1989: The Struggle to Create Post-Cold War Europe* (Princeton, 2009).
30. Padraic Kenney, *A Carnival of Revolution: Central Europe 1989* (Princeton, 2002).
31. Timothy Garton Ash, *The Polish Revolution: Solidarity*, 3rd ed. (New Haven, 2002).
32. Ignac Romsics, *From Dictatorship to Democracy: The Birth of the Third Hungarian Republic, 1988–2001* (Boulder, 2007).
33. Robin E. H. Sheperd, *Czechoslovakia: The Velvet Revolution and Beyond* (Houndmills, 2000).
34. Peter Sinai-Davies, *The Romanian Revolution of December 1989* (Ithaca, 2005).
35. Ronald Grigor Suny, *The Revenge of the Past: Nationalism, Revolution and the Collapse of the Soviet Union* (Stanford, 1993). Belarus and the Ukraine also belonged to the CIS.
36. John P. Dunlop, *The Rise of Russia and the Fall of the Soviet Empire* (Princeton, 1993).
37. Adam Roberts and Timothy Garton Ash, eds., *Civil Resistance and Power Politics: The Experience of Non-violent Action from Gandhi to the Present* (Oxford, 2009).
38. See the essays in "Das Jahr 1989 als Zäsur der Kommunismusgeschichte," *Jahrbuch für historische Kommunismusforschung*, 2009.
39. Svetlana Savranskaya, Thomas Blanton, and Vladislav Zubok, eds., *Masterpieces of History: The Peaceful End of the Cold War in Eastern Europe, 1989* (Budapest, 2010).
40. Jacek Wieclawski, "The Eastern Enlargement of the European Union: Fears, Challenges, and Reality," *Globality Studies Journal*, No. 15, March 18, 2010, globality.cc.stonybrook.edu/?p=118.
41. Charles King, *Extreme Politics: Nationalism, Violence, and the End of Eastern Europe* (Oxford, 2010).
42. Konrad H. Jarausch, ed., *United Germany: Debating Processes and Prospects* (New York, 2013).

43. Claus Offe, *Varieties of Transition: The East European and the East Germen Experience* (Cambridge, MA, 1997).

44. Milada Anna Vachudova, *Europe Undivided: Democracy, Leverage and Integration after Communism* (New York, 2005).

45. Maier, *Dissolution*, 285–329.

46. Francis Fukuyama, *The End of History and the Last Man* (New York, 1992), ix–xxiii, 39–51; and Eric J. Hobsbawm, *Age of Extremes: The Short Twentieth Century, 1914–1991* (London, 1994).

47. Daniel N. Nelson, "Political Convergence: An Empirical Assessment," *World Politics* 30 (1978), 411–32.

48. Geir Lundestad, *The United States and Western Europe since 1945: From "Empire" by Invitation to Transatlantic Drift* (Oxford, 2003).

49. Francois Furet, *The Passing of an Illusion: The Idea of Communism in the Twentieth Century* (Chicago, 1999).

50. Stefan Wolle, *Die heile Welt der Diktatur: Alltag und Herrschaft in der DDR, 1971–1989* (Berlin, 1998), 69–83.

26. TRANSFORMING THE EAST

1. Peter S. Green, "Two Rivals Vying for Control of Poland's Steel Group," *New York Times*, December 20, 2002.

2. Sabrina P. Ramet, ed., *Central and Southeast European Politics since 1989* (Cambridge, 2010), 9–36. Cf. Nancy M. Wingfield's chapter in the third edition of Joseph Rothschild, *Return to Diversity: A Political History of East Central Europe since World War II* (New York, 2000), 265–302.

3. Richard Schroeder, *Die wichtigsten Irrtümer über die deutsche Einheit*, 2nd ed. (Freiburg, 2007), versus Daniela Dahn, *Wehe dem Sieger! Ohne den Osten, kein Westen*, 2nd. ed. (Reinbeck, 2011).

4. Milada Vachudova, *Europe Undivided: Democracy, Leverage, and Integration after Communism* (New York, 2005), 1–9.

5. Jürgen Habermas, *Die Nachholende Revolution: Kleine Polititsche Schriften* (Frankfurt, 1990), vol. 7; and Ralf Dahrendorf, *Reflections on the Revolution in Europe: In a Letter Intended to Have Been Sent to a Gentleman in Warsaw* (New York, 1990).

6. Padraic Kenney, *The Burdens of Freedom: Eastern Europe since 1989* (New York, 2006); and Günther Heydemann and Karel Vodicka, eds., *Vom Ostblock zur EU: Systemtransformationen 1990–2012 im Vergleich* (Göttingen, 2013).

7. Thomas Kostelecky, *Political Parties after Communism: Developments in East Central Europe* (Baltimore, 2002), 8–38.

8. Elisabeth Bakke, "Central and East European Party Systems since 1989," in *Central and Southeast European Politics*, 64–90.

9. Kostelecky, *Political Parties*, 39–75.

10. Anna Grzymala-Busse, *Rebuilding Leviathan: Party Competition and State Exploitation in Post-Communist Democracies* (Cambridge, 2007).

11. Vachudova, *Europe Undivided*, 63–222.

12. Konstanty Gebert, "Poland since 1989: Muddling Through, Wall to Wall," Carol Skalnik Leff, "Building Democratic Values in the Czech Republic since 1989," and Andras Bozoki and Eszter Simon, "Hungary since 1989," in *Central and Southeast European Politics*, 139–81, 204–32.

13. Aurel Braun, "Facing the Twenty-first Century: Lessons, Questions, and Tendencies," Erica Harris, "Slovakia since 1989," Lavinia Stan, "Romania: In the Shadow of the Past," and Maria Spirova, "Bulgaria since 1989," in *Central and Southeast European Politics*, 182–203, 379–420, 536–52.

14. John Keane, *Vaclav Havel: Political Tragedy in Six Acts* (New York, 2000).

15. Karl Kaser, "Economic Reforms and the Illusion of Transition," in *Central and Southeast Politics*, 91–110.

16. Anders Aslund, *Building Capitalism: The Transformation of the Former Soviet Bloc* (Cambridge, 2002).

17. Wolfgang Seibel, *Verwaltete Illusionen: Die Privatisierung der DDR-Wirtschaft durch die Treuhandanstalt und ihre Nachfolger, 1990–2000* (Frankfurt, 2005); and Aslund, *Building Capitalism*, 255–303.

18. Aslund, *Building Capitalism*, 396–440.

19. Hermann Smith-Sivertsen, "The Baltic States," in *Central and Southeast European Politics*, 447–72.

20. Barry Eichengreen, *The European Economy since 1945: Coordinated Capitalism and Beyond* (Princeton, 2007), 406–13.

21. Kaser, "Economic Reforms," 100ff.

22. Ivan Berend, *Central and Eastern Europe, 1944–1993: Detour from the Periphery to the Periphery* (Cambridge, 1996).

23. Konrad H. Jarausch, ed., *United Germany: Debating Processes and Prospects* (New York, 2013), 1–21.

24. Berend, *Central and Eastern Europe*, 341–49.

25. Daina S. Eglitis and Tana Lace, "Stratification and the Poverty of Progress in Post-Communist Latvian Capitalism," *Acta Sociologica* 52 (2009), 329–49.

26. John S. Micgiel, ed., *Perspectives on Political and Economic Transitions after Communism* (New York, 1997), 197–212.

27. Myra Marx Ferree, "Feminist Encounters: Germany, the EU and Beyond," in *United Germany*, 171–79.

28. Geoffrey Evans, "The Social Bases of Political Divisions in Post-Communist Eastern Europe," *Annual Review of Sociology* 32 (2006), 245–70.

29. Aslund, *Building Capitalism*, 304–47.

30. Michael Illner, "The Changing Quality of Life in a Post-Communist Country: The Case of the Czech Republic," *Social Indicators Research* 43 (1998), 141–70.

31. Sebastian M. Herrmann et al., eds., *Ambivalent Americanizations: Popular and Consumer Culture in Central and Eastern Europe* (Heidelberg, 2008).

32. Friederike Kind-Kovács and Jessie Labov, eds., *Samizdat, Tamizdat, and Beyond: Transnational Media during and after Socialism* (New York, 2013).

33. Christa Wolf, *City of Angels or The Overcoat of Dr. Freud* (New York, 2013). Cf. Thomas Goldstein, "Writing in Red: The East German Writers' Union and the Role of Literary Intellectuals in the German Democratic Republic, 1971–1990" (PhD dissertation, University of North Carolina, 2010).

34. Peter Gross, *Entangled Evolutions: Media and Democratization in Eastern Europe* (Washington, 2002), 158–74.

35. Lavinia Stan, ed., *Transitional Justice in Eastern Europe and the Former Soviet Union: Reckoning with the Communist Past* (Milton Park, 2009), 12–14.

36. Ibid., 247–70. Cf. Roman David, *Lustration and Transitional Justice: Personnel Systems in the Czech Republic, Hungary and Poland* (Philadelphia, 2011).

37. Maria Todorova and Szusza Gille, eds., *Post-Communist Nostalgia* (New York, 2010), 1–14.

38. Detlef Pollack, Jörg Jacobs, Olaf Müller, and Gerd Pickel, eds., *Political Culture in Post-Communist Europe: Attitudes in New Democracies* (Aldershot, 2003).
39. Sabrina P. Ramet, *Thinking about Yugoslavia: Scholarly Debates about the Yugoslav Breakup and the Wars in Bosnia and Kosovo* (Cambridge, 2005).
40. Marie-Janine Calic, *Geschichte Jugoslawiens im 20. Jahrhundert* (Munich, 2010), 340–44.
41. Louis Sell, *Slobodan Milosevic and the Destruction of Yugoslavia* (Durham, 2002); and Cathie Carmichael, "Brothers, Strangers and Enemies: Ethno-nationalism and the Demise of Communist Yugoslavia," in Dan Stone, ed., *Oxford Handbook of Postwar European History* (Oxford, 2012), 546–62.
42. Sabrina P. Ramet, *The Three Yugoslavias: State-Building and Legitimation, 1918–2005* (Washington, 2006).
43. James Gow, *The Serbian Project and Its Adversaries: A Strategy of War Crimes* (Montreal, 2003). Cf. Isabelle Delpla, Xavier Bougarel, and Jean-Louis Fournel, eds., *Investigating Srebrenica: Institutions, Facts, Responsibilities* (New York, 2014).
44. Geert Hinrich Ahrens, *Diplomacy on the Edge: Containment of Ethnic Conflict and the Minorities Working Group of the Conferences on Yugoslavia* (Washington, 2006).
45. David L. Phillips, *Liberating Kosovo: Coercive Diplomacy and U.S. Intervention* (Cambridge, MA, 2012).
46. Ray Salvatore Jennings, "Serbia: Evaluating the Bulldozer Revolution," in Katryn Stoner and Michael McFaul, eds., *Transitions to Democracy: A Comparative Perspective* (Baltimore, 2012).
47. Charles Ingrao and Thomas A. Emmert, eds., *Confronting the Yugoslav Controversies: A Scholars' Initiative* (West Lafayette, IN, 2009).
48. Berend, *Central and Eastern Europe*, 301ff. Cf. Christopher Hann, ed., *Postsozialismus: Transformationsprozesse in Europa und Asien aus ethnologischer Perspektive* (Frankfurt, 2002).
49. Ian Bremmer, *The J-Curve: A New Way to Understand Why Nations Rise and Fall* (New York, 2006).
50. See the country essays in Ramet, *Central and Southeast European Politics*, 111–472.
51. Jarausch, *United Germany*, 1–21. Cf. Claus Offe, *Varieties of Transition: The East European and East German Experience* (Cambridge, MA, 1997).
52. Vachudova, *Europe Undivided*, 257–59; and Heydemann and Vodicka, *Vom Ostblock*, 329–80.

27. GLOBAL CHALLENGES

1. Michael Hardt and Antonio Negri, "What the Protesters in Genoa Want," and Alessandra Stanley and David E. Sanger, "Italian Protester Is Killed by Police at Genoa Meting," *New York Times*, July 20 and 21, 2001.
2. Anthony Giddens, *The Consequences of Modernity* (Cambridge, 1991), 64; and idem, *Europe in the Global Age* (Cambridge, 2007), 6–9.
3. Jagdish Bhagwati, *In Defense of Globalization* (Oxford, 2004).
4. Timothy S. Murphy, *Antonio Negri: Modernity and the Multitude* (Cambridge, 2012); and Jorge Heine and Ramesh Thakur, eds., *The Dark Side of Globalization* (New York, 2011).
5. Peter Berger, "Many Globalizations: The Cultural Dynamics of Globalization," in Howard Wiarda, ed., *Globalization: Universal Trends, Regional Implications* (Lebanon, NH, 2011), 23–34.

6. Ivan Berend, *An Economic History of Twentieth Century Europe: Economic Regimes form Laissez-Faire to Globalization* (Cambridge, 2006), 278–300.

7. Ibid., 325f., and Robert Gilpin, *The Challenge of Global Capitalism: The World Economy in the 21st Century* (Princeton, 2000), 18–28.

8. Gilpin, *Challenge of Global Capitalism*, 31–34; and Peter Marsh, *The New Industrial Revolution: Consumers, Globalization and the End of Mass Production* (New Haven, 2012).

9. Paul S. Adams, "Europe and Globalization: Challenges and Alternatives," in Howard J. Wiarda, ed., *Globalization: Universal Trends, Regional Implications* (Boston, 2007), 103–28.

10. Scott deCarlo, "The World's Biggest Companies," *Forbes*, February 4, 2008; and Peter Dicken, "Economic Globalization: Corporations," in George Ritzer, ed., *The Blackwell Companion to Globalization* (Oxford, 2007), 291–306.

11. Timo Fleckenstein, *Institutions, Ideas and Learning in Welfare State Change: Labor Market Reforms in Germany* (Basingstoke, 2011).

12. Paul Copeland and Dimitris Papadimitriou, eds., *The EU's Lisbon Strategy: Evaluating Success, Understanding Failure* (Basingstoke, 2012).

13. Andreas Wirsching, *Der Preis der Freiheit: Geschichte Europas in unserer Zeit* (Munich, 2012), 226–69.

14. Sandra Chaney, *Nature of the Miracle Years: Conservation in West Germany, 1945–1975* (New York, 2008).

15. Sara Nofri, *Environment in the European Press: A Multilingual Comparison* (Wiesbaden, 2013).

16. Melanie Arndt, *Tschernobyl: Auswirkungen des Reaktorunfalls auf die Bundesrepublik Deutschland und die DDR* (Erfurt, 2011); and Sara Ann McGill, *Chernobyl Disaster* (New York, 2009).

17. *Eurobarometer 69.2: National and European Identity, European Elections, European Values, and Climate Change*, March–May 2008 (ICPSR 25021).

18. Christopher Rootes, ed., *Acting Locally: Local Environmental Mobilizations and Campaigns* (London, 2008).

19. Maria Lee, *EU Environmental Law: Challenges, Change and Decision-Making* (Oxford, 2005).

20. Steve Yearley, "Globalization and the Environment," in *Blackwell Companion to Globalization*, 239–53.

21. Christof Mauch and Kiran Klaus Patel, eds., *The United States and Germany in the Twentieth Century: Competition and Convergence* (Washington, 2010), 180–93.

22. Leslie Page Moch, *Moving Europeans: Migration in Western Europe since 1650*, 2nd ed. (Bloomington, 2003).

23. Sven Kunisch, Stephan Boehm, and Michael Boppel, eds., *From Grey to Silver: Managing the Demographic Change Successfully* (Berlin, 2011), 3–21; and Nicole Kramer, "Altern als Thema der Zeitgeschichte," *Zeithistorische Forschungen* 10 (2013), 455–63.

24. Ulrich Herbert, *Geschichte der Ausländerpolitik in Deutschland: Saisonarbeiter, Zwangsarbeiter, Gastarbeiter, Flüchtlinge* (Munich, 2001). Cf. Rita Chin, *The Guest Worker Question in Postwar Germany* (Cambridge, 2007).

25. Christina Boswell and Andrew Geddes, *Migration and Mobility in the European Union* (Basingstoke, 2011), 150–75.

26. Anna Triandafyllidou and Ruby Gropas, eds., *European Immigration: A Sourcebook* (Aldershot, 2007), 1–17. A special case were the new Jewish immigrants from Russia that were welcomed by the Federal Republic of Germany as atonement for the Holocaust.

27. Sarah Thomsen Vierra, "At Home in Almanya? Turkish-German Spaces of Belonging in the Federal Republic of Germany, 1961–1990" (PhD dissertation, University of North Carolina, 2011).

28. Anthony M. Messina, *The Logics and Politics of Post–World War II Migration to Western Europe* (Cambridge, 2007), 54–96.

29. Konrad H. Jarausch, *After Hitler: Recivilizing Germans, 1945–1995* (New York, 2005), 230–66; and the forthcoming volume edited by Cornelia Wilhelm on migration, memory, and diversity (New York, 2015).

30. Simon Reeve, *One Day in September: The Full Story of the 1972 Munich Olympics Massacre and the Israeli Revenge Operation "Wrath of God"* (New York, 2000).

31. Bruce Hoffman, *Inside Terrorism*, rev. ed. (New York, 2006). Cf. Tzvetan Todorov, *The Fear of Barbarians: Beyond the Clash of Civilizations* (Chicago, 2010).

32. Edgar Wolfrum, *Rot-Grün an der Macht: Deutschland, 1998–2005* (Munich, 2013), 279–324.

33. Ibid., 402–56.

34. Joan Wallach Scott, *The Politics of the Veil* (Princeton, 2007); Gilles Kepel, *Beyond Terror and Martyrdom: The Future of the Middle East* (Cambridge, MA, 2008), 172–256.

35. Ibid.; and C. Gus Martin, ed., *The Sage Encyclopedia of Terrorism* (Thousand Oaks, CA, 2011).

36. David Spence, ed., *The European Union and Terrorism* (London, 2007), 1–29.

37. Franz Eder and Martin Senn, eds., *Europe and Transnational Terrorism: Assessing Threats and Countermeasures* (Baden-Baden, 2009).

38. Paul Nolte, *Was ist Demokratie? Geschichte und Gegenwart* (Munich, 2012).

39. Judy Dempsey, "'Enraged Citizens' Movement Rattles German Politics," *New York Times*, May 16, 2011.

40. Hagen Schulz-Forberg and Bo Strath, *The Political History of European Integration: The Hypocrisy of Democracy-through-Market* (London, 2010).

41. Hara Kouki and Eduardo Romanos, eds., *Protest beyond Borders: Contentious Politics in Europe since 1945* (New York, 2011), 86–102.

42. Wirsching, *Preis der Freiheit*, 308–47.

43. Tony Blair, *A Journey: My Political Life* (New York, 2010), 313–20; and Wolfrum, *Rot-Grün an der Macht*, 528ff.

44. John Dunn, *Democracy: A History* (New York, 2005), 149–88; and Gerhard Loewenberg, *On Legislatures: The Puzzle of Representation* (Boulder, 2011).

45. Andrew Chadwick and Philip N. Howards, eds., *Routledge Handbook of Internet Politics* (London, 2009); and Evgeny Morozov, *The Net Delusion: The Dark Side of Internet Freedom* (New York, 2011).

46. William I. Robinson, "Theories of Globalization," in *Blackwell Companion to Globalization*, 125–43.

47. Konrad H. Jarausch, ed., "Zwischen 'Reformstau' und 'Sozialabbau': Anmerkungen zur Globalisierungsdebatte in Deutschland, 1973–2003," in idem, *Ende der Zuversicht? Die Siebziger Jahre als Geschichte* (Göttingen, 2008), 330–49; and Wirsching, *Preis der Freiheit*, 226–347.

48. Göran Therborn and Habibul Haque Khondker, eds., *Asia and Europe in Globalization: Continents, Regions and Nations* (Leiden, 2006), 275–309.

49. Daniel S. Hamilton and Joseph P. Quinlan, *Globalization and Europe: Prospering in the New Whirled Order* (Washington, 2008).

50. Maria Joao Rodrigues, ed., *Europe, Globalization and the Lisbon Agenda* (Cheltenham, 2009); Lionel Jospin, *My Vision of Europe and Globalization* (Cambridge, 2002); and Pascal Lamy and Jean-Pisany-Ferry, *The Europe We Want* (London, 2002).

28. PROSPECTS FOR THE TWENTY-FIRST CENTURY

1. Robert Kagan, "Power and Weakness," *Policy Review*, June 1, 2002; and idem, *Of Paradise and Power: America and Europe in the New World Order* (New York, 2003).
2. Jürgen Habermas and Jacques Derrida, "February 15, or What Binds Europeans Together: A Plea for a Common Foreign Policy, Beginning in the Core of Europe," *Constellations* 10, Nr. 3 (2003).
3. Edward W. Said, *Orientalism* (New York, 1978), 1–28; Dipesh Chakrabarty, *Provincializing Europe: Postcolonial Thought and Historical Difference*, 2nd ed. (Princeton, 2007).
4. Jeremy Rifkin, *The European Dream: How Europe's Vision of the Future Is Quietly Eclipsing the American Dream* (New York, 2004).
5. Dan Stone, *Goodbye to All That: The Story of Europe since 1945* (Oxford, 2014).
6. John Headley, *The Problem with Multiculturalism: The Uniqueness and Universality of Western Civilization* (New Brunswick, 2012).
7. Jasper M. Tautsch, "The Invention of the 'West,'" *Bulletin of the German Historical Institute in Washington* 53 (Fall 2013), 89–102; and the forthcoming study by Michael Kimmage.
8. Jeffrey Anderson, G. John Ikenberry, and Thomas Risse, eds., *The End of the West? Crisis and Change in the Atlantic Order* (Ithaca, 2008).
9. Victoria de Grazia, *Irresistible Empire: America's Advance through Twentieth Century Europe* (Cambridge, MA, 2006); and David Ellwood, *The Shock of America: Europe and the Challenge of the Century* (Oxford, 2012), 1–10.
10. Andrew Kohut and Bruce Stokes, *America against the World: How We Are Different and Why We Are Disliked* (New York, 2006), 220–25.
11. Dominic Sachsenmaier, "Global History and Critiques of Western Perspectives," *Comparative Education* 42 (2006), 451–70.
12. Samuel P. Huntington, *The Clash of Civilizations and the Remaking of the World Order* (New York, 1996), 19ff.
13. Sam Moyn, *The Last Utopia: Human Rights in History* (Cambridge, MA, 2010).
14. Walter Laqueur, *After the Fall: The End of the European Dream and the Decline of a Continent* (New York, 2011), 180ff.
15. T. R. Reid, *The United States of Europe: The New Superpower and the End of American Supremacy* (New York, 2004), 88–144.
16. Ibid., 144–76; and Richard Berthoud and Maria Iacovou, eds., *Social Europe: Living Standards and Welfare States* (Cheltenham,2004).
17. James J. Sheehan, *Where Have All the Soldiers Gone? The Transformation of Modern Europe* (Boston, 2008).
18. Ralf Roth, ed., *Städte im europäischen Raum: Verkehr, Kommunikation und Urbanität im 19. Und 20. Jahrhundert* (Stuttgart, 2009).
19. Peter Clark, *European Cities and Towns, 400–2000* (Oxford, 2009).
20. Malgorzata Pakier and Bo Strath, eds., *A European Memory? Contested Histories and Politics of Memory* (New York, 2010).
21. Rifkin, *European Dream*, 358ff.; and Reid, *United States of Europe*, 227ff.
22. G. John Ikenberry, "Explaining Crisis and Chance in Atlantic Relations," in *End of the West*, 1–27. Cf. Paul Nolte, *Transatlantische Ambivalenzen: Studien zur Sozial- und Ideengeschihte des 18. Bis 20. Jahrhunderts* (Munich, 2014).
23. Mary Nolan, *The Transatlantic Century: Europe and America, 1890–2010* (Cambridge, 2012), 1–9, 356–73.

24. Steven Hill, "Ignore America's Europe-bashing—It's Nothing New," *The Guardian,* September 2, 2012; and Robert Marquard, "Is Romney's Europe-bashing Well Placed?" *Christian Science Monitor,* January 11, 2012.
25. Ellwood, *Shock of America,* 488–519; and Kohut and Stokes, *America against the World,* 22–40.
26. Konrad H. Jarausch, "Drifting Apart: Cultural Dimensions of the Transatlantic Estrangement," in Hermann Kurthen, Antonio Menendez, and Stefan Immerfall, eds., *Safeguarding German-American Relations in the New Century* (Lanham, 2006), 17–32; and Kohut and Stokes, *America against the World,* 41–205.
27. Mark Leonard, *Why Europe Will Run the 21st Century* (London, 2005).
28. Timothy Garton Ash, *Free World: America, Europe and the Surprising Future of the West* (New York, 2004), 71–83; Steven Erlanger, "Conflicting Goals Complicate an Effort to Forge a Trans-Atlantic Trade Deal," *New York Times,* June 12, 2012.
29. Sabrina P. Ramet and Christine Ingebritsen, eds., *Coming in from the Cold War: Changes in U.S.-European Interactions since 1980* (Oxford, 2002).
30. Dieter Mahncke, Alicia Amos, and Christopher Reynolds, eds., *European Foreign Policy: From Rhetoric to Reality?* (Brussels, 2004).
31. Gergana Noutcheva, *European Foreign Policy and the Challenge of Balkan Accession: Conditionality, Legitimacy and Compliance* (Hoboken, NJ, 2012).
32. Birol A. Yesilada, *EU-Turkey Relations in the 21st Century* (Abingdon, UK, 2012).
33. Trang Phan and Michel Guillou, *Francophonie et mondialisation: Histoire et institutions des origines à nos jours* (Paris, 2011).
34. Yenkong Ngangjoh-Hodu and Francis A.S.T. Matambalya, *Trade Relations between the EU and Africa: Development, Challenges and Options beyond the Cotonou Agreement* (London, 2010).
35. Jan van der Harst and Pieter C. M. Swieringa, eds., *China and the EU: Concord or Conflict?* (Maastricht, 2012).
36. Zhongqi Pan, ed., *Conceptual Gaps in China-EU Relations: Global Governance, Human Rights and Strategic Partnerships* (Basingstoke, 2012).
37. Zaki Laidi, ed., *EU Foreign Policy in a Globalized World: Normative Power and Social Preferences* (London, 2008).
38. Jan Zielonka, "Europe as a Global Actor: Empire by Example?" *International Affairs* 84 (2008), 471–84.
39. Sir Malcom Rifkin, "Britain and the EU: An Ever-Closer Union?" speech, May 6, 2013, http://www.euractiv.com. Cf. Michael Geary and Kevin A. Lees, "The Growing EU-UK Gulf," *National Interest,* January 28, 2013.
40. Finn Laursen, *The EU's Lisbon Treaty: Institutional Choices and Implementation* (Burlington, 2012).
41. Philip Arestis and Malcolm Sawyer, eds., *The Euro Crisis* (Basingstoke, 2012).
42. Federiga Bindi and Irina Angelescu, eds., *The Foreign Policy of the European Union: Assessing Europe's Role in the World* (Washington, 2012).
43. Richard Tilly, Paul J. J. Welfens, and Michael Heise, eds., *50 Years of EU Economic Dynamics: Integration, Financial Markets and Innovation* (Berlin, 2007).
44. Deborah Herlocker, "The Influence of the Erasmus Exchange Program on the Development of a Common European Identity" (PhD dissertation, University of North Carolina, 2005).
45. Hartmut Kaelble, *A Social History of Europe, 1945–2000: Recovery and Transformation after Two World Wars,* rev. ed. (New York, 2013). Cf. Ariana Brill, *Abgrenzung und Hoffnung: "Europa" in der deutschen, britischen und amerikanischen Presse, 1945–1980* (Göttingen, 2014).

46. Darko Bandic and Dusan Stoianovic, "Little Joy in Croatia as It Enters the EU," *ABC News*, June 17, 2013; and Ed Dolan, "Here's Why Latvia's Decision to Join the Euro Makes Sense," *Wall Street Journal*, June 16, 2013.
47. Sophie Meunier and Kathleen R. McNamara, eds., *Making History: European Integration and Institutional Change at Fifty* (Oxford, 2007).
48. James Anderson and James Goodman, "Regions, States and the EU: Modernist Reaction or Postmodern Adaptation?" *Review of International Political Economy* 2 (1995), 600–631.
49. Jan Zielonka, *Europe as Empire: The Nature of the Enlarged European Union* (Oxford, 2006).
50. See the forthcoming study "Germany and the Future of Europe" by J. D. Bindenagel.
51. Joschka Fischer, "From Confederacy to Confederation," Berlin, May 12, 2000; and idem, *Scheitert Europa? Europa am Scheideweg* (Cologne, 2014).

POSTSCRIPT: A CHASTENED MODERNITY

1. Richards Plavnieks, "Nazi Collaborators on Trial during the Cold War: The Cases against Viktors Arajs and the Latvian Auxiliary Security Police" (PhD dissertation, University of North Carolina, 2013); personal communication from Irmgard Mueller; and Andre Weckmann, *Wie die Würfel fallen: Ein Roman aus dem Elsass* (Kehl, 1981). Cf. Mary Fulbrook, *Dissonant Lives: Generations and Violence through the German Dictatorships* (Oxford, 2011).
2. Mark Mazower, *Dark Continent: Europe's Twentieth Century* (New York, 1999), versus Richard Vinen, *A History in Fragments: Europe in the Twentieth Century* (London, 2000).
3. Editorial, *London Times*, January 1, 1901; Shiv Visvanathan, "A Letter to the 21st Century," *Economic and Political Weekly*, January 8, 2000.
4. Eric Hobsbawm, *Age of Extremes: The Short Twentieth Century, 1914–1991* (London, 1994). Cf. Martin Sabrow, *Zeitgeschichte schreiben: Von der Verständigung über die Vergangenheit in der Gegenwart* (Göttingen, 2014), 160–93.
5. Eric Weitz, *A Century of Genocide: Utopias of Race and Nation* (Princeton, 2003); and Norman Naimark, *Stalin's Genocides* (Princeton, 2010).
6. Elizabeth Pond, *The Rebirth of Europe* (Washington, 1999).
7. Chris Lorenz and Berber Bevenage, eds., *Breaking up Time: Negotiating Borders between Present, Past and Future* (Göttingen, 2013); and Robert Hassan, *Empires of Speed: Time and the Acceleration of Politics and Society* (Leiden, 2012).
8. Peter N. Stearns and Herrick Chapman, *European Society in Upheaval: Social History since 1750*, 3rd. ed. (New York, 1992). Cf. Jürgen Kocka and Alan Mitchell, eds., *Bourgeois Society in 19th Century Europe* (Oxford, 1993).
9. Theodore H. von Laue, *The World Revolution of Westernization: The Twentieth Century in Global Perspective* (New York, 1987).
10. Francois Furet, *The Passing of an Illusion: The Idea of Communism in the Twentieth Century* (Chicago, 1999).
11. Günther Heydemann und Eckhard Jesse, eds., *Diktaturvergleich als Herausforderung: Theorie und Praxis* (Berlin, 1998).
12. Ronald Inglehart, *Modernization and Postmodernization: Cultural, Economic and Political Change in 43 Countries* (Princeton, 1997).
13. Ulrich Beck and Christoph Lau, "Second Modernity as a Research Agenda: Theoretical and Empirical Explorations in the 'Meta-Change' of Modern Society," *British Journal of Sociology* 56 (2005), 525–57.

14. Sophia Marshman, "Bauman on Genocide—Modernity and Mass Murder: From Classification to Annihilation?" in Michael Hviid Jacobson and Poul Poder, eds., *The Sociology of Zygmunt Bauman* (Aldershot, 2008), 75–96. Cf. Ulrich Herbert, *Geschichte Deutschlands im 20. Jahrhundert* (Munich, 2014), 1247–51.
15. Martin Doerry, *Übergangsmenschen: Die Mentalität der Wilhelminer und die Krise des Kaiserreichs* (Munich, 1986); and Jürgen Osterhammel, *The Transformation of the World: A Global History of he 19th Century* (Princeton, 2014).
16. Roger Chickering, *The Great War and Urban Life in Germany: Freiburg, 1914–1918* (Cambridge, 2007).
17. Eric Weitz, *Weimar Germany: Promise and Tragedy* (Princeton, 2007).
18. Heinrich August Winkler, *Geschichte des Westens. Die Zeit der Weltkriege, 1914–1945* (Munich, 2011), 1197–1214.
19. Martin Thomas, Bob Moore, and L. J. Butler, eds., *Crises of Empire: Decolonization and Europe's Imperial States, 1918–1975* (London, 2008).
20. John Lewis Gaddis, *The Cold War* (London, 2006).
21. Tony Judt, *Postwar: A History of Europe since 1945* (New York, 2005), 777–800.
22. Andrew Moravcsik, *The Choice for Europe: Social Purpose and State Power from Messina to Maastricht* (Ithaca, 1998).
23. James J. Sheehan, *Where Have All the Soldiers Gone? The Transformation of Modern Europe* (Boston, 2008).
24. Anthony J. Nicholls, *Freedom with Responsibility: The Social Market Economy in Germany, 1918–1963* (Oxford, 1994). Cf. Thomas Piketty, *Capital in the Twenty-first Century* (Cambridge, MA, 2014).
25. Geoff Eley, *Forging Democracy: The History of the Left in Europe, 1750–2000* (Oxford, 2002).
26. Steve Milder and Konrad H. Jarausch, "Renewing Democracy: The Rise of Green Politics in West Germany," *German Politics and Society*, forthcoming in 2015.
27. Stefan Ludwig Hoffmann, ed., *Human Rights in the Twentieth Century* (New York, 2011).
28. Colin Crouch, *Post-Democracy* (New York, 2004).
29. Stephen Philip Kramer, "The Return of History in Europe," *Washington Quarterly*, Fall 2012, 81–91.
30. Wolfgang Streeck, *Gekaufte Zeit: Die vertagte Krise des demokratischen Kapitalismus* (Berlin, 2013), and Dan Stone, *Goodbye to All That: The Story of Europe since 1945* (Oxford, 2014), 291–94.
31. Tony Judt, *Ill Fares the Land* (New York, 2010).
32. "U.S. President Obama at the Brandenburg Gate in Berlin," World Security Network, June 21, 2013. Cf. Mary Nolan, *The Transatlantic Century: Europe and the United States, 1890–2010* (Cambridge, 2012).

INDEX

Czechoslovakia (*continued*)
democracy in, 141; minorities in, 303–4;
partition of, 303–6; reform of, 600; separation of, 687, 701
Czech Republic, 527, 687, 701, 704

Dada, 182
Dahrendorf, Ralf, 574–75
Dalí, Salvador, 198
D'Annunzio, Gabriele, 162, 164
Danzig. *See* Gdańsk
Darré, Walter, 263, 345
Dawes Plan (1924), 150, 218, 266
Dayton Accords (1995), 715–16. *See also* Yugoslavia: break up of
Debussy, Claude, 186
decartelization, 416, 463. *See also* Potsdam
Conference
decolonization, 782–83; in Africa, 488–90;
causes of, 482, 483–87, 490–91; challenges
of independence, 491–95; debates about,
481–82; patterns of, 489–90; results of, 482,
494–99, 504–5; successes of, 493, 498; white
exodus, 500
de Gasperi, Alcide, 418, 423, 751
de Gaulle, Charles, 315, 325, 350, 413, 423, 489,
517, 518–19, 596, 626, 647, 650, 782
deindustrialization, 620–23, 637, 722; consequences of, 622–23, 636; struggle against, 624
Delors, Jacques, 522
demilitarization, after World War II, 416, 463
democracy, 162, 165–66, 206, 228, 459, 471,
740; cyber-democracy, 743–44; democracy
deficit, 531, 741; failures of, 142–44, 154,
267; grassroots, 602–3, 740–41, 742; and
human rights, 786–87; new democracies,
140–41, 152–153; people's democracy,
433–47, 471; reform of, 411, 424–25, 531,
743–44; restoration of, 401, 411–15, 423, 425
democratization, 109, 125–26, 130; in Eastern
Europe, 697–701
denazification, 416, 463; Soviet style of, 432,
435, 451
Denikin, Anton, 123, 244
Derrida, Jacques, 607, 748, 769
d'Estaing, Giscard, 519, 521, 626
de-Stalinization, 257–58, 441–45. *See also*
Khrushchev; Secret Speech
détente, 640–41, 653, 654, 655, 658–62, 670. *See
also* Cold War
developmental dictatorships: communist, 493;
right-wing, 493–94. *See also* decolonization

dictatorship of the proletariat, 126, 143, 239,
257, 260, 312, 459; in Eastern Europe, 437,
471. *See also* democracy: people's democracy
Dien Bien Phu, 488
Dietrich, Marlene, 187
digitalization, 561, 637
Dimitrov, Georgi, 436
disarmament: after the world wars, 138, 292;
nuclear, 476, 604, 646, 661–62
Dix, Otto, 188, 198
Döblin, Alfred, 191
Dollfuss, Engelbert, 300, 301
Dönitz, Karl, 377, 392, 409
Dual Alliance, 58, 60, 68, 77. *See also* World
War I: alliances in
Dual Monarchy, 33, 87. *See also* Habsburg
Empire
Dubček, Alexander, 600–601
Dulles, John Foster, 138, 473, 511, 643
Duma, 108, 109. *See also* Russian Empire
Dunkirk, 324
Durkheim, Emile, 4
Dutschke, Rudi, 594, 595–96
Dzerzhinsky, Felix, 123

East Germany (GDR), 432, 435–36, 466–67,
676; civil society in, 438; de facto recognition
of, 652; demonstrations in, 678–79; election
in, 680–81; exodus from, 674, 676–77; June
17 (1953) revolt in, 442; rearmament of,
467–68; Socialist Unity Party (SED) of,
435, 466–67, 676, 678, 681; unification with
FRG, 680–81, 688, 702, 719. *See also* Eastern
Europe; West Germany
Eastern Europe, 152, 430, 471, 692–93, 696,
699–701; collapse of communism in, 667–78,
673–674, 682; communist repression in,
432–33, 437–38; consumerism in, 445–49,
543; culture in, 439, 555–56, 709; dissent
in, 441–42, 672, 709; economy in, 436, 440,
445, 446–47, 450, 539, 619–20, 623–24, 671,
701–5; in the EU, 527; liberation of, 433–34;
nationalism in, 88, 687–88; postcommunist
parties in, 698–99; protest in, 588, 598–602;
society in, 547, 605–6, 705–9; Soviet domination of, 427–48, 429–30, 432, 436–37,
449–50; standard of living in, 445, 446–47,
706–7
Ebert, Friedrich, 142, 265
economic boom, 536, 546, 561
education, 574–75, 577–58, 727; early childhood, 576; in Eastern Europe, 575; higher,

576–77; and overcrowding, 592–93; poly-technic training, 575; reform of, 525, 575–76; secondary, 576
EFTA, 517, 519
Egypt, 30, 61, 328, 375, 471, 484, 488–89, 494, 658
Ehmke, Horst, 569
Ehrenburg, Ilya, 443
Einstein, Albert, 52, 197, 279, 642
Eisenhower, Dwight D., 380, 383, 391, 392, 410–11, 428, 473, 489, 643
Eisenhüttenstadt, 624, 695
Eisenstein, Sergei, 103, 258
El Alamein, Battle of (1942), 375
Eliot, T. S., 202, 606
Elysée Treaty (1963), 519, 530, 647
"empire by invitation," 420, 457, 478, 557, 648, 692. See also Americanization; Cold War
Enabling Act (1933), 277
energy sources: coal and steel crisis, 621; nuclear, 507, 514, 588, 729, 786; oil, 614, 616–17; renewable, 732
English Channel: blockade of, 83. See also naval warfare
Enigma, 379
Entente, 49, 60–61, 77, 79, 86, 88, 91–92. See also World War I: alliances in
environment, 731–32, 786; climate change, 729–30; degradation of, 497–98, 728–29; environmental movements, 605, 730
equalization of burdens law, 539. See also welfare state: German model of
Erasmus Program, 525, 529, 768
Erdogan, Recep Tayyip, 763
Erhard, Ludwig, 416, 514, 536–37, 567, 569, 580
espionage: in Cold War, 469–70; U-2 planes, 470, 475; in World War II, 379
Ethiopia, 161, 175, 296, 484, 640
ethnic cleansing: in Bosnia, 715; in World War II, 345–46, 352–56, 462–63
Euratom, 507, 514, 515
eurocrisis, 528–29, 767, 787
Europe, 6–13, 16, 764, 787–88; criticism of, 7, 482, 748–49, 754; defense of, 557–58, 749; destruction of, 395, 400, 402–3; differences from the U.S., 754–57, 760; division of, 410, 453, 464, 476, 783; hegemony of, 11, 42–45, 215, 482; identity of, 509–10, 529, 757, 768–69; impact of imperialism, 38, 44–45, 499–503; narratives of, 774, 780–84; reconstruction of, 220–21, 401–2, 536, 562;

recovery of, 783–84; reuniting of, 526, 687; role of, 748, 762–66; self-destruction of, 781, 782; soft power of, 760–61
"Europe of the fatherlands," 518, 647
European Central Bank (ECB), 524, 529, 725, 767; deficit criteria of, 524; euro, 524–25, 767
European Coal and Steel Community (ECSC), 511–12
European Community (EC), 519–21
European Defense Community (EDC), 422, 468, 507, 512–14
European Economic Community (EEC), 507, 516, 567
European integration, 422, 507; antecedents of, 509; crises of, 512–13, 521, 528; debates about, 507–8, 526, 532; Euroskepticism, 508, 766, 787; functionalist approach to, 513; successes of, 516–17, 529, 530
European Monetary System (EMS), 519, 524, 784
European Parliament, 516, 521–23, 527–28, 741, 767
European Union (EU), 522–24, 771, 784; attraction of, 699, 762; constitution of, 527–28; enlargement of, 526–27, 687, 763; environmental protection in, 730–31; exit from, 766; foreign policy of, 762, 767–68; further integration of, 526–29, 766; as postmodern polity, 770–72; science programs of, 525, 727; successes of, 768–70
Eurosclerosis, 519, 619
Evian Accords (1962), 489
existentialism, 405, 549

Falaise, 383
Falkenhayn, Erich von, 84, 93
Falkland Islands, Battle of (1914), 84
Fallada, Hans, 226
fascism, 162, 165, 172–73, 176–77, 178, 180, 195, 234; and gender, 164–65; ideology of, 156–57, 164–65, 170, 178–79; opposition to, 177–78; origins of, 156; as a transnational movement, 169–70, 176–77, 180
fascism (in Italy), 156, 157, 163–65; life under, 170–74; opposition to, 168–69; Partito Nazionale Fascista (PNF), 166–68; seizure of power, 166–70; terror under, 168–69, 173–74. See also Mussolini, Benito
Fashoda Crisis (1898), 41, 60–61
Ferguson, Niall, 20
Finland, 309, 320, 349, 409; independence of, 122, 138; neutrality of, 414, 526

immigration, 732–34; attitudes toward, 501, 732–33, 735; EU restrictions on, 734, 735–36; non-European, 500–501; and social integration, 734–35

imperialism, 21, 23–26, 38–40; "blowback" of, 499–503; and Christianization, 36–37; bureaucracy and, 37, 39; civilizing mission of, 25, 28–29, 31, 36; criticism of, 20–21, 41; culture of, 36, 38–42; definitions of, 22–23; economy of, 24, 27–28, 35–36, 50; and exploitation, 27–28, 34–35; impact of, 22, 34, 37–38, 44; landed empires, 32–34; neoimperialism, 492; overseas empires, 30–32, 484; patterns of, 26–30; and rivalry, 25–26, 56, 60–62; society under, 28, 35, 40–41

India, 27, 30, 457, 471–72, 485–86, 497–98, 764

Indonesia, 335, 471, 486, 492

industrialization, 7–8; nationalization of industry, 413, 425, 439, 466, 474, 477, 539, 547, 565, 621, 626; smokestack, 447, 539; Soviet, 236, 245–50; of warfare, 92

influenza pandemic (1918), 213–14

intergovernmentalism, 525. *See also* EU

International Building Exhibition (IBA), 535, 571

international law, 51, 69–70

International Monetary Fund, 407, 493, 702

international order, 10–11, 47–48, 130; alliances, 58, 60, 70; crises of, 49, 59–64, 290; democratic conception of, 311–12; the Hague convention, 52, 70; post-1945 reconstruction, 419–23; sources of hostility, 53–59, 150–51, 311; ties of peace, 49–53

Intershops, 447, 543

Iraq War (2003), 737–38

Ireland, 145–46

Iron Curtain speech (1946), 464

Islam, fundamentalist, 736–37

irredentism, 79, 161

Italy, 159–60, 162–63, 166–69, 417–18, 425, 464, 635; backwardness of, 158–62; democracy in, 159–60, 166; and Germany, 174–75, 176; imperial ambitions of, 161, 174–75, 296; protests in, 596; in World War I, 68–69, 79, 87, 161–62; in World War II, 328

Izetbegović, Bakir, 715

Izvolsky, Alexander, 61

Japan, 67, 498; invasion of Manchuria, 293; surrender of, 408; war with China, 335; in World War II, 336–38, 349, 408

Jaruzelski, Wojciech, 674, 682

Jaurès, Jean, 53, 67

Jewish councils, 357. *See also* Holocaust

Joffre, Joseph, 77

John Paul II, Pope, 674

Joyce, James, 191

July Crisis (1914), 63–64, 71

Jünger, Ernst, 99, 191, 364

Jutland, Battle of (1916), 85

Kádár, János, 445, 600

Kadets, 116. *See also* Russia

Kafka, Franz, 190–91

Kagan, Robert, 748, 759

KAL 007 Flight, 656–57

Kamenev, Lev, 115, 119, 244, 245, 251

Kandinsky, Wassily, 190

Kapp Putsch, 134, 265

Karadžić, Radovan, 715, 717

Kautsky, Karl, 53

Keitel, Wilhelm, 279, 315, 392

Kekkonen, Urho, 640

Kelsen, Hans, 228

Kelly, Petra, 605, 656

Kemal, Mustafa, 52

Kennan, George, 458, 461, 664

Kennedy, John F., 475–76, 646

Kenyatta, Jomo, 495

Kerensky, Alexander, 114, 115–16, 119–20

Kesselring, Albert, 381

Keynes, John Maynard, 139, 211, 212, 228–29, 785

Keynesianism, 210–11, 615, 616, 626, 637; neo-Keynesianism, 562, 569

Khmer Rouge, 496

Khrushchev, Nikita, 257, 441, 442–43, 446, 473–75, 646; overthrow of, 448

Kierkegaard, Søren, 549

Kipling, Rudyard, 25

Kirov, Sergei, 251

kitchen debate (1959), 446. *See also* Cold War

Kitchener, Herbert, 27, 41, 60

Klaus, Václav, 698, 701

Klee, Paul, 198

Klemperer, Victor, 262, 283, 437

Klima, Ivan, 600

Klimt, Gustav, 186

Kluck, Alexander von, 77

Kocka, Jürgen, 5

Koestler, Arthur, 253, 437

Kohl, Helmut, 619, 627, 631, 660, 667, 680–81, 743

Kolchak, Aleksandr, 123

Kollwitz, Käthe, 198